**FRIENDS
OF ACPL**

D1241174

PRIVATE WEALTH

CFA Institute Investment Perspectives Series is a thematically organized compilation of high-quality content developed to address the needs of serious investment professionals. The content builds on issues accepted by the profession in the CFA Institute Global Body of Investment Knowledge and explores less established concepts on the frontiers of investment knowledge. These books tap into a vast store of knowledge of prominent thought leaders who have focused their energies on solving complex problems facing the financial community.

CFA Institute is the global association for investment professionals. It administers the CFA® and CIPM curriculum and exam programs worldwide; publishes research; conducts professional development programs; and sets voluntary, ethics-based professional and performance-reporting standards for the investment industry. CFA Institute has more than 95,000 members, who include the world's 82,000 CFA charterholders, in 134 countries and territories, as well as 135 affiliated professional societies in 56 countries and territories.

www.cfainstitute.org

Research Foundation of CFA Institute is a not-for-profit organization established to promote the development and dissemination of relevant research for investment practitioners worldwide. Since 1965, the Research Foundation has emphasized research of practical value to investment professionals, while exploring new and challenging topics that provide a unique perspective in the rapidly evolving profession of investment management.

To carry out its work, the Research Foundation funds and publishes new research, supports the creation of literature reviews, sponsors workshops and seminars, and delivers online webcasts and audiocasts. Recent efforts from the Research Foundation have addressed a wide array of topics, ranging from private wealth management to quantitative tools for portfolio management.

www.cfainstitute.org/foundation

PRIVATE WEALTH

Wealth Management in Practice

Stephen M. Horan, CFA

WILEY

John Wiley & Sons, Inc.

Copyright © 2009 by CFA Institute. All rights reserved.

Published by John Wiley & Sons, Inc., Hoboken, New Jersey.
Published simultaneously in Canada.

No part of this publication may be reproduced, stored in a retrieval system, or transmitted in any form or by any means, electronic, mechanical, photocopying, recording, scanning, or otherwise, except as permitted under Section 107 or 108 of the 1976 United States Copyright Act, without either the prior written permission of the Publisher, or authorization through payment of the appropriate per-copy fee to the Copyright Clearance Center, Inc., 222 Rosewood Drive, Danvers, MA 01923, (978) 750-8400, fax (978) 646-8600, or on the web at www.copyright.com. Requests to the Publisher for permission should be addressed to the Permissions Department, John Wiley & Sons, Inc., 111 River Street, Hoboken, NJ 07030, (201) 748-6011, fax (201) 748-6008, or online at http://www.wiley.com/go/permissions.

Limit of Liability/Disclaimer of Warranty: While the publisher and author have used their best efforts in preparing this book, they make no representations or warranties with respect to the accuracy or completeness of the contents of this book and specifically disclaim any implied warranties of merchantability or fitness for a particular purpose. No warranty may be created or extended by sales representatives or written sales materials. The advice and strategies contained herein may not be suitable for your situation. You should consult with a professional where appropriate. Neither the publisher nor author shall be liable for any loss of profit or any other commercial damages, including but not limited to special, incidental, consequential, or other damages.

For general information on our other products and services or for technical support, please contact our Customer Care Department within the United States at (800) 762-2974, outside the United States at (317) 572-3993 or fax (317) 572-4002.

Wiley also publishes its books in a variety of electronic formats. Some content that appears in print may not be available in electronic books. For more information about Wiley products, visit our web site at www.wiley.com.

ISBN 978-0-470-38113-7

Printed in the United States of America.

10 9 8 7 6 5 4 3 2 1

CONTENTS

PART II: INVESTMENT MANAGEMENT
FOR TAXABLE PRIVATE CLIENTS

FOREWORD

Industry reports are clear; globally, the ranks of the high-net-worth individual (HNWI) have grown faster than increases in economic output. India and the Pacific Rim have experienced the most pronounced growth. Although recent declines in asset prices will certainly temper HNWI growth, the secular trend of wealth creation that drives increases in the high-net-worth population remains intact. Additionally, all investors are being asked to assume greater responsibility for the management of their financial future, particularly as it relates to retirement planning.

As a result, the demand for wealth management services is growing immensely, and building a competitive private wealth management practice requires a program of education and training. Many organizations offer training of various levels of sophistication for advisers serving this market. We like to think the CFA Program, started in 1963, is chief among them.

The increasing demand for wealth management services has also increased the supply of educational materials in this area. Here again, CFA Institute has been at the forefront of developing content for practitioners—with this book being just one example.

Included are materials published by CFA Institute and the Research Foundation of CFA Institute that meet the highest standards for quality and relevance. And to help guide the reader, the 23 individual pieces are grouped in four sections that address different concerns in the private wealth area: life-cycle investing, investment management for taxable private clients, tax-advantaged savings accounts, and after-tax performance. Each area addresses issues that are as unique as the clients that private wealth managers serve. And each area highlights approaches for managing these unique needs.

Being a compilation of materials from the Research Foundation of CFA Institute, the *Financial Analysts Journal*, and *CFA Institute Conference Proceedings Quarterly*, this book taps into the vast store of knowledge of some of the most prominent thought leaders—ranging from Nobel Prize winners, to academics, to practitioners—in private wealth who have focused their energies on solving the complex problems facing individual investors. We are grateful these authors have found a fertile home for their ideas at CFA Institute and the Research Foundation of CFA Institute.

I am very pleased, therefore, to present *Private Wealth: Wealth Management in Practice* the first in our CFA Institute Investment Perspectives Series. I know you will find it a useful guide and resource in meeting the challenges of private wealth management.

ROBERT R. JOHNSON, CFA
Deputy CEO and Managing Director
CFA Institute

INTRODUCTION

The management of private client assets is comprehensive and complex. Institutional asset managers often have focused mandates to manage a pool of financial assets (often in the same asset class or subasset class) for the benefit of an end investor, as in the case of a mutual fund manager or pension fund manager. The purview of the wealth manager, however, extends beyond a particular asset class or even financial assets in general. It encompasses a broad range of implied assets and liabilities in an individual's or family's comprehensive portfolio that affect the ultimate disposition of the financial assets.

For some investors, implied assets include the value embedded in a stream of social security or pension payments as they approach retirement. Conceptually, the value of these cash flows can be estimated and their risk described. For younger investors, estimating the value and describing the risk of their future earning stream may be significant. These assets are certainly not tradable. They nonetheless have value (often times relatively significant value) and are germane to overall life-cycle planning and asset allocation analysis.

Without a doubt, each solution is unique. It depends on individual goals, preexisting risk exposures and tolerances, and investment constraints—all of which are often correlated with the client's wealth level. The fundamental wealth management process, however, is generally applicable even if the ultimate solutions and outcomes vary considerably by client. Moreover, optimal solutions derive from an understanding of the complex interactions between investments, taxes, estate planning, and other issues.

To illustrate how complex these interactions can become, consider an incredibly simple case. A 65-year-old single woman has just retired. She has no bequest motive and is extremely risk averse. She plans to spend the rest of her life residing in a rented apartment, reading, writing, painting, strolling on the beach, and traveling. Her only assets are her state-sponsored retirement benefits, a tax-deferred retirement account worth $1 million, and a taxable money market account worth $1 million. What is the safest investment strategy that she can pursue to maximize her spendable after-tax income for as long as she lives?

The risk to her standard of living posed by uncertain longevity and inflation can be addressed by annuitizing part of her wealth, and market risk can be minimized by investing in inflation-protected default-free bonds. But there is still the substantial risk of future tax increases. Should she invest in tax-exempt bonds to avoid uncertainty about tax increases? Conceptually, inflation-protected tax-exempt bonds or annuities are candidates for dealing with these risks, but they are not yet available as retail products. So, the wealth manager faces the problem of incomplete markets, an understanding of which lends insights for financial innovation.

Next, the wealth manager must assess how much risk the client can accept to accomplish her goals. But this decision depends in part on the tax characteristics of the investments, which influences the choice of accounts where those assets might be located. The choice of tax-deferred retirement accounts has estate planning implications and may affect how her state-sponsored retirement benefits are taxed as well.

This book is a thematically organized collection of some of the best wealth management thinking contained in the annals of CFA Institute and the Research Foundation of CFA Institute. Some of the material represents insightful guidance on common problems, such as managing concentrated stock positions. Other authors have built on classic conceptual frameworks of legendary thinkers, such as Paul Samuelson and Harry Markowitz, giving new application to their pioneering ideas and testifying to the power of adhering to fundamental principles. Still other authors have pushed the boundaries of traditional thinking by offering new paradigms and ways of thinking about the issues confronting the growing ranks of individuals and families that have accumulated wealth for which they bear ultimate management responsibility.

With the proper tools, opportunities for the wealth manager to add value abound. This book provides those tools. The skeleton of the book is organized around three chapters commissioned by the Research Foundation of CFA Institute. Each chapter develops an integrated framework with broad application. Selected articles from the *Financial Analysts Journal* and *CFA Institute Conference Proceeding Quarterly* are then used to either develop these themes more fully or extend the analysis in yet more practical ways.

Part I examines life-cycle investing. Robert Merton and Paul Samuelson set the stage with musings about the state of financial planning in general. In "The Future of Retirement Planning," Dr. Merton discusses the forces that precipitated the shift toward defined-contribution retirement plans and predicts the evolution of innovative financial and insurance products that will manage individual risk and accommodate common behavioral tendencies. Dr. Samuelson argues that retirement risk can best be managed through a common pool of diversified securities in "Is Personal Finance a Science?"

With that backdrop, Roger Ibbotson; Moshe Milevsky; Peng Chen, CFA; and Kevin Zhu in their chapter "Lifetime Financial Advice: Human Capital, Asset Allocation, and Insurance" develop a framework to address the fundamental problem of life-cycle finance—allocating the value of one's financial and implied assets over one's lifespan. The problem involves the management of many risks (mortality risk and longevity risk not least among them) subject to constraints imposed by exogenous factors, such as the nature of one's human capital.

The remaining works in Part I build on these concepts and introduce other possible solutions. Zvi Bodie, Jonathan Truessard, and Paul Willen, for example, propose a methodological framework to develop contracts that meet consumers' life-cycle needs. Mark Warshawsky advocates life-care annuities, which combine a life annuity with long-term care insurance. The economic efficiency of this product stems from the correlation between mortality risk and healthy lifestyles, which effectively curbs the adverse selection problem that would arise if each product were sold separately. Jason Scott outlines the advantage of the longevity (or deferred) annuity, which efficiently manages longevity risk without the disadvantages of a traditional immediate annuity. Laurence Kotlikoff outlines problems with using spending targets in retirement planning. Moshe Milevsky and Chris Robinson derive a simple model to estimate sustainable spending rates without resorting to Monte Carlo analysis. Finally, Michael Stutzer develops an asset allocation model that reconciles expected utility maximization models with shortfall probability minimization models.

The second part addresses issues confronting high-net-worth investors. In the chapter "Investment Management for Taxable Private Investors," Jarrod Wilcox, CFA; Jeffrey Horvitz; and Dan diBartolomeo develop a holistic framework that avoids many criticisms of modern portfolio theory while using computational techniques that investment professionals are familiar with. They pay particular attention to tax-efficient asset allocation and portfolio management techniques, such as tax-loss harvesting and concentrated stock management. They also develop a framework for implementation that allows the wealth management firm to address the problem of providing customized solutions to a heterogeneous clientele.

Robert Gordon, Jeffrey Horvitz, Scott Welch, Andrew Berkin, and Jia Ye develop the themes of tax-loss harvesting and managing low-basis stock positions further. Clifford Quisenberry, CFA, illustrates how some of these concepts manifest themselves in a core/satellite investment strategy, and Martin Leibowitz illustrates how taxes interact with inflation to increase the after-tax equity risk premium for taxable investors.

Part III develops an analytical framework and rules of thumb for the ubiquitous investor facing decisions involving tax-advantaged savings accounts, such as 401(k) plans and Roth IRAs. The model developed by Stephen Horan, CFA, in the chapter "Tax-Advantaged Savings Accounts and Tax-Efficient Wealth Accumulation" is applied to a wide range of decisions, such as choosing between different types of plans, Roth IRA conversions, asset location, and tax-efficient withdrawal strategies for investors facing progressive tax rates on taxable withdrawals. William Reichenstein, CFA, extends these concepts into an asset allocation setting.

Because investors can use only their after-tax wealth to fulfill their spending, dynastic, and philanthropic goals, performance evaluation tools that measure growth in after-tax wealth are important. In the final part, James Poterba and Lee Price, CFA, describe the issues and challenges involved in estimating after-tax performance and propose methodologies. James Peterson; Paul Pietranico, CFA; Mark Riepe, CFA; and Fran Xu, CFA; identify mutual fund characteristics that drive a fund's tax drag, including portfolio risk, investment style, and recent net redemptions.

We are thrilled to present this resource to the wealth management community and hope it serves as the foundation for future innovation in financial products and analytical frameworks that address the needs of the growing population of individual investors.

Stephen M. Horan, CFA
Zvi Bodie

PART I

LIFE-CYCLE INVESTING

CHAPTER 1

THE FUTURE OF RETIREMENT PLANNING

Robert C. Merton

The next generation of retirement products will provide the user-friendliness and simplicity of defined-benefit plans, but they will come in the form of increasingly sophisticated defined-contribution plans. The tools and technology needed to design such products are available in the marketplace and need only be adapted to retirement applications.

With the move to defined-contribution plans, we, the financial services industry, are asking individuals to make complex financial management decisions that they have not had to make in the past and that, for the most part, they are not adequately prepared to make. In addition, I believe we are presenting these decisions in formats that make them difficult for individuals—even those who are generally well educated—to resolve.

I will begin this presentation with a few remarks about defined-benefit retirement plans, particularly how they went wrong and what we can learn from their flaws. I will then discuss defined-contribution plans, which have become the *de facto* alternative to defined-benefit plans. Unfortunately, traditional defined-contribution plans have a number of features that prevent them from being the long-term answer for employer-sponsored retirement plans. Thus, I will discuss a next-generation solution deriving from defined-contribution plans. Finally, I will discuss financial management technology and the tools available today that can be used to address and help solve the shortcomings of current retirement products.

DEFINED-BENEFIT RETIREMENT PLANS

Most expert observers agree that corporate defined-benefit (DB) plans are on their way out. The trend in that direction was emphasized in particular when IBM announced in early 2006 that it intended to close its defined-benefit plan to both existing and new employees. IBM is

Reprinted from *The Future of Life-Cycle Saving and Investing*, The Research Foundation of CFA Institute (October 2007):5–18.

an employee-centric, financially strong company with an overfunded DB plan, and yet the DB plan is being shut down. Some observers say that defined-benefit plans have become too expensive for the corporations to maintain; others say they are too risky. I think the simplest explanation for what happened to defined-benefit plans is that they were mispriced, not three or five years ago but from the outset.

For example, assume that the liabilities in a defined-benefit pension plan have the equivalent duration of 10 years and a risk-free rate of 5 percent. Assume, too, that the plan used a blended expected return on the asset portfolio of 9 percent, not risk adjusted (with assets including risky securities). If liabilities that should have been discounted at 5 percent with a 10-year life span are instead discounted at 9 percent, the result is two-thirds of the present value. Thus, for every $1.00 of cost a corporation is expecting from a plan, the cost is actually $1.50.

If a corporation is negotiating with its employees and it offers what it mistakenly believes is $1.00 of benefits that are really worth $1.50, then employees are likely to choose the benefits offered over cash, even if they do not know the actual value of the benefits. As an analogy, consider a corporate automobile perk that allows employees to choose either a Toyota Camry or a Bentley. Which will they choose? Will the outcome be random? I do not think so. Even if they have no idea of the actual cost of each, most people are likely to pick the $300,000 Bentley over a $30,000 Camry, and just so with generous benefits versus cash compensation.

From the very beginning, providers and sponsors should have recognized that the accounting treatment of these plans was systematically underpricing the cost of benefits. Because of this underpricing, I can say with confidence that we will not go through a cycle that brings us back to defined-benefit plans, at least not to plans with such a pricing structure. Defined-benefit plans have some admirable features, and they may be used again, but we will not return to them with these benefits at this price.

Although defined-benefit plans have been underpriced from the beginning, the reason they are being shut down now rather than 10 years ago is path dependent. During the 1990s, the stock market was up 9 out of 10 years. Therefore, funding for such underpriced plans appeared not to be an issue. But the 2000–02 market crash combined with globally falling interest rates changed that unrealistic outlook, which is why the plans are being reconsidered now.

DEFINED-CONTRIBUTION RETIREMENT PLANS

The use of defined-contribution plans has become the default strategy following the decline in defined-benefit plans. Although defined-contribution plans solve the problem for the plan sponsor by (1) making costs predictable and (2) taking risk off the balance sheet, they place a tremendous burden of complex decision making on the user.

For example, assume the objective function is that employees hope to maintain the same standard of living in their retirement that they enjoyed in the latter part of their work lives. If that is the goal, then a defined-benefit type of payout is quite attractive. In a defined-contribution scenario, however, a 45-year-old will have contributions coming in for 20 years or more and a 35-year-old for 30 years prior to retirement, and each will need to decide the size of these contributions, as well as the types of investments to make with these funds, in order ultimately to provide the required standard of living at the age of 65.

Finding and executing a dynamic portfolio strategy to achieve such a goal is an extremely complex problem to solve, even for the best financial minds. Yet, through the use of defined-contribution plans, the financial services industry is, in effect, asking employees of all sorts—from brain surgeons, to teachers, to assembly line workers—to solve just such a problem. The situation is not unlike that of being a surgical patient who, while being wheeled into the operating room, has the surgeon lean down and say, "I can use anywhere from 7 to 17 sutures to close you up. Tell me whatever number you think is best, and that is what I will do." Not only is that a frightening decision for a patient to be faced with, but it is one that most patients are, at best, poorly qualified to make.

The Next Generation of Retirement Planning

Let me turn to what I think might be a good next generation for defined-contribution plans. If we accept that one of the prospects that most frightens individuals is the possibility of outliving their assets, then the objective function of establishing a standard of living in retirement that approximates the standard of living individuals enjoyed in the latter part of their careers is an appropriate one. Furthermore, if we consider the behavior of most participants in defined-contribution plans, we realize that most people do not enjoy financial planning. After all, most participants do not change their contribution allocations after first establishing them. Therefore, considering individuals' fear of outliving assets and their disinclination to do financial planning, how should the next generation of plans be designed?

First, if the objective function is an appropriate standard of living in retirement, then the plan should be a system that integrates health care, housing, and inflation-protected annuities for general consumption. Health and housing are substantial factors in the retiree's standard of living that are not well tracked by the U.S. Consumer Price Index or by any other simple inflation index and should be treated as separate components in providing for an overall standard of living. Furthermore, in order to receive a real annuity at the time of retirement, individuals must expect to pay real prices. Thus, during the accumulation period, real mark-to-market prices should be used. But where do we find such mark-to-market prices? Well, we can approximate them. Insurers, in particular, have the expertise to develop them. What I suggest is that, rather than establishing arbitrary interest rates for the long run, plan developers should use actual market prices derived from actual annuities and mortality experience and mark them to market with respect to real interest rates and not to arbitrary projections. For example, if a plan is based on a 4 percent interest rate and the actual rate turns out to be 2 percent, then the retirees will not have the amount of money they had counted on.

In addition, plans need to be portable. They need to be protected against all credit risks, or at least against the credit risk of the employer. Plans also need a certain degree of robustness, and that robustness must be appropriate to the people who use them. Consider another analogy. If I am designing a Formula 1 race car, I can assume that it will be driven by a trained and experienced Formula 1 driver, so I can build in a high degree of precision because I know the car will not be misused in any way. But if I am designing a car that the rest of us drive every day, I have to be more concerned about robustness than a sophisticated level of precision. When designing a car for the rest of us, I have to assume that the owner will sometimes forget to change the oil or will sometimes bang the tires into the curb. I have to assume that it will be misused to some degree, so its design must be robust enough to withstand less than optimal behavior and yet still provide the intended outcomes. In applying this analogy to financial plan design, one probably should not assume that users will revise their savings rates in the optimal or recommended fashion.

Qualities of Plan Design: Simplicity and Constancy

What I have in mind is a defined-contribution plan that satisfies the goals of employers while also providing the outcomes of defined-benefit plans, which do such a good job of meeting the needs of retirees. Users should be given choices, but the choices should be ones that are meaningful to them, not the choices that are typically given today, such as what mixture of equities and debt to include in a portfolio. I do not think such choices are helpful for most people.

To use the automobile analogy again, we should be designing plans that let people make their decisions based on a car's miles per gallon, a factor that makes sense to them, rather than an engine's compression ratio, which is a degree of information that most people cannot use effectively. We need to design products that are based on questions that most people find reasonable, such as the following: What standard of living do you desire to have? What standard of living are you willing to accept? What contribution or savings rate are you willing or able to make? Such questions embed the trade-off between consumption during work life and consumption in retirement, and they make more sense to people than questions about asset allocation—or compression ratios.

Besides creating a simple design with only a handful of choices—but choices that are relevant—we need a design that does not change, at least in the way that users interact with it. An unchanging design leads to tools that people will be more likely to learn and use. In fact, a design that is unchanging is almost as important as a design that is simple.

For example, I have been driving for almost 50 years, and during that time the steering wheel in cars has not changed, even though automobile designers could have replaced steering wheels with joysticks. They have been careful to keep the car familiar so that users like me do not have to relearn how to drive each time we buy a new car.

The design of the accelerator is also emblematic of this constancy in design. Depressing and releasing the accelerator requires the same action and provides the same tactile experience that it did 50 years ago. But the technology triggered by the accelerator is entirely different today. Fifty years ago when a driver pressed on the accelerator, that action actually forced metal rods up to the carburetor, opening up passages to allow air and gas to mix and combust and thus send more energy through the engine. Today, the tactile experience is the same for the driver, but the accelerator is not moving metal rods. The processes activated by the accelerator are now electronic. And yet, automobile manufacturers have spent large sums of money making that accelerator feel the same as it did 50 years ago.

The lesson to be learned is that something simple and consistent is easier for people to learn and remember than something complicated and changing. The goal is to be innovative without disturbing the user's experience because planning for retirement is a complicated matter that should not be made more difficult by providing tools that are difficult to use.

Let me return to my automobile analogy. Driving a car is a complex problem. If I wrote down all the information needed to operate a car so that a driver could go from the financial district in Boston to Logan International Airport, I would have a tome full of instructions. It would have to explain the use of the wheel, the gearshift, the accelerator, the brakes, the mirrors, the turn signals, and more. Just getting the car in motion and onto a busy thoroughfare is

3 1833 05764 0515

a complicated coordination problem. Getting to the airport is another level of complexity alto-gether. And the journey itself is filled with uncertainties. The driver must be alert at all times because, for example, a pedestrian may try to cross the street against the light or a portion of the route may be closed for repairs, and the driver must be prepared to react to each of these uncertainties.

The trip to the airport is difficult enough as it is, but what if the driver is told at the beginning of the drive to the airport, "You must aim the car in the right direction at the start of your trip. After that, you cannot turn the wheel." Knowing the complexities involved in the trip ahead, such constraints make it almost inconceivable that the driver will reach the destination in a satisfactory manner. And yet, most of the models that are used to develop defined-contribution plans implicitly assume that numerous decisions are fixed. That is not an optimal design at all.

We must, therefore, design a system that is user friendly, one that people, given time, can become familiar with and thus willing to use—a system in which the designers do the heavy lifting so that users need only make lifestyle decisions that they understand and that the system then translates into the investment actions needed to achieve the users' goals. The optimal strategies of the system should guide users to arrive at their target retirement goals smoothly. The system will maximize the prospects of achieving a desired standard of living subject to a risk constraint of a minimum life income amount in retirement, but optimiza-tion is not simply about ensuring a desired level of retirement income but also about the effi-ciency or effectiveness in achieving that goal. Just as it is possible to save too little for retirement, it is also possible to save too much and face the regret of forgone consumption opportunities during the many years *before* retirement. Despite these complexities, I am opti-mistic that such systems are doable, not with futuristic tools but with technology and tools that are available today.

How do I think this next generation of defined-contribution plans will be devel-oped? For one thing, I foresee them developing as corporate plans through plan sponsors because, although the defined-benefit plans are a legacy, I believe employers will con-tinue to provide retirement assistance in some manner, whether that assistance comes in the form of a 403(b) or a 401(k). One important role employers can play is that of gatekeepers.

Despite the doubts that are sometimes expressed by employees about their employers, when it comes to retirement planning and life-cycle products, people tend to trust their employers far more than they do third-party financial service providers. And employers, despite the criticism sometimes aimed at them, generally want the best for their employees. So, employers can perform a crucial function as reliable gatekeepers when it comes to provid-ing retirement products for their employees.

TECHNOLOGY AND TOOLS FOR CREATING PRODUCTS

The paradox of the type of system I have just described is that the simpler and easier it is for retirees to use, the more complex it is for its producer. The dynamic trading and risk assess-ment needed for the next-generation plan require sophisticated models, tools, and trading capability, none of which needs to be explained to the individual.

Interestingly, the mean–variance portfolio model is still the core of most professional investment management models, even for sophisticated institutions. Certainly, it has been updated since its first use in the 1950s, but it is a tribute to Harry Markowitz and William Sharpe that it is still at the core of thinking about risk and return in practice. But to design the next generation of retirement products, designers must consider explicitly some of the other dimensions of risk.

Human Capital

The first dimension is human capital, and the response to include it may seem obvious. But it becomes less obvious how it should be done the more closely it is observed. For example, assume that a university professor and a stockbroker have the same present value of their human capital and the same financial capital. Their risk tolerance is also the same. When deciding which of the two should hold more stocks in their portfolio, most people intuitively respond that the stockbroker should. After all, stockbrokers typically know a lot more about stocks than professors do. But if we consider their situations more closely, we realize that the stockbroker's human capital is far more sensitive to the stock market than the professor's. Therefore, to achieve the same total wealth risk position, the stockbroker should actually put less of his or her financial wealth into stocks. Most models today take into account the value of human capital, but few consider the risk of human capital or how human capital is related to other assets, and that situation needs to change.

Wealth vs. Sustainable Income Flows

The second dimension that needs to be considered is the use of wealth as a measure of economic welfare. To illustrate, consider two alternative environments faced by the individual: One has assets worth $10 million; the other has assets worth $5 million. The environment with $10 million can earn an annual riskless real rate of 1 percent; the one with $5 million can earn an annual riskless real rate of 10 percent. Which environment is preferable? Of course, if all wealth is to be consumed immediately, the $10 million alternative is obviously better. At the other extreme, suppose the plan is to consume the same amount in perpetuity. A few simple calculations reveal that the $5 million portfolio will produce a perpetual annual real income of $500,000 and that the $10 million portfolio will produce only $100,000. So, with that time horizon for consumption, the $5 million environment is equally obviously preferable. The "crossover" time horizon for preference between the two is at about 10 years. Thus, we see that wealth alone is not sufficient to measure economic welfare.

How many advice engines, even sophisticated ones, take this changing investment-opportunity environment dimension into account? Many such engines quote an annuity (i.e., an income amount) as an end goal, but in doing so, they take an estimated wealth amount and simply apply the annuity formula with a fixed interest rate to it, as if there were no uncertainty about future interest rates. In other words, they do not distinguish between standard of living and wealth as the objective. Sustainable income flow, not the stock of wealth, is the objective that counts for retirement planning.

Imagine a 45-year-old who is thinking in terms of a deferred lifetime annuity that starts at age 65. The safe, risk-free asset in terms of the objective function is an inflation-protected lifetime annuity that starts payouts in 20 years. If interest rates move a little bit, what happens to the value of that deferred real annuity? It changes a lot. If I report the risk-free asset the way typical 401(k) accounts are reported—namely, as current wealth—the variation reported in wealth every month will be tremendous. But if I report it in annuity (or lifetime income) units, it is stable as a rock.

Peru has developed a Chilean-type pension system. A large percentage of the assets—between 40 and 60 percent—are held in one-year (or less) Peruvian debt, with limited international investment. Such a structure does not make much sense for a pension plan. For one, the duration of the bonds should be considerably longer. But every month, the balance is reported on a mark-to-market basis to all plan participants. Imagine the communication challenge of investing in a bond with a 40-year duration, instead, and reporting the resulting enormously volatile monthly balance and explaining why it is actually risk free.

How plans are framed and how their values are reported (wealth versus annuity income units) is thus not trivial. The proper unit of account selected is essential for conveying what is risky and what is not.

Prepackaged Liquidity

Derivative securities can be designed to replicate the payoffs from dynamic trading strategies in a retirement plan. This is done by, in effect, running the Black–Scholes derivation of option pricing "backwards." Thus, instead of finding a dynamic trading strategy to replicate the payout of a derivative, the financial services firm creates a derivative that replicates the dynamic strategy desired and then issues that derivative as a prepaid liquidity and execution contract for implementing the strategy. As an example, the dynamic trading strategy for which such prepackaged trading liquidity can be created might be a systematic plan for changing the balance between equity and debt holdings in a prescribed way over time.

Housing Risk

Housing and housing risk are another important dimension, and reverse mortgages are entirely pertinent to this topic. If one is trying to lock in a standard of living for life, owning the house he or she lives in is the perfect hedge. In implementing this aspect of the retirement solution, a reverse mortgage provides an importantly useful tool. A reverse mortgage works within the U.S. tax code to strip out that part of the value of a house not needed for retirement-housing consumption without putting the user at any leveraged risk with respect to the consumption of that house. It is a practical way to decompose a complex asset and use the value to enhance one's standard of living in retirement. It can also be a far more efficient way of creating a bequest than holding onto a house and leaving it to heirs. After all, one does not have to be an expert to know that it is probably far from optimal bequest policy, from the point of view of the heirs' utility, to receive the value of the house as a legacy at some uncertain time in the future—perhaps next year, perhaps in 30 years. I am hopeful that this market will continue to grow rapidly in size and efficiency.

Behavioral Finance and Regret Insurance

For those who believe in its findings, behavioral finance also belongs in the design of life-cycle products. As an example, consider loss aversion, or fear of regret: It appears that loss aversion dysfunctionally affects investors' choices. It inhibits them from doing what is in their best interests. How might we mitigate this problem? Is it possible to create a new financial product, called "regret insurance"? If such a thing is possible, what would it look like?

Consider the following scenario. Assume that a person is broadly invested in the stock market but, for some rational reason, decides to sell. The investor, however, fears that immediately after she sells, the market values will rise. She is frozen by her fear of regret, the regret of selling too low and missing an opportunity to enhance her assets. Fortunately, she can mitigate this situation by purchasing regret insurance. In this case, she buys a policy that guarantees the sale of her stock portfolio at its highest price during the following two years. After two years pass, the investor and the insurer will examine the daily closing price for the portfolio, and the insurer will buy the portfolio for its highest daily closing price during the two years. For the cost of a set premium, the investor is guaranteed an absolute high and is thereby freed of uncertainty and the likelihood of regret.

Such insurance can work for buyers as well as sellers. Suppose an investor wants to buy into the stock market, but he fears that prices will fall after the purchase and he will miss out on better prices. To mitigate his regret, he purchases an insurance policy that allows him to buy the market at the lowest price recorded during the previous two years.

Some people might say that this idea of regret insurance sounds too complicated to produce. How, they might ask, would an insurer determine the risk and then establish a reasonable price? I would submit that such products are already being used in the form of lookback options, which provide exactly the kind of insurance just described. In the exotic options industry, which is quite large, lookback options are frequently issued, which illustrates my general point that the technology and the mathematical tools are already in place to develop the next generation of retirement products. The learning-curve experiences of nearly three decades of trading, creating, pricing, and hedging these types of securities are in place for someone entering the retirement solutions business. It is simply a matter of using market-proven technology in a way that it is not now being used.

CONCLUDING ILLUSTRATION

One can see from the previous hypothetical example how the identified dysfunctional financial behavior induced by behavioral regret might be offset by the introduction of a well-designed financial product (regret insurance). And if successful, the impact of that cognitive dysfunction on an individual's financial behavior and on equilibrium asset prices can be offset. Note that this change occurs not because of "corrective" education or other means of modifying the individual's internal behavioral makeup but, instead, because an external means is introduced that causes the "net" behavior of the individual to be "as if" such a correction had taken place.

I want to close with a personal, real-world example that illustrates the same dynamics of interplay between the cognitive dissonance of the individual and the corrective effect of the creation and implementation of a financial product or service designed to offset the distortions in financial behavior that would otherwise be obtained, in this case with respect to efficient refinancing of housing mortgages, instead of regret.

In 1999, I took out a mortgage on my apartment, although I do not remember what the interest rate was. Three years later, the same broker who handled my mortgage called me and offered to reduce my mortgage payments by $400 a month. The offer sounded too good to be true, so I asked what the closing costs would be. He replied that the lender would cover all the closing costs. I then surmised that there must be an embedded option to refinance in my mortgage and that now the lender was trying to get that option out of the mortgage by its generous refinance offer. But the broker assured me that the new mortgage would give me the identical right to refinance whenever I wanted. Furthermore, the lender was not extending the payment period, and all the other terms of the old mortgage would remain intact, except that I would now be paying $400 less per month. Even though the deal sounded too good to be true, he convinced me that it was on the level, so I agreed to the refinancing. He came to my office, we signed and he notarized the contract (without my attorney being involved), and the deal has been just as beneficial as he had said.

My guess is that the broker had been given incentives to monitor mortgages like mine for possible refinancing because if he did not get to me, a competitor would. Better to cannibalize your own business by pursuing refinancing than to have the business taken away altogether. Furthermore, my mortgage was probably sold into the capital markets, so his employer, as the originator, would not lose. Certainly, this supposition does not go counter to the way the world works, and thus I ended up being a beneficiary of the competition of the system.

The point of my story is that I turned out to be an excellent illustration of behavioral finance in action. After all, how can someone who does not know the interest rate on his mortgage determine whether he should optimally refinance it? But because of the way the market has developed, the same company that gave me the mortgage gave me a better deal at no cost. I thus ended up behaving like Rational Man in refinancing my mortgage but not because I became "educated" about optimal refinancing models (which I already knew), learned what my interest rate was (which I still do not know), and then optimally exercised. Instead, innovation of financial services together with technology for low transaction costs and market competition allowed me to act "as if" I had. In the process, capital market prices for mortgages were being driven closer to those predicted by the efficient market hypothesis of neoclassical finance. The next generation of retirement products will surely be designed to accommodate and offset such typically suboptimal human behavior.

QUESTION AND ANSWER SESSION

Question: How do you see us moving from defined-benefit plans to something more sophisticated than today's simple defined-contribution plans?

Merton: Most companies want to provide good benefits for their employees. After all, providing efficient benefits is an effective way to pay people, besides its reflecting on a company's reputation. The compensation system of the company is a key strategic issue, and benefits are becoming an ever-larger element of compensation.

That is why such decisions are moving from the CFO to the CEO. They are strategic, and they have considerable implications for the success of the company. Furthermore, companies do not want "smoke and mirrors" for solutions. They do not want to be told that a plan solution will take care of retirement by earning equity market returns virtually risk free, at least over the long run, or by beating the market itself by 1, 2, or 5 percentage points. There are no simple-fix "free-lunch" solutions. That is how we got into trouble with the defined-benefit plans.

Employees, too, need to be told to adjust their expectations. Get used to driving a Camry, not a Bentley, or be prepared to spend $300,000 to get the Bentley instead of $30,000 for the Camry. Contribution rates will be whatever is required to achieve goals, and individuals will have to make choices—for example, accept lower wages and higher contribution rates or plan to pay supplemental amounts for additional retirement benefits. They should also expect to make some substitution between the level of retirement consumption and consumption in their working years.

Question: You mentioned that mean–variance is still the norm for modeling, yet the new products you describe have returns that are not normally distributed. Do you believe that many future financing concerns will be addressed by these complex, nonnormally distributed products?

Merton: Yes. But individuals do not need to be aware of this sea change. Individuals do not have to understand the nonlinearities and complexities of option investment strategies or regret insurance. All they are doing is buying a contract that allows them to achieve their targeted replacement of income.

Like the driver of an automobile, individuals do not have to know how the product works. But someone has to know because someone has to be a gatekeeper. Such products cannot be black boxes into which money is poured. But the surgeon, the teacher, and the assembly line worker will not be doing the due diligence. If the plan sponsor is not the one to look under the hood and find out how a product works and decide that it is legitimate, then some other similar mechanism must be established.

Mean–variance portfolio theory is, as I said, at the core of what's done with asset management for personal finance, asset allocation, mutual funds, and so forth. But the technology to do risk assessment, valuation, and the dynamic strategies I have alluded to, including trying to replicate a 20-year deferred real annuity that is not publicly traded, is market-proven technology that is used every day by Wall Street firms, fixed-income trading desks, capital markets groups, hedge funds, and so forth. Such financial technology is not something that I have plucked off a professor's idea list. It is in use, and more of it is being created all the time. What I am talking about is a new application of market-proven technologies, and that is why I am confident that the products that I have mentioned are implementable. To be truly an effective solution, the design of such systems, however, must be scalable and cost-effective.

Question: Are you proposing that this new generation of individual retirement investors do not need to understand the risks involved in their plans?

Merton: I am not opposed to people being informed about the investments in their plans, but I think they ought to be informed about things that are useful to them. Disclosing the details of financial technology to nonprofessionals is unlikely to make them any better prepared. What they need to know is that gatekeepers have been established to assure the quality of a plan's design.

Question: So, you believe a gatekeeper has to be established? In the defined-benefit scenario, corporations did not play that role.

Merton: Plan sponsors did play that role in defined-benefit plans, although not always well. They are still playing that role, and I think they view themselves as such. I do not think they are walking away and closing their defined-benefit plans and telling their employees to go open an IRA.

Corporations have a certain fiduciary duty. Any company that creates a 401(k) plan needs to assure that it is not bogus. If it is, the company is responsible. The company does not guarantee returns, but it must perform due diligence to assure that the plan is sound. One of the strengths of a defined-benefit plan is that it is managed in-house, and the company is responsible for the payouts promised. Defined-contribution plans are outsourced, so plan sponsors have to be more diligent. The one thing I know that does not work is to send surgeons, teachers, and assembly line workers back to school to teach them about duration, delta hedging, and other financial technical details so that they can have a retirement account. Someone else has to take that role. The plan sponsor is probably the natural gatekeeper.

Question: If we need some instruments that are currently not traded, is there a role for government to issue, for example, longevity bonds, so we can derive more information on that type of instrument?

Merton: Absolutely. The creation of TIPS (Treasury Inflation-Protected Securities) and their equivalents was an enormous event, especially for those of us who lived through the big inflation problems with retirement accounts in the late 1970s and early 1980s. As far as I know, only one company—I think it was Aetna working with the Ford Motor Company pension program—wrote an index instrument back then, but it capped the protection at a specific level. Having government-sponsored TIPS and the inflation swap markets that have developed around them means that there will be a lot of ways to develop underlying instruments. Government can play a role.

Certainly, it would be delightful if we had some way of trading longevity efficiently and observing the pricing functions for it. We are not yet there. Still, given the existing environment, I think it is better to use the best estimates from the markets on the cost of longevity risk. In the case of inflation indexing, even though long-dated deferred annuities are not, as far as I know, available at any kind of reasonable prices, one can use well-known dynamic strategies to approximate the returns to such annuities. Such strategies are used all the time in capital market transactions and are done on the other side of these swap transactions to come close to replicating that.

But even if our level of precision for such replications were eight digits, if much of the actual data for other elements of the retirement solution are accurate only to one digit, we do not accomplish a lot by imposing that extra precision. If we get one piece of this problem to a rather precise point, then we know at least one of the elephants in the parlor. For example, in the early phase of retirement accumulation, people do not know what their income will be during the next 30 or so years before they retire. They do not know whether they will be married or divorced. They do not know how many children they will have. They do not know how the tax code will change. We all deal with a host of uncertainties. The idea that we should spend enormous resources making precise one dimension out of all those uncertainties is neither efficient nor cost-effective.

People do, however, need greater precision as they approach retirement because that is when they know much more accurately what they need. They know their income, their marital status, their dependent status. That is also when lifetime annuities become available. Could annuities be more efficient in design and price? No question about it. But they are available, and both design and cost will improve considerably.

Consider another analogy. If you intend to sail from Southampton, United Kingdom, to New York City, you want to aim the boat so that you are not going to Miami, but you do not need a lot of precision at the outset because you can tack as needed to keep a reasonable course. But as you approach New York Harbor, you do not want to be off even by 50 yards. The same concept applies with life-cycle products. A lot of things happen to people during the 30 years leading up to retirement—many more than they, or we, can predict in advance. What individuals need is a mechanism that allows their retirement planning to adjust to all of these uncertainties as they impinge on them. With the right mechanism, they can adjust their retirement planning and make it more precise as they approach their destination so that, at the end, they can have a lifetime, guaranteed annuity in the amount needed to sustain their lifestyle in retirement.

Now, the guarantee may be, in effect, that of a AA insurance company rather than that of a AAA company. But the guarantee of a AA insurance company is almost always good enough. I am proposing a model that is different from one in which an individual approaches retirement and purchases a variable annuity about which the insurer says, "If the stock market earns 4 percent a year over the Treasury bond yield for the next 15 years, you will be in fat city." Market risks are a far bigger factor than AA credit risk.

If a stronger guarantee is worth it, institutions may effectively collateralize it. I see such immunization occurring in the United Kingdom, and it may be headed to the United States. Perhaps we will have longevity bonds that are used to immunize against systematic longevity risks. If there is enough worry about the credit of an insurance company, then the annuity need not be run from the general account. The insurer can create SPVs (special-purpose vehicles) in which it can fund the annuities with the right-duration real bonds or with longevity bonds, if those appear.

Although retirement planning today presents a big, challenging problem, it also offers big opportunities. I am excited and optimistic about the prospects ahead. A lot of financial technology exists to help us address the problem.

REFERENCES

Merton, Robert C. 2003. "Thoughts on the Future: Theory and Practice in Investment Management." *Financial Analysts Journal*, vol. 59, no. 1 (January/February):17–23.

———— 2006. "Allocating Shareholder Capital to Pension Plans." *Journal of Applied Corporate Finance*, vol. 18, no. 1 (Winter):15–24.

———— 2006. "Observations on Innovation in Pension Fund Management in the Impending Future." *PREA Quarterly* (Winter):61–67.

Merton, Robert C., and Zvi Bodie. 2005. "The Design of Financial Systems: Towards a Synthesis of Function and Structure." *Journal of Investment Management*, vol. 3, no. 1 (First Quarter):1–23.

CHAPTER 2

IS PERSONAL FINANCE
A SCIENCE?

Paul A. Samuelson

Personal finance is an inexact science. For example, life-cycle retirement mutual funds are based on the unproven belief that long-horizon investments represent less risk than do short-horizon investments. And although a single, enormous, public Social Security index fund diversified among domestic and foreign stocks and bonds will produce better retirement savings for the majority of people than will private accounts, such a fund would put numerous people out of jobs. Fortunately, some advancements have been made in recent years.

My assigned presentation title is ill expressed. Its wording might seem to be asking, "Is personal finance an *exact* science?" And, of course, the answer to that is a flat no. If this disappoints anyone in the audience, now is a good moment to rectify your miscalculation by leaving.

What I do hope to address is what kind of inexact science personal finance is. Actually, the earliest political economy—in Aristotle or even the Holy Scriptures—began as the management of the household. You cannot be more low-down personal than that.

My Harvard mentor Joseph Schumpeter, in a crescendo of brainstorming, went so far as to claim that solving the numerical problems of economics—one pig for three hens rather than two or four—was the effective Darwinian evolutionary selection force that made humans become human. Descartes opined, "I think; therefore, I am." Schumpeter out-opined Descartes by asserting, "Because we humanoid primates had to struggle with personal finance, we became human."

In our introductory economics textbooks, Robinson Crusoe always played a starring role—and rightly so. Some 10,000 years ago, agriculture broadly defined was the only existent industry. Each farm and hunting family had little reason to trade with their 20–50 known neighbors—neighbors who were virtual clones of themselves.

Reprinted from *The Future of Life-Cycle Saving and Investing*, The Research Foundation of CFA Institute (October 2007):1–4.

I do not jest. As recently as around 1970, one of my innumerable sons spent his summer away from Milton Academy with his "new" temporary mother on a farm in lower Austria. That is a region where no marriage took place before the female candidate proved her fertility by becoming pregnant. Virtually all that the family consumed was grown on their peasant farm. Slaughtering the hog was the big event of the summer—pure personal finance once again.

But alas, devil nicotine ended that bucolic scenario of self-sufficiency. My son's "new" brother became hooked on cigarette smoking. This requires cash. And to get cash, you must shift to some cash crop for the first time. That is how and why personal finance became perforce *market oriented* as it is today almost everywhere.

I spoke of elementary textbooks. My McGraw-Hill bestseller, *Economics: An Introductory Analysis*, came out back in 1948.[1] For the 50-year celebration of it, I had to reread this brainchild. What I discovered was that, apparently, mine was the first primer ever to devote a full chapter to personal finance—including Series E savings bonds, diversified mutual funds, and how much more income sons-in-law earned who were doctors and lawyers as compared with clergymen, dishwashers, cabdrivers, or stenographers. Fifty years later, I was pleasantly surprised to reread much in the new facsimile edition of that 1948 original, like the following words:

> Of course America's post-1935 social security system, which was formulated in depression times to intentionally discourage saving and to coax into retirement job-hoggers, will have to be abandoned in the future as a pay-as-you-go non-actuarial financial system. Such systems begin with seductively favorable pension rates that are transitional only, and must mandate stiffer contributions in future stationary or declining demographic states.

This was apparently one of my first initiations into overlapping-generation economics. You might say that in my small way, I was then being John the Baptist to latter-day Larry Kotlikoff, who is known deservedly around Central Square as "Mr. Generational Accounting."

Life-cycle finance à la Franco Modigliani recognizes that as mammals, we all do begin with a free lunch. As mortals, we are all going to die. But prior to that event, with few exceptions, we will need to be supported in retirement years by personal finance. And as we used to think before Reagan and the two Bushes, old-age pensions might come partly out of Social Security *public* finance.

My brief words here will focus on personal life-cycle finance. That is a domain full of, shucks, ordinary common sense. Alas, *common* sense is not the same thing as *good* sense. Good sense in these esoteric puzzles is hard to come by.

Here is a recent example. Life-cycle retirement mutual funds are a current rage. Fund A is for the youngster in this audience who will be retiring in 2042; Fund B is for 2015 retirees. Funds A and B both might begin with, say, 65 percent in risky stocks and 35 percent in allegedly safer bonds. But even without anyone having to make a phone call, Fund B will move earlier than Fund A to pare down on risky stocks and goose up exposure to safe bonds.

The logic for this is simple—as simple as that $2 + 2 = 4$ and that the next 9 years is a shorter horizon period than the next 36 years. The law of averages, proven over and over in Las Vegas or even at the ballpark, allegedly tells us that riskiness for a pooled sample of, say, 36 items is only half what it is for a pooled sample of only 9 horizon items—the well-known $\sqrt{n}$ verity, or maybe *fallacy*.

Milton Friedman is assuredly no dummy. Just ask him. Maybe he would recall from his course in statistics that the ratio of $\sqrt{9}$ (i.e., 3) to $\sqrt{36}$ (i.e., 6) measures how less risky stocks are, in the sense that the long-horizon portfolio endures only half the stock riskiness of the short-horizon portfolio. Do not copy down my fuzzy arithmetic. It is only blue smoke, sound, and fury signifying nothing.

I have triplet sons. I will call them Tom, Dick, and Harry to protect their privacy. All three are risk-averse chips off the old block: Unless the mean gains of a portfolio exceed its mean losses, they will avoid such an investment. However, Tom is less paranoid than Dick, whereas Harry is even more risk averse than Dick. Nevertheless, all three will shun life-cycle funds. For each of their 25 years until retirement, each will hold constant the fractional weight of risky equities. Tom's constant is $\frac{3}{4}$; Dick's is $\frac{1}{2}$; suspicious Harry stands at only $\frac{1}{4}$.

How do I know that? Because in my family we eat our own cooking. I have written numerous learned papers denying that the correct law of large numbers vindicates the commonsense erroneous notions about risk erosion when investment horizons grow from 1 to 10 or from 100 to 10,000.

Mine has been the Lord's work. But it has brought me no second Nobel Prize—not even when I go on to write articles using only one-syllable words to rebut the many pure mathematicians who believe that all of us should seek only to maximize our portfolio's long-term growth rates.[2] Georges Clemenceau said that wars are too important to leave to generals. I say, applied math is too important to be left to pure math types!

I do not seem to have made many converts saved from error, however. I console myself by repeating over and over Mark Twain's wisdom: "You will never correct by *logic* a man's error if that error did not get into his mind by logic."

With Zvi Bodie on this program, I can hurry on to new personal finance topics. Housing will be one. Why housing in a personal finance seminar? I will leave it to Yale University's Bob Shiller or Wellesley College's Karl (Chip) Case, but not before articulating my 1958 point that, money aside, people's homes are an ideal contrivance for converting working-age savings into retirement-day dissaving.

President George W. Bush has advocated—so far unsuccessfully—that those of us covered by Social Security should be allowed to transfer into our own accounts our fair share of what has been paid into the public fund on our account. That way, the long-term sure-thing surplus yield of common stocks over bonds can be a wind at our back augmenting our golden years of retirement. Besides, as Libertarians say, "It's our money, not the government's."

Do not shoot the piano player—I am only quoting from White House handouts.

I am not a prophet. I cannot guarantee that, risk corrected, stocks will outperform bonds from 2006 to 2050. However, if the U.S. electorate wants to drink from that whiskey bottle and bet on that view, private accounts are not the efficient way to implement such a plan. Ask Massachusetts Institute of Technology's Peter Diamond for sermons on this topic.

A century of economic history about private and public financial markets strongly nominates that one huge public diversified indexed Social Security fund, using both stocks and bonds and both domestic and foreign holdings, will produce for the next generations better retirement pensions along with better sleep at night. One of its unique virtues is beneficial mutual insurance–reinsurance among adjacent generations.

Of course, this sensible—"good sense" sensible—proposal is too efficient ever to be adopted. To adopt it would free some millions of financial employees to transfer into useful plumbing, beer brewing, and barbering jobs.

Never forget the old saw, "Insurance is sold, not bought." The same goes for stocks, bonds, and lottery coupons. Borrowing from Abraham Lincoln, I can say that God must love those common folk that behavior scientist economists write about because She made so many of them.

Fortunately, there have been some good social inventions. If the poet Browning were to ask me, "Did you once see Shelley plain?" I would have to answer no. But I did see up close my Harvard graduate school buddy Bill Greenough. It was his Harvard PhD thesis that invented for TIAA-CREF the *variable lifetime annuity* invested efficiently in common stocks. And early on, I did write blurbs for Jack Bogle's successful launching of Vanguard's no-load rock-bottom fee S&P 500 Index stock mutual funds.

Along with the hero who invented the wheel and the heroes who discovered how to make cheese cheese and how to make cider hard cider, in my Valhalla of famous heroes, you will find the names of Greenough and Bogle.

My final words are cut short by this audience's well-fed drowsiness. I will leave as a question for later discussion: Will hedge funds make our golden years more golden, or will the new concoctions of option engineers, instead of reducing risks by spreading them optimally (in fact, by making possible about 100 to 1 over leveraging), result in microeconomic losses for pension funds and, maybe someday, even threaten the macro system with lethal financial implosions?

Good teachers always end their lectures with a question.

NOTES

1. Paul A. Samuelson, *Economics: An Introductory Analysis* (New York: McGraw-Hill Book Company, 1948).
2. Paul A. Samuelson, "Why We Should Not Make Mean Log of Wealth Big Though Years to Act Are Long," *Journal of Banking & Finance*, vol. 3, no. 4 (December 1979):305–307.

CHAPTER 3

LIFETIME FINANCIAL ADVICE: HUMAN CAPITAL, ASSET ALLOCATION, AND INSURANCE

Roger G. Ibbotson
Moshe A. Milevsky
Peng Chen, CFA
Kevin X. Zhu

In determining asset allocation, individuals must consider more than the risk–return trade-off of financial assets. They must take into account human capital and mortality risk in the earlier life-cycle stages and longevity risk in the later life-cycle stages. The authors show how to integrate these factors into individual investors' asset allocations through a systematic joint analysis of the life insurance a family needs to protect human capital and how to allocate the family's financial capital. The proposed life-cycle model then addresses the transition from the accumulation to the saving phases—in particular, the role (if any) of immediate payout annuities.

FOREWORD

Life-cycle finance is arguably the most important specialty in finance. At some level, all institutions exist to serve the individual. But investing directly by individuals, who reap the rewards of their successes and suffer the consequences of their mistakes, is becoming a

---

Reprinted from The Research Foundation of CFA Institute (April 2007).

dramatically larger feature of the investment landscape. In such circumstances, designing institutions and techniques that allow ordinary people to save enough money to someday retire—or to achieve other financial goals—is self-evidently a worthwhile effort, but until now, researchers have devoted too little attention to it.

The central problem of life-cycle finance is the spreading of the income from the economically productive part of an individual's life over that person's whole life. As with all financial problems, this task is made difficult by time and uncertainty. Merely setting aside a portion of one's income for later use does not mean that it will be there—in real (inflation-adjusted) terms—when it is needed. No investment is riskless if the "run" is long enough. In addition, there is the ordinary risk that the realized return will be lower than the expected return. Finally, no one knows how long he or she is going to live. The need to provide for oneself in old age—when the opportunity to earn labor income is vastly diminished—introduces a kind of uncertainty into life-cycle finance that is not present, or at least not as visible, in institutional investment settings.

The risk that one will outlive one's money is best referred to as "longevity risk." The traditional way that savers have managed this risk is by purchasing life annuities or by having annuitylike cash flow streams purchased for them through defined-benefit (DB) pension plans. (Social Security can also be understood, at least from the viewpoint of the recipient, as an inflation-indexed life annuity.) DB pension plans are declining in importance, however, and a great many workers do not have such a plan. Thus, individual saving and individual investing, including saving and investing through defined-contribution plans, are increasing in importance. For most workers, these efforts provide the only source of retirement income other than Social Security.

It makes sense that annuities would be widely used by workers as a way to replace the guaranteed lifetime income security that once was provided by pensions. But annuities are not as well understood, not as popular, and not as competitively priced, given the increased need for them, as one would hope.

Life insurance is, in a sense, the opposite of an annuity. The purchaser of an annuity bets that he or she will live a long time. The purchaser of life insurance bets that he or she will die soon. Both products have optionlike payoffs, the values of which are conditional on the actual longevity of the purchaser. Life insurance also is seldom used in financial planning, perhaps because, as with annuities, its option value is poorly understood. I do not mean that most people do not have some life insurance—they do. But like annuities, life insurance is not often well integrated into the financial planning process. Why not?

In *Lifetime Financial Advice: Human Capital, Asset Allocation, and Insurance*, four distinguished authors—Roger G. Ibbotson; Moshe A. Milevsky; Peng Chen, CFA; and Kevin X. Zhu—attempt to solve this puzzle. They note that the largest asset that most human beings have, at least when they are young, is their human capital—that is, the present value of their expected future labor income. Human capital interacts with traditional investments, such as stocks, bonds, and real estate, through the correlation structure. But human capital interacts in even more interesting and profitable ways with life insurance and annuities because these assets have payoffs linked to the holder's longevity. The authors of *Lifetime Financial Advice* present a framework for understanding and managing all of these assets holistically.

Ibbotson's earlier work (with numerous co-authors) has documented the past returns of the major asset classes, thus revealing the payoffs received for taking various types of risk, and has presented an approach to forecasting future asset class returns. The asset classes that Ibbotson and his associates are best known for studying are stocks, bonds, bills, and consumer goods (inflation). Knowledge of the past and expected returns of these asset classes, and knowledge of the degree by which realized returns might differ from expected returns, is what makes conventional asset allocation possible. But it is not the whole story. The present chapter finishes the story and makes scientific *financial planning*, which goes beyond conventional asset allocation, possible for individuals by adding in human capital and human capital–contingent assets (life insurance and annuities). With all these arrows in the quiver, an investment adviser can *guarantee* a target standard of living, rather than merely minimize the likelihood of falling below the target, which is all that can be accomplished with conventional asset allocation.

As the Baby Boomers begin to retire, their many trillions of dollars of savings and investments are shifting from accumulation to decumulation, making the ideas and techniques described in *Lifetime Financial Advice* timely and necessary. We hope and expect that researchers will continue to follow this path in the future by placing a much greater emphasis on life-cycle finance than in the past. We intend that upcoming Research Foundation chapters will reflect the heightened emphasis on life-cycle finance. The present chapter is an unusually complete and theoretically sound compendium of knowledge on this topic. We are exceptionally pleased to present it.

Laurence B. Siegel
Research Director
The Research Foundation of CFA Institute

INTRODUCTION

We can generally categorize a person's life into three financial stages. The first stage is the growing up and getting educated stage. The second stage is the working part of a person's life, and the final stage is retirement. This chapter focuses on the working and the retirement stages of a person's life because these are the two stages when an individual is part of the economy and an investor.

Even though this chapter is not really about the growing up and getting educated stage, this is a critical stage for everyone. The education and skills that we build over this first stage of our lives not only determine who we are but also provide us with a capacity to earn income or wages for the remainder of our lives. This earning power we call "human capital," and we define it as the present value of the anticipated earnings over one's remaining lifetime. The evidence is strong that the amount of education one receives is highly correlated with the present value of earning power. Education can be thought of as an investment in human capital.

One focus of this chapter is on how human capital interacts with financial capital. Understanding this interaction helps us to create, manage, protect, bequest, and especially, appropriately consume our financial resources over our lifetimes. In particular, we propose ways to optimally manage our stock, bond, and so on, asset allocations with various types of insurance products. Along the way, we provide models that potentially enable individuals to customize their financial decision making to their own special circumstances.

On the one hand, as we enter the earning stage of our lives, our human capital is often at its highest point. On the other hand, our financial wealth is usually at a low point. This is the time when we began to convert our human capital into financial capital by earning wages and saving some of these wages. Thus, we call this stage of our lives the "accumulation stage." As our lives progress, we gradually use up the earning power of our human capital, but ideally, we are continually saving some of these earnings and investing them in the financial markets. As our savings continue and we earn returns on our financial investments, our financial capital grows and becomes the dominant part of our total wealth.

As we enter the retirement stage of our lives, our human capital may be almost depleted. It may not be totally gone because we still may have Social Security and defined-benefit pension plans that provide yearly income for the rest of our lives, but our wage-earning power is now very small and does not usually represent the major part of our wealth. Most of us will have little human capital as we enter retirement but substantial financial capital. Over the course of our retirement, we will primarily consume from this financial capital, often bequeathing the remainder to our heirs.

Thus, our total wealth is made up of two parts: our human capital and our financial capital. Recognizing this simple dichotomy dramatically broadens how we analyze financial activities. We desire to create a diversified overall portfolio at the appropriate level of risk. Because human capital is usually relatively low risk (compared with common stocks), we generally want to have a substantial amount of equities in our financial portfolio early in our careers because financial wealth makes up so little of our total wealth (human capital plus financial capital).

Over our lifetimes, our mix of human capital and financial capital changes. In particular, financial capital becomes more dominant as we age so that the lower-risk human capital represents a smaller and smaller piece of the total. As this happens, we will want to be more conservative with our financial capital because it will represent most of our wealth.

Recognizing that human capital is important means that we also want to protect it to the extent we can. Although it is not easy to protect the overall level of our earnings powers, we can financially protect against death, which is the worst-case scenario. Most of us will want to invest in life insurance, which protects us against this mortality risk. Thus, our financial portfolio during the accumulation stage of our lives will typically consist of stocks, bonds, and life insurance.

We face another kind of risk after we retire. During the retirement stage of our lives, we are usually consuming more than our income (i.e., some of our financial capital). Because we cannot perfectly predict how long our retirement will last, there is a danger that we will consume all our financial wealth. The risk of living too long (from a financial point of view) is called "longevity risk." But there is a way to insure against longevity risk, which is to purchase annuity products that pay yearly income as long as one lives. Providing that a person or a couple has sufficient resources to purchase sufficient annuities, they can insure that they will not outlive their wealth.

This chapter is about managing our financial wealth in the context of having both human and financial capital. The portfolio that works best tends to hold stocks and bonds as well as insurance products. We are attempting to put these decisions together in a single framework. Thus, we are trying to provide a theoretical foundation—a framework—and practical solutions for developing investment advice for individual investors throughout their lives.

In this section, we review the traditional investment advice model for individual investors, briefly introduce three additional factors that investors need to consider when making investment decisions, and propose a framework for developing lifetime investment advice for individual investors that expands the traditional advice model to include the additional factors that we discuss in the section.

The Changing Retirement Landscape

According to the "Survey of Consumer Finances" conducted by the U.S. Federal Reserve Board (2004), the number one reason for individual investors to save and invest is to fund spending in retirement. In other words, funding a comfortable retirement is the primary financial goal for individual investors.

Significant changes in how individual investors finance their retirement spending have occurred in the past 20 years. One major change is the increasing popularity of investment retirement accounts (IRAs) and defined-contribution (DC) plans. Based on data from the Investment Company Institute, retirement assets reached $14.5 trillion in 2005. IRAs and DC plans total roughly half of that amount—which is a tremendous increase from 25 years ago. Today, IRAs and DC plans are replacing traditional defined-benefit (DB) plans as the primary accounts in which to accumulate retirement assets.

Social Security payments and DB pension plans have traditionally provided the bulk of retirement income in the United States. For example, the U.S. Social Security Administration reports that 44 percent of income for people 65 and older came from Social Security income in 2001 and 25 percent came from DB pensions. As Figure 3.1 shows, according to Employee Benefit Research Institute reports, current retirees (see Panel B) receive almost 70 percent of their retirement income from Social Security and traditional company pension plans whereas today's workers (see Panel A) can expect to have only about one-third of their retirement income funded by these sources (see GAO 2003; EBRI 2000). Increasingly, workers are relying on their DC retirement portfolios and other personal savings as the primary resources for retirement income.

The shift of retirement funding from professionally managed DB plans to personal savings vehicles implies that investors need to make their own decisions about how to allocate retirement savings and what products should be used to generate income in retirement. This shift naturally creates a huge demand for professional investment advice throughout the investor's life cycle (in both the accumulation stage and the retirement stage).

This financial advice must obviously focus on more than simply traditional security selection. Financial advisers will have to familiarize themselves with longevity insurance products and other instruments that provide lifetime income.

In addition, individual investors today face more retirement risk factors than did investors from previous generations. First, the Social Security system and many DB pension plans are at risk, so investors must increasingly rely on their own savings for retirement spending. Second, people today are living longer and could face much higher health-care costs in retirement than members of previous generations. Individual investors increasingly seek professional advice also in dealing with these risk factors.

Traditional Advice Model for Individual Investors

The Markowitz (1952) mean–variance framework is widely accepted in academic and practitioner finance as the primary tool for developing asset allocations for individual as well as institutional investors. According to modern portfolio theory, asset allocation is determined by constructing mean–variance-efficient portfolios for various risk levels.[1] Then, based on the investor's risk tolerance, one of these efficient portfolios is selected. Investors follow the asset allocation output to invest their financial assets.

The result of mean–variance analysis is shown in a classic mean–variance diagram. Efficient portfolios are plotted graphically on the *efficient frontier*. Each portfolio on the frontier represents

FIGURE 3.1   How will you pay for retirement?

A. Current Workers

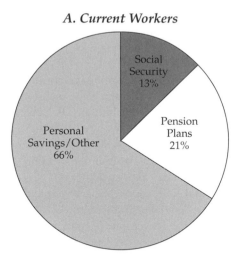

B. Current Retirees

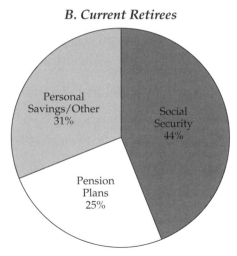

Source: Based on data from EBRI (2001).

the portfolio with the smallest risk for its level of expected return. The portfolio with the smallest variance is called the "minimum variance" portfolio, and it can be located at the left side of the efficient frontier. These concepts are illustrated in Figure 3.2, which uses standard deviation (the square root of variance) for the x-axis because the units of standard deviation are easy to interpret.

This mean–variance framework emphasizes the importance of taking advantage of the diversification benefits available over time by holding a variety of financial investments or asset classes. When the framework is used to develop investment advice for individual investors, questionnaires are often used to measure the investor's tolerance for risk.

Unfortunately, the framework in Figure 3.3 considers only the risk–return trade-off in financial assets. It does not consider many other risks that individual investors face throughout their lives.

FIGURE 3.2   Mean–Variance-Efficient Frontier

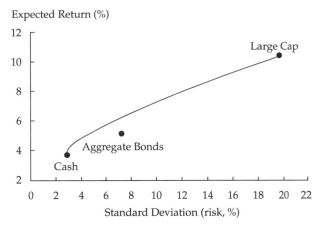

Note: "Large Cap" refers to large-capitalization stocks.

FIGURE 3.3   Traditional Investment Advice Model

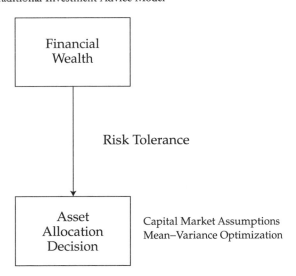

Three Risk Factors and Hedges

We briefly introduce three of the risk factors associated with human capital that investors need to manage—wage earnings risk, mortality risk, and longevity risk—and three types of products that should be considered hedges of those risks. Note that these risk factors, or issues, are often neglected in traditional portfolio analysis. Indeed, one of the main arguments in this chapter is that comprehensive cradle-to-grave financial advice cannot ignore the impact and role of insurance products.

Human Capital, Earnings Risk, and Financial Capital

The traditional mean–variance framework's concentration on diversifying financial assets is a reasonable goal for many institutional investors, but it is not a realistic framework for individual investors who are working and saving for retirement. In fact, this factor is one of the main observations made by Markowitz (1990). From a broad perspective, an investor's total wealth consists of two parts. One is readily tradable financial assets; the other is human capital.

Human capital is defined as the present value of an investor's future labor income. From the economic perspective, labor income can be viewed as a dividend on the investor's human capital. Although human capital is not readily tradable, it is often the single largest asset an investor has. Typically, younger investors have far more human capital than financial capital because young investors have a longer time to work and have had little time to save and accumulate financial wealth. Conversely, older investors tend to have more financial capital than human capital because they have less time to work but have accumulated financial capital over a long career.

One way to reduce wage earnings risk is to save more. This saving converts human capital to financial capital at a higher rate. It also enables the financial capital to have a longer time to grow until retirement. The value of compounding returns in financial capital over time can be very substantial.

And one way to reduce human capital risk is to diversify it with appropriate types of financial capital. Portfolio allocation recommendations that are made without consideration of human capital are not appropriate for many individual investors. To reduce risk, financial assets should be diversified while taking into account human capital assets. For example, the employees of Enron Corporation and WorldCom suffered from extremely poor overall diversification. Their labor income and their financial investments were both in their own companies' stock. When their companies collapsed, both their human capital and their financial capital were heavily affected.

There is growing recognition among academics and practitioners that the risk and return characteristics of human capital—such as wage and salary profiles—should be taken into account when building portfolios for individual investors. Well-known financial scholars and commentators have pointed out the importance of including the magnitude of human capital, its volatility, and its correlation with other assets into a personal risk management perspective.[2] Yet, Benartzi (2001) showed that many investors invest heavily in the stock of the company they work for. He found for 1993 that roughly a third of plan assets were invested in company stock. Benartzi argued that such investment is not efficient because company stock is not only an undiversified risky investment; it is also highly correlated with the person's human capital.[3]

Appropriate investment advice for individual investors is to invest financial wealth in an asset that is not highly correlated with their human capital in order to maximize diversification benefits over the entire portfolio. For people with "safe" human capital, it may be appropriate to invest their financial assets aggressively.

Mortality Risk and Life Insurance

Because human capital is often the biggest asset an investor has, protecting human capital from potential risks should also be part of overall investment advice. A unique risk aspect of an investor's human capital is mortality risk—the loss of human capital to the household in the unfortunate event of premature death of the worker. This loss of human capital can have a devastating impact on the financial well-being of a family.

Life insurance has long been used to hedge against mortality risk. Typically, the greater the value of human capital, the more life insurance the family demands. Intuitively, human capital affects not only optimal life insurance demand but also optimal asset allocation. But these two important financial decisions—the demand for life insurance and optimal asset allocation—have, however, consistently been analyzed *separately* in theory and practice. We have found few references in either the risk/insurance literature or the investment/finance literature to the importance of considering these decisions jointly within the context of a life-cycle model of consumption and investment. Popular investment and financial planning advice regarding how much life insurance one should carry is seldom framed in terms of the riskiness of one's human capital. And optimal asset allocation is only lately being framed in terms of the risk characteristics of human capital, and rarely is it integrated with life insurance decisions.

Fortunately, in the event of death, life insurance can be a perfect hedge for human capital. That is, term life insurance and human capital have a negative 100 percent correlation with each other in the "living" versus "dead" states; if one pays off at the end of the year, the other does not, and vice versa. Thus, the combination of the two provides diversification to an investor's total portfolio. The many reasons for considering these decisions and products jointly become even more powerful once investors approach and enter their retirement years.

Longevity Risk and the Lifetime-Payout Annuity

The shift in retirement funding from professionally managed DB plans to DC personal savings vehicles implies that investors need to make their own decisions not only about how to allocate retirement savings but also about what products should be used to generate income throughout retirement. Investors must consider two important risk factors when making these decisions. One is financial market risk (i.e., volatility in the capital markets that causes portfolio values to fluctuate). If the market drops or corrections occur early during retirement, the portfolio may not be able to weather the added stress of systematic consumption withdrawals. The portfolio may then be unable to provide the necessary income for the person's desired lifestyle. The second important risk factor is longevity risk—that is, the risk of outliving the portfolio. Life expectancies have been increasing, and retirees should be aware of their substantial chance of a long retirement and plan accordingly. This risk is faced by every investor but especially those taking advantage of early retirement offers or those who have a family history of longevity.

Increasingly, all retirees will need to balance income and expenditures over a longer period of time than in the past. One factor that is increasing the average length of time spent in retirement is a long-term trend toward early retirement. For example, in the United States, nearly half of all men now leave the workforce by age 62 and almost half of all women are out of the workforce by age 60. A second factor is that this decline in the average retirement age has occurred in an environment of rising life expectancies for retirees. Since 1940, falling mortality rates have added almost 4 years to the expected life span of a 65-year-old male and more than 5 years to the life expectancy of a 65-year-old female.

Figure 3.4 illustrates the survival probability of a 65-year-old. The first bar of each pair shows the probability of at least one person from a married couple surviving to various ages, and the second bar shows the probability of an individual surviving to various ages. For married couples, in more than 80 percent of the cases, at least one spouse will probably still be alive at age 85.

Longevity is increasing not simply in the United States but also around the world. Longevity risk, like mortality risk, is independent of financial market risk. Unlike mortality

FIGURE 3.4   Probability of Living to 100

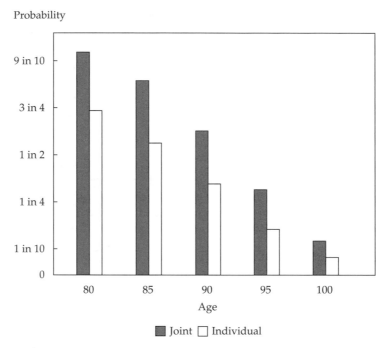

Source: Society of Actuaries, 1996 U.S. Annuity 2000 table.

risk, longevity risk is borne by the investor directly. Also unlike mortality risk, longevity risk is related to income needs and so, logically, should be directly related to asset allocation.

A number of recent articles—for example, Ameriks, Veres, and Warshawsky (2001); Bengen (2001); Milevsky and Robinson (2005); Milevsky, Moore, and Young (2006)—have focused financial professionals' as well as academics' attention on longevity risk in retirement. A growing body of literature is trying to use traditional portfolio management and invest-ment technology to model personal insurance and pension decisions. But simple retirement planning approaches ignore longevity risk by assuming that an investor need only plan to age 85. It is true that 85 is roughly the life expectancy for a 65-year-old individual, but life *expec-tancy* is only a measure of central tendency or a halfway point estimate. Almost by definition, half of all investors will exceed their life expectancy. And for a married couple, the odds are more than 80 percent that at least one spouse will live beyond this milestone. If investors use an 85-year life expectancy to plan their retirement income needs, many of them will use up their retirement resources (other than government and corporate pensions) long before actual mortality. This longevity risk—the risk of outliving one's resources—is substantial and is the reason that lifetime annuities (payout annuities) should also be an integral part of many retirement plans.

A lifetime-payout annuity is an insurance product that converts an accumulated invest-ment into income[4] that the insurance company pays out over the life of the investor. Payout annuities are the opposite of life insurance. Consumers buy life insurance because they are afraid of dying too soon and leaving family and loved ones in financial need. They buy payout annuities because they are concerned about living too long and running out of assets during their lifetime.

Insurance companies can afford to provide this lifelong benefit by (1) spreading the longevity risk over a large group of annuitants and (2) making careful and conservative assumptions about the rate of return they will earn on their assets. Spreading or pooling the longevity risk means that individuals who do not reach their life expectancy, as calculated by actuarial mortality tables, subsidize those who exceed it. Investors who buy lifetime-payout annuities pool their portfolios together and collectively ensure that everybody will receive payments as long as each lives. Because of the unique longevity insurance features embedded in lifetime-payout annuities, they can play a significant role in many investors' retirement portfolios.

An Integrated Framework

This chapter was inspired by the need to expand the traditional investment advice framework shown in Figure 3.3 to integrate the special risk factors of individual investors into their investment decisions. The main objective of our study was to review the existing literature and develop original solutions—specifically:

1. To analyze the asset allocation decisions of individual investors while taking into consideration human capital characteristics—namely, the size of human capital, its volatility, and its correlation with other assets.
2. To analyze jointly the decision as to how much life insurance a family unit should have to protect against the loss of its breadwinner and how the family should allocate its financial resources between risk-free (bondlike) and risky (stocklike) assets within the dynamics of labor income and human capital.[5]
3. To analyze the transition from the accumulation (saving) phase to the distribution (spending) phase of retirement planning within the context of a life-cycle model that emphasizes the role of payout annuities and longevity insurance because of the continuing erosion of traditional DB pensions.

To summarize, the purpose here is to parsimoniously merge the factors of human capital, investment allocation, life insurance, and longevity insurance into a conventional framework of portfolio choice and asset allocation. We plan to establish a unified framework to study the total asset allocation decision in accumulation and retirement, which includes both financial market risk as well as other risk factors. We will try to achieve this goal with a minimal amount of technical modeling and, instead, emphasize intuition and examples, perhaps at the expense of some rigor. In some cases, we will provide the reader with references to more advanced material or material that delves into the mathematics of an idea. Furthermore, we provide some of the technical material in appendices.

We are specifically interested in the interaction between the demand for life insurance, payout annuities, and asset allocation when the correlation between the investor's labor income process and financial market returns is not zero. This project significantly expands our earlier works on similar topics.[6] First, we analyze portfolio choice decisions at both the preretirement stage and in retirement, thus presenting a complete life-cycle picture. Second, instead of focusing on traditional utility models, we explore lifetime objective functions and various computational techniques when solving the problem. Third, we include a comprehensive literature review that provides the reader with background information on previous contributions to the field.

The rest of the chapter is organized into two general segments. This first segment, which includes the sections on Human Capital and Asset Allocation Advice and Human Capital, Life Insurance, and Asset Allocation, investigates the advice framework in the accumulation stage. Specifically, the former segment analyzes the impact of human capital on the asset allocation decision, while the latter segment presents the combined framework that includes both the asset allocation decision and the life insurance decision. We present a number of case studies to illustrate the interaction between the two decisions and the effects of various factors.

The second segment, which includes the sections on Retirement Portfolio and Longevity Risk, Asset Allocation and Longevity Insurance, and When to Annuitize, investigates the retirement stage. In the piece on Retirement Portfolio and Longevity Risk, we analyze the risk factors that investors face in retirement. We focus our discussion on longevity risk and the potential role that lifetime-payout annuities can play in managing longevity risk. In the section on Asset Allocation and Longevity Insurance, we present the model for constructing optimal asset allocations that include lifetime-payout annuities for retirement portfolios.[7] In When to Annuitize, we discuss the timing of the annuitization decision (i.e., when investors should annuitize their assets).

The final section provides an overall summary of the framework and recommendations from the accumulation stage through the retirement stage and discusses implications of our work.

HUMAN CAPITAL AND ASSET ALLOCATION ADVICE

In determinations of the appropriate asset allocation for individual investors, the level of risk a person can afford or tolerate depends not only on the individual's psychological attitude toward risk but also on his or her total financial situation (including the types and sources of income). Earning ability outside of investments is important in determining capacity for risk. People with high earning ability are able to take more risk because they can easily recoup financial losses.[8] In his well-known *A Random Walk Down Wall Street,* Malkiel (2004) stated, "The risks you can afford to take depend on your total financial situation, including the types and sources of your income exclusive of investment income" (p. 342). A person's financial situation and earning ability can often be captured by taking the person's human capital into consideration.

A fundamental element in financial planning advice is that younger investors (or investors with longer investment horizons) should invest aggressively. This advice is a direct application of the human capital concept. The impact of human capital on an investor's optimal asset allocation has been studied by many academic researchers. And many financial planners, following the principles of the human capital concept, automatically adjust the risk levels of an individual investor's portfolio over the investor's life stages. In this section, we discuss why incorporating human capital into an investor's asset allocation decision is important. We first introduce the concept of human capital; then, we describe the importance of human capital in determining asset allocation. Finally, we use case studies to illustrate this role of human capital.

What Is Human Capital?

An investor's total wealth consists of two parts. One is readily tradable financial assets, such as the assets in a 401(k) plan, individual retirement account, or mutual fund; the other is human capital. Human capital is defined as the economic present value of an investor's future labor income. Economic theory predicts that investors make asset allocation decisions to maximize their lifetime utilities through consumption. These decisions are closely linked to human capital.

Although human capital is not readily tradable, it is often the single largest asset an investor has. Typically, younger investors have far more human capital than financial capital because they have many years to work and they have had few years to save and accumulate financial wealth. Conversely, older investors tend to have more financial capital than human capital because they have fewer years ahead to work but have accumulated financial capital. *Human capital should be treated like any other asset class;* it has its own risk and return properties and its own correlations with other financial asset classes.

Role of Human Capital in Asset Allocation

In investing for long-term goals, the allocation of asset categories in the portfolio is one of the most crucial decisions (Ibbotson and Kaplan 2000). However, many asset allocation advisers focus on only the risk–return characteristics of readily tradable financial assets. These advisers ignore human capital, which is often the single largest asset an investor has in his or her personal balance sheet. If asset allocation is indeed a critical determinant of investment and financial success, then given the large magnitude of human capital, one must include it.

Intuitive Examples of Portfolio Diversification Involving Human Capital

Investors should make sure that their total (i.e., human capital plus financial capital) portfolios are properly diversified. In simple words, investment advisers need to incorporate assets in such a way that when one type of capital zigs, the other zags. Therefore, in the early stages of the life cycle, financial and investment capital should be used to hedge and diversify human capital rather than used naively to build wealth. Think of financial investable assets as a defense and protection against adverse shocks to human capital (i.e., salaries and wages), not an isolated pot of money to be blindly allocated for the long run.

For example, for a tenured university professor of finance, human capital—and the subsequent pension to which the professor is entitled—has the properties of a fixed-income bond fund that entitles the professor to monthly coupons. The professor's human capital is similar to an inflation-adjusted, real-return bond. In light of the risk and return characteristics of this human capital, therefore, the professor has little need for fixed-income bonds, money market funds, or even Treasury Inflation-Protected Securities (real-return bonds) in his financial portfolio. By placing the investment money elsewhere, the total portfolio of human and financial capital will be well balanced despite the fact that if each is viewed in isolation, the financial capital and human capital are not diversified.

In contrast to this professor, many *students* of finance might expect to earn a lot more than their university professor during their lifetimes, but their relative incomes and bonuses will fluctuate from year to year in relation to the performance of the stock market, the industry they work in, and the unpredictable vagaries of their labor market. Their human capital will be almost entirely invested in equity, so early in their working careers, their financial capital should be tilted slightly more toward bonds and other fixed-income products. Of course, when they are young and can tolerate the ups and downs in the market, they should have some exposure to equities. But all else being equal, two individuals who are exactly 35 years old and have exactly the same projected annual income and retirement horizon should not have the same equity portfolio structure if their human capital differs in risk characteristics.

Certainly, simplistic rules like "100 minus age should be invested in equities" have no room in a sophisticated, holistic framework of wealth management.

It may seem odd to advise future practitioners in the equity industry *not* to "put their money where their mouths are" (i.e., not to invest more aggressively in the stock market), but in fact, hedging human capital risks is prudent risk management. Indeed, perhaps with some tongue in cheek, we might disagree with famed investor and stock market guru Peter Lynch and argue that you should *not* invest in things you are familiar with but, rather, in industries and companies you know nothing or little about. Those investments will have little correlation with your human capital. Remember the engineers, technicians, and computer scientists who thought they knew the high-technology industry and whose human capital was invested in the same industry; they learned the importance of the human capital concept the hard way.

Portfolio allocation recommendations that do not consider the individual's human capital are not appropriate for many individual investors who are working and saving for retirement.

Academic Literature

In the late 1960s, economists developed models that implied that individuals should optimally maintain constant portfolio weights throughout their lives (Samuelson 1969, Merton 1969). An important assumption of these models was that investors have no labor income (or human capital). This assumption is not realistic, however, as we have discussed, because most investors do have labor income. If labor income is included in the portfolio choice model, individuals will optimally change their allocations of financial assets in a pattern related to the life cycle. In other words, the optimal asset allocation depends on the risk–return characteristics of their labor income and the flexibility of their labor income (such as how much or how long the investor works).

Bodie, Merton, and Samuelson (1992) studied the impact of labor income flexibility on investment strategy. They found that investors with a high degree of labor flexibility should take more risk in their investment portfolios. For example, younger investors may invest more of their financial assets in risky assets than older investors because the young have more flexibility in their working lives.

Hanna and Chen (1997) explored optimal asset allocation by using a simulation method that considered human capital and various investment horizons. Assuming human capital is a risk-free asset, they found that for most investors with long horizons, an all-equity portfolio is optimal.

In our modeling framework, which we will present in a moment, investors adjust their financial portfolios to compensate for their risk exposure to nontradable human capital.[9] The key theoretical implications are as follows: (1) younger investors invest more in stocks than older investors; (2) investors with safe labor income (thus safe human capital) invest more of their financial portfolio in stocks; (3) investors with labor income that is highly correlated with the stock markets invest their financial assets in less risky assets; and (4) the ability to adjust labor supply (i.e., higher flexibility) increases an investor's allocation to stocks.

Empirical studies show, however, that most investors do not efficiently diversify their financial portfolios in light of the risk of their human capital. Benartzi (2001) and Benartzi and Thaler (2001) showed that many investors use primitive methods to determine their asset allocations and many of them invest heavily in the stock of the company for which they work.[10] Davis and Willen (2000) estimated the correlation between labor income and equity market returns by using the U.S. Department of Labor's "Current Occupation Survey." They found that human capital has a low correlation (-0.2 to 0.1) with aggregate equity markets. The implication is that the typical investor need not worry about his or her human capital being

FIGURE 3.5   Human Capital and Asset Allocation

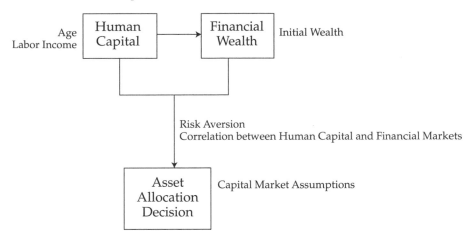

highly correlated with the stock market when making asset allocation decisions; thus, most investors can invest the majority of their financial wealth in risky assets.[11]

Empirical studies have also found that for the majority of U.S. households, human capital is the dominant asset. Using the U.S. Federal Reserve Board's 1992 "Survey of Consumer Finances," Lee and Hanna (1995) estimated that the ratio of financial assets to total wealth (including human capital) was 1.3 percent for the median household. Thus, for half of the households, financial assets represented less than 1.3 percent of total wealth. The 75th percentile of this ratio was 5.7 percent. The 90th percentile was 17.4 percent. In short, financial assets represented a high percentage of total wealth for only a small proportion of U.S. households. The small magnitude of these numbers places a significant burden on financial advisers to learn more about their clients' human capital, which is such a valuable component of personal balance sheets.

Figure 3.5 shows the relationships among financial capital, human capital, other factors (such as savings and the investor's aversion to risk), and the asset allocation of financial capital.

Human Capital and Asset Allocation Modeling

This section provides a general overview of how to determine optimal asset allocation while considering human capital. Appendix 3A contains a detailed specification of the model, which is the basis of our numerical examples and case studies.

Human capital can be calculated from the following equation:

$$HC(x) = \sum_{t=x+1}^{n} \frac{E[h_t]}{(1 + r + v)^{t-x}},$$ (3.1)

where

x = current age
$HC(x)$ = human capital at age x
h_t = earnings for year t adjusted for inflation before retirement and after retirement, adjusted for Social Security and pension payments
n = life expectancy
r = inflation-adjusted risk-free rate
v = discount rate[12]

In the model, we assume there are two asset classes.[13] The investor can allocate financial wealth between a risk-free asset and a risky asset (i.e., bonds and stocks). We assume the investor has financial capital W_t at the beginning of period t. The investor chooses the optimal allocation involving the risk-free asset and the risky asset that will maximize expected utility of total wealth, which is the sum of financial capital and human capital, $W_{t+1} + H_{t+1}$. We assume the investor follows the constant relative risk aversion (CRRA) utility function. In our case, it is

$$U = \frac{(W_{t+1} + H_{t+1})^{1-\gamma}}{1 - \gamma} \qquad (3.2)$$

for $\gamma \neq 1$ and

$$U = \ln(W_{t+1} + H_{t+1}) \qquad (3.3)$$

for $\gamma = 1$. In Equations 3.2 and 3.3, γ is the coefficient of relative risk aversion and is greater than zero.

In the model, labor income and the return of risky assets are correlated. The optimization problem the investor faces is expressed in detail in Appendix 3A.

The investor's human capital can be viewed as a "stock" if both the correlation with a given financial market index and the volatility of labor income are high. It can be viewed as a "bond" if both correlation and volatility are low. In between these two extremes, human capital is a diversified portfolio of stocks and bonds, plus idiosyncratic risk.[14] We are quite cognizant of the difficulties involved in calibrating these variables that were pointed out by Davis and Willen (2000), and we rely on some of their parameters for our numerical examples in the following case studies.

Case Studies

In the cases, we look at some specific parameters and the resulting optimal portfolios. In the first case, we treat future labor income as certain (i.e., there is no uncertainty in the labor income). The model indicates that human capital in this case is a risk-free asset (as in the case of our professor). Then, we add uncertainty into consideration. Specifically, we treat human capital as a risky asset.

For example, let us assume that we have a male U.S. investor whose annual income is expected to grow with inflation and there is no uncertainty about his annual income—which is $50,000. He saves 10 percent of his income each year. He expects to receive Social Security payments of $10,000 each year (in today's dollars) when he retires at age 65. His current financial wealth is $50,000, of which 40 percent is invested in a risk-free asset and 60 percent is invested in a risky asset. Finally, he rebalances his financial portfolio annually back to the initial portfolio allocation. Human capital was estimated by using Equation 3.1.

Financial capital for the examples, in contrast to human capital, can be easily parameterized on the basis of the evolution of returns over time. Table 3.1 provides the capital market assumptions that are used in this computation for this and other cases in this section and the section on Human Capital, Life Insurance, and Asset Allocation.

Figures 3.6 and 3.7 illustrate the relationships of financial capital, human capital, and total wealth (defined as the sum of financial capital and human capital) that investors might expect over their working (preretirement) years from age 25 to age 65. For example, under our assumptions and calculation of human capital, for a male investor who is 25 years old, Figure 3.6 shows that his human capital is estimated to be about $800,000; Figure 3.7 shows that it represents 94 percent of his total wealth and far outweighs his financial capital at that

TABLE 3.1   Capital Market Return Assumptions

Asset	Compounded Annual Return	Risk (standard deviation)
Risk free (bonds)	5%	—
Risky (stocks)	9	20%
Inflation	3	—

Note: These capital market assumptions are comparable to the historical performance of U.S. stocks and bonds from 1926 to 2006, after adjusting for investment expenses the investor would have to pay. According to Ibbotson Associates (2006), the compounded annual return for that period was 10.36 percent for the S&P 500 Index (with a standard deviation of 20.2 percent), 5.47 percent for U.S. government bonds, and 3.04 percent for inflation.

FIGURE 3.6   Expected Financial Capital, Human Capital, and Total Wealth over Life Cycle with Optimal Asset Allocation

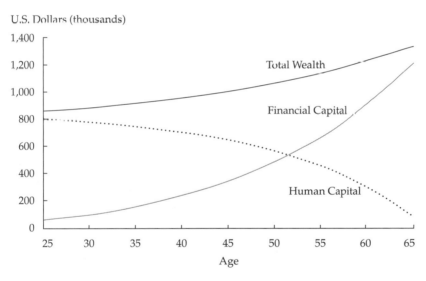

age. His financial capital is only $50,000. As the investor gets older and continues to make savings contributions, these monies plus the return from the existing portfolio increase the proportion of financial capital. At age 65, Figure 3.6 shows the human capital decreasing to $128,000 (to come from future Social Security payments) and the financial portfolio peaking just above $1.2 million.

Case #1. Human Capital as a Risk-Free Asset

In this case, we assume that there is no uncertainty about the investor's annual income, so his human capital is a risk-free asset because it is the present value of future income. He is age 25 with annual income of $50,000 and current financial wealth of $50,000. The coefficient of relative risk aversion for this investor is assumed to be 5.5 (i.e., $\gamma = 5.5$).

Figure 3.8 shows the optimal asset allocation of this investor's financial capital from age 25 to 65. As can be seen, the allocation of financial wealth to risk-free assets increases

FIGURE 3.7   Financial Capital and Human Capital as Share of Total Wealth over Life Cycle

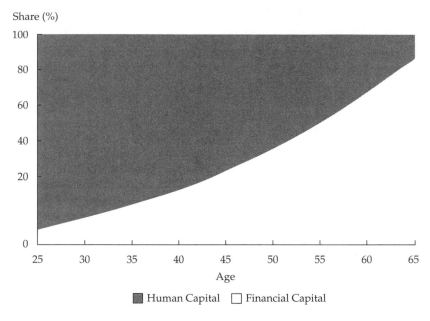

FIGURE 3.8   Case #1: Optimal Asset Allocation to the Risk-Free Asset over Life Cycle

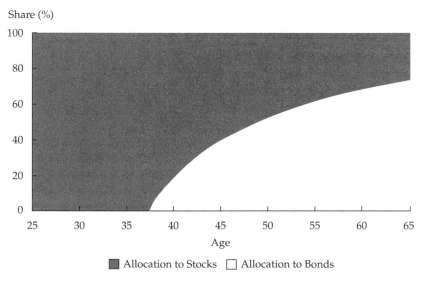

Note: Risk tolerance level at 5.5.

over time. In other words, the investor increases allocations to the risk-free asset in order to maintain a desired risk exposure in the total wealth portfolio. Households will tend to hold proportionately less of the risk-free financial asset when young (when the value of human capital is large) and tend to increase the proportion of financial wealth held in the risk-free financial asset as they age (as the amount of human capital declines).

Now, let's analyze the risk exposure of the investor's total portfolio at different ages in this case. When considering human capital, to keep the desired risk exposure of his total portfolio at the level indicated by $\gamma = 5.5$, the investor will choose a 100 percent stock asset allocation because he already has 94 percent of his total wealth (represented by his human capital) invested in bonds. Investing 100 percent in stocks is the closest we can get his total portfolio to the target desired risk exposure level without borrowing. When the investor is 45, his total wealth consists of about 40 percent financial assets and 60 percent human capital; the asset allocation for his financial assets is about 60 percent stocks and 40 percent bonds. At age 65, he ends up with a financial portfolio of 27 percent stock and 73 percent bonds.

This simple example illustrates that when an investor's human capital is riskless, the investor should invest more in stocks than an investor closer to retirement, and when an investor gets older, his or her human capital will decrease and financial capital will increase. Thus, the investor should gradually scale back the amount invested in stocks.

Unfortunately, although investors are almost always given the discretion to change their allocations to various assets and account managers usually even maintain a website for this purpose, empirical studies (e.g., Ameriks and Zeldes 2001) suggest that only a small minority of investors actually make any adjustments.

Case #2. Human Capital as a Risky Asset

In Case #1, we assumed that human capital was 100 percent risk free. But only a small portion of investors would have this kind of "safe" human capital. Labor income is uncertain for most investors for a number of reasons, including the possibilities of losing one's job or being laid off. The uncertainty in labor income makes human capital a risky asset.

But the riskiness varies by individual; for example, a business owner, a stock portfolio manager, a stockbroker, and a schoolteacher have different risk profiles in their human capital. To incorporate human capital in total wealth, we need to consider the unique risk and return characteristics of each individual's human capital.

There are two basic types of risk for an investor's human capital. The first type can be treated as risk related to other risky assets (such as stocks). The second type is risk uncorrelated with the stock market. Let's look at the two types and how they affect optimal asset allocation.

To analyze the impact of the two types of human capital risk on the investor's allocation of financial capital, we constructed the following two scenarios. In Scenario 1, human capital is risky and highly correlated with the stock market ($\alpha_h = 0.2$, where α_h is the volatility of the shocks to the labor income, and $\rho_{hs} = 0.5$, where ρ_{hs} is the correlation between shocks to labor income and shocks to the risky asset's returns). In Scenario 2, human capital is risky but it is uncorrelated with the stock market ($\alpha_h = 0.2$ and $\rho_{hs} = 0$).

Figure 3.9 shows the optimal asset allocations of financial capital in the two scenarios. The assumptions used in Case 1 prevail except for the assumption about volatility and correlation between human capital and the stock market.

Let's start by analyzing the first type of risk (Scenario 1), in which the human capital risk is highly correlated with the risk of other risky financial assets. A simple example of this scenario would be the perfect correlation of labor income with the payoffs from holding the aggregate stock market—for example, a stockbroker or a stock portfolio manager. In this situation, our hypothetical investor will use his financial assets to balance his human capital risk. The stockbroker's human capital is far more sensitive to the stock market than a schoolteacher's. If a stockbroker and a schoolteacher have the same total wealth and similar risk

FIGURE 3.9   Case #2: Proportion of Risk-Free Asset in Scenarios 1 and 2

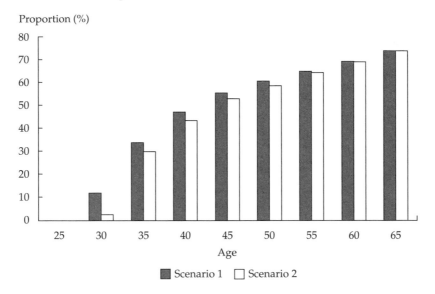

tolerances, human capital theory recommends that the stockbroker invest a smaller portion of his financial assets in the stock market than the schoolteacher because the stockbroker has implicitly invested his human capital in the stock market. For young investors with equitylike human capital, the financial assets should be invested predominantly in fixed-income assets. Because the value of one's human capital declines with age, the share of risk-free assets in the stockbroker's portfolio will also decline and the share of risky assets in the portfolio of financial assets will rise until retirement.

Now, let's consider Scenario 2, in which the investor's labor income is risky but not correlated with the payoffs of the risky assets (i.e., is independent of financial market risk). In this case, the investor's optimal financial asset allocation follows, by and large, the same pattern as the case in which the investor's human capital is risk free—especially when the risk of human capital is small (variance in the income over time is small). The reason is that, similar to the risk-free asset, human capital is uncorrelated with financial market risk. When the risk of human capital increases, however, the investor should reduce overall risk in the financial portfolio. In other words, if your occupational income (and future prospects for income) is uncertain, you should refrain from taking too much risk with your financial capital.

Case #3. Impact of Initial Financial Wealth

The purpose of this case is to show the impact of different amounts of current financial wealth on optimal asset allocation. Assume that we hold the investor's age at 45 and set risk preference at a moderate level (a CRRA risk-aversion coefficient of 4). The correlation between shocks to labor income and risky-asset returns is 0.2, and the volatility of shocks to labor income is 5 percent. The optimal allocations to the risk-free asset for various levels of initial financial wealth are presented in Figure 3.10.

Figure 3.10 shows that the optimal allocation to the risk-free asset increases with initial wealth. This situation may seem to be inconsistent with the CRRA utility function because the CRRA utility function implies that the optimal asset allocation will not change with the amount of wealth the investor has. Note, however, that "wealth" here includes both financial

FIGURE 3.10   Case #3: Optimal Asset Allocation to the Risk-Free Asset at Various Financial Wealth Levels

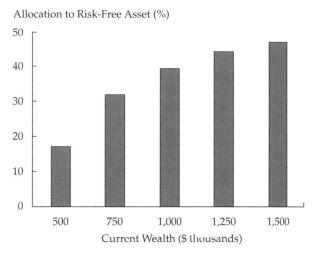

Allocation to Risk-Free Asset (%)

Current Wealth ($ thousands)

wealth and human capital. In fact, this situation is a classic example of the impact of human capital on optimal asset allocation. An increase in initial financial wealth not only increases total wealth but also reduces the percentage of total wealth represented by human capital. In this case, human capital is less risky than the risky asset.[15] When initial wealth is low, human capital dominates total wealth and asset allocation. As a result, to achieve the target asset allocation of a moderate investor—say, an allocation of 60 percent to the risk-free asset and 40 percent to the risky asset—the closest allocation is to invest 100 percent of financial wealth in the risky asset because human capital is illiquid. As initial wealth rises, the asset allocation gradually approaches the target asset allocation that a moderately risk-averse investor desires.

In summary, for a typical investor whose human capital is less risky than the stock market, the optimal asset allocation is more conservative the more financial assets the investor has.

Case #4. Correlation between Wage Growth Rate and Stock Returns

In this case, we examine the impact of the correlation between shocks to labor income and shocks to the risky asset's returns. In particular, we want to evaluate asset allocation decisions for investors with human capital that is highly correlated with stocks. Examples are an investor's income that is closely linked to the stock performance of her employer's company or an investor's compensation that is highly influenced by the financial markets (e.g., the investor works in the financial industry).

Again, the investor's age is 45 and the coefficient of relative risk aversion is 4. The amount of financial capital is $500,000. The optimal asset allocations to the risk-free asset for various correlations are presented in Figure 3.11.

As Figure 3.11 shows, the optimal allocation becomes more conservative (i.e., more assets are allocated to the risk-free asset), with increasing correlation between income and stock market returns. One way to look at this outcome is that a higher correlation between human capital and the stock market results in less diversification and thus higher risk for the total portfolio (human capital plus financial capital). To reduce this risk, an investor must invest more financial wealth in the risk-free asset. Another way to look at this result is in terms of *certainty equivalents* (or utility equivalents) of wealth. The higher the uncertainty (or

FIGURE 3.11   Case #4: Optimal Asset Allocation to the Risk-Free Asset at Various
Correlation Levels

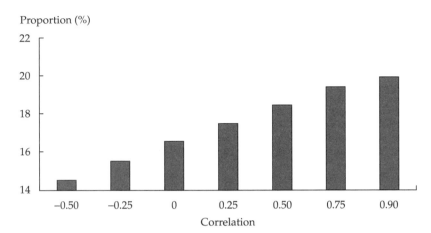

volatility), all else being equal, the lower the certainty-equivalent value. In utility terms, with
increasing correlation and rising volatility, this investor is actually poorer!

Implications for Advisers

A financial adviser or consultant should be aware of the following issues when developing a
long-term asset allocation plan for typical individual investors:

1. Investors should invest financial assets in such a way as to diversify and balance out their
   human capital.
2. A young investor with relatively safe human capital assets and greater flexibility of labor
   supply should invest more financial assets in risky assets, such as stocks, than an older
   investor should, perhaps even with leverage and debt. The portion of financial assets
   allocated to stocks should be reduced as the investor gets older. Also, if the stock market
   performs well, the investor's financial capital will grow, and again, the implication is to
   reduce the portion of financial assets invested in stocks.
3. An investor with human capital that has a high correlation with stock market risk should
   also reduce the allocation to risky assets in the financial portfolio and increase the allocation to assets that are less correlated with the stock market.[16]

In short, the risk characteristics of human capital have a significant impact on optimal
financial portfolio allocation. Therefore, to effectively incorporate human capital into making
the asset allocation decision, financial advisers and consultants need to determine (1) whether
the investor's human capital is risk free or risky and (2) whether the risk is highly correlated
with financial market risk.

Summary

Human capital is defined as the present value of future labor income. Human capital—not
financial assets—is usually the dominant asset for young and middle-aged people.

Many academic researchers have advocated considering human capital when developing
portfolio allocations of an investor's financial assets. That is, investors should invest their
financial assets in such a way as to diversify and balance their human capital.

In addition to the size of the investor's human capital, its risk–return characteristics, its relationship to other financial assets, and the flexibility of the investor's labor supply also have significant effects on how an investor should allocate financial assets. In general, a typical young investor would be well advised to hold an all-stock investment portfolio (perhaps even with leverage) because the investor can easily offset any disastrous returns in the short run by adjusting his or her future investment strategy, labor supply, consumption, and/or savings. As the investor becomes older, the proportion of human capital in total wealth becomes smaller; therefore, the financial portfolio should become less aggressive.

Although the typical U.S. investor's income is unlikely to be highly correlated with the aggregate stock market (based on results reported by Davis and Willen 2000), many investors' incomes may be highly correlated with a specific company's market experience. Company executives, stockbrokers, and stock portfolio managers (whose labor income and human capital are highly correlated with risky assets) should have financial portfolios invested in assets that are little correlated with the stock market (e.g., bonds).

HUMAN CAPITAL, LIFE INSURANCE, AND ASSET ALLOCATION

In the previous section, we discussed how human capital plays an important role in developing the appropriate investment recommendations for individual investors. In addition, recognition is growing among academics and practitioners that the risk and return characteristics of human capital (wage and salary profiles) should be taken into account when building portfolios for the individual investor. Therefore, we expanded the traditional investment advice framework to include not only an investor's financial capital but also human capital. To illustrate the effect of human capital in the expanded framework, we used case studies in which the human capital characteristics were quite different.

In this section, we study another (perhaps even more important) risk aspect of human capital—*mortality risk*.[17] And we further expand the framework developed in the previous section to include the life insurance decision. We first explain the rationale for examining the life insurance decision together with the asset allocation decision. We develop a unified model to provide practical guidelines on developing optimal asset allocation and life insurance allocation for individual investors in their preretirement years (accumulation stage). We also provide a number of case studies in which we illustrate model allocations that depend on income, age, and tolerance for financial risk.

Life Insurance and Asset Allocation Decisions

A unique aspect of an investor's human capital is mortality risk—the family's loss of human capital in the unfortunate event of the investor's premature death. This risk is huge for many individual investors because human capital is their dominant asset.

Life insurance has long been used to hedge against mortality risk. Typically, the greater the value of the human capital, the more life insurance the family demands. Intuitively, human capital affects not only optimal asset allocation but also optimal life insurance demand. These two important financial decisions have consistently been analyzed separately, however, in theory and practice. We found few references in the literature to the need to consider these decisions jointly and within the context of a life-cycle model of consumption and investment. Popular investment and financial planning advice regarding how much life insurance one should acquire is never framed in terms of the riskiness of one's human capital.

FIGURE 3.12   Relationships among Human Capital, Asset Allocation, and Life Insurance

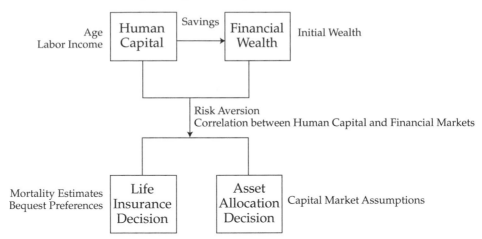

And the optimal asset allocation decision has only lately come to be framed in terms of the risk characteristics of human capital. Rarely is the asset allocation decision integrated with life insurance decisions.

Motivated by the need to integrate these two decisions in light of the risk and return characteristics of human capital, we have analyzed these traditionally distinct lines of thought together in one framework. These two decisions must be determined jointly because they serve as risk substitutes when viewed from an individual investor's portfolio perspective.

Life insurance is a perfect hedge for human capital in the event of death. Term life insurance and human capital have a negative 100 percent correlation with each other. If one pays off at the end of the year, then the other does not, and vice versa. Thus, the combination of the two provides great diversification to an investor's total portfolio. Figure 3.12 "updates" Figure 3.5 to illustrate the types of decisions the investor faces when jointly considering human capital, asset allocation, and life insurance decisions together with the variables that affect the decisions.

Human Capital, Life Insurance, and Asset Allocation

We discussed the literature on human capital and asset allocation extensively in the previous section, so in this section, we concentrate on the link between life insurance and human capital. A number of researchers have pointed out that the lifetime consumption and portfolio decision models need to be expanded to take into account lifetime uncertainty (or mortality risk). Yaari's 1965 paper is considered the first classical work on this topic. Yaari pointed out ways of using life insurance and life annuities to insure against lifetime uncertainty. He also derived conditions under which consumers would fully insure against lifetime uncertainty (see also Samuelson 1969; Merton 1969). Like Yaari, Fischer (1973) pointed out that earlier models either dealt with an infinite horizon or took the date of death to be known with certainty.

Theoretical studies show a clear link between the demand for life insurance and the uncertainty of human capital. Campbell (1980) argued that for most households, the uncertainty of labor income dominates uncertainty as to financial capital income. He also developed solutions based on human capital uncertainty to the optimal amount of insurance a household should purchase.[18] Buser and Smith (1983) used mean–variance analysis to model life insurance demand in a portfolio context. In deriving the optimal insurance demand and the optimal allocation between risky and risk-free assets, they found that the optimal amount of insurance depends on two components: the expected value of human capital and the risk–return characteristics of the insurance contract. Ostaszewski (2003) stated that life insurance—by addressing the uncertainties and inadequacies of an individual's human capital—is the business of human capital "securitization."

Empirical studies of life insurance adequacy have shown that underinsurance, however, is prevalent (see Auerbach and Kotlikoff 1991). Gokhale and Kotlikoff (2002) argued that questionable financial advice, inertia, and the unpleasantness of thinking about one's death are the likely causes.

Zietz (2003) has provided another excellent review of the literature on insurance.

Description of the Model

To merge considerations of asset allocation, human capital, and optimal demand for life insurance, we need a solid understanding of the actuarial factors that affect the pricing of a life insurance contract. Note that, although numerous life insurance product variations exist—such as term life, whole life, and universal life, each of which is worthy of its own financial analysis—we focus exclusively on the most fundamental type of life insurance policy—namely, the *one-year, renewable term policy*.[19]

On a basic economic level, the premium for a one-year, renewable term policy is paid at the beginning of the year—or on the individual's birthday—and protects the human capital of the insured for the duration of the year.[20] (If the insured person dies within that year, the insurance company pays the face value to the beneficiaries soon after the death or prior to the end of the year.) Next year, because the policy is renewable, the contract is guaranteed to start anew with new premium payments to be made and protection received.

In this section, we provide a general approach to thinking about the joint determination of the optimal asset allocation and prudent life insurance holdings. Appendix 3B contains a detailed specification of the model that is the basis for the numerical examples and case studies later in the section.

We assume there are two asset classes. The investor can allocate financial wealth between a risk-free asset and a risky asset (i.e., bonds and stocks). Also, the investor can purchase a term life insurance contract that is renewable each period. The investor's objective is to maximize overall utility, which includes utility in the investor's "live" state and in the investor's "dead" state, by choosing life insurance (the face value of a term life insurance policy) and making an asset allocation between the risk-free and risky assets.[21] The optimization problem can be expressed as follows:

$$\max_{(\theta_x, \, \alpha_x)} E[(1 - D)(1 - \bar{q}_x) U_{alive}(W_{x+1} + H_{x+1}) + D(\bar{q}_x) U_{dead}(W_{x+1} + \theta_x)], \qquad (3.4)$$

where

θ_x = amount of life insurance

α_x = allocation to the risky asset

D = relative strength of the utility of bequest, as explained in Appendix 3B

$\bar{q}_x$ = subjective probabilities of death at the end of the year $x + 1$ conditional on being alive at age x

$1 - \bar{q}_x$ = subjective probability of survival

W_{x+1} = wealth level at age $x + 1$, as explained in Appendix 3B

H_{x+t} = human capital

and $U_{alive}(\cdot)$ and $U_{dead}(\cdot)$ are the utility functions associated with the alive and dead states. The model is repeated in Equation 3B.2 and described in detail in Appendix 3B.

We extend the framework of Campbell (1980) and Buser and Smith (1983) in a number of important directions. First, we link the asset allocation decision to the decision to purchase life insurance in one framework by incorporating human capital. Second, we specifically take into consideration the effect of the bequest motive (attitude toward the importance of leaving a bequest) on asset allocation and life insurance.[22] Third, we explicitly model the volatility of labor income and its correlation with the financial market. Fourth, we also model the investor's subjective survival probability.

Human capital is the central component that links both decisions. Recall that an investor's human capital can be viewed as a stock if both the correlation with a given financial market subindex and the volatility of the labor income are high. Human capital can be viewed as a bond if both the correlation and the volatility are low. In between those two extremes, human capital is a diversified portfolio of stocks and bonds, plus idiosyncratic risk. Again, we rely on some of the Davis–Willen (2000) parameters for our numerical case examples. It is important to distinguish between, on the one hand, correlations and dependence when considering human capital and aggregate stock market returns (such as return of the S&P 500 Index) and, on the other hand, correlations of human capital with individual securities and industries. Intuitively, a middle manager working for Dow Corning, for example, has human capital returns that are highly correlated with the performance of Dow Corning stock. A bad year or quarter for the stock is likely to have a negative effect on financial compensation.

The model has several important implications. First, as expressed in Equation 3.4, it clearly shows that both asset allocation and life insurance decisions affect an investor's overall utility; therefore, the decisions should be made jointly.[23] The model also shows that human capital is the central factor. The impact of human capital on asset allocation and life insurance decisions is generally consistent with the existing literature (e.g., Campbell and Viceira 2002; Campbell 1980). One of our major enhancements, however, is the explicit modeling of correlation between the shocks to labor income and financial market returns. The correlation between income and risky-asset returns plays an important role in both decisions. All else being equal, as the correlation between shocks to income and risky assets increases, the optimal allocation to risky assets declines, as does the optimal quantity of life insurance. Although the decline in allocation to risky assets with increasing correlation may be intuitive from a portfolio theory perspective, we provide precise analytic guidance on how it should be implemented. Furthermore, and contrary to intuition, we show that a higher correlation with any given subindex brings about the second result—that is, reduces the demand for life insurance. The reason is that the higher the correlation, the higher the discount rate used to estimate human capital from future income. A higher discount rate implies a lower amount of human capital—thus, less insurance demand.

Second, the asset allocation decision affects well-being in both the live (consumption) state and the dead (bequest) state whereas the life insurance decision affects primarily the bequest state. Bequest preference is arguably the most important factor, other than human capital, in evaluating life insurance demand.[24] Investors who weight bequest as more important (who have a higher D) are likely to purchase more life insurance.

Another unique aspect of our model is the consideration of subjective survival probability, $1 - \bar{q}_x$. The reader can see intuitively that investors with low subjective survival probability (i.e., those who believe they have a high mortality rate) will tend to buy more life insurance. This "adverse selection" problem is well documented in the insurance literature.[25]

Other implications are consistent with the existing literature. For example, our model implies that the more financial wealth one has—all else being equal—the less life insurance one demands. More financial wealth also indicates more conservative portfolios when human capital is "bondlike." When human capital is "stocklike," more financial wealth calls for more aggressive portfolios. Naturally, risk tolerance also has a strong influence on the asset allocation decision. Investors with less risk tolerance will invest conservatively and buy more life insurance. These implications will be illustrated in the case studies.

We emphasize at this point that our analysis completely ignores the non-human-capital aspects of insurance purchases. For example, a wide variety of estate planning, business succession, and tax minimization strategies might increase demand for insurance much more than the level we have derived in our models. These aspects are beyond the scope of our analysis.

Case Studies

To illustrate the predictions of the model, we analyze the optimal asset allocation decision and the optimal life insurance coverage for five different cases. We solve the problem via simulation; the detailed solving process is presented in Appendix 3B.

For all five cases, we assumed the investor can invest in two asset classes. We used the capital market assumptions given in Table 3.1 of the previous section, which can be summarized as follows: compound annual geometric mean returns for bonds of 5 percent and for stocks of 9 percent, standard deviation of stock returns of 20 percent, and an inflation rate of 3 percent.

In these case studies, the investor is female. Her preference toward bequest is one-fourth of her preference toward consumption in the live state.[26] She has no special information about her relative health status (i.e., her subjective survival probability is equal to the objective actuarial survival probability). Her income is expected to grow with inflation, and the volatility of the growth rate is 5 percent.[27] Her real annual income is $50,000, and she saves 10 percent each year. She expects to receive a Social Security payment of $10,000 each year (in today's dollars) when she retires at age 65. Her current financial wealth is $50,000. She is assumed to follow constant relative risk aversion (CRRA) utility with a risk-aversion coefficient of γ. Finally, we assume that her financial portfolio is rebalanced and the term life insurance contract renewed annually.[28] These assumptions remain the same for all cases. Other parameters, such as initial wealth, will be specified in each case.

Case #1. Human Capital, Financial Asset Allocation, and Life Insurance Demand over the Lifetime

In this case, we assumed that the investor has a CRRA, γ, of 4. Also, the correlation between the investor's income and the market return of the risky asset is 0.20.[29] For a given age, the amount of insurance this investor should purchase can be determined by her consumption/bequest preference, risk tolerance, and financial wealth. Her expected financial wealth, human capital, and the derived optimal insurance demand over the investor's life from age 25 to age 65 are presented in Figure 3.13.

Several results of modeling this investor's situation are worth noting. First, human capital gradually decreases as the investor gets older and her remaining number of working years becomes smaller. Second, the amount of her financial capital increases as she ages as a result of growth of her existing financial wealth and the additional savings she makes each year. The allocation to risky assets decreases as the investor ages because of the dynamic between

FIGURE 3.13   Case #1: Human Capital, Financial Asset Allocation, and Insurance Demand over Lifetime

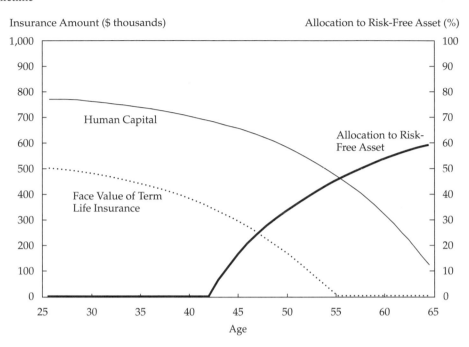

human capital and financial wealth over time. Finally, the investor's demand for insurance decreases as she ages. This result is not surprising because the primary driver of insurance demand is human capital, so the decrease in human capital reduces insurance demand.

These results appear to be consistent with conventional financial planning advice to reduce insurance holdings later in life, even though mortality risk itself has increased. In fact, one of the widespread misunderstandings about insurance, especially among young students of finance, is that a person needs large amounts of life insurance only when facing the greatest chance of death (i.e., only for older people). To the contrary, the magnitude of loss of human capital at younger ages is far more important than the higher probability of death at older ages.

Case #2. Strength of the Bequest Motive

This case shows the impact of the bequest motive on the optimal decisions about asset allocation and insurance. In this case, we assume that the investor is age 45 and has an accumulated financial wealth of $500,000. The investor has a CRRA coefficient of 4. The optimal allocations to the risk-free asset and insurance for various bequest preferences are presented in Figure 3.14.

In this case, insurance demand increases as the bequest motive strengthens (i.e., as D gets larger). This result is expected because an investor with a strong bequest motive is highly concerned about her heirs and has an incentive to purchase a large amount of insurance to hedge the loss of human capital. In contrast, Figure 3.14 shows almost no change in the proportional allocation to the risk-free asset at different strengths of bequest motive. This result indicates that asset allocation is primarily determined by risk tolerance, returns on the risk-free and risky assets, and human capital. This case shows that the bequest motive has a strong effect on insurance demand but little effect on optimal asset allocation.[30]

FIGURE 3.14   Case #2: Optimal Insurance Demand and Allocation to the Risk-Free Asset by Strength of Bequest Preference

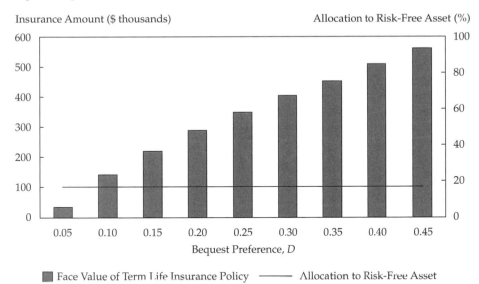

FIGURE 3.15   Case #3: Optimal Insurance Demand and Allocation to the Risk-Free Asset by Risk-Aversion Level

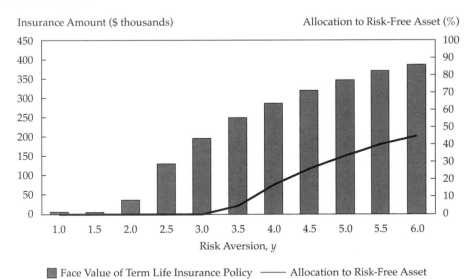

Case #3. The Impact of Risk Tolerance

In this case, we again assume that the investor is age 45 and has accumulated financial wealth of $500,000. The investor has a moderate bequest preference level (i.e., $D = 0.2$). The optimal allocations to the risk-free asset and the optimal insurance demands for this investor for various risk-aversion levels are presented in Figure 3.15.

As expected, allocation to the risk-free asset increases with the investor's risk-aversion level—the classic result in financial economics. Actually, the optimal portfolio is 100 percent in stocks for risk-aversion levels less than 2.5. The optimal amount of life insurance follows a similar pattern: Optimal insurance demand increases with risk aversion. For this investor with moderate risk aversion (a CRRA coefficient of 4) and the human and financial assumptions that we have made, optimal insurance demand is about $290,000, which is roughly six times her current income of $50,000.[31] Therefore, conservative investors should invest more in risk-free assets and buy more life insurance than aggressive investors should.

Case #4. Financial Wealth

For this case, we hold the investor's age at 45 and her risk preference and bequest preference at moderate levels (a CRRA coefficient of 4 and bequest level of 0.2). The optimal asset allocation to the risk-free asset and the optimal insurance demands for various levels of financial wealth are presented in Figure 3.16.

First, Figure 3.16 shows that the optimal allocation to the risk-free asset increases with initial wealth, which was discussed extensively in the section on Human Capital and Asset Allocation Advice.

Second, optimal insurance demand decreases with financial wealth. This result can be intuitively explained through the substitution effects of financial wealth and life insurance. In other words, with a large amount of wealth in hand, one has less demand for insurance because the loss of human capital will have much less impact on the well-being of one's heirs. In Figure 3.16, the optimal amount of life insurance decreases from more than $400,000 when the investor has little financial wealth to almost zero when the investor has $1.5 million in financial assets.

In summary, for an investor whose human capital is less risky than the stock market, the more substantial the investor's financial assets are, the more conservative optimal asset allocation is and the smaller life insurance demand is.

FIGURE 3.16   Case #4: Optimal Insurance Demand and Allocation to the Risk-Free Asset by Level of Financial Wealth

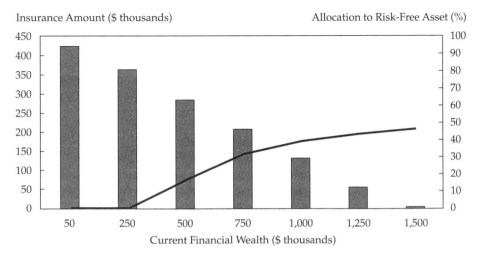

Insurance Amount ($ thousands)   Allocation to Risk-Free Asset (%)

Current Financial Wealth ($ thousands)

■ Face Value of Term Life Insurance Policy   —— Allocation to Risk-Free Asset

Case #5. Correlation between Wage Growth Rate and Stock Returns

In this case, we want to evaluate the life insurance and asset allocation decisions for investors with a high correlation between the risky asset and the investors' income. This kind of correlation can happen when an investor's income is closely linked to the stock performance of the company where the investor works or when the investor's compensation is highly influenced by the financial market (e.g., the investor works in the financial industry).

Again, the investor's age is 45 and she has a moderate risk preference and bequest preference. Optimal asset allocation to the risk-free asset and insurance demand for various levels of correlations in this situation are presented in Figure 3.17.

The optimal allocation becomes more conservative (i.e., more allocation is made to the risk-free asset) as income and stock market return become more correlated, which is similar to the results described in the previous section. The optimal insurance demand decreases as the correlation increases. Life insurance is purchased to protect human capital for the family and loved ones. As the correlation between the risky asset and the income flow increases, the *ex ante* value of human capital to the surviving family decreases. This lower valuation on human capital induces a lower demand for insurance. Also, less money spent on life insurance indirectly increases the amount of financial wealth the investor can invest, so the investor can invest more in risk-free assets to reduce the risk associated with her total wealth.[32]

Another way to think about these results is to consider the certainty (or utility) equivalent of risky human capital, which can be thought of as the economic present value of a cash flow stream. The higher the correlation with other financial assets and the higher the volatility of the cash flow stream, the lower the certainty-equivalent value and, therefore, the lower the demand for insurance.

In summary, as wage income and stock market returns become more correlated, optimal asset allocation becomes more conservative and the demand for life insurance falls.

FIGURE 3.17   Case #5: Optimal Insurance Demand and Allocation to the Risk-Free Asset by Correlation Level

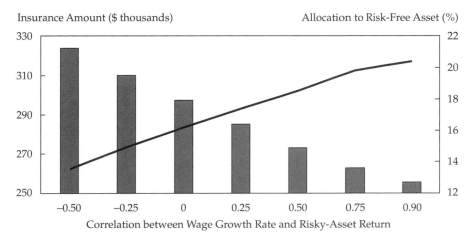

Insurance Amount ($ thousands)   Allocation to Risk-Free Asset (%)

Correlation between Wage Growth Rate and Risky-Asset Return

■ Face Value of Term Life Insurance Policy   —— Allocation to Risk-Free Asset

Summary

We have expanded on the basic idea that human capital is a "shadow" asset class that is worth much more than financial capital early in life and that it also has unique risk and return characteristics. Human capital—even though it is not traded and is highly illiquid—should be treated as part of a person's endowed wealth that must be protected, diversified, and hedged.

We demonstrated that the correlation between human capital and financial capital (i.e., whether the investor resembles more closely a bond or a stock) has a noticeable and immediate effect on the investor's demand for life insurance—in addition to the usual portfolio considerations. Our main argument is that the two decisions—quantity of life insurance and asset allocation—cannot be solved in isolation. Rather, they are aspects of the same problem.

We developed a unified human capital–based framework to help individual investors with both decisions. The model provided several key results:

- Investors need to make asset allocation decisions and life insurance decisions jointly.
- The magnitude of human capital, its volatility, and its correlation with other assets significantly affect the two decisions over the life cycle.
- Bequest preferences and a person's subjective survival probability have significant effects on the person's demand for insurance but little influence on the person's optimal asset allocation.
- Conservative investors should invest relatively more in risk-free assets and buy more life insurance.

We presented five case studies to demonstrate the optimal decisions in different scenarios.

RETIREMENT PORTFOLIO AND LONGEVITY RISK

In the previous two sections, we studied human capital and its impact on asset allocation and life insurance decisions for investors in the accumulation stage (i.e., when people are generally saving money prior to retirement). In the next three sections, we shift our attention to the retirement stage.

In this section, we investigate the risk factors that investors face when making decisions about saving for and investing their retirement portfolios. We illustrate the common mistakes that investors experience when making their asset allocation and spending decisions in retirement. Through the use of Monte Carlo simulation techniques, we illustrate the longevity risk that investors face and the potential benefits of including lifetime-payout annuities in retirement portfolios.

Three Risk Factors in Retirement

A typical investor has two goals in retirement. The primary goal is to ensure a comfortable life style during retirement. In other words, investors would like to enjoy roughly the same life style in retirement that they had before (or a better one). Second, they would like to leave some money behind as a bequest. Three important risks confront individuals when they are making saving and investment decisions for their retirement portfolios: (1) financial market risk, (2) longevity risk, and (3) the risk of not saving enough (spending too much). Part of the third risk is the risk of inflation.

Financial Market Risk

Financial market risk, or volatility in the capital markets, causes portfolio values to fluctuate in the short run even though they may appreciate in the long run. If the market drops or corrections occur early during retirement, the individual's portfolio may not be able to weather the stress of subsequent systematic withdrawals. Then, the portfolio may be unable to generate the income necessary for the individual's desired life style or may simply run out of money before the individual dies.

Investors often ignore financial market risk by assuming a constant rate of return from their retirement portfolio (i.e., no market volatility). As a result, they make inappropriate asset allocations and product selections. For an illustration of the impact of the constant-return assumption, consider the following case. Assume that a 65-year-old investor has $1 million invested in a 60 percent stock/40 percent bond portfolio (hereafter, 60/40).[33] He would like to have $75,000 a year worth of income in retirement. Social Security and his defined-benefit (DB) pension plan will provide about $25,000 of this annual retirement income. Thus, he needs his investment portfolio to generate $50,000 each year from age 65 for the remainder of his life. Assuming that the compounded annual nominal returns for stocks and bonds are, respectively, 9 percent and 5 percent, the estimated average compounded annual nominal return on the portfolio is 7.4 percent. We assume inflation to be 3.0 percent.

Figure 3.18 shows the wealth and income levels projected for the constant returns in this case.[34] If we assume that the future return is constant, each year the portfolio will generate a 6.14 percent compounded return after expenses and fees, or roughly 3.14 percent after inflation. The $1 million portfolio will be able to sustain a withdrawal of more than $50,000 a year in real terms for the investor's life expectancy and beyond. In other words, with constant returns, the investor will meet his income needs and not run out of money.

Market return, however, is not the same every year. In some periods, the portfolio returns will be much lower than 6.14 percent and may even be negative—as occurred in

FIGURE 3.18   Projected Wealth

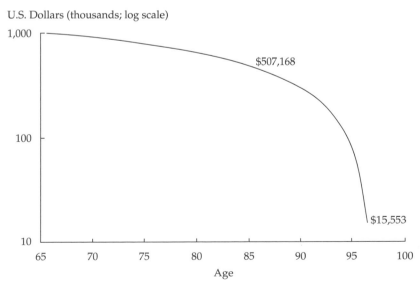

Note: 65-year-old male investor; $1 million; 60/40 portfolio.

2000, 2001, and 2002. So, although 6.14 percent may be a reasonable average assumption, it is unrealistic for the investor to make decisions based purely on the average return. Doing so underestimates the risk, and investors are generally risk averse by nature.

To show the impact of the entire return spectrum, we used a Monte Carlo simulation. Monte Carlo simulation is a technique to evaluate the outcome of portfolios over time by using a large number of simulated possible future return paths. In this case, the returns were randomly generated from a normal distribution with a 6.14 percent compounded average return and a 13 percent standard deviation.[35]

Panel A of Figure 3.19 presents the Monte Carlo analysis results for the same case used in Figure 3.18. This analysis shows a 10 percent chance that this portfolio will be depleted by age 82, a 25 percent chance it will be depleted by age 88, and a 50 percent chance it will be depleted by age 95. When considered in light of the uncertain life spans of investors, this result reveals a much larger risk than many investors would accept. Panel B of Figure 3.19 shows the wealth produced by a nonannuitized 60/40 portfolio plus Social Security and DB plan payments of $25,000 a year.

Longevity Risk

Longevity risk is the risk of living longer than planned for and outliving one's assets. With life expectancies continuing to increase, retirees—especially those who retire early or have a family history of long lives—must be aware of the possibility of a long lifetime and adjust their plans accordingly.

Americans are living longer, on average, than ever before. The probability that an individual retiring at age 65 will reach age 80 is greater than 70 percent for females and greater than 62 percent for males. For a married couple, the odds reach nearly 90 percent that at least one spouse will live to age 70. As Figure 3.4 illustrated, in more than 80 percent of cases, at least one spouse will still be alive at age 85.

Simple retirement planning approaches ignore longevity risk by assuming the investor needs to plan only to age 85. It is true that 85 years is roughly the life expectancy for an individual who is 65 years old, but life expectancy is only the average estimate. Roughly half of investors will live longer than life expectancy. Therefore, investors who have used an 85-year life expectancy to plan their retirement income needs may find they have used up their retirement resources (other than government and corporate pensions) long before actual mortality. This longevity risk is substantial.

Risk of Spending Uncertainty

Investors may not save enough to adequately fund their retirement portfolios. Retirees are increasingly relying on investment income from their own portfolios, such as defined-contribution (DC) plans and individual retirement accounts, to fund their retirements. The ambiguity in this situation is that investors cannot determine exactly what they will earn between now and retirement. Moreover, they may not have the discipline to save adequately.

The evidence is that most investors do not save enough (Benartzi and Thaler 2001). A large proportion of investors do not even fund their 401(k) plans enough to use the match that their employers provide. If an employer provides a 50 percent match, then for each dollar an investor puts into her or his 401(k) plan, the employer puts in 50 cents. This immediate 50 percent "return" should not be given up by any rational employee, but it often is.

Although most savings can generate only normal capital market returns, savings are critical to meet retirement needs. To expect investment returns to compensate for a savings shortfall is

FIGURE 3.19   Nonannuitized Portfolio

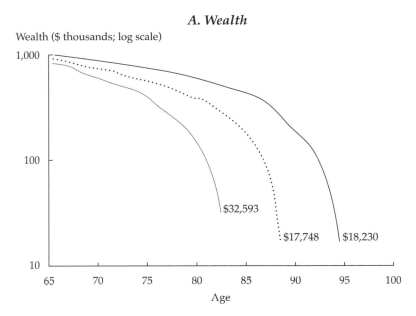

A. Wealth

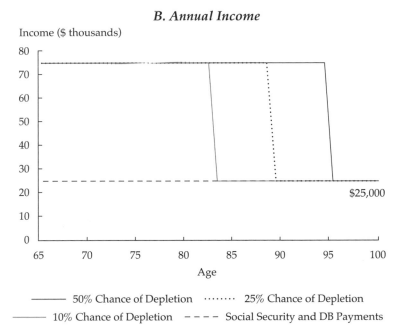

B. Annual Income

not reasonable. To the contrary, investment returns allow the savings to multiply several times over the course of a retirement.

Controlling the Three Risks

Financial risk can be mitigated by using modern portfolio theory, which provides methods to reduce portfolio risk by capturing the long-term diversification benefits among investments.

Insurance products can hedge away longevity risk. The risk of inadequate savings is primarily a behavioral issue.

For financial market risk, investors can turn to the rich literature and models of modern portfolio theory. Although financial market risk cannot be completely eliminated, investors can take advantage of the benefits of diversifying among various investments by following long-term asset allocation policies. The Markowitz mean–variance model is widely accepted as the gold standard for asset allocation.

Mean–variance optimization is a first step, but it considers only the risk and return trade-off in the financial market. It does not consider the longevity risk that people face during retirement.

DB pension plans provide longevity insurance by supplying their plan participants with income that cannot be outlived. In many cases, this income is also adjusted for inflation, which provides a further hedge against unexpected shocks to inflation. Fewer and fewer U.S. workers, however, are being covered by DB plans.

Because living a long life means needing more resources to fund longer-term income needs, rational investors will have to turn to sources other than DB plans. One approach is to take on more financial risk, if the investor can tolerate the risk, in the hopes of gaining more return. This plan can be accomplished by selecting an aggressive asset allocation policy (typically by using more stocks than the usual 60 percent and/or by adding higher-risk assets, such as hedge funds).

Rational investors will also want to hedge away the financial aspect of longevity risk because this type of risk exposure offers no potential reward.[36] In other words, investors should be willing to pay an insurance premium to hedge away the longevity risk. This approach is similar to the concept of homeowner insurance, which protects against hazard to one's home. Lifetime annuities (payout annuities) provide investors with this type of longevity insurance. And lifetime annuities should be an integral part of many retirement plans precisely because of the real and substantial longevity risk—which should be treated just as seriously as the risks of disability, critical illness, and premature death.

Recently, behavioral economists have developed some innovative ways to help investors overcome the myopic behavior of spending today instead of saving for retirement. For example, Thaler and Benartzi (2004) pioneered the "Save More Tomorrow" (SMarT) program. SMarT takes advantage of the behavioral theory that people heavily weight current consumption over future (retirement) consumption. The program encourages workers to save some portion of their future *raises*, not their current income, in their 401(k) plans. In this plan, when they receive their raises, their savings rates go up but they still get to take home part of the extra compensation for immediate consumption. The plan is palatable because raises are in the future and people are less averse to trading future consumption for savings than to trading current consumption in order to save.

Longevity Risk and Sources of Retirement Income

Social security, DB pension plans, and personal savings (including DC savings) are the main sources of retirement income for Americans.[37] In this section, we look closely at the effectiveness of various sources in managing longevity risk.

Social Security and DB Pension Plans

Traditionally, Social Security and DB pension plans have provided the bulk of retirement income. For example, the U.S. Social Security Administration has reported that 39 percent of the income of persons 65 and older came from Social Security income in 2001 and 18 percent came from DB pensions (see GAO 2003). According to Employee Benefit Research Institute reports, current retirees receive about 60 percent of their retirement income from Social Security and traditional company pension plans, whereas today's workers can expect to have only about one-third of their retirement income funded by these sources (EBRI 2000).

Longevity insurance is embedded in U.S. government–funded Social Security and DB pension benefits because the benefits are paid out for as long as the beneficiary (and, typically, the beneficiary's spouse) lives. In DB pension plans, the employer (as plan sponsor) agrees to make future payments during retirement and is responsible for investing and managing the pension plan assets, thus bearing the investment and longevity risks. Because a DB pension plan typically covers a large number of employees, the overall longevity risk of the plan is significantly mitigated for the employer.

In the past two decades, a shift has been going on from DB plans to DC plans.[38] Over the past 20 years, the percentage of private-sector workers who participate in a DB plan has decreased and the percentage of such workers who participate in a DC plan has consistently increased. Today, the majority of active retirement plan participants are in DC plans, whereas most plan participants were in DB plans 20–30 years ago.

DC Plans and Other Personal Savings

Because workers increasingly must rely on their DC retirement portfolios and other personal savings as their primary sources of retirement income, workers must now bear longevity risk. DC plans contain no promise by an employer or the government that money will be available during retirement.

In addition to being exposed to longevity risk as never before, today's workers who are saving for retirement through DC plans have to manage this risk themselves. Personal savings are used to fund retirement income in two ways. First, a retiree may receive a lump sum directly from the plan as a cash settlement and then invest and withdraw from the portfolio during retirement. This plan is typically referred to as a "systematic withdrawal strategy." Second, a retiree may receive a lump sum and preserve the assets by purchasing a lifetime annuity with some or all of the proceeds to provide a stream of income throughout retirement. This plan is typically referred to as "annuitization."

Annuitization and systematic withdrawals (from an invested portfolio) have different advantages and risks for retirees. A life annuity, whether received from an employer-sponsored pension plan or purchased directly through an insurance company, ensures that a retiree will not run out of income no matter how long he or she lives. If a retiree dies soon after purchasing an annuity, however, he or she will have received considerably less than the lump sum a systematic withdrawal strategy would provide. With payout annuities, the investor will also be unable to leave that asset as a bequest, and the income from the annuity may not be adequate to pay for unexpected large expenses.

Retiring participants who systematically withdraw lump sums have the flexibility of preserving or drawing down those assets as they wish, but they risk running out of assets if they live longer than expected, if assets are withdrawn too rapidly, or if the portfolio suffers poor investment returns. Payout annuities offer a means to mitigate much of the financial uncertainty that accompanies living to a very old age but may not necessarily be the best approach for all retirees. For example, an individual with a life-shortening illness might not be concerned about the financial needs that accompany living to a very old age.

Longevity Risk and Payout Annuities

Because mean–variance optimization addresses only the risk and return trade-offs in the financial markets, we focus our attention on the importance of longevity insurance. We touch on the difference between fixed- and variable-payout annuities and then move on to address the proper allocation of retiree income between conventional financial assets and payout annuity products that help to manage longevity risk.

Living a long life means more resources are needed to fund longer-term income needs. On the one hand, rational investors may decide to take on more financial risk in hopes of gaining more return. On the other hand, rational investors would also want to hedge away the financial aspect of longevity risk because there is no potential financial reward for this type of risk exposure. In other words, investors should be willing to pay an insurance premium to hedge away longevity risk. Lifetime-payout annuities provide investors with this type of longevity insurance.

A lifetime-payout annuity is an insurance product that converts an accumulated investment into income that the insurance company pays out over the life of the investor. Payout annuities are the opposite of life insurance. Investors buy life insurance because they are afraid of dying too soon and leaving family and loved ones in financial need. They buy payout annuities because they are concerned about living too long and running out of assets during their lifetime. Insurance companies can provide this lifelong benefit by spreading the longevity risk over a large group of annuitants and making careful and conservative assumptions about the rate of return to be earned on their assets.

Spreading or pooling the longevity risk means that individuals who do not reach their life expectancy (as calculated by actuarial mortality tables) subsidize those who exceed it. Investors who buy lifetime-payout annuities pool their portfolios and collectively ensure that everybody will receive payments as long as they live. Because of the unique longevity insurance features embedded in lifetime-payout annuities, they can play a significant role in many investors' retirement portfolios.

The two basic types of payout annuities are fixed and variable. A fixed-payout annuity pays a fixed nominal dollar amount each period. A variable annuity's payments fluctuate in accord with the performance of the fortunes of the underlying investments chosen by the buyer of the annuity. Payments from a lifetime-payout annuity are contingent on the life span of the investor. Other payout options are available, however, that might guarantee that payments will be made for a specified period of time or might offer refund guarantees. For examples, see Appendix 3C.

If an investor buys a life annuity from an insurance company, the investor is transferring the longevity risk to the insurance company, which is in a far better position than an individual to hedge and manage those risks. But of course, the investor pays a price. Should an investor self-insure against longevity risk?

Fixed-Payout Annuity

Figure 3.20 illustrates the payment stream from an immediate fixed annuity. With an initial premium or purchase amount of $1 million, the annual income payments for our 65-year-old male would be $6,910 a month, or $82,920 a year.[39] The straight line represents the annual payments before inflation. People who enjoy the security of a steady and predictable stream of income may find a fixed annuity appealing. The drawback of a fixed annuity, however, becomes evident over time. Because the payments are the same year after year, purchasing power is eroded by inflation as the annuitant grows older. The curved line in Figure 3.20

FIGURE 3.20   Income from Fixed Annuity

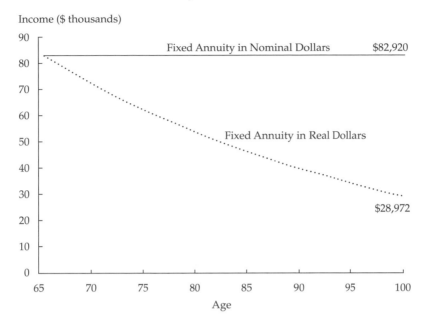

represents the same payment stream after taking into account a hypothetical 3 percent inflation rate.[40] Although the annuitant receives the same payment amount, that payment no longer purchases as much as it used to.

Despite the benefits of longevity insurance and fixed nominal payout amounts, a portfolio that consists solely of fixed lifetime annuities has several drawbacks. First, as noted, is decline in the value of the payments over time because of inflation. Second, one cannot trade out of the fixed-payout annuity once it has been purchased.[41] This aspect may be a problem for investors who need or prefer liquidity. Finally, when an investor buys a fixed annuity, the investor locks in payments based on the current interest rate environment. Payout rates from today's fixed-payout annuities are near historical lows because of current low interest rates. Our 65-year-old male might have received as much as $11,500 a month in the early 1980s in exchange for a $1 million initial premium. In 2003, that same $1 million bought only $6,689 a month. These drawbacks do not mean that fixed annuities are a poor investment choice. On the contrary, as we will show, fixed annuities can be a crucial part of a well-diversified retirement income portfolio.

Variable-Payout Annuities

A variable-payout annuity is an insurance product that exchanges accumulated investment value for annuity units that the insurance company pays out over the lifetime of the investor. The annuity payments fluctuate in value depending on the investments held; therefore, disbursements also fluctuate. To understand variable-payout annuities, think of a mutual fund whose current net asset value (NAV) is $1 per unit. The unit fluctuates each day. On any given day in any given week, month, or year, the price may increase or decrease relative to the previous period. With a variable annuity, instead of receiving fixed annuity payments, the investor receives a fixed number of fund units. Each month, the insurance company converts

FIGURE 3.21   Income from 100 Percent Immediate Variable Annuity

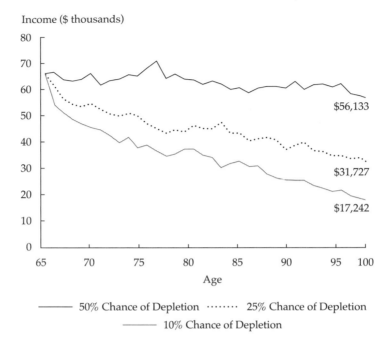

the fund units into dollars based on the NAV at the end of the month to determine how much to pay the investor. Therefore, the cash flow from the variable-payout annuity fluctuates with the performance of the funds the investor chooses.

Figure 3.21 illustrates the annuity payment stream, in real terms, from a 60/40 portfolio and a life-only payment option in an immediate variable annuity. We conducted a Monte Carlo simulation to illustrate the various payment scenarios. The simulation was generated for the case of the same investor discussed earlier from historical return statistics for stocks, bonds, and inflation for 1926–2006; a $1 million initial portfolio; and a 3 percent assumed investment return (AIR).[42] The initial payment at age 65 is estimated to be $66,153 a year.[43] The three lines in the chart show the 10th, 25th, and 50th percentiles. As Figure 3.21 demonstrates, there is a 10 percent chance that annual inflation-adjusted annuity payments will fall below $17,300 if the investor reaches 100, a 25 percent chance that they will be around $32,000 or lower, and a 50 percent chance that they will fall below $57,000.

Asset Allocation, Payout Annuities, and Disciplined Savings

Figure 3.22 shows the probability of success for two retirement income strategies—one using 100 percent systematic withdrawal from a 60/40 portfolio without any lifetime annuity (as depicted in Figure 3.18) and a second strategy using a payout annuity (25 percent fixed annuitization, 25 percent variable annuitization) and 50 percent systematic withdrawal from the same 60/40 portfolio. The systematic withdrawal strategy with no annuity has a higher risk of causing the portfolio to fall short of funding the required income need. The probability of success begins to drop before age 80 and falls to a low of 42 percent by age 100. The combination strategy is a far better strategy for increasing the odds of meeting income goals

FIGURE 3.22   Probability of Meeting Income Goal: Payout Annuities vs. Systematic Withdrawal

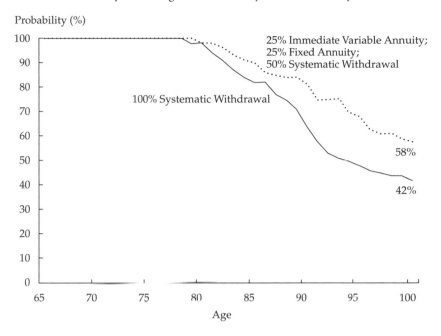

over this investor's lifetime. Although the probability of not being able to meet the income goal 100 percent of the time remains, the shortfall comes at a later stage in life and the success rate remains the highest.

For retirees, such a combination of types of annuitization and systematic withdrawal could help manage the financial risks and the income needs they face during retirement. But what is the best combination of various types of annuities and systematic withdrawal? The next section explores the solution to the challenge of an asset allocation in retirement that includes both conventional asset classes and immediate payout annuity products.

Summary

In this section, we presented the three risk factors that investors face when making retirement portfolio decisions: financial market risk, longevity risk, and the risk of spending too much (which includes inflation risk). We focused on the role that lifetime-payout annuities should play in a retirement portfolio to alleviate both financial market and longevity risks. First, we demonstrated that traditional wealth-forecasting techniques that use a constant-return assumption can lead investors to believe they face little or no risk in funding retirement income needs. We then used a Monte Carlo simulation to illustrate more realistically the market risks in systematic withdrawal from a mutual fund portfolio, and we compared the results of withdrawal strategies with the benefits of payout annuities. Our analysis made clear that combining immediate fixed and variable life annuities with conventional investment instruments, such as mutual funds, is the optimal solution to providing retirement income.

This section demonstrated that an immediate payout annuity is an effective way to manage longevity risk in retirement. Buying a lifetime-payout annuitization is not, however, an all-or-nothing decision; the investor can choose how much to allocate between mutual fund accounts and annuitization. Combining nonannuitized assets with annuitized assets can help investors manage financial market risk, longevity risk, and bequest desires. In the next section, we present a model to develop an optimal asset allocation that includes fixed- and variable-payout annuities.

ASSET ALLOCATION AND LONGEVITY INSURANCE

In this segment, we explore the idea of the optimal allocation to payout annuities in an investor's retirement portfolio. Our objective is to arrive at precise recommendations regarding how much of a retiree's portfolio income should contain longevity insurance in the form of pension (life) annuities and how much of the portfolio (and income) should be allocated to non-longevity-insured products, such as systematic withdrawal plans. The aim includes creating a comprehensive asset and product allocation strategy that addresses the unique requirements of today's, and tomorrow's, retirees.

As an investor ages, mortality risk (i.e., the risk that premature death will destroy the family's source of human capital) is replaced by longevity risk—the risk that the individual will outlive the time he or she has expected and planned to live. We argue that this risk also can be hedged by using an instrument that is the opposite of life insurance, namely, life annuities. In this section, we discuss how modern portfolio theory (MPT), which was originally designed for financial asset classes, can be merged with a similar framework for life annuities. We start by explaining the concept of mortality credit and then develop a simple one-period model with some numerical examples and some case studies. In the next section, we delve in more detail into the optimal timing of annuitization.

In addition to the usual risk and return information from the financial markets, a model for the optimal demand for longevity insurance and life annuities requires inputs for the relative strength of the retiree's bequest motives, subjective health status, and liquidity restrictions. We discuss all of these in detail. Recall from earlier sections that asset allocation is traditionally, in MPT, determined by constructing efficient portfolios for various risk levels (Markowitz 1952; Merton 1971). Then, based on the investor's risk tolerance, one of the efficient portfolios is chosen.

MPT is widely accepted as the primary tool for developing asset allocation recommendations. Its effectiveness is questionable, however, when dealing with asset allocations for individual investors in retirement because longevity risk is not considered in the classical framework. In this section, we review the need for longevity insurance during retirement and establish a framework for studying total asset allocation decisions in retirement, which includes conventional asset classes and immediate payout annuities.

Benefits of Longevity Insurance: Mortality Credits

Most retirees are hesitant to voluntarily purchase immediate annuities with their IRA (individual retirement account), 401(k), or other liquid wealth because they fear losing control and/or believe they can "do better" with other investment alternatives. Recent data from the LIMRA International research organization suggest that fewer than 5 percent of retirees who have a traditional variable annuity (VA) in accumulation choose to annuitize and derive income. When people within a traditional defined-benefit pension plan are offered the option of switching into a defined-contribution pension plan and giving up the implicit life annuity, most turn the offer down. Clearly, some confusion exists about the mechanics and benefits of these instruments. In the following section, we illustrate the benefits of annuitization and longevity insurance with a simple story, which also positions the income annuity product firmly within the realm of investment risk and return.

The 95-Year-Old Tontine Deal

Imagine five 95-year-old women who live in the United States and are interested in creating an investment club—but a club that is different from the usual kind. Each of the women invests $100 in a pool, but only survivors at the age of 96 can split the proceeds. While they are waiting to reach their 96th birthdays, the five women decide to put the money in a local bank's one-year certificate of deposit (CD) that is paying 5 percent interest for the year.

So, what will happen next year? According to statistics compiled by the U.S. Social Security Administration, there is a roughly 20 percent chance that a member of the investment club will die during the next year and, of course, an 80 percent chance that all will survive. And although virtually anything can happen to the women during the next 12 months of waiting, the probability implies that, *on average,* four 96-year-olds will survive to split the $525 pool at year end. Note that each survivor will receive $131.25 as her total return on the original investment of $100. The 31.25 percent investment return contains 5 percent of the bank's money and a healthy 26.25 percent of "mortality credits." These credits represent the capital and interest "lost" by the deceased and "gained" by the survivors.

The catch, of course, is that the *nonsurvivor* forfeits her claim to the funds. And although the heirs of the nonsurvivor's demise might be frustrated with the outcome, the survivors receive a superior investment return. More importantly, *all of them* are able to manage their lifetime income risk in advance without having to worry about what the future will bring. This story translates the benefits of longevity insurance into investment rates of return.

The story can be taken one step further. Suppose the investment club decides to invest the $500 in the stock market or some risky NASDAQ high-technology fund instead of a safe 5 percent CD for the next year. What happens if the value of the stock or high-tech fund falls 20 percent during the next year? How much will the surviving club members lose? If you think the answer is "nothing," you are absolutely correct. The four survivors divide the $400 among themselves so each receives her original $100 back.

Such is the power of mortality *credits.* They subsidize losses on the downside and enhance gains on the upside. In fact, one can argue that when adding longevity insurance to a diversified portfolio, an investor (or annuitant) can actually afford and tolerate more financial risk.

Of course, real life annuity contracts do not work in the way described in the story. Our hypothetical tontine contract is renewable each year, and the surviving 96-year-olds can take their mortality credits and go home. In practice, annuity contracts are for life and the mortality credits are spread and amortized over many years of retirement. The basic *insurance economics* of the annuity, however, are exactly as described for the hypothetical tontine. The next section will explore the mechanics and age-related effect of mortality credits, but for now, readers should keep in mind that mortality credits increase as the tontine members grow older.

The Payout Annuity's Insurance against Longevity Risk

The main lesson from the tontine story is that longevity risk can be hedged away with lifetime-payout annuities. A lifetime-payout annuity is an insurance product that exchanges an accumulated investment into payments that the insurance company pays out over a specified time—in this case, over the lifetime of the investor. Payout annuities are the exact opposite of traditional life (or more aptly named "premature death") insurance.

As discussed in the section called Retirement Portfolio and Longevity Risk, the two basic types of payout annuities are fixed annuities and variable annuities. A fixed-payout annuity pays a fixed dollar amount each period, perhaps with a cost-of-living adjustment, in real or nominal terms. A variable-payout annuity's payments fluctuate in value depending on the investments held, so disbursements also fluctuate. The payment from a lifetime-payout annuity is contingent on the life span of the investor. When the investor dies, his or her estate will no longer receive any payments unless a special guarantee period or estate benefit was purchased at the same time as the annuity. Such arrangements are normally paid for by reducing the benefit stream.

A substantial amount of literature has recently been written on the costs and benefits of life annuities. Space constraints prevent us from providing a comprehensive review, but the relevant academic literature can be roughly partitioned into three categories.

The first strand consists of literature on the theoretical insurance economics of life annuities. It investigates the equilibrium supply and demand of life annuities in the context of a complete market and utility-maximizing investors. This literature includes the classic work by Yaari (1965) and works by Richard (1975), Brugiavini (1993), Yagi and Nishigaki (1993), and Milevsky and Young (2002). Broadly, the main conclusions of these investigators are that life annuities should play a substantial role in a retiree's portfolio.

The empirical annuity literature examines the actual pricing of these products and whether consumers are getting their money's worth when they buy life annuities. This strand includes a sequence of papers by Brown, Warshawsky, Mitchell, and Poterba in various combinations.[44]

A third and final strand is the attempt to create normative models to help investors decide how much to annuitize, when to annuitize, and the appropriate asset mix within annuities. These authors include Kapur and Orszag (1999), Blake, Cairns, and Dowd (2000), and Milevsky (2001).

We have tried to abstract from the complications one would encounter in reality by developing in this section a simple framework for analyzing the risk and return trade-off between one-period, tontine-like annuities and conventional asset classes.

Optimal Asset Allocation Mix with Payout Annuities

Smart asset allocation decisions that take advantage of the benefits of diversifying among different asset classes are an effective tool for managing and reducing market risk. Therefore, to help investors find the appropriate allocation of their savings in retirement, we must incorporate fixed- and variable-payout annuities into the traditional asset allocation models.

Classical asset allocation models used by popular software vendors and advisory services use information on the investor's time horizon and level of risk aversion to determine the appropriate asset mix. But to incorporate payout annuities and retirement dynamics in asset allocation, a proper model requires more information.

We have developed a model for optimally allocating investment assets within and between two distinct categories—annuitized assets and nonannuitized assets. The annuitized assets include fixed and variable immediate annuities. The nonannuitized assets could include all types of investment instruments—for example, mutual funds, stocks, bonds, and U.S. Treasury bills that do not

FIGURE 3.23   Trade-Off between Bequest and Consumption

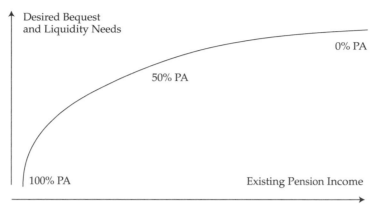

Note: PA = payout annuities.

contain a mortality-contingent income flow. In addition, a proper model must take into account the following decision factors:

- investor's risk tolerance,
- investor's age,
- investor's subjective probability of survival,
- objective probability of survival,
- relative weights the investor places on personal spending and creating an estate value, and
- risk and return characteristics of risky and risk-free assets.

Regarding the trade-off between bequest (the desire to leave a bequest) and consumption (the need for liquidity in assets), the model developed in the next section incorporates classical economic models of consumer behavior. Figure 3.23 provides a graphical illustration of the trade-off between the desire for bequest and liquidity needs in light of an existing pension income. The greater the desire for creating an estate, or the higher the bequest value, the lower the demand (or need for) payout annuities (PA). The reason is that life annuities trade off longevity insurance against the creation of an estate.

Model Asset Allocation with Lifetime-Payout Annuities

We start by assuming that a rational, utility-maximizing investor is choosing the allocation of his retirement portfolio to maximize his utility. We also assume that the investor has four investment products to choose among: a risk-free asset, a risky asset, an immediate fixed annuity (IFA), and an immediate variable annuity (IVA). This model can be easily expanded to incorporate more assets.[45]

The model is formulated in a one-period framework, which makes the life annuity more of a tontine, but the underlying idea is the same regardless of the number of periods in the model. With four categories to choose from, the investor is looking at the traditional asset allocation problem. How does this rational, utility-maximizing individual go about selecting the right mix of risky and risk-free assets and of traditional financial instruments and immediate annuities?

Table 3.2 summarizes the assumed returns from the four investment products conditioned on the alive state versus the dead state. From a mathematical point of view, we have the

TABLE 3.2   Returns to Four Investment Choices

Asset	Alive State	Dead State
Risk-free asset (T-bills)	$R = 5\%$	$R = 5\%$
Risky asset (U.S. equity)	$X = 9\%$	$X = 9\%$
Immediate fixed annuity	$(1 + R)/p - 1$	0
Immediate variable annuity	$(1 + X)/p - 1$	0

Note: $R =$ return to the risk-free asset, $X =$ return to the risky asset, $p =$ objective probability of survival.

following problem: Find the asset allocation weights, denoted by a_1, a_2, a_3, a_4, that maximize the objective function

$$E[U(W)] = \bar{p} \times A \times E[U(a_1wR + a_2wX + a_3wR/p + a_4wX/p)]$$
$$+ (1 - \bar{p}) \times D \times E[U(a_1wR + a_2wX)], \qquad (5.1)$$

subject to $a_1 + a_2 + a_3 + a_4 = 1$ and $a_i > 0$.

In this model, we use the following notation:

- A denotes the relative strength placed on the utility of consumption.
- D denotes the relative strength placed on the utility of bequest. The sum of A and D is assumed to be 1, so there is only one free variable. Individuals with no utility of bequest will be assumed to have $D = 0$.
- p denotes the objective probability of survival, which is the probability that is used by the insurance company to price immediate annuities.
- $\bar{p}$ denotes the subjective probability of survival. The subjective probability of survival may not match the objective (annuitant) probability. In other words, a person might believe he or she is healthier (or less healthy) than average. This circumstance would affect the expected utility but not the payout from the annuity, which is based on objective (annuitant) population survival rates.
- X denotes the (1 plus) random return from the risky asset.
- R denotes the (1 plus) risk-free rate.
- The expression $E[U(a_1wR + a_2wX + a_3wR/p + a_4wX/p)]$ denotes the utility from the live state.
- The expression $E[U(a_1wR + a_2wX)]$ denotes utility from the dead state. (Notice that the annuity term, which divides by the probability of survival, does not appear in the dead state because the annuity does not pay out in the dead state.)
- The function $U(\cdot)$ denotes the standard utility function for end-of-period wealth.

The model can handle cases of both constant relative risk aversion (CRRA) and decreasing relative risk aversion as well as other functional forms that are consistent with loss aversion.

Because the weights a_1 through a_4 sum to 1, we essentially have only three weights to solve because $a_4 = 1 - (a_1 + a_2 + a_3)$. An important factor to consider in solving the utility maximization is that, as functions of (a_1, a_2, a_3), both $E[U(W)]$ and its derivatives are defined by integrals that cannot be performed analytically; they must be performed numerically.

The technical problem to be solved is to maximize the expected utility $E[U(W)]$ as a function of the weights a_1, a_2, and a_3, where $a_1 \geq 0$, $a_2 \geq 0$, $a_3 \geq 0$, and $a_1 + a_2 + a_3 \leq 1$.

Now, although $E[U(W)]$ is a nonlinear function of the three free parameters (a_1, a_2, a_3), it is *strictly* concave; hence, one need only find a local maximum to find the global maximum.

Numerical Examples and Case Studies

To understand the intuition and results of the model, we examine several cases to gauge the effect of changing parameters on the optimal allocation. We start with the individual and capital market assumptions that will remain the same for all three cases. All cases will assume that the individual is a 60-year-old male who would like to allocate his portfolio among the two investment asset classes and the two mortality-contingent classes. The return, r_f, from the risk-free asset class (T-bills, termed "cash" in the tables and figure) is shown in Table 3.2 with no volatility. The return from the risky asset is lognormally distributed with a mean return value, R, of 9 percent and a standard deviation, SD, of 20 percent. (These return and risk assumptions are the same as those used for the cases studies in the sections on Human Capital and Asset Allocation Advice and Human Capital, Life Insurance, and Asset Allocation.)

For the objective mortality parameter, we use a table provided by the U.S. Society of Actuaries called the Individual Annuity Mortality (IAM) 2000 basic table. The basic table provides the probabilities of survival for a healthy population of potential annuitants. The subjective probability of survival may be lower (or higher) than the numbers indicated by the IAM 2000. The utility preferences are taken from the CRRA family, with a CRRA coefficient of γ. Finally, a 20-year horizon represents the one period. In other words, the individual intends to reallocate (rebalance) assets after 20 years. In practice, of course, investors should rebalance their portfolios much before the 20-year horizon, which requires a dynamic, multiperiod model.

Case #1. Total Altruism and Complete Bequest Motive

In this case, the investor's utility is derived entirely from bequests. That is, the weight of his utility of bequest is assumed to be 1 and the weight of his utility of consumption is 0: $D = 1$ and $A = 0$. The objective probability of survival is 65 percent (roughly equal to the survival probability of a 60-year-old male in the next 20 years), and the subjective probability is the same 65 percent. In other words, we are assuming that the investor does not have any private information about his or her mortality status that would lead him to believe he is healthier or less healthy than average men of his age.

Based on these input parameters, the model produces the optimal allocations, by risk aversion, given in Table 3.3.

A few things are evident from Table 3.3. First, immediate annuities receive no allocation because the investor cares only about leaving a bequest. The intuition for this result can be traced back to a classic paper by Yaari (1965). If consumers are 100 percent altruistic, they will not waste the asset by annuitizing. Second, the allocation to stocks gradually decreases as the investor's risk aversion increases. Thus, because the investor has no consumption motive, the allocation task is the traditional choice of risk-free versus risky assets. For example, for investors with a relative risk-aversion level of 2, the optimal allocation is 21 percent to the risk-free asset and 79 percent to equity.

This case can be viewed as an illustration for extraordinarily wealthy individuals for whom the size of the portfolio far exceeds consumption needs. For such individuals, bequest becomes the dominant factor. Annuities do not receive any allocation because longevity insurance is not needed and annuities prevent leaving any money to heirs.

TABLE 3.3 Optimal Allocations for Case #1: Complete Bequest Motive

Risk Aversion	Cash	Equity	IFA	IVA	Total Risk Free	Total Risky	Total Traditional	Total Annuity
1.0	0%	100%	0%	0%	0%	100%	100%	0%
1.5	0	100	0	0	0	100	100	0
2.0	21	79	0	0	21	79	100	0
2.5	37	63	0	0	37	63	100	0
3.0	49	51	0	0	49	51	100	0
3.5	57	43	0	0	57	43	100	0
4.0	63	37	0	0	63	37	100	0
4.5	68	32	0	0	68	32	100	0
5.0	71	29	0	0	71	29	100	0
5.5	74	26	0	0	74	26	100	0
6.0	76	24	0	0	76	24	100	0

Notes: Male, age = 60, 65 percent objective and subjective survival probability, 100 percent bequest, 20-year horizon, R_f = 5 percent, R = 9 percent, SD = 20 percent. In the column headings, IFA stands for immediate fixed annuity and IVA stands for immediate variable annuity.

Case #2. No Bequest Motive

This case maintains the same age and gender, survival probability, and time horizon but completely eliminates the strength of bequest; that is, $A = 1$ and $D = 0$. In other words, 100 percent of the utility weight is placed on "live" consumption. The optimal allocations to the assets among various risk-aversion levels are presented in Table 3.4.

Because the returns on annuities are always higher than the returns on traditional assets—conditional on the retiree being alive—the immediate annuities receive 100 percent of the allocation in this case. The allocation to the immediate variable annuity gradually decreases, whereas the allocation to the immediate fixed annuity increases as the risk aversion of the investor increases.

This case can be used as an illustration for investors who would like to maximize their lifetime consumption and have no interest in leaving any money behind. (They are sometimes known as the "die broke" crowd.) All the savings should be used to purchase annuities. Overall, the optimal allocation between risky and risk-free assets (in this case, they are an immediate fixed annuity and an immediate variable annuity) is almost identical to that of Case #1. For investors with a risk-aversion level of 2, for example, the optimal allocation is 21 percent to the immediate fixed annuity and 79 percent to the immediate variable annuity.

Case #3. Bequest Motive of 20 Percent and Consumption Motive of 80 Percent

In this variation, the strength of the bequest motive is raised from $D = 0$ to a more realistic $D = 0.2$. In other words, 80 percent of the utility weight is placed on alive-state consumption. The optimal allocations to the assets for various risk-aversion levels are presented in Table 3.5. Figure 3.24 depicts the allocations graphically.

TABLE 3.4   Optimal Allocations for Case #2: No Bequest Motive

Risk Aversion	Cash	Equity	IFA	IVA	Total Risk Free	Total Risky	Total Traditional	Total Annuity
1.0	0%	0%	0%	100%	0%	100%	0%	100%
1.5	0	0	0	100	0	100	0	100
2.0	0	0	21	79	21	79	0	100
2.5	0	0	37	63	37	63	0	100
3.0	0	0	49	51	49	51	0	100
3.5	0	0	57	43	57	43	0	100
4.0	0	0	63	37	63	37	0	100
4.5	0	0	68	32	68	32	0	100
5.0	0	0	71	29	71	29	0	100
5.5	0	0	74	26	74	26	0	100
6.0	0	0	77	23	77	23	0	100

Note: Male, age 60, 65 percent survival, 0 percent bequest, 20-year horizon, $R_f = 5$ percent, $R = 9$ percent, $SD = 20$ percent.

TABLE 3.5   Optimal Allocations for Case #3: Bequest Motive 20 Percent, Consumption Motive 80 Percent

Risk Aversion	Cash	Equity	IFA	IVA	Total Risk Free	Total Risky	Total Traditional	Total Annuity
1.0	0%	34%	0%	66%	0%	100%	34%	66%
1.5	0	50	0	50	0	100	50	50
2.0	13	48	8	31	21	79	61	39
2.5	25	42	12	20	37	63	67	33
3.0	35	37	14	14	49	51	72	28
3.5	43	33	14	10	57	43	76	24
4.0	50	29	13	8	63	37	79	21
4.5	55	26	13	6	68	32	81	19
5.0	59	24	12	5	71	29	83	17
5.5	62	22	12	4	74	26	84	16
6.0	65	20	11	3	76	24	86	14

Note: Male, age 60, 65 percent survival, 20 percent bequest, 20-year horizon, $R_f = 5$ percent, $R = 9$ percent, $SD = 20$ percent.

FIGURE 3.24   Optimal Allocations: Bequest Motive 20 Percent, Consumption Motive 80 Percent

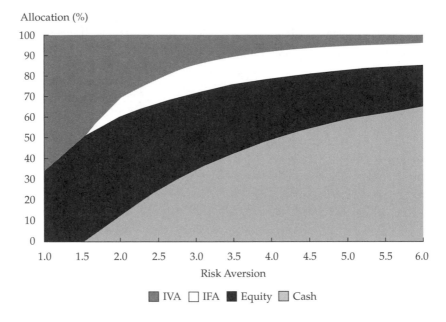

There are several interesting allocation results in this case. First, unlike the previous two cases, all four of the asset classes are represented in the optimal allocations. The reason is that immediate annuities are more suitable than traditional assets for consumption and traditional investments are more suited for bequest motives in this one-period framework. In general, the higher the bequest motive of an investor, the more the investor should allocate to traditional investments and the less to immediate annuities.

Second, the allocations between risky (both IVA and equity) and risk free (cash and IFA) are almost identical to those in Case #1 and Case #2 at comparable risk-aversion levels. This result indicates that the changes in the investor's bequest and consumption motives do not have a significant impact on the investor's behavior regarding risk. The optimal allocation between risky and risk-free assets is determined by the investor's risk tolerance.

Third, the allocation to annuities decreases as the investor's risk aversion increases. In other words, investors who are more averse to market risk will avoid immediate life annuities. This outcome makes intuitive sense: The investor can get little or no utility from immediate annuity investments if he or she dies shortly after the purchase. With traditional investments, some utility will be left for the heirs. Apparently, the higher aversion to market risk increases the implicit weight on the utility of bequest. For an investor with a risk-aversion level of 2, the optimal allocation is 13 percent cash, 48 percent equity, 8 percent IFA, and 31 percent IVA.

Summary

This section was motivated by investors' need to manage longevity risk together with financial risk. We introduced a model that merges financial market risk *and* longevity risk in analyzing the economic trade-off of investments.

Our main qualitative insight is as follows. The natural asset allocation spectrum consists of investments that go from safe (fixed) to risky (variable). The product allocation spectrum ranges from conventional savings vehicles to annuitized payout (pension) instruments. The asset and product spaces are separate dimensions of a well-balanced financial portfolio; yet, the product/asset allocation must be analyzed jointly.

Formally, we presented a mathematical one-period model to analyze the optimal allocations within and between payout annuities and traditional asset classes. The numerical results confirm that the optimal allocations among assets are influenced by such factors as age, risk aversion, subjective probability of survival, utility of bequest, and the expected risk and return trade-offs of various investments. We also found that the global allocation between risky and risk-free assets is influenced only by the investor's risk tolerance; it is not significantly affected by the subjective probability of survival or the utility of consumption versus the utility of bequest.

In some sense, we are advocating a classical economic "separation theorem" argument. The first step of a well-balanced retirement plan is to locate a suitable global mix of risky and risk-free assets independently of the assets' mortality-contingent status. Then, once a comfortable balance has been struck between risk and return, the annuitization decision should be viewed as a second-step "overlay" that is placed on top of the existing asset mix. And depending on the strength of the investor's bequest motives and subjective health assessments, the optimal annuitized fraction will follow. These assume that the payout annuities contain only longevity insurance without any other options (i.e., benefit riders).

Of course, retirement is not one point or period in time. In the next section, we analyze the impact of aging on the optimal timing of annuitization.

WHEN TO ANNUITIZE

In the previous two sections, we made the point that payout annuities, either variable or fixed, have a rightful place in an individual investor's optimal retirement portfolio.[46] We argued that, depending on an individual investor's bequest motive versus the investor's desire for consumption, the investor should have a substantial portion of total wealth allocated to annuities that provide some form of guaranteed income for life.

The same principles that govern the allocation of financial assets should govern product allocation. For example, as much as 75 percent of desired (retirement) income can and should be longevity insured. Of course, for those investors with lucrative defined-benefit (DB) pensions and/or Social Security benefits, a large portion of retirement income may already contain longevity insurance. These investors have no need to acquire more. Individuals who do not have longevity insurance prior to retirement, however, should be interested in acquiring some protection against outliving their resources.

Table 3.6 illustrates the extent to which Americans' retirement income is currently longevity insured. A typical retiree has diverse sources of income. Many are entitled to a Social Security payment, a number of them have DB pensions, and some have income from other annuities. All of these assets are longevity insured; they cannot be outlived, although their real purchasing power might decline over time. Other sources of retirement income, such as employment, interest income, dividends, and systematic withdrawal from market funds, are not longevity insured. Note from Table 3.6 that at advanced ages, 80 percent of an average retiree's income is longevity insured. And although these numbers are population averages, they do confirm that longevity insurance is not an esoteric concept. For the average American,

TABLE 3.6   Average Longevity-Insured Portion of
Income for U.S. Population, 2004

Age Group	Portion Insured
65–69	49.9%
70–74	62.4
75–79	70.4
80–84	75.1
85+	80.1

Source: Employee Benefit Research Institute (EBRI 2006).
Note: Longevity-insured assets are Social Security, DB
pensions, and annuities.

longevity-insured assets are the foundation of his or her retirement income. Another pattern in Table 3.6 is that as the age in the U.S. retiree age group decreases, so does the percentage of income that contains longevity insurance, probably as a result of the reduced coverage of U.S. workers by DB pension plans.

In light of the dwindling longevity insurance shown in Table 3.6, the question—and the focus of this section—is exactly *when* and *how* individual investors should go about purchasing income annuities or longevity insurance policies if they do not have them already. Intuitively, purchasing an (irreversible) immediate income annuity at the age of 30, 40, or even 50 makes little sense for a variety of reasons. First of all, the mortality credits—the *raison d'être* of annuitization, which we explained in the previous section—are miniscule at these ages. Moreover, real world transaction costs, fees, and expenses would easily eliminate the effect of mortality-insurance pooling. The empirical data tell the same story as our intuition: The implied longevity yields from payout annuities computed at the age of 50 by the methodology developed in Milevsky (2005b) are substantially lower than the relevant risk-free rates.

Here is a slightly more rigorous way to think about this issue. At the age of 50, the unisex mortality rate (i.e., the probability of a man or woman dying within one year) in the United States is approximately 0.4 percent, or 4 deaths per 1,000 people in that age group, according to the Retirement Pension (RP) 2000 (pensioners, nonprojected) mortality table provided by the Society of Actuaries. Thus, if the underlying pricing interest rate for the annuity in the economy is 5 percent, then annuitization at age 50 would add only 42 bps of return (i.e., mortality credits). These mortality credits are relatively insensitive to the pricing rate or the underlying interest rate in the economy. At a 7 percent pricing rate, the mortality credits would be 43 bps, and at a 10 percent pricing rate, they would be 44 bps. In fact, to a crude first order of approximation, the mortality credits are slightly higher than the mortality rates themselves, as per the following Taylor series expansion:

$$\text{Mortality credits} = \frac{1+R}{1-q_x} - (1+R) \approx q_x(1+q_x) + Rq_x(1+q_x) > q_x, \qquad (3.5)$$

where R denotes the pricing rate and q_x is the mortality credit at age x.

Moreover, although an additional 42 bps of investment return is not something to be taken lightly, few of these mortality credits are likely to accrue to the annuitant (or tontine

TABLE 3.7   Value of Unisex Mortality Credits

Age of Annuitant	Spread above Pricing Interest Rate
55	35 bps
60	52
65	83
70	138
75	237
80	414
85	725
90	1,256
95	2,004
100	2,978

Source: The IFID Centre calculations.

Note: Assuming a 40 percent weight to male mortality and a 60 percent weight to female mortality; 6 percent net interest.

participant) once insurance company profits, commissions, and transaction costs are taken into account. More importantly, any insurance company that must set aside equity capital on the order of 5–10 percent of annuity reserves will demand a return on equity on the order of 10–20 percent, which creates a drag of yet another 50–200 bps, even for the most efficient, low-cost providers unless they are not-for-profit organizations or, perhaps, a government entity. Moreover, if we consider the Individual Annuity Mortality (IAM) 2000 basic table instead of the higher mortality rates (i.e., less antiselection) in the RP2000 table, the pure mortality credits at age 50 drop to about 30 bps.[47]

Table 3.7 displays the mortality credits at increasing ages under the assumption of a unisex mortality table that averages the q values in Equation 3.5 with a 40 percent weight to male mortality and a 60 percent weight to female mortality. These numbers were generated from the annuitant mortality table (the RP2000), which includes the antiselection effect one would experience with such a group. Notice how only after age 65 do the credits exceed 100 bps. Note also that at higher ages, they are substantial.

Mortality credits can also be viewed as the threshold investment return required to beat the income from the annuity during the year in question. If a so-called self-annuitizer can earn the pricing rate, R, plus whatever is left of the mortality credits in Equation 3.5 after transaction costs, the person is better off not annuitizing at age 50 but waiting until age 51 to consider the decision. The following equation makes this point algebraically:

$$a_{x+1} = a_x \left(\frac{1 + R}{1 - q_x} \right) - 1, \tag{3.6}$$

where the actuarial symbol a_x denotes the annuity factor, or the cost of $1 of income per year for life starting at age x, under a valuation rate of R. Similarly, a_{x+1} denotes the annuity factor at age $x + 1$.

Equation 3.6 is an actuarial identity based on the definition of the annuity factor. From a financial point of view, it implies the following: If the quantity a_x can be invested to earn a total return of $(1 + R)/(1 - q_x)$ or greater, the investor at age x can consume the same dollar the annuity would have provided and still have enough funds to purchase an identical income annuity at age $x + 1$, under the assumption the q and R values do not change from one year to the next. In that case, why would the investor ever annuitize at the age of x?

Thus, when the individual investor has no bequest motive (i.e., does not care about leaving any inheritance) and experiences zero transaction costs, he or she should definitely annuitize at age 50 (or even earlier) simply to gain access to the 42 bps, despite its meagerness. But in the real world, this situation never happens. Although a 50-year-old investor may claim to have no bequest motives, the investor's preferences may change over the remaining 30–40 years of his or her life. Annuitizing totally at age 50 kills the option of acting on any bequest preference that develops.

Another problem with premature annuitization is that when the immediate annuity is of the fixed nominal (or even real) type—which currently represents 90 percent of income annuities sold in the United States—the individual investor is selecting an *asset allocation* together with an annuitization *allocation*.[48] The asset class underlying the annuity is essentially fixed-income assets with a predetermined duration and sensitivity to interest rates. This is precisely where the irreversible nature of real world annuities, as opposed to pure tontines, affects the optimal age and process by which to annuitize. Given that this contract is for life, the annuitant must now commit to a fixed-income asset allocation that can never be altered. A typical investor would surely want to rebalance and reallocate wealth to different asset classes over time, but the locked-in nature of the contract impedes the ability to rebalance.

An inability to rebalance is costly from a utility perspective and reduces the appeal of annuitization at all ages, as argued by Browne, Milevsky, and Salisbury (2003). Stated differently and in the language of Equation 3.5, although we would like to gain access to the mortality credit portion, q_x, we might not desire the return, R, that comes with it.

Indeed, in a perfect world, one could offset, hedge, or strip away the undesired exposure to bonds by shorting an appropriate fixed-income portfolio with an equal and opposite duration, but for the simple individual investor, the transaction costs would be prohibitive. By annuitizing prematurely into a fixed immediate annuity, not only are investors forced into an undesired bond allocation today, but they are forced to maintain this suboptimal allocation for the rest of their natural lives. Consider, for example, an investor who rationally wants to maximize her discounted lifetime utility by holding 100 percent equities—or given the hedging characteristics of human capital, perhaps even more—in her personal portfolio. Forcing her to hold bonds, even with the ongoing mortality credits, might be worse for her in a utility-adjusted sense than for her to hold the desired equities without the mortality credits.

In fact, even when an individual investor has access to low-cost immediate variable annuities that can be rebalanced among a variety of traditional asset class, such as stocks, bonds, cash, real estate, and commodities, an inherent loss of flexibility comes from restricting choices to a given company's family of investment accounts—which is an inevitable by-product of real world annuities.

All utility-destroying restrictions negate the mortality credits at younger ages. This point has recently been made rigorously by Milevsky and Young (2007). They found little theoretical justification for annuitization prior to the ages of 65–70.

Financial economists and pension economists who argue the benefits of annuities and their mortality credit subsidies, as per Equation 3.5, are really discussing pure tontines that can be renegotiated at the end of some arbitrary and fictitious time period. These products—if they actually existed—would contain the *real option* to change one's mind, preferences, and strategy at the end of the period.

A related issue is annuitizing at a young age but with income payments starting at an advanced age.[49] Is this akin to annuitizing prematurely, or is it enough that income starts at an advanced age? Would the same logic apply as in the case of mortality credits?

If the delayed annuity is 100 percent reversible (i.e., the investor can cash out at market value at any time prior to the income commencement date), then we would argue that annuitization has not really taken place. The purchase of the delayed annuity at age 30, 40, or even 50 is effectively a fixed-income allocation with an embedded call option to annuitize. The call option's underlying state (stochastic) variable is the changing mortality tables used to price annuities or population hazard rate (rate of mortality). Because the investor can fully reverse the decision, possibly subject to a market value adjustment based on the new level of interest rates, no pooling of mortality risk occurs until the income annuity begins paying. The value of the embedded call option to annuitize—hence, the relative appeal of this type of product compared with a straight bond—would depend critically on the specifics, such as the implied mortality rates in the contract relative to current annuity rates. The devil is in the details, and it is impossible to pass judgment on the relative merits of such a product in the absence of the contract parameters.[50] Is the mortality table fixed at the time of purchase or dependent on population mortality at the time of annuitization? Is the strike price of this option to annuitize currently in the money or far out of the money? At best, it could be a surrogate for a desired bond allocation; at worst, it would be an overpriced and unnecessary call option.

In fact, we would argue that a traditional DB pension plan is effectively a staggered purchase of fixed-income strips, plus the mortality call options. (Even if the delayed annuity is not cashable in a mark-to-market sense, as long as there is some cash value that accrues over time and can be accessed at some point—perhaps at death, disability, or retirement—the same comments would apply.) Oddly, what we are saying is that an investor in a DB pension plan is not really accruing or accumulating income annuities but, rather, is buying an option to annuitize based on some mortality table. The decision to annuitize takes place at retirement when the retiree decides to *not* take the lump sum option, which is available in most DB pension plans.

Now, in contrast, if the delayed annuity is 100 percent irreversible with zero cash value and no survivor benefit, then we would concede that to start accumulating these credits at a young age might be optimal, provided the concerns about transaction costs did not negate the mortality credits. This concept is the advanced-life delayed annuity product explored in Milevsky (2005a). In this approach, a small premium is paid on an ongoing basis in exchange for a mortality-contingent income that starts at an advanced age. Note, however, that the threshold for beating the implied return from the delayed annuity at younger ages would still be quite low, even if the income did not start until an advanced age. Another factor to consider would be the embedded option on a given mortality table (i.e., the commitment to use current rates regardless of what happens to aggregate mortality), which might also increase the relative value of such a strategy/product. Again, the devil is in the details, so generalizing about the merits of such products is quite difficult, especially after taking into account fees, commissions, and profit margins.

Thus—despite the preponderance of theoretical arguments in favor of annuitization— we are hesitant to advocate a single optimal age at which an investor should convert his or her savings account into an irreversible income annuity. Given the many trade-offs involved in this decision and numerous sources of uncertainty, we *are* comfortable with suggesting that prior to age 60 is too early whereas waiting until the age of 90 is too late. (At the advanced age of 90, the unisex mortality rate, q_{90}, of 15 percent leads to mortality credits of 1,850, which are insurmountable on any investment frontier.)

For these reasons, a body of literature is emerging that suggests that investors should annuitize slowly, as in a dollar-cost-averaging (DCA) strategy.[51] Depending on contract and policy features, this process would start at, for example, age 65–70 and continue until age 80 or 85, until the entire amount of desired annuity income was actually annuitized. Milevsky and Young (2007) proved the optimality of a staggered purchase option that annuitizes a small fraction on an ongoing basis. That result does not come from any attempt to speculate on interest rates or to time the shape of the yield curve. Rather, it is the natural result of balancing out the competing risks we described earlier.

There are two exceptions to this general rule, however, although both are rare. One is a situation in which long-term interest rates are extraordinarily high. The second may occur if consumers have solid reasons to believe that they are much healthier than the average annuitant. Of course, that judgment will be harder for people to make than whether they are much healthier than other people of the *same age*.

In summary, a number of previous research papers have been devoted to emphasizing the important role of income/payout annuities in the optimal portfolio of an individual investor. We have repeated the arguments that allocation to income annuities (and insurance) is just as important as allocation to financial instruments—stocks, bonds, cash, and so on. The theoretical arguments in favor of annuitization are so powerful that an entire body of economic literature has emerged under the title of "the annuity puzzle" that seeks to discover the reasons so few consumers actively and consciously embrace these instruments. Nevertheless, we remain unsure of the precise age at which this product allocation should take place. All we can offer is a range.

Additional reasons exist to delay annuitization. First, the retiree maintains complete control of her funds, which means that she maintains liquidity. She can meet emergencies or unforeseen cash crunches—for long-term care, for example—from a nonannuitized pool of money. Second, the retiree retains the option to annuitize at some later time. Why pay for something today if you can probably pay for it in 10 years with no real increase in cost and no diminishment in the benefits of the purchase?

An additional factor is inflation. Most of today's annuities are inadequate in protecting against inflation.[52] Maintaining control of the funds allows you to hedge the inflation risk by purchasing assets that tend to increase in inflationary periods. Annuitization is akin to purchasing a bond with amortized principal and souped-up coupons. The coupons are higher than normal because the bond is completely nontransferable and goes with you to the grave. Unexpected inflation—together with a general increase in interest rates—wreaks havoc on bond prices. The same thing goes for annuities. Today's annuity products do not offer such attractive features as commutability (which would allow policyholders to withdraw cash from their immediate annuities), but the chances are good that future annuity products will.

Even though annuities are not traded in the marketplace, they lose theoretical value when interest rates increase. And all investors would do well to keep in mind that inflation is not permanently dead. In fact, the spread between yields on real and nominal bonds has been 2–3 percent in recent years. In other words, investors are expecting, roughly speaking, at least 2–3 percent inflation a year over the next 30 years. At 2 percent, $1 will be worth only half as much, in today's dollars, 30 years from now. And if a 65-year-old couple does not worry that far ahead, they should not be purchasing a life annuity in the first place.

Finally, a major reason for deferring annuitization as long as prudently possible (and perhaps even not doing so) is the bequest motive. Putting all one's money into a pure life annuity leaves nothing for one's estate. With a straight life annuity, payments cease with the buyer's death. In the worst-case scenario, which many people fear, the investor hands over $100,000 to an insurance company that promises monthly checks for the rest of the investor's life, and then, a few months later, the investor dies. The monthly checks stop coming, the rest of the $100,000 belongs to the insurance company, and the investor's estate gets nothing.[53]

The whole idea of annuity purchases involves the pooling of risk. The living are subsidized by the dying. In fact, participants in qualified retirement plans must obtain written permission from their spouses if they want to elect a single-life annuity payment. The longer someone defers annuitization, the greater the chances that the person will die prior to purchasing the life annuity, in which case, the estate inherits the proceeds of the account. Although taxes will complicate the amount, marginal tax rates are far less than 100 percent, so something will always be left over if it was not annuitized.

SUMMARY AND IMPLICATIONS

We have shown how individuals should make financial decisions throughout their lives involving more than merely asset allocation. The key to the process is the recognition that individuals have human capital as well as financial capital. This human capital contributes substantial earnings during the accumulation stage of a life cycle but should be at least partially protected with life insurance. As individuals age, human capital is depleted, but as they save, human capital is converted into financial capital. As individuals invest, this financial capital grows to replace the future consumption needs of the investor. During the retirement stage of the life cycle, the income from the human capital needs to be replaced with pensions, Social Security payments, and the returns and principal from the financial capital.

In providing an approach to making the financial decisions that individuals face, we specifically modeled personal situations in the context of the financial markets and the stock, bond, life insurance, and annuity products available to investors. Our models suggest optimal purchases of these products together with optimal financial asset allocation mixes for individuals when such variables are put in as the individuals' projected earnings stream, savings rate, retirement needs, assumed market risks and returns, and mortality tables.

Accumulation Stage

We first considered a person's accumulation stage—that is, the individual's working life, which is typically from about age 25 to age 65. The individual or family consumes part of this income and saves the rest. Saving converts human capital into financial capital. The investor faces three main risks during these years: market risk, mortality risk, and savings risk. The market risk concerns what types of returns the markets will generate on financial capital. The mortality risk concerns the potential demise of the wage earner and the resulting cessation of wage income for the family. The savings risk concerns the extent to which the individual and family are able to generate sufficient savings flow into their financial capital to adequately provide for the retirement stage of their lives.

Market risk is controlled by selecting an optimal asset allocation mix, in the context of the individual's wealth in human and financial capital, from the available products. We modeled human capital as mostly fixed and bondlike, so the optimal whole portfolio (human capital plus financial capital) requires picking only the appropriate financial asset allocation. The human capital part itself can be protected with life insurance. Finally, the savings risk is controlled by selecting an appropriate savings rate, which can be solved for.

During the accumulation stage of their lives, investors generally take their human capital as a given, although some may decide to shift their careers to meet their consumption or other financial needs. Human capital is typically a large quantity at the start of a career because it reflects the present value of all the future income that individuals are expected to earn. This human capital is bondlike (i.e., earning a relatively stable, although usually growing, and predictable income stream). Most individuals have little financial capital early in their careers. Any small amount of financial capital should be invested almost entirely in equitylike investments so that the individual's overall asset allocation (human and financial capital) has both an equity and a fixed-income component.

As individuals progress through their careers, their human capital declines. More and more of their earned income has already been achieved, and less and less of it is available for future consumption and saving. Ideally, individuals have already saved some of this income so that it will be available as part of their financial portfolio. As their financial capital becomes a greater proportion of their total wealth, financial asset allocation will begin to shift from almost all equities to a larger and larger proportion of bonds. By retirement, individuals hold most of their wealth as financial capital; therefore, the allocation of their financial assets should have a large bond component to balance the mix of their total capital.

The changes in the proportions of human capital and financial capital that occur as individual's age affect insurance needs as well as asset allocation. Early in their careers, when individuals have much human capital, protecting much of this capital with life insurance is reasonable. As individuals age, they have less human capital to protect, so less life insurance is needed. During retirement, individuals have little human capital left but some life insurance may still be desirable to ensure that a minimum level of wealth can be transferred as bequests.

During the accumulation stage, actual asset allocations and the amount of life insurance to be purchased depend not only on age but also on the progression of individual careers. These decisions depend also on the amount of financial capital that individuals have at any given time. The more financial capital an individual has, the less life insurance he or she needs to buy to protect human capital but also the more the individual needs to protect the financial capital by making conservative financial investments. If the individual is risk averse, he or she will want to protect *both* human capital and financial capital in the accumulation stage. This can be done by buying more life insurance and adding more bonds into the financial asset portfolio.

Finally, the type of work that individuals do affects their needs for life insurance and their asset allocations. Individuals who work in low-risk (bondlike) professions (e.g., tenured teachers) especially need to protect their otherwise low-risk human capital by buying sufficient life insurance. Individuals who work in careers that have earnings that are highly correlated with the stock market or the economy (e.g., stockbrokers, commissioned sales people) should view their human capital as more equitylike and attempt to reduce their overall risk by holding more bonds in their financial portfolios.

We have presented models to solve for the actual suggested amounts of life insurance that an individual (or family) should buy as well as what an investor's asset allocation mix should be throughout this accumulation stage. These models use inputs that are both specific to individual cases and marketwide. The individual-specific inputs are an individual's age, gender, family status, annual earned income, expected growth in income, the variability of the earned income, and its correlation with the stock market or risky assets in a portfolio. The inputs also include the individual's consumption, expected retirement age, pension benefits, retirement needs, risk aversion, and bequest desires. The marketwide inputs include expected returns for the stock and bond markets, their correlation with each other, their standard deviations, and estimated management fees and transaction costs in managing a portfolio. Predicted Social Security levels and structure are also inputs, together with mortality rates and life insurance fees. The outputs are the individual's suggested life insurance amounts, financial asset allocations, and savings rates.

In summary, during the accumulation stage, the following directions are suggested for individual investors:

1. The older the individual is, the less life insurance is needed and the more bonds should be included in the asset allocation.
2. The higher the initial financial wealth is, the less life insurance is needed but the more bonds should be included in the asset allocation.
3. The more risk averse an investor is, the more life insurance is needed and the more bonds should be in the asset allocation.
4. The more desire the individual has to make bequests to beneficiaries, the more life insurance is needed, but this bequest desire has little impact on asset allocation.
5. The more an individual's earning power is sensitive to the economy and the stock market, the less life insurance is needed but the more bonds are needed in the asset allocation.

Retirement Stage

After an individual reaches retirement age, most of the individual's human capital has been used up; that is, he or she will no longer be earning income on a regular basis. The individual may have a defined-benefit (DB) pension plan and Social Security benefits, and possible other sources of earned income, but much of his or her retirement consumption will probably have to be drawn from the principal and the return generated from his or her financial portfolio.

During this stage of their lives, retirees face three risks that are somewhat different from the three risks they faced in the accumulation stage. They still face market risk, probably at an even greater level than earlier because most of their capital is now financial capital. They also face longevity risk, which is the risk of outliving their assets. Finally, as they approach the end of their lives, they face a bequest risk—the risk that they may not be able to leave the desired amounts to their beneficiaries. (They may have always faced this risk, but the probabilities that they will need to make a bequest have gone up.)

Individuals control market risk by attempting to choose optimal financial asset allocations. They can control longevity risk by purchasing immediate annuities, which pay out income each year for the rest of their lives. They can collectively manage the asset allocation to include stocks, bonds, and fixed and variable annuities. Finally, they can lock in any bequests that they want to ensure by buying life insurance.

One way to meet retirement needs is to have saved sufficient amounts during the accumulation stage and invested this financial portfolio in stocks and bonds. When retirement income is needed, the investor can make systematic withdrawals from this portfolio. This procedure is likely to be successful if the investor lives to the age predicted for the person by mortality tables. Because roughly half of investors (or couples, including spouses) live past their life expectancies, however, they incur longevity risk. For long-lived investors, their systematic withdrawals from stock and bond portfolios may deplete their financial portfolios.

Not all people will have saved enough to ensure their retirement by systematically withdrawing from their stock and bond portfolios. Another way to meet retirement needs is to hedge longevity risk by purchasing immediate payout annuities. Fixed-payout annuities pay a constant stream of income for as long as the retiree lives. The fixed payout is usually expressed as a percentage of the amount of the annuity purchased. Variable-payout annuities pay out a variable stream based on the fluctuating value of an annuity portfolio so that in an up market, for example, the payout increases.

We showed how an investor can assemble a combined portfolio of stocks, bonds, and fixed-payout and variable-payout annuities. Such a portfolio can increase the probability that an individual or couple will have sufficient yearly income to maintain their standard of living throughout their life span, no matter how long they live.

A retiree is also concerned about making bequests to beneficiaries. There is always a trade-off between insuring against longevity risk and the likelihood of leaving substantial monies to beneficiaries. As in the accumulation stage, investors can ensure that bequests can be made by buying life insurance. We specifically depicted the individual's trade-off between reducing longevity risk and fulfilling bequest desires. In general, buying payout annuities reduces bequest amounts but life insurance directly protects bequests.

In putting together an optimal portfolio that includes stocks, bonds, fixed annuities, variable annuities, and life insurance, an adviser must take into account the investor's risk aversion and the returns and risk that the markets are expected to provide. Advisers can model the returns on stock and bond markets, netting out anticipated fees and transaction costs. They can do the same for the annuity products. Annuities are usually quoted net of fees, with the expected return on fixed annuities directly observable. The expected returns on variable annuities are not directly observable because the principal is expected to rise or decline with market movements.

If individuals expect Social Security payments or have a DB pension, advisers can think of them as already owning some annuities. Social Security is usually indexed to inflation, whereas pension benefits generally resemble a fixed annuity. Once a value is assigned to these existing "annuities," they can partially meet the demand for annuity products in the overall portfolio mix.

We used two types of inputs to model the optimum mix of stocks, bonds, and fixed and variable annuities. The first set of inputs came from the specific individual retiree (or couple). These included the gender, age, financial wealth, probability of living beyond their expected mortality, risk tolerance, and consumption and bequest desires. The second set of assumptions concerned the financial markets. We estimated stock and bond expected returns, standard deviations, correlation structure, and fee levels. The same was necessary, together with considering the mortality tables of the general population, for the fixed and variable annuity products.

Solving for the optimal asset allocation of stocks, bonds, and fixed and variable annuities is only part of the problem. Advisers also need to determine *when* to start purchasing annuities for a portfolio. The problem is complicated because the purchase of a payout annuity is an irreversible decision and because the transaction costs, fees, and expenses of an annuity can easily dominate the effects of mortality pooling. In addition to costs and expenses, insurance companies have to worry about the moral hazard of individuals trying to reverse their policies when they perceive that their life expectancies have shortened. For all these reasons, reversing a payout annuity entails large penalties.

So, when or at what age should an individual invest in a payout annuity? Consider the simple case of fixed-payout annuities. The rate (after costs) should exceed the fixed payments one would receive on a bond because the investor is being paid a mortality credit to cover the fact that the principal of the annuity is never repaid and the stream of income stops when the investor dies. If bequests are unimportant, then the earlier the individual invests in an annuity, the better. But most people have some bequest desires—or will develop some in the future. The irreversibility of an annuity, however, locks in the asset allocation, thus giving the investor little control if his or her circumstances change. The extreme case is premature death: The annualized income stream stops, and the annuity becomes worthless.

The benefits of annuities in reducing longevity risk diminish, however, if the individual waits too long to purchase the annuity. Given the trade-offs, we suggest waiting until after retirement to buy payout annuities and staggering the purchases.

Our models optimize the retirement asset allocation to include stocks, bonds, and fixed- and variable-payout annuities, together with sufficient life insurance to help protect the bequests that retirees want to make. Specific asset allocation findings for the retirement stage of investing are as follows:

1. Including payout annuities in a retirement asset allocation reduces the probability of outliving assets (e.g., reduces longevity risk).
2. Fixed-payout annuities substitute for bonds, and variable-payout annuities substitute for stocks, although more aggressive equity mixes can be invested in once longevity risk has been diminished.
3. Payout annuities protect against longevity risk; life insurance protects bequests that can be made. In general, the more annuities purchased, the less capital is left over for bequests.
4. Payout annuities should generally be purchased after retirement with staggered purchases because annuities are irreversible purchases that partially lock in investors' asset allocations and reduce bequests.

Modeling the Life Cycle

We have suggested ways that investors can make stock, bond, life insurance, and payout annuity decisions over their life cycles. We addressed both the accumulation stage and the retirement stage in several sections.

The models presented here can be used to make specific recommendations. During the accumulation stage (generally from about age 25 to 65), the models can suggest optimal financial asset allocations (stock and bond mixes) and life insurance purchases. During the retirement stage, the models can suggest asset allocations to stocks, bonds, and fixed- and variable-payout annuities. When bequest desires are included, life insurance levels can also be suggested.

To implement these models for specific individuals, the adviser will need some personal information about the individuals as inputs. This information includes the investor's gender, age, family status, earnings, financial wealth, consumption and savings patterns, risk aversion, anticipated retirement age, bequest desires, and subjective life expectancy. It is also necessary for the adviser to know the expected growth and variability of the individual's earnings and the correlation of the earnings with stock and bond markets. In addition, the adviser needs to know something about the products available in the marketplace. Inputs include stock and bond expected returns, standard deviations of returns, payout annuity fixed rates, payout annuity variable expected returns and risks, costs and fees, the correlation structure among the product categories, and objective mortality rates.

Individuals face a complex set of investment decisions that continually change throughout their life cycles. We believe that research has come a long way in addressing these practical problems that investors face. We hope that the concepts and financial models presented here can help investors meet their consumption, retirement, and bequest needs.

APPENDIX 3A: HUMAN CAPITAL AND THE ASSET ALLOCATION MODEL

The term "human capital" often conveys a number of different and, at times, conflicting ideas in the insurance, economics, and finance literature. We define human capital as "the financial, economic present value of net incomes that depend on a number of subjective or market pricing factors." In general, the net incomes are wages or salaries before retirement and pension payments after retirement.

Measuring the Present Value of Human Capital

Let the symbol h_t denote the random (real, after-tax) income that a person will receive during the discrete time period (or year) t; then, in general, the expected discounted value of this income flow, $DVHC$, at the current time, t_0, is represented mathematically by

$$DVHC = \sum_{t=1}^{n} \frac{E[h_t]}{(1 + r + v)^t},$$ (3A.1)

where n is the number of periods over which we are discounting, r is the relevant risk-free discount rate, and v is a (subjective) parameter that captures illiquidity plus any other potential risk premium associated with one's human capital. In Equation 3A.1, the expectation $E[h_t]$ in the numerator converts the random income into a scalar. Note that in addition to expectations (under a physical, real-world measure) in Equation 3A.1, the denominator's v, which accounts for all broadly defined risks, obviously reduces the t_0 value of the expression $DVHC$ accordingly.

And depending on the investor's specific job and profession, he or she might be expected to earn the same exact $E[h_t]$ in each time period t, yet the random shocks to incomes, $h_t - E[h_t]$, might have very different statistical characteristics vis-à-vis the market portfolio; thus, each profession or job will induce a distinct "risk premium" value for v, which will then lead to a lower discounted expected value of human capital. Therefore, because we are discounting with an explicit risk premium, we feel justified in also using the term "financial economic value of human capital" to describe $DVHC$.

Similarly, in the discussions in the sections on Human Capital and Asset Allocation Advice and on Human Capital, Life Insurance, and Asset Allocation, when we focus on the correlation or covariance between human capital and other macroeconomic or financial factors, we are, of course, referring to the correlation between shocks $h_t - E[h_t]$ and shocks to or innovations in the return-generating process in the market. This correlation can induce a (quite complicated) dependence structure between *DVHC* in Equation 3A.1 and the dynamic evolution of the investor's financial portfolio.[54]

Model Specification: Optimal Asset Allocation with Human Capital

We assume that the investor is currently age x and will retire at age y. The term "retirement" is simply meant to indicate that the human capital income flow is terminated and the pension phase begins. We further assume that the financial portfolio will be rebalanced annually. We do not consider taxes in our models. The investor would like to know what fraction of his or her financial wealth should be invested in a risky asset (stock).

In the model, an investor determines the allocation to the risky asset, α_x, to maximize the year-end utility of total wealth (human capital plus financial wealth). The optimization problem can be expressed as

$$\max_{(\alpha_x)} E[U(W_{x+1} + H_{x+1})], \tag{3A.2}$$

subject to the budget constraints

$$W_{x+1} = (W_x + h_x - C_x)[\alpha_x e^{\mu_s - (1/2)\sigma_s^2 + \sigma_s Z_s} + (1 - \alpha_x)e^{r_f}], \tag{3A.3}$$

where e is the exponent, 2.7182, and

$$0 \leq \alpha_x \leq 1. \tag{3A.4}$$

The symbols, notations, and terminology used in the optimal problem are as follows:

α_x = allocation to the risky asset.

W_t = financial wealth at time t. The market has two assets—one risky and one risk free. This assumption is consistent with the two-fund separation theorem of traditional portfolio theory. Of course, the approach could be expanded to multiple asset classes.

r_f = return on the risk-free asset.

S_t = value of the risky asset at time t. This value follows a discrete version of a geometric Brownian motion:

$$S_{t+1} = S_t \exp\left(\mu_S - \frac{1}{2}\sigma_S^2 + \sigma_S Z_{S,t+1}\right), \tag{3A.5}$$

where μ_S is the expected return and σ_S is the standard deviation of return of the risky asset. $Z_{S,t}$ is a random variable. $Z_{S,t} \sim N(0, 1)$.

h_t = value of labor income. In our numerical cases, we assume that h_t follows a discrete stochastic process specified by

$$h_{t+1} = h_t \exp(\mu_h + \sigma_h Z_{h,t+1}), \tag{3A.6}$$

where $h_t > 0$; μ_h and σ_h are, respectively, the annual growth rate and the annual standard deviation of the income process and $Z_{h,t}$ is a random variable. $Z_{h,t} \sim N(0, 1)$.

Based on Equation 3A.6, for a person at age x, income at age $x + t$ is determined by

$$h_{x+t} = h_x\left[\prod_{k=1}^{t} \exp(\mu_h + \sigma_h Z_{h,k})\right]. \tag{3A.7}$$

We further assume that correlation between labor income innovation and the return of the risky asset is ρ. That is,

$$\text{corr}(Z_S, Z_h) = \rho. \tag{3A.8}$$

Mathematically, the relationship between Z_S and Z_h can be expressed as

$$Z_h = \rho Z_S + \sqrt{1 - \rho^2}\, Z, \tag{3A.9}$$

where Z is a standard Brownian motion independent of Z_S and Z_h.

H_t = value of human capital at time t. It is the present value of future income from age $t + 1$ to life expectancy. Income after retirement is the payment from pensions.

Based on Equation 3A.7, for a person at age $x + t$, the present value of future income from age $x + t + 1$ to life expectancy, denoted as T, is determined by

$$H_{x+t} = \sum_{j=t+1}^{T} \left\{ h_{x+j} \exp\left[-(j - t)(r_f + \eta_h + \zeta_h) \right] \right\}, \tag{3A.10}$$

where η_h is the risk premium (discount rate) for the income process and captures the market risk of income and ζ_h is a discount factor in human capital evaluation to account for the illiquidity risk associated with one's job. We assumed a 4 percent discount rate per year.[55]

Based on the capital asset pricing model, η_h can be evaluated by

$$\begin{aligned} \eta_h &= \frac{\mathrm{cov}(Z_h, Z_S)}{\mathrm{var}(Z_S)}(\mu_S - r_f) \\ &= \rho[\mu_S - (e^{r_f} - 1)]\frac{\sigma_h}{\sigma_S}. \end{aligned} \tag{3A.11}$$

Furthermore, the expected value of H_t, which is $E[H_{x+t}]$, is defined as the human capital a person has at age $x + t + 1$.

C_t = consumption in year t. For simplicity, C_t is assumed to equal C (i.e., constant consumption over time).

The power utility function (constant relative risk aversion) is used in our numerical examples. The functional form of the utility function is

$$U(W) = \frac{W^{1-\gamma}}{1 - \gamma} \tag{3A.12}$$

for $W \geq 0$ and $\gamma \neq 1$ and

$$U(W) = \ln(W) \tag{3A.13}$$

for $W \geq 0$ and $\gamma = 1$. The power utility function is used in the examples for $U(\cdot)$.

We solved the problem via simulation. We first simulated the values of the risky asset by using Equation 3A.5. Then, we simulated Z_h from Equation 3A.9 to take into account the correlation between income change and return from the financial market. Finally, we used Equation 3A.6 to generate income over the same period. Human capital, H_{x+t}, was calculated by using Equations 3A.7 and 3A.10. If wealth level at age $x + 1$ was less than zero, we set the wealth equal to zero; that is, we assumed that the investor had no remaining financial wealth. We simulated this process N times. The objective function was evaluated by using

$$\frac{1}{N} \sum_{n=1}^{N} U[W_{x+1}(n) + H_{x+1}(n)]. \tag{3A.14}$$

In the numerical examples, we set N equal to 20,000.

APPENDIX 3B: LIFE INSURANCE AND THE ASSET ALLOCATION MODEL

We describe here the basic pricing mechanism of life insurance and, more importantly, provide the detailed model that underlies the numerical results and examples in the section on Human Capital, Life Insurance, and Asset Allocation.

Pricing Mechanism for One-Year, Renewable Term Life Insurance

The one-year renewable term policy *premium* is paid at the beginning of the year and protects the human capital of the insured for the duration of the year. (If the insured person dies within that year, the insurance company pays the *face value* to the beneficiaries soon after the death or prior to the end of the year.) In the next year, the contract is guaranteed to start anew with new premium payments to be made and protection received; hence the word "renewable."

The policy premium is obviously an increasing function of the desired face value, and the two are related by the following simple formula:

$$P = \frac{q}{1+r}\theta. \tag{3B.1}$$

The premium, P, is calculated by multiplying the desired face value, θ, by the probability of death, q, and then discounted by the interest rate factor, $1 + r$. The theory behind Equation 3B.1 is the well-known *law of large numbers*, which guarantees that probabilities become percentages when individual probabilities are aggregated. Note the implicit assumption in Equation 3B.1: Although death can occur at any time during the year (or term), the premium payments are made at the beginning of the year, and the face values are paid at the end of the year. From the insurance company's perspective, all of the premiums received from the group of N individuals of the same age (i.e., having the same probability of death) are commingled and invested in an *insurance reserve* earning a rate of interest r so that at the end of the year, $PN(1 + r)$ is divided among the qN beneficiaries.

No savings component or investment component is embedded in the premium defined by Equation 3B.1. To the contrary, at the end of the year, the survivor loses any claim to the pool of accumulated premiums because all funds go directly to the beneficiaries.

As the individual ages, his or her probability of death increases (denoted by adding the subscript x to the probability, q_x). In this case, the same face amount (face value) of life insurance, θ, will cost more and will induce a higher premium, P_x, per Equation 3B.1. Note that in practice, the actual premium is *loaded* by an additional factor, $1 + \lambda$, to account for commissions, transaction costs, and profit margins. So, the actual amount paid by the insured is closer to $P(1 + \lambda)$, but the underlying pricing relationship driven by the law of large numbers remains the same.

Also, from a traditional financial planning perspective, the individual conducts a budgeting analysis to determine his or her life insurance demands (i.e., the amount the surviving family and beneficiaries need, in present value terms, in order to replace wages lost as a result of death). That quantity is taken as the required face value in Equation 3B.1, which then produces a premium. Alternatively, one can think of a budget for life insurance purchases, and the face value is then determined by Equation 3B.1.

In our model and the related discussion, we "solve" for the optimal age-varying amount of life insurance, θ_x (which then provides the age-varying policy payment, P_x), that maximizes the welfare of the family by taking into account the investor's or family's risk preferences and attitudes toward leaving a bequest as well as replacing lost income.

Model Specification: Optimal Asset Allocation, Human Capital, and Insurance Demands

The model specification in the section on Human Capital, Life Insurance, and Asset Allocation is an extension of the model of optimal asset allocation with human capital provided in Appendix 3A and discussed in the section on Human Capital and Asset Allocation Advice.

We start with assuming that the investor is currently age x and will retire at age Y. The term "retirement" as we use it here is simply meant to indicate that the income flow from human capital terminates and the pension phase begins. We further assume that the financial portfolio will be rebalanced annually and that the life insurance—which is assumed to be the one-year, renewable term policy—will be renewed annually. (We do not consider taxes in our models.)

In the model, the investor determines the amount of life insurance to demand, θ_x (that is, the face value of the policy, or "death benefit"), together with the allocation to the risky asset, α_x, that will maximize the year-end utility of the investor's total wealth (human capital plus financial wealth) weighted by the "alive" and "dead" states. The optimization problem can be expressed as

$$\max_{(\theta_x, \, \alpha_x)} E[(1 - D)(1 - \bar{q}_x)U_{alive}(W_{x+1} + H_{x+1}) + D(\bar{q}_x)U_{dead}(W_{x+1} + \theta_x)], \qquad (3B.2)$$

which is Equation 3.4, subject to the following budget constraints:

$$W_{x+1} = [W_x + h_x - (1 + \lambda)q_x\theta_x e^{-r_f} - C_x][\alpha_x e^{\mu_S - (1/2)\sigma_S^2 \sigma_S Z_S} + (1 - \alpha_x)e^{r_f}], \qquad (3B.3)$$

$$\theta_0 \le \theta_x \le \frac{(W_x + h_x - C_x)e^{r_f}}{(1 + \lambda)q_x}, \qquad (3B.4)$$

and

$$0 \le \alpha_x \le 1. \qquad (3B.5)$$

Equation 3B.4 requires the cost (or price) of the term insurance policy to be less than the amount of the client's current financial wealth, and the investor is required to purchase a minimum insurance amount ($\theta_0 > 0$) in order to have minimum protection from the loss of human capital. The symbols, notations, and terminology used in the optimal problem are as follows:

θ_x = face value or death benefit of life insurance.

α_x = allocation to risky assets.

D = relative strength of the utility of bequest. Individuals with no utility of bequest will have $D = 0$.

q_x = *objective* probability of death at the end of the year $x + 1$ conditional on being alive at age x. It is used in pricing insurance contracts.

$\bar{q}_x$ = *subjective* probability of death at the end of the year $x + 1$ conditional on being alive at age x; $1 - \bar{q}_x$ denotes the subjective probability of survival. The subjective probability of death may be different from the objective probability. In other words, a person might believe he or she is healthier (or less healthy) than population average. This belief would affect expected utility but not the pricing of the life insurance, which is based on an objective population survival probability.

λ = fees and expenses (i.e., actuarial and insurance loading) imposed and charged on a typical life insurance policy.

W_t = financial wealth at time t. The market has two assets—one risky and one risk free. This assumption is consistent with the two-fund separation theorem of traditional portfolio theory. Of course, the approach could be expanded to multiple asset classes.

r_f = return on the risk-free asset.

S_t = value of the risky asset. This value follows a discrete version of a geometric Brownian motion:

$$S_{t+1} = S_t \exp\left(\mu_S - \frac{1}{2}\sigma_S^2 + \sigma_S Z_{S,t+1}\right), \tag{3B.6}$$

where μ_S is the expected return, σ_S is the standard deviation of return of the risky asset, and $Z_{S,t}$ is a random variable; $Z_{S,t} \sim N(0,1)$.

h_t = value of labor income. In our numerical cases, we assume that h_t follows a discrete stochastic process specified by

$$h_{t+1} = h_t \exp(\mu_h + \sigma_h Z_{h,t+1}), \tag{3B.7}$$

where $h_t > 0$; μ_h and σ_h are, respectively, the annual growth rate and the annual standard deviation of the income process; and $Z_{h,t}$ is a random variable. $Z_{h,t} \sim N(0,1)$.

Based on Equation 3B.7, for a person at age x, income at age $x + t$ is determined by

$$h_{x+t} = h_x \left[\prod_{k=1}^{t} \exp(\mu_h + \sigma_h Z_{h,k}) \right]. \tag{3B.8}$$

ρ = correlation between changes in labor income and the return of the risky asset; that is,

$$\text{corr}(Z_S, Z_h) = \rho. \tag{3B.9}$$

Mathematically, the relationship between Z_S and Z_h can be expressed as

$$Z_h = \rho Z_S + \sqrt{1 - \rho^2} Z, \tag{3B.10}$$

where Z is a standard Brownian motion independent of Z_S and Z_h.

H_t = human capital value at time t. It is the present value of future income from age $t + 1$ to life expectancy. Income after retirement is the payment from pensions.

Based on Equation 3B.8, for a person at age $x + t$, the present value of future income from age $x + t + 1$ to life expectancy denoted as T is determined by

$$H_{x+t} = \sum_{j=t+1}^{T} \{h_{x+j} \exp[-(j - t)(r_f + \eta_h + \zeta_h)]\}, \tag{3B.11}$$

where η_h is the risk premium (discount rate) for the income process and captures the market risk of income and ζ_h is a discount factor in human capital evaluation to account for the illiquidity risk associated with one's job. In the numerical examples, we assume a 4 percent discount rate per year.[56]

Based on the capital asset pricing model, η_h can be evaluated by

$$\begin{aligned} \eta_h &= \frac{\text{cov}(Z_h, Z_S)}{\text{var}(Z_S)}[\mu_S - (e^{r_f} - 1)] \\ &= \rho[\mu_S - (e^{r_f} - 1)]\frac{\sigma_h}{\sigma_S}. \end{aligned} \tag{3B.12}$$

Furthermore, the expected value of H_t, which is $E(H_{x+t})$, is defined as the human capital a person has at age $x + t + 1$.

C_t = consumption in year t. For simplicity, C_t is assumed to equal C (i.e., constant consumption over time).

The power utility function (constant relative risk aversion) is used in our numerical examples. The functional form of the utility function is

$$U(W) = \frac{W^{1-\gamma}}{1-\gamma} \tag{3B.13}$$

for $W \geq 0$ and $\gamma \neq 1$ and

$$U(W) = \ln(W) \tag{3B.14}$$

for $W \geq 0$ and $\gamma = 1$. The power utility function is used in the examples for both $U_{alive}(\cdot)$ and $U_{dead}(\cdot)$, which are the utility functions associated with, respectively, the alive and dead states.

We solved the problem via simulation. We first simulated the values of the risky asset by using Equation 3B.6. Then, we simulated Z_h from Equation 3B.10 to take into account the correlation between income change and return from the financial market. Finally, we used Equation 3B.7 to generate income over the same period. Human capital, H_{x+t}, was calculated by using Equations 3B.8 and 3B.11. If wealth level at age $x + 1$ was less than zero, then we set the wealth equal to zero; that is, we assumed that the investor has no remaining financial wealth. We simulated this process N times. The objective function was evaluated by using

$$\frac{1}{N} \sum_{n=1}^{N} U_{alive}[W_{x+1}(n) + H_{x+1}(n)] \tag{3B.15}$$

and

$$\frac{1}{N} \sum_{n=1}^{N} U_{dead}[W_{x+1}(n) + \theta_x]. \tag{3B.16}$$

In the numerical examples, we set N equal to 20,000.

APPENDIX 3C: PAYOUT ANNUITY VARIATIONS

The section on Retirement Portfolio and Longevity Risk describes the two basic types of payout annuities—fixed and variable. In this appendix, we discuss some variations in payout annuities.

Single-Life and Joint-Life Annuities

When considering retirement security, retirees must consider the retirement income needs of their spouses. For example, if a married couple converts their savings into a single-life payout annuity on the husband, then at his death, the wife will experience a 100 percent decline in annuity income. This issue can be solved by purchasing joint-life annuities.

A joint-life annuity is structured to provide income for as long as either member of a couple is alive. Because a joint-life payout annuity makes payments much longer, on average, than a single-life payout annuity, the joint option reduces the income payment each year. Depending on the couple's preferences, the annuity can be designed to provide the same income after the death of a spouse or provide a reduced level of income.

Table 3C.1 illustrates the difference in terms of payments for a fixed-payout annuity for a single-life annuity for a man, a single-life annuity for a woman, and a joint payout with

TABLE 3C.1   Immediate Fixed-Payout Annuity Payments

Payment	Single Male	Single Female	Joint
Annual payment	$7,848	$7,392	$6,492

Source: Ibbotson Associates, based on industry quotes in June 2005.

Note: Initial premium or purchase amount of $100,000; age 65 years for male and female.

100 percent survivor benefit. The payment amount is calculated for an initial premium or purchase amount of $100,000. For a 65-year-old man, the payment would be $654 per month. For a 65-year-old woman, the payment would be $616 per month. For a joint payout with 100 percent survivor benefit, the payment would fall to $6,492 per year.

Payment-Period Guarantees

Another variation in annuitization is payment-period guarantees. Some retirees who wish to purchase annuities may be concerned that early death could result in only a short period of annuity payment. These retirees would like a portion of their original premium payment to be made available to their heirs. This arrangement can be achieved by purchasing payout annuities with payment-period guarantees. These guarantees provide a minimum number of monthly payments regardless of the age of the annuitant's death or offer a partial return of premium at death.

Choosing a guarantee period decreases the amount of income paid out each period to the retiree. Table 3C.2 presents a comparison of the payment differences for no guarantee in the contract, for a 10-year guarantee period, and for a 20-year guarantee period.

Guaranteed Payment Floors

Guaranteed payment floors may be added to immediate variable annuities. They guarantee that the monthly payment will not drop below a certain percentage of the first payment (for example, 80 percent). The goal is to provide a minimum monthly payment without giving up the potential increase in payments provided by a variable annuity. A guaranteed minimum income benefit is typically offered as an optional feature or rider to a variable annuity contract for an additional charge, generally ranging from 0.30 percent to 0.75 percent of the contract's account value.

TABLE 3C.2   Immediate Fixed-Payout Annuities with Period Guarantees

Guarantee Period	Single Male	Single Female	Joint
No guarantee	$7,848	$7,392	$6,492
10-year guarantee	7,584	7,236	6,492
20-year guarantee	6,960	6,828	6,360

Source: Ibbotson Associates, based on industry quotes in June 2005.

Note: Initial premium or purchase amount of $100,000; age 65 years for male and female.

ACKNOWLEDGMENTS

We would like to thank the Research Foundation of CFA Institute for its support in making this chapter possible. We especially appreciate the assistance, support, and encouragement of Research Director Larry Siegel. We also want to acknowledge Michael Henkel, Thomas Idzorek, Sherman Hanna, Jin Wang, Huaxiong Huang, and Robert Kreitler for many helpful discussions regarding some of the underpinnings of this work. We would also like to acknowledge the assistance provided by research associates and staff at the IFID Centre and Ibbotson Associates. Finally, we want to thank Alexa Auerbach and the editorial staff members of CFA Institute for extensive editing assistance.

NOTES

1. In addition to Markowitz (1952), see Merton (1969, 1971).
2. For example, Bodie, Merton, and Samuelson (1992); Campbell and Viceira (2002); Merton (2003).
3. Meulbroek (2002) estimated that a large position in company stock held over a long period is effectively, after accounting for the costs of inadequate diversification, worth less than 50 cents on the dollar.
4. In this chapter, we use various terms synonymously to represent *lifetime-payout annuity*— lifetime annuity, payout annuity, and immediate annuity.
5. How much an investor should consume or save is another important decision that is frequently tied to the concept of human capital. In this chapter, we focus on only the asset allocation and life insurance decisions; therefore, our model has been simplified by the assumption that the investor has already decided how much to consume or save. Our numerical cases assume that the investor saves a constant 10 percent of salary each year.
6. For example, Chen and Milevsky (2003); Huang, Milevsky, and Wang (2005); Chen, Ibbotson, Milevsky, and Zhu (2006).
7. We believe we are the first to analyze longevity risk in the broader asset allocation framework and develop the optimal allocation to payout annuities. Ibbotson Associates has been granted a patent on developing optimal allocations that include traditional assets and payout annuities (patent number 7120601).
8. Educational attainments and work experience are the two most significant factors determining a person's earning ability.
9. See Merton (1971); Bodie, Merton, and Samuelson (1992); Heaton and Lucas (1997); Jagannathan and Kocherlakota (1996); Campbell and Viceira (2002).
10. Heaton and Lucas (2000) showed that wealthy households with high and variable business income invest less in the stock market than similarly wealthy households without that sort of business income, which is consistent with the theoretical prediction.
11. Although this might be true in aggregate, it can vary widely among individuals.
12. The discount rate should be adjusted to the risk level of the person's labor income (see Appendix 3A).
13. The model was inspired by an early model by Campbell (1980) that seeks to maximize the total wealth of an investor in a one-period framework. The total wealth consists of the investor's financial wealth and human capital. In this section, we focus on the asset allocation decision for investors' financial capital instead of the life insurance decision in Campbell's paper.

14. Note that when we make statements such as "this person's human capital is 40 percent long-term bonds, 30 percent financial services, and 30 percent utilities," we mean that the unpredictable shocks to future wages have a given correlation structure with the named subindices. Thus, as in our previous example, the tenured university professor could be considered to be a 100 percent real-return (inflation-indexed) bond because no shocks to his wages would be linked to any financial subindex.

15. In this case, income has a real growth rate of 0 percent and a standard deviation of 5 percent, yet the expected real return on stocks is 8 percent and the standard deviation for stock returns is 20 percent.

16. For example, all else being equal, alternative assets with low correlations with the stock market (e.g., commodities, certain hedge funds) can be attractive for these investors.

17. The section on Human Capital, Life Insurance, and Asset Allocation is partly based on material in Chen, Ibbotson, Milevsky, and Zhu (2006).

18. Economides (1982) argued in a corrected model that Campbell's approach underestimated the optimal amount of insurance coverage. Our model takes this correction into consideration.

19. One-year, renewable term life insurance is used throughout this chapter. Appendix 3B provides a description of the pricing mechanism of this insurance policy. Although an analysis is beyond the scope of this chapter, we believe that all other types of life insurance policies are financial combinations of term life insurance with investment accounts, added tax benefits, and embedded options.

20. In this description, we are obviously abstracting somewhat from the realities of insurance pricing, but to a first-order approximation, the descriptions capture the essence of actuarial cost.

21. We assume that the investor makes asset allocation and insurance purchase decisions at the start of each period. Labor income is also received at the beginning of the period.

22. Bernheim (1991) and Zietz (2003) showed that the bequest motive has a significant effect on life insurance demand.

23. The only scenarios in which the asset allocation and life insurance decisions are not linked are when the investor derives his or her utility 100 percent from consumption or 100 percent from bequest. Both are extreme—especially the 100 percent from bequest.

24. A well-designed questionnaire can help elicit individuals' attitudes toward bequest, even though a precise estimate may be hard to obtain.

25. The actuarial mortality tables can be taken as a starting point. Life insurance is already priced to take into account adverse selection.

26. That is, we set D equal to 0.2 in the model.

27. The salary growth rate and the volatility were chosen mainly to show the implications of the model. They are not necessarily representative.

28. The mortality and insurance loading is assumed to be 12.5 percent.

29. Davis and Willen (2000) estimated the correlation between labor income and equity market returns by using the U.S. Department of Labor's "Current Occupation Survey." They found that the correlation between equity returns and labor income typically lies in the interval from −0.10 to 0.20.

30. In this model, subjective survival probability and the bequest motive have similar impacts on the optimal insurance need and asset allocation. When subjective survival probability is high, the investor will buy less insurance.

31. This result is close to the typical recommendation made by financial planners (i.e., purchase a term life insurance policy that has a face value four to seven times one's current annual income). See, for example, Todd (2004).

32. See Case #3 for a detailed discussion of the wealth impact.

33. All dollar amounts presented in this section are in real dollars (i.e., inflation-adjusted amounts).

34. All illustrations in this chapter are net of fees and expenses. Fee amounts were obtained from Morningstar Principia as of March 2006. They are 1.26 percent for mutual funds and 2.40 percent for variable annuities.

35. In this chapter, we generated 2,000 return paths. Each path contained 35 years (from age 65 to age 100).

36. Living a long life is desirable, of course, from many aspects; we are focusing here only on the financial aspect of longevity.

37. The section on Asset Allocation and Longevity Insurance provides summary statistics on the sources of retiree income.

38. The U.S. Department of Labor has reported that private-sector employers sponsored only approximately 56,000 tax-qualified DB plans in 1998, down from more than 139,000 in 1979. The number of tax-qualified DC plans sponsored by private employers more than doubled over the same period—from approximately 331,000 to approximately 674,000 (see GAO 2003).

39. This rate is the quote obtained in July 2006 for a 65-year-old male living in Illinois with $1 million to spend. The quote was obtained from www.immediateannuities.com.

40. The average inflation rate in the United States from 1926 to 2006 was 3.04 percent.

41. Payout annuities are available that do allow the investor to withdraw money from them, but the investor typically has to pay a surrender charge or market value adjustment charge. Furthermore, this flexibility applies only during the period of the annuity when payments are guaranteed regardless of life status.

42. The AIR is an initial interest rate assumption that is used to compute the amount of an initial variable annuity payment. Subsequent payments will either increase or decrease depending on the relationship of the AIR to the actual investment return.

43. All initial payments for immediate payout annuities were obtained from www.immediateannuity.com on 12 June 2005 for an assumed 65-year-old female living in Illinois and a $100,000 premium.

44. Poterba (1997); Mitchell, Poterba, Warshawsky, and Brown (1999); Brown and Poterba (2000); Brown (2001); Brown and Warshawsky (2001).

45. The section on Asset Allocation and Longevity Insurance is partly based on material in Chen and Milevsky (2003).

46. See related papers by Chen and Milevsky (2003) and Ameriks, Veres, and Warshawsky (2001). For more theoretical papers that made the same arguments, see the classic by Yaari (1965) and the recent extension by Davidoff, Brown, and Diamond (2005).

47. Remember that a large number of mortality tables are used by actuaries in the insurance industry. The RP2000 table is meant to capture the behavior (i.e., mortality) of general members of a DB pension plan, whereas the IAM tables are meant to cover a (healthier) group of individuals who tend to purchase life annuities.

48. According to LIMRA International estimates, approximately $150 million of retail premiums [not including the 403(b) market] went to variable-income annuities and approximately $2 billion went to fixed-income annuities in 2004.

49. Several insurance companies have rolled out products that allow investors to annuitize at a young age but with payment starting at an older age.

50. See the paper by Milevsky and Abaimova (2005) for an attempt to analyze a type of product that offers this call option in defined-contribution pension plans.

51. DCA in general is a suboptimal investment strategy and has been shown to be mean–variance inefficient by a number of writers.

52. Annuities are available that protect from inflation—the so-called real annuities—but they are relatively more expensive than plain annuities.

53. If the contract has a guarantee period (which, of course, must be paid for), the monthly payments will continue until the guarantee period is over. So in this case, the estate, children, or loved ones do get something.

54. For a more rigorous and mathematically satisfying treatment of the ongoing interaction between human capital and market returns as it pertains to the purchase of life insurance in a continuous-time framework, see Huang, Milevsky, and Wang (2005).

55. The 4 percent discount rate translates into about a 25 percent discount on the overall present value of human capital for a 45-year-old with 20 years of future salary. This 25 percent discount is consistent with empirical evidence on the discount factor between restricted stocks and their unrestricted counterparts (e.g., Amihud and Mendelson 1991). Also, Longstaff (2002) reported that the liquidity premium for the longer-maturity U.S. T-bond is 10–15 percent of the value of the bond.

56. See the discussion of this issue in Appendix 3A.

REFERENCES

Ameriks, John, and Stephen Zeldes. 2001. "How Do Household Portfolio Shares Vary with Age?" Working paper, Columbia University.

Ameriks, John, Robert Veres, and Mark J. Warshawsky. 2001. "Making Retirement Income Last a Lifetime."*Journal of Financial Planning*, Article 6 (December): www.journalfp.net.

Amihud, Yakov, and Haim Mendelson. 1991. "Liquidity, Asset Prices, and Financial Policy." *Financial Analysts Journal*, vol. 47, no. 6 (November/December):56–66.

Auerbach, Alan J., and Laurence Kotlikoff. 1991. "Life Insurance Inadequacy—Evidence from a Sample of Older Widows." NBER Working Paper 3765 (July).

Benartzi, Shlomo. 2001. "Excessive Extrapolation and the Allocation of 401(k) Accounts to Company Stock."*Journal of Finance*, vol. 56, no. 5:1747–1764.

Benartzi, Shlomo, and Richard H. Thaler. 2001. "Naive Diversification Strategies in Defined Contribution Saving Plans."*American Economic Review*, vol. 91, no. 1 (March):79–98.

Bengen, William P. 2001. "Conserving Client Portfolios during Retirement, Part IV."*Journal of Financial Planning*, Article 14 (May): www.journalfp.net.

Bernheim, B. Douglas. 1991. "How Strong Are Bequest Motives? Evidence Based on Estimates of the Demand for Life Insurance and Annuities."*Journal of Political Economy*, vol. 99, no. 5 (October):899–927.

Blake, David, Andrew J.G. Cairns, and Kevin Dowd. 2000. "PensionMetrics: Stochastic Pension Plan Design during the Distribution Phase." Working paper, Pensions Institute (November).

Bodie, Zvi, Robert C. Merton, and William F. Samuelson. 1992. "Labor Supply Flexibility and Portfolio Choice in a Life Cycle Model."*Journal of Economic Dynamics & Control*, vol. 16, nos. 3–4 (July/October):427–449.

Brown, J.R. 2001. "Private Pensions, Mortality Risk, and the Decision to Annuitize."*Journal of Public Economics*, vol. 82, no. 1 (October):29–62.

Brown, J.R., and J. Poterba. 2000. "Joint Life Annuities and Annuity Demand by Married Couples."*Journal of Risk and Insurance*, vol. 67, no. 4 (December):527–553.

Brown, J.R., and M.J. Warshawsky. 2001. "Longevity-Insured Retirement Distributions from Pension Plans: Market and Regulatory Issues." NBER Working Paper 8064.

Browne, S., Moshe A. Milevsky, and T.S. Salisbury. 2003. "Asset Allocation and the Liquidity Premium for Illiquid Annuities."*Journal of Risk and Insurance*, vol. 70, no. 3 (September):509–526.

Brugiavini, Agar. 1993. "Uncertainty Resolution and the Timing of Annuity Purchases."*Journal of Public Economics*, vol. 50, no. 1 (January):31–62.

Buser, Stephen A., and Michael L. Smith. 1983. "Life Insurance in a Portfolio Context."*Insurance, Mathematics & Economics*, vol. 2, no. 3:147–157.

Campbell, Ritchie A. 1980. "The Demand for Life Insurance: An Application of the Economics of Uncertainty."*Journal of Finance*, vol. 35, no. 5 (December):1155–1172.

Campbell, John, and Luis Viceira. 2002. *Strategic Asset Allocation—Portfolio Choice for Long-Term Investors*. New York: Oxford University Press.

Chen, Peng, and Moshe A. Milevsky. 2003. "Merging Asset Allocation and Longevity Insurance: An Optimal Perspective on Payout Annuities."*Journal of Financial Planning*, vol. 16, no. 6 (June):52–62.

Chen, Peng, Roger G. Ibbotson, Moshe A. Milevsky, and Kevin X. Zhu. 2006. "Human Capital, Asset Allocation, and Life Insurance."*Financial Analysts Journal*, vol. 62, no. 1 (January/February):97–109.

Davidoff, Thomas, Jeffrey R. Brown, and Peter A. Diamond. 2005. "Annuities and Individual Welfare."*American Economic Review*, vol. 95, no. 5 (December):1573–1590.

Davis, Stephen J., and Paul Willen. 2000. "Occupation-Level Income Shocks and Asset Returns: Their Covariance and Implications for Portfolio Choice." Working paper, University of Chicago Graduate School of Business.

EBRI. 2000. "Retirement Confidence Survey." Washington, DC: Employee Benefit Research Institute.

———. "Retirement Confidence Survey." Washington, DC: Employee Benefit Research Institute.

———. "Retirement Confidence Survey." Washington, DC: Employee Benefit Research Institute.

Economides, Nicholas. 1982. "Demand for Life Insurance: An Application of the Economics of Uncertainty: A Comment."*Journal of Finance*, vol. 37, no. 5 (December):1305–1309.

Federal Reserve Board. 2004. "Survey of Consumer Finances" (www.norc.org/projects/scf/homepage.htm).

Fischer, S. 1973. "A Life Cycle Model of Life Insurance Purchases."*International Economic Review*, vol. 14, no. 1 (February):132–152.

GAO. 2003. "Report to Congressional Requesters: Private Pensions." U.S. General Accounting Office (July): www.gao.gov/new.items/d03810.pdf.

Gokhale, Jagadeesh, and Laurence J. Kotlikoff. 2002. "The Adequacy of Life Insurance."*Research Dialogue*, no. 72 (July): www.tiaa-crefinstitute.org.

Hanna, Sherman, and Peng Chen. 1997. "Subjective and Objective Risk Tolerance: Implications for Optimal Portfolios."*Financial Counseling and Planning*, vol. 8, no. 2:17–25.

Heaton, John, and Deborah Lucas. 1997. "Market Frictions, Savings Behavior, and Portfolio Choice."*Macroeconomic Dynamics*, vol. 1, no. 1 (March):76–101.

———. 2000. "Portfolio Choice and Asset Prices: The Importance of Entrepreneurial Risk."*Journal of Finance*, vol. 55, no. 3 (June):1163–1198.

Huang, H., A. Moshe Milevsky, and Jin Wang. 2005. "Portfolio Choice and Life Insurance." Research report, IFID Centre (September): www.ifid.ca.

Ibbotson Associates. 2006. *Stocks, Bonds, Bills, and Inflation 2006 Yearbook*. Chicago: Ibbotson Associates.

Ibbotson, Roger G., and Paul D. Kaplan. 2000. "Does Asset Allocation Policy Explain 40, 90, or 100 Percent of Performance?" *Financial Analysts Journal*, vol. 56, no. 1 (January/February): 26–33.

Jagannathan, Ravi, and N.R. Kocherlakota. 1996. "Why Should Older People Invest Less in Stocks Than Younger People?" *Federal Reserve Bank of Minneapolis Quarterly Review*, vol. 20, no. 3 (Summer):11–23.

Kapur, Sandeep, and J. Michael Orszag. 1999. "A Portfolio Approach to Investment and Annuitization during Retirement." Mimeo, Birkbeck College, London (May).

Lee, Hye Kyung, and Sherman Hanna. 1995. "Investment Portfolios and Human Wealth." *Financial Counseling and Planning*, vol. 6:147–152.

Longstaff, Francis A. 2002. "The Flight-to-Liquidity Premium in U.S. Treasury Bond Prices." NBER Working Paper 9312 (November).

Malkiel, Burton G. 2004. *A Random Walk Down Wall Street*. 8th ed. New York: Norton & Company.

Markowitz, Harry M. 1952. "Portfolio Selection." *Journal of Finance*, vol. 7, no. 1 (March):77–91.

———. 1990. *Portfolio Selection*. 2nd ed. Oxford, U.K.: Blackwell Publishers.

Merton, Robert C. 1969. "Lifetime Portfolio Selection under Uncertainty: The Continuous-Time Case." *Review of Economics and Statistics*, vol. 51, no. 3 (August):247–257.

———. 1971. "Optimum Consumption and Portfolio Rules in a Continuous-Time Model." *Journal of Economic Theory*, vol. 3, no. 4 (December):373–413.

———. 2003. "Thoughts on the Future: Theory and Practice in Investment Management." *Financial Analysts Journal*, vol. 59, no. 1 (January/February):17–23.

Meulbroek, Lisa. 2002. "Company Stock in Pension Plans: How Costly Is It?" Working Paper 02-058, Harvard Business School (March).

Milevsky, Moshe A. 2001. "Spending Your Retirement in Monte Carlo." *Journal of Retirement Planning*, vol. 4 (January/February):21–29.

———. 2005a. "Advanced Life Delayed Annuities: Pure Longevity Insurance with Deductibles." *North American Actuarial Journal*, vol. 9, no. 4 (October):109–122.

———. 2005b. "The Implied Longevity Yield: A Note on Developing an Index for Payout Annuities." *Journal of Risk and Insurance*, vol. 72, no. 2 (June):301–320.

Milevsky, Moshe A., and Anna Abaimova. 2005. "Variable Payout Annuities with Downside Protection: How to Replace the Lost Longevity Insurance in DC Plans." Research report, IFID Centre (October): www.ifid.ca.

Milevsky, Moshe A., and Chris Robinson. 2005. "A Sustainable Spending Rate without Simulation." *Financial Analysts Journal*, vol. 61, no. 6 (November/December):89–100.

Milevsky, Moshe A., and Virginia R. Young. 2002. "Optimal Asset Allocation and the Real Option to Delay Annuitization: It's Not Now-or-Never." Pensions Institute Working Paper 0211 (September): www.pensions-institute.org/workingpapers/wp0211.pdf.

———. 2007. "Annuitization and Asset Allocation." *Journal of Economic Dynamics and Control* (http://linkinghub.elsevier.com/retrieve/pii/S0165188906002041).

Milevsky, Moshe A., Kristen Moore, and Virginia R. Young. 2006. "Asset Allocation and Annuity-Purchase Strategies to Minimize the Probability of Financial Ruin." *Mathematical Finance*, vol. 16, no. 4 (October):647–671.

Mitchell, Olivia S., James M. Poterba, Mark J. Warshawsky, and Jeffrey R. Brown. 1999. "New Evidence on the Money's Worth of Individual Annuities." *American Economic Review*, vol. 89, no. 5 (December):1299–1318.

Ostaszewski, Krzysztof. 2003. "Is Life Insurance a Human Capital Derivatives Business?" *Journal of Insurance Issues*, vol. 26, no. 1:1–14.

Poterba, James. 1997. "The History of Annuities in the United States." NBER Working Paper 6001 (April).

Richard, Scott F. 1975. "Optimal Consumption, Portfolio and Life Insurance Rules for an Uncertain Lived Individual in a Continuous Time Model." *Journal of Financial Economics*, vol. 2, no. 2 (June):187–203.

Samuelson, Paul A. 1969. "Lifetime Portfolio Selection by Dynamic Stochastic Programming." *Review of Economics and Statistics*, vol. 51, no. 3 (August):239–246.

Thaler, Richard, and Shlomo Benartzi. 2004. "Save More Tomorrow: Using Behavioral Economics to Increase Employee Savings." *Journal of Political Economy*, vol. 112, no. 1, Part 2 (February):S164–S187.

Todd, Jerry D. 2004. "Integrative Life Insurance Needs Analysis." *Journal of Financial Service Professionals* (March).

Yaari, M.E. 1965. "Uncertain Lifetime, Life Insurance, and the Theory of the Consumer." *Review of Economic Studies*, vol. 32, no. 2 (April):137–150.

Yagi, T., and Y. Nishigaki. 1993. "The Inefficiency of Private Constant Annuities." *Journal of Risk and Insurance*, vol. 60, no. 3 (September):385–412.

Zietz, Emily N. 2003. "An Examination of the Demand for Life Insurance." *Risk Management & Insurance Review*, vol. 6, no. 2 (September):159–191.

CHAPTER 4

THE THEORY OF OPTIMAL LIFE-CYCLE SAVING AND INVESTING

Zvi Bodie
Jonathan Treussard
Paul Willen

How much should a family save for retirement and their kids' college education? How much insurance should they buy? How should they allocate their portfolio among different assets? The modern theory of household financial planning provides the right analytical framework and key insights, and recent work has extended the theory to account for such real-world problems as borrowing and short-sale constraints. But a gap still remains between what people do and what theory says they should do—a gap partially attributable to the institutional and intellectual complexity of theoretically optimal plans. Many of these shortcomings can be addressed by innovative financial products made feasible by recent advances in financial technology.

Life-cycle saving and investing are today a matter of intense concern to millions of people around the world. The most basic questions people face are

- How much of their income should they save for the future?
- What risks should they insure against?
- How should they invest what they save?

Many of these questions are answered for people—in whole or in part—by government, trade unions, employers, and other institutions. In this paper, we argue that economic theory offers important insights and guidelines to policymakers in government, to the financial

Reprinted from *The Future of Life-Cycle Saving and Investing,* The Research Foundation of CFA Institute (October 2007):19 37.

services firms that produce life-cycle financial products, to the advisers who recommend to their clients which products to buy, and to educators who are trying to help the public make informed choices.

The literature is vast and complex, and we will not attempt to survey or summarize it all in this paper. Instead, we lay out the basic analytical framework using a few relatively uncomplicated models and focus on several key concepts. This analytical framework could serve as a valuable guide to financial services firms in helping them to develop and explain products in terms that are understandable to the layman.

In the first section of this paper, we introduce the life-cycle model of consumption choice and portfolio selection. We emphasize the central role of consumption in life-cycle planning, and we highlight the use of financial assets as means to transfer consumption from points in the individual's life cycle when consumption has relatively little value to points when consumption has relatively more value. The second section highlights five concepts from the life-cycle model that are directly relevant to the practice of life-cycle planning: (1) the notion of a lifetime budget constraint, (2) the relevance of contingent claims in life-cycle planning, (3) the trade-off imposed by varying costs of consumption over one's lifetime, (4) the role of risky assets, and (5) the asset allocation decision over the life cycle. In the third section, we recognize the complexity of life-cycle planning and the relevance of financial frictions at the individual level, and accordingly, we argue that it is the role of specialized firms to engineer and deliver life-cycle products that meet the needs of households. The final section contains our concluding remarks.

THEORETICAL INTRODUCTION

The starting point for analysis of life-cycle portfolio choice is a model of the evolution of an investor, which one can think of as an event tree.[1] Figure 4.1 illustrates an event tree for a fictional investor who lives for three periods: youth, prime earning years, and retirement. In addition to aging, events occur that affect the investor. In Period 2, he earns either high or low income, and in Period 3, he enjoys either good or bad health. Figure 4.1 shows income and, in retirement, expenses associated with the different outcomes. We assume that our investor earns no income in retirement and faces no health expenses before retirement. A financial plan, in this context, tells an investor how much to save or borrow, how to invest any savings—not just today (in Period 1) but in the future (in Period 2)—and how much the investor should withdraw in retirement (Period 3). That plan could also depend on contingencies: Along the high-income path, our investor may want to save more; along a bad health path, our investor may want to withdraw less to prepare for high bills.

Suppose, for simplicity, that the only investment opportunity is to save or borrow at 0 percent interest. The lines labeled "advice" in Figure 4.1 reflect a simple proposed financial plan: Save $10,000 a year when young, save $20,000 a year during prime earning years, and withdraw $50,000 a year in retirement. It is easy to verify that this plan works. Savings at retirement equal $750,000, which, divided up over the remaining 15 years, allows withdrawals of $50,000 a year.

How good is this proposal? Standard approaches to financial planning would focus on whether the investor could afford to save enough or whether the $50,000 would be enough in retirement. What does the life-cycle theory say about this proposal? We distill the following three principles from the life-cycle approach.

FIGURE 4.1   The Life-Cycle Model: An Event Tree

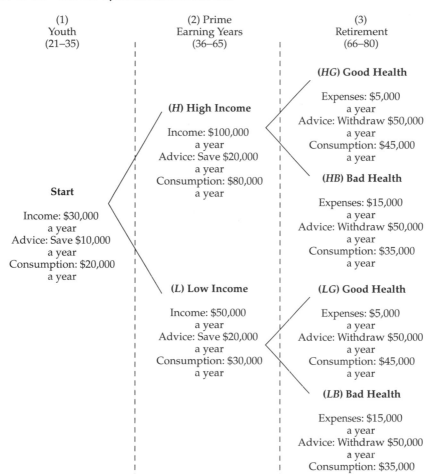

Principle 1: Focus not on the financial plan itself but on the consumption profile that it implies

In this example, we can easily calculate consumption (shown in Figure 4.1) because it equals income less savings during working years and withdrawals less health expenses in retirement.[2]

Principle 2: Financial assets are vehicles for moving consumption from one location in the life cycle to another

Suppose, for example, our investor wanted to increase consumption in youth. By reducing savings in youth and leaving it unchanged in prime earning years, our investor can transfer consumption from retirement to youth.

By reducing savings in youth and raising savings in middle age, our investor can transfer consumption from prime earning years to youth.[3]

Principle 3: A dollar is more valuable to an investor in situations where consumption is low than in situations where consumption is high

In Figure 4.1, for example, the life-cycle model says that if we offered to give a dollar to our investor but said he must choose when he wanted it, our investor would want the money in youth, when his consumption is lowest. The law of diminishing returns is at work here: An additional dollar is a lot more valuable to a recent college graduate than to a 55-year-old executive.

So, what does the life-cycle model tell us about the advice in Figure 4.1? Looking at the implied consumption over the life cycle, we notice huge variations. According to our third principle above, a dollar is much more valuable when consumption is low than when it is high. And so we can improve on this plan by trying to move consumption from situations with high consumption to situations with low consumption.

- Consumption in youth ($20,000) is much lower (and thus more valuable) than it is on average in prime earning years ($55,000). By saving less in youth and more in prime earning years, our investor could transfer consumption from low-value situations to high-value situations and make himself better off.
- Consumption in situations HG and HB ($40,000 on average) is much lower (and thus more valuable) than in situation H ($80,000). By saving more in situation H, our investor could transfer consumption from low-value situations to high-value situations and make himself better off.
- Consumption in situations LG and LB ($40,000 on average) is higher (and thus less valuable) than in situation L ($30,000). By saving less in situation L, our investor could transfer consumption from low-value situations to high-value situations and make himself better off.

Now, suppose we introduce health insurance. And suppose health insurers offered a contract that says that for every dollar you invest, you receive $2 if your health is bad in retirement. If you borrow a dollar in prime earning years and invest in this stylized form of health insurance, what happens? Your consumption in prime earning years remains the same but falls by $1 when your health is good (because you have to repay the loan) and increases by $1 when your health is bad (because you receive the $2 for having bad health less the loan repayment). Thus, health insurance transfers consumption resources from situations where your health is good to situations where your health is bad. For example, in Figure 4.1, consumption is higher (and thus less valuable) in good health situations than in bad ones, so our investor can make himself better off by buying insurance.

FIVE KEY CONCEPTS

With the overview of the life-cycle model complete, we now highlight five of the most important insights produced by the theory of life-cycle planning: (1) the notion of a lifetime budget constraint, (2) the relevance of contingent claims in life-cycle planning, (3) the trade-off imposed by varying costs of consumption over one's lifetime, (4) the role of risky assets, and (5) the asset allocation decision over the life cycle.

Insight 1: The Lifetime Budget Constraint

One of the great early insights in financial planning follows directly from Principle 2 above: Under certain conditions, household consumption over the life cycle depends entirely on the present discounted value of lifetime income and not on the evolution of income itself. More specifically, suppose two investors have some financial wealth and also expect some stream of labor income over their remaining working life.[4] Now, calculate the discounted present value of their future income, which we call "human wealth," and add it to their savings and call the sum "total wealth." According to the life-cycle model, under certain conditions, if two investors have the same total wealth, then their consumption decisions over the life cycle will be the same, regardless of the shape of their actual income profile.

To understand why we can ignore the profile of income across dates and random outcomes, return to Principle 2, which says that we can use financial assets to transfer consumption from one situation to another. A loan is a financial asset that allows you to increase consumption today in exchange for reducing consumption by the amount of the loan plus interest at a future date. What is the maximum amount an investor can consume today? It is her current savings plus the maximum amount she can borrow. What is the maximum amount she can borrow? It is, theoretically, the present discounted value of her future labor income. Thus, total wealth, as defined in the previous paragraph, measures the maximum amount an investor can transfer to the present. Now that our investor has transferred everything to the present, she can decide when to spend it, and using the same technology, she can transfer her wealth to the situations where she wants to consume. It is important to stress that the idea of transferring all lifetime income to the present is purely a hypothetical construct used as a way to measure lifetime resources using a single metric.

The importance of the lifetime budget constraint is that it shows that financial wealth is only one part of the wealth that matters to an investor. Total wealth equals the sum of both financial wealth and human wealth. For most households—basically for almost all households in which the income earner is not old—human wealth dwarfs financial wealth. Table 4.1 shows the ratio of human wealth to income measured using real-world data for various groups in the population. To see the importance of human wealth, consider a 35-year-old male college graduate earning $100,000 and owning $400,000 in financial wealth. Consider also an heir who plans to remain out of the labor force his entire life and has $3 million in financial wealth. One might think that these two investors have nothing in common, but according to one version of the life-cycle model, they should, in fact, consume exactly the same amounts. Note that according to Table 4.1, the college graduate's human wealth is 25.9 times his current income, or in this case, $2.59 million, to which we add financial wealth of $400,000 to get total wealth of $2.99 million, almost exactly the same as the heir.

We can also incorporate future expenses into the lifetime budget constraint. For example, suppose an investor knows that she will send two kids to college at given dates in the future. If we know how much that education will cost, we can simply subtract the present value of future education costs from current total wealth, just as we added future income.[5]

Insight 2: The Importance of Constructing "Contingent Claims"

Previously, we argued that investors can use financial assets to transform their income and expense streams into the equivalent of financial wealth, but we were unspecific as to how. Now, we focus on how investors can actually affect these transformations. First, the easy case: If future income and expenses are certain, then investors can transform them into additions and subtractions from current wealth by simply borrowing and/or saving the appropriate amount. For example, if one knows that one will earn $100,000 five years from now and the interest rate is 5 percent, one can raise current liquid financial wealth by borrowing $78,350 and paying back the money plus $21,650 in interest from future earnings.

TABLE 4.1 Human Wealth Measured as a Fraction of Current Income

	Initial Age				
Item	25	35	45	55	65
High school graduates					
Men	29.7	19.1	12.8	8.2	—
	(= 718,530/24,199)	(= 629,378/33,005)	(= 439,494/34,301)	(= 219,269/26,814)	—
Women	27.9	16.6	11.9	8.6	—
	(= 379,592/13,606)	(= 317,191/19,159)	(= 202,351/16,997)	(= 101,256/11,784)	—
College graduates					
Men	47.4	25.9	15.9	8.7	—
	(= 1,483,412/31,297)	(= 1,483,295/57,264)	(= 1,212,542/76,385)	(= 691,057/79,566)	—
Women	32.9	20.1	13.3	7.0	—
	(= 881,762/26,808)	(= 792,354/39,424)	(= 580,133/43,506)	(= 266,430/38,064)	—
Male college graduates					
Retire at 55	39.3	20.0	9.9	—	—
	(= 1,231,486/31,297)	(= 1,144,728/57,264)	(= 757,535/76,385)	—	—
Retire at 75	51.0	28.6	18.6	12.2	7.0
	(= 1,597,261/31,297)	(= 1,636,299/57,264)	(= 1,418,165/76,385)	(= 967,398/79,566)	(= 432,870/61,491)
Male advanced degree holders	51.0	28.1	16.7	9.2	—
	(= 1,651,729/32,386)	(= 1,709,956/60,773)	(= 1,431,000/85,798)	(= 866,733/94,627)	—

Source: Authors' calculations based on data from the Panel Study of Income Dynamics.

Note: Human wealth is measured as a multiple of current income. For example, a 25-year-old male college graduate has human wealth equal to 47.4 times his current income.

But in practice, things are not so easy. The main problem with calculating the lifetime budget constraint is random outcomes. To see why random outcomes are a problem, return to Figure 4.1. Following the logic above, our investor can convert his future labor income into current financial wealth by borrowing. But how much should he borrow? Along the "high-income" path, he earns $100,000 a year. So, if we assume an interest rate of zero, he could borrow $100,000 today and pay it back, say, at age 45. But suppose he does not get the high-income outcome but, instead, earns "low income." Then, at age 45, his income would not be sufficient to pay off the loan. Another alternative would be to borrow $75,000, the average of his two income draws, but he would still have insufficient funds.

What if financial markets offered a security that paid off $1 only if our investor got the low-income outcome and another security that paid off $1 only if our investor got the high-income outcome? Then, our investor could convert his future income along the low-income path into current income by shorting $50,000 of the low-income asset and similarly convert his income along the high-income path using the high-income asset. We call these assets that pay off contingent on some future event "contingent claims."[6]

If contingent claims are so useful, one might ask why we do not observe them. And the answer is that we do, although they rarely ever appear in the form we described. Let us revisit the case of health insurance. Earlier, we described a stylized contract that paid off only in bad health states. In its most familiar form, however, health insurance is a contract that pays the investor's medical bills both in good and bad health states in exchange for a payment today. Accordingly, health insurance—as we observe it—is not a contingent claim per se because it pays off in both outcomes. Nonetheless, it is easy to construct a contingent claim using this common form of health insurance and the riskless bond. For example, if you want a claim contingent on the bad health outcome, then borrow $5,000 and buy health insurance. In the bad health event, you receive $10,000 ($15,000 less the loan repayment), and in the good health event, you get nothing because the health insurance payoff and the loan repayment cancel each other out. One can similarly construct a claim contingent on the good outcome.[7]

Contingent claims help with another serious problem: inflation. Suppose our investor knows for sure that he will earn $100,000 next year, but he is uncertain about inflation. Suppose that inflation could either be zero or 10 percent. Thus, our investor's real income next year actually does vary randomly: Along one path, he receives $100,000 in real spending power, and along the other, he receives $90,000. According to Principle 2, our investor will want to shift consumption from the low-inflation event to the high-inflation event. If we create inflation-contingent claims, our investor will be able to do just that. It is for this reason that economists have long advocated and spearheaded the creation of inflation-indexed bonds, marketed as TIPS or Treasury Inflation-Protected Securities.[8]

We have now, we hope, convinced the reader of the value of contingent claims in life-cycle financial planning. But before we go on, we should discuss the limits to the use of contingent claims. First, contingent claims work well when both parties can verify the event in question and neither party can affect or has better information about the likelihood of the event occurring. For example, it is easy to verify the price of General Motors Corporation (GM) stock. And for the most part, investors who either have better information or who can affect the price are legally forbidden from trading, so we see a large variety of claims contingent on the level of GM stock (futures, options, etc.). But earlier, we proposed that an investor would buy claims contingent on the level of his labor income. First, because income is not always easy to verify (the investor would have an incentive to hide some income and claim that he earned only $50,000 when he actually earned $100,000 so as to allow him to pay back only $50,000) and because a worker has some control over how much he earns (again, our investor has an incentive to earn less because he would then have to repay less), income-linked contingent claims present practical problems.[9] Second, the creation of contingent claims requires that we clearly understand the risks investors face, and neither record keeping nor econometric techniques have yet rendered measurement of these risks trivial.

Insight 3: The Prices of Securities Matter!

In discussing contingent claims, we have shown how households can eliminate variation in consumption across different random events by transferring consumption from outcomes with high consumption to outcomes with low consumption by buying and selling consumption in those different outcomes using contingent claims. But we have said nothing about the price of contingent claims, and as everyone knows, prices usually play a central role in determining how much of something someone wants to buy or sell.

To illustrate some of the issues with the pricing of contingent claims, we consider an investor who faces two equally probable outcomes in the future: In outcome H, she consumes $100,000, and in outcome L, she consumes $50,000. Table 4.2 provides information for this example. To analyze this problem, we will need two concepts from probability theory. First, we measure the "expected" level of consumption, which we get by weighting different outcomes by their probability and summing. The expected consumption for our investor is $75,000. But many different consumption profiles yield the same expected consumption (for example, $75,000 with certainty), and risk-averse investors are not indifferent among them. Our investor, if risk averse, would certainly prefer $75,000 with certainty. But we can go further and actually measure how much she prefers other consumption profiles by measuring the "certainty equivalent consumption level"—the level of certain consumption that would make her as happy as the random consumption in question. For a particular level of risk aversion, we calculate that our investor would be as happy with $70,710 with certainty as with the $100,000 and $50,000 with equal probability.[10]

Now, a financial planner comes along to help her out. The financial planner has at his disposal a set of contingent claims, one paying $1 in outcome H and another paying $1 in outcome L. What strategy should he propose to the investor? Let us start with a baseline case where both contingent claims cost the same: 50 cents. The financial planner proposes to the investor that she short $25,000 of outcome H income by shorting the contingent claim and that she go long $25,000 of outcome L income by purchasing the outcome L contingent claim. The cost of the state L contingent claims ($12,500) is exactly offset by the gains from shorting the outcome L contingent claim, meaning that the long–short portfolio costs nothing. What happens to consumption? The investor now consumes $75,000 in both outcomes. This strategy, therefore, shifts consumption from the high outcome to the low outcome—just what we said financial assets were supposed to do. And the certainty equivalent level of consumption, trivially equal to the actual level of consumption, $75,000, is much higher than the initial level. So, the financial planner provided good advice.

Now, we change the world a little and set the prices of the contingent claims unequally at 40 cents for the H outcome and 60 cents for the L outcome. Suppose the planner provides the same advice (called "Strategy 1" in the table). The plan still provides the same certain level of consumption, but a slight problem exists: Because the price of the H state consumption has fallen relative to the L state, the revenue from the sale of H state consumption no longer offsets the cost of the added L state consumption. The investor now needs to come up with $5,000 to execute the strategy. We assume that the investor does not have that money

TABLE 4.2   Understanding the Role of the Prices of Contingent Claims

Item	H	L
Scenario		
Probability	50%	50%
Initial consumption	$100,000	$50,000
Expected consumption	$75,000	
Certainty equivalent	70,710	
Baseline prices		
Price of contingent claim	50¢	50¢
Strategy	Sell $25,000	Buy $25,000
Cost	−$12,500	$12,500
New consumption	75,000	75,000
Expected consumption	$75,000	
Certainty equivalent	75,000	
Alternative prices		
Price of contingent claim	40¢	60¢
Strategy 1	Sell $25,000	Buy $25,000
Cost	−$10,000	$15,000
New consumption	75,000	75,000
Expected consumption	$75,000	
Certainty equivalent	75,000	
Strategy 2	Sell $30,000	Buy $20,000
Cost	−$12,000	$12,000
New consumption	70,000	70,000
Expected consumption	$70,000	
Certainty equivalent	70,000	
Strategy 3	Sell $12,500	Buy $8,333
Cost	−$5,000	$5,000
New consumption	87,500	58,333
Expected consumption	$70,833	
Certainty equivalent	71,440	

and confine ourselves to self-financing strategies. The planner regroups and provides Strategy 2, a self-financing strategy that yields certain consumption of $70,000. By selling more of the cheap state H claims and buying fewer of the expensive state L claims, our investor can achieve certain consumption of $70,000 without adding any money. Has the planner earned his money? No. Recall that certainty equivalent consumption for the initial consumption profile exceeded $70,000.

Not all investors will respond to asset prices in the same way. Differences in risk aversion, for example, play a big role. Risk aversion measures the willingness of an investor to tolerate variation in consumption across random outcomes. In Strategies 2 and 3, we argue that our investor is willing to accept a substantial increase in variation of consumption in exchange for a small increase in expected consumption. But that conclusion follows only because of the specific choice of risk aversion that we made. A household with higher risk aversion might opt for the sure consumption. Another issue that has drawn significant attention from economists is "habits." Some have argued that households are particularly unwilling to tolerate reductions in consumption. In this case, for example, suppose that our investor currently consumes $70,000 a year and is unwilling to tolerate any reduction in consumption. Then, for her, the only plausible option would be to accept the lower expected level of consumption that accompanies the strategy of achieving riskless consumption. To add to the challenge of portfolio choice in this situation, we point out that the investor knows that higher consumption may restrict her choices in the future and, therefore, may restrict consumption now so that she can take risky bets in the future.[11]

So far, both strategies proposed by the planner have caused problems—one because it required substantial additional funds and the other because it did not provide any benefit. Does this mean that financial planning cannot help this investor? No. Strategy 3 offers a bundle of contingent claims that manages to raise the investor's certainty equivalent consumption without requiring additional investment. What is unique about this plan among the ones we have looked at so far is that it does not provide a certain level of consumption.

The earlier examples illustrate that the optimal plan depends on the prices of the contingent claims. With either set of prices, it was possible to eliminate variability from consumption. But in only one of the cases was this advisable. The difference between the two scenarios is that in the baseline, there was no risk premium (and thus no incentive for the investor to take on risk) and in the alternative, there was a risk premium. To see the difference, calculate the returns on a riskless bond that pays $1 in both outcomes and an equity-type security that pays $1 in state L and $2 in state H. In the baseline scenario, the price of this bond would be $1, making the return zero; the price of this equity would be $1.50 with an expected payoff of $1.50, so it also has a return of zero. In the alternative scenario, the return on the riskless bond is still zero, whereas the equity security now costs $1.40 with the same expected payoff of $1.50, meaning that it returns 7 percent more than the riskless bond.

Insight 4: Risky Assets in the Life-Cycle Model

One of the most important insights of the life-cycle model concerns the benefits of risky assets. In the life-cycle model, we view risky assets as a way to move money across different outcomes at a given time, not as a way to transfer resources across time. Let us illustrate this point with an example.

Consider an investor who lives for two years, this year and a "next year" in which there are two possible outcomes: "good times" and "bad times." Our investor can invest in a bond that pays 5 percent regardless of the outcome and a stock that increases 30 percent in good times and falls 5 percent in bad times. Figure 4.2 illustrates this event tree. Standard investment advice would view the two assets as different ways to save for the future—to transfer money to the future. In the life-cycle model, we divide their roles. We do so by constructing a portfolio composed of $100 of stock financed by a $100 short position in the bond. This portfolio costs nothing today and, as Figure 4.2 shows, pays $25 in good times and –$10 in bad times. In other words, one can use this portfolio to convert $10 in bad times into $25 in good times (circled Transaction 2 in the figure). To transfer money across time, one uses the bond that, for example, allows the investor to transfer $100 today for $105 in both states in the future (circled Transaction 1 in the figure).

FIGURE 4.2   The Role of Risky Assets in the Life-Cycle Model

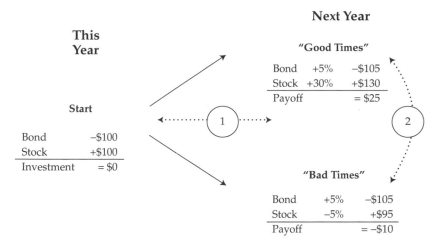

Suppose our investor wants to decide whether to invest $100 in the stock or bond. Our analysis shows that a $100 investment in the stock is a combination of a $100 investment in the bond and the portfolio described above. In other words, the investor is exchanging $100 today for $105 in the future and exchanging $10 in bad times for $25 in good times. According to our logic, we view investing $100 in the bond as exchanging $100 today for $105 next year but transferring nothing from bad times to good times. Thus, the difference in the two investment options has to do not with transferring resources across time—both investments achieve that—but with transferring resources across outcomes.

Therefore, the decision to invest in the stock revolves around whether the investor is willing to give up $10 in bad times in exchange for $25 in good times. If we imagine, for the purposes of discussion, that the two outcomes are equally probable, then this seems like an exceptionally good deal. But we should recall that a goal of financial planning is to smooth consumption across outcomes, so we need to know whether our investor wants to transfer income from bad times to good times. At first glance, one might imagine that our investor would want to transfer income just the opposite way if, for example, "good times" meant employment and "bad times" meant joblessness.

Insight 5: Asset Allocation over the Life Cycle

One of the great early discoveries of the theory of life-cycle financial planning was an understanding of the evolution of the optimal level of risk exposure as an investor ages. Despite the prevailing folk wisdom (and advice from some practitioners and academics) that investors should reduce the proportion of their portfolio invested in risky assets as they age, Merton (1969) and Samuelson (1969) showed that, for standard preferences,[12] it is optimal for individuals to maintain a constant fraction of their total wealth (human capital plus financial wealth) invested in equities at all ages.

The above may suggest that the life-cycle theory has little advice on asset allocation other than to choose the right proportion once. In fact, because of the influence of labor income, the proportion of financial wealth invested in risky assets can vary dramatically over the life cycle. This issue was taken up by Bodie, Merton, and Samuelson (1992), who considered life-cycle investors with risky wages and a degree of choice with respect to the labor–leisure decision. The model's results indicate that the fraction of an individual's financial wealth optimally invested in equity should "normally" decline with age for two reasons. First, because human capital is usually less risky than equity and because the value of human capital usually declines as a proportion of an individual's total wealth as one ages, an individual may need to invest a large share of his or her financial wealth in risky assets to get sufficient overall risk exposures. Second, the flexibility that younger individuals have to alter their labor supply allows them to invest more heavily in risky assets. The opposite result, however, is also possible. For people with risky human capital, such as Samuelson's businessmen or stock analysts, the optimal path may be to start out early in life with no stock market exposure in one's investment portfolio and increase that exposure as one ages.

NEW FINANCIAL PRODUCTS

In this section, we map the key concepts from the life-cycle model into a methodological framework for the successful production of consumer-oriented structured life-cycle contracts. This approach, which recognizes that individuals do not have the ability to engineer for themselves contingent claims packaged in the form they most desire, owes much to Merton's development of the theory of financial intermediation.[13] The production of life-cycle products is successful if

1. the state-contingent consumption promised by the life-cycle product effectively satisfies the needs of the individual and
2. the financial intermediary has the adequate production/risk management infrastructure in place for the consumer-oriented life-cycle product to be technologically feasible.

An analogy is that of the automobile industry. The customer is offered a standard product with optional features. Then, it is the automobile manufacturer's responsibility to fill the order received. Similarly, the development of financial products should start with designing standard products that serve primarily to secure a certain standard of living in retirement with various options.

In particular, the technology applied to this approach is entirely nested within the contingent claims analysis (CCA) framework developed by Merton (e.g., 1992). In accordance with the CCA methodology, the process that allows a financial intermediary to successfully engineer, market, and deliver optimal life-cycle products to its customers is best viewed as a production process that consists of three sets of tasks, as illustrated in Figure 4.3.

Stage 1

This stage requires the financial firm to determine its production-cost schedule (i.e., the cost of state-contingent consumption). These costs fall under two categories: the cost of certain future consumption provided by the market prices of inflation-protected bonds and the cost of state-specific consumption implied by the market prices of such securities as options (e.g., Breeden and Litzenberger 1978). State-contingent prices, also known as Arrow–Debreu prices (Arrow 1953; Debreu 1959), allow one to gauge the objective trade-off of consuming in different states of the world; thus, they are critical inputs in the process of designing optimal life-cycle consumption programs. These prices are instrumental in guaranteeing that the life-cycle

FIGURE 4.3   Using the Life-Cycle Model to Address Consumer Needs

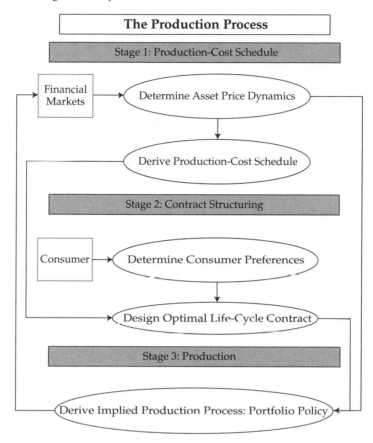

contract satisfies the individual's budget constraint. A critical aspect of this stage is that it requires no knowledge of the financial intermediary's future customers and their preferences.

Stage 2

This is a contract-structuring stage during which, using the schedule of state prices, the financial firm structures the product that best satisfies the customer's tastes given the individual's lifetime wealth and planning horizon. For anticipated spending items with a well-defined time structure, and for which successful funding is a high priority—such as securing a comfortable standard of living in retirement and being in a position to send children to college—the financial firm should guarantee a floor given a particular flow of contributions. To the extent that the individual has wealth in excess of that required to finance necessities, modern finance theory (e.g., Vasicek 1977; Cox and Huang 1989; and Merton 1992) indicates that optimal discretionary spending over the life cycle is functionally identical to a derivatives contract on the growth-optimum portfolio.[14] By acknowledging the effects of consumption habit formation (e.g., Dybvig 1995; Bodie, Detemple, Otruba, and Walter 2004) on individual well being, "consumption ratcheting" features may play a central role in the design of consumer-oriented life-cycle products.

Stage 3

After the contract is finalized, the financial intermediary initiates production by dynamically replicating the payoffs promised to the customer. This is done via hedging in financial markets.[15] Although the financial intermediary replicates the guaranteed payments as closely as possible, it must also raise risk capital from investors to assure customers that their payments will not be subject to residual risk (e.g., the risk that the intermediary may default on its obligation to deliver the promised amounts).[16] Consumers should not have to become investors in the debt or equity of the financial intermediary.

CONCLUSION

As products and services for addressing the financial risks of retirement change, so do the varieties of institutions available to provide support to the elderly. Today, many diverse retirement income systems coexist around the world, each relying in varying proportions on one or more of the following institutional forms:

- support from family or community,
- pension plans sponsored by employers and/or labor unions,
- social insurance programs run by governments, and
- personal savings in the form of real and financial assets—equity in one's home or business, savings accounts, insurance contracts, mutual funds, and so on.

Many experts agree, however, that the mix of these institutional forms will change significantly in the next few years. Change is particularly to be expected in the industrialized countries, such as the United States, the United Kingdom, Australia, Western Europe, and Japan, where the rapid aging of the population reflects both that people are living longer and that they are having fewer children. In these economies, people will find they can rely less on family and government support than in the past and must, instead, turn to financial markets and related institutions by saving and investing for their own retirement. Even in emerging markets, new demographic and economic realities have prompted the beginning of widespread retirement system reforms, as seen in the pension reform movements of Latin America, Eastern Europe, and more recently, Asia.

In response to global population aging and financial deregulation, governments and financial firms are seeking to create new institutions and services that will provide the desired protection against the financial consequences of old age, illness, and disability and will insulate people against both inflation and asset price fluctuations. New opportunities are to be expected for older persons to continue employment, perhaps on a part-time basis, and to convert their assets, particularly housing wealth, into spendable income. For better or for worse, these developments mean that people are being given more individual choice over their own asset accumulation and drawdown processes. Because these new financial instruments transfer more responsibility and choice to workers and retirees, the challenge is to frame risk–reward trade-offs and to cast financial decision making in a format that ordinary people can understand and implement.

ACKNOWLEDGMENTS

The authors thank Phil Dybvig, Debbie Lucas, and participants at this conference for helpful comments and suggestions.

NOTES

1. In finance, the event tree has become a workhorse tool—most importantly, the Cox–Ross–Rubinstein (1979) binomial model.
2. This insight goes back to Fisher (1930) and Modigliani and Brumberg (1954, 1979).
3. Moving consumption over the life cycle is at the heart of life-cycle planning. As Irving Fisher put it, the intent of life-cycle planning theory is to "modify [the income stream received by the individual] by exchange so as to convert it into that particular form most wanted by [this individual]" (Fisher 1930, Chapter 6).
4. The lifetime budget constraint is presented in Fisher (1930), Modigliani and Brumberg (1954), and Modigliani (1986). This concept of a lifetime budget constraint has been generalized and successfully applied to life-cycle planning under uncertainty, starting most notably with Cox and Huang (1989), and has been central to the development of finance theory over the past decade or so.
5. See, for instance, CollegeSure savings funds.
6. Also called Arrow–Debreu securities after the seminal work of Arrow (1953) and Debreu (1959). See also Arrow (1971) and the recent work by Sharpe (2006).
7. This type of reasoning is the essence of production technology supporting the creation of contingent claims, in theory and in practice, going back to Black and Scholes (1973), Merton (1973), and Cox, Ross, and Rubinstein (1979). This is the core of modern financial engineering as it applies to life-cycle planning.
8. See, for instance, Fischer (1975) and Bodie (2003) for the role of inflation-protected bonds in life-cycle plans.
9. These problems are related to moral hazard and the resulting borrowing constraint literature, such as He and Pages (1993) and El Karoui and Jeanblanc-Picque (1998), who extended the study of human capital in life-cycle planning to address the important real-world problems caused by the limited ability of people to borrow against future income.
10. This type of calculation, known as certainty equivalent analysis, is explained at http://en.wikipedia.org/wiki/Certainty_equivalent. Certainty equivalent measures have been used to compare investment strategies since at least Merton and Samuelson (1974).
11. For a discussion of these issues, see Dybvig (1995).
12. In particular, Samuelson (1969) and Merton (1969) studied individuals with constant relative risk aversion. For more details, see http://en.wikipedia.org/wiki/Risk_averse#Relative_risk_aversion.
13. This approach is exposed in Chapter 14 of Merton (1992).
14. The growth-optimum portfolio minimizes the expected time to reach a prespecified wealth target under the assumption of continuously reinvested gains. The composition of the growth-optimum portfolio is subjective in that it depends on expected rates of return on stocks.
15. For example, Detemple, Garcia, and Rindisbacher (2003, 2005) offer a flexible mathematical technology to determine the precise portfolio policy supporting optimal life-cycle products.
16. Risk capital is defined in Merton and Perold (1993).

REFERENCES

Arrow, K. 1953. "The Role of Securities in the Optimal Allocation of Risk-Bearing." *Econometrie* [translated and reprinted in *Review of Economic Studies* (1964), vol. 31, no. 2:91–96].

———. 1971. "Insurance, Risk, and Resource Allocation," Chapter 5 in *Essays in the Theory of Risk-Bearing*. Chicago: Markham Publishing Company.

Black, F., and M. Scholes. 1973. "The Pricing of Options and Corporate Liabilities." *Journal of Political Economy*, vol. 81, no. 3 (May/June):637–654.

Bodie, Z. 2003. "Thoughts on the Future: Life-Cycle Investing in Theory and Practice." *Financial Analysts Journal*, vol. 59, no. 1 (January/February):24–29.

Bodie, Z., R. Merton, and W. Samuelson. 1992. "Labor Supply Flexibility and Portfolio Choice in a Life Cycle Model." *Journal of Economic Dynamics and Control*, vol. 16:427–449.

Bodie, Z., J. Detemple, S. Otruba, and S. Walter. 2004. "Optimal Consumption-Portfolio Choices and Retirement Planning." *Journal of Economic Dynamics and Control*, vol. 28:1115–1148.

Breeden, D., and R. Litzenberger. 1978. "Prices of State-Contingent Claims Implicit in Option Prices." *Journal of Business*, vol. 51, no. 4 (October):261–651.

Cox, J., and C. Huang. 1989. "Optimal Consumption and Portfolio Policies When Asset Prices Follow a Diffusion Process." *Journal of Economic Theory*, vol. 49, no. 1 (October):33–83.

Cox, J., S. Ross, and M. Rubinstein. 1979. "Option Pricing: A Simplified Approach." *Journal of Financial Economics*, vol. 7, no. 3 (September):229–263.

Debreu, G. 1959. *Theory of Value*. New Haven, CT: Yale University Press.

Detemple, J., R. Garcia, and M. Rindisbacher. 2003. "A Monte Carlo Method for Optimal Portfolios." *Journal of Finance*, vol. 58, no. 1 (February):401–446.

———. 2005. "Intertemporal Asset Allocation: A Comparison of Methods." *Journal of Banking and Finance*, vol. 29, no. 11 (November):2821–2848.

Dybvig, P. 1995. "Dusenberry's Ratcheting of Consumption: Optimal Dynamic Consumption and Investment Given Intolerance for Any Decline in Standard of Living." *Review of Economic Studies*, vol. 62, no. 2 (April):287–313.

El Karoui, N., and M. Jeanblanc-Picque. 1998. "Optimization of Consumption with Labor Income." *Finance and Stochastics*, vol. 2, no. 4:409–440.

Fischer, S. 1975. "The Demand for Index Bonds." *Journal of Political Economy*, vol. 83, no. 3 (June):509–534.

Fisher, I. 1930. *The Theory of Interest*. New York: Macmillan Company.

He, H., and H. Pages. 1993. "Labor Income, Borrowing Constraints, and Equilibrium Asset Prices." *Economic Theory*, vol. 3, no. 4:663–696.

Merton, R. 1969. "Lifetime Portfolio Selection under Uncertainty: The Continuous-Time Case." *Review of Economics and Statistics*, vol. 51, no. 3 (August):247–257.

———. 1973. "Theory of Rational Option Pricing." *Bell Journal of Economics and Management Science*, vol. 4, no. 1 (Spring):141–183.

———. 1992. *Continuous-Time Finance*. Malden, MA: Blackwell.

Merton, R., and A. Perold. 1993. "Management of Risk Capital in Financial Firms." In Chapter 8 of *Financial Services: Perspectives and Challenges*. Edited by S.L. Hayes III. Cambridge, MA: Harvard Business School Press:215–245.

Merton, R., and P. Samuelson. 1974. "Fallacy of the Log-Normal Approximation to Optimal Portfolio Decision-Making over Many Periods." *Journal of Financial Economics*, vol. 1, no. 1 (May):67–94.

Modigliani, F. 1986. "Life Cycle, Individual Thrift, and the Wealth of Nations." *American Economic Review*, vol. 76, no. 3 (June):297–313.

Modigliani, F., and R. Brumberg. 1954. "Utility Analysis and the Consumption Function: An Interpretation of Cross-Section Data." In *Post Keynesian Economics*. Edited by K. Kurihara. New Brunswick, NJ: Rutgers University Press.

———. 1979. "Utility Analysis and Aggregate Consumption Functions: An Attempt at Integration." In *Collected Papers of Franco Modigliani*, vol. 2, Edited by A. Abel. Cambridge, MA: MIT Press.

Samuelson, P. 1969. "Lifetime Portfolio Selection by Dynamic Stochastic Programming." *Review of Economics and Statistics*, vol. 51, no. 3 (August):239–246.

Sharpe, W. 2006. "Retirement Financial Planning: A State/Preference Approach." Working paper.

Vasicek, O. 1977. "An Equilibrium Characterization of the Term Structure." *Journal of Financial Economics*, vol. 5, no. 2 (November):177–188.

CHAPTER 5

IS CONVENTIONAL FINANCIAL PLANNING GOOD FOR YOUR FINANCIAL HEALTH?

Laurence J. Kotlikoff

Economics teaches that households save, insure, and diversify in order to miti-gate fluctuations in their living standards over time and across contingencies (i.e., practice consumption smoothing). But for households, setting spending targets that are consistent with consumption smoothing is incredibly difficult, and even small targeting mistakes (on the order of 10 percent) can lead to enormous mistakes in recommended saving and insurance levels and to major disruptions (on the order of 30 percent) in living standards in retirement or widow(er)hood. Conventional planning's use of spending targets also distorts its portfolio advice because the standard Monte Carlo simulations assume that households make no adjustment whatsoever to their spending regardless of how well or how poorly they do on their investments. But consumption smoothing dictates such adjustments and, indeed, precludes running out of money (i.e., ending up with literally zero consumption). It is precisely the range of these adjustments that households need to understand to assess their portfolio risk.

Economic theory predicts, and casual observation confirms, that households seek to main-tain their living standards (smooth their consumption) as they age and face life's various contingencies. Seeking a stable living standard and actually achieving one, however, are two very different things. We cannot insure against aggregate shocks, including economic

Reprinted from *The Future of Life-Cycle Saving and Investing,* The Research Foundation of CFA Institute (October 2007):55–71.

downturns, natural disasters, and epidemics, nor can we buy actuarially fair insurance against a range of individual shocks, such as job loss, excessive longevity, and disability. And we generally lack the self-control to save and insure adequately even given attractive opportunities to do so.

These concerns with consumption smoothing are well known and have been amply studied.[1] But another problem—namely, the computation challenge posed by consumption smoothing—has received little attention, which is surprising because consumption mistakes could well swamp these other considerations. Certainly, the calculations required to minimize consumption disruptions over time and across states of nature are highly complex. Just consider the number and range of current and future variables involved in consumption smoothing: The list includes household demographics; labor earnings; retirement dates; federal, state, and local taxes; U.S. Social Security benefits; pension benefits; regular and retirement assets; borrowing constraints; rules for retirement account contributions and withdrawals; home ownership; mortgage finance; economies in shared living; the relative costs of children; changes in housing; choice of where to live; the financing of college and weddings; gifts made or received; inheritances; paying for one's dream boat; and so on. And each of these variables demands consideration under each and every survival contingency.[2]

Taxation by itself is a factor worthy of a high-speed computer processor. Figuring out the federal and state taxes when both spouses are alive and in each future survivor state (years in which one spouse is deceased) requires determining whether they will itemize their deductions, whether they will receive any of the many potentially available tax credits, whether they will have to pay the Alternative Minimum Tax, whether they will pay taxes on their Social Security benefits, whether they will be contributing to or withdrawing from retirement accounts, and whether they will be in high or low tax brackets. And as if this list were not bad enough, determining future taxes introduces a nasty simultaneity problem. We cannot figure out the future taxes until we know the current spending (which determines, in part, the future taxable capital income), but we cannot figure out the current spending without knowing the future taxes (which determines, in part, what the couple has available to spend).

Computing Social Security benefits is another nightmare. With 2,528 separate rules in the *Social Security Handbook,* figuring out what retirement, dependent, survivor, divorce, mother, father, and child benefits one will receive can be maddening, particularly in light of the system's complex average indexed monthly wage and primary insurance amount benefit formulae as well as its ancillary adjustments to the primary insurance amount. These adjustments include the earnings test, the early retirement reduction factors, the delayed retirement credit, the recomputation of benefits, the family benefit maximum, the windfall elimination and offset formulae for workers with noncovered employment, and the phase-in to the system's ultimate age 67 normal retirement age.[3] How many households can even list all these interrelated factors, let alone process them accurately?

The standard fallback in economics is that households do not need to know all the details or have PhDs in math to make correct life-cycle decisions. Indeed, we economists view the mathematical formulation of optimal intertemporal choice as simply descriptive modeling. "Households," we tell ourselves, "do not do the math but act *as if* they do. Yes, households will make mistakes, but these mistakes will be small and average out."

Unfortunately, studies of saving and insurance adequacy and portfolio diversification— including Kotlikoff, Spivak, and Summers (1982); Auerbach and Kotlikoff (1987, 1991);

Bernheim, Carman, Gokhale, and Kotlikoff (2003); Bernheim, Forni, Gokhale, and Kotlikoff (2000, 2003); and Bernheim, Berstein, Gokhale, and Kotlikoff (2006)—belie this proposition. Vast numbers of households save, insure, and avoid risk either far too much or far too little. The fact that households make both types of mistakes and that, as a consequence, generate *average* behavior that, on its face, is not extreme offers little professional consolation. The medical community would not declare that heart disease has been cured if half of peoples' hearts beat too fast and the other half too slow.

The other professional fallback is that households that look financially sick are, in fact, financially healthy but simply have unusual preferences or prior beliefs about future events. Thus, a household that invests only in cash can be viewed as being extremely risk averse and also convinced that deflation is around the corner. Because preferences and priors are taken as economic primitives that are above reproach, there is no scientific basis for classifying extreme financial behavior as financial pathology. Imagine the medical profession declaring cancer a perfectly healthy manifestation of genetic free will.

Perhaps it is time to identify financial disease according to the financial pain it engenders. Based on this criterion, we are, generically speaking, financially quite sick. Indeed, the ravages of financial pathology are clearly seen among today's elderly, one-third of whom are wholly dependent or almost wholly dependent on Social Security.

Many households seek to cure their financial ills by turning to the financial planning industry for advice. In so doing, they effectively let financial planners or financial planning software decide what their preferences are and how they should be maximized. For such households, the study of their financial behavior may simply boil down to understanding what planners or software they are using and what these planners or programs are leading them to do.

If conventional financial planning corresponds closely to what economics prescribes, then households taking this advice will improve their financial health. But what if conventional financial planning generates recommendations that are far afield from proper consumption smoothing? In this case, "financial planning" will represent a cure-all, not real penicillin, and potentially leave one in worse financial shape.

In this paper, I examine one aspect of conventional financial planning: namely, the requirement that households set their own retirement and survivor spending targets. I show that from the perspective of consumption smoothing (the goal of achieving a stable living standard), even small targeting mistakes, on the order of 10 percent, can lead to enormous mistakes in recommended saving and insurance levels and to major living standard disruptions (on the order of 30 percent) at retirement. Given the computational difficulties involved in achieving proper consumption smoothing on one's own, targeting mistakes of 10 percent or greater appear inevitable.

In soliciting spending targets, the traditional approach asks households to tally up all of their current expenditures and to use this level of spending as a target for retirement and survivor spending with some adjustment for changes in spending needs. The goal here seems to be that of consumption smoothing (i.e., to achieve the same living standard before and after retirement and in survivor states).

The rub, however, is that the current level of spending, which underlies the targeting, may be higher or lower than the sustainable level. Given the computation problems referenced earlier, this is almost inevitable. If current spending is higher than the sustainable level, the targets will be set too high. In this case, households will be told to save and insure more than is consistent with consumption smoothing. If current spending is lower than the sustainable level, the targets will be set too low. In this case, households will be advised to save and insure less than is consistent with consumption smoothing.

If the target is set too high, the household will be told to oversave and overinsure and will end up with a lower living standard prior to retirement and a higher one after retirement and in survivor states. If the target is set too low, the household will be told to undersave and underinsure and will end up with a higher living standard prior to retirement and a lower one after retirement and in survivor states. Both types of targeting mistakes will lead to consumption disruption rather than consumption smoothing.

This conclusion depends, of course, on whether the household takes the advice being given. Telling households that are currently overspending to substantially cut their current living standard may lead them to ignore the advice, decide to retire later, or accept a much lower future living standard. And telling households that are currently underspending to start spending at what they perceive as crazy rates may lead them to discount financial planning altogether.

Why can small targeting mistakes lead to such bad financial advice and such large disruptions in living standard when the household retires or loses a head or spouse/partner? First, in the case of retirement, the targeting mistake is being made for roughly 30 years—from roughly age 65 to roughly age 95. In the case of survivorship, the targeting mistake is being made for all of the survivor's potential remaining years. Second, spending more (less) than one should in retirement and survivor states means spending less (more) than one should prior to retirement in states when no one is deceased, which magnifies the living standard disruption (gap) beyond the original targeting mistake. Finally, the oversaving (undersaving) and overinsuring (underinsuring) associated with targeting for living standards that are too high (low) lead to higher (lower) taxes and insurance premium payments than would otherwise be paid. This induces further cuts (increases) in the preretirement living standard than would otherwise arise.

As I will show, targeted spending also underlies and undermines conventional financial planning's portfolio advice, potentially leading households to take on much more investment risk than is prudent. What households need to assess in considering risky investments is the variability of their future living standards. But standard planning assumes households will spend precisely their targeted amounts year after year regardless of the returns they receive unless and until they run out of money. This approach focuses attention on the probability of the plan (i.e., the target) working rather than on the spending consequences of it not. Because riskier investing can raise the probability of a plan's "success," households may be encouraged to take more risk than is appropriate. They may also get the idea that adjusting their portfolios rather than their lifestyle is the prudent response to low returns.

METHODOLOGY

Maximizing and preserving one's living standard is the hallmark of consumption smoothing—the economic approach to financial planning. Although conventional financial planning attempts to achieve consumption smoothing by having households set targets based on their current spending, this practice is essentially guaranteed to provide poor saving, insurance, and investment advice and to promote consumption disruption rather than consumption smoothing.

One might then wonder whether a better approach would be to use the conventional planning methodology but adjust the spending target to equalize living standards across one's working life, retirement, and widow(er)hood. Such target practice can, in theory, work. But doing so for any given set of assumptions could take hours, not seconds. The reason for the added complexity is that many, if not most, households are borrowing constrained, meaning that they or their financial planner would need to simultaneously set and adjust spending targets for each borrowing-constrained interval.[4] When one adds to this picture return uncertainty, we are no longer talking hours but weeks because the household would need to solve not for one spending path but for all possible (and potentially borrowing-constrained) spending paths that would arise under each path of return realizations.

The only practical way to handle these problems mathematically is via dynamic programming, developed in the early 1950s by Richard Bellman. Specifically, one formulates a general plan for consumption smoothing in the last period (the maximum age of life), which I will call T. It then uses the period T plan to formulate a plan for the next to last period (i.e., $T-1$). The $T-1$ plan is used to formulate the $T-2$ plan and so forth, back to the current time period, which I will call 0. This Time 0 plan is then used to determine how much to spend, save, and insure in the current year.

Although mathematicians, economists, and engineers are well versed in dynamic programming, the architects of traditional financial planning software are not. Or if they are, they are constrained by their superiors to keep things simple, which, in this context, means failing to elicit much of the information—such as the path of future labor earnings, prospective changes in housing, and plans for retirement account withdrawals—needed to generate an accurate dynamic program.

RESULTS

A dynamic programming model, as described above, is used to generate sample consumption-smoothing results for a prototypical family. These results are then compared with those given by a conventional targeting approach. First, I will review some general features of the consumption-smoothing results.

The amount of recommended consumption expenditures needed to achieve a given living standard varies from year to year in response to changes in the household's composition. It also rises when the household moves from a situation of being liquidity constrained to one of being unconstrained (i.e., not needing or wanting to borrow). Finally, as mentioned, recommended household consumption will change over time if users intentionally specify that they want their living standard to change.

The simultaneity issue with respect to taxes mentioned earlier is just one of two such issues that needs to be considered. The second is the joint determination of life insurance holdings of potential decedents and survivors. Widows and widowers may need to hold life insurance to protect their children's living standard through adulthood and to cover bequests, funeral expenses, and debts (including mortgages) that exceed the survivor's net worth inclusive of the equity on her or his house.

But the more life insurance is purchased by the potential decedent, the less life insurance survivors will need to purchase, if one assumes they have such a need. Thus, survivors will pay less in life insurance premiums and have less need for insurance protection from their decedent spouse/partner. Hence, one cannot determine the potential decedent's life insurance holdings until one determines the survivor's holdings. But one cannot determine the survivor's holdings until one determines the decedent's holdings.

Dealing with the tax and life insurance simultaneity issues as well as the borrowing and nonnegative life insurance constraints all within a single dynamic program seems well beyond the computing power of a desktop personal computer, particularly given the speed required for a commercial product.

The difficulty, time, and luck required to solve this simultaneous consumption-smoothing, borrowing-constrained, saving, life insurance, and tax problem may explain why financial planning software producers have universally adopted the computationally trivial targeted-spending approach. As indicated, this approach puts the onus on the household heads and spouses/partners of doing literally millions of complex calculations in their heads in order to set their targets appropriately. Because none of us has computer chips implanted in our brains, let alone the right neuronware, the chance of making at least small targeting mistakes is extremely high.

CONSUMPTION SMOOTHING VS. MIS-TARGETING SPENDING

Consider a middle-aged, middle-class, married household with two children. Both spouses are age 40 in 2005. One child is age 10, and one is age 7. The couple lives in California. The husband earns $75,000 a year, and the wife, $50,000. Neither spouse has a pension or a retirement account, but the couple does have $75,000 in regular assets. The couple owns a $300,000 home with a $125,000 20-year mortgage with monthly payments of $1,250. Property taxes, homeowners' insurance, and maintenance total $6,000 a year. The couple plans to spend $25,000 in today's dollars on college tuition and other expenses for each child for four years. Each spouse will retire at age 65 and begin collecting Social Security benefits in that year. Past "covered" earnings (i.e., used to determine Social Security benefits) for the husband (wife) were $37,500 ($25,000) in 1987 when he (she) was 22, and they grew by 4 percent each year through 2004. The couple expects inflation to run at 3 percent annually and to earn a 6 percent nominal rate of return on savings. The remaining inputs are the economies in shared living and the relative cost of children. Based on previous work, I assumed that two can live as cheaply as 1.6, that to provide the same living standard to a child as to an adult costs only 70 percent as much, and that taxes and Social Security provisions in the future are those suggested by current law.

Consumption Smoothing

Table 5.1 shows annual recommendations for selected years for the consumption-smoothing case. All values in these and other tables are in 2005 dollars. Note that the couple's living standard per equivalent adult, given in the last column, equals $31,337. This amount remains constant through 2060, when each spouse reaches age 95, assuming they both live that long. The recommended total consumption expenditure, in contrast, initially equals $71,852 but declines in 2014 and again in 2017 as the two children reach age 19 and are assumed to leave the household. In 2017 and thereafter, recommended total consumption expenditure equals $50,139. For 2005, the recommendation for consumption smoothing would be $484,947

TABLE 5.1   Consumption Smoothing Annual Recommendations (in constant 2005 dollars)

Year	H's Age	W's Age	Consumption	Saving	H's Life Insurance	W's Life Insurance	Living Standard per Adult
2005	40	40	$71,852	$ 1,440	$484,947	$128,554	$31,337
2006	41	41	71,852	1,678	479,364	131,024	31,337
2007	42	42	71,852	1,906	467,677	132,826	31,337
2008	43	43	71,852	2,117	452,332	135,409	31,337
2009	44	44	71,852	2,309	435,512	139,488	31,337
2010	45	45	71,852	2,458	425,461	144,822	31,337
2011	46	46	71,852	2,597	415,998	151,089	31,337
2012	47	47	71,852	2,701	407,888	158,198	31,337
2013	48	48	71,852	2,767	401,155	166,140	31,337
2014	49	49	61,455	−12,770	388,883	169,766	31,337
2015	50	50	61,455	−12,895	377,052	173,952	31,337
2016	51	51	61,455	−13,057	365,666	178,683	31,337
2017	52	52	50,139	−27,760	333,541	165,914	31,337
2018	53	53	50,139	−2,930	301,025	152,962	31,337
2019	54	54	50,139	−2,849	268,095	139,801	31,337
2020	55	55	50,139	−2,775	234,700	126,405	31,337
2021	56	56	50,139	22,250	207,122	112,783	31,337
2022	57	57	50,139	22,525	179,143	98,908	31,337

Note: H = husband; W = wife.

and $128,554 in term life insurance holdings for the husband and wife, respectively. Over time, recommended holdings decline.

Table 5.2 details the couple's total spending, which includes consumption, special expenditures on college, life insurance premiums, and housing. Note that real housing expenditures (expenditures valued in 2005 dollars) decline over time as the assumed 3 percent rate of inflation reduces the purchasing power of nominal mortgage payments. Once the mortgage is fully paid off, housing expenses are $6,000 a year. These expenses are property taxes, maintenance, and homeowners' insurance, all three of which remain fixed in real terms. Term life insurance premiums first rise and then fall as the household ages. This reflects the increase with age in premium per dollar of coverage as well as the decline over time in recommended life insurance holdings.

Table 5.3 displays selected years of the couple's regular asset balance sheet. It shows four things. First, households never exceed their debt limit, which in this case is zero. Second, all assets and income are spent (i.e., the household dies broke if the head and spouse/partner make it to their maximum ages of life). Third, a household's living standard per equivalent adult is smooth over any interval of years within which the household

TABLE 5.2   Consumption Smoothing Total Spending (in constant 2005 dollars)

Year	H's Age	W's Age	Consumption	Special Expenditures	Housing Expenditures	Life Insurance Premiums	Total Spending
2005	40	40	$71,852	$0	$20,563	$ 983	$93,398
2006	41	41	71,852	0	20,139	1,093	93,084
2007	42	42	71,852	0	19,727	1,198	92,777
2008	43	43	71,852	0	19,327	1,302	92,481
2009	44	44	71,852	0	18,939	1,408	92,199
2010	45	45	71,852	0	18,562	1,538	91,952
2011	46	46	71,852	0	18,196	1,678	91,726
2012	47	47	71,852	0	17,841	1,831	91,524
2013	48	48	71,852	0	17,496	2,000	91,348
2014	49	49	61,455	25,000	17,161	2,140	105,756
2015	50	50	61,455	25,000	16,836	2,288	105,579
2016	51	51	61,455	25,000	16,521	2,445	105,421
2017	52	52	50,139	50,000	16,214	2,422	118,775
2018	53	53	50,139	25,000	15,917	2,373	93,429
2019	54	54	50,139	25,000	15,628	2,301	93,068
2020	55	55	50,139	25,000	15,348	2,203	92,690
2021	56	56	50,139	0	15,075	2,119	67,333
2022	57	57	50,139	0	14,811	2,008	66,958

Note: H = husband; W = wife.

is not borrowing constrained. Fourth, if consumption, and thus the living standard, is increased in any year, the household will die in debt. This implies that the living standard is maximized.

Mis-Targeting Spending

Now suppose that in 2005, this household is spending not $71,852 on consumption but 10 percent more (less), namely, $79,037 ($64,667). Furthermore, suppose that this household uses its current consumption to set its retirement and survivor consumption spending levels but that in setting these targets, it appropriately adjusts for changes in the household's demographic over time and across survivor states. In this case, the household will specify a retirement consumption target that is 10 percent greater (smaller) than $50,139, or $55,153 ($45,125). It will also specify survivor consumption spending targets that are 10 percent higher (lower), on a year-by-year basis, than those generated in this consumption-smoothing run.

TABLE 5.3 Consumption Smoothing Regular Asset Balance Sheet (in constant 2005 dollars)

Year	H's Age	W's Age	Income	Total Spending	Taxes	Saving	Regular Assets
2044	79	79	$51,191	$56,139	$3,783	−$8,732	$162,454
2045	80	80	50,937	56,139	3,686	−8,888	153,566
2046	81	81	50,678	56,139	3,584	−9,045	144,521
2047	82	82	50,415	56,139	3,479	−9,203	135,317
2048	83	83	50,147	56,139	3,369	−9,362	125,955
2049	84	84	49,874	56,139	3,257	−9,522	116,433
2050	85	85	49,597	56,139	3,140	−9,683	106,750
2051	86	86	49,314	56,139	3,020	–9,845	96,905
2052	87	87	49,028	56,139	2,896	−10,007	86,898
2053	88	88	48,736	56,139	2,768	−10,171	76,727
2054	89	89	48,440	56,139	2,637	−10,336	66,390
2055	90	90	48,139	56,158	2,502	−10,521	55,869
2056	91	91	47,833	56,253	2,363	−10,784	45,085
2057	92	92	47,518	56,338	2,219	−11,039	34,046
2058	93	93	47,197	56,392	2,070	−11,266	22,780
2059	94	94	46,869	56,368	1,917	−11,417	11,363
2060	95	95	46,536	56,139	1,760	−11,363	0

Note: H = husband; W = wife.

How will these targeting mistakes affect the household's living standard, consumption expenditure, saving, life insurance holdings, assets, and taxes over its life cycle? The answers are provided in Tables 5.4 through 5.7. To start, the household's living standard is shown in Table 5.4. The fifth column, labeled CS for consumption smoothing, indicates that the household's living standard per equivalent adult is $31,337 each year. This is the amount of consumption spending that a single adult would need to earn to enjoy the same living standard as she or he enjoys living in the household.

The fourth column presents the household's living standard path if it overtargets retirement and survivor spending by 10 percent and is thus directed to oversave and overinsure. The result is a $26,289 living standard prior to retirement and a $34,439 living standard after retirement. The ratio of the latter to the former amount is 1.31, indicating that the targeting mistake causes a 31 percent disruption in living standard at retirement. This is a huge discrepancy given the maintained assumption that the household seeks to smooth its living standard.

In the case that the household undertargets retirement and survivor spending by 10 percent, it will spend more before retirement and less thereafter than in the consumption-smoothing case. But as Column 6 shows, the preretirement living standard for this household is not

TABLE 5.4 Consumption and Saving Recommendations: Consumption Smoothing vs. Mis-Targeting, Living Standard (in constant 2005 dollars)

Year	H's Age	W's Age	Living Standard			Percentage Difference in Living Standard Relative to CS	
			+10%	CS	−10%	+10%	−10%
2005	40	40	$26,289	$31,337	$32,673	−16.1%	4.3%
2010	45	45	26,289	31,337	32,673	−16.1	4.3
2015	50	50	26,289	31,337	32,673	−16.1	4.3
2020	55	55	26,289	31,337	32,673	−16.1	4.3
2025	60	60	26,289	31,337	39,109	−16.1	24.8
2030	65	65	34,439	31,337	28,159	9.9	−10.1
2035	70	70	34,439	31,337	28,159	9.9	−10.1
2040	75	75	34,439	31,337	28,159	9.9	−10.1
2045	80	80	34,439	31,337	28,159	9.9	−10.1
2050	85	85	34,439	31,337	28,159	9.9	−10.1
2055	90	90	34,439	31,337	28,159	9.9	−10.1
2060	95	95	34,439	31,337	28,159	9.9	−10.1

Notes: H = husband; W = wife. CS references consumption smoothing, +10 percent references a 10 percent positive targeting mistake; −10 percent references a 10 percent negative mistake.

constant. Instead, it rises from $32,673 to $39,109 because of the binding of the household's liquidity constraint—the assumption is that the household cannot take on any debt beyond the original mortgage balance, which is a constraint that most households operate under. After retirement, the household's living standard drops to $28,159. The ratio of $28,159 to $39,109 is 0.72, indicating that the household suffers a 28.0 percent reduction in its living standard with respect to its pre- and postretirement spending. Again, we see a major disruption at retirement in the household's living standard because of mis-targeting.[5]

Because the overspending household was, by assumption, enjoying a 2005 living standard of $34,471 (10 percent higher than $31,337) when it visited its financial planner or used conventional financial planning software, it would have been advised to cut its current living standard by 23.7 percent (1 − 26,289/34,471) to meet its target. The underspending household was enjoying a $28,203 living standard (10 percent lower than $31,337). It would have been told to raise its spending by 15.8 percent (32,673/28,203 − 1). These are big adjustments. It is also ironic that the overspending household is being led to underspend and the underspending household is being led to overspend.

Clearly, adjusting upward is easier than adjusting downward. Hence, the underspending household is more likely than the overspending household to take the mistaken advice. Thus, the household that may be most concerned with maintaining its living standard in retirement will be led by standard financial planning to experience a 28.0 percent drop in its living standard when it retires—precisely what it is trying so hard to avoid. Of course, households could well be making targeting mistakes from a situation of currently spending the correct amount: All they need to do is make mistakes in adding up their current expenditures or miscalculate the appropriate demographic adjustments. I refer here to the adjustment for the absence of children in retirement or the absence of a spouse in widow(er)hood. Adjusting for this change in the number and sizes of mouths to feed requires thinking through economies in shared living and the relative cost of children. These are not easy considerations even for very well educated households.

If ±10 percent mistakes occur with equal likelihood, the spread in preretirement living standards for two otherwise identical households could easily be 48.8 percent—the difference in the $26,289 and $39,109 preretirement living standards of households that set their spending targets 10 percent too high and 10 percent too low, respectively. The corresponding postretirement spread in living standards is 22.3 percent. For a source of age-specific consumption inequality, this seems like a good place to look.

Mistakes in Consumption, Saving, and Insurance Recommendations

Table 5.5 and Table 5.6 report saving and life insurance recommendations for the three cases. The proportionate consumption differences across the cases are the same as for the living standard differences just discussed. Hence, here I focus on saving and insurance recommendations. As one can quickly see, the differences are tremendous. In 2005, for example, the +10 percent saving recommendation is $11,955 compared with −$810 in the −10 percent case. At age 60, the two saving recommendations are $38,818 and $19,711, respectively. At 75, they are −$13,891 and −$4,240.

TABLE 5.5 Consumption and Saving Recommendations: Consumption Smoothing vs. Mis-Targeting, Saving (in constant 2005 dollars)

Year	H's Age	W's Age	Recommended Consumption			Recommended Saving		
			+10%	CS	−10%	+10%	CS	−10%
2005	40	40	$60,278	$71,852	$74,915	$11,955	$ 1,440	−$ 810
2010	45	45	60,278	71,852	74,915	13,146	2,458	520
2015	50	50	51,555	61,455	64,074	−3,619	−12,895	−13,923
2020	55	55	42,062	50,139	52,276	4,798	−2,849	−3,000
2025	60	60	42,062	50,139	62,575	38,818	31,423	19,711
2030	65	65	55,102	50,139	45,054	−10,168	−6,594	−3,189
2035	70	70	55,102	50,139	45,054	−11,894	−7,350	−3,719
2040	75	75	55,102	50,139	45,264	−13,891	−8,112	−4,240
2045	80	80	55,102	50,139	45,054	−16,083	−8,888	−4,758
2050	85	85	55,102	50,139	45,054	−18,611	−9,683	−5,278
2055	90	90	55,102	50,139	45,054	−21,356	−10,521	−5,805
2060	95	95	55,102	50,139	45,054	−16,262	−11,363	−6,343

Notes: H = husband; W = wife. CS references consumption smoothing, +10 percent references a 10 percent positive targeting mistake; −10 percent references a 10 percent negative mistake.

TABLE 5.6   Life Insurance Recommendations: Consumption Smoothing vs. Mis-Targeting, Life
Insurance (in constant 2005 dollars)

Year	H's Age	W's Age	Husband's Life Insurance			Wife's Life Insurance		
			+10%	CS	−10%	+10%	CS	−10%
2005	40	40	$814,600	$484,947	$106,436	$460,405	$128,554	$0
2010	45	45	690,432	425,461	112,015	414,861	144,822	0
2015	50	50	582,515	377,052	119,611	384,669	173,952	0
2020	55	55	399,515	234,700	9,982	296,195	126,405	0
2025	60	60	220,819	92,366	0	186,569	55,269	0
2030	65	65	63,139	0	0	85,191	0	0
2035	70	70	85,191	0	0	63,139	0	0
2040	75	75	45,822	0	0	45,822	0	0
2045	80	80	32,261	0	0	32,261	0	0
2050	85	85	22,807	0	0	22,807	0	0
2055	90	90	17,603	0	0	17,603	0	0
2060	95	95	0	0	0	0	0	0

Notes: H = husband; W = wife. CS references consumption smoothing, +10 percent references a
10 percent positive targeting mistake; −10 percent references a 10 percent negative mistake.

Life insurance recommendations in the ±10 percent cases are equally day and night.
In 2005, the +10 percent targeting mistake leads to a recommendation of $814,600 in life
insurance for the husband whereas the −10 percent targeting mistake leads to a recommendation of only $106,436. Both of these values are far away from $484,947—the
desired consumption-smoothing amount. For the wife, the +10 percent mistake leads to a
$460,405 term life insurance recommendation for 2005. In contrast, the −10 percent mis-
take leads to a recommendation of zero life insurance. The recommended consumption-
smoothing amount in this case is $128,554. The dramatically higher level of life insurance
in the +10 percent case entails dramatically higher life insurance premiums. For example,
at age 50, the +10, consumption-smoothing, and −10 households pay premiums of
$4,017, $2,288, and $497, respectively. Table 5.7 shows equally wild disparities in assets
and tax payments across the three cases. At retirement, the household with the +10 percent
targeting mistake holds $488,412 in assets. This is 1.8 times the consumption-smoothing
assets holdings of $270,715 and 3.4 times the $144,405 for −10 percent holdings. Because
higher asset levels imply higher taxable asset income, taxes are highest for the +10 percent
household and lowest for the −10 percent household. At age 65, the high, middle, and low
tax payments are $7,078, $4,737, and $2,640, respectively. As indicated, these discrepancies
in tax and insurance premium payments exacerbate the consumption disruption at retirement and at widow(er)hood that arises from mis-targeting future retirement and survivor
spending.

TABLE 5.7 Assets and Taxes: Consumption Smoothing vs. Mis-Targeting (in constant 2005 dollars)

Year	H's Age	W's Age	Assets			Taxes		
			+10%	CS	−10%	+10%	CS	−10%
2005	40	40	$ 89,205	$ 78,690	$ 76,440	$32,411	$32,411	$32,411
2010	45	45	152,732	89,159	76,548	34,100	33,114	32,916
2015	50	50	186,022	71,558	51,470	36,735	34,776	34,421
2020	55	55	176,192	22,188	0	38,540	35,812	35,403
2025	60	60	335,873	144,250	66,660	42,868	39,309	38,082
2030	65	65	488,412	270,715	144,405	7,078	4,737	2,640
2035	70	70	423,520	235,480	126,865	6,542	4,488	2,674
2040	75	75	367,143	196,448	106,706	5,914	4,136	2,623
2045	80	80	291,190	153,566	83,951	5,188	3,686	2,493
2050	85	85	203,311	106,750	58,602	4,442	3,140	2,290
2055	90	90	101,868	55,869	30,633	3,421	2,502	2,018
2060	95	95	0	0	0	1,839	1,760	1,679

Notes: H = husband; W = wife. CS references consumption smoothing, +10 percent references a 10 percent positive targeting mistake; −10 percent references a 10 percent negative mistake.

Sensitivity of Consumption Disruption to Assumptions

Consumption disruption caused by mis-targeted spending is likely to be greater for older households because they have fewer years over which to adjust their preretirement spending to avoid the difficulty of spending too much or too little in retirement. Households that are liquidity constrained are likely to set their spending targets too low because their current spending is limited by the availability of their liquid funds. If they retain these targets after their liquidity constraint is relaxed, they will, of course, be induced to undersave and under-insure for the future. Households earning low rates of return will experience larger consumption disruptions because larger adjustments to current spending will be needed to fund a given targeting mistake. Finally, households with higher maximum ages of life will face larger disruptions because one needs to fund targeting mistakes for more potential retirement and survivorship years.

PORTFOLIO "ADVICE"

Conventional planning's use of spending targets also distorts its portfolio advice. Given the household's retirement spending target and portfolio mix, conventional planning runs Monte Carlo simulations that determine the household's probability of running out of money. These simulations typically assume that households make no adjustment whatsoever to their spending as a result of doing well or poorly on their investments. But consumption smoothing dictates such adjustments and precludes letting oneself get into the position of completely running out of money (i.e., ending up with literally zero consumption). It is precisely the range of these living standard adjustments that households need to understand to assess their portfolio's risk. Conventional portfolio analysis not only answers the wrong question; it may also improperly solicit risk taking because riskier investments may entail a lower chance of financial exhaustion thanks to their higher mean.

To see this point in its starkest form, take, as an example, a single 60-year-old man named Joe whose only economic resource is $500,000 in assets. Assume Joe's maximum age of life is 95 and that he faces no taxes of any kind. Suppose Joe sets his spending target at $30,000 a year. Also assume that Joe holds only a properly laddered portfolio of TIPS— Treasury Inflation-Protected Securities (i.e., inflation-indexed bonds)—yielding 2 percent after inflation. These bonds are essentially riskless and permit Joe to consume, at most and at least, $20,413 in today's dollars each year. What is Joe's probability of meeting his target— $30,000—each year? It is zero, of course, because spending $30,000 will drive Joe broke unless he fortuitously dies beforehand.

Now, suppose that Joe invests in an S&P 500 Index fund of large-cap stocks rather than in TIPS. Since 1926, the real return on large caps has averaged 9.16 percent on an annual basis.[6] If Joe is able to earn this return for sure, he will be able to spend $48,264 a year. But large-cap stocks are risky, with a standard deviation of, say, 20 percent. Nonetheless, there is still almost a 60 percent chance that Joe will be able to spend $30,000 a year. So, if Joe uses a standard Monte Carlo portfolio analyzer, he will find that investing in TIPS fails completely to meet his goal but that investing in stocks gives him a chance to meet his goal. Joe may view this as a good bet given the way this investment outcome information is being presented.

Suppose then that Joe invests all his assets in large caps and then experiences in the next three years the large-cap returns (including dividends) recorded in 2000, 2001, and 2002— specifically, −9.1 percent, −11.9 percent, and −22.1 percent. Will Joe continue to spend $30,000 a year and remain in the stock market given that his wealth after three years has dropped from $500,000 to $238,013? Probably not. At that point, Joe may well switch to holding just TIPS and be forced to live from that point on at about a third of his desired yearly spending rate. In not showing such large and sudden adverse potential living standard adjustments, standard financial planning seems to be encouraging more risk taking than is appropriate. This concern is heightened by the prospect of many households being induced as part of the same planning exercise to set their future spending targets at higher levels than are appropriate.

CONCLUSION

Economics teaches us that we save, insure, and diversify in order to mitigate fluctuations in our living standards over time and across contingencies. Although the goals of conventional financial planning appear consonant with such consumption smoothing, the actual practice of conventional planning is anything but. Conventional planning's disconnect with economics begins with its first step, namely, forcing households to set their own retirement and survivor spending targets. Setting spending targets that are consistent with consumption smoothing is incredibly difficult, which makes large targeting mistakes almost inevitable. But as shown here, even small targeting mistakes, on the order of 10 percent, can lead to enormous mistakes in recommended saving and insurance levels and to major disruptions (on the order of 30 percent) in living standards in retirement or widow(er)hood.

There are three reasons why small targeting mistakes lead to such bad saving and insurance advice and such large consumption disruptions. First, the wrong target spending level is being assigned to each and every year of retirement and widow(er)hood. Second, planning to spend too much (little) in retirement and widow(er)hood requires spending too little (much) before those states are reached, which magnifies the living standard differences. Third, both saving and insuring the wrong amounts affect tax and insurance premium payments, further exacerbating consumption disruption.

Conventional planning's use of spending targets also distorts its portfolio advice. Given a household's spending target and its portfolio mix, standard practice entails running Monte Carlo simulations to determine the household's probability of running out of money. These simulations assume that households make no adjustment whatsoever to their spending regardless of how well or how poorly they do on their investments. But consumption smoothing dictates such adjustments and, indeed, precludes running out of money (i.e., ending up with literally zero consumption). It is precisely the range of these living standard adjustments that households need to understand to assess their portfolio risk. Conventional portfolio analysis not only answers the wrong question; it may also improperly encourage risk taking because it focuses on the fact that riskier investments may entail a lower chance of financial exhaustion (thanks to their higher mean) rather than on the risk or worst-case scenario.

Purveyors of financial advice have an ethical, if not a fiduciary, responsibility to ensure that the advice they provide is sound. Financially protecting one's family is a very serious business that requires careful analysis and a real commitment of time. It also requires posing and correctly answering the right question—namely, How can I preserve my family's living standard through time and in unforeseen, but not unforeseeable, circumstances?

Perhaps a final medical analogy will help explain the situation. None of us would go to a doctor for a 60-second checkup, nor would we elect surgery performed by a meat cleaver over surgery with a scalpel. And any doctor who provided such services would quickly be drummed out of the medical profession. Financial planning, like brain surgery, is an extraordinarily precise business. Small mistakes and the wrong tools can just as easily undermine as improve financial health.

NOTES

1. As an example, see http://post.economics.harvard.edu/faculty/laibson/papers.html for a long list of excellent papers by David Laibson and his colleagues contributing to the field of behavioral finance.

2. Survival contingencies are distinguished by which spouse/partner dies and when he or she dies. The reason is that the survivor will inherit different amounts of wealth, collect different amounts of life insurance, and receive different levels of Social Security survivor and retirement benefits depending on the age at which his or her spouse/partner dies.

3. Unfortunately, the handbook is remarkably uninformative about many details of these adjustments, particularly the order in which they are applied. Several of the old-timers knocking about in the U.S. Social Security Administration's Office of the Actuary know these details, but when they go, this information may literally disappear. One might

think that the computer code that generates the hundreds of billions of dollars worth of actual Social Security benefit payments would be easy to check regarding such matters. But this code is, as I have been told, documented very poorly and written in an ancient computer language, namely, COBOL, that no one at the Social Security Administration apparently understands. Furthermore, it cannot necessarily be reproduced from scratch because many Social Security rules were apparently made administratively.

4. Bernheim, Berstein, Gokhale, and Kotlikoff (2006) found that roughly three-fifths of Boston University participants in a study of saving and insurance adequacy were borrowing constrained.

5. A small, but growing, body of research is examining living standard changes at retirement. Bernheim, Skinner, and Weinberg (2001), for example, provide evidence that living standards drop, on average, at retirement by 14 percent, with a median drop of 12 percent.

6. This is the average of annual real returns rather than the geometric mean, based on data in Ibbotson's 2005 yearbook.

REFERENCES

Auerbach, Alan J., and Laurence J. Kotlikoff. 1987. "Life Insurance of the Elderly: Adequacy and Determinants." In *Work, Health, and Income among the Elderly.* Washington, DC: The Brookings Institution.

———. 1991. "The Adequacy of Life Insurance Purchases." *Journal of Financial Intermediation*, vol. 1, no. 3 (June):215–241.

Bernheim, B. Douglas, Jonathan Skinner, and Steven Weinberg. 2001. "What Accounts for the Variation in Retirement Wealth among U.S. Households?"*American Economic Review*, vol. 91, no. 4 (September):832–857.

Bernheim, B. Douglas, Solange Berstein, Jagadeesh Gokhale, and Laurence J. Kotlikoff. 2006. "Saving and Life Insurance Holdings at Boston University—A Unique Case Study."*National Institute Economic Review,* vol. 198, no. 1 (October):75–96.

Bernheim, B. Douglas, Katherine Carman, Jagadeesh Gokhale, and Laurence J. Kotlikoff. 2003. "Are Life Insurance Holdings Related to Financial Vulnerabilities?"*Economic Inquiry*, vol. 41, no. 4 (October):531–554.

Bernheim, B. Douglas, Lorenzo Forni, Jagadeesh Gokhale, and Laurence J. Kotlikoff. 2000. "How Much Should Americans Be Saving for Retirement?"*American Economic Review*, vol. 90, no. 2 (May):288–292.

———. 2003. "Mismatch between Life Insurance Holdings and Financial Vulnerabilities— Evidence from the Health and Retirement Survey."*American Economic Review*, vol. 93, no. 1 (March): 354–365.

Kotlikoff, Laurence J., Avia Spivak, and Lawrence Summers. 1982. "The Adequacy of Savings."*American Economic Review*, vol. 72, no. 5 (December):1056–1069.

CHAPTER 6

THE LIFE CARE ANNUITY

Mark J. Warshawsky

Life care annuities address inefficiencies in the market by combining a life annuity and long-term care insurance, thus blending the longevity risk (and adverse selection) of annuity buyers with the morbidity/disability risk of those denied long-term care insurance. Life care annuities attempt to produce a self-sustaining pooling equilibrium superior to that of the two separate consumer populations.

A life care annuity (LCA) is the combination of a life annuity and long-term care insurance (LTCI). In return for the payment of a premium (either in a lump sum or collected over time), the LCA provides a stream of fixed-income payments for the lifetime of the named annuitant.[1] In return for higher premium charges, a co-annuitant, usually the spouse, can be added; payments in this case would continue until the death of the second-to-die co-annuitant. In addition, the LCA provides an extra stream of payments if the annuitant (and/or the co-annuitant) requires long-term care. The annuitant qualifies for the long-term care payment if he or she is cognitively impaired or is unable to perform at least two of the six recognized activities of daily living (ADLs), such as walking or eating without substantial human assistance. These ADL triggers are the same triggers used in the LTCI policies qualified under current tax law.

Because this second segment of the LCA is intended to function as comprehensive LTCI, the additional layer of payments to the disabled annuitant must be sufficient to cover the extra expenses incurred for home health care or nursing home care, generally as soon as possible after the disability commences and for as long as those care needs continue. For that reason, the inclusion of yet another layer of "pop-up" disability payments in the LCA may be advisable in case a disability is severe (e.g., impairment in four ADLs) or lasts a particularly long time (e.g., two years). When the extent of needed care is great, costs will increase. Moreover, long-term care costs have been increasing more rapidly than consumer prices in general, and LTCI should reflect this fact.

The desired level of payments in the first segment of the LCA (the life annuity segment) will depend on the financial resources of the annuitant; on the existence and size of other life annuity income, such as a defined-benefit (DB) pension and Social Security; and on the

Reprinted from *The Future of Life-Cycle Saving and Investing,* The Research Foundation of CFA Institute (October 2007):103–106.

annuitant's desired standard of living in retirement. And importantly, the amount devoted to the life annuity should consider the investor's risk tolerance and personal preferences for bequests, *inter vivos* gifts, and other needs and desires for which a life annuity is not the best-suited vehicle.[2]

What is the motivation for the integration of a life annuity and LTCI—separate insurance products that are widely available and have been marketed for decades? The integration is intended to address inefficiencies in the separate markets for those products. For example, empirical research has shown that immediate life annuities are as much as 10 percent more expensive than they would be without adverse selection (Friedman and Warshawsky 1990; Mitchell, Poterba, Warshawsky, and Brown 1999). Adverse selection exists because individuals with long life expectancies seek to purchase life annuities whereas other individuals tend not to. A large improvement in utility could be achieved by the annuitization of assets at fair actuarial value in retirement rather than at the prices distorted by adverse selection.

At the same time, according to Kemper, Murtaugh, and Spillman (1995), current underwriting practices prevent 25 to 33 percent of the retiring population (ages 65 to 75) from purchasing individual LTCI policies. That is, individuals with impaired health, or with lifestyles perceived by the insurer to be unhealthy, cannot purchase LTCI.[3] The conclusion is that if LTCI were easier to purchase, it would be much more widely held. Brown and Finkelstein (2004) demonstrated, using simulation analysis, substantial demand by individuals above the lowest two or three wealth deciles to pay for actuarially fairly priced private LTCI coverage on top of Medicaid. (Of course, Medicaid coverage itself provides significant consumer welfare because of its LTCI coverage.)

Finally, the LCA combination is motivated by the observed positive correlation between mortality and poor health and lifestyle.

These observations and findings led to the proposal for an integrated product that would offer a life annuity and an LTCI policy at a lower cost, and with wider eligibility, than could be provided by the two types of policies offered separately. The LCA blends the longevity risk of annuity buyers with the morbidity/disability risk of those desiring, but denied access to, LTCI coverage. The product thus appeals to two populations simultaneously. The proposal is an application of economic theory—a practical attempt to produce a self-sustaining pooling equilibrium that is superior to the separate equilibrium currently in existence.

The proposal rests on three hypotheses that we tested:

1. The life expectancy of voluntary purchasers of an integrated product will be less than that of voluntary purchasers of life annuities.
2. The population eligible for, and most likely to be attracted to, the integrated product will be larger than the populations attracted to and eligible for the two products issued separately.
3. With minimal medical underwriting, the cost of the integrated product will be less than the sum of the costs of the two products sold separately.[4] Note that "minimal underwriting" means that only those who would go immediately into claim status for LTCI benefits (e.g., those who are already nursing home residents) would be rejected for the LCA.[5]

The basic integrated product that we modeled was an immediate LCA that paid $1,000 (nominal) a month for the lifetime of a 65-year-old individual (of either sex) with a 10-year

TABLE 6.1   Premiums at Age 65 for Income Annuity with Disability Benefits: Current LTC Underwriting Practice vs. Minimal Underwriting

Item	$1,000 Monthly Life Annuity Only	$2,000 Monthly 2–3 ADL Disability Benefit	$1,000 Monthly 4+ ADL Disability Benefit	Combined Premium
All persons	$139,098	$15,950	$3,155	$158,203
Prospective purchasers				
Current LTC underwriting	$145,041	$13,900	$2,843	$161,784
Minimal underwriting only	139,827	13,723	2,777	156,326
Nonpurchasers				
Current LTC underwriting	$119,051	$22,866	$4,207	$146,124
Minimal underwriting only	104,147	122,764	21,293	248,203

Source: Murtaugh, Spillman, and Warshawsky (2001).

Note: All numbers are without inflation protection.

guaranteed period. The disability payment was an additional $2,000 (nominal) a month if 30 days had passed after the annuitant had two ADL impairments or had been cognitively impaired for at least 90 days *plus* another $1,000 (nominal) a month if the annuitant had four ADL impairments. The balance between the life annuity and LTCI segments is important in achieving the pooling equilibrium; few people rejected for LTCI would want to buy pure life annuity products, but a guaranteed period added to the annuity component of the LCA makes it more attractive to this population.

We found that for this basic integrated product, the single-payment premium at age 65 would be $156,326. As Table 6.1 shows, that price is about $5,000 less than the two products sold separately.

This proposal also has a public policy context. On the annuity side, employer provision of retirement income support for workers has moved toward the defined-contribution plan form, in which a life annuity distribution is not required—indeed, is not often offered. Therefore, the individual plan participant must search in the voluntary individual annuity market if he or she is interested in coverage by a life annuity at retirement. Even for those workers covered by a DB pension plan, mandatory annuitization has become less common; therefore, the scope of adverse selection has increased. Moreover, mandatory annuitization is not featured in many Social Security reform proposals.

On the long-term care side, the U.S. Congress, concerned about apparent abuses of the Medicaid spend-down requirement and by the runaway cost of the program to the federal and state governments, has recently tightened eligibility for the long-term care benefits of Medicaid. Indeed, research by Brown and Finkelstein (2004) demonstrated that, even without considering concerns about gaming the Medicaid system, Medicaid has had a substantial crowding-out effect on private LTCI coverage. Hence, as Medicaid eligibility is tightened, the need for private LTCI coverage will increase among lower and lower ranges of the income and wealth distribution. Despite the need, the preferred solutions of the insurance industry have been sales of individual LTCI policies at young ages or employer provision of the benefit, where underwriting is not a significant factor. These approaches, however, have not taken deep root.

Moreover, in the life-cycle planning of a household, there is a natural focal point for the LCA—namely, when the household is approaching or has just begun retirement and is seriously considering, given finite resources, the rest of the household's financial future.

New product designs in the private sector should respond to changing private and public factors in pragmatic ways. And the product providers need to be accommodated and perhaps encouraged by public policy. The LCA is a step in the right direction.

NOTES

1. The income payments may be fixed in nominal or real terms; a *real* annuity is the more expensive form.
2. Guarantee periods (in which the annuity will be paid to beneficiaries for a fixed period of time even if the annuitant dies), cash refunds, and various liquidity features of many individual life annuity products currently marketed may, however, meet some of these preferences and needs.
3. This finding is corroborated by observation in the insurance industry of the high rejection rate of applications for LTCI policies by older applicants.
4. For more details, see Murtaugh, Spillman, and Warshawsky (2001).
5. An alternative formulation would allow coverage for even these people, but it would have to be delayed two or three years for them.

REFERENCES

Brown, Jeffrey R., and Amy Finkelstein. 2004. "The Interaction of Public and Private Insurance: Medicaid and the Long-Term Care Insurance Market." NBER Working Paper No. 10989 (December).

Friedman, Benjamin, and Mark J. Warshawsky. 1990. "The Cost of Annuities: Implications for Saving Behavior and Bequests."*Quarterly Journal of Economics*, vol. 105, no. 1 (February):135–154.

Kemper, Peter, Christopher Murtaugh, and Brenda Spillman. 1995. "Risky Business."*Inquiry*, vol. 32, no. 3 (Fall):271–284.

Mitchell, Olivia, James Poterba, Mark J. Warshawsky, and Jeffrey R. Brown. 1999. "New Evidence on the Money's Worth of Individual Annuities."*American Economic Review*, vol. 89, no. 5 (December):1299–1318.

Murtaugh, Christopher, Brenda Spillman, and Mark J. Warshawsky. 2001. "In Sickness and in Health: An Annuity Approach to Financing Long-Term Care and Retirement Income." *Journal of Risk and Insurance*, vol. 68, no. 2 (June):225–254.

CHAPTER 7

THE LONGEVITY ANNUITY: AN ANNUITY FOR EVERYONE?

Jason S. Scott

As of 2005, U.S. individuals had an estimated $7.4 trillion invested in IRAs and employer-sponsored retirement accounts. Many retirees will thus face the difficult problem of turning a pool of assets into a stream of retirement income. Purchasing an immediate annuity is a common recommendation for retirees trying to maximize retirement spending. The vast majority of retirees, however, are unwilling to annuitize all their assets. This research demonstrates that a "longevity annuity," which is distinct from an immediate annuity in that payouts begin late in retirement, is optimal for retirees unwilling to fully annuitize. For a typical retiree, allocating 10–15 percent of wealth to a longevity annuity creates spending benefits comparable to an allocation to an immediate annuity of 60 percent or more.

The aging of the U.S. population and the demise of the defined-benefit (DB) plan are two major trends reshaping the retirement landscape. As of this writing, the oldest of the Baby Boomers have already turned 60. The aging of that generation will create an unprecedented explosion in the retiree population. The assets available to these new retirees are also undergoing significant change. The past two decades have seen a substantial shift from DB-funded pensions toward a reliance on IRA and 401(k) accounts to fund retirement. As of 2005, Americans had approximately $7.4 trillion invested in IRAs and employer-sponsored defined-contribution plans, compared with $1.9 trillion in employer-sponsored DB plans (Investment Company Institute 2006). This shift has raised a critical question for many newly minted retirees: "How can I convert accumulated assets into retirement income?"

Reprinted from the *Financial Analysts Journal* (January/February 2008):40–48.

Note: The views expressed herein are those of the author and not necessarily those of Financial Engines.

An immediate annuity is a common recommendation—from practitioners and academics alike—to maximize retirement income from a given pool of assets. In a typical immediate annuity contract, an insurance company promises to make regular monthly or annual payments for the life of the individual in exchange for a one-time premium payment.

More than four decades have passed since economic theory first concluded that individuals who wish to maximize guaranteed spending in retirement should convert all their available assets to an immediate annuity (see Yaari 1965). Yet, few retirees allocate *any* dollars to an immediate annuity, much less fully annuitize.[1] Given retirees' reluctance to make annuity purchases, I extend the theoretical analysis by considering the question, "Which annuity should I buy with *a fraction* of my assets?"

The gulf between theory and behavior is so wide that numerous academic studies have analyzed the "annuity puzzle."[2] An important aspect is that virtually all of the previous analyses assumed that the fundamental annuity contract available is an immediate annuity. However, a new type of annuity contract, a "longevity annuity," has recently been introduced.[3] Longevity annuities are essentially immediate annuity contracts without the initial payouts. That is, a longevity annuity involves an up-front premium with payouts that begin in the future. For example, an age-85 longevity annuity can be purchased at age 65 with payouts commencing only when *and if* the purchaser reaches age 85.

Researchers are starting to consider longevity annuities. Milevski (2005) assessed the potential for employees to use periodic contributions to their pension plan to purchase longevity annuity payouts. Milevsky identified as barriers to implementation the piecemeal purchase and the potential for a gap in timing between purchase and payouts to exceed 30 years.[4] Hu and Scott (2007) demonstrated that longevity annuities are generally preferable to immediate annuities because of the many well-documented behavioral biases in decision making. As I will show, longevity annuities not only have a behavioral advantage, but they also have a purely rational advantage. In particular, longevity annuities maximize the insurance benefit per premium dollar. For that reason, longevity annuities, especially those that start payouts late in life, may indeed qualify as an annuity for everyone.

WHAT MAKES INSURANCE VALUABLE?

Before diving into the issue of longevity risk and annuities, I start with a basic question: What makes insurance valuable? First, consider the answer in a simple setting. Suppose a driving enthusiast absolutely must have a car. Furthermore, suppose this driver has no access to insurance to replace the car if an accident occurs. To self-insure, he must set aside enough money for a replacement car in case of an accident. The money he sets aside he cannot spend.

Access to car insurance completely changes the situation. Now, the motorist has to set aside only the cost of insurance. Any remaining dollars he can now safely spend on other things. The size of this windfall to the driver depends crucially on the insurance cost relative to the replacement cost. (Throughout this example, all claims are assumed to be for the full value of the car.) For example, assume the car has a replacement cost of $20,000. Suppose the driver has an excellent driving record and only a 5 percent chance of making an insurance claim. If insurance is sold at cost, then the car insurance price is $1,000.[5] In this case, purchasing insurance allows the driver $19,000 in additional spending relative to self-insurance. So, at this price, the insurance provides $19 of additional spending per $1 of insurance premium.

If the driver has a history of wrecking cars, the chance of totaling the car is now much higher, so the price for car insurance also rises. Suppose the chance of an accident has increased fivefold, to 25 percent. The cost of insurance also rises fivefold, to $5,000. Now, purchasing insurance allows only $15,000 in additional spending. The spending improvement per premium dollar has been reduced to just $3. Although insurance still makes sense, the benefit relative to self-insurance is less compelling.

In the extreme case of a reckless driver with a 95 percent chance of totaling the car, the insurance cost may rise to a staggering $19,000. The spending benefit per premium dollar has shrunk to a paltry 5 cents. If the insurance price is cost plus a profit premium, it could actually exceed the replacement cost for this driver.

Analyzing the spending improvement per premium dollar helps individuals select from competing insurance contracts. Suppose an individual has an additional dollar she is willing to allocate to insurance. What insurance contract should she select? When the alternative is self-insurance, the answer is simple. She should allocate the extra insurance dollar to the insurance contract that frees up the most spending. In other words, she should select the insurance product with the highest spending improvement per premium dollar. To simplify the exposition, I refer to this quantity as the "spending improvement quotient," or Q. Specifically,

$$Q = \text{Spending improvement quotient}$$
$$= \frac{\text{Self-insurance costs} - \text{Insurance costs}}{\text{Insurance costs}}. \quad (7.1)$$

In the car insurance examples, the insurance cost was simply the car replacement cost reduced to reflect the chance of an insurance payout. If the probability of an insurance payout is denoted by P, then the spending improvement quotient simplifies to:

$$Q = \frac{\text{Self-insurance costs} - (P \times \text{Self-insurance costs})}{P \times \text{Self-insurance costs}}$$
$$= \frac{1 - P}{P}. \quad (7.2)$$

This result is intuitive. To evaluate the potential insurance benefit, one simply considers the likelihood of a payout. If an insurance payout is unlikely, insurance is generally cheap relative to self-insurance and insurance can provide substantial benefits. If an insurance payout is highly likely, insurance cannot be provided at much of a discount to self-insurance. In such conditions, insurance provides little benefit.

These fundamental concepts apply to all insurance contracts, including longevity insurance. Focusing on high-value, or high-Q, insurance is the key to maximizing the benefit per premium dollar.[6]

TURNING IRAs INTO INCOME

With the dramatic increases in IRA and 401(k) plan balances, a common problem facing retirees will be turning those assets into income. To illustrate how insurance concepts apply to the retirement income problem, I analyze the problem faced by a newly retired individual. This retiree is 65 years old and has a $1 million IRA available to fund retirement spending.

Before tackling the full retirement problem, consider the simpler problem of funding spending for a single year 20 years in the future. For the retiree, this would correspond to funding spending at age 85. If the retiree wants a guaranteed payout in 20 years time, an obvious investment choice is a zero-coupon bond. The price today for a bond that pays $1 in

20 years, B_{20}, depends on the prevailing interest rates. Assuming interest rates are 2.5 percent at all maturities, spending in 20 years will cost:[7]

$$B_{20} = \text{Price today of a zero-coupon bond paying out \$1 in 20 years}$$
$$= \frac{1}{(1.025)^{20}}$$
$$= \$0.61.$$

Each dollar the retiree wants to spend at age 85 can be initially secured for a 61 cent investment in a 20-year zero-coupon bond.

Securing spending with bonds is analogous to setting aside the full replacement cost of the car. With self-insurance, the money is set aside whether or not the insurance event occurs. Similarly, the dollar from the zero-coupon bond is available whether or not the retiree actually lives to spend it.

An alternative to using bonds is an annuity contract. Suppose the retiree can purchase an annuity contract today that has a one-time payout in 20 years. The annuity contract differs from the bond in that the payout is contingent on survival. Given the similarities in payout structure, I will call this single-payment annuity a "zero-coupon annuity."

How much does a $1 payout in 20 years cost when using a zero-coupon annuity? As in the car insurance example, the price for longevity insurance depends on the probability of a payout. For longevity insurance, the payout probability is the chance of the retiree surviving 20 years to qualify for the payout. If S_{20} is the 20-year survival probability, then the zero-coupon annuity price, A_{20}, is

$$A_{20} = \text{Price today of a zero-coupon annuity paying \$1 in 20 years, if alive}$$
$$= S_{20} \times B_{20}.$$
(7.3)

If the retiree is male, the 20-year survival probability appropriate for annuity pricing is about 52 percent.[8] Even with some insurance market–related frictions, a zero-coupon annuity offers spending in 20 years at nearly a 50 percent discount to self-insurance in the bond market.

As in the car insurance example, a spending improvement quotient for the 20-year zero-coupon annuity can be calculated. In this case, the Q is

$$Q_{20} = \frac{\text{Self-insurance costs} - \text{Insurance costs}}{\text{Insurance costs}}$$
$$= \frac{B_{20} - A_{20}}{A_{20}}$$
$$= \frac{1 - S_{20}}{S_{20}}$$
$$= 0.94.$$

That is, the future spending that costs $1.94 to secure in the bond market costs only $1.00 in the annuity market. Thus, every annuity dollar allocated to finance spending at age 85 frees up 94 cents for additional spending.

The preceding analysis indicates that annuity-based spending at age 85 can be secured at a substantial discount to bond-based spending. The same analysis applies to spending each year throughout retirement. Figure 7.1 displays the results from repeating the Q-analysis for each age between 65 and 100. The range of spending improvements is surprising. The potential insurance

FIGURE 7.1   Spending Improvement Quotient, *Q:* Zero-Coupon Annuity Payments

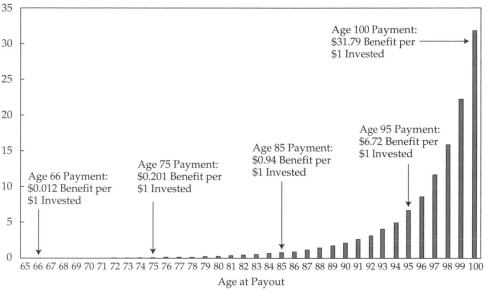

benefit for spending at age 66 is a paltry 1 cent per premium dollar. Given the previous examples, the reason for this result is obvious. People who purchase annuities at age 65 almost always live to collect the payment at age 66. In this situation, potential insurance benefits are extremely limited. In contrast, the age-100 payment has a *Q*-value of 31.79. Funding spending at age 100 with an annuity costs only pennies on the dollar compared with the cost of a bond. For this individual, the insurance benefit of the age-100 zero-coupon annuity is approximately *2,500 times* the insurance benefit provided by the age-66 zero-coupon annuity.

Abstracting from the details of Figure 7.1, the message is clear. Longevity insurance provides substantial benefits for late-life spending but much smaller benefits for near-term spending.[9] This observation explains both the problem with immediate annuities and the potential of longevity annuities. Both immediate and longevity annuities can be thought of as bundles of zero-coupon annuities. An age-85 longevity annuity, for example, bundles together each of the zero-coupon annuities from age 85 onward. Similarly, immediate annuities represent a bundle of all the zero-coupon annuities. The difference between the two types of annuities is that immediate annuities add near-term, low-value annuity payments to the bundle. The resulting blended average *Q*-value for the immediate annuity is 0.56.[10] In contrast, the *Q*-value for the age-85 longevity annuity, at 2.93, is more than five times higher.

LONGEVITY ANNUITIES TO MAXIMIZE SPENDING

For each dollar the retiree shifts from bonds to immediate annuities, 56 cents is available for additional spending. If all assets were shifted to an immediate annuity, spending would increase by 56 percent relative to a bond-based spending program.

But what if the retiree is uncomfortable with a 100 percent allocation to annuities? How should retirees allocate the dollars they are willing to annuitize? Figure 7.1 provides the basis for an answer. For the first dollar annuitized, the best spending improvement can be had by purchasing the age-100 zero-coupon annuity. Indeed, putting all annuity wealth into the age-100 annuity is tempting. After all, look at the spending boost! The retiree needs spending in every year, however, not just at age 100. Even though he cannot focus all spending on age-100 annuities, the first bonds that should be substituted with annuities should be bonds earmarked for age-100 spending. Assuming the retiree wishes to allocate more dollars to annuities, the next-highest surplus-producing annuity will be the age-99 annuity followed by the age-98 annuity.

The optimal bundle of zero-coupon annuities to purchase thus depends on the amount of assets the retiree is willing to annuitize. Notice that all optimal bundles are longevity annuities because optimal strategies entail sequentially adding earlier and earlier zero-coupon annuities. If he is willing to annuitize only a few dollars, then the longevity annuity that begins payments at age 100 is optimal. If more dollars are available for annuitization, a longevity annuity that begins payouts at age 99 is in order. The start age for the longevity annuity payments will continue to be reduced until the annuity allocation is exhausted. Surprisingly, only retirees interested in fully annuitizing their assets should select an immediate annuity. All other retirees should opt for the longevity annuity that exhausts their willingness to annuitize.[11]

Figure 7.2 illustrates the difference between allocating dollars to immediate annuities and allocating dollars to longevity annuities. Allocations to immediate annuities result in a constant 56 cents additional spending per dollar annuitized. Thus, the available spending when an immediate annuity is used increases linearly from a base of $41,416 with a pure bond portfolio to a maximum of $64,645 with a 100 percent annuity allocation. The curve corresponds to the spending achievable with longevity annuities. The longevity annuity's curvature stems from the fact that the initial dollars are spent on high-Q, age-100 payments. Additional dollars

FIGURE 7.2   Longevity Annuity Spending vs. Immediate Annuity Spending

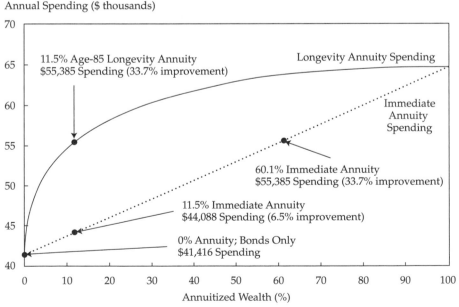

Note: $1 million in assets, age 65, male.

are then spent on successively lower-Q payments. Diminishing returns cause the slope of the longevity annuity curve to gradually flatten as the annuity allocation increases.

The longevity annuity's spending curve shares both the beginning and ending points with the immediate annuity spending line. The two strategies emanate from the same point because 0 percent annuitized corresponds to bond-only income for both. With 100 percent annuitized, a longevity annuity has a payment start date that is immediate. Thus, the two annuity options also share the 100 percent annuitized point. At *every point between* 0 percent and 100 percent annuitized, however, the longevity annuity provides higher spending levels per dollar annuitized.

To grasp the leverage available from longevity annuities, consider the age-85 longevity annuity (i.e., the longevity annuity that begins to make payments at age 85).[12] Suppose the retiree with the $1 million funds spending prior to age 85 with bonds and funds spending after age 85 with a longevity annuity. Using the bond and annuity prices derived previously, he finds that an 11.5 percent allocation to an age-85 longevity annuity will generate annual payouts of $55,385 starting at age 85. Allocating the balance of the portfolio to zero-coupon bonds generates $55,385 in annual income prior to age 85. Thus, this combination has increased annual spending throughout retirement by 33.7 percent relative to using a bond-only portfolio.

If an immediate annuity were used instead, the same 11.5 percent annuity allocation would increase spending only by 6.5 percent. To achieve a comparable spending increase with immediate annuities, the retiree would have to allocate more than 60 percent of his portfolio to annuity purchases. Convincing a retiree to annuitize 60 percent of assets would be extremely challenging irrespective of the potential benefit. Annuitizing 11.5 percent of assets might prove much more palatable, especially if this modest allocation allowed guaranteed spending to increase by more than a third. The ability of longevity annuities to deliver a majority of the annuitization benefits for a relatively small portfolio allocation makes them a powerful tool to help retirees effectively turn assets into income.

ROBUSTNESS ANALYSIS

The preceding analysis made three key assumptions to allow evaluation of the relative efficiency of longevity annuities. Those assumptions were the mortality rates for retirees, the prevailing interest rates for bond investments, and the formula by which insurance companies turn mortality and interest rates into annuity prices. This section explores the impact of altering these key assumptions.

The robustness analysis consists of analyzing six cases, each with a different set of core assumptions. The results for each case are reported in Table 7.1.

Case 1 assumes the retiree is male, prevailing interest rates are 2.5 percent, and annuity prices are determined by using the theoretical model described in the preceding paragraphs. Thus, Case 1 corresponds to the situation previously explored in detail. Given those assumptions, an 11.5 percent allocation to an age-85 longevity annuity provides more than five times the spending improvement of the immediate annuity (33.7 percent vs. 6.5 percent).

In Case 1, the retiree was assumed to be a man. Women, however, have different mortality rates. Given that mortality plays a critical role in annuity pricing, Case 2 repeats the analysis for a female retiree. An improved mortality rate has increased the annuity costs in general, but longevity annuities still provide substantial benefits relative to immediate annuities. For this retiree, the spending increase with a longevity annuity is 4.35 times as big as with an immediate annuity.

TABLE 7.1 Robustness Analysis: Interest Rate, Mortality, and Annuity Pricing Assumptions for *Age-85 Longevity Annuity* vs. *Immediate Annuity*

	Theoretical Bond/ Annuity Prices				Actual Bond/ Annuity Prices	
	Case 1	Case 2	Case 3	Case 4	Case 5	Case 6
Assumption						
Mortality: male (M) vs. female (F)	M	F	M	F	M	F
Interest rates: real 2.5% rate vs. nominal 5% rate (%)	2.5	2.5	5.0	5.0	~5.0[a]	~5.0[a]
Bond-only spending from $1 million ($)	41,416	41,416	57,557	57,557	58,841	$58,841
Age-85 longevity annuity results						
Optimal annuity allocation (%)[b]	11.5	15.3	8.2	10.9	7.9	10.4
Spending improvement (%)	33.7	27.9	21.9	18.3	21.5	18.2
Immediate annuity results[c]						
Annuity allocation (%)	11.5	15.3	8.2	10.9	7.9	10.4
Spending improvement (%)	6.5	6.4	3.3	3.3	3.1	3.1
Longevity annuity benefit multiple[d]	5.23	4.35	6.61	5.52	6.91	5.84

[a]The Treasury yield curve on 13 July 2006 ranged from 5.0 percent to 5.27 percent.
[b]The "optimal annuity allocation" is the annuity allocation required to equalize income across all retirement years. Income from ages 65 through 84 is bond funded. Thereafter, annuities fund income.
[c]The "immediate annuity results" reflect immediate annuity prices estimated from age-67 longevity annuity price quotes.
[d]This multiple is the ratio of longevity annuity spending improvement to immediate annuity spending improvement.

Case 1 and Case 2 assume an interest rate of 2.50 percent. As of this writing, this interest rate corresponds to the real rate of interest available from government inflation-indexed bonds. If the dollars the retiree is trying to secure each year in retirement are inflation-indexed dollars, then this real interest rate is appropriate for the calculations. Some retirees, however, may opt for fixed spending that does not increase with inflation. For this situation, using nominal interest rates in the calculations is appropriate. As of this writing, nominal interest rates are approximately 5.00 percent. Case 3 and Case 4 thus repeat the analysis using the nominal rate of interest. Although the specific numbers have changed, the relative strength of longevity annuities remains.[13] For these cases, the spending improvement for the longevity annuity relative to the immediate annuity increases by a factor of 6.61 for a male retiree and 5.52 for a female retiree.

The analysis up to this point has been somewhat theoretical to help pinpoint the key reasons longevity annuities provide substantial advantages. An important point, however, is that benefits from longevity annuities can be readily achieved by retirees in the real world. As of this writing, at least three insurance companies are offering longevity annuities. Metropolitan Life Insurance Company (MetLife) introduced longevity annuities in 2004 under the product name Retirement Income Insurance. In March 2006, The Hartford Financial Service Group introduced a longevity annuity product named The Hartford Income Security. Presidential Life Insurance Company also offers a longevity annuity product. Although all of the products provide a straightforward way of securing fixed nominal payouts in retirement, none offers the ability to generate inflation-protected payouts.[14] Theoretical versus actual pricing comparisons can thus be made only for annuities with fixed nominal payouts.

Actual bond and annuity prices can be obtained to assess the validity of the preceding analysis in the real world. In July 2006, MetLife provided a longevity annuity price quote for a 65-year-old wishing to purchase an age-85 longevity annuity.[15] In addition to annuity prices, bond yields are required to perform this analysis. U.S. Treasury yield data were obtained on 13 July 2006. At that time, the yield curve for government securities ranged from 5 percent to 5.27 percent.

Case 5 and Case 6 report the results when actual bond and annuity prices were used. For a male retiree, a modest 7.9 percent longevity annuity allocation allows spending to increase by 21.5 percent. A comparable allocation to an immediate annuity increases spending only by 3.1 percent. For this real-world case, the spending improvement from longevity annuities is 6.91 times the spending improvement achieved from immediate annuities.

The results from using actual prices are comparable to those achieved with theoretical pricing assumptions (Case 3 and Case 4). If anything, actual prices suggest that the size of the longevity annuity advantage is slightly underestimated in the theoretical pricing model.

Although actual prices confirm the longevity annuity advantage over an immediate annuity, note that neither annuity has met with large-scale economic success. So, whether recently introduced longevity annuities will ultimately increase the popularity of annuities or will result in yet another annuity puzzle remains to be seen.[16]

This robustness analysis has considered the influence of three critical assumptions: mortality rates, interest rates, and annuity pricing formulas. Although the particulars of the analysis do indeed depend on these three factors, the advantage of longevity annuities was robust across all of these permutations. In some sense, the robustness is not surprising. The key to longevity annuity benefits is the realization that purchasing income conditional on survival *must* get cheaper as the chance of survival declines. Because cheaper insurance corresponds to more valuable insurance, longevity annuities allow retirees to concentrate their annuity dollars on high-value insurance. This fundamental advantage of longevity annuities should be robust across virtually all scenarios.

CONCLUSION

Millions of retirees will face the problem of translating their accumulated assets into retirement income. Retirees hoping to increase their retirement spending are often counseled, by academics and practitioners alike, to consider immediate annuities. Unfortunately, the theoretical foundation for an immediate annuity relies on the willingness of the retiree to fully annuitize. In practice, virtually no retirees voluntarily annuitize their entire portfolios. This chapter has extended the theory by answering the key question of which annuity to buy with a *portion* of one's assets.

The answer to this question is somewhat surprising. By focusing on the fundamental properties that make insurance valuable, I have demonstrated that longevity annuities maximize guaranteed retirement spending per dollar annuitized. Retirees willing to annuitize only a portion of their assets should prefer some form of longevity annuity. In fact, the first few dollars annuitized with a longevity annuity provide such substantial benefits that many retirees should find these annuities desirable. A sample calculation, with actual annuity prices, found that a 65-year-old male retiree could increase his guaranteed spending by more than 21 percent by allocating less than 8 percent of his portfolio to an age-85 longevity annuity. This spending improvement was almost *seven times* the spending improvement from a comparable immediate annuity allocation.

So, the answer to the question, Is the longevity annuity an annuity for everyone? is a *qualified* yes. The qualifications stem from the many individual-specific considerations, such as a retiree's wealth, health, and desire to leave a bequest, that are important to the annuitization decision. For example, a retiree without liquid wealth is clearly a poor candidate for a longevity annuity purchase.[17] In addition, a wealth level probably exists that is so high that spending and longevity considerations are irrelevant. For retirees with wealth levels between these extremes, however, longevity annuities can play an important role in maximizing retirement spending. Similar caveats apply to retirees in poor health. A retiree with no prospect of surviving beyond age 85 should not be interested in a longevity annuity. A retiree with assets set aside to support post-85 spending will find, however, that a longevity annuity provides comparable spending at a lower cost irrespective of their current health level. Finally, the desire to leave behind an estate may motivate some retirees to avoid annuities. However, because the longevity annuity outlay typically absorbs only 10–20 percent of assets, the bequest motive would have to be powerful indeed to eliminate all demand for longevity annuities. Therefore, qualifications to the yes answer are certainly in order, but they appear to be more the exception than the rule. In fact, as Baby Boomers increasingly enter retirement with a 401(k) balance rather than a corporate income promise, this analysis suggests that most will find that a modest longevity annuity purchase can substantially increase their spending in retirement.

APPENDIX 7A: PUBLIC POLICY CONSIDERATIONS

A straightforward economic analysis demonstrates the desirability of longevity annuities. Large-scale adoption of longevity annuities may depend critically, however, on public policy decisions. Two important policy issues that could increase the use of longevity annuities are the current rules regarding minimum required distributions and the inclusion of a longevity annuity option in employer-sponsored plans.

First, the current IRS rules regarding minimum required distributions (MRDs) create a barrier to the adoption of longevity annuities. Annuities that begin payouts after age 70 currently run afoul of the MRD rules. For example, an age-65 retiree who uses his IRA to purchase an age-85 longevity annuity cannot make the MRD at age 70 because no annuity payments are scheduled until age 85. Even if only a portion of the IRA is used to make the longevity annuity purchase, future market declines or withdrawals can still result in insufficient funds to make the MRD. Recognizing this issue, insurance companies do not currently allow longevity annuities with late-life start dates to be purchased with IRA or 401(k) assets.[18]

Requiring that IRA and 401(k) dollars be distributed and taxed prior to a late-dated longevity annuity purchase creates a substantial barrier to longevity annuity utilization.

The second policy issue relates to the significant role inertia plays in the effectiveness of corporate pension plans. Numerous studies have documented that many employees follow the path of least resistance when making decisions regarding their corporate pension. The Pension Protection Act of 2006 (PPA) is landmark legislation in that it encourages employers to "automate" their pension plans with reasonable defaults so that the path of least resistance is likely to lead to a prosperous retirement. Examples of newly made default decisions include automatic enrollment, automatic savings escalations, and automatic portfolio management. Thus, an employee who fails to make any proactive decision is automatically enrolled in the pension plan, contributes at a reasonable level, and is invested in a reasonably diversified portfolio. The PPA was silent, however, on ways to automate the translation of pension assets into income.

Because the benefit per dollar annuitized is dramatic, at least for the late-dated longevity annuities, a longevity annuity with a sufficiently late start date might be an ideal default candidate to help automate the income phase of retirement. The cost might be as little as 5–15 percent of assets, but the longevity protection benefit would be substantial.

ACKNOWLEDGMENTS

I would like to thank Wei-Yin Hu, David Ramirez, Andrea Scott, and John Watson for many excellent comments and suggestions.

NOTES

1. For example, LIMRA International (2007) estimated sales of fixed immediate annuities to be $5.9 billion for 2006.
2. See Brown and Warshawsky (2004) for a summary of explanations for the annuity puzzle, which included a bequest motive, the influence of Social Security, annuity pricing, and irreversibility of the annuity purchase. The full-annuitization prediction is robust, however, to most of these explanations.
3. Longevity annuities are also referred to as "delayed payout" annuities because in them, the annuity payments are delayed relative to an immediate annuity.
4. These two concerns can be mitigated by a longevity annuity lump-sum purchase at retirement. Milevsky also identified as potential problems payout gaps in excess of 10 years for inflation-protected products and the lack of a death benefit. Although inflation protection is not a feature of currently available longevity annuities, these products do allow individuals to select a "no death benefit" option.
5. If the insurance company sells a similar policy to numerous drivers with comparable risk profiles, the average cost of a policy will equal $20,000 × 0.05, or $1,000.
6. Note that an expected utility analysis is a more general approach to evaluating insurance options. Using Q simplifies the analysis by assuming that an individual's response is independent of the insurance purchase (e.g., when a crash happens, the same outlay occurs irrespective of whether the individual self-insured or purchased insurance).
7. This interest rate roughly corresponds to the real rate of interest as of this writing.

8. Social Security population average mortality tables indicate a 40 percent survival probability. Survival based on the GAR-94 mortality tables (with generational adjustments) is 51.58 percent. The annuity-pricing survival rate is higher than the average mortality rate for two reasons. First, annuity purchasers are generally healthier than average. Second, insurance companies have to cover the cost of doing business. Given the reserves and adjustments built into the GAR-94 tables, they should be a reasonable choice for estimating annuity prices.

9. This general result is independent of the desired spending pattern (e.g., fixed real, fixed nominal, increasing, decreasing, etc.). Irrespective of the pattern, annuitized wealth optimally supports late-retirement spending whereas nonannuitized wealth should be directed at early retirement spending. See Scott, Watson, and Hu (2007) for a detailed discussion of this result.

10. The Q-value for an immediate annuity can be calculated by comparing a bundle of zero-coupon bonds with a bundle of zero-coupon annuities. Using bonds to purchase \$1 of spending each year in retirement costs $B_0 + B_1 + \cdots + B_{35} = \$1 + \$0.976 + \cdots + \$0.421 = \$24.145$. Using annuities to purchase \$1 of spending each year in retirement costs $A_0 + A_1 + \cdots + A_{35} = \$1 + \$0.9636 + \cdots + \$0.0129 = \$15.469$. The spending improvement achieved by shifting bond-based to annuity-based spending is thus 0.56.

11. Interested readers can refer to Scott et al. (2007) for more details on optimal annuitization.

12. This longevity annuity is highlighted because it is the longevity annuity with the latest starting age that is readily available in the market.

13. Fixed nominal payments imply that the retiree is spending more during early retirement and less during late retirement. Because less wealth is used to fund spending after age 85, the amount optimally allocated to an age-85 annuity decreases.

14. Some products do allow the retiree to select a payout option that includes fixed annual payout increases once benefits begin. Although not perfectly hedging inflation, this option allows a retiree to prepare for some degree of average anticipated inflation.

15. For a male retiree, a \$100,000 premium purchased monthly payments of \$7,730 starting at age 85, which implies that each dollar of annual income starting at age 85 costs approximately \$1.10 (assuming no within-year mortality and 5 percent interest rates). An age-67 longevity annuity price quote implied a per dollar annuity cost of \$10.24. The price per dollar spending when an immediate annuity was used was estimated by taking the age-67 longevity annuity and adding \$1 and \$0.94 to account for, respectively, the age-65 and the age-66 payments.

16. Public policy changes that would encourage the use of longevity annuities are explored in Appendix 7A.

17. The potentially perverse incentives associated with Medicaid assistance may cause retirees with little wealth to prefer immediate consumption over longevity insurance.

18. More generally, any assets subject to MRDs are precluded from purchasing a longevity annuity which initiates payouts after age 70.

REFERENCES

Brown, J.R., and M.J. Warshawsky. 2004. "Longevity-Insured Retirement Distributions from Pension Plans: Market and Regulatory Issues." In *Public Policies and Private Pensions*. Edited by W.G. Gale, J.B. Shoven, and M.J. Warshawsky. Washington, DC: Brookings Institution Press.

Hu, W., and J.S. Scott. 2007. "Behavioral Obstacles in the Annuity Market." *Financial Analysts Journal*, vol. 63, no. 6 (November/December):71–82.

Investment Company Institute. 2006. "The U.S. Retirement Market, 2005." *Research Fundamentals*, vol. 15, no. 5 (July): http://www.ici.org/pdf/fm-v15n5.pdf.

LIMRA International. 2007. "LIMRA Reports Record Sales for U.S. Individual Annuities." Press release (21 March): http://www.limra.com/Pressroom/PressReleases/pr032107.aspx.

Milevsky, M.A. 2005. "Real Longevity Insurance with a Deductible: Introduction to Advanced-Life Delayed Annuities (ALDA)." *North American Actuarial Journal*, vol. 9, no. 4 (October):109–122.

Scott, J.S., J.G. Watson, and W. Hu. 2007. "Efficient Annuitization: Optimal Strategies for Hedging Mortality Risk." Pension Research Council Working Paper 2007-9.

Yaari, M.E. 1965. "Uncertain Lifetime, Life Insurance, and the Theory of the Consumer." *Review of Economic Studies*, vol. 32, no. 2 (April):137–150.

CHAPTER 8

A SUSTAINABLE SPENDING RATE WITHOUT SIMULATION

Moshe A. Milevsky and Chris Robinson

Financial commentators have called for more research on sustainable spending rates for individuals and endowments holding diversified portfolios. We present a forward-looking framework for analyzing spending rates and introduce a simple measure, stochastic present value, that parsimoniously meshes investment risk and return, mortality estimates, and spending rates without resorting to opaque Monte Carlo simulations. Applying it with reasonable estimates of future returns, we find payout ratios should be lower than those many advisors recommend. The proposed method helps analysts advise their clients how much they can consume from their savings, whether they can retire early, and how to allocate their assets.

> "Retirees Don't Have to Be So Frugal: A Case for Withdrawing Up to 6 Percent a Year"
> —Jonathan Clements
> *Wall Street Journal* (17 November 2004)

Retirees and endowment and foundation trustees share a common dilemma: How much can we spend without running out of money during our lifetime? Sustainable withdrawal and spending rates have been the subject of sporadic academic research over the years. The issue has developed new urgency, however, as the wave of North American Baby Boomers approaches retirement and seeks guidance on "what's next" for their retirement savings. Complicating the issue is the likelihood that Baby Boomers can expect to live for a long (but random) time in retirement as medical advances stretch human lifetimes.

For endowments and foundations, this topic has a 30-year history going back to a special session at the American Economics Association devoted to spending rates, in which Tobin (1974) cautioned against consuming anything other than dividends and interest income.[1] Also in the

---

Reprinted from the *Financial Analysts Journal* (November/December 2005):89–100.

1970s, Ennis and Williamson (1976) analyzed appropriate asset allocation in conjunction with a given spending policy. More recently, Altschuler (2000) argued that endowments are actually "too stingy" and are not spending enough; Dybvig (1999) discussed how a pseudo portfolio insurance scheme used in asset allocation can protect a desired level of spending; and Hannon and Hammond (2003) discussed the impact of the recent (poor) market performance on the ability to sustain payouts.

In the parallel retirement planning arena, Bengen (1994); Ho, Milevsky, and Robinson (1994); Cooley, Hubbard, and Walz (1998, 2003); Pye (2000); Ameriks, Veres, and Warshawsky (2001); and Guyton (2004) have run financial experiments incorporating historical, simulated, and scrambled returns to quantify the sustainability of various *ad hoc* spending policies and consumption rates for retired individuals. These results usually advocated withdrawals in the 4–6 percent range of initial capital depending on age and asset allocation and then increasing at the rate of inflation and/or contingent on market performance.

The problems with the growing number of these and similar studies based on Monte Carlo simulations—which are intellectually motivated by the "game of life" simulations envisioned by Markowitz (1991)—are that they (1) are difficult to replicate, (2) conduct only a minimal number of simulations, and (3) provide little pedagogical intuition on the financial trade-off between retirement risk and return.[2]

Arnott (2004, p. 6) claimed that "our industry pays scant attention to the concept of sustainable spending, which is key to effective strategic planning for corporate pensions, public pensions, foundations, and endowments—even for individuals." Financial advisors continue to test the sustainability of spending strategies, but the financial literature lacks a coherent modeling framework on which to base the discussion.

We provide an intuitive and consistent planning model by deriving an analytic relationship between spending, aging, and sustainability in a random portfolio environment. We introduce the concept of stochastic present value (SPV) and an expression for the probability that an initial corpus or investment (nest egg) will be depleted under a fixed consumption rule when both rates of return and time until death are stochastic. And, in contrast to almost all other authors who have tackled this problem, we do not depend on Monte Carlo simulations or historical (bootstrap) studies. Instead, we base the analysis on the SPV and a continuous-time approximation under lognormal returns and exponential lifetimes.

In the case of a foundation or endowment with an infinite horizon (perpetual consumption), this formula is exact. In the case of a random finite future lifetime (the situation of a retiree), the formula is based on moment-matching approximations, which target the first and second moments of the "true" stochastic present value. The results are remarkably accurate when compared with more costly and time-consuming simulations.

We provide numerical examples to demonstrate the versatility of the closed-form expression for the SPV in determining sustainable withdrawal rates and their respective probabilities. This formula, which can easily be implemented in Excel, produces results that are within the standard error of extensive Monte Carlo simulations.[3]

THE RETIREMENT FINANCES TRIANGLE

The main qualitative contribution of this chapter can be understood by reference to the triangle in Figure 8.1. It provides a graphical illustration of the relationships among the three most important factors in retirement planning: spending rates, investment asset allocation,

FIGURE 8.1   Retirement Finances Triangle

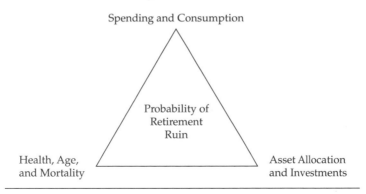

and mortality (determined by gender and age). We link these three factors in one parsimonious manner by using the "probability of retirement ruin," where "ruin" is defined as outliving one's resources, as a risk metric to gauge the relative impact of each factor and trade-offs between them.

We evaluate the stochastic present value of a given spending plan at a given age under a given portfolio allocation at the initial level of wealth to determine the probability that the plan is sustainable. Increasing the age of the retiree at retirement, reducing the spending rate, or increasing the portfolio return will each shift the mass of the SPV closer to zero (which means reducing the area inside the triangle) and thus generate a higher probability that an initial nest egg will be enough to sustain the plan. Reducing the age at retirement, increasing the spending rate, or reducing the portfolio return will shift the mass of the SPV away from zero—increasing the area inside the triangle—and will thus increase the probability of ruin.

STOCHASTIC PRESENT VALUE OF SPENDING

The SPV concept is borrowed from actuaries in the insurance industry, who use a similar idea to compute the distribution of the present value of mortality-contingent liabilities, such as pension annuities and life insurance policies. At any given time, an insurance company is thus able to quantify the amount of reserves needed today to fulfill all future liabilities with 99 percent or 95 percent certainty.

The same idea can be applied to retirement planning. Retirees can use an SPV model to compute the size of the retirement portfolio they need in order to draw down a specified annual amount while not incurring more than a specified probability of running out of money during their lifetime.

In the language of stochastic calculus, the probability that a diffusion process that starts at a value of w will hit zero prior to an independent "killing time" can be represented as the probability that a suitably defined SPV is greater than the same w. Imagine that you invest a lump sum of money in a portfolio earning a real (after-inflation) rate of return of R percent a year and you plan to consume/spend a fixed real dollar each and every year until some horizon denoted by T. If the horizon and investment rate of return are certain, the present value (PV) of your consumption at initial time zero, t_0, is

$$PV = \sum_{i=1}^{T} \frac{1}{(1 + R)^i}$$
$$= \frac{1 - (1 + R)^{-T}}{R},$$

(8.1)

which is the textbook formula for an *ordinary simple annuity* of \$1. In a deterministic world, if you start retirement with a nest egg greater than the PV in Equation 8.1 times your desired annual consumption, your money will last for the rest of your T-year life. If you have less than this amount, you will be "ruined" at some age prior to death.

For example, if $R = 7$ percent and $T = 25$, the required nest egg is 11.65 (the PV in Equation 8.1) times your real consumption. If you have more than this lump sum of wealth at retirement, your plans are sustainable. If you start your retirement years with 10 times your desired real annual consumption, then you will run out of money in 17.79 years. Note that as T goes to infinity, which is the endowment case, the PV converges to the number $1/R$. At $R = 0.07$, the resulting PV is 14.28 times the desired consumption.

Human beings have an unknown life span, and retirement planning should account for this uncertainty. Table 8.1 illustrates the probabilities of survival based on mortality tables from the U.S.-based Society of Actuaries. For example, a 65-year-old female has a 34.8 percent chance of living to age 90; a 65-year-old male has a 23.7 percent chance of living to age 90. Although the oft-quoted statistic for life expectancy is somewhere between 78 and 82 years in the United States, this statistic is relevant only at the time of birth. If pensioners reach their retirement years, they may be facing 25–30 more years of life with substantial probability because conditional life expectancy increases with age.

Should a 65-year-old plan for the 75th percentile or 95th percentile of the end of the mortality table? What T value should be used in Equation 8.1? The same questions apply to investment return R. The average real investment returns from a broadly diversified portfolio of U.S. equity during the past 75 years have been in the vicinity of 6–9 percent, according to Ibbotson Associates (2004), but the year-by-year numbers can vary widely. So, again, what number should be used in Equation 8.1?

The aim is not to guess or take point estimates but, rather, to actually account for this uncertainty within the model itself. In a lecture at Stanford University, Nobel Laureate

TABLE 8.1   Conditional Probability of Survival at Age 65

To Age:	Female	Male
70	93.9%	92.2%
75	85.0	81.3
80	72.3	65.9
85	55.8	45.5
90	34.8	23.7
95	15.6	7.7
100	5.0	1.4

Source: Society of Actuaries RP-2000 Table (with projection).

William F. Sharpe amusingly called the (misleading) approach that uses fixed returns and fixed dates of death "financial planning in fantasyland."

So, in contrast to the deterministic case—in which both the horizon and the investment return are certain—when both of these variables are stochastic, the analog to Equation 8.1 is *stochastic present value*, defined as

$$SPV = \frac{1}{(1 + \tilde{R}_1)} + \frac{1}{(1 + \tilde{R}_1)(1 + \tilde{R}_2)} + \cdots + \frac{1}{\prod\limits_{j=1}^{\tilde{T}}(1 + \tilde{R}_j)}$$

$$= \sum_{i=1}^{\tilde{T}} \prod_{j=1}^{i}(1 + \tilde{R}_j)^{-1}, \tag{8.2a}$$

where the new variable $\tilde{T}$ denotes the random time of death (in years) and the new variable $\tilde{R}_j$ denotes the random investment return during year j. (For the infinitely lived endowment or foundation, $\tilde{T} = \infty$.)

The intuition behind Equation 8.2a is as follows. Looking forward, a retiree must sum up a random number of terms, in which each denominator is also random. The first item discounts the first year of consumption at the first year's random investment return. The second item discounts the second year's consumption (if the individual is still alive) at the product (the compounded rate) of the first and second years' random investment return. And so on.

If the investment return frequency is infinitesimal, the summation sign in Equation 8.2a converges to an integral and the product sign is converted into a continuous-time diffusion process. The continuous-time analog of Equation 8.2a can be written as follows:

$$SPV = \int_0^\infty \text{prob}\,(\tilde{T} > t)R_t^{-1}dt, \tag{8.2b}$$

where R_t denotes the *total* cumulative investment return (which is random) from the initial time, t_0, until time t. The exponent of -1 discounts the \$1, conditional on survival, back to t_0.

The SPV defined by either Equation 8.2a in discrete time or Equation 8.2b in continuous time can be visualized as shown in Figure 8.2. The stochastic present value is a random variable with a probability density function (PDF) that depends on the risk–return parameters of the underlying investment-generating process and the random future lifetime. The x-axis

FIGURE 8.2   SPV of Retirement Consumption

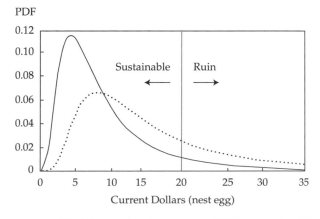

of Figure 8.2 is initial wealth, from which a person intends to consume $1 each year until death. For example, if one starts with an endowment of $20 and intends to consume $1 (after inflation) a year, the probability of sustainability is equal to the probability that the SPV is less than $20. This probability corresponds to the area under the curve to the left of the line at $20 on the x-axis. The probability of ruin is the area under the curve to the right of the $20 line. (Recall that the area under any curve on the graph totals 100 percent.) For any given case, a move to the left on the curve is equivalent to a decision to consume a higher proportion of wealth each year—because the individual is starting with a smaller nest egg and consuming one dollar—so, the probability that the plan is sustainable declines.

The precise shape and parameters governing the SPV depend on the investment and mortality dynamics, but the general picture is remarkably consistent and similar to Figure 8.2. The SPV is defined over positive numbers, is right skewed, and is equal to zero at zero.

The two distinct curves in Figure 8.2 denote different cases. The solid-line curve that has more of its area to the left of the $20 line represents a scenario with a lower risk of ruin or shortfall. The dotted-line curve is a higher-risk case. For example, the solid curve could be a woman age 65 and the dotted curve could be a woman age 50. For the same portfolio (size and asset allocation), the woman age 65 has a lower probability of shortfall for any given consumption level because she has a shorter remaining life span for that consumption. Or the two curves could represent different people at the same age consuming the same amount but with different asset allocations; the allocation for the solid curve provides the lower risk of failing to earn enough to sustain the desired consumption level. What we want to know is the actual shape of Figure 8.2.

The analytic contribution of this chapter is implementation of a closed-form expression for the SPV defined by Equation 8.2b under the assumption that the total investment return, R_t, is generated by a lognormal distribution—that is, an exponential Brownian motion. This classical assumption has many supporters—from Merton (1975) to Rubinstein (1991). But even from an empirical perspective, Levy and Duchin (2004) found that the lognormal assumption "won" many of the "horse races" when plausible distributions for historical returns were compared. Furthermore, many popular optimizers, many asset allocation models, and much oft-quoted common advice are based on the classical Markowitz–Sharpe assumptions of log-normal returns. Therefore, for the remainder of this chapter, we follow this tradition.[4]

ANALYTIC FORMULA FOR SUSTAINABLE SPENDING

Three important probability distributions allow us to derive a closed-form solution for sustainability. The first is the ubiquitous lognormal distribution, the second is the exponential lifetime distribution, and the last one is the—perhaps lesser-known—reciprocal gamma distribution. These three distributions merge together in the SPV. They allow us to solve the problem when investment return and date of death are risky or stochastic variables.

Lognormal Random Variable

The *investment total return*, R_t, between time t_0 and time t is said to be lognormally distributed with a mean of μ and standard deviation of σ if the expected total return is

$$E(R_t) = e^{\mu t}, \tag{8.3a}$$

the expected log return is

$$E[\ln(R_t)] = (\mu - 0.5\sigma^2)t, \tag{8.3b}$$

the log volatility is

$$E\{SD[\ln(R_t)]\} = \sigma\sqrt{t}, \tag{8.3c}$$

and the probability law can be written as

$$\text{prob}[\ln(R_t) < x] = N[(\mu - 0.5\sigma^2)t, \sigma\sqrt{t}, x], \tag{8.3d}$$

where $N(\cdot)$ denotes the cumulative normal distribution.

For example, a mutual fund or portfolio that is expected to earn an inflation-adjusted continuously compounded return of $\mu = 7$ percent a year with a logarithmic volatility of $\sigma = 20$ percent has a $N(0.05, 0.20, 0) = 40.13$ percent chance of earning a negative return in any given year. But if the expected return is a more optimistic 10 percent a year, the chances of losing money are reduced to $N(0.08, 0.20, 0) = 34.46$ percent. Note that the expected value of lognormal random variable R_t is $e^{\mu t}$ but the median value (that is, geometric mean) is a lower $e^{(\mu - 0.5\sigma^2)t}$. By definition, the probability that a lognormal random variable is less than its median value is precisely 50 percent. The gap between expected value $e^{\mu t}$ and median value $e^{(\mu - 0.5\sigma^2)t}$ is always greater than zero, proportional to the volatility, and increasing in time. We will return to the *mean versus median* distinction later.

Exponential Lifetime Random Variable

The *remaining lifetime* random variable denoted by the letter T is said to be exponentially distributed with mortality rate λ if the probability law for T can be written as

$$\text{prob}(T > s) = e^{-\lambda s}. \tag{8.4a}$$

The expected value of the exponential lifetime random variable is equal to and denoted by

$$E(T) = \frac{1}{\lambda}, \tag{8.4b}$$

whereas the median value—which is the 50 percent mark—can be computed from

$$\text{Median}(T) = \frac{\ln(2)}{\lambda}. \tag{8.4c}$$

Note that the expected value is greater than the median value. For example, when $\lambda = 0.05$, the probability of living for at least 25 more years is $e^{-(0.05)(25)} = 28.65$ percent and the probability of living for 40 more years is $e^{-(0.05)(40)} = 13.53$ percent. The expected *lifetime* is $1/0.05 = 20$ years, and the median lifetime is $\ln(2)/0.05 = 13.86$ years.

Although human aging does not conform to an exponential or constant force of mortality assumption—which means that death would occur at a constant rate—for the purposes of estimating a sustainable spending rate, it does a remarkably good job when properly calibrated.

Reciprocal Gamma Random Variable

A random variable denoted by X is the *reciprocal gamma* (RG) variable distributed with parameters α and β if the probability law for X can be written as

$$\text{prob}(X \in dx) = \frac{x^{-(\alpha+1)}e^{(-1/x\beta)}}{\Gamma(\alpha)\beta^\alpha}dx. \tag{8.5}$$

Equation 8.5, which is the probability density function of the RG distribution, has two degrees of freedom, or free parameters, and is defined over positive numbers. The two defining (α, β) parameters must be greater than 0 for the PDF to properly integrate to an area under the curve value of 1. In fact, the parameter α must be greater than 1 for the expectation to be defined and must be greater than 2 for the standard deviation to be defined.

The denominator of Equation 8.5 includes a gamma function, $\Gamma(\alpha)$, that is defined and can be computed recursively as

$$\Gamma(\alpha) = \Gamma(\alpha - 1)(\alpha - 1). \tag{8.6}$$

The expected (mean) value—that is, first moment—of the RG distribution is

$$E(X) = [\beta(\alpha - 1)]^{-1}, \tag{8.7a}$$

and the second moment is

$$E(X^2) = [\beta^2(\alpha - 1)(\alpha - 2)]^{-1}. \tag{8.7b}$$

For example, within the context of this chapter, a typical parameters pair would be $\alpha = 5$ and $\beta = 0.03$. In this case, the expected value of the RG variable would be $1/[(0.03)(4)] = 10$.

The structure of the RG random variable is such that the probability an RG random variable is *greater* than some number x is equivalent to the probability that a gamma random variable is *less* than $1/x$. This fact is important (and quite helpful) because the gamma random variable is available in all statistical packages.

MAIN RESULT: EXPONENTIAL RECIPROCAL GAMMA

Our primary claim is that if one is willing to assume lognormal returns in a continuous-time setting, the stochastic present value in Figure 8.2 is the reciprocal gamma distributed in the limit. In other words, the probability that the SPV is greater than the initial wealth or nest egg, denoted by w, is

$$\text{prob}[SPV > w] = \text{GammaDist}\left(\frac{2\mu + 4\lambda}{\sigma^2 + \lambda} - 1, \frac{\sigma^2 + \lambda}{2}\Big|\frac{1}{w}\right), \tag{8.8}$$

where GammaDist$(\alpha, \beta|\cdot)$ denotes the cumulative distribution function of the gamma distribution (in Microsoft Excel notation) evaluated at the parameter pair (α, β). The familiar μ and σ are the return and volatility parameters from the investment portfolio, and λ is the mortality rate. The expected value of the SPV is $(\mu - \sigma^2 + \lambda)^{-1}$.

For example, start with an investment (endowment, nest egg) of $20 that is expected to earn a 7 percent real return in any given year with a volatility (standard deviation) of 20 percent a year.[5] A 50-year-old (of any gender) with a median future life span of 28.1 years intends to consume $1 after inflation a year for the rest of his or her life. If the median life span is 28.1 years, then by definition, the probability of survival for 28.1 years is exactly 50 percent; so, the "implied mortality rate" parameter is $\lambda = \ln(2)/28.1 = 0.0247$. According to Equation 8.8, the probability of retirement ruin, which is the probability that the stochastic present value of $1 consumption is greater than $20, is 26.8 percent. In the language of Figure 8.2, if we evaluate the SPV at $w = 20$, the area to the right has a mass of 0.268 units. The area to the left—the probability of sustainability—has a mass of 0.732 units.[6]

In the random life span of $\lambda > 0$, our result is approximate, albeit correct to within two moments of the true SPV density. We will show that this issue is not significant. In the infinite horizon case of $\lambda = 0$, our result is *not an approximation*. It is a theorem that the SPV defined by Equation 8.2b is, in fact, the reciprocal gamma distributed.[7]

NUMERICAL EXAMPLES

Our base case is a newly retired 65-year-old who has a nest egg of $1,000,000 which must last for the remainder of this individual's life. In addition to pensions, the retiree wants $60,000 a year in real dollars from this nest egg (which is $6 per $100 in the terms commonly used in practice). The $60,000 is to be created via a systematic withdrawal plan that sells off the required number of shares/units each month in a reverse dollar-cost-average strategy. These numbers are prior to any income taxes, and our results are for pretax consumption needs; in addition, we are not distinguishing between tax-sheltered and taxable plans, which is a different important issue.

The retiree wants to know whether the stochastic present value of the desired $60,000 income a year is *probabilistically less* than the initial nest egg of $1,000,000. If it is, the retiree's standard of living is sustainable. If the SPV of the consumption plan is larger than $1,000,000, however, the retirement plan is unsustainable and the individual will be "ruined" at some point, unless of course, he or she reduces consumption.

Table 8.2 provides an extensive combination of consumption/withdrawal rates for various ages based on our model in Equation 8.8 and based on exact mortality rates instead of the exponential approximation. The rates assume an all-equity portfolio with expected return of 7 percent and volatility of 20 percent. The time variable is determined by the first columns in Table 8.2—retirement age, the median age at death (based on actuarial mortality tables), and the implied hazard rate, λ, from this median value. The entries show the risk of ruin for annual spending rates ranging from $2 to $10 per $100 initial nest egg.

The first rows of Table 8.2 are for an endowment or foundation with an infinite horizon. The "exact" probability of ruin is derived directly from Equation 8.2b and ranges from a low of 15 percent ($2 spending) to a high of 92 percent ($10 spending).[8] According to Table 8.2, if the example person retiring at age 65 invests the $1,000,000 nest egg in this all-equity portfolio and withdraws the desired $60,000 a year, the exact probability of ruin is 25.3 percent.

The approximate answer from an estimated reciprocal gamma (ERG) formula based on an exponential future lifetime is, at 26.2 percent probability of ruin, slightly higher than the exact outcome. The gap between these two percentages is only 0.9 percentage points, however, which boosts our confidence in the model in Equation 8.8. Indeed, the differences throughout Table 8.2 between the results from using the model's assumption of exponential mortality—calibrated to the true median life span—and those from using the exact mortality table are reasonably small and do not materially change the assessment of the retiree's position. Figure 8.3 illustrates for the base case with a range of consumption rates the approximation error from using the ERG formula when the "true" future lifetime random variable is more complicated.

For low consumption rates, the ERG formula slightly overestimates the probability of ruin and thus gives a more pessimistic picture. At higher consumption rates, the exact probability of ruin is higher than the approximation. Notice the relatively small gap between the two curves, which at its most is no more than 3–5 percent. The two curves are at their closest when the spending rate is between $5 and $7 per original $100.

TABLE 8.2 Reciprocal Gamma Approximation for Ruin Probability vs. Exact Results Using Correct Mortality Table

Retirement Age	Median Age at Death	Hazard Rate, λ		Real Annual Spending per $100 of Nest Egg								
				$2.0	$3.0	$4.0	$5.0	$6.0	$7.0	$8.0	$9.0	$10.0
NA	Infinity	0.00%	Approx.:	15.1%	30.0%	45.1%	58.4%	69.4%	77.9%	84.4%	89.1%	92.5%
			Exact.:	15.1	30.0	45.1	58.4	69.4	77.9	84.4	89.1	92.5
			Diff.:	0.0	0.0	0.0	0.0	0.0	0.0	0.0	0.0	0.0
50	78.1	2.47	Approx.:	4.27	10.27	18.0	26.8	35.8	44.6	52.8	60.3	66.9
			Exact.:	3.04	9.10	17.8	27.7	37.8	47.2	55.5	62.6	68.5
			Diff.:	1.2	1.2	0.3	-0.9	-2.0	-2.6	-2.7	-2.3	-1.6
55	83.0	2.48	Approx.:	4.26	10.23	18.0	26.7	35.7	44.5	52.7	60.2	66.8
			Exact.:	2.83	8.95	18.0	28.7	39.6	49.9	59.0	66.7	73.0
			Diff.:	1.4	1.3	0.0	-2.0	-3.9	-5.4	-6.3	-6.5	-6.3
60	83.4	2.96	Approx.:	3.48	8.54	15.3	23.1	31.4	39.7	47.6	55.0	61.7
			Exact.:	1.82	6.36	13.7	22.9	32.9	42.7	51.7	59.6	66.4
			Diff.:	1.7	2.2	1.6	0.2	-1.5	-3.0	-4.1	-4.6	-4.6
65	83.9	3.67	Approx.:	2.64	6.68	12.27	18.9	26.2	33.7	41.1	48.3	54.9
			Exact.:	1.02	4.03	9.43	16.8	25.3	34.1	42.7	50.5	57.4
			Diff.:	1.6	2.7	2.8	2.1	0.9	-0.4	-1.5	-2.2	-2.5
70	84.6	4.75	Approx.:	1.61	4.73	8.95	14.2	20.1	26.5	33.0	39.5	45.8
			Exact.:	0.48	2.20	5.71	11.0	17.6	24.9	32.4	39.6	46.4
			Diff.:	1.3	2.5	3.2	3.2	2.6	1.6	0.6	-0.1	-0.6
75	85.7	6.48	Approx.:	1.07	2.90	5.69	9.32	13.6	18.5	23.6	29.0	34.4
			Exact.:	0.18	0.98	2.89	6.10	10.5	15.8	21.7	27.7	33.7
			Diff.:	0.9	1.9	2.8	3.2	3.1	2.6	1.9	1.2	0.7
80	87.4	9.37	Approx.:	0.52	1.47	3.00	5.10	7.71	10.8	14.2	18.0	21.9
			Exact.:	0.05	0.34	1.16	2.76	5.20	8.43	12.3	16.6	21.1
			Diff.:	0.5	1.1	1.8	2.3	2.5	2.3	1.9	1.4	0.8

NA = not applicable.

Notes: Mean arithmetic portfolio return = 7 percent; standard deviation of return = 20 percent; mean geometric portfolio return = 5 percent. Differences may not be exact because of rounding.

FIGURE 8.3   Approximation vs. Exact Probability That Given Spending Rate Is Not Sustainable

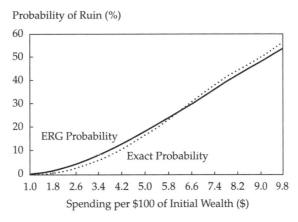

Note: Age = 65; mean arithmetic portfolio return = 7 percent; standard deviation of return = 20 percent.

Regardless of whether one uses the exact or the approximate methodology, a 25 percent chance of retirement ruin is unacceptable to most retirees. Table 8.2 indicates, however, that lowering the desired consumption or spending plan by $10,000 to a $50,000 systematic withdrawal plan can reduce the probability of ruin to 16.8 percent (in the exact method) or 18.9 percent (in the approximation). And if the spending plan is further reduced to $40,000, the probability of ruin shrinks to 9.4 percent (exact) and 12.3 percent (approximate). If the same individual were to withdraw $90,000, the probability of ruin would be 50.5 percent (exact) or 48.3 percent (approximate). The retiree or the financial planner can determine whether these odds are acceptable vis-à-vis the retiree's tolerance for risk.

To understand the intuition behind the numbers, recall that the mean or expected value of the SPV of $1 of real spending is $1/(\mu - \sigma^2 + \lambda)$, where μ and σ are the investment parameters and λ is the mortality rate parameter induced by a given median remaining lifetime. For a 65-year-old of either sex, the median remaining lifetime is 18.9 years (83.9 median age of death in Table 8.2 minus actual age of 65) according to the RP-2000 Society of Actuaries mortality table. To obtain the 50 percent probability point with an exponential distribution, we solve for $e^{-18.9\lambda} = 0.5$, which leads to $\lambda = \ln(2)/18.9 = 0.0367$ as the implied rate of mortality. The mean value of the SPV for $\mu = 7$ percent and $\sigma = 20$ percent works out to $1/(0.07 - 0.04 + 0.0367)$, which is an average of $15 for the SPV per dollar of desired consumption. Thus, if the retiree intends to spend $90,000 a year, it should come as no surprise that a nest egg of only 11 times this amount is barely sustainable on average. Note that the expected value of the SPV decreases in μ and λ and increases in σ. Higher mean is good, higher volatility is bad, and the benefit of a higher mortality rate comes from reducing the length of time over which the withdrawals are taken.

EFFECTS OF INVESTMENT STRATEGIES

We are not entering the debate about what are the "right" values for return expectations because our work makes no contribution to answering that important but contentious question. But we can use our model to show the effect of various portfolio composition and return assumptions. The portfolio in Table 8.2 is an all-equity portfolio with mean return of 7 percent and volatility of 20 percent. As expected, if the mean return is higher or the volatility lower, with all else held constant, the sustainability improves, and vice versa. What happens, however, if we change both parameters in the same direction, which is what we normally expect in an efficient financial market?

Consider a common portfolio that is 50 percent equity and 50 percent bonds, which we will say has a mean arithmetic return of 5 percent and volatility of 12 percent. Table 8.3 shows the probabilities of unsustainable spending for various ages and spending rates per $100 of nest egg for such a balanced portfolio.

Consider first the base case of a newly retired 65-year-old who has a nest egg of $1,000,000, from which the retiree wants $60,000 a year. In this case, Table 8.3 shows that the risk of ruin is a bit lower, at 24 percent, than it was for the all-equity portfolio but not much lower. Most retirees would be unhappy with that chance. Again, cutting consumption lowers the probability of ruin; a reduction to $40,000 would lower the chance of ruin to a more acceptable 9 percent. If the person waits until age 70 to retire and wants to withdraw $60,000 a year as planned, the risk of ruin drops to 17.6 percent.

In general, for cases that are toward the lower left of Tables 8.2 and 8.3, the probability of ruin falls somewhat with a lower-risk/lower-return portfolio. In contrast, for cases that are toward the upper right of the tables, the risk of ruin is higher with a lower-risk/lower-return portfolio. The reason for these opposing effects lies in the nature of the consumption pattern. If a retiree wants a lot of income from a portfolio, relative to the size of the portfolio and/or relative to his or her expected remaining lifetime, then the risk of shortfall can be reduced only by gambling on a high-risk/high-return portfolio. Changing to a high-risk/high-return portfolio does not give the retiree a satisfactory reduction in the risk of ruin, however, because the values in the upper right of Table 8.2 are all unacceptably high from any point of view. If the retiree will settle for a more reasonable level of consumption—say, no more than $6 per $100 at age 65—the more balanced portfolio also reduces the risk of ruin. (Note that for Table 8.3, we reduced volatility by 8 percent but return by only 2 percent. Changes in return have more effect than changes in volatility.)

This message is particularly unsettling for endowments that are required to pay out in perpetuity. Their payout rates are almost always in the range of 4–6 percent of principal. But the odds of maintaining the real value of that payout are poor for either a balanced or an all-equity portfolio, with the probability of ruin ranging from 45 percent to 84 percent, depending on the payout and the asset allocation. An endowment can always maintain a payout of some percentage of the market value of assets in perpetuity, but our results are saying that the *real value* of whatever is paid out will probably have to be reduced, thus providing less and less real value for student scholarships, research projects, or whatever is funded by the endowment. Lest the reader think this judgment is simply a case of unreasonably pessimistic investment return assumptions, consider the following. Even with a long-run real return expected to be 9 percent with a standard deviation of 16 percent—a remarkable performance if anyone could maintain it over the long run—the risk of ruin for a perpetual endowment is 9.5 percent for a perpetual payout of real $4 per $100 of principal today. The risk of ruin rises to 19.6 percent if the payout is $5 and to 32.4 percent if the payout is $6.

In Table 8.4, we pose the question of which action helps the base-case 65-year-old more—reducing consumption or changing the investment portfolio. The "Portfolio" column headings consist of possible combinations of mean and volatility to represent various investment strategies; they range from low risk and low return to high risk and high return. Down the side is consumption per $100 of nest egg. At every level of consumption, Table 8.4 shows

TABLE 8.3   Ruin Probability Approximation for Balanced Portfolio of 50 Percent Equity and 50 Percent Bonds

Retirement Age	Median Age at Death	Hazard Rate, λ	Real Annual Spending per $100 of Initial Nest Egg									
			$2.00	$3.00	$4.00	$5.00	$6.00	$7.00	$8.00	$9.00	$10.00
Endowment	Infinity	0.00%	6.7%	24.9%	49.0%	70.0%	84.3%	92.5%	96.6%	98.6%	99.4%
50	78.1	2.47	1.8	6.4	14.0	24.0	35.2	46.3	56.8	66.0	73.8
55	83.0	2.48	1.8	6.3	14.0	24.0	35.1	46.2	56.7	65.9	73.7
60	83.4	2.96	1.5	5.2	11.6	20.1	29.9	40.1	50.0	59.1	67.2
65	83.9	3.67	1.1	4.0	9.0	15.8	24.0	32.8	41.8	50.5	58.5
70	84.6	4.75	0.8	2.8	6.3	11.4	17.6	24.7	32.2	39.8	47.2
75	85.7	6.48	0.5	1.7	3.9	7.2	11.4	16.3	21.9	27.8	33.9
80	87.4	9.37	0.3	0.9	2.0	3.8	6.2	9.1	12.5	16.3	20.5

Note: Mean arithmetic portfolio return = 5 percent; standard deviation of return = 12 percent; mean geometric portfolio return = 4.28 percent.

163

TABLE 8.4   Probability of Ruin for Various Portfolios at Age 65

Consumption per $100 of Nest Egg	Portfolio: Mean Arithmetic Return and [Volatility]				
	4% [10%]	5% [12%]	6% [15%]	7% [17%]	8% [20%]
$2.00	1.5%	1.1%	1.3%	1.2%	1.6%
$3.00	5.0	4.0	4.1	3.8	4.5
$4.00	11.1	9.0	8.8	8.0	8.8
$5.00	19.1	15.8	15.1	13.7	14.4
$6.00	28.4	24.0	22.5	20.4	20.8
$7.00	38.2	32.8	30.6	27.7	27.6
$8.00	47.8	41.8	38.8	35.3	34.7

that the choice of investment portfolio does not matter much. At levels of $2 or $3 per $100, any portfolio gives a low probability of ruin. At $4 per $100, the individual's tolerance for risk could begin to affect the portfolio choice. Once the consumption rises to $5 per $100, the probabilities of ruin would be unacceptable to most retirees. No matter what reasonable portfolio is chosen, asset allocation will not turn a bad situation into a good one.

Another interesting insight comes from examining the interplay between the three main parameters in our formula. Increasing the fixed mortality rate, λ, by 100 bps—which reduces the median future lifetime from $\ln(2)/\lambda$ to $\ln(2)/(\lambda + 0.01)$—obviously reduces the probability of retirement ruin, all else being equal. The same reduction can also be achieved by increasing the portfolio return by 200 bps together with increasing the portfolio variance by 100 bps. Recall that the (α, β) parameter arguments in Equation 8.8 can be expressed as a function of $(\mu + 2\lambda)$ and $(\sigma^2 + \lambda)$. Thus, having a longer life span is interchangeable with decreasing the portfolio return or increasing portfolio variance.

Another perspective on the issue can be gained by fixing a "ruin tolerance" level and then inverting Equation 8.8 to solve for the level of spending that satisfies the given probability. Leibowitz and Henriksson (1989) advanced this idea within the context of a static portfolio asset allocation. Browne (1995, 1999) and then Young (2004) solved the dynamic versions of this portfolio control problem for a finite and a random time horizon, respectively. The inversion process is relatively easy because a number of software packages have a built-in function for the inverse of the gamma function in which the argument is the probability rather than the spending rate.

Table 8.5 takes this inverted approach by solving for the sustainable spending rate that results in a given probability of ruin for the same set of possible portfolios used in Table 8.4. On the one hand, if a 65-year-old retiree is willing to assume or "live with" a ruin probability of only 5 percent (Panel B), which means that he desires a 95 percent chance of sustainability, the most he can consume from a balanced portfolio with mean return of 5 percent and volatility of 12 percent is $3.24 per initial nest egg of $100. On the other hand, if he is willing to tolerate a 10 percent chance of ruin (Panel A), the maximum consumption level increases from $3.24 to $4.17 per $100. The higher the ruin-tolerance level, the more he can consume.[9] An increase in return or a decrease in volatility always raises sustainable consumption, but if risk and return tend to move together in the long run, as is generally observed in practice, changes in asset allocation will not have a major effect.

TABLE 8.5   Sustainable Spending Rate That Results in a Given Probability of Ruin for Various Portfolios at Different Retirement Ages

		Portfolio: Arithmetic Return, [Volatility], and (Geometric Return)					
Current Age	Hazard Rate	3.00% [10.00%] (2.50%)	4.00% [10.00%] (3.50%)	5.00% [12.00%] (4.28%)	6.00% [15.00%] (4.88%)	7.00% [17.00%] (5.56%)	8.00% [20.00%] (6.00%)
A. Probability of ruin 10%							
Endowment	0.00%	$1.22	$1.95	$2.24	$2.22	$2.37	$2.20
50	2.47	2.54	3.20	3.52	3.55	3.72	3.56
55	2.48	2.55	3.21	3.52	3.55	3.72	3.57
60	2.96	2.81	3.47	3.79	3.82	3.99	3.84
65	3.67	3.20	3.85	4.17	4.20	4.38	4.23
70	4.75	3.79	4.44	4.75	4.80	4.97	4.82
75	6.48	4.74	5.38	5.70	5.75	5.92	5.77
80	9.37	6.33	6.96	7.28	7.33	7.51	7.37
B. Probability of ruin 5%							
Endowment	0.00%	$0.99	$1.64	$1.86	$1.76	$1.84	$1.64
50	2.47	1.95	2.52	2.77	2.73	2.84	2.64
55	2.48	1.96	2.53	2.77	2.74	2.84	2.65
60	2.96	2.15	2.72	2.96	2.93	3.04	2.85
65	3.67	2.44	3.00	3.24	3.22	3.32	3.13
70	4.75	2.88	3.43	3.67	3.66	3.76	3.58
75	6.48	3.58	4.12	4.37	4.36	4.47	4.28
80	9.37%	4.76	5.29	5.54	5.53	5.65	5.46

CONCLUSION AND NEXT STEPS

Our analysis using the stochastic present value provides an analytic method for assessing the sustainability of retirement plans and offers new insights into, in particular, retirement longevity risk.

The distinction between Monte Carlo simulations and the analytical techniques promoted in this chapter is more than simply a question of academic tastes.[10] Although simulations will continue to have a legitimate and important role in the field of wealth management, our simple formula can serve as a test and calibration tool for more complex simulation. It can also explain the link between the three fundamental variables affecting retirement planning: spending rates, uncertain longevity, and uncertain returns. The formula makes clear that increasing the mortality hazard rate—which is equivalent to aging—while holding the probability of ruin constant has the same effect as increasing the portfolio rate of return and decreasing the portfolio volatility. An implication is that females, who are expected to live three to five years longer than males, on average, and thus have a lower rate of death at any given age, should be spending less in order to maintain the same (low) probability of ruin that males need.

Even with the most tolerant attitude toward the risk of ruin, a retiree should be spending no more than, with the notation used in this chapter, $(\mu - \sigma^2 + \lambda)$ percent of the initial nest egg, where λ is $\ln(2)$ divided by the median future lifetime. This spending rate should be sustainable, on average, because the expected value of $1 consumption for life is $(\mu - \sigma^2 + \lambda)^{-1}$.

Here is another way to think about average sustainability. Note that $\mu - \sigma^2$ is even lower than the (continuously compounded) geometric mean $\mu - 0.5\sigma^2$. If the arithmetic mean return is 7 percent, then the geometric mean return is $\mu - 0.5\sigma^2 = 5$ percent and the quantity $\mu - \sigma^2 = 3$ percent, for $\sigma = 20$ percent volatility. Thus, a retiree who is satisfied with average sustainability can plan to spend only 3 percent plus an additional 0.693 divided by her or his median remaining lifetime. A median of 10 more retirement years can add 6.9 percentage points to spending; a median of 20 and 30 more retirement years adds, respectively, 3.5 percentage points and 2.3 percentage points. For an endowment or foundation, $\lambda = 0$ and, therefore, average sustainability can be achieved only by spending no more than 3 percent of contributed capital. Of course, if the assumed 20 percent volatility can be reduced by further diversification, these static spending rates can obviously be increased. But then again, using a higher volatility might be a prudent hedge against model misspecification—specifically, the "jump and crash" risk that is not adequately captured in a lognormal distribution.

We want to stress that we are not advocating ruin minimization as a normative investment strategy. Notwithstanding its inconsistency with rational utility maximization, Browne (1999) and Young have both documented the uncomfortably high degrees of leverage such a dynamic policy might entail. Rather, we believe that the probability of retirement ruin is a useful risk metric that can help retirees understand the link between their desired spending patterns, retirement age, and the current composition of their investment portfolios.

Indeed, the concept of a stochastic present value of a retirement plan can be used beyond the limited scope of computing probabilities of ruin. For example, one can use this idea to investigate the impact of including payout annuities or nonlinear instruments in a retiree's (or endowment's) portfolio. Similarly, the SPV can be used to compare the relative tax efficiency of various asset location decisions for retirement income products and the role of life annuities in increasing the sustainability of a given spending rate. For example, we have found that including zero-cost collars in the retiree's portfolio (i.e., selling out-of-the-money calls whose funds are then used to purchase out-of-the-money puts) shifts the SPV toward zero, which reduces the probability of ruin and increases the sustainability of the portfolio. In summary, we urge the financial industry to focus on designing products that maximize income sustainability over a random retirement horizon.

ACKNOWLEDGMENTS

We would like to thank Jin Wang and Anna Abaimova for research assistance and Tom Salisbury and Kwok Ho, with whom we had very helpful discussions during the development of this research.

NOTES

1. The National Association of College and University Business Officers endowment survey conducted in 2004 showed that the median endowment spending rate in 2003 was 5.0 percent of assets, with the 10th percentile being 4.0 percent and the 90th percentile being 6.4 percent.

2. Using several free Web-based simulators, we ran some case studies and found wide variations in the suggested "nest egg" needed to support a comfortable retirement. A similar concern about the variation in simulation outcomes—which was misinterpreted as a criticism of the Monte Carlo method—was echoed recently by McCarthy (2002/2003).

3. The spreadsheet is available by selecting this chapter from the November/December contents page on the *FAJ* website at www.cfapubs.org.

4. We provide an analysis of the effect of this assumption in an online technical appendix.

5. We discuss the question of reasonable return distribution assumptions later.

6. The more technically inclined readers might want more than simply a formula. A proof that Equation 8.8 is the proper distribution of the stochastic present value is based on moment-matching techniques and the partial differential equations for the probability of ruin based on Equation 8.2b. We believe that a variant of this result can be traced back to Merton. For more details, proofs, and restrictions, see Milevsky (1997), Browne (1999), or Milevsky (forthcoming 2006)—specifically, the actuarial, financial, and insurance references contained in this last article.

7. For those readers who remain unconvinced that what is effectively the "sum of lognormals" can converge to the inverse of a gamma distribution, we suggest they simulate the SPV for a reasonably long horizon and conduct a Kolmogorov–Smirnov goodness-of-fit test of the inverse of these numbers against the gamma distribution with the parameters given by $\alpha = (2\mu + 4\lambda)/(\sigma^2 + \lambda) - 1$ and $\beta = (\sigma^2 + \lambda)/2$. As long as the volatility parameter, σ, is not abnormally high relative to the expected return, μ, they will get convergence of the relevant integrand.

8. By "exact" probability of ruin, we mean the outcome from using a complete actuarial mortality table starting at age 65 to discount all future cash flows rather than using the exponential lifetime approximation. See Huang, Milevsky, and Wang (2004) for more details about the accuracy of such an approximation based on partial differential equation (PDE) methods.

9. A variant of this "probabilistic spending" rule was designed by one of the authors and was recently implemented by the Florida State Board of Administration for its billion-dollar Lawton Chiles Endowment Fund. Each year, the trustees of the fund compute the probability of preserving its real value and then adjust spending up or down accordingly. See www.sbafla.com/pdf/funds/LCEF_TFIP_2003_02_25.pdf for more information.

10. For example, Whitehouse (2004) described the benefits of analytic PDE-based solutions over Monte Carlo simulations.

REFERENCES

Altschuler, G. 2000. "Endowment Payout Rates Are Too Stingy." *Chronicle of Higher Education* (31 March):B8.

Ameriks, J., M. Veres, and M. Warshawsky. 2001. "Making Retirement Income Last a Lifetime." *Journal of Financial Planning* (December):60–76.

Arnott, R.D. 2004. "Editor's Corner: Sustainable Spending in a Lower-Return World." *Financial Analysts Journal,* vol. 60, no. 5 (September/October):6–9.

Bengen, W.P. 1994. "Determining Withdrawal Rates Using Historical Data." *Journal of Financial Planning*, vol. 7, no. 4 (October):171–181.

Browne, S. 1995. "Optimal Investment Policies for a Firm with a Random Risk Process: Exponential Utility and Minimizing the Probability of Ruin." *Mathematics of Operations Research*, vol. 20, no. 4 (November):937–958.

————. 1999. "The Risk and Reward of Minimizing Shortfall Probability." *Journal of Portfolio Management*, vol. 25, no. 4 (Summer):76–85.

Cooley, P.L., C.M. Hubbard, and D.T. Walz. 1998. "Retirement Spending: Choosing a Withdrawal Rate That Is Sustainable." *Journal of the American Association of Individual Investors*, vol. 20, no. 1 (February):39–47.

————. 2003. "Does International Diversification Increase the Sustainable Withdrawal Rates from Retirement Portfolios?" *Journal of Financial Planning* (January):74–80.

Dybvig, P.H. 1999. "Using Asset Allocation to Protect Spending." *Financial Analysts Journal*, vol. 55, no. 1 (January/ February):49–62.

Ennis, R.M., and J.P. Williamson. 1976. "Spending Policy for Educational Endowment." Research Publication Project of the Common Fund.

Guyton, J.T. 2004. "Decision Rules and Portfolio Management for Retirees: Is the 'Safe' Initial Withdrawal Rate Too Safe?" *Journal of Financial Planning* (October):50–60.

Hannon, D., and D. Hammond. 2003. "The Looming Crisis in Endowment Spending." *Journal of Investing*, vol. 12, no. 3 (Fall):9–20.

Ho, K., M. Milevsky, and C. Robinson. 1994. "How to Avoid Outliving Your Money." *Canadian Investment Review*, vol. 7, no. 3 (Fall):35–38.

Huang, H., M.A. Milevsky, and J. Wang. 2004. "Ruined Moments in Your Life: How Good Are the Approximations?" *Insurance: Mathematics and Economics*, vol. 34, no. 3 (June):421–447.

Ibbotson Associates. 2004. *Stocks, Bonds, Bills and Inflation: 2004 Yearbook*. Chicago, IL: Ibbotson Associates.

Leibowitz, M.L., and R.D. Henriksson. 1989. "Portfolio Optimization with Shortfall Constraints: A Confidence-Limit Approach to Managing Downside Risk." *Financial Analysts Journal*, vol. 45, no. 2 (March/April):34–41.

Levy, H., and R. Duchin. 2004. "Asset Return Distributions and the Investment Horizon." *Journal of Portfolio Management*, vol. 30, no. 3 (Spring):47–62.

Markowitz, H.M. 1991. "Individual versus Institutional Investing."*Financial Services Review*, vol. 1, no. 1:1–8.

McCarthy, Ed. 2002/2003."Puzzling Predictions." *Bloomberg Wealth Manager* (December/ January):39–54.

Merton, R. 1975. "An Asymptotic Theory of Growth under Uncertainty." *Review of Economic Studies*, vol. 42, no. 3:375–393. Reprinted in 1992 as Chapter 17 in *Continuous-Time Finance*, revised edition, Blackwell Press.

Milevsky, M.A. 1997. "The Present Value of a Stochastic Perpetuity and the Gamma Distribution." *Insurance: Mathematics and Economics*, vol. 20, no. 3:243–250.

————. Forthcoming 2006. *The Calculus of Retirement Income: Financial Models for Pensions and Insurance*. Cambridge University Press.

Pye, G. 2000. "Sustainable Investment Withdrawals." *Journal of Portfolio Management*, vol. 26, no. 3 (Summer):13–27.

Rubinstein, M. 1991. "Continuously Rebalanced Investment Strategies." *Journal of Portfolio Management*, vol. 18, no. 1 (Fall):78–81.

Tobin, J. 1974. "What Is Permanent Endowment Income?" *American Economic Review*, vol. 64, no. 2:427–432.

Whitehouse, Kaja. 2004. "Tool Tells How Long Nest Egg Will Last." *Wall Street Journal* (31 August):2.

Young, V.R. 2004. "Optimal Investment Strategy to Minimize the Probability of Lifetime Ruin." *North American Actuarial Journal*, vol. 8, no. 4:106–126.

CHAPTER 9

ASSET ALLOCATION WITHOUT UNOBSERVABLE PARAMETERS

Michael Stutzer

Some asset allocation advice for long-term investors is based on maximization of expected utility. Most commonly used investor utilities require measurement of a risk-aversion parameter appropriate to the particular investor. But accurate assessment of this parameter is problematic at best. Maximization of expected utility is thus not only conceptually difficult for clients to understand but also difficult to implement. Other asset allocation advice is based on minimizing the probability of falling short of a particular investor's long-term return target or of an investable benchmark. This approach is easier to explain and implement, but it has been criticized by advocates of expected utility. These seemingly disparate criteria can be reconciled by measuring portfolio returns relative to the target (or benchmark) and then eliminating the usual assumption that the utility's risk-aversion parameter is not also determined by maximization of expected utility. Financial advisors should not be persuaded by advocates of the usual expected-utility approach.

Advice about desirable quantitative asset allocations for long-term investors is abundant. The quantitative route to investor-specific advice requires the following three steps:

1. The advisor chooses a criterion function to optimize, which depends on some investor-specific information (e.g., attitude toward risk).
2. Historical time series of asset returns are used in computer optimization algorithms to estimate optimized portfolio asset allocations—one allocation for each possible set of investor-specific information.
3. Investor input is used to obtain the investor's specific portfolio asset allocation.

Reprinted from the *Financial Analysts Journal* (September/October 2004):38–51.

For example, for a financial advisor who relies on modern portfolio theory (MPT), the first step is to choose the mean–variance criterion function, $\mu - \gamma\sigma^2$, where μ denotes the mean, σ^2 denotes the variance of a portfolio's return distribution, and γ is a parameter that is intended to measure the investor's aversion to high variance of returns (which the theory assumes to be the appropriate measure of investor risk). In the second step, historical time series of asset returns supply the values of μ and σ^2, which the advisor then uses in an optimization algorithm to estimate portfolio asset allocations along the mean–variance-efficient frontier. Finally, the advisor must specify a value of risk-aversion parameter γ, which is required to recommend a specific efficient portfolio asset allocation. Investor input is used to determine the appropriate value of γ.

Although quantitative financial software can provide scientifically valid assistance with Steps 1 and 2, computer software for a similarly valid implementation of Step 3 is hard to locate. For example, Siegel (2002) produced a 200-year time series of real (i.e., inflation-adjusted) asset returns to estimate mean–variance-efficient frontiers at various possible investor horizons and provided a table listing the recommended stock allocations associated with four values of γ. He categorized the risk tolerance associated with these four values as "ultraconservative," "conservative," "moderate," and "risk taking." This approach is commonly used to implement Steps 1 and 2 of the asset allocation advice process. But Siegel was silent about the critical Step 3. How is an advisor to determine the exact value of γ suitable for a particular investor? An *ad hoc* assignment of specific ranges of γ to the four risk-tolerance categories does not solve the problem of assigning a particular investor to one of those categories.

Moreover, it is by no means obvious that the mean–variance criterion is always the appropriate way to implement Step 1. Siegel wrote:

> The focus of every long-term investor should be the growth of purchasing power— monetary wealth adjusted for the effect of inflation. (p. 11)

But remember that the growth rate of purchasing power—that is, inflation-adjusted, *real* wealth—is a random variable. If the long-term investor's sole focus is the maximum extremely long term (i.e., only asymptotically realized) growth rate of real wealth, Step 1 of the process should specify the expected growth rate of wealth as the criterion rather than Siegel's mean–variance criterion. The excellent survey by Hakansson and Ziemba (1995) noted that the expected-growth-rate-of-wealth criterion is equivalent to the expected-log-utility criterion and has been advocated by many as a suitable criterion for long-term asset allocation (e.g., Thorp 1975). Moreover, if the investor has some concerns about higher-order moments of the growth rate of real wealth, the criterion chosen in Step 1 could be the expected constant relative risk-aversion (CRRA) utility of wealth at the end of the investor's horizon (see Equation 9.2 or the maximization expression in Problem 9.3 in the following section), which is probably the most widely used alternative utility function. The log utility is a special case of CRRA utility that is produced by a limiting lower value for its curvature parameter, γ. To illustrate this conventional method of asset allocation, I will later use Siegel's dataset to apply expected-CRRA-utility maximization to a simple but illustrative asset allocation problem.

Step 3 of the process still requires accurate assessment of a CRRA investor's risk-aversion parameter, however, which will determine what is conventionally defined to be the investor's *coefficient* or *degree* of relative risk aversion, $1 + \gamma$. Best practice for determining this parameter will be discussed later, and I will show that it is highly problematic.

Moreover, two thoughtful and esteemed leaders in the growing field of behavioral finance, Rabin and Thaler (2001), stated that any method to measure a coefficient of relative risk aversion is doomed to failure. They concluded:

> Indeed, the correct conclusion for economists to draw, both from thought experiments and from actual data, is that people do not display a consistent coefficient of relative risk aversion, so it is a waste of time to try to measure it. (p. 225)

Thus, another asset allocation criterion—one that does not require assessment of an individual's risk-aversion parameter—is examined, namely, minimizing the probability of falling short of an investor's expressly desired target return on real wealth. Olsen (1997) provided evidence that fund managers try to avoid falling short of their expressly stated benchmarks (a goal that may sometimes be forced on managers by those who hire them). For other investors, Olsen and Khaki (1998), citing Yates's (1992) behavioral findings, asserted:

> Much recent empirical evidence suggests that perceived risk is primarily a function of loss and the possibility of realizing a return below some target or aspiration level. (p. 58)

Reichenstein (1986) cited other behavioral research supporting this conception of risk. Shortfall (or its complement, outperformance) probability has also been incorporated into quantitative asset allocation models (e.g., Leibowitz and Henriksson 1989; Leibowitz and Langetieg 1989; Leibowitz, Bader, and Kogelman 1996; Browne 1999). In addition, it has been the basis for analyses of the extensively debated time diversification issue (Milevsky 1999).[1]

So, I will discuss implementing Step 1 of the process with target-shortfall-probability minimization (or target-outperformance-probability maximization). This criterion does not require assessment of an investor's risk-aversion parameter, but it does require identification of the investor's target return. Motivated by Siegel's advice to focus on the long-term growth of real wealth, I will illustrate specifically how to use shortfall minimization to implement the three-step asset allocation process. I will then reconcile the seemingly disparate asset allocation criteria of expected CRRA utility and minimizing (maximizing) the probability of falling short of (exceeding) an investor's target or benchmark. Finally, I will reexamine the criticisms of other uses of shortfall probability lodged by influential advocates of expected utility and argue that these criticisms do not apply to the target-shortfall-probability criterion I describe.[2]

CONVENTIONAL USE OF CRRA UTILITY

The criterion function chosen in Step 1 of this asset allocation process is maximization of the expected CRRA utility of end-of-holding-period inflation-adjusted wealth. To motivate the computer optimization algorithm used in Step 2 of the process, a short mathematical study of the problem is required.[3] Let $R_{p,t}$ denote the gross real return (1 plus the net real return) from holding a portfolio with a vector of asset allocation (value-weighted) proportions or weights denoted by p_t between periods $t-1$ and t. The real market value of the portfolio at the end of H periods is the real invested wealth, W_H:

$$W_H = W_0 \prod_{t=1}^{H} R_{p,t}. \tag{9.1}$$

The expected CRRA utility of wealth at the end of H periods, $E[U(W_H)]$, is:

$$
\begin{aligned}
E[U(W_H)] &= E\left[U\left(W_0\prod_{t=1}^{H}R_{p,t}\right)\right] \\
&= E\left[-\left(W_0\prod_{t=1}^{H}R_{p,t}\right)^{-\gamma}\right] \\
&= -(W_0)^{-\gamma}E\left[\left(\prod_{t=1}^{H}R_{p,t}\right)^{-\gamma}\right],
\end{aligned}
\tag{9.2}
$$

where γ is the investor's risk-aversion parameter, which determines the investor's constant coefficient of relative risk aversion, and W_0 is the investor's initial wealth.

Now consider the problem of choosing possibly-time-varying portfolio asset allocation weight vectors, $p_1, p_2, \ldots, p_H$, to maximize Equation 9.2. Inspection of Equation 9.2 immediately shows that the solution will *not* depend on the investor's initial wealth, W_0, because the variable part of Equation 9.2 is premultiplied by the same constant, W_0. Accordingly, we can set $W_0 = 1$ without loss of generality.

To proceed, we must make assumptions about the nature of the joint returns of the assets used to form the portfolio returns. The simplest asset allocation problem, which I use as the basis for both the (strictly illustrative) quantitative example in this chapter and the common advice to keep portfolios rebalanced to constant allocation weights, arises when the joint assets' return process is independently and identically distributed (IID) across time. When returns are IID, the problem of maximizing Equation 9.2 by choosing possibly-time-varying allocation weight vectors reduces to the problem of choosing a single weight vector to maximize the following single-period expected CRRA utility:[4]

$$
\max_{p} E(-R_p^{-\gamma}).
\tag{9.3}
$$

In summary, the possibly-time-varying asset allocation weights that maximize the expected CRRA utility of real wealth at the end of the holding period (Equation 9.2) will not depend on the investor's initial wealth. When the assets' joint returns are IID across time, Equation 9.2 will be maximized by initially choosing a vector of value-weighted optimal-asset-allocation proportions or weights that maximizes the expression in Problem 9.3 and then *rebalancing the portfolio at the beginning of each subsequent period back to those initial weights*. The italics are to emphasize that simply buying and holding a fixed stock portfolio until the end of period H is not optimal; rather, each asset's *proportion* of total portfolio value must be kept fixed. Thus, some funds will always have to be moved from assets that have recently done relatively well to assets that have recently done relatively worse. One has to sell some assets "high" in order to buy some other assets "low."[5]

Because no one knows for certain what the exact asset return distribution is, Step 2 of the asset allocation process often proceeds by following Kroll, Levy, and Markowitz (1984) in using T past periods' historical returns to maximize the following historical-time-average estimator of Problem 9.3:

$$
\max_{p} \frac{1}{T}\sum_{t=1}^{T} - R_{pt}^{-\gamma}.
\tag{9.4}
$$

The output of Step 2 is an optimal set of portfolio asset allocations, one for each positive value of γ.

The third (and final) step of the asset allocation process attempts to obtain an accurate value for the investor's risk-aversion parameter, which will enable recommendation of a specific asset allocation for that investor. Later, I discuss a published questionnaire that has been used for this purpose and illustrate its implications for the simplest asset allocation problem, described here.

The simplest asset allocation problem is to recommend a fractional weight, p, to invest in a single risky asset (e.g., a domestic stock index) with the rest of the portfolio $(1 - p)$ invested at an *ex ante* constant real interest rate. Siegel argued that for U.S. investors, U.S. Treasury Inflation-Indexed Securities (commonly called TIPS) provide a vehicle for the "rest" of the assets and assumed (for simplicity in his Figure 2-7) that TIPS can be used to earn a constant real rate of 3.5 percent a year. To relate my results to his, I also adopt this assumption in the numerical examples. Strictly for pedagogical purposes, I also assume that the IID annual return process for the risky asset has the familiar binomial form frequently used in teaching: The stock index is as likely to go up, with a real gross total rate of return of $u > 1$ a year, as to go down, with a real gross total return of $d < 1$ a year.[6]

Siegel's 200-year historical time series of real stock returns has an (arithmetic) average annual real return of 8.27 percent (resulting in an inflation-adjusted equity premium of 8.27 percent -3.5 percent $= 4.77$ percent), with a standard deviation of 18.18 percent. For this illustration, I chose a value for u of 1.2645 and for d of 0.9009 to match the statistics of Siegel's data.[7] Therefore, the asset allocation problem (Problem 9.3) for this example is

$$\max_{p} \frac{1}{2}\{-[1.2645p + 1.035(1 - p)]^{-\gamma}\}$$
$$+ \frac{1}{2}\{-[0.9009p + 1.035(1 - p)]^{-\gamma}\}. \tag{9.5}$$

The γ-dependent solutions of Problem 9.5 for stock allocation weight p are presented in Table 9.1.

Without using the information that the stock return process is binomial, the previous argument was that Problem 9.3 can be used to produce Table 9.1. Substituting Siegel's 200 years of historical inflation-adjusted stock returns into Problem 9.4 and numerically maximizing produced results that are fairly close to the exact binomial-process results from Problem 9.5 shown in Table 9.1.

Table 9.1 indicates that the recommended stock allocation depends critically on a relatively precise estimate of the investor's risk aversion to determine the investor's coefficient of relative risk aversion, $1 + \gamma$. Increasing the degree of relative risk aversion from 2 to 4, for example, decreases the recommended stock allocation from 79 percent of portfolio value to 39 percent, with significant implications for the mean and standard deviation of the portfolio's

TABLE 9.1   Conventional CRRA-Utility Maximizing: Asset Allocation and Performance

CRRA $1 + \gamma$	Stock Weight, p	Mean Return	Standard Deviation
10	15%	4.2%	2.8%
8	19	4.4	3.5
6	26	4.7	4.7
4	39	5.1	6.2
3	52	6.0	9.5
2	79	7.3	14.3
1.5	106	8.5	19.2
1 (log utility)	160	11.1	29.1

real returns. Low values of $1 + \gamma$ lead to recommended stock allocations greater than 100 percent, which is predicated on the feasibility of investing all of the investor's wealth in stock and borrowing at the (assumed constant) TIPS real interest rate to invest more (or shorting TIPS) until the end of the holding period. Because this strategy is unlikely in practice, the focus from now on will be on stock allocation fractions below 100 percent.[8]

Table 9.1 also shows that the means of the expected-utility-maximizing portfolios' real returns are directly related to their volatilities, as would also be the case for mean–variance utility-maximizing portfolios in realistic problems with more than one risky asset.

The sensitivity of the asset allocation recommendation to seemingly small changes in curvature parameter γ underscores the need for Step 3 of the asset allocation process: The advisor must estimate an accurate value of γ appropriate for a particular investor. In the questionnaire intended to measure an individual's γ value that was devised by Barsky, Juster, Kimball, and Shapiro (1997), one of the key questions is as follows:

> Suppose that you are the only income earner in the family, and you have a good job guaranteed to give you your current (family) income every year for life. You are given the opportunity to take a new and equally good job, with a 50–50 chance it will double your (family) income, and a 50–50 chance that it will cut your (family) income by a third. Would you take the new job? (p. 540)

A respondent's answers to this and similar questions, in conjunction with calculations involving expected utility (Problem 9.3), permit the questioner to estimate an interval containing the respondent's coefficient of relative risk aversion. For example, a respondent who answers "no" to the quoted question and another that substitutes "20 percent" for "a third" have a value of $1 + \gamma$ that exceeds 3.76 (Barsky et al., Table I). Barsky et al. polled more than 11,000 respondents between the ages of 51 and 61. About two out of every three respondents answered "no" to the question (Barsky et al., Table IIA); the authors estimated that the average respondent had a coefficient of relative risk aversion close to 12 (Table XI).

Hanna, Gutter, and Fan (2001) made slight modifications to the questions, to make them more appropriate to long-run (i.e., retirement) investment planning, and gave a Web-based questionnaire to 390 younger respondents. The authors still found that more than two out of three respondents had a coefficient of relative risk aversion above 3.76; their average respondent had a coefficient value close to 8.

From Table 9.1, these experimental estimates indicate that better than two out of every three investors should not allocate more than 39 percent of portfolio wealth to stocks, with the rest allocated to TIPS.[9]

SHORTFALL-PROBABILITY MINIMIZATION

An investor who wants to earn an inflation-adjusted return of at least 4.5 percent a year, which is only 100 bps higher than the TIPS return assumed in the example, would probably prefer a substantially higher stock allocation than 39 percent. To see why, suppose Figure 9.1 is shown and explained to this investor. Figure 9.1 shows the familiar decreasing shortfall-probability curves for underperforming the 4.5 percent target real rate of return. Specifically, one curve in Figure 9.1 plots the horizon-dependent probability that a particular rebalanced asset allocation's cumulative return will fall short of a hypothetical account that grows at a constant gross (1 plus its net) inflation-adjusted rate of return of $r = 1.045$ a year.[10] Figure 9.1 shows that an investor who wants to minimize the probability of falling short of this particular target wealth

FIGURE 9.1   Shortfall Probabilities: Target Real Rate of Return of 4.5 Percent

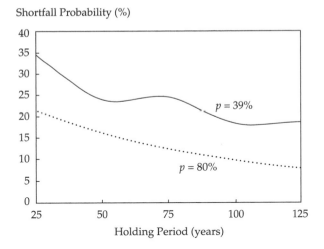

path needs to invest more than 39 percent in stocks. An 80 percent stock allocation has a shortfall probability of 21 percent at a 25-year horizon, with the probability falling to 16 percent at a 50-year horizon. (Later, I show that a stock allocation weight slightly higher than the plotted 80 percent will minimize the long-run shortfall probability.) Both probabilities are (relatively) significantly lower than would be achieved by a 39 percent allocation to stocks. Hence, the odds are about 5:1 (i.e., about a 5/6 versus 1/6 chance) that an 80 percent stock allocation will result in a growth rate of wealth exceeding 4.5 percent a year over a 50-year holding period, which accumulates to a target inflation-adjusted wealth of $1.045^{50} \approx \$9.03$ for every \$1.00 initially invested.

Table 9.1 shows, however, that CRRA investors with a coefficient of risk aversion higher than 4 would prefer a 39 percent stock allocation to an 80 percent allocation. So, if financial advisors use the questionnaire answers alone to implement Step 3 of the CRRA asset allocation process, they will advise more than two-thirds of their clients to invest no more than 39 percent in stocks.[11] In fact, calculations with the expected utility (Problem 9.5) show that those investors should prefer investing *nothing* in stocks (i.e., everything in TIPS) to investing 80 percent in stocks, which would guarantee that they would have absolutely no chance of meeting or beating a 4.5 percent growth rate (or any other growth rate higher than the TIPS rate of 3.5 percent), *even though the 80 percent stock allocation will result in only a 10 percent probability of underperforming TIPS at a 50-year horizon.*

Problems with Assessing the Risk-Aversion Parameter

The questionnaires used as best practice for assessing a risk-aversion parameter indicate that for a large majority of investors, financial advisors should recommend long-term stock allocations that are more conservative than the shortfall-probability analysis implies. A reason may lie in the scale of the risks. Because wealth has a positive growth trend, the different possible long-term asset allocations result in unavoidably different *large-scale* risks to the investor at long horizons, but the Barsky et al. and Hanna et al. questions involve smaller-scale risks (e.g., doubling income versus cutting it by some percentage)—not a long-term allocation's potential to increase income by a factor of nine or more. Hence, the questions involve a risk scale more appropriate to shorter-term investments. Is risk aversion fixed, or does it vary by scale of the risk? According to the conventional expected-CRRA-utility theory that underlies the questionnaire, a conventional CRRA investor has a *fixed* γ, one that does not vary with the scale of risks considered by the investor. In practice, however, Rabin and Thaler concluded that γ could vary, at least over some scale of differing investment opportunities:

> Data sets dominated by smaller-scale investment opportunities are likely to yield much higher estimates of risk aversion than data sets dominated by larger-scale investment opportunities. Indeed, the correct conclusion to draw, both from thought experiments and from actual data, is that people do not display a consistent coefficient of risk aversion, so it is a waste of time to try to measure it. (pp. 224–225)

Moreover, advice based on conventional CRRA long-run asset allocation cannot be "saved" by increasing the scale of the risks in the questionnaire. As noted, conventional CRRA expected-utility theory implies that changes in the scale of risks posed should *not* change the risk-aversion parameter as estimated from the questionnaire; if such changes to the questions do result in lower estimates of γ, *the underlying conventional CRRA hypothesis is wrong.*

Another questionable area is the reliability of individual respondents' answers on the questionnaires. For example, if an individual were to retake the questionnaire later, the answers might be different, so the interval estimate for the individual's γ would be different. Simultaneously administering another questionnaire whose choices had been seemingly innocuously altered (e.g., changing the probabilities or sizes of the gains or losses in a way that would permit similar interval γ estimates to be made) might also yield a different interval estimate for γ.

The two survey studies cited here did not address this issue, but Yook and Everett (2003) submitted six different qualitative risk-tolerance questionnaires to 113 part-time MBA students at Johns Hopkins University. The questionnaires were used by some major brokerages and mutual funds to provide asset allocation advice for clients. Yook and Everett standardized the risk-tolerance information provided by the questionnaires in a way that assigned the number 0 to the least risk-tolerant respondent of each questionnaire and the number 100 to the most risk tolerant. If different questionnaires provided similar information about respondents' risk tolerances, the authors expected the 0–100 scores for the respondents to be highly correlated. Yet, the 15 possible pairwise comparisons among the six questionnaires yielded an average pairwise Pearson correlation coefficient of only 56 percent. As a result, the authors concluded:[12]

> the 0.56 average correlation coefficient is much lower than what we should expect it to be to warrant the use of the questionnaire method without qualm. This low correlation may manifest the artificiality inherent in the risk-questionnaire design. (Yook and Everett, text above Table 1)

Moreover, advice based on conventional expected-utility asset allocation is not likely to be any less problematic if a different utility function is adopted. Rabin (2000) considered the use of *any* concave utility of wealth to be highly problematic:

> The problems with assuming that risk attitudes over modest and large stakes derive from the same utility-of-wealth function relate to a longstanding debate in economics. Expected-utility theory makes a powerful prediction that economic actors don't see an amalgamation of independent gambles as significant insurance against the risk of those gambles; they are either barely less willing or barely more willing to accept risks when clumped together than when apart. (p. 1287)

When returns are IID, wealth at the end of horizon H results from the time-averaged sum (the "amalgamation") of the independent, single-period, log gross portfolio returns (the "independent gambles") earned beforehand.[13] The longer the horizon, the larger the "stakes."

Eliminating the Risk-Aversion Parameter

As an alternative to the use of Table 9.1 in asset allocation, Step 2 of the proposed target-shortfall-probability-minimizing long-term asset allocation produces the data in Table 9.2.[14] For each feasible target rate of return on real wealth (the assumption is that short selling and borrowing at the assumed inflation-adjusted TIPS rate over a long horizon are not possible), Table 9.2 reports the asset allocation required to minimize the suitably long-run probability of falling short of the target. In general, the higher the target return, the higher the minimum probability of a target shortfall.[15]

A financial advisor could use Table 9.2 to explain the unavoidable trade-off between feasible real return targets and the probabilities of achieving them. For example, a 5 percent target could increase each $1.00 of initially invested wealth by a real gross rate of return of 1.05 each year, which would accumulate to a whopping inflation-adjusted 1.05^{50} or $11.48 over 50 years. According to Table 9.2, the probability-maximizing way to beat this long-run target requires an all-stock portfolio, and even that will result in a 24 percent (i.e., almost 1 in 4) chance of falling short of it after 50 years. In contrast, a 3.7 percent real return target (20 bps higher than the assumed return on TIPS) dictates a 37 percent weight in stocks and corresponds to a much lower cumulative inflation-adjusted multiple, 1.037^{50} or 6.15 after 50 years. Table 9.2 shows that this strategy involves only a 6 percent (i.e., about 1:17) chance that the lower multiple will not be achieved (i.e., a 94 percent probability that it will be achieved).

The financial advisor should explain that the Table 9.2 data illustrate an unavoidable fundamental trade-off: High-growth portfolios are generally more volatile than low-growth portfolios. And although their higher growth helps them exceed a target return, their higher volatilities increase the chance that they will not reach the target.

Step 3, the final step of the asset allocation process, entails an interactive feedback session between the advisor (or a computer-based analytical system) and the investor. The investor considers the fundamental trade-offs between target returns (or the investor's equivalent target wealth levels) and the probabilities of falling short of them (or complementary probabilities of exceeding them) at various horizons. Based on this assessment, the investor who initially wanted a high target return might revise the return expectations downward because a lower target is associated

TABLE 9.2   Shortfall-Probability Minimizing: Asset Allocation and Performance

Target Return (percent)	Stock Weight, p	Minimum Shortfall Probability	
		25 Years	50 Years
5.0	101%	35%	24%
4.5	83	24	16
4.0	58	24	10
3.7	37	11	6
3.5	0	0	0

with a lower probability of shortfall. If the investor must fund a fixed inflation-adjusted liability that is expected on some future date, the advisor can explain that the investor should also expect to invest a higher fraction of income to compensate for the lower target return. This trade-off might prompt the investor to again reconsider other feasible targets, savings fractions, and so on, until a satisfactory return target is established. Finally, the investor is advised to select the optimal asset allocation associated with the satisfactory return target.

Don't put the cart before the horse. An advisor who adopts a conventional γ-dependent mean–variance or other expected-utility criterion in Step 1 of the asset allocation process might argue that explanations of the trade-offs shown in Table 9.2 and/or the mean–variance statistics in Table 9.1 can be used to help the financial advisor measure an investor's γ. For example, an investor who receives the explanation of Table 9.2 might decide to adopt a target real rate of return of 4.0 percent and thus invest 58 percent in stocks. Table 9.1 indicates that an investor who wishes to maximize expected CRRA utility and who has a (supposedly) constant coefficient of risk aversion that is slightly less than 3 would also choose to allocate 58 percent to stocks. Hence, the financial advisor might be tempted to infer that 3 is "the" value of γ that can reliably be used to recommend an asset allocation for this investor. Similarly, a financial advisor who adopts a mean–variance utility might be tempted to present the trade-off information in Table 9.2 to an investor to "reverse engineer" a value for the appropriate mean–variance utility's required risk-aversion parameter.

In realistic situations, however (that is, when multiple risky asset classes are available), an advisor's attempts to use shortfall probability as auxiliary information in Step 3 may lead to results that are internally inconsistent with the expected-utility or mean–variance criterion adopted in Step 1. To see why, suppose there is one other asset class in addition to domestic stocks and TIPS—for example, an international stock index fund. To elicit a value for the investor's target real rate of return, a financial advisor could expand Table 9.2 to include international stock and use the table to explain the asset allocation trade-offs. For illustration, assume this explanation has been made and that the corresponding recommendation to minimize target shortfall probability is to invest 50 percent in domestic stocks, 20 percent in international stocks, and the rest (30 percent) in TIPS. The required three-asset allocation analogous to Table 9.1 will probably not show even a *single* value of $1 + \gamma$ that would lead *by conventional expected-CRRA-utility maximization* to these three specific percentages.

The attempt to reverse engineer a γ value in this example would fail, but this failure should not be mourned, because it prevents the financial advisor from placing the cart (Step 3) before the horse (Step 1). The recommended asset allocation must be internally consistent with the optimization criterion used to produce that allocation. Investors may well find shortfall (or outperformance) probabilities to be useful and informative because they rationally want to minimize (maximize) the target shortfall (outperformance) probabilities instead of being forced to use the expected-utility or mean–variance criterion that the advisor adopted in Step 1.

For example, that mean–variance investors care *only* about the mean and variance of their future wealth and that they maximize the criterion $\mu - \gamma\sigma^2$ are *axiomatic*. A mathematical theoretical implication of this is that the investor, to select a specific combination of mean and variance and specific asset allocation that will generate it, needs to know *only* the mean–variance wealth trade-offs on the efficient frontier permitted by the investment opportunity set. For that investor to also need to know various target shortfall or outperformance statistics is inconsistent, unless those statistics provide absolutely no information other than what is already provided by the asset means and variances.

Yet, even legendary mean–variance-analysis advocate William Sharpe recommends the use of the Financial Engines website, which contains the following example of how an investor can use its probabilistic assessments:[16]

> For example, a person with a 40 percent chance of achieving an income goal of $50,000 may find that tolerable if they have a 95 percent chance of achieving an income of $40,000 (in other words, their long-term downside income is $40,000).[17]

Unless portfolio returns are either normally distributed or from some other two-moment family of distributions, the quote provides more information than can be obtained from the mean and variance associated with the return distribution of the asset allocation being analyzed. Thus, although the criterion inherent in the quote does not exactly state the shortfall (outperformance) probability criterion developed in this chapter, it certainly is similarly motivated.

RECONCILIATION OF METHODS

The previous section illustrated how a financial advisor might use Table 9.2, in conjunction with input from an investor client, to recommend a specific long-run shortfall-probability-minimizing asset allocation. How were those target return–dependent asset allocations found? A theoretical extension of the results in Stutzer (2000, 2003) shows that the optimal long-term asset allocations can be found by solving the following problem:

$$\max_{p} \max_{\gamma} E\left[-\left(\frac{R_p}{r}\right)^{-\gamma}\right]. \tag{9.6}$$

Problem 9.6 differs from the conventional use of CRRA utility (Problem 9.3) by the presence of the target (gross) return per year, r, as well as the inner maximization over γ prior to maximizing over stock weight p. For the $r = 1.045$ gross return target used to produce Figure 9.1, Problem 9.6 is the following simple modification of Problem 9.5:

$$\max_{p} \max_{\gamma} \frac{1}{2}\left\{-\left[\frac{1.2645p + 1.035(1 - p)}{1.045}\right]^{-\gamma}\right\}$$
$$+ \frac{1}{2}\left\{-\left[\frac{0.9009p + 1.035(1 - p)}{1.045}\right]^{-\gamma}\right\}. \tag{9.7}$$

Numerically solving Problem 9.7 in a spreadsheet yields $p = 82.7$ percent, as indicated in Table 9.2 (to the nearest percentage), which is close to the 80 percent allocation used for illustrative purposes in Figure 9.1. The optimized value of γ associated with the optimal $p = 82.7$ percent is approximately 0.9, but this should *not* be taken to imply that the investor with a 4.5 percent target return has a constant coefficient of relative risk aversion of 1.9. Through the inner maximization over γ in Problem 9.7, the investor uses a *different* (inner-maximizing) value of γ to evaluate each specific p. So, although the 4.5 percent target investor does use a value of $\gamma \approx 0.9$ when evaluating the expected utility of a $p = 82.7$ percent allocation, this same investor uses an inner-maximized value of $\gamma \approx 1.3$ when evaluating the alternative (suboptimal) $p = 39$ percent allocation used to produce Figure 9.1. Simply put, an investor ranks the desirability of the various asset allocations by using the following function of p:

$$\max_{\gamma} E\left[-\left(\frac{R_p}{r}\right)^{-\gamma}\right] \equiv \max_{\gamma} \frac{1}{2}\left\{-\left[\frac{1.2645p + 1.035(1 - p)}{1.045}\right]^{-\gamma}\right\}$$
$$+ \frac{1}{2}\left\{-\left[\frac{0.9009p + 1.035(1 - p)}{1.045}\right]^{-\gamma}\right\}. \tag{9.8}$$

The other long-term allocations in Table 9.2 were produced by successively substituting each alternative target gross return for the number 1.045 in Problem 9.7 and then solving it by using the maximizing routine in a spreadsheet.

In summary, conventional expected-CRRA-utility maximization and long-run target-shortfall-probability minimization can be reconciled by eliminating the conventional assumption that expected utility should be only partially maximized (i.e., maximized only over the possible asset allocations), rather than totally maximized over both the asset allocations and the positive values of γ. This unconventional use of expected-utility theory (conventional expected-utility maximization holds the risk-aversion parameter fixed) is an application of theoretical results proven in Stutzer (2000, 2003). An analyst who (mis)specifies a conventional power utility function for a long-run investor who is seeking to minimize a target shortfall probability should find that the utility function's risk-aversion "parameter" is not a fixed constant but, instead, a variable that depends on the investor's target and the investment opportunity set.

MODIFICATIONS FOR REALISTIC SITUATIONS

Some modifications of the computations are recommended for the realistic applications faced by practicing advisors. First, the numerical example dealt with only two assets, one of which was assumed to result in a constant real return (i.e., a constant real interest rate). In practice, advisors will consider a diverse group of assets, none of which earn a constant real rate of return. But despite the diversity of available asset classes, advisors should strive to avoid recommendations involving a large number of asset classes. Because of the inherent uncertainty in the use of historical return series, an analyst considering a large number of asset classes will be forced to make overly specific and possibly small percentage recommendations (e.g., invest 3 percent in South Korean stocks, 2 percent in Colorado real estate investment trusts, etc.). Such specifics convey an unrealistic degree of precision.

Second, the example investor's target was a purely hypothetical account growing at a *fixed* real rate of return. The advisor should make sure the investor understands that such an account is *not* an investable benchmark and, therefore, cannot be matched with certainty. In practice, however, investors might designate an investable benchmark (e.g., an S&P 500 Index mutual fund or exchange-traded fund), which can be matched by investing 100 percent in it. In either case, the advisor needs to find the asset allocation with the best chance of actually beating the noninvestable target or investable benchmark.

When the assets' returns are jointly IID, only simple modifications to Problem 9.6 are needed. With the nth asset's real return in historical period t denoted by R_{nt}, an N-asset portfolio's real return with constantly rebalanced asset (value-weighted) proportions $w_1, \ldots, w_{N-1}$ is denoted

$$R_{pt} = \sum_{n=1}^{N-1} w_n(R_{nt} - R_{Nt}) + R_{Nt}. \tag{9.9}$$

If an investable benchmark is designated, the advisor denotes its return in historical period t by R_{bt}. After entering the historical data in a spreadsheet or computer program, the advisor simply uses the numerical maximizer to solve the following simple generalization of Problem 9.4:

$$\max_{w_1,\ldots,w_{N-1}} \max_{\gamma} \frac{1}{T}\sum_{t=1}^{T} -\left(\frac{R_{pt}}{R_{bt}}\right)^{-\gamma}. \tag{9.10}$$

That is, the advisor substitutes the designated benchmark return, R_b, for r in Problem 9.6 and then uses the historical average to estimate the expected value in that formula. As in using any portfolio optimizer, the advisor can constrain the weights in Problem 9.10 to be nonnegative if short selling is precluded. A problem is that numerical solutions may be extreme when highly correlated assets are present. This may also happen when mean–variance-optimizing software is used. This problem provides another reason to restrict attention to a limited number of broad, disparate asset classes whose returns are not highly correlated with one another.

Also, to ensure that a numerical solution to Problem 9.10 does indeed exist, a rebalanced portfolio of the assets needs to be available that, when given enough time, *can* beat the investor's target or designated benchmark portfolio. Thus, the rebalanced portfolio's expected log gross return should exceed the target or benchmark's expected log return (Stutzer 2003). In practice, with historical return data subject to these provisos, a numerical solution to Problem 9.10 has been easily obtained by using a spreadsheet optimizer. A valid solution finds a positive value for γ.

The assumption that returns are IID may not approximate the actual situation well enough, however, for Problem 9.10 to be applied with confidence that the recommendations will yield the best allocation. For example, Siegel's (pp. 38–39) examination of stocks' historical real returns led him to assume that future stock returns would be mean reverting rather than IID. He thus concluded that advisors should recommend considerably higher stock allocations than would otherwise be the case. Fortunately, Problem 9.10 can be modified to accommodate non-IID returns (Foster and Stutzer 2002). The required formula still involves maximizing over all possible values of a risk-aversion parameter, but it is more complicated than Problem 9.10. Instead, advisors can estimate asset allocation–dependent shortfall-probability curves (like those in Figure 9.1) directly. To do so, one first fixes asset allocation weights (i.e., a specific rebalanced portfolio); then, one applies a straightforward technique of bootstrapping with moving blocks (e.g., see Hansson and Persson 2000) to simulate numerous future return scenarios for the portfolio and the designated benchmark. From the scenarios, one tabulates the fraction of times the portfolio's cumulative return at horizon H falls short of the designated benchmark's cumulative return. This fraction is the estimate of the portfolio's shortfall probability at horizon H. By repeating this procedure for other portfolios (i.e., other asset allocation weights), a computer program searches for the specific asset allocation weights with the lowest shortfall probability at H. Long-run investors should adopt an asset allocation that minimizes the shortfall probabilities for suitably large values of H.

REEXAMINING THE ARGUMENTS

Given the behavioral evidence favoring target shortfall criteria and the implementational advantages of shortfall-probability minimization, a reexamination of the typical arguments made *in favor of* the conventional use of expected utility and *against* the use of shortfall probability will be useful.

The normative case for conventional use of expected utility is grounded in the Von Neumann–Morgenstern (1980) axioms for decision making in risky situations. Von Neumann and Morgenstern started from the postulate that a decision maker is able to rank-order the desirability (i.e., from most desirable to least desirable) of different probability distributions of wealth ("wealth lotteries") resulting from the various feasible decisions. They posed seemingly sensible axioms that decision makers might adhere to when composing this rank order. They proved that a decision maker acting in accord with those axioms acts as if he or she had adopted *some* utility function and had then rank-ordered the probability distributions in accord with the size of their respective expected utilities. Hence, the decision maker's top-ranked decision should be the one that leads to the distribution of wealth with the highest expected utility.

The problem with this and other axiomatic "rationalizations" for expected-utility maximization is that axioms that appear to be reasonable on first examination do not always remain so after closer examination. For example, much reconsideration has been given to Von Neumann and Morgen-stern's crucial "independence axiom," without which there can be *no* conventional expected utility. Machina (1987) summarized the evidence showing that most individuals' choices violate this axiom and hence cannot be consistent with expected-utility maximization. Moreover, Rabin and Rabin and Thaler pointed out the paradoxical behavior toward differently scaled risks by anyone who does maximize an expected *concave* utility—such as Problem 9.3 with $\gamma > 0$, as in the example I discussed.

In light of these negative findings about expected-utility maximization, the case against the use of shortfall probabilities is not compelling. Much of it appears to be associated with early arguments made by Samuelson (1963).[18] The following reexamination of Samuelson's arguments against shortfall probability will show that they either are overstated or do not apply to the criterion of minimizing *target* shortfall probability.

Samuelson correctly noted that in repeated betting situations analogous to long-run asset allocation, even though the probability of falling short of some wealth target (which could be mere wealth preservation) is low, "the improbable loss will be very great indeed if it does occur" (p. 110). Although technically correct, this statement might lead readers to believe that minimizing the shortfall probability will induce *excessively risky* behavior (presumably, by failing to adequately weigh the prospect of great but improbable shortfalls). But Samuelson also noted the obvious point that the probability of *outperformance* is the complement of the shortfall probability, so minimizing shortfall probability is the same as maximizing outperformance probability. Hence, readers might just as well believe that a criterion of target-outperformance-probability maximization is flawed because the improbable gain will be very great indeed if it does occur, inducing excessively *conservative* behavior!

The truth is that neither claim is relevant. What determines the risk borne by a shortfall-probability-minimizing (equivalently, an outperformance-probability-maximizing) investor is the specific target the investor wants to beat *and* the investment opportunity set the investor uses to try to beat it. The illustrative asset allocation example summarized in Table 9.2 shows that the full range of risk behavior is possible. To prove that not all target-shortfall-probability minimizers should prefer an 80 percent stock allocation to a 39 percent stock allocation depicted in Figure 9.1, Figure 9.2 depicts the same evaluation for a more conservative investor, one who is willing to accept a 3.7 percent target real growth rate, which is 80 bps below the target adopted by the investor using Figure 9.1 and only a mere 20 bps above the (assumed completely risk-free) TIPS rate of 3.5 percent. Figure 9.2 shows that this more conservative investor would prefer investing 39 percent in stocks to investing 80 percent in stocks.

Moreover, Samuelson's expected-concave-utility criterion is not a reasonable alternative. This method evaluates each decision in accord with the size of the probability-weighted average of a *fixed* concave utility function's values at each possible wealth outcome. The concavity yields diminishing marginal utility increments for successively larger wealth outcomes. Although this procedure may appear to be more reasonable than focusing on the probability of falling short of some target, keep in mind that it is the source of the highly problematic and paradoxical behavior toward differently scaled risks identified by Rabin and Rabin and Thaler.

Samuelson's other criticism of outperformance probability applies only to criteria that he formulated in the following way:

> the ordering principle of selecting between two actions in terms of which has the greater probability of producing a higher result does not even possess the property of being transitive. (Samuelson 1969, p. 246)

FIGURE 9.2   Shortfall Probabilities: Target Real Rate of Return of 3.7 Percent

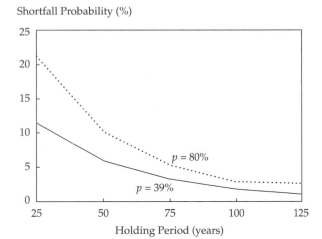

In the context of asset allocation, Samuelson is worried about the following possibility. Suppose an investor decides to prefer portfolio p's asset allocation to that of portfolio p' if there is a better than 50 percent chance (i.e., better than even odds) that the value of portfolio p at the end of, say, $H = 40$ years will exceed that of portfolio p'. The investor then uses the same criterion to decide whether portfolio p' is better than a third portfolio p''. Hypothetical examples can be constructed in which an investor will prefer portfolio p to portfolio p' and prefer portfolio p' to portfolio p'' but will prefer portfolio p'' to portfolio p. This "intransitivity" is widely held to be irrational, and rightly so. *But it cannot occur when using the criterion formulated here.*

To see how it cannot occur with shortfall minimization as I have described it, suppose that at some specific horizon H, portfolio p has a higher probability of outperforming an account growing at a target gross rate of return than portfolio p' has (for instance, 70 percent for portfolio p versus 60 percent for portfolio p'). And suppose that portfolio p' has a higher probability of outperforming this target than portfolio p'' has (say, 60 percent versus 55 percent). Then, portfolio p obviously has a higher probability of outperforming the target than portfolio p'' has (i.e., 70 percent versus 55 percent). Hence, transitivity will hold no matter what H is, and the analysis has already showed that an investor who wants to maximize the long-run probability of outperforming a target gross return of, say, $r = 1.045$ should assign a rank order to each portfolio p in accord with the size of Problem 9.8, which is a function of p. A rank order produced in accord with the size of *any* function's value is automatically transitive.

From this analysis, one can quickly see that the problem with Samuelson's formulation of an outperformance-probability criterion is its lack of a benchmark (i.e., an account growing at rate r or, alternatively, an investable portfolio of risky assets) to measure outperformance probabilities against. Samuelson's critique was apparently motivated largely by probabilistic arguments reputedly used by some advocates for expected-growth-rate maximization (i.e., the expected-log-utility criterion, not target-based or benchmark-based outperformance probability).

A third possible criticism of shortfall probability may be grounded in the work of Rubinstein (1991) and of Browne, among others, who found that significant probabilities of underperforming investor targets can persist for a long, long time—especially when maximizing the expected growth rate of wealth (i.e., expected log utility). Figure 9.1 illustrates the nature of this persistence in the simple asset allocation problem. But because an 80 percent stock allocation is close to the allocation that minimizes the long-run probability of falling short of the ambitious $r = 1.045$ growth target, Figure 9.1 also shows that the persistence of shortfall probabilities is unavoidable when the target is ambitious; moreover, it would only be worse if some other criterion function were used to choose a stock allocation. Figure 9.2 shows that the persistence is lower when target r is lower. Generally, the solution to Problem 9.6 selects the asset allocation that minimizes the long-run probability of falling short of the investor's target gross return, so the shortfall probabilities will persist even longer when a different asset allocation is selected by a different criterion function.

In summary, possible intransitivities and persistence of shortfall probabilities might be used to critique arguments advocating that *all* investors should maximize the mean growth rate of wealth (i.e., maximize expected log utility). But neither argument provides a relevant critique of target-shortfall-probability minimization as described here.

CONCLUSIONS

A financial advisor's prescriptive use of either mean–variance or expected-utility-maximizing asset allocation is hampered by several difficulties. One is determining a value for the required risk-aversion parameter that is appropriate for the client. Another difficulty is explaining the rationale for maximizing these criteria. And a paradox arises when the same concave utility function is used to evaluate differently scaled risks. These difficulties can be (at least partly) alleviated by prescribing an asset allocation that minimizes the long-run probability of falling short of a target return—an inflation-adjusted rate of return. The target rate of return is determined by the advisor in consultation with the investor, who has seen and understood the tradeoff between possible target rates of return and the probabilities of falling short of (and of outperforming) the targets.

Surprisingly, the seemingly disparate conventional maximization of expected CRRA utility and the minimization of long-run target shortfall probability can be reconciled by *completely maximizing the expected CRRA utility of the ratio of the portfolio's return to the investor's target return*. This maximization requires unconventionally maximizing the expected utility by selection of both the portfolio's asset allocation weights *and* the utility's risk-aversion parameter (as opposed to conventional maximization over the weights alone with the use of some fixed value of the risk-aversion parameter). This unconventional formulation of minimizing long-run target shortfall probability retains the framework of expected-utility maximization while eliminating the conventional but problematic requirement that the advisor fix a value of the risk-aversion parameter that is most appropriate for the investor. Instead, in an interactive feedback process, the advisor and the investor mutually determine the most appropriate target rate of return or investable benchmark the investor wants to beat.

Criticisms of the use of shortfall probability are either overstated or not applicable to target-shortfall-minimization (target-outperformance-maximization) probability as described here. Theorists who believe that this criterion is inferior to risk-aversion-parameter-dependent expected utility need to reevaluate that position in light of the implementation and the risk-scaling problems highlighted in this chapter.

ACKNOWLEDGMENTS

The author thanks Tom Rietz for information about questionnaire-based risk-aversion estimates. This work benefited from a large number of questions and comments offered by participants in numerous academic and practitioner forums around the world.

NOTES

1. Because I focus solely on the asset allocation advice for long-term investors, I do not address the controversial subject of time diversification.
2. Moreover, any future critiques of this criterion must be considered in light of the new and surprisingly devastating criticisms in Rabin (2000) and Rabin and Thaler that apply to *all* conventional expected-concave-utility-of-wealth criteria favored by Samuelson (1963, 1969).
3. Mossin (1968) used a more complicated dynamic programming method to study this problem. A later influential paper by Samuelson (1969) used a different criterion function—the time-additive sum of single-period CRRA utilities of *consumption during the holding period*. Mossin's end-of-holding-period utility of wealth did not permit withdrawals for consumption until the end of the holding period. Hence, the derivations in Samuelson (1969) do not apply to the problem studied in this paper, although they do lead to similar results.
4. A simple proof follows. Set $W_0 = 1$ in Equation 9.2, which produces the equivalent criterion function of $-E\left[\left(\prod_{t=1}^{H} R_{p,t}\right)^{-\gamma}\right]$. When returns are independently distributed, we can move the expectation operator inside the product to yield $-\prod_{t=1}^{H} E(R_{p,t}^{-\gamma})$. We immediately see that the portfolio weights that maximize this function will be the weights that minimize $\prod_{t=1}^{H} E(R_{p,t}^{-\gamma})$. Moreover, because the logarithmic function is monotonically increasing, the same weight vectors will also minimize $\log \prod_{t=1}^{H} E(R_{p,t}^{-\gamma}) \equiv \sum_{t=1}^{H} \log E(R_{p,t}^{-\gamma})$. Because this problem is additively separable, the first-order necessary condition for any *particular* p_t will not include any of the other p_t's. As a result, p_t can be found simply by minimizing $E(R_{p,t}^{-\gamma})$. If we make use of the assumption that portfolio returns are independently distributed across the H equal-length periods, we can remove the subscript t from p_t in this problem, producing $E(R_p^{-\gamma})$. Multiplying by $E(R_p^{-\gamma})$ by -1 converts it into the one-period maximization in the chapter (Problem 9.3).
5. In practice, rebalancing may also be a useful strategy for maximizing other criterion functions, even when a more elaborate dynamic strategy could, in theory, do better (e.g., when portfolio returns are not IID). Buetow, Sellers, Trotter, Hunt, and Whipple (2002) documented some of the general benefits of rebalancing.
6. Later, I describe how the analysis should be modified to address realistic applications with multiple assets, more realistic return processes, and a situation in which no asset earns a constant real rate of return.
7. Matching the average real stock return requires the solution of one equation in the two unknowns, u and d; matching the standard deviation requires the solution of another equation in the two unknowns. The assumed values of u and d are the only ones satisfying both equations. They are reported to only four decimal places in the text, but more accurate floating point values were used in the computations. Because of this discrepancy, readers may be unable to exactly duplicate the calculations that yielded the tables here but should get close enough to determine whether they are doing them correctly.
8. Restricting investors to using stocks and *non-inflation-indexed* bonds, Siegel derived a mean–variance-efficient stock allocation of 115 percent for an investor with a 30-year horizon and what he described as "moderate risk tolerance" (p. 38). This high percentage occurred because his 200-year series of inflation-adjusted stock returns has some of the properties typical of series generated from a mean-reverting process rather than an IID process. As a result, the 30-year cumulative real returns presented in his series have lower volatility than would occur if returns were IID and were thus more favorably appraised by his mean–variance criterion than IID returns would be. When the possibility of allocating assets

to TIPS (earning an assumed real rate of 3.5 percent a year) was added, the mean–variance-efficient "tangency" portfolio (of only the stocks and non-inflation-indexed bonds) for an investor with a horizon of 10 years still allocated 185 percent to stocks; hence, it was 85 percent short in bonds. A mean–variance utility-maximizing investor's risk-aversion parameter would then determine only the relative split of wealth between that portfolio and TIPS. Siegel thus concluded, "Stocks should constitute the overwhelming proportion of all long-term financial portfolios" (p. 361). Because my purpose was to use the simplest possible asset allocation problem to illustrate the crucial implementational differences between conventional mean–variance and expected-utility criteria and the target-shortfall-probability criterion, I did not use the controversial hypothesis that real stock returns are in fact (rather than simply historically appearing to be) generated by a mean-reverting process. But later, I do describe the modifications required to adapt the computations to incorporate mean reversion and/or other apparent deviations from the example's IID assumption.

9. Of course, implicit in Table 9.1 is an assumption that the investor is concerned only about inflation-adjusted invested wealth at one point in time (i.e., H years in the future). Siegel made this assumption, as have many others in applications of portfolio choice theory. Because Siegel's focus was (and my focus is) on asset allocation advice for long-term investors, horizon H might be thought of as the number of years until the investor will retire or die. In the case of retirement perhaps (and surely in the case of death), the advice should not be too dependent on knowing the particular value of H! Fortunately, advice based on Table 9.1 does not depend at all on H, although such need not be the case when returns are non-IID.

10. For each stock weight p, let R_p^u denote the portfolio's gross (1 plus its net) return when the stock goes up and R_p^d denote the portfolio's gross return when the stock goes down. For a horizon length T, shortfall occurs when there are x or fewer up moves—that is, when $x R_p^u (T - x) R_p^d \leq 1.045^T$. Hence, the probability of shortfall is computed by evaluating the cumulative binomial distribution (with probability of an up move equal to 1/2) at the highest integer x satisfying this inequality. This calculation can be easily accomplished in a spreadsheet.

11. Technically, some of these individuals might have revealed a coefficient of risk aversion between 3.76 and 4.00 by this single answer, although the questionnaire provides no way to tell.

12. I thank Michele Gambera of Morningstar for providing this reference. Although the six questionnaires did not attempt to estimate an investor's risk tolerance in the quantitative way described by Barsky et al. and Hanna et al., the results indicate that an analogous study of reliability is warranted, one in which different questionnaires pose quantitatively different wealth lotteries.

13. That is, $W_H \equiv W_0 \prod_{t=1}^{H} R_{pt} \equiv W_0 e^{(\Sigma_{t=1}^{H} \log R_{pt}/H)H}$.

14. The next section describes how this table was produced and how it could be produced in more realistic problems.

15. The relationship between target return and probability in Table 9.2 is only weakly (rather than strictly) monotonic because of the discrete, binomial distribution process used to model the stock return. The relationship would be strictly monotonic had an absolutely continuous (e.g., lognormal) distribution been assumed in the calculations, and one would obtain a strictly increasing relationship between the target return and the (minimized) probability of falling short of it at any horizon H.

16. The Financial Engines website (www.financialengines.com) describes Sharpe as "Founder Bill Sharpe" and describes his role as follows: "One of the fathers of Modern Portfolio

Theory, Nobel laureate Dr. Sharpe has helped some of the nation's largest pension fund managers invest billions of dollars of retirement money. When he realized that he could offer this help to individuals through an advice technology platform, he started Financial Engines. Financial Engines combines Dr. Sharpe's pioneering investment methodology with scalable technology to provide all investors with cost-effective, expert advice."

17. This sentence was found in the "Common Questions" section of www.financialengines. com as part of the answer to the question: "What is a good Forecast?" In the quote, the "Forecast" is the 40 percent probability of outperforming the investor's $50,000 target (i.e., "income goal").

18. Arguments in Samuelson (1963) were repeated in numerous later articles; see Samuelson 1969; Merton and Samuelson 1974; Samuelson 1979.

REFERENCES

Barsky, R.B., F.T. Juster, M.S. Kimball, and M.D. Shapiro. 1997. "Preference Parameters and Behavioral Heterogeneity: An Experimental Approach in the Health and Retirement Study." *Quarterly Journal of Economics*, vol. 112, no. 2 (May):537–579.

Browne, Sid. 1999. "The Risk and Rewards of Minimizing Shortfall Probability." *Journal of Portfolio Management*, vol. 25, no. 4 (Summer):76–85.

Buetow, Gerald W., Ronald Sellers, Donald Trotter, Elaine Hunt, and Willie A. Whipple. 2002. "The Benefits of Rebalancing." *Journal of Portfolio Management*, vol. 28, no. 2 (Winter):23–32.

Foster, F. Douglas, and Michael Stutzer. 2002. "Performance and Risk Aversion of Funds with Benchmarks: A Large Deviations Approach." Working paper, University of Colorado Finance Department.

Hakansson, Nils H., and William T. Ziemba. 1995. "Capital Growth Theory." In *Handbooks in Operations Research and Management Science: Finance*, vol. 9. Edited by Robert A. Jarrow, Vojislav Maksimovic, and William T. Ziemba. Amsterdam: North Holland.

Hanna, Sherman D., Michael S. Gutter, and Jessie X. Fan. 2001. "A Measure of Risk Tolerance Based on Economic Theory." *Financial Counseling and Planning*, vol. 12, no. 2:1–8.

Hansson, Bjorn, and Mattias Persson. 2000. "Time Diversification and Estimation Risk." *Financial Analysts Journal*, vol. 56, no. 5 (September/October):55–62.

Kroll, Yoram, Haim Levy, and Harry Markowitz. 1984. "Mean–Variance versus Direct Utility Maximization." *Journal of Finance*, vol. 39, no. 1 (March):47–61.

Leibowitz, Martin, and R. Henriksson. 1989. "Portfolio Optimization with Shortfall Constraints: A Confidence-Limit Approach to Managing Downside Risk." *Financial Analysts Journal*, vol. 45, no. 2 (March/April):34–41.

Leibowitz, Martin, and Terence Langetieg. 1989. "Shortfall Risk and the Asset Allocation Decision: A Simulation Analysis of Stock and Bond Profiles." *Journal of Portfolio Management*, vol. 16, no. 1 (Fall):61–68.

Leibowitz, Martin, Lawrence Bader, and Stanley Kogelman. 1996. *Return Targets and Shortfall Risks*. Chicago, IL: Irwin.

Machina, Mark J. 1987. "Choice under Uncertainty: Problems Solved and Unsolved." *Economic Perspectives*, vol. 1, no. 1 (Summer):121–154.

Merton, Robert, and Paul Samuelson. 1974. "Fallacy of the Log-Normal Approximation to Optimal Portfolio Decision-Making over Many Periods." *Journal of Financial Economics*, vol. 1, no. 1 (May):67–94.

Milevsky, Moshe. 1999. "Time Diversification: Safety First and Risk." *Review of Quantitative Finance and Accounting*, vol. 12, no. 3 (May):271–281.

Mossin, Jan. 1968. "Optimal Multiperiod Portfolio Policies." *Journal of Business*, vol. 41, no. 2 (April):215–229.

Olsen, Robert A. 1997. "Investment Risk: The Experts' Perspective." *Financial Analysts Journal*, vol. 53, no. 2 (March/ April):62–66.

Olsen, Robert A., and Muhammad Khaki. 1998. "Risk, Rationality, and Time Diversification." *Financial Analysts Journal*, vol. 54, no. 5 (September/October):58–63.

Rabin, Matthew. 2000. "Risk Aversion and Expected-Utility Theory: A Calibration Theorem." *Econometrica*, vol. 68, no. 5 (September):1281–92.

Rabin, Matthew, and Richard Thaler. 2001. "Anomalies: Risk Aversion." *Journal of Economic Perspectives*, vol. 15, no. 1 (Winter):219–232.

Reichenstein, William. 1986. "When Stock Is Less Risky Than Treasury Bills." *Financial Analysts Journal*, vol. 42, no. 6 (November/December):71–75.

Rubinstein, Mark. 1991. "Continuously Rebalanced Investment Strategies." *Journal of Portfolio Management*, vol. 18, no. 1 (Fall):78–81.

Samuelson, Paul A. 1963. "Risk and Uncertainty: A Fallacy of Large Numbers." *Scientia*, vol. 98, no. 4 (April/May):108–113.

———. 1969. "Lifetime Portfolio Selection by Dynamic Programming." *Review of Economics and Statistics*, vol. 51, no. 3 (August):239–246.

———. 1979. "Why We Should Not Make Mean Log of Wealth Big Though Years to Act Are Long." *Journal of Banking and Finance*, vol. 3, no. 4:305–307.

Siegel, Jeremy J. 2002. *Stocks for the Long Run*. 3rd ed. New York: McGraw-Hill.

Stutzer, Michael. 2000. "A Portfolio Performance Index." *Financial Analysts Journal*, vol. 56, no. 3 (May/June):52–61.

———. 2003. "Portfolio Choice with Endogenous Utility: A Large Deviations Approach." *Journal of Econometrics*, vol. 116, nos. 1–2 (September–October):365–386.

Thorp, Edward O. 1975. "Portfolio Choice and the Kelly Criterion." In *Stochastic Optimization Models in Finance*. Edited by W.T. Ziemba and R.G. Vickson. New York: Academic Press.

Von Neumann, John, and Oskar Morgenstern. 1980. *Theory of Games and Economic Behavior*. (First published in 1944.) Princeton, NJ: Princeton University Press.

Yates, Frank. 1992. *Risk-Taking Behavior*. New York: John Wiley & Sons.

Yook, Ken C., and Robert Everett. 2003. "Assessing Risk Tolerance: Questioning the Questionnaire Method." *Journal of Financial Planning*, vol. 25, no. 8 (August): www.fpanet.org/journal/articles/2003_Issues/jfp0803-art7.cfm.

PART II

INVESTMENT MANAGEMENT FOR TAXABLE PRIVATE CLIENTS

CHAPTER 10

INVESTMENT MANAGEMENT FOR TAXABLE PRIVATE INVESTORS

Jarrod Wilcox, CFA
Jeffrey E. Horvitz
Dan diBartolomeo

FOREWORD

Investment management for taxable individuals is immensely complex. This complexity arises from the tax code, the naturally varied needs and wants of individuals and families, and the densely layered management and brokerage structure of the financial services industry. Yet, little rigorous research has been done on private wealth management. In fact, when David Montgomery and I wrote "Stocks, Bonds, and Bills after Taxes and Inflation," which appeared in the Winter 1995 *Journal of Portfolio Management*, we received a number of letters from financial planners and others concerned with private asset management, saying that, as far as the letter writers knew, we had addressed matters of concern to them for the first time. (It wasn't true, but that was their perception.) These managers toiling away on behalf of individual investors and their families are, of course, responsible for more assets than any other category of manager (most wealth is held by individuals, not pensions, foundations, or endowments), but, rightly or wrongly, they felt neglected and unguided in their pursuit of the goals common to all investors: higher returns, lower risk, and reasonable costs.

In *Investment Management for Taxable Private Investors*, a trio of distinguished authors—Jarrod Wilcox, Jeffrey E. Horvitz, and Dan diBartolomeo—do much to correct this imbalance. They begin by noting that private investors are much more diverse than institutional investors. This assertion is perhaps contrary to intuition. But viewed from the perspective of a private asset manager who is juggling the varied risk tolerances, cash flow needs, and balance

Reprinted from The Research Foundation of CFA Institute (January 2006).

sheet complexities of a family of private wealth holders, institutional investors do, indeed, all look pretty much the same. Taxation, at both the federal and state level in the United States, or in comparable jurisdictions in other countries, adds a thick layer of difficulty, which is exemplified by the fact that the U.S. Internal Revenue Code (just that one jurisdiction) is 9,000 pages long.

The authors begin with a strong review of finance theory, and to the usual litany of core concepts, they add stochastic growth theory, which has a grand history in the formal literature of finance but which has been little used. They note that because financial theory is an intentional oversimplification of reality, it is an even greater oversimplification when applied to private wealth management.

In the next section of the chapter, the authors review the principal asset classes and strategies that are used to benefit the private investor, with special attention paid to taxes and to maximizing after-tax returns. They also comment on the varied wealth levels, consumption patterns, and attitudes the private asset management practitioner is likely to encounter.

A particularly valuable section of the chapter deals with the organizational challenges faced by a private wealth management firm or practice. Providing customized investment services to a diverse population of choosy clients is difficult and costly. The authors describe a "portfolio manufacturing" approach that allows the firm to address this challenge profitably.

In the concluding section, the authors turn to the specialized problems of asset location, concentrated portfolios, and benchmarking. Asset location is the question of whether a given investment is (considering all factors, including other assets held by the investor) most tax efficient in a taxable or tax-deferred account. The asset location problem is made more complicated by the proliferation of types of tax-deferred accounts and by frequent tax law changes. In addition, portfolios that are concentrated in a single stock or industry are common among private investors and present a special challenge; liquidating the position all at once is not typically tax efficient, and some asset owners do not want it liquidated. Wilcox, Horvitz, and diBartolomeo describe several approaches to reducing the risk caused by such a concentrated position. Finally, the problems of establishing suitable benchmarks and of conducting progress evaluations for private wealth portfolios are addressed.

Just about all of us are private investors at some level. Thus the lessons in this chapter are valuable to all of us—not only to providers of private asset management services but also to consumers of them. For these reasons, the Research Foundation is extremely pleased to present *Investment Management for Taxable Private Investors*.

Laurence B. Siegel
Research Director
The Research Foundation of CFA Institute

PREFACE

The amount of published research in finance is large, but the amount of work devoted to issues that are important to private investors is a small percentage of the total, and the amount that is available pales in comparison to the needs of investors. Nevertheless, we wish to acknowledge the pioneering work of a handful of people who made overall contributions to the concepts and practice of managing investments for private investors. Their work was an inspiration for our investigations.

Early academic theoretical work by George Constantinides demonstrated that decisions about recognizing capital gains could be treated as option valuation problems. Another early influence on work in this field was William Fouse, who argued compellingly at the end of the 1960s that index funds were more tax efficient than the actively managed funds of the day. More recently, William Reichenstein, John Shoven, and several others began the study of tax-deferred savings accounts. David Stein, Robert Arnott, and Jean Brunel have written extensively on improving after-tax returns—in particular, on how active management can be modified for private (taxable) investors. In a sense, their intellectual godfather was Robert Jeffrey (1993), a demanding private wealth client who stimulated management firms focusing on institutional investors to come up with something better than what was then available for taxable investors.[1]

Despite the efforts of such authors, we believe that the taxable investor could be much better served by the investment community than it has been, and we commend the Research Foundation of CFA Institute for its efforts to redress this imbalance. This chapter was motivated by the taxable investor's needs:

- Private investors are much more diverse than institutional investors. The differences are related primarily to their amount of wealth, their needs, and their desires (which usually change over time) for consumption and to leave a legacy, their tax posture (which can vary from year to year), and how they personally value changes in wealth.
- Finance theory involves much simplification of real-world problems, and this simplification is even more pronounced when theory is applied to private investors.
- For individual investors, taxation is one of the most important aspects of investment performance, policy, and strategy—as important as pretax risk and return. The U.S. tax code is complex, however, and contains both traps and opportunities. How it applies and how it affects each private investor can be highly specific to circumstances that may change significantly over time.
- Investment professionals cannot adequately serve the private investor without customizing services toward a "market of one." Whether this customization is highly personal or nearly automated, it cannot be a "one size fits all" approach. The standardized rules and methods that can work well for the institutional investor are likely to fail the private investor.

Organization and Topics

We began with some ideas we wanted to get across with respect to obtaining better after-tax returns. As the chapter progressed, however, we realized that the needs of the professional investment manager who is used to serving institutional clients were much broader than we had previously thought. For example, how does one deal with investors who, unlike institutional investors, have limited life spans and, consequently, a somewhat predictable pattern of changing needs? How does the professional investment management organization cope with the order-of-magnitude increases in customization and complexity required for truly responsive private wealth management? Specifically, what does one do to cope with such tricky problems as a large concentrated position in low-cost-basis stock? What does the world look like from the wealthy investor's viewpoint, and what changes in attitude are required of the professional manager with an institutional background? To address this wide range of topics, we divided the chapter into four parts:

I   A Conceptual Framework for Helping Private Investors,
II   Private Wealth and Taxation,
III Organizing Management for Private Clients, and
IV   Special Topics (location, concentrated risk, and benchmarking).

Although each section of the chapter was written by a designated author or authors, we read, edited, and discussed one another's work extensively. The section responsibilities were as follows:

- Jarrod Wilcox, CFA: Sections called Introduction and Challenge Section, Theory and Practice in Private Investing, and Life-Cycle Investing, and Appendices 10A and 10B;
- Jeffrey Horvitz: Sections called Lifestyle, Wealth Transfer, and Asset Classes; Overview of Federal Taxation of Investments; Techniques for Improving After-Tax Investment Performance; and Assessment and Benchmarking for Private Wealth; and
- Dan diBartolomeo: Sections called Institutional Money Management and the High-Net-Worth Investor and Portfolio Management as a Manufacturing Process.

The section on Individual Retirement Plans and Location was jointly authored by Dan diBartolomeo and Jeffrey Horvitz, and all three authors wrote the section called On Concentrated Risk. We hope the reader enjoys reading the chapter as much as we enjoyed collaborating in the synthesis of its ideas.

The reader will discover in this chapter useful information, presented with a minimum of mathematics, on the following topics:[2]

- challenges in investing private wealth;
- proper application of academic theory to practical private wealth management;
- life-cycle planning for various stages of wealth, life expectancy, and desires for wealth transfer;
- differing needs by wealth level;
- the U.S. federal taxation of investments;
- obtaining a tax alpha—or achieving the best practical after-tax returns;
- adapting institutional money management for serving high-net-worth investors;
- private portfolio management as a manufacturing process;
- individual retirement plans and the issue of which securities to locate in them;
- combining risk management with tax concerns in dealing with concentrated risk positions.

In several sections, the reader will see data such as maximum applicable rates and other statutory numbers in the tax code in braces, { }. We have used data that were applicable *at the time this chapter was written,* and the braces are to remind the reader that tax rates and tax code metrics may become out of date because they are subject to legislative change. The reader is cautioned not to assume that the numbers in braces will be in effect in the future.

ACKNOWLEDGMENTS

We wish to express our appreciation to the Research Foundation of CFA Institute for encouraging us to prepare this treatment of topics of special interest to investment professionals serving private clients. We also wish to give special thanks to Robert Gordon, Steven Gaudette, and David Boccuzzi, who were kind enough to read the draft and suggest changes, and to Milissa Putman for excellence in document preparation.

Dan diBartolomeo
Jeffrey E. Horvitz
Jarrod Wilcox, CFA
Massachusetts
August 2005

PART I   A CONCEPTUAL FRAMEWORK FOR HELPING PRIVATE INVESTORS

The first section points to some of the perhaps difficult attitudinal changes needed for an investment advisor or management organization to successfully work with wealthy private clients—including a willingness to accept customization and deal with complexity and a more proactive view of fiduciary responsibility than is needed when working with institutional clients. The section on Theory and Practice in Private Investing draws from and adapts useful academic theories to the task of managing private money while cautioning against the many mistakes that may be made if theory is not applied with sufficient consideration of the real complexities involved. The last section in Part I applies these concepts to construct a consistent approach to lifetime investing that is flexible enough to deal properly with the differences in age and financial outcomes advisors meet in private investors.

INTRODUCTION AND CHALLENGE

The client, a U.S. businessman, was astonished to see that his investment advisory firm had mistakenly rebalanced his family's stock portfolio in the same way as for portfolios of its tax-exempt pension fund accounts. The resulting enormous tax bill was this investor's introduction to the culture gap that can sometimes exist between professionals serving institutional and private investors. An even wider gulf separates most academic research from the empirical world of private investors. Pragmatic professional investors often find the teachings of theoretical finance inapplicable.

Academics, professional institutional investors, and private investors—all have insights that can contribute to effective management of private wealth. Our purpose in this chapter is to provide an integrated view aimed at enhancing the value of the services professional investment managers and advisors provide to private investors.

Challenges in Investing Private Wealth

Private investors differ widely in their needs not only from tax-exempt institutions but also from one another—and even from themselves at different points in their lives. Consequently, effective private wealth investing requires a high degree of *customization*. Largely because of taxation, investing private wealth is also *complex*. And private investors usually need help from those willing to take *fiduciary responsibility*. Each of these factors poses significant challenges for the professional investment manager.

Need for Customization

Private investors differ from tax-exempt investors, and from each other, in many ways that affect best investment practice. Under a progressive income tax regime like that in the United States, different investors have different marginal income tax rates. They also live in different states, paying different state tax rates. Capital gains taxes differ from taxes on ordinary income; capital gains taxes are levied on the profit, but usually only upon liquidation of the security position.

One private investor may have a life expectancy of 10 years; another, of 30 years. Goals for possible wealth transfer before or at the end of life also differ widely. Some want to pass wealth on to their children; others want to support a charitable cause. Some just want to make sure that they do not outlive their wealth. For some investors, the issue of a proper balance between current income and capital appreciation may be a delicate intergenerational family matter; for others, it may be a matter of indifference—except for tax considerations. Private investors have different sizes of portfolios, so an investment management structure that is too costly for one is inexpensive for another.

Private investors differ in their risk attitudes and in their desires for active management. They may have extensive business interests or low-cost-basis stocks that need special diversification. Some investors want to be very involved in the details of their wealth management in order to keep a feeling of control of their personal capital; some are content to delegate. Private investors may be in the wealth accumulation and savings mode or in the wealth preservation and spending mode.

The needs of tax-exempt entities are much more homogeneous and more amenable to standardized approaches than the needs of private investors. The first challenge for institutional investment managers, then, is to focus on the investor's individual needs. Doing this properly requires special knowledge and an approach and cost structure that allow considerable customization—not only for the extraordinarily wealthy but also for the much larger group of investors who need and are willing to pay for professional services.

Inherent Complexity

Even after adequate customization has been defined, the investment professional's job remains much more complex than would be a similar role serving a pension fund. Private investors, perhaps mostly for tax reasons, often have a complex system of "buckets" in which wealth of different types and tax efficiency is located. These buckets may be as basic as a bank account and a retirement plan or as complicated as a wealthy family's business, a taxable personal portfolio, multiple trusts for the owners and their children, various limited partnerships, and a private foundation. Different investment policies may be appropriate for different buckets, depending on tax rules, family members' needs, and the planned end-of-life disposition of wealth. The investor needs coordinated investment policies and procedures among the buckets.

For each bucket, the system of tax rules may be complex and highly nonlinear, even for an investor of moderate wealth. Depending on nation (or even state) of domicile, an investor holding a simple common stock portfolio may face different taxes on dividends, short-term capital gains, and long-term capital gains. Complex rules govern the extent to which net losses can be carried forward into future years, the potential for tax-loss harvesting, and the need to avoid "wash sale" penalties. Finally, wealth transfer taxes, such as estate and gift taxes, have their own complicated requirements that can influence what the optimal decisions are in earlier years.

This complexity implies that practices learned elsewhere for gaining extra return while managing risk may give investment managers the wrong answer. For example, attempting to add to expected pretax return by active management may, instead, reduce after-tax return. The application of mean–variance optimization as usually practiced may give a poor answer to the question of what to do with a concentrated position of low-cost-basis stock or how to best take advantage of opportunities for deferring taxes through loss realization.

The challenge for professional managers is to take this complexity seriously, to quantify the value to be added by giving it due attention, and to balance that value against the benefits from devoting resources to other activities—for example, forecasting security returns or communicating with clients.

Fiduciary Responsibility

An institutional investment manager may be involved mostly in some combination of the quest for returns superior to a benchmark and the quest to control tracking error around a benchmark. Adequate fiduciary responsibility for this manager is relatively easy: The scope of the assignment and the complexity of the client's needs are limited, and the investment sophistication of the client is relatively high—not so in working with private clients. In many such cases, the investment advisor's responsibility extends to advice on how much risk to take and on generating after-tax returns, help in selecting not only securities but also other investment managers, and long-term financial planning. The stakes, at least for the client, are high. And the amount of accurate investment knowledge clients have may be very low.

Some private clients lack information about investments, are distrustful of financial matters, and may be too conservative for their own good. Others, particularly those who have created wealth in a conventional business career, mistakenly believe their personal experience to be transferable to the arena of the liquid securities markets and are overconfident. These attitudes are often reinforced by the popular media, with their emphasis on financial heroes who have experienced unusually good results, and even by professional investment research, which is generally optimistically biased and gives too much importance to recent developments. The popular investment press is filled with "do-it-yourself" articles implying that investing is both simple and obvious. But most clients need help of a type that they do not know enough about to request. In general, to fulfill their fiduciary responsibility, investment professionals must be proactive with private clients.

The importance of this challenge deserves what might at first seem to be a digression on ethics—that is, achieving good business through good practice.

Good Practice in Working with Private Clients

In serving private clients, especially if one comes from the world of competitive investment performance, the ethical standards that stand out relate to (1) the costs of customizing versus its value and (2) the possible short-term loss of revenues through educating clients about realistic long-term expectations.

CFA Institute maintains that ethical standards are good business. Consider these excerpts from the list of standards to which holders of the Chartered Financial Analyst designation are expected to adhere, together with our queries:[3]

> When Members and Candidates are in an advisory relationship with a client, they must:
> a. Make a reasonable inquiry into a client's or prospective client's investment experience, risk and return objectives, and financial constraints prior to making any investment recommendation or taking investment action and must reassess and update this information regularly.
> b. Determine that an investment is suitable to the client's financial situation and consistent with the client's written objectives, mandates, and constraints before making an investment recommendation or taking investment action.
> c. Judge the suitability of investments in the context of the client's total portfolio.

Query: Does not this standard mean that after-tax returns and their associated risks should be the focus for private investors rather than pretax returns and risks? How important is tracking error relative to absolute risk?

Performance Presentation. When communicating investment performance information, Members or Candidates must make reasonable efforts to ensure that it is fair, accurate, and complete.

Misrepresentation. Members and Candidates must not knowingly make any misrepresentations relating to investment analysis, recommendations, actions, or other professional activities.

Query: Is it enough to say that "past performance is not a guarantee of future success," or should investment managers educate clients with regard to the modest extent to which performance history is evidence of future success? Should discussion of product features that are attractive in the short run be balanced by explanations of the less favorable implications for longer-term and after-tax outcomes?

Meeting such requirements set forth by the CFA Institute Standards of Professional Conduct is particularly challenging when true suitability requires costly customization and record keeping for the most-effective tax management and when most private clients require education if they are to avoid damaging decisions. Private clients need education to avoid misunderstanding the significance of performance data, and they need it to help them understand the long-term implications of such appealing product features as high current income or downside protection.

Private clients with smaller portfolios have not been able to obtain some of the customized treatment we advocate, although this situation is beginning to change with the advent of greater computer automation. They have also been hard to convince to pay directly for advice because so much of the support for their financial planning comes through sales commissions. The result has been conflicts of interest that make client education and full fiduciary responsibility problematic. Said another way, private investors are more expensive than institutional clients for a financial services company to serve well. Either the fees for excellent professional services will be high, possibly prohibitively so for investors of moderate wealth (as they are today), or the investment professional must adopt methods that are both likely to bring about good investment outcomes and are cost-effective to implement. As improved tools bring down the cost of lifetime financial planning, risk management, and tax management, however, and as managers learn to communicate the value of these processes, the opportunity for profitable fiduciary responsibility seems likely to increase.

Case Example

The case mentioned in the section's opening was real. In the early 1980s, a large family fund was invested with a high-flying quantitative boutique manager given the assignment of maintaining a rather passive but highly quantitatively managed stock portfolio. The combination of a charismatic chief executive, leading-edge technologies, and a terrific track record had attracted many new accounts to this boutique. One of them was just a little different. In contrast to other accounts handled by the firm, this account was tax sensitive. The firm, however, was more investment centered than client centered in the management of the portfolios in its care. The portfolio manager had developed a number of computerizations of formerly manual processes. He favored passive portfolios with a computerized procedure for rebalancing the portfolios back toward their benchmarks. On the fateful day of the first rebalancing of the family fund, the identifier of the account was not excluded from a computer file to be read by a computerized trading program. The consequence was a massive and unnecessary tax bill.

Summary

The professional investor who is used to managing institutional portfolios faces special challenges when serving private investors:

- the need for customization because of differences in investor situations,
- a huge increase in complexity caused by taxation rules and interlinked portfolios, and
- broader fiduciary responsibilities for private clients, who may be poorly informed and who may need more all-inclusive help than institutional clients.

Good practice in working with private clients requires an ethical standard that

- goes beyond choosing suitable securities to encompass specific attention to after-tax returns and absolute versus relative risk and
- proactively avoids misrepresentation by including investor education in the job—for example, by pointing out how difficult it is to project past performance rather than by merely providing an accurate performance record.

These requirements make private investors more expensive to service than institutional clients and encourage the development of cost-effective ways to meet private clients' needs.

THEORY AND PRACTICE IN PRIVATE INVESTING

Private investors face far more complex decisions than do untaxed, long-lived institutions. Classical financial models, with their heroically simplified assumptions, cannot hope to present a complete picture of what private investors face, and using the models can even lead to worse results than using old-fashioned, less-theory-driven investment methods. This section addresses six key concepts of current finance theory as applied pragmatically to private investors:

1. the quasi-efficient market,
2. utility theory as applied to risk,
3. Markowitz portfolio optimization,
4. the capital asset pricing model (CAPM),
5. option valuation models, and
6. stochastic growth theory.

The Quasi-Efficient Market

Empirical academic research has amply confirmed that the liquid public securities markets are mostly efficient, in that the prices of securities incorporate publicly available information, so that it is difficult to make abnormal profits. We do not have to accept idealized theories of *perfect* instantaneous incorporation of new information to accept the stubborn empirical fact that security returns are hard to forecast. It is the "nearly" qualifier on return independence that gives employment to investment analysts and talented strategists and traders. But investors are well advised to base their strategies around a default position that presumes they will not be able to forecast most price fluctuations.

We *can* say that over long periods of time, stocks are likely to outperform bonds, but we cannot say with much confidence whether the stock market will go up tomorrow or which stock will have the best returns. It is hard to admit, but at any moment, much of what we know and much of what we have just learned is already incorporated in prices, at least for the heavily traded public markets. For the private investor who wishes to both outperform the market and delegate investing to someone else, the forecasting task has two layers. The investor must first choose a superior manager; then, the manager must choose the right security at the right time. The initial layer of the problem, selecting an above-average manager, is nearly of the same uncertainty and difficulty as the second layer of the problem—above-average security selection and timing. Competition among investment managers to exploit modest pockets of market inefficiency with which to earn above-average returns without excessive risk (the second layer), and thereby attract clients (the first layer), is intense.

Not only is the market for skillful managers itself competitive, with the more successful managers likely to attract so many clients that the initial extra-profitable investing niche is outgrown, but it is made murkier for the private investor by the confusion between good pretax and good after-tax return performance. To those who believe there is at least a modest statistical possibility of successfully investing with investment managers who exhibit a streak of high performance, we suggest that they consider the drag on after-tax performance from the increased effective tax rates triggered by turnover. While not wanting to discourage the pursuit of above-average returns through better forecasts within areas of market inefficiency, we believe that adding value to private client portfolios is far easier through reducing effective tax rates and through after-tax control of risk appropriate to the client's lifestyle needs and aspirations than it is through beating the market.

Utility Theory and Investment Risk Taking

More than a century ago, economic theories became popular that were based in the law of diminishing marginal utility with increasing wealth known with certainty. The reach of this concept was greatly extended after World War II, when it began to be used as a way to describe the fact that money received with certainty was preferable to a risky process with the same expected value. Utility curves mapped utility as a function of wealth. The utility of wealth known with certainty was presumed to lie on the curve, whereas the utility of mean expected values of an uncertain outcome between two possibilities was supposed to lie on a lower straight line connecting the two points. Different degrees of curvature represented different degrees of risk aversion. A utility function of declining risk aversion with increasing wealth could be represented by curves that got flatter as wealth increased.

Although utility curves can be used to construct illuminating theories, their use in practical application for private investors is problematic. Individuals have difficulty expressing the shape of their utility curves, and their responses can vary depending on the framing of questions and the time period involved. Even in simple cases, they usually cannot convert their utility curves for terminal wealth after many periods into the utility curve they would need for the single current period.

Therefore, advisors need a method for specifying connections between appropriate utility functions for the short run to produce optimal utility in the long run. The mean–variance optimization approach is an important building block in this direction but one that does not need to explicitly reference utility to be useful in practice.

Markowitz Mean–Variance Portfolio Optimization

Markowitz (1959) devised an approach for thinking about diversification based on maximizing a risk-adjusted expected portfolio return. More concretely, the expected portfolio return is expressed as the sum of individual security expected returns weighted by their proportions in the portfolio. The portfolio return variance is the sum of the elements of a weighted return covariance matrix. Each element in the matrix represents the risk contribution of a pair of securities. This contribution is the product of the proportions of each security in the portfolio, their standard deviations of return, and the correlation coefficient of their returns. Maximizing the risk-adjusted expected return constructed in this manner is known as portfolio mean–variance optimization.

The *efficient frontier* is the set of portfolios for which at a given risk, no higher expected return is to be had. The maximization of the Markowitz mean–variance objective consists of selecting that point on the efficient frontier that corresponds to the best outcome given the investor's trade-off between expected return and variance (or risk aversion). For a fairly wide variety of plausible utility curves, maximizing a linear function of mean expected return and variance can approximate maximizing utility, as long as the possible outcomes are not too extremely separated. This capability is simply the consequence of being able to fit a quadratic curve closely to any smooth curve within a local region.

For the private investor, taking taxes into account is especially important when providing inputs to the model. Examples are given in Appendix 10A and Appendix 10B.

Correctly specified, kept up to date, and restricted to the kinds of problems for which it is suited, period-by-period mean–variance optimization produces excellent long-term results. To avoid misusing it, the investment manager or advisor should be familiar with several potential pitfalls:

- misspecifying the input variables,
- focusing on the wrong kind of variance,
- not controlling for errors in inputs,
- overly narrow scope,
- inadequacy of return variance as a risk measure,
- need to update risk-aversion parameters, and
- significant links between periods.

If not handled with care, each of these issues can be more of a problem for private taxable investors than for institutional, tax-exempt investors. Brunel (2002) offered a view of the difficulties similar to this list but was less optimistic with regard to the potential for overcoming them.

Misspecifying the Input Variables

Taxable investors should use *after-tax* returns and risks as inputs to a Markowitz mean–variance analysis. An individual's tax-advantaged accounts, such as pension plans, should be treated as separate asset classes. For example, bonds held in an individual retirement account (and, consequently, having a low effective tax rate because of tax deferral) should be treated as a different asset class from bonds held in a taxable account. Returns from stocks {taxed at a 15 percent rate} are more tax advantaged than returns from taxable bonds {taxed at a 35 percent rate}; consequently, using pretax returns distorts the optimization for taxable investors.

Similar tax effects apply to estimates of risk. Taxation affects risk management because the government often acts as a risk-sharing partner. Here is a simplified example. Suppose an investment has an equal risk of a 15 percent gain or a 5 percent loss, and suppose the capital gains tax rate is 20 percent. Pretax, the mean gain will be 5 percent and the forecasted standard deviation will be 10 percent. After tax, the mean gain will be 4 percent and the standard deviation will be 8 percent (both have been reduced by 1/5). But rather than standard deviation, what is used in the optimizing calculation is the *variance* (standard deviation squared). The after-tax mean is 4/5 of the pretax mean, but the after-tax variance is only 16/25 of the pretax risk. Counterintuitively, the attractiveness of the risky asset relative to a risk-free asset is *increased* by taxation. As the applicable tax rate increases, generally, one should, all other things being equal, have a greater preference for assets with greater pretax risk. Of course, the qualification is that the taxable investor have enough unrealized gains elsewhere in the portfolio, or in the near future, to effectively use tax losses.

Focusing on the Wrong Kind of Variance

Institutional portfolio management often proceeds in stages, with long-term asset allocation leading to portions of the portfolio being farmed out to specialized investment managers within each asset class. To measure skill and to prevent the manager from deviating from the assigned mandate, the institution may place considerable emphasis on risk relative to a benchmark. This risk is typically measured as the squared standard deviation of differences in return from the benchmark, and it is inserted into mean–variance optimization in place of the absolute return variance. Such relative risk is of far less interest to private investors, however, who must be concerned with their portfolio as a whole. Because a focus on tracking error penalizes investment managers who reduce total portfolio risk, too much concern with relative risk and too little emphasis on absolute risk is a particular trap in professional management of private wealth.

Easily overlooked is the possibility of future tax changes, both through changes in tax law and through the investor's individual tax posture. Ideally, this "risk" should be incorporated in estimating after-tax risk and return; in other words, the potential for future changes in tax treatment is itself a source of after-tax return variance.

Not Controlling for Errors in Inputs

After a few years of attempting practical application, investment practitioners recognized that when mean–variance optimization is applied to large numbers of assets, the optimization problem as originally posed is unduly sensitive to errors in the input assumptions. And estimating effective tax rates aggravates the problem of uncertain inputs.

Fortunately, methods have been devised for managing at least the part of the problem that grows rapidly as the number of assets analyzed for the portfolio grows. These methods include (1) simplifying the covariance matrix by decomposing it into a smaller number of statistical common factors, (2) shrinking estimates toward prior beliefs not evident in the particular sample or model from which the original estimates were drawn (Ledoit 1999), and (3) trying out multiple assumptions and averaging the resulting optimal output proportions (Michaud 2001). Such methods are not necessary for an allocation among a few broad asset classes, but they are vital when dealing with numerous securities, as in the application of mean–variance optimization to day-to-day portfolio management.

Overly Narrow Scope

Institutional investors using Markowitz optimization usually do so for both conventional and alternative assets classes but almost always limit use to those classes with easily quantifiable market values. Private investors, however, are concerned with their total financial picture, which extends beyond liquid financial assets. Implied assets that may need to be taken into account include the value of a house or houses, perhaps a private family business, discounted stock options, unvested stock or stock options, and the capitalized saving stream from employment. Implied liabilities may include a home mortgage and the present value of any net spending (e.g., spending in excess of employment income), such as in retirement. To exclude these implied assets and liabilities is to assume that they do not vary in a way that would affect ideal holdings in marketable securities. Whether the extra effort required to include implied assets and liabilities is worthwhile will depend on the individual case.

Inadequacy of Variance as a Risk Measure

Markowitz recognized that investors object only to downside risk, not to upside risk. Usually, the relative downside risks of diversified portfolios are adequately ranked by their relative variances or, equivalently, by the square root of variance (standard deviation). However, return variance may not adequately capture the adverse impact of either strongly skewed returns for a large portion of the portfolio, as when using a put option on the stock market, or a rare but catastrophic outcome, as when heavy market losses force the sale of a large illiquid asset, such as a business. Therefore, additional downside risk measures may be useful in some cases. Downside risk is also often introduced through the complexities of the tax code when realized losses, some carrying high short-term tax rates, must be imperfectly matched against future realized gains, either considerably later or at a lower long-term capital gains rate. An alternative to ad hoc downside risk measures is suggested later in this section when we discuss expected logarithmic return.

Need to Update Risk-Aversion Parameters

Markowitz mean–variance optimization is often used as an aid in financial planning or asset allocation over long time horizons—five years being fairly typical. In the interim period, the professional advice is usually to rebalance back toward that strategic allocation when returns of asset classes move asset weights too far away from desired proportions. Of course, that advice should be tempered by tax considerations.

An important aspect is that, unless the full asset allocation analysis is redone more frequently than every five years, rebalancing does not deal with the fact that appropriate risk aversion may change as a function of substantial changes in wealth. This issue is particularly acute for private investors who experience major personal losses. Institutional investors, which are usually more professionally diversified, probably do not often get into a position where they are forced by losses to become more conservative to avoid disastrous shortfalls.

Significant Links between Periods

Transaction costs, although they imply an impact beyond the period in which they are incurred, are generally small enough that one can simply amortize the cost over the estimated prospective holding period. The savings in effective capital gains tax rates from compounding unrealized gains through long-term holdings (tax deferral) can be treated the same way. At times, however, planning that is more explicitly *multiperiod* is advisable. For example, a large tax payment may reduce discretionary wealth so much that potential changes in risk-aversion trade-offs need to be taken into account. An example is given in Appendix 10B.

The Capital Asset Pricing Model

The CAPM attempts to describe a security market in equilibrium. It assumes that each investor is a Markowitz mean–variance optimizer and that all investors process the same information in the same way; they differ only in their aversion to risk, expressed as return variance. Another key assumption is that each investor can lend or borrow at the same risk-free interest rate. The model also assumes either no taxes or that all investors are subject to the same tax rates. The CAPM implies that, among other things, a passive index fund holding the entire market of risky securities in proportion to their respective market values will be more efficient than any other portfolio.

The CAPM's assumptions are clearly unrealistic. For example, the same capitalization-weighted portfolio of risky assets cannot be optimal for both taxable and nontaxable investors. The practical issue, however, is not the realism of the assumptions but whether the model's predictions can be put to good use. Although extensive empirical research does not support several of the CAPM's predictions, it has found that market index funds, although not per-fectly optimal, are good choices for taxable investors. The broad diversification of index port-folios, the low fees, and the low turnover (which allows capital gains taxes to be deferred for long periods) are a combination that has many desirable properties for the private investor.

Option Valuation Theory

Option securities convey the right, but not the obligation, to buy or sell a given underlying security at a given price and at (European option) or until (American option) a given time. The original Black–Scholes option valuation model is based on the insight that a stock option payoff can be replicated with a continuously changing basket of long and short positions involving only cash, bonds, and the underlying stock. The assumptions behind the model were not completely realistic, but the model's accuracy has been sufficient to produce a pro-found change in the way we understand option valuation: Option values depend on return variance in the underlying stock and are not generally a material function of expected return for the stock.

All private investors subject to capital gains taxes can benefit from a basic understanding of option valuation because the right but not the obligation to sell at a loss creates a tax bene-fit. The investor has an option to sell or not to sell, and so to realize a gain or loss throughout the holding period of the security. For any given tax lot, this option has a value that depends on the variance of the underlying security. Across a portfolio of various tax lots for the same security, the value of a portfolio of such options is enhanced by dispersion in the ratios of cost to price. The combined value of these individual security option portfolios is enhanced to the degree that the underlying risks are imperfectly correlated across stocks, so the option value can be obtained without the corresponding increase in portfolio variance that would result from systematic market risk.

Because of the option to realize a capital gain or loss, a taxable investor is (1) less hurt by portfolio risk than are tax-exempt investors, (2) better off owning multiple tax lots of the same stock bought at different prices, and (3) able to derive benefit from stock-specific risk (volatility). The result is a lower effective tax rate and higher expected after-tax returns.

Investment professionals who have spent their careers working with tax-exempt portfolios—where specific risks of individual stocks are something to be avoided—may be surprised at the idea of encouraging specific risk. The idea of cultivating dispersion in tax-lot ratios of price to cost may be even more foreign. Yet, the benefits to private investors in reducing effective tax rates through tax-loss harvesting can be material. This benefit supports the use of portfolios that are large in terms of more variety in security names, more tax lots, and more emphasis on a diversified list of relatively less correlated returns. In practice, these criteria can be met by a portfolio of many diversified small-capitalization stocks bought at different times to obtain cost variety.

Stochastic Growth Theory

In addition to the core concepts of finance discussed up to this point, we have long advocated stochastic growth theory as a useful approach to setting the risk-aversion parameter in mean–variance optimization for short time periods in such a way that they produce better long-term results (Wilcox 2003). The insights of this theory tell us that when one maximizes expected log return on *discretionary* wealth each period, the result tends to maximize median long-term total wealth. Rubinstein (1976) proposed a similar approach for incorporating investor preferences into market pricing theory.

Log return is calculated each period as the natural logarithm of the quantity 1 plus the conventional arithmetic return. To calculate compound return over multiple periods, subtract 1 from the antilog of the sum of the individual log returns. It can be shown that maximizing the expected log return in individual periods tends to maximize the median compound result in the long run.

The idea of maximizing expected log return on the total portfolio for individual periods to get the best compounding result has a long history, beginning with Bernoulli in the 1700s. Applied to the total portfolio in unmodified form, the approach does not account for the needs of conservative investors, but applying it to only the portion of the portfolio that is discretionary (i.e., that the investor can afford to lose) is a different matter. This limited approach will maximize the median growth of the discretionary wealth away from the shortfall point. It also imposes an extreme penalty if the portfolio's value comes near the shortfall point. By setting the shortfall point high enough, any degree of additional conservatism can be produced.

A Taylor series is a mathematical device for expressing a nonlinear function of some quantity as the sum of an infinite series of terms of increasing powers of the quantity. When expected log return is expressed as a Taylor series of the difference between outcomes and the expected arithmetic return, the result provides great insight into the impact of statistical characteristics of conventional arithmetic returns, such as mean, variance, skewness, and kurtosis. Each successive term provides incremental information about events of smaller probability but greater influence on compounding returns if they should occur.

For investors of limited human lifetimes, four terms are sufficient to consider in making current investment decisions. The advisor thereby takes into account not only the variance used in Markowitz mean–variance optimization but also excess downside risk represented by negative skew and so-called fat-tailed (high-kurtosis) return distributions.

In most practical cases involving diversified investment portfolios, the effects of even these third (skewness) and fourth (kurtosis) return moments are tiny and can be ignored. Then the objective of maximizing expected log return on discretionary wealth can be approximated using a formula derived from simplifying (for small to moderate expected arithmetic returns) only the first two terms of its Taylor series representation (Wilcox):

$$\text{Expected log return} \cong LE(1 - T^*) - \frac{L^2 V(1 - T^*)^2}{2}, \tag{10.1}$$

where

  L = ratio of total assets to discretionary wealth
  E = pretax mean return
  T^* = effective tax rate
  V = pretax return variance

Maximizing this function provides an approach to analyzing financing decisions. But in the more typical case where no changes in the ratio of total assets to discretionary wealth are permitted, this objective can also be achieved approximately by dividing it by the resulting constant leverage, L, and maximizing

$$E(1 - T^*) - \frac{LV(1 - T^*)^2}{2}. \tag{10.2}$$

This objective is simply *Markowitz mean–variance optimization with after-tax means and variances and with the trade-off for risk aversion set to $L/2$*, or half the ratio of assets to discretionary wealth. In other words, rather than asking the investor to identify a subjective aversion to near-term risk, the advisor, assuming a goal of maximizing long-term median outcomes, objectively determines an optimum aversion to this risk based on the investor's specification of a shortfall point.

Figure 10.1 illustrates this idea for a wealthy family.[4] The family's capitalized net spending rate is shown as an implied liability that must be subtracted from total assets to derive discretionary wealth. The ratio of assets to discretionary wealth, L, is the implicit leverage (noted as 2.6) that determines how conservative the investor needs to be to realize best long-term median results while avoiding the shortfall point.

FIGURE 10.1 Investor Balance Sheet

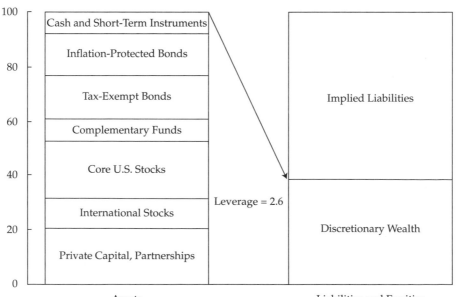

This "discretionary wealth" approach to mean–variance optimization also implies a risk-control discipline for investors who experience large losses that they do not think they will soon recoup. That is, the method forces increased conservatism as the portfolio value approaches the shortfall point. Used this way, the process for updating risk aversion is akin to constant proportion portfolio insurance (CPPI) but with the critical difference that, given an already determined leverage, risk aversion is managed at a level that optimizes expected growth away from the shortfall point.[5]

Summary

Financial theory oversimplifies the problems of private investors. It provides a starting point, but to be useful, it must be adapted carefully and extensively. The main ideas and adaptations are as follows:

- Most ideas and data available to the public are already well priced, which makes picking stocks, timing markets, and picking good managers problematic for most investors. This situation increases the relative importance of risk and tax management. Investors face a trade-off between risk and return, but specifying it for private investors through utility theory, which is idealized and relates to a single period, is often impractical.
- Markowitz mean–variance optimization is the best tool we have for balancing risk and return efficiently, but its correct implementation requires careful study.
- Option valuation theory teaches us that the choice of when to realize a taxable gain or loss is valuable and is enhanced by dispersion in returns and ratios of market value to cost basis.
- Stochastic growth theory helps us understand how to correctly balance return and risk to achieve long-term goals without triggering shortfalls along the way.

LIFE-CYCLE INVESTING

Should investors have different portfolios when they are young, in middle age, and old? Should one's life-cycle pattern of asset allocations depend on how wealthy one is? Do a person's plans for disposition of wealth at the end of life make any difference? Intuition suggests that the answer to each of these questions is "yes," but investors and investment advisors need to be able to quantify these effects. The purpose of this section is to provide a structured and quantitative approach to answering these questions.

Although investment advisors may have their personal, subjective opinions, as advisors, they do not have a professional basis for telling clients how they should trade off current spending against future wealth. Advisors can, however, use simulations to show clients the possible distributions of outcomes under various assumptions about savings, spending, and possible investment results. Such simulations are best constructed period by period, with assumptions that reflect the best investment allocations the investment professional can construct for each point in the life cycle and contingent on the results to that point.

The key element in applying best-practice simulations is the *time series of implied balance sheets* (refer to Figure 10.1 in the previous section) showing the relationship of discretionary wealth to assets. Discretionary wealth is what is left over after implied and tangible financial assets have been added and after implied and tangible financial liabilities have been subtracted.[6] In this context, "discretionary" implies "what the investor would not like to give up but the loss of which would not be considered disastrous." The sequence of balance sheets, including the evolution in the implied leverage on discretionary wealth, is used period by period for asset allocation decisions. The review of evolving leverage should lead to better informed decisions—whether they are made qualitatively or quantitatively through mean–variance optimization. As the investor goes from youth to maturity to middle age to retirement to old age, the ratio of discretionary wealth to total assets will determine appropriate levels of investment aggressiveness.

Interaction of Life Cycle and Wealth

As a first cut, Table 10.1 shows a broad (there are many exceptions to it) characterization of typical best policies by wealth class and age. Note especially the *interaction* between age and wealth, which together are the key factors for an appropriate investment posture.

A surprise might be the conservative entries in the "young" column. The negative present value of a retirement spending stream liability plus possible liabilities for housing, children's college, and so on, may keep discretionary wealth low or negative until employment-related implied assets and financial assets build up. Then, the investor can make the transition from a conservative to a balanced strategy or from a balanced to an aggressive investment strategy. Many people, "the rest of us" row, may never accumulate enough discretionary wealth, even including implied assets from employment, to move beyond conservative or very conservative ideal portfolios.

Perhaps most investors would be classed as "prosperous." Also, those who are classed initially as high-net-worth (HNW) investors but later do poorly with their investments will need a second evolution in asset allocation (i.e., back to greater conservatism) as they move from employment and net savings to retirement and net spending. Unless they save significantly and have favorable investment returns, coupled with a restrained standard of living in retirement, these HNW investors will find their ratios of discretionary wealth to assets declining.

For those other HNW investors who do well with their investments, the situation may be quite different. Investors who significantly increase their proportion of discretionary assets to total wealth as they approach retirement (or even the end of life) can become more aggressive. This conclusion is contrary to the usual textbook recommendation (and also to the old saw that the equity allocation percentage should be 100 minus the investor's age), but it may be appropriate if investment prospects are likely to result in more wealth than will be needed over the investors' lives.

The extremely wealthy, shown in the top row of Table 10.1, can usually maintain discretionary wealth at high levels for their entire lifetime and can always invest aggressively.

A time-sequenced set of balance sheets has far greater value for life-cycle customization if it includes not only conventional investments and debts but also *implied* assets and liabilities.

TABLE 10.1   Typical Best Policies by Stage and Wealth Class

Wealth Class	Young	Middle Age	Old
Very wealthy	Aggressive	Aggressive	Aggressive
High net worth	Balanced	Aggressive	Balanced/aggressive
Prosperous	Conservative	Balanced	Conservative
The rest of us	Conservative	Conservative	Very conservative

FIGURE 10.2   New High-Net-Worth Investor's Balance Sheet

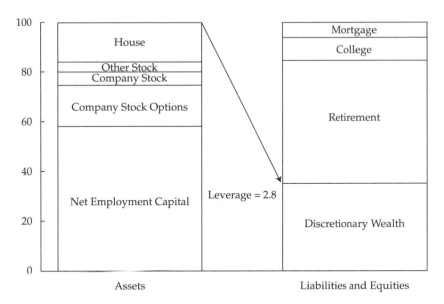

Portion (%)

Consider the general case: On the negative side, the present value of the implied liability for spending in retirement has a relatively modest value when one is young because of time discounting (and perhaps because of limited early lifestyle aspirations). It usually rises to a peak close to retirement and then may gradually diminish as future life expectancy shortens. On the positive side, implied employment assets (i.e., the present value of future savings during employment) build up through time and then diminish as retirement approaches.

To make the concept of employment-related implied assets clearer, Figure 10.2 shows the implied balance sheet for a newly HNW executive in his mid-30s. He is not yet truly wealthy, but he has considerable implied wealth from employment. The wealth is composed of unvested stock and stock options plus the capitalization of his stream of savings during employment—all discounted not only with respect to time but for the ongoing probability of loss of employment. For simplicity, Figure 10.2 omits the valuation of life insurance and the implied liabilities for capital gains taxes.

Case Example

Juan inherits nothing but funding for a college education. He earns an engineering degree and a master's degree in business administration. Saving prudently, he gradually increases his saving rate as his salary and bonuses increase. His implied employment assets (i.e., the present value of his future savings during employment) also build up through time. By age 34, and based on his current lifestyle, Juan believes he has his minimum current retirement goals covered. To keep the example simple, assume that Juan never marries and will have no children. He carries minimal life insurance. (These simplifications allow this discussion to avoid the complicated issue of valuing life insurance, which has little value to Juan.)

Figure 10.3 shows the paths of Juan's employment assets and retirement liabilities, together with more conventional investment assets, from age 20 to age 85. His capitalized

FIGURE 10.3   Hypothetical Real Balance Sheet Series

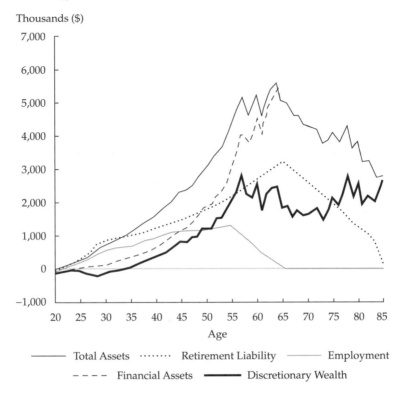

savings stream from future employment continues to rise until he is 55. From that point until retirement at age 65, his implied employment assets decline as the savings period shortens. Because of prudent savings, aided by moderate investment performance, however, his financial assets rise steadily and, by his retirement, are larger than his implied employment assets.

After 55, Juan's financial assets continue to grow for some years but with much greater fluctuation than previously—for two reasons. First, growth of his financial assets (shown in Figure 10.3 after taxes and after inflation) is now dominated by investment returns rather than new savings. Second, his increased discretionary wealth permits all of his financial wealth to be invested in an equity portfolio rather than in less-volatile investments. Between age 55 and age 65, he does experience a rapidly *declining* present value of future employment, together with a rapidly *rising* present value of capitalized retirement spending (assuming a life expectancy of 85 years), which combine to bring discretionary wealth down from a peak of more than $2.5 million to a little less than $1.5 million in constant dollars.

Retired with no dependents, Juan sticks to his original prudent retirement lifestyle of spending an average of $250,000 after taxes and inflation for the next 20 years. He mentally sets aside a significant sum for medical expenses in the last years of his life. His investments gradually decline with his withdrawals from about $4.8 million to about $2.8 million. He leaves his estate to charity.

The key determinant of portfolio policy for Juan was the ratio of discretionary wealth to total assets. Figure 10.4 shows how Juan's well-considered investment allocations evolved during his life on the basis of changes in this ratio. From age 20 through 33, the present value of

FIGURE 10.4   Hypothetical Ratio of Discretionary Wealth to Total Assets

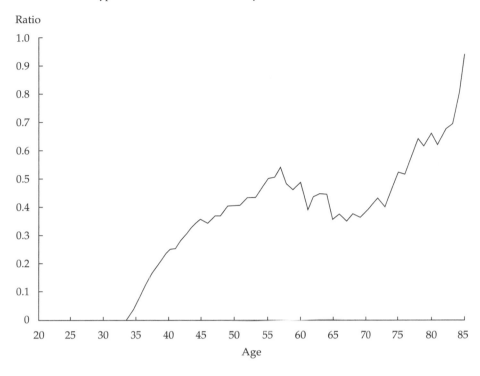

Juan's retirement spending plan is greater than his total assets, even including the present value of future savings capitalized. In working out the investment returns during this period, the example assumes that because Juan is facing a shortfall relative to the present value of money needed for retirement, he allocates no money to stocks until discretionary wealth becomes positive. A different investor might think that any losses on the stock market could be made up by a contingent increased rate of savings, but Juan does not feel that he has that flexibility. (Valuing flexibility is discussed in the next section.)

From age 34 to age 56, Juan gradually increases his allocation to equities, with 100 percent allocation during his peak prosperity in terms of discretionary wealth as a fraction of total assets. This period is before the present value of his retirement liability begins to be important. Juan favors actively managed funds, and for simplicity, the assumption is that, on average, he has no unrealized capital gains or losses each year.

After a peak in discretionary wealth relative to prosperity in middle age, Juan becomes a bit more conservative; he retreats to a balanced stock/bond portfolio as the present value of his remaining employment declines and the present value of retirement spending increases. After about age 75, however, he realizes that his investment returns are more than keeping up with the gradually declining present value of his retirement spending. That is, with his increasing age, his fraction of discretionary wealth to total assets begins increasing again as the present value of retirement spending begins to shrink. In other words, Juan is not likely to outlive his funds and he has no fixed obligations. This development allows funds to once again be invested in an aggressive portfolio, although one from which he can receive adequate cash flow.

This example shows how good investment policy can change over an investor's life cycle. It is clear that a rule of thumb such as "the percentage of equity should be equal to 100 minus the investor's age" will not generally work for many HNW (and most all very wealthy) investors, who may be able to handle even more risk as they get older. For the other end of the age spectrum, there is a strong argument that those young people with little wealth and without the flexibility to increase their savings if investments turn sour should be very conservative. More generally, the oft-touted virtues of the stock market do not apply to those with few financial resources, even though long-run *average* returns of stocks are indeed higher than long-run bond returns. Those on the edge of financial disaster cannot afford to take much risk.

Flexibility of Employment Earnings and Consumption Spending

What happens if discretionary wealth falls to zero or even becomes negative? People in this situation have to readjust their thinking—even if it is painful—about what they must earn or can spend. The desirability of flexibility in employment earnings, consumption, and financial requirements means that portfolio investment is actually a subproblem within a broader set of choices that, if considered in complete detail, would involve complicated mathematics.

To simplify the investment problem, however, rather than make it more complex, the investment advisor might show a wealthy investor who initially requires capitalizing $1 million a year in a spending allowance that perhaps, in an emergency, he or she could live on less, perhaps 80 percent of that amount. Then, the 20 percent difference can be capitalized as a flexibility asset by discounting it not only for time but also for the subjectively estimated probability that this flexibility will actually be used. Having flexibility among future employment, consumption, and savings has a quasi-option value that, in itself, is a type of asset. Rather than ignoring flexibility, when it is material relative to discretionary wealth, the advisor can take it into account as an asset-like feature. Treatment of flexibility as a crudely valued option asset oversimplifies a complex situation, but it is better than leaving flexibility out of the investment plan altogether.

Because large and sudden shocks to consumption are painful, arriving at a given increment of discretionary wealth by saving small amounts over long periods is much easier than arriving by saving large amounts over a short period. *Flexibility favors the young investor because it allows him or her to be more aggressive in allocation to stocks and other risky assets.* Nevertheless, this protection is limited, and the default position should be that young investors of limited means and heavy financial responsibilities should be conservative.

Remaining Lifetime Risks

Outliving one's assets may not be a concern for the very wealthy, but it is a pressing concern to investors of moderate wealth, even some who would be classified as HNW investors. The investment that addresses the risk of outliving one's savings is an annuity.

The question of whether an annuity is appropriate for a client depends on both life situation and price. Whether annuities are overpriced depends not only on provider profits and costs for marketing but also on tax issues. For example, in the United States, the taxation of distributions from annuities is figured by subtracting the original contribution of principal, and then, on the negative side, all gains are taxed at ordinary income tax rates. One does not get the benefit of lower capital gains tax rates. On the positive side, annuities provide the benefits of genuine risk pooling. For high-tax-bracket individuals, and with the currently low U.S. dividend and capital gains tax rates, one can argue that self-insurance through investing is competitive with annuities.

Without something like an annuity, how can the investor best manage the risk arising from an uncertain remaining life span? The investor could, from the beginning, plan for a longer life than actuarially expected. That approach would build in an additional safety cushion by reducing discretionary wealth. A better approach is to construct several lifespan scenarios. After converting them to different implied liabilities for future retirement expenditures, using the discretionary wealth method will result in different appropriate risk tolerances for each scenario. The greater impact on risk tolerance of the longer-life scenarios as compared with shorter-life scenarios will produce a more conservative result. *Uncertainty about length of life is properly reflected in a more conservative investment portfolio.*[7]

Disposition of Excess Wealth

Wealth transfers involving gifts and estates is the domain of experts in tax law, but once the alternatives have been identified, they can be analyzed in the framework put forward in this section. The after-tax cash flow streams can be reduced to implied and explicit assets and liabilities, and the resulting sequence of balance sheets and their implications for asset allocation by location can be analyzed in a Markowitz mean–variance framework.

Even if the investor should have little faith in, or ability to implement, a full-fledged algorithmic solution to planning disposition of wealth, the effort to put the problem into the sequence of implied balance sheets will lead to a firmer grasp of the nature of the decisions he or she needs to make.

Summary

Combining stochastic growth theory with the notion of avoiding interim shortfalls leads us to a framework for

- managing discretionary wealth as the key to avoiding shortfalls and achieving long-term financial goals and
- expanding the investor's balance sheet to include implied liabilities, such as capitalized retirement, lifestyle maintenance, and taxes for unrealized capital gains, and to include implied assets, such as capitalized employment-related savings and unvested benefits.

The resulting framework for financial planning, which should be contingent on both age and financial outcomes, guides life-cycle investing, which involves

- summarizing current optimal risk attitudes in the ratio of assets to discretionary wealth,
- subjecting plans to a disciplined review and revision as discretionary wealth and the investment environment change, and
- clarifying the need to address flexibility, end-of-life risk reduction, and plans for excess wealth disposition.

PART II   PRIVATE WEALTH AND TAXATION

In this part, the sections aim to convey the viewpoint of the wealthy investor toward financial matters. What matter most, at least in comparison with institutional investors, are taxation and provisions for transferring wealth to others. The section on Lifestyle, Wealth Transfer, and Asset Classes is a general description of attitudes and circumstances. The Overview of Federal Taxation of Investments describes in considerable detail how the U.S. tax code affects the wealthy investor, with particular attention to capital gains taxes and the estate tax. Techniques for Improving After-Tax Investment Performance describes important strategies for improving after-tax returns.

LIFESTYLE, WEALTH TRANSFER, AND ASSET CLASSES

In the late 1950s, one of the most popular shows on television was "The Millionaire." Each episode was a short story in which an emissary, Michael Anthony, delivered to an unsuspecting recipient a $1 million check from John Beresford Tipton, an eccentric multimillionaire. For the recipient, this gift was a dramatic, life-changing event, for better or for worse, like sweeping a state lottery is today.

Half a century later, millionaires are commonplace and billionaires are common enough to fill more than two-thirds of the Forbes 400 list, which surely undercounts the actual number. Such is the result of a combination of inflation, general growth in wealth (at least in nominal terms), and a change in the distribution of wealth, with an increasing concentration at the upper ranges.

According to the World Wealth Report 2005 published by Merrill Lynch and Capgemini, more than 8 million people had assets greater than $1 million, excluding their primary residences, in 2004. The report categorized this wealth as high-net-worth (HNW) individuals ($1 million to $5 million), midtier millionaires ($5 million to $30 million), and ultra-HNW individuals (more than $30 million). It estimated that worldwide the numbers are 7,445,800 HNW individuals, 774,800 midtier millionaires, and 77,500 ultra-HNW individuals. Although the category limits are somewhat subjective, note that each higher category has roughly a tenth the number of people in the category below it.

Wealth of the HNW Household

U.S. Internal Revenue Service (IRS) statistics show that the top 10 percent threshold of adjusted gross income (AGI) for 2002 was $92,663.[8] The top 1 percent threshold of AGI was $285,424, which was 10 times the median AGI. Federal income tax filers of more than $1 million of AGI, which is the top 0.13 percent, numbered 168,608.

According to 1997 data, the top 1 percent of households holds approximately 30 percent of all the wealth in the United States, and the top 5 percent holds about 55 percent of all the wealth (Quadrini and Rios-Rull 1997). Using 1998 data from the Federal Reserve's Survey of Consumer Finances, Montalto (2001) reported that 4.5 percent of U.S. households at that time, about 4.6 million, had assets, including their primary residences, of $1 million or more. More than 80 percent of these HNW (greater than $1 million) households were headed by someone at least 45 years old. For the HNW group, financial assets (e.g., cash, stocks, bonds, mutual funds) and nonfinancial assets (e.g., real estate and business interests) each constitute about half (mean share) of the net assets. The World Wealth Report 2005 estimated that there are about 2.5 million people in the United States with assets, excluding their primary residences, greater than $1 million.

Investors with a financial net worth ranging from $1 million to $5 million, excluding primary residences, are typically limited to using mutual funds or directly owning public stocks and bonds. They have limited access to the kind of products, such as private equity, that institutions can use. Many will be somewhere in the upper ranges of tax rates, for both income and estate taxes.

The group from about $5 million to $30 million has the wherewithal to invest in stocks and bonds through individual accounts and to have some limited participation in alternative asset classes, mostly through expensive retail investment partnerships or some funds of hedge funds. The vast majority are likely to be in the top marginal tax brackets and are potentially subject to substantial estate tax. The trend is for families at the higher end of this range to work in multifamily offices to achieve the economy of scale necessary to have access to institutional advice and investment opportunities.

Families and individuals with more than $30 million in assets are likely to have some combination of family investment office, financial advisor, and sophisticated tax planner. This group will have varying mixes of concentrated direct investments and more diversified institutional kinds of investments. They also have enough liquid wealth to invest in most of the alternative asset classes, such as hedge funds, private equity, venture capital, and institutional real estate. Despite the typically unattractive tax treatment of hedge funds, hedge fund strategies (collectively) represent the most popular alternative asset classes for this group.

Families and individuals with more than $100 million start to look and act more like institutional investors. They often have their own family offices, with some investment professionals, and have access to the majority of institutional investment products, including such illiquid investments as private equity and venture capital partnerships. Their asset allocations and investment strategies are fully as sophisticated as those of most institutional investors. They can afford the best investment advice from institutional consultants and tax attorneys. They can rarely afford in-house money managers until their investment assets approach about $1 billion, however, in which case directly employing in-house managers for specific asset classes can become economical.

At the top end are those with wealth in the billions (even tens of billions). The Forbes 400 list for 2004 probably undercounts the number of mega-rich and underestimates the wealth reported, but even so, it lists *278 billionaires*. For the majority of billionaires (or billionaire families), wealth is often concentrated in directly owned or controlled businesses but substantial liquid wealth is left for other investments. These rare investors are highly individualized but typically function as institutional investors with respect to their diversified financial investments.

Whether the levels of wealth are *qualitatively* different is not clear, although common sense would suggest so. Perhaps jumps in functional wealth are characterized by a log function; perhaps increments such as $1 million, $10 million, $100 million, $1 billion, and $10 billion are useful wealth "plateaus" or categories. An alternative view is that a completely different functional relative-wealth plateau may be achieved when the annual return on the wealth approximates the total wealth of the category just below it. If such plateaus correctly characterize the relative desirability of wealth, this factor has obvious implications for the implied shape of the utility curve corresponding to each plateau. In contrast to these wealth/utility categorizations, an investment-oriented categorization of wealth might take into account the widening choices of asset classes and investment vehicles that become practical and available as wealth levels increase. (Wealth levels as they relate to categories of consumption are discussed indirectly in the next section.)

With the range of wealth so extreme, identifying and discussing the "average" HNW investor is difficult. The goals, needs, and financial aspirations of the diverse but small number of HNW investors vary widely (much more than for those in or below the upper middle class, where more homogenous financial circumstances are the norm). But one thing the HNW all have in common is that taxes have a significant effect on their ability to retain and increase their wealth.

Consumption, Spending, and Risk Management

For most people, spending and consumption are essentially the same thing, but for the very wealthy, consumption is usually much less than total spending. Their basic needs for consumption—that is, clothing, food, shelter, and so on—are easily met and exceeded. For the very wealthy, even luxury wants are easily satisfied. A portion of their spending in excess of consumption is devoted to a variety of expensive consumer durables—luxury housing, second homes, yachts, airplanes, works of art, high-end jewelry. These expenditures are highly discretionary and are related to investment returns, but they are not necessarily *consumption*, at least not in amount equal to the expenditure. Pointing to the highly discretionary nature of luxury spending, Ait-Sahalia, Parker, and Yogo (2004) found, "By contrast [with basic goods] the consumption of luxuries is both more volatile and more correlated with excess [stock market] returns" (p. 2961). In fact, some nonconsumption expenditures on goods such as homes or works of art may even appreciate and have the potential to create an inflation hedge. For the extremely wealthy, to completely dissipate one's wealth by spending is hard.

In assessing an HNW client's risk tolerance, the important difference between total spending and consumption should be explicitly recognized in terms of how much risk can be tolerated. The following simple categorization of spending needs and desires is an aid in this assessment:

1. Basic necessities (food, basic housing, basic clothing, utilities, transportation, medical/ insurance coverage)
2. Lifestyle maintenance (education, entertainment, dining out, child care, family vacations)
3. Luxury consumption (luxury travel, luxury clothes, domestic staff, luxury furnishings)
4. Noninvestment assets (luxury primary home, second home, yacht, private airplane, art, antiques)
5. Savings and investments (bank accounts, employee stock and options, pensions, whole life insurance, stocks, bonds, alternative investments)

A sixth category, which is not as rare as one might think, is the goal of making money as an end in itself, either for ego, prestige, or a sense of "winning."

Most of these elements must be funded with *after-tax money*. Expenditures require cash. Many clients and advisors become confused by thinking that *income* is required to maintain lifestyle. In fact, cash is the medium for purchasing goods and services, and cash is not identical with income. Income—consisting of salary, interest, and dividends—is taxed either heavily (salary and interest) or moderately (dividends) and may not be the most tax-efficient way to fund expenditures. In some instances, taxable income is generated that has no accompanying cash ("phantom income") as when a partnership has taxable income but does not distribute cash.

Today, to the extent that investments provide the main source for expenditures, capital appreciation and dividends are among the most effective methods of generating cash.[9] Sales of securities at or below cost can generate cash with no current tax at all. Distinguishing the need for cash rather than "income" will help an advisor craft an optimal investment program.

Shortfall Constraints

The topic of shortfall constraints for institutional investors, most of which are tax exempt, has been well developed by Leibowitz (1992). The immunization of liabilities through asset matching is another topic that has been well developed for the tax-exempt investor. For the majority of individuals, who spend most of what they earn, these concepts have little application because their savings are too limited to provide resources for asset/liability matching or immunization; moreover, they often have financial liabilities but little in the way of financial assets. For the HNW investor, however, a tax-adjusted adaptation of these institutional techniques will be of value in securing the financial well being of the investor and family.

For private investors, the advisor has to take into account not only the magnitude and probability of a shortfall but also the personal *importance* (personal negative utility) of the shortfall. This problem is different from the situation facing most tax-exempt investors. They are concerned with shortfalls measured in dollars to match known liabilities and little concerned with large differences in marginal utility. For most individuals, such differences are important: Not being able to make a child's college tuition payment is very different from not being able to trade in a 100-foot yacht for a 150-foot yacht. An advisor could develop shortfall-constraint analyses separately for each expenditure category—for example, the five categories listed previously.

Because many of the "liabilities" of the wealthy investor are related to consumption—in particular, the "conspicuous consumption" described by Veblen (1994)—they may not be easily deferred without unpleasant disruptions in lifestyle. So, the ability to weather temporary reductions in investment wealth, investment-related income, or salary income may be more than a dollar-and-cents issue. For the highly discretionary categories of expenditures, the importance of a temporary reduction should be less than for more basic needs. Adequate risk analysis needs to take into account the consequences as well as the likelihood and magnitude of the potential loss. Permanent losses of wealth can have emotional consequences, as well as economic consequences, that adversely affect self-esteem and social prestige.

In modeling or analyzing taxable portfolios, especially in light of shortfall constraints, the advisor needs to be aware of some peculiar potential tax implications. Portfolios with poor performance will usually have proportionately more losses than gains. Thus, the opportunity to offset losses with gains within or outside these investment portfolios may be limited or nonexistent. Conventional approaches to modeling after-tax returns usually give full credit to tax losses, but poorly performing portfolios may not allow the use of these losses, in which case, conventional estimates of the tax benefits are overstated. Unusable losses create a tax asymmetry whereby portfolios with net losses are functionally pretax and thus larger than the equivalent tax-exempt portfolios, but portfolios with net gains are after tax and thus smaller than the equivalent tax-exempt portfolios. In other words, portfolio analysis should be based on effective, not nominal, tax rates, which may be idiosyncratic to the circumstances of the specific investor.

Shrinking (Finite) Time Horizons

As investors get older, their investment horizons shrink, which has important investment and tax implications. The *actuarial* life expectancy is not fixed at birth but is conditional upon having reached greater age, so the life expectancy of a person at age 10 is less than that of a person who has reached age 60. Obviously, *life span*—that is, the maximum length of life—has a practical upper limit; life span is not infinite, but nonetheless, a person who outlives the actuarial tables and runs out of money has a serious problem. Consequently, planning needs to take into account the longest possible survival, not actuarial life expectancy alone. Conventional actuarial practice is to forecast life expectancy *on average for large sets of people*, which can be done with high accuracy. With a sample size of one individual, the average life expectancy is simply the wrong measure of what people have to worry about.

The average investor's risk tolerance may decrease as life span and investment horizon decrease, but very wealthy investors with bequest goals for their wealth may have an increasing risk tolerance because they are not investing for consumption during their own lifetimes but, rather, to bequeath money to charities or subsequent generations. In the case of a surviving spouse, particularly one who is substantially younger than the investor, the problem can be thought of as an extended life expectancy of the investor.

When the investment horizon becomes shorter as a consequence of shorter life expectancy, the rational course of action for most investors is to minimize the recognition of taxable gains. The gains will almost always incur less tax at death than during a person's lifetime, with the remaining value of the investment assets left for the estate tax. The asset mix should reflect not only any end-of-life changes in risk tolerance, but also the tremendous advantages of tax deferral and the potential to avoid tax entirely for estates below the threshold for estate tax exemption.[10]

The estate tax applies, if at all, to the fair market value, which is the sum of the tax basis plus all unrecognized gains, although there are some differences between the treatment of private investments and the treatment of publicly traded securities. (Private investments are another matter because of the possibility of discounts from gross fair market value based on factors such as illiquidity, minority discounts, and restrictions on transferability.) At the time of death, any unrecognized capital gains escape capital gains tax, but the amount of the unrecognized gain is part of the estate assets subject to the estate tax.

The amount saved by not realizing gains during the investor's lifetime is calculated as

$$(1 - \text{Estate tax rate}) \times (\text{Unrealized gain} \times \text{Capital gains tax rate}).$$

For other types of estate planning (e.g., leaving money to one's spouse), the tax-deferral period can be enhanced, which adds value.

The Estate Tax and Wealth Transfer

Although the topic of estate planning is complex, extensive, and outside the scope of this chapter, some important points need to be made because the goal of many investment programs for HNW investors includes leaving wealth to family members, charities, and others. The estate tax and the gift tax are every bit as much a tax on investments as are income and capital gains taxes but are given little attention in the investment literature.

The estate tax potentially applies to approximately the wealthiest 2 percent of taxable households in the United States. Some estate planners have called it the only "voluntary" tax in the United States, meaning that people have so many ways to avoid paying estate tax that an estate is relatively rarely subject to it. Although this statement is true to an extent, the estate tax applies to a significant portion of the HNW population. Small estates may incur no estate tax at all, and a step-up in basis to fair market value at time of death means that a subsequent sale at the same fair market value has no capital gain. Thus, investments with unrealized gains held until death are functionally tax exempt. One of the many oddities of the tax law is that individuals with estates that are not above the exemption receive much better tax treatment at death than when the investor was alive; at death, all the potential tax liability on unrecognized gains is completely wiped away forever.

The tax law is favorable for transfers of assets between spouses. Assets can be transferred to a spouse during life or at death with no immediate tax implication. This aspect creates an important opportunity for tax deferral. The probability function of joint survivorship of a married couple is different from the actuarial life expectancy of either spouse alone; joint actuarial life is longer. Therefore, the investment planning horizon can be far longer than the earliest-to-die estimate of a married couple. Assets left to a spouse, either directly or through a trust (e.g., a qualified terminal income property trust), need not be taxed until the death of the surviving spouse. Modeling across the investment horizon needs to take these path dependencies into account because they have serious tax implications and thereby affect after-tax returns and terminal wealth.

By adding many years to potential tax deferral, the advantageous differential between pretax and after-tax compounding, discussed in the section on Techniques for Improving After-Tax Investment Performance, can be dramatically enhanced. When combined with the estate tax exemption, this potential may allow a substantial pool of untaxed investment assets. The estate tax exemption for each spouse still applies, but any assets in excess of the first-to-die exemption will carry over at the decedent's cost basis.

Horvitz and Wilcox (2003) showed that the mechanism of tax deferral is differential compounding; the difference between pretax and after-tax terminal wealth is a nonlinear function of time and the differential in pretax and after-tax compounding rates. Leaving investment assets untaxed to a surviving spouse extends the time for that compounding difference, often for many years, and at the same time provides a larger base for interest and/or dividends for current income.

Investors with children often wish to provide support to them during the investor's lifetime and with a bequest upon death. Under current tax treatment, the gift tax during the investor's life is always less expensive than the estate tax for the same dollars transferred because the tax on gifts applies to the amount transferred whereas the estate tax is paid on the gross amount, leaving only the net available for transfer.[11] With a gift, however, the investor does give up control of the funds and the right to use the money. To transfer $100,000 net as a gift at a 50 percent gift tax rate requires $150,000 pretax, whereas the same $100,000 transferred from a taxable estate at the same rate requires $200,000. Appreciated property transferred by gift does not receive a step-up in basis. If sold at a gain by the transferee, tax is due on the difference between the donor's basis and what is received on sale; if sold at a loss, the difference is the lesser of the difference between the donor's basis and (1) the sale price or (2) the fair market value at the time of transfer.

Another option is to separate assets into "artificial" components, such as a "life estate" and "remainder." The life estate is computed as an actuarial function based on the investor's presumed lifetime and a statutory discount rate that creates a present value for tax purposes; the difference is the remainder interest. If the investment assets can earn more than the discount rate, the net value will accrue without additional gift or estate tax. Such techniques have implications for the kinds of assets to be partitioned into the life and remainder interests. For example, one technique is to retain a life interest in an investment with a high expected return while making a gift or sale of the remainder interest and valuing the life interest by using the applicable federal rate, which is set by the IRS and reflects low-risk rates of return. The excess return from the actual investment will accrue to the remainder interest. There are many variations of these apportionments.

The techniques for handling gifts and bequests are too varied and complex to cover in this chapter, but readers should understand the availability of ways to minimize current tax treatment—and possibly avoid it entirely. Planning for spousal and intergenerational transfers should be made part of any investment program and should take into account the tax treatment of funds upon transfer or disposition, asset location (discussed in the first section of Part IV), and the implication of tax deferral for periods extending beyond the investment horizon of the investor.

Complete investment planning means integrating family assets—the assets held by the investor, the investor's parents (if an inheritance is anticipated), the spouse, and the investor's children. It means taking into account the time horizons for each of these family members. For optimal integration of investment planning, the advisor should consider locating specific types of assets in the hands of certain family members while regarding the entire portfolio as an integrated, diversified whole.

For investors who intend to make charitable bequests, proper tax management can result in investment returns approaching those of tax-exempt investors. The reason is simple: To the extent that investment gains are deferred upon death or *inter vivos* disposition, they are never taxed, which effectively results in a tax-free return. This effect is true whether the investor/descendant makes the bequest or whether the assets are left to a spouse who then makes the bequest. Investors who intend to donate substantial amounts of their wealth to charity should be particularly sensitive to the value of tax deferral and tax-managed investing to maximize the effective rate of return and the terminal value of the assets to be transferred. Investors who make donations during their lifetime benefit from a deduction equal to the fair market values, so lifetime donations of highly appreciated securities are an effective alternative to bequests; they eliminate capital gains while providing a potential deduction against high-rate ordinary income. Donations do reduce wealth but not dollar for dollar—which can be another reason to maximize tax deferral.

Case Example

Mary, a divorced 50-year-old living in upstate New York, inherits a trust of some $2 million cash from her parents; it supplements the $350,000-a-year salary she earns as a corporate executive. Mary saves part of her salary income and part of her trust distributions for her children. The trust is administered by a professional bank trust department as trustee. The terms of the trust are that Mary is to receive the greater of (1) all the distributable net income or (2) 5 percent of the asset value for life, with the remainder to be held in trust for the benefit of her two children and further descendants when she dies.

The bank assigns a trust administration officer and an investment officer to the account. The trustee decides on a conventional asset allocation of 60 percent stocks and 40 percent bonds. The trustee's investment department has a list of about 100 stocks from the S&P 500 Index that it follows and approves for the trust accounts, but the investment officers have discretion to vary the proportions of the specific security holdings. The assigned investment officer generally follows the standard stock list and buys and sells stocks to stay with that list. The bond portfolio is a diversified selection of New York state municipal bonds. All these decisions appear to be prudent and unassailable by fiduciary standards.

Unfortunately, Mary's income makes her subject to the alternative minimum tax (AMT), so the nominal coupon from the municipal bonds produces less income after taxes than she would have received if she had been invested in higher-yielding taxable bonds. If the investment officer had used higher-yielding taxable bonds, some of the AMT effect could have been mitigated. The trustee has failed to consider Mary's tax situation outside the trust factors and simply assumed that tax-exempt bonds are better than taxable bonds for high-bracket taxpayers. Next, municipal issuers in New York experience financial difficulties that cause the municipal bonds to drop in credit rating and in value. The trustee has focused solely on the tax exemption in Mary's state of domicile (to keep the exemption for state tax purposes) and failed to diversify these municipal bond holdings. Moreover, the stock strategy he has selected is subject to turnover as the recommended list changes, which eliminates any real value for tax deferral.

Because of the high annual recognition of capital gains and the payout of municipal income instead of taxable income (which would have been nominally more), the life-estate interest is favored over the remainder interest, so the remainder interest diminishes more than anticipated and more than either Mary or her parents would have wanted. Because the trust is under the generation-skipping transfer tax exemption, no estate tax will be due on the death of Mary or her descendants, which makes the remainder interest extremely valuable from an estate tax perspective and is consistent with Mary's (and her parents') goals of leaving money to the next generation without estate tax. The trustee has been wasting this valuable opportunity.

By failing to take into account Mary's total tax picture as integrated with the trust, the trustee has ignored her intentions for saving for her children and their children. By focusing on simplistic tax management and working from the premise of what the trust department "usually does" (instead of what Mary needs), the trustee is, in fact, doing a poor job while still looking professional.

Gross-to-Net Investment Returns

Gross investment returns must absorb four key factors if they are to provide long-term purchasing power. The factors are the "Four Horsemen of the Investment Apocalypse" that can devastate purchasing power:

1. investment expenses (for example, management fees, transaction and custody costs),
2. taxes (income and estate taxes),
3. inflation, and
4. consumption.

Consumption, the ultimate purpose of wealth accumulation for most people, must come after the first three factors are satisfied. More than anything else, the long-term erosion of purchasing power (which is the functional definition of wealth) is the most serious problem for the HNW investor faced with the interplay of taxation and inflation.

Investment Expenses

The tax rules can be complex with respect to deducting investment expenses. Generally, direct transaction costs (e.g., commissions) and indirect transaction costs (e.g., the market impact of trading) reduce the net gain that will be taxed. Manager fees may have various tax treatments; they can reduce capital gains or, in some instances, result in a deduction against ordinary income because itemized deductions are subject to limits as a percentage of adjusted gross income. The effect is to increase the marginal tax rate approximately in the amount of the percentage limitation.

Manager fees are almost always a percentage of assets under management and their effect on net returns is easily calculated by subtracting the fee rate from the gross rate of return. Transaction costs are much harder to identify, but they are mostly a function of activity (i.e., turnover). High levels of activity can seriously reduce gross return, yet individuals commonly pay little attention to turnover. In fact, many investors would be appalled at paying a manager a fee for "doing nothing," even if it is the best thing to do.

Impact of Taxation and Inflation

For investments to preserve purchasing power, they have to return more than the inflation rate *after* deducting management fees, costs, and taxes. Using U.S. tax rates applicable at the time (not today's rates) and actual inflation rates for 1925–2004, Ibbotson Associates (2005)

TABLE 10.2   Annualized Compound Returns, 1925–2004 (net of taxes and inflation)

U.S. Asset	Return
Stocks	4.8%
Municipal bonds	1.3
Government bonds	0.8
Treasury bills	−0.9

Source: Ibbotson Associates (2005).

found the compound annual returns, net of taxes and inflation for that period, for the U.S. asset classes shown in Table 10.2.[12]

The difference for the Ibbotson data between the long-term pretax, preinflation returns and after-tax, postinflation annualized returns was about 4.5 percent for bonds and about 5.4 percent for stocks. For taxable investors, one may reasonably ask whether their "long run" will be long enough to reliably use static percentage asset allocations to bonds when faced with taxes and inflation and the possibility of multidecade periods of loss.

Fixed Income   The U.S. bond markets, adjusted for taxes and inflation rates existing at the time of the study reported in Table 10.2, show extremely long trends of gaining and losing purchasing power—trends that go for decades. A growth of net purchasing power went on for about 20 years from 1925 until the beginning of World War II, followed by about 35 years of loss in net purchasing power. This remarkable loss of value was then followed by the great bond bull market from the early 1980s to the present, which nearly tripled the net purchasing power of long-term (more than 20 years) bondholders. These long trending effects on net purchasing power are the result of the confluence of market conditions, inflation eras, and tax regimes. No one factor completely accounts for the results. The conventional wisdom that taxable investors should *always* hold bonds as a permanent part of their investment portfolios—irrespective of expected returns, expected taxes, and expected inflation—should be questioned, especially for long-term wealthy investors.

Treasury Inflation-Indexed Securities (commonly called TIPS) provide inflation protection, but somewhat less than one might think because the inflation component is also taxed annually at high ordinary income rates. Thus, these securities are most suitable for tax-sheltered retirement accounts. Depending on the changing state of yields, inflation, and tax rates, TIPS may not always completely maintain purchasing power unless held in a tax-sheltered vehicle.

In Table 10.2, the long-term after-tax results for municipal bonds are slightly better than the results for U.S. government bonds, but diversification with municipal bonds can be difficult without going to bonds outside the state of residence of the investor, which eliminates the exemption for state tax purposes. A portfolio of single-state bonds is subject to much more risk than a multi-state portfolio. Treasuries, taxed at the federal level, are not subject to any state or local income taxes, but normally yield less than bonds with lower credit ratings. Municipal bonds often come with call features that make them worth less than noncallable taxable bonds. They are also often more mispriced and expensive to trade than their taxable counterparts. The longer maturities of municipal bonds are often more attractive to taxable investors than is the short end of the market.

The permanent, strong diversification benefit of fixed-income investments is not always reliable; when bond returns are positively correlated with stocks for extended time periods, as during periods of high inflation, their diversification benefit is reduced. The place of fixed-income instruments, particularly long-dated bonds for wealthy investors with high proportions of discretionary wealth, must be carefully considered because of their potentially low after-tax returns, modest diversification benefits, and exposure to the erosion of purchasing power resulting from inflation.

Stocks U.S. stocks have provided long-term protection of net purchasing power, but long periods have occurred when even stocks lost purchasing power for the taxable investor. Until the end of WWII, the stock market was characterized by jagged multiyear ups and downs with a long trend up in net purchasing power. From roughly the end of WWII until about the mid-1960s, the U.S. market experienced 20 years of mostly upward movement in net purchasing power. For about the next 20 years, a long trend of seriously diminished net purchasing power occurred. In fact, an investor in the S&P 500 in 1967 did not recover purchasing power until about 13 years later. The loss of purchasing power during that period, peak to trough, was about 25 percent. This period was followed by the great bull market beginning in the early 1980s that resulted in a stunning surge in net purchasing power.

The dividend component used to be unattractive to investors in high tax brackets, but with recent changes to the tax law, the return from stocks, whether from dividends or long-term capital gain, is taxed at the same rate. The remaining advantage of long-term capital gains is the potential for tax deferral.[13]

Cash Although cash may sometimes be king, it does not provide a good hedge against inflation. Historically, T-bills have returned slightly above the inflation rate *pretax*, but because the return is taxed as ordinary income, T-bills will almost always return less than inflation after taxes. The result is a slow hemorrhaging in purchasing power that becomes unsustainable after long periods of time.

Alternative Asset Classes Space does not allow more than a cursory treatment of the many other asset classes. (A somewhat fuller overview can be found in the section called Overview of Federal Taxation of Investments.) Most hedge funds engage in investment activities that are highly tax inefficient.

Most arbitrage strategies are inherently short term in nature and involve some degree of U.S. Internal Revenue Code Section 1256 contracts, in which taxes may not be deferred and which mandate tax allocation of gains to 60 percent long-term capital gains and 40 percent short-term capital gains. At today's rates, {15 percent and 35 percent} respectively, this requirement results in an effective federal tax rate of 23 percent. Hedge funds engaged in very active trading in long or short security strategies usually generate large proportions of short-term gain and loss, which usually have the worst kind of tax treatment. Private equity and venture capital generally have favorable tax treatment because the capital gains tend to be long term. In addition, certain fees and expenses (e.g., management fees) may be a deduction against ordinary income. Real estate is subject to a higher tax rate for long-term capital gains than are many other types of asset classes, although depreciation can shield current income. Unless the deferral period is long, however, the savings may not be important, especially because the depreciation must be recaptured at high tax rates. Hard assets such as timber, gold, oil, and gas have generally favorable tax characteristics. Timber is literally a growing asset, with the potential for relatively long tax deferral of gains that accrue and a depletion formula that temporarily shelters income. Oil and gas investments can have favorable depreciation and depletion deductions.

Access to the alternative investments is limited to the very wealthiest investors unless the investor uses intermediaries who, for a substantial fee, provide commingled investment vehicles for HNW investors in the lower wealth ranges. In analyzing funds of funds or other pooled conduits for investors who cannot meet the minimum investment requirements for direct access, the advisor needs to understand the impact of the overlay management fees and additional carried interest paid to the intermediary. In some cases, the fees, particularly the management fees, can eviscerate most of the financial advantages of the asset class.[14]

Other specialized products attempt to replicate the investment performance of an asset class, such as hedge funds, by using structured financial products. They pay a return based on the performance of a specialized index, much like conventional stock index futures, without a direct investment in the underlying assets, and they purportedly capture the systematic risk and return of the asset class. For example, the investor might enter into an arrangement to purchase a warrant that will pay the total return of a basket of hedge funds. Supposedly, the return will be treated as all long-term capital gains rather than a pass-through of income taxed at the higher rate that would have occurred had the investment been made directly in the hedge funds.

Such products and the indices on which they are based raise substantial concerns for the taxable investor. The details are beyond the scope of this chapter, but consider the following. First is the cost. Second is the potential, depending on the structure, for unintended adverse tax treatment. For example, the "constructive ownership" rules might apply if the arrangement gives the investor almost exactly the same return (and risk) as the underlying investment. In this case, the IRS will recast the transaction as if it were owned directly and will assess nondeductible penalty interest on any underpayment of tax. Third is the difficult question of whether a given index accurately captures the performance of the asset class. The question pertains to issues of survivorship bias, representativeness (bias) in the managers included, stale pricing, and so on.

Another pragmatic issue that arises with a synthetic fund of funds is the fee expansion caused by the asymmetrical performance fees. Hedge fund managers typically get "2 + 20" (that is, a 2 percent fee plus 20 percent of the profits). Consider the result with two managers, each of whom is half of a fund of funds. Manager A makes 40 percent, whereas Manager B loses 40 percent. Because of the performance fees paid to Manager A, the net fee is a hefty 6 percent [that is, $0.02 + (0.4 \times 0.2 \times 0.5)$].

Noninvestment Assets   As noted previously, many expenditures are not consumption, nor are they investments in the sense of having as the primary purpose maximizing risk-adjusted investment returns. Examples of noninvestment assets include homes, vacation homes, yachts, antiques, and works of art.

Certain other types of assets may have investment characteristics but are not structured or intended solely to maximize risk-adjusted return. For example, insurance implicitly has investment characteristics, but its primary purpose is to protect against a major liability or to provide contingency protection rather than to increase wealth. Life insurance proceeds are generally exempt from tax, but that characteristic does not necessarily make them good investments, although many people seem to use insurance as a form of forced saving. Certain types of insurance products create tax-advantaged investment "wrappers," but at a cost.[15] These products have characteristics of both tax shelters and noninvestment assets.

Employment skills also represent an important asset for most people; salary is often the largest single component of their current income. In any financial planning, the investor needs to take into account the entire package of assets, liquid and nonliquid, pure investment and noninvestment. This approach is also true for offsetting gains and losses with complex rules that affect the particular tax treatment.

Summary

The key points to check in evaluating the investment needs of the HNW investor are as follows:

- Ascertain the major components of expenditure liability and categorize them from necessity to highly discretionary.
- Ascertain how much in the way of expenditures is required and, of that amount, how much is consumption and how much is nonconsumption spending.
- Ascertain the investment horizon, not of the investor alone but also of the others who may rely on or succeed in the ownership of the investment assets (e.g., family members, charities).
- Consider the entire family wealth picture in terms of the (current and long-term) intentions of the investor and the opportunity to locate assets in the most optimal way among family members.
- Consider charitable intentions carefully in terms of the high value for tax deferral.
- Carefully consider the interplay between taxation and inflation as they affect net investment returns relating to maintaining long-term purchasing power.
- Finally, when making allocations among asset classes, take into account fees and costs, taxes, inflation, and consumption—not simply optimization of gross returns.

OVERVIEW OF FEDERAL TAXATION OF INVESTMENTS

U.S. taxable investors must be acutely aware of the federal tax code, which is mind numbing in its complexity. It carries many traps for the unwary but also opportunities to improve after-tax investment performance. This section attempts to give an overview of relevant major elements of U.S. taxation; the tens of thousands of pages of tax code, regulations, and rulings and the many court cases interpreting those statutory provisions make adequate coverage of everything impossible. Other countries have tax laws that differ in material ways from those of the United States, but to the extent that elements of those tax laws have similar structures (e.g., taxing income differently from capital gains, taxing only realized gains), much of the investment-related analytical framework in this section is applicable, with minor modifications, to other countries.

Because each individual investor's circumstances are likely to result in particular, if not unique, tax issues, and because those circumstances may vary from year to year, investors should seek tax advice that is specific to their circumstances rather than relying on these general principles. The experienced tax practitioner reading this overview will undoubtedly find many arcane exceptions to the general concepts and principles, but for most situations taxable investors will encounter, this simplified framework of taxation can help guide investment choices.

The reader should keep the following points in mind:

1. What most people think of as a tax rate is largely an idiosyncratic function of the investor's mix of types of incomes and deductions and the dollar amount of each; therefore, the investor's effective rate is only somewhat related to the published tax rates.
2. Many investments have return components that receive different tax treatments, which makes it difficult to generalize accurately about the tax efficiency of asset classes.

3. The income tax is only one tax that investors need to be aware of; in particular, the estate tax can be a critical factor in evaluating investment strategies. Other relevant taxes include the alternative minimum tax (AMT), state and local taxes, and foreign taxes.

4. The constantly changing tax laws are a source of significant risk and uncertainty.

The Mechanism of Income Taxation

The federal tax code applied to investments is primarily a profit-sharing mechanism that usually requires payment on investment returns that are actually (or, in some cases, "constructively"— that is, deemed for tax purposes as if actually) received. An important exception to this principle is the tax treatment of certain derivative instruments. For example, U.S. IRC (Internal Revenue Code) Section 1256 contracts are taxed as 60 percent long-term capital gains and 40 percent short-term capital gains when sold or deemed to have been sold (and marked-to-market) on the last day of the calendar year.[16] Another example is the estate tax, which is based on the fair market value of assets irrespective of the amount of unrealized profit.

Understanding that tax is a profit-sharing mechanism is an important insight for understanding the relationship of tax to investments, in that it is not much different from any private profit-sharing arrangement. Effectively, the government "owns" a certain share of the profits from investments, but the government cannot control the timing of the disposition of the investments or when it will receive its share. Unlike the taxpayer, the government has no capital at risk, although its profits will vary proportionately with the investor's. The mechanism of federal taxation is nearly identical to the typical "carried interest" of a general partner in a private equity or venture capital fund except for who controls the timing of tax realizations.[17]

Income, such as interest or dividends, is usually shared between the government and the investor when it is received. Profits on appreciated securities are usually taxed upon sale. Some dispositions or transfers, such as gifts or contributions to a joint venture, may not be taxed at the time of transfer, but the tax is simply deferred. Usually, publicly traded securities cannot be exchanged for other similar securities without paying taxes as if the securities were sold, but certain kinds of private investments can be exchanged for other "like kind" investments and the tax is deferred (see IRC Section 1031). The rules for tax-free exchanges or other dispositions are complex.

Quantifying the amount of tax involves three factors. First is the *tax rate*—the factor that most people think of when it comes to taxation. For most high-net-worth investors the tax rate is the highest marginal tax rate, although lower rates are applied on a sliding scale to taxpayers with low-to-moderate taxable income in any particular calendar year. Because the tax rates and other statutory values in the tax code may become out of date (as they are subject to legislative change), the maximum applicable rates and other statutory numbers *as of the time this chapter was written* are shown in braces, { }. The reader is cautioned not to assume that the numbers in braces will be in effect in the future.

The second factor is the *character* of income to be taxed. Usually, the nature of the underlying investment and the holding period determine the character of the income for tax purposes. Character includes capital gained (both long term and short term), tax-exempt income (which may be exempt from federal and/or state taxes), profits from collectibles, and recapture of depreciation or amortization from investments such as real estate or oil and gas. The investor must pay close attention to the character of income, which determines which rates and which rules about offset apply. Many, if not most, investments have components of taxable income and profits consisting of more than one character. For example, bonds may be taxable both as to interest payments (ordinary income) and price appreciation (capital gains) if sold before maturity.

The third factor is the set of complex rules for *netting* of gains and losses or netting of income and expenses or deductions, which results in the amount to which the tax rate is applied. Netting is functionally the way taxable income is defined and, in many ways, is more significant than the rate itself. The net income calculation entails complex adjustments to gross income involving allowable deductions, exemptions, limitations on deductions and exemptions, application of the formidable AMT, and rules involving the order of offsetting income of different character.

The interplay of these three factors—rate, character, and netting—with the complex rules governing each of them, make it challenging to calculate tax on investments, to estimate and plan in each calendar year, and to maximize after-tax investment return by minimizing taxes. A particularly difficult step is to optimally structure a long-term investment portfolio about which one has much certainty as to the year-by-year tax treatment.

The highest stated rate for federal income tax purposes is {35 percent} for ordinary income, but it is not the maximum effective rate, which is higher. Two main features of the current tax system create this quirk and illustrate the problem of defining "income." The limitation on itemized deductions and on the personal exemption has the effect of making the tax rate higher.[18] The reason is that above the applicable threshold, every dollar of additional income entails a partial reduction in deductions.[19] Deductions are a reduction of taxable income that is first subject to limits based on the specific type of deduction; then, whatever is left over is limited to the excess above a threshold determined as a percentage of the income, which itself must be in excess of a dollar-amount threshold. Effectively, deductions can be "wasted" as income goes up; the effective marginal rate of earning the next dollar is high if it causes the loss of existing deductions.

Alternative Minimum Tax

Related to the problem in limiting deductions is the AMT. Essentially, it is a parallel calculation in which various deductions, exclusions, and credits that would have reduced adjusted gross income (AGI) are added back to calculate a new taxable amount subject to a rate of {0 percent, 26 percent, or 28 percent} depending on the dollar level of income of the taxpayer. For many wealthy investors, the {28 percent} rate is likely to apply. The details of calculating the AMT are too lengthy to deal with here, but one point to keep in mind is that for taxpayers with significant amounts of long-term capital gains and/or tax-exempt income but small amounts of ordinary income, the effect of the AMT is to diminish the tax benefits of long-term capital gains or tax-exempt income. The reason is that any deductions that are already available will be mostly wasted by having inadequate taxable income against which they can be used.

The tax rules are in a nearly constant state of change. Rate, character, and netting are subject to frequent legislative changes (and new interpretations) by both the Internal Revenue Service and the U.S. Tax Court. On complex matters of taxation, the IRS is continually issuing regulations, private letter rulings, technical advice memoranda, and so on, many of which are issued years after the underlying tax rule became effective—and sometimes even after the rule has been replaced. Congress tinkers with tax rates so frequently that history is barely a guide to even the upper and lower ranges of possible tax rates. The political risk of changes, favorable and unfavorable, in tax law is an overlooked aspect of risk management for taxable investors.[20] The high risk of change in the tax law creates an actual volatility of after-tax returns (usually affecting approximately yearly time horizons) that is rarely taken into account by investors as a source, not unlike market volatility, of quantifiable risk.

Treatment of Losses

The IRS has specific, complex rules about the treatment of capital losses on investments. The character of the income usually, but not always, determines the ordering of the application of losses, whereas the principles of netting quantify the net taxable amount.

The approach in the tax law generally is to require losses to first offset gains of the same character; remaining net losses are used to offset gains of different character. For example, short-term capital losses must first offset short-term gains; then, any unused losses are applied against any net long-term gains (long-term gains less any long-term losses); and finally, any remaining losses can be used to offset up to {$3,000} of ordinary income. Any remaining losses after this can be carried forward to the next year but must be used in the same sequence. Generally, net losses can be carried forward without a time limitation, but they cannot be carried back to adjust taxable income in prior years and cannot be deferred (to avoid using up net short-term losses against net long-term gain, for example). Losses carried forward usually must be used to offset gains in the current year, even if those gains would have been taxed at a lower rate than the rate applicable to the previous losses.[21]

Short-term capital gains are pernicious, in that gains are taxed at the same rate as ordinary income but if the portfolio has excess short-term capital *losses*, they must first be used to offset *long-term* capital gains, which produces an effective waste of tax loss because the long-term capital gains would otherwise be taxed at a much lower rate than the short-term capital gains.

Investment interest expense can be used to offset only investment income, not professional fees and salaries, portfolio income, or dividends. Although excess (net of investment income) investment interest expense cannot be deducted, it can be carried forward to be used in future years. Because the rates for net capital gains and dividends are lower than ordinary income tax rates, capital gains and dividends are not normally used to offset investment interest, although the taxpayer can make an election to do so. Investment interest cannot be used to offset tax-exempt income from municipal bonds. Usually investment losses from passive investment activities (those in which the taxpayer is not actively involved) can be used to offset income or gains only from other passive investment activities.

Special loss limitations known as "wash sale" rules are particularly important for most investors. If an investor sells a security at a loss, that loss may not be recognized if the investor purchases the same or a substantially identical security 30 days before or 30 days after the day of the trade. Although this problem has no perfect solution, commonly used methods to mitigate the restriction include doubling up on shares, waiting the 30 days to repurchase identical shares, and buying shares of a different issuer with similar characteristics (this can also include selling mutual fund shares and replacing them with the shares of a functionally similar mutual fund).

Tax Treatment of Different Asset Classes

Different asset classes are subject to different types of tax treatment and are affected differently by all three of the quantifying factors—rate, character, and netting. The following subsections provide examples of the general tax treatment of certain asset classes.

Fixed Income

The tax treatment of bonds should be simple, but it is not. Generally, the return from fixed-income securities comes in the form of price changes (appreciation or loss) and interest income. The majority of bonds pay interest, which is taxed at ordinary income rates, but many variations can be found among bonds, each of which has its own special tax characteristics. Most bonds create long-term capital gains (or losses) or short-term capital gains (or losses) if sold before maturity. Some of the more common types of bonds are briefly described here:

- Zero-coupon bonds create annual tax liabilities for imputed but unpaid interest.
- U.S. Treasury instruments are taxable for federal purposes but not taxable for state income tax purposes.
- U.S. Saving Bonds (Series EE/E, HH/H, and I) are exempt from state and local taxes, and federal tax is deferred.
- U.S. government agency bonds are taxable at the federal level. Many, but not all, are exempt from state and local taxes (see Table 10.3).
- Municipal bonds are generally tax exempt at the federal level but are exempt from state income tax only if the bonds were issued in the same state in which the investor resides. Certain types of private-purpose municipal bonds are functionally taxable at the federal level because they may cause the taxpayer to be subject to the AMT {26 percent or 28 percent}. Bonds sold at a premium or discount to the adjusted purchase price will incur capital gains or losses.
- Mortgage-backed bonds (and other asset-backed bonds) usually pay a mixture of taxable interest and untaxed principal amortization.
- U.S. (and certain non-U.S.) corporate bonds create ordinary income as to the interest component.[22]
- Non-U.S. bonds, corporate or sovereign, are generally taxed the same as corporate bonds.

TABLE 10.3   Agency Bonds Exempt and Not Exempt from State and Local Taxes

Not Exempt
Government National Mortgage Association (GNMA or Ginnie Mae)
Federal National Mortgage Association (FNMA or Fannie Mae)
Federal Home Loan Mortgage Corporation (FHLMC or Freddie Mac)
Exempt
Federal home loan banks
Federal farm credit banks
Student Loan Marketing Association
Separate Trading of Registered Interest and Principal of Securities (STRIPS)
Resolution Funding Corporation (REFCORPS)
Financing Corporation (FICO)

Notes: The distinction as to whether agency bonds are exempt or not from state and local taxes depends on whether the agency is the primary debtor. The nonexempt agencies purchase and repackage private loans for resale. The exempt agencies directly issue securities to the public to raise money for their governmental purposes.

- Interest from Treasury Inflation-Indexed Securities (commonly called TIPS) is taxed as ordinary income, but TIPS are also taxed currently as ordinary income for the inflation-related adjustments to the principal value. The gross adjustment to principal directly changes the cost basis, dollar for dollar.
- Bonds purchased at a premium or discount to face value have a variety of tax treatments, some optional and some not. Also, the treatment of amortized premiums and discounts may depend on the type of bond or how it was purchased or sold. Here are some of the main types:

    1. bond with original issue discount or premium,
    2. municipal bond,
    3. government bond issued before 1982,
    4. bond with original maturity less than one year,
    5. bond with a market discount (sold for less than face value), and
    6. bond with a market premium (sold for more than face value).[23]

Clearly, the investor's after-tax return from fixed-income investments is more complicated than simply the nominal rate of return of the bond; it is a function of the character of the income (which may be derived from one or more return components of the bond), the netting (e.g., application of the AMT), and the applicable tax rate for each component. A particular investment portfolio that has attractive after-tax returns in one calendar year may be more or less attractive in subsequent calendar years depending on the particularities of the investor's tax position as it relates to other items of income, loss in the future, and changes in the three tax factors.

Stocks

Stocks generate returns from dividends and from price changes. Dividends used to be taxed as ordinary income (for most high-net-worth investors, at the highest marginal rate), but tax changes have reduced the tax to the same rate as the rate on long-term capital gains {15 percent}, subject to the complex restrictions to prevent trading simply for tax benefits of the wash sale rules.[24] The current wash sale rules are (1) for common stock, the investor must have held the stock for more than 60 days during the 120-day period beginning 60 days before the ex-dividend date and (2) for preferred stock, the investor must have held it for 90 days during the 180-day period beginning 90 days before the ex-dividend date. Note that a put or in-the-money call restarts the holding period, which must be tested each record date.

Capital gains and losses for stocks depend importantly on the holding period. Short-term capital gains rates (historically, the same as ordinary income rates) apply to securities held for 12 months or less. Long-term capital gains rates, at {15 percent}, are significantly lower than short-term rates, at {35 percent}. Thus, capital gains can be taxed much more favorably (i.e., long term) for as little as a one-day difference in holding period. During the last quarter of the 20th century, long-term rates went back and forth between 20 percent and 28 percent. For a brief time, the law included an 18 percent rate for securities held five years or more. Such changes are evidence of the instability, and hence volatility risk, of the tax component of net returns.

Accurate and detailed record keeping is critical to identifying the specific tax lots to be sold so as to maximize long-term capital gains and minimize short-term capital gains. If investors do not have adequate records to identify the specific tax lot of stock sold, they must use the "first-in, first-out" method. Average cost for allocating the tax basis across different security lots can be used for most mutual fund shares.

Mutual Funds and Exchange Traded Funds

Mutual funds are a type of pass-through entity. With minor exceptions, net capital gains and dividends from the securities held by a mutual fund are distributed each year to the fund's shareholders. In addition to intentional turnover that creates capital gains, or merger and acquisition activity that creates involuntary capital gains within a fund, large redemptions by shareholders can create liquidations of securities that result in involuntary capital gains. At the end of the year, those investors remaining in the fund will have to pay taxes on their pro rata share of the capital gains, even if they did not redeem any shares themselves. For mutual funds that have embedded net gains, new investors must also recognize these gains as distributed or at year-end. This recognition can create unexpected tax problems. Losses cannot be taken by the taxpayer unless fund shares are sold; however, they are netted against gains within the mutual fund. Investors who use dividend reinvestment plans and who have sold shares at a loss may be subject to wash sale rules if the sales were not carefully timed. For large investors, some mutual funds will make in-kind distributions; this approach saves on transaction costs, but for tax purposes, in-kind distributions will be deemed sales and will be taxable.

Exchange traded funds (ETFs) are publicly traded securities that usually hold a basket of stocks, such as an index, but can also be actively managed. The tax treatment is a cross between treatment of a single stock and treatment of a mutual fund. Because of the way ETFs are structured and traded, the market price is close to the net asset value, and when shares are sold, the investor recognizes a capital gain or loss. Turnover within the funds and dividends or interest are taxable to the shareholders. Unlike mutual funds, however, the redemptions by other shareholders do not create tax recognition for the remaining investors. As a result, ETFs can defer capital gains distributions more efficiently than mutual funds—a significant advantage.

Neither mutual funds nor ETFs are well suited for tax-loss harvesting controlled by the private investor because the volatility of these portfolios is less than the volatility of the underlying stocks, although the fund manager can use tax-loss harvesting within the fund. The tax lots available for harvesting are only the shares in the fund, not the individual securities held within the funds. Tax-loss harvesting is more effective with separately managed accounts.

Real Estate

Investment real estate profits are taxed in multiple ways: Net rents are treated as ordinary income, long-term capital gains are taxed at a special intermediate rate, and the recapture of previously taken depreciation expense is taxed at a third rate (IRC Section 1250). Real estate (or mortgages) held by a real estate investment trust (REIT) is generally treated in a manner similar to the treatment of a mutual fund. The tax characteristics of the underlying investments are carried through to the shareholder; that is, no tax is paid by the REIT, which must distribute substantially all its income annually. Real estate partnerships, like all partnerships, are pass-through entities that pay no tax themselves, but tax is paid by the partners, generally in proportion to their partnership interests, and the original character of the income is unchanged. Although tax-free exchanges can sometimes be accomplished with real estate held by a partnership, directly held real estate is best suited to tax-free exchanges (IRC Section 1031). Personal residences are treated differently from personal vacation homes, and both have tax treatments that are significantly different from the treatment of real estate held for investment purposes.

Collectibles

Profits on collectibles, such as works of art, are subject to either short-term capital gains tax {35 percent} or a special long-term capital gains rate {28 percent}. The netting of gains and losses against other types of capital gains is unfavorable if collectibles are sold at a loss but favorable if they are sold at a gain.

Private Equity and Venture Capital

Private equity and venture capital funds (including funds of funds) are typically limited partnerships that are treated as pass-through entities; the tax characteristics of the underlying investments are carried through to the investor (i.e., no tax is paid at the partnership level). The management fees charged by investment partners may sometimes be deductible as an expense against ordinary income, whereas the net gains are usually long-term capital gains because of the longer holding periods of the underlying illiquid investments.[25]

Hedge Funds

Hedge funds are also treated as pass-through entities; most hedge fund gains come in the form of short-term capital gains, however, because of the funds' high-velocity trading or use of derivatives (e.g., IRC Section 1256 contracts, which are taxed at a statutory 60 percent long-term rate and 40 percent short-term rate when sold or deemed sold at marked-to-market values at the end of the year). Some hedge funds treat their activities as a business and qualify as "traders." Net income is taxed at the higher ordinary income rates, but the expenses of trading and operations can be deducted against gross trading profits. Traders making an IRC Section 475 election, which requires mark-to-market recognition of income, can receive even more favorable treatment of expenses and losses. To qualify as traders, some hedge funds may claim aggressive tax status that may not be sustainable if challenged by the IRS. For investors who are not traders, fund expenses are subject to the limitation on deductions of {2 percent} of AGI and interest expenses are a separate itemized deduction.

Before investing with a hedge fund, the prudent investor should thoroughly understand the prospective tax treatment of the fund—for example, by looking at the historical tax returns of the fund and considering IRS challenges to tax positions taken by the fund. Multistrategy funds, particularly so-called global macro funds, are usually more difficult to assess prospectively because the tax character of the underlying investment strategies is likely to vary greatly over time.

Individuals as Businesses or Traders

It is not easy for most individuals to qualify as traders because the IRS takes a strict approach to accepting trader status. To qualify, taxpayers generally need to show that their trading activities are done almost daily and for a livelihood, that the number of trades and dollar amounts are significant, that significant time is spent trading, and that the holding periods are short.

Derivatives

A variety of derivative financial instruments receive special statutory tax treatment. Generally, these instruments are exchange traded options and futures (including IRC Section 1256 contracts) sold by securities dealers in the normal course of their business and traded in the public markets. Most derivatives that typical investors encounter are either taxed at the short-term capital gains rate if sold during the year or taxed as IRC Section 1256 contracts with 60 percent considered long-term capital gains and 40 percent considered short-term capital gains, for a blended effective rate of {23 percent}. Nondealer futures contracts are usually treated as if they had the same character as the underlying investment would have had if held directly by the investor.

Synthetic Hedges and "Constructive Ownership"

A wide variety of techniques, with all sorts of variations, are available for attempting either the conversion of ordinary income or short-term capital gains into long-term capital gains or for creating the effect of a sale without the tax consequences. The tax rules are complex and must be analyzed in the context of the specific transaction.

If a security position is so completely hedged that substantially all of the risk is removed, the IRS may recharacterize it as a sale and tax will be due as if it were sold. Guidance on how much the investor must remain at risk to avoid having the transaction deemed a constructive sale is limited.

Derivative contracts can be used in various ways to create more favorable tax treatment than that given the underlying investment. Sometimes, intermediary pass-through entities are created to hold a highly taxed investment; then, investors purchase derivative instruments that have the same or very similar pretax total returns, with the gains of the derivative instrument taxed as long-term capital gains. But when derivatives are used to create such synthetic hedges with nearly identical economics to the underlying investment assets, the IRS tries to ignore the overlay for tax purposes. So, an investor may be deemed to have constructive ownership, which can result in a tax treatment as if the asset underlying the derivative instrument were, in fact, directly owned by the investor. Gain in excess of any underlying long-term capital gains will then be treated as ordinary income, and nondeductible interest will be charged on the underpayment of tax.

Estate and Gift Taxes

The estate tax (or "death tax") follows a different principle and has a different function from income taxation. The estate tax is applied to the fair market value of assets irrespective of whether unrealized gains or losses are involved. Intense debate is going on as this chapter is being written about either eliminating the estate tax entirely or raising the exemption amount high enough that only the very wealthiest estates will be subject to it. The 2005 estate tax exemption is $1,500,000, and the exemption is scheduled to rise to $3,500,000 by 2009.[26]

Related to the estate tax is the generation skipping transfer (GST) tax. This onerous tax functions as a two-step estate tax and affects estates left to grandchildren, either directly or in trust. Assets left to a grandchild are treated as if left to the decedent's child who then immediately died and left the same assets to his or her child. The estate tax, if any is due, is paid on the estate and then taxed again on the net amount. For example, if the estate tax was 45 percent and an estate was over the exemption by $1 million, the first layer of tax would be $450,000 (leaving $550,000), and the second layer (because of the GST) would be an additional 45 percent of the $550,000.

Related to the estate tax and the GST tax is the gift tax, which is applied to certain transfers during the taxpayer's lifetime. Under current law, each taxpayer is allowed to "gift" *inter vivos* (during life) up to {$11,000} per recipient to an unlimited number of recipients and has a cumulative lifetime exclusion of {$1 million}. Payment of a gift tax can mitigate or even eliminate the application of the estate tax. Previously, the estate and gift amounts excluded from tax were linked as a unified credit, but they no longer are.

Appreciated assets get a step-up in cost basis, so for estates not subject to tax, all *unrealized* gains become permanently tax free. Unrealized losses from assets that have gone down in value are lost permanently, however, except to the extent that an estate subject to tax is that much less valuable. The new tax basis is the fair market value at the time of the heir's death.

For transfers by gift rather than inheritance, the rules about cost basis for gifts other than cash are complex.[27] Appreciated property generally has a tax basis equal to the tax basis in the hands of the transferor. The new tax basis for assets that have decreased in value, however, is the fair market value at the time of transfer. In some instances, unrealized losses are wasted in the gifting of depreciated property. For gifts or inheritances on which estate or gift taxes are paid, the tax is allocated on a pro rata basis between the original tax basis (cost) and the appreciation, to create a new basis in the hands of the transferee. Transfers to a spouse are exempt from any gift tax but retain the adjusted basis of the transferor for tax purposes. Transfers to a spouse can also be made through a qualified terminal interest property (QTIP) trust, which can restrict the spouse's power to appoint the principal but allows the spouse to have lifetime income. Estate tax is due upon the death of the surviving spouse. *A QTIP trust can be very valuable in extending the deferral of unrecognized gains.*

The federal estate tax is perhaps the most important overlooked tax in investment planning and should receive far more attention from investors and their advisors than it currently receives. As onerous as the estate tax is and as complex as the rules involving estate and gift taxes may be, careful planning can often eliminate or substantially mitigate the tax burden, albeit usually at the expense of control during the investor's lifetime.

States also have estate taxes that should not be ignored in investment planning. Historically, the states and federal government essentially shared the estate tax that was collected through a system of tax credits for estate tax payments. Because of recent changes in the federal estate tax, states have been receiving less money and are rapidly moving to amend their estate taxes to make up the difference. Most of these changes will result in a combined federal and state estate tax that is significantly higher than the federal tax alone.

The federal estate tax law provides an opportunity to artificially create and partition the *income* streams from the *remainder* streams that are provided by an asset or investment. The income stream may be based on the actual return (an income trust) or some defined percentage return (a "unitrust"), usually called a "life estate." The remainder interest may be determined when the investor (or others) dies or for a fixed period of years. The variations are numerous; most are known by acronyms [e.g., GRAT (grantor retained annuity trust), GRUT (grantor retained unitrust), GRIT (grantor retained income trust)]. Counterparts give either the income stream or the remainder to a charity for the investor to take a current charitable deduction [e.g., CRUT (charitable retained unitrust), CLAT (charitable lead annuity trust), CRAT (charitable retained annuity trust)]. These vehicles have potential for arbitraging the tax rates of the components and also for arbitraging the statutory discount rate used to value the transferred component compared with the actual return on the investment. In some respects, these vehicles are the tax equivalent of derivative financial instruments and can be analyzed accordingly.

Tax-Sheltered Saving Accounts

The federal government provides tax incentives for various retirement and other savings accounts. Rather than cover each one in detail, because they are subject to legislative change, an overview of their general characteristics is in order.

Tax-sheltered accounts can be analyzed on the basis of whether the amounts deposited are before or after tax and whether the withdrawal of amounts is taxable or nontaxable. Accounts funded with after-tax money (e.g., Roth individual retirement accounts) can usually be withdrawn tax free, but accounts funded with pretax money [e.g., a regular IRA or 401(k)] are usually taxed at ordinary income rates on the full amount of distributions, both principal and profits, when withdrawn.

In any event, their central feature is that while the money is held in the account, it compounds without current taxation. Only when the current and future tax rates are different does an opportunity arise not only to compound tax free but also to have an arbitrage of the different tax rates. For very wealthy investors, the amount of money that can be put into these accounts may not be significant. For investors willing to use tax-deferred investments, such as tax-managed index funds that are subject to only a {15 percent} tax rate, Roth IRA accounts may not add value, especially if the estate is not likely to be taxed.

Deciding which types of assets should be held in a tax-sheltered account and which should be held outside is complicated and highly conditional on such factors as expected changes in future applicable tax rates. (This topic is discussed more fully in the section on Individual Retirement Plans and Location.) Generally, investments that produce mostly current income and/or ordinary income subject to high tax rates should be held in a tax-sheltered account; other assets can be held outside. When considering where to put fixed-income securities, advisors and investors should keep in mind the penalties for early withdrawals from tax-sheltered accounts. Most investors' fixed-income holdings are intended to provide security, and using the money if it is needed may require withdrawals at inopportune times.

State Taxation

With 50 state taxing jurisdictions (plus many local tax jurisdictions), this section cannot thoroughly discuss the tax regimes in each.[28] When potential after-tax returns are calculated, state taxes can be used as a deduction against income for federal tax purposes; however, these deductions are subject to important limitations (e.g., the itemized deduction limitation). In quantifying the applicable marginal tax rate for calculating the combined federal and state tax applicable to investment returns, an advisor should take into account the deduction of state tax from federal tax, which is subject to various limitations.[29] In other words, an investor cannot simply add the two tax rates together.

International Taxation

Like the United States, other developed countries usually have some tax on returns from publicly traded companies domiciled in the country. Dividends and interest may be subject to withholding taxes that, in theory, can be recovered, in whole or in part, by U.S. taxpayers if the subject country has a tax treaty with the United States that allows recovery. The paperwork for recovering these withholding taxes can be burdensome. When investors are considering professional investment managers, they should inquire about the ability of the manager to recover non-U.S. withholding taxes. Generally, taxes in other countries that are not recovered can be taken as a credit or deduction against income. Certain non-U.S. jurisdictions are considered tax havens and do not tax foreign nationals' investments domiciled there. The effectiveness of these tax havens is under constant attack by the IRS, however, and their value is questionable for most investors.

Key Tax Questions in Analyzing Investments

The major points of this section can be summarized by considering the key questions related to taxes that the investor or investment advisor should ask when analyzing an investment.

First, what is the *character* of the components of expected return:

- ordinary income;
- dividends;
- long-term capital gains;
- short-term capital gains;
- asset class–specific tax rates—collectibles, real estate, recaptured depreciation, oil and gas depletion allowances, and so on;
- federal tax exemption;
- state/local tax exemption;
- foreign income subject to withholding?

Second, given the character of the income, the AMT, and the limitation on deductions, what will be the effective marginal tax rate for the nth dollar of return?

Third, what deductions, expenses, or offsets are available to reduce the tax on the investment return? Does this investment make the most efficient use of those potential benefits? Will the taxpayer be subject to the AMT, and if so, how will being subject to the AMT affect the net treatment of taxable income?

Fourth, especially for periods of fewer than 12 months, what is the anticipated holding period of the investment?

Fifth, how will potential future changes in tax rates affect the after-tax risk and return attractiveness of the investment?

Finally, how will the long-term attractiveness of the investment be affected by the application of the estate tax?

TECHNIQUES FOR IMPROVING AFTER-TAX INVESTMENT PERFORMANCE

The taxable investor in the United States has many options for improving after-tax return by decreasing the effect of the tax bite. Many investors do not take full advantage of what is available to them by law, however, and their advisors or investment managers do not pay close enough attention to the need to manage toward the lowest effective tax rates. This section first presents an overview of the most obvious and relevant techniques for improved after-tax investing by U.S. investors, followed by a summary of some of the less-used techniques. The presentations are not a substitute for specific advice from tax professionals that takes into account the unique circumstances of the investor, and many technical details must be lost in such an overview.

Tax-Lot Management

The first essential step in any tax-aware investment program is adequate record keeping. Although not required by law, keeping the lot-by-lot price, quantity, date, and associated commission costs of investments is in the investor's interest. In selling securities, it allows the investor to identify which specific lot was sold. When multiple purchases are made of the same security, each purchase has an associated cost or tax basis. By identifying the specific lot(s) for disposition, the investor can minimize current recognition of gains by picking those tax lots with the least associated tax liability. If the records are not adequate and each trade cannot be properly identified with a specific tax lot, an investor is required to use first-in, first-out accounting, with the earliest-acquired lot's tax basis used first. For mutual funds held by a broker or institutional custodian, the investor may use the average cost basis, but this approach is not as tax effective as specific lot accounting. The U.S. Internal Revenue Service (IRS) does, however, let the investor direct a broker or mutual fund (in writing) to always deliver for sale the highest-cost-basis stock first without making the specific identification at the time of each trade.

Holding 12 Months for Long-Term Capital Gains

Nothing adds value to the private investor's portfolio so simply and effectively as holding securities for at least 12 months to qualify for long-term capital gains treatment. At current U.S. tax rates of {35 percent} for ordinary income and short-term capital gains versus {15 percent} for long-term capital gains, literally 20 percent (35 percent − 15 percent) of all profits are at stake in the holding-period decision.[30] In other words, the investor keeps 85 percent of the profits after paying long-term capital gains tax but only 65 percent of the profits after paying tax as ordinary income or short-term capital gains. To make up such a difference, an investor would need a rate of return 31 percent higher for the same investment—all for merely changing the holding period. An 8.0 percent return subject to long-term capital gains tax is equivalent to about a 10.5 percent pretax return subject to ordinary income tax or short-term capital gains rates. State and local taxes can make this difference even greater.

Unlike recognizing short-term gains, selling a security at a short-term *loss* in less than 12 months provides no disadvantage. Because short-term capital losses must first be used to offset short-term capital gains, however, then offset long-term capital gains, and only at this point offset (a limited amount of) ordinary income, the effective rate at which the losses are used is dependent on the nature of the other gains.

Table 10.4 provides a simple example of the powerful effect of the holding-period differences on terminal wealth. Such differences make it hard to justify short-term trading for the ordinary taxable investor. Those who believe that they can successfully overcome the tax disadvantage by phenomenal results may wish to seek qualification as a business (or "trader") for the

TABLE 10.4   Additional Wealth from $10,000 Invested after Different Return and Tax Rates Applied

Return and Tax	5 Years	10 Years	20 Years
Rate of return = 5%			
15% LTCG tax	$2,310	$ 5,160	$12,990
35% STCG tax	1,730	3,770	8,960
Rate of return = 10%			
15% LTCG tax	$5,040	$12,610	$41,120
35% STCG tax	3,700	8,770	25,240

Notes: LTCG = long-term capital gains; STCG = short-term capital gains.

purpose of trading securities, at least so that expenses, which otherwise cannot be deducted, can offset profits that will be treated as ordinary income.

Investment managers who reach a negative view about a security they have purchased within 12 months may be concerned that the client will complain if the stock goes down but the manager has held it in order to get long-term capital gains treatment. A clear understanding with the client from the beginning as to the tax benefits that are certain with near-term stock price changes but are highly uncertain with a stock sale may mitigate this dilemma for the manager.

For investors who anticipate a short-term holding period (e.g., have a near-term strong bullish or bearish market sentiment), the tax burden can sometimes be mitigated by using futures contracts or listed options. For example, rather than buying the S&P 500 Index itself for fewer than 12 months, the investor can buy the futures contract, which will be taxed at a statutory rate of {60 percent} long-term capital gains and {40 percent} short-term capital gains for a blended rate of {23 percent}, which is less than the short-term capital gains rate of {35 percent}. A further explanation of tax choices for investment horizons of less than one year, one to five years, and more than five years is given in Gordon and Rosen (2001).

Tax-Loss Harvesting

Tax-loss harvesting is the voluntary sale of a security at a loss for the express purpose of currently recognizing the loss for tax purposes. In most circumstances, taking such losses is in anticipation of using them to offset gains in the same tax year, but sometimes, it may be worthwhile to warehouse losses that can be carried forward into future tax years, especially if those losses are expected to evaporate in the future. One of the key problems with taking current losses solely for tax purposes is the difficulty of replacing the sold security immediately. The "wash sale" rules (although more detailed than given here) generally require that the same, similar, or functionally equivalent security cannot be purchased 30 days before or after the sale if the loss is to be recognized for tax purposes (see also the Overview of Federal Taxation of Investments).

A loss taken now saves taxes if, and only if, the investor has offsetting taxable gains. Special rules require that losses offset gains in a particular order, even if high-tax-rate short-term capital losses wind up offsetting low-tax-rate long-term capital gains. Unused losses can be carried forward indefinitely into the future. To the extent that losses can be used to offset gains and save taxes, more net-of-tax money is available for repurchasing the same or substitute securities, but when a repurchased or substitute security is sold in the future, the difference will result in a recapture of the loss (subject to certain exceptions to be discussed).

Whether current recognition of capital losses is used to offset current gains elsewhere in the portfolio or losses are "banked" as tax-loss carryforwards to be used against future gains, many investors do not understand that taxes saved now by taking losses are usually simply postponed. Although net losses may be carried forward to use in future years, taking the loss provides no utility if the investor has no prospects of other gains for offset, now or in the future. In other words, losses are not valuable in their own right. When a tax loss is taken and a substitute security is purchased at a lower cost, a new tax cost basis is established at the lower cost. The result is the possibility for an even larger gain that may have to be recognized in the future.

A simple example will clarify what happens. Suppose an investor purchases stock in Company XYZ for $100 and a year later, it is trading at $80. The investor sells it for a loss of $20, which offsets some other long-term capital gains the investor received. At a long-term capital gains rate of 15 percent, the investor would save $3 in taxes that would otherwise have had to be paid. With $80 of sales proceeds plus $3 of tax savings, the investor could reinvest a total of

$83 in another security (or wait 30 days and buy XYZ again); the $83 would become the new cost basis for tax purposes. The investor would have additional purchasing ability of 3.75 percent ($3 ÷ $80) because of the tax savings, so (at the $80 market price) she could buy 3.75 percent more shares of XYZ than she had before. But the new tax basis of $83.00 is $17.00 less than the original basis of $100.00. If the repurchased securities appreciate, any new gain will include the $17.00 reduction in basis that came about as part of the tax-loss harvesting.

If the investor never sells the substitute stock and her estate is not subject to estate tax, either because the estate is less than the amount of the estate tax exemption or because the estate is going to charity, the government never recaptures the tax savings from the loss. The government also may not recapture it from investors who are subject to the estate tax because the estate tax is based on the gross fair market value irrespective of the amount of unrealized gain. In the example, the investor's estate on which taxes will be due (if taxes *are* due) may become somewhat larger because the investor may be able to advantageously reinvest the tax savings from the tax-loss harvesting; in this case, the government partially recoups the earlier tax savings.

Arnott, Berkin, and Ye (2001) simulated tax-loss harvesting by using S&P 500 stocks and a 35 percent tax rate. They found:

> *A great deal of loss harvesting is possible in the first few years; the earnings on the associated tax savings lead to an immediate and dramatic increase in relative portfolio value. After the first five years or so, the pace of gain added begins to diminish rather sharply. Yet, even after 25 years, the tax alpha is still adding about 0.5% per year to portfolio wealth, an alpha that most active managers can't add reliably pre-tax, let alone after tax. (pp. 13–14)*

When they took deferred taxes into account, they found "a much more moderate early benefit, but it quickly compounds and builds over time" (p. 14). Even after 25 years, the tax alpha was still almost 50 basis points a year. At the 2005 lower tax rates, this tax alpha would be lower but would not be erased. When a 20 percent tax rate was used, the authors still found a median increase in terminal wealth of 8 percent after 25 years.

Using a similar methodology but with 2003 tax rates and various stock indexes, Stein (2004b) found essentially similar results—with postliquidation tax alphas averaging around 40 basis points a year in Year 10 to Year 30. As expected, the particular simulation results were affected by tax rates, length of holding period, market return, and volatility.

But tax-loss harvesting should not be taken lightly or done too frequently. Done incorrectly and without regard for the recapture and the transaction costs of selling and rebuying, the unwary investor can experience undetectable losses that result in a slow hemorrhage of wealth. No tests or measures will directly show the effect, but it will surely erode value. On balance, it is better to err on the side of conservatism by forgoing some possible current tax savings so as not to incur transaction costs that might ultimately prove to be more than the present value of the tax saved from harvesting. That is not to say that tax-loss harvesting should be restricted to year-end actions. Gordon and Rosen discussed timing and suggested techniques for mitigating the effect of the wash sale rules that otherwise prohibit taking losses if the same (or essentially the same) security is purchased 30 days before or after the trade date. These techniques include

- doubling up on shares,
- doubling up forward conversion, and
- writing out-of-the-money puts.

A rigorous analytic procedure for determining the absolute optimum strategy for tax-loss harvesting is not yet available for practical use, but choosing policies that clearly add value is not difficult. For example, a constraint that must be satisfied is that the net present value of tax deferral exceed the round-trip transaction cost of selling and buying a replacement security. The calculation of this breakeven threshold is more subtle than it sounds, however, because the net tax savings depend on the likelihood of increased consequent taxes at a later point in time. This likelihood depends, in turn, on such myriad factors as average turnover rate, life expectancy, and whether an estate tax will be due.

If one always realizes a loss when the net benefit is only slightly above zero, the cumulative effect on terminal wealth will be only slightly above zero. Consequently, a better policy is to wait until the loss is larger. Determining how much larger analytically requires determining when to exercise a complicated tax option. Monte Carlo simulation allows one to try out various tax-loss harvesting strategies, however, to see how the strategies would perform in a range of market conditions and assumed future tax-paying contexts. The strategies can be made contingent on the size of the individual loss, the volatility of the stock, its return correlations with the market as a whole, the presence or absence of loss carryforwards, and so on.

Tax Deferral and Turnover

The effect of minimizing turnover was well documented by Jeffrey and Arnott (1993). Their focus was on turnover as a proxy for average gain recognition; that is, average turnover of 20 percent implies that, on average, approximately 1/5 of the portfolio has gain or loss recognition in any given year. Obviously, not all turnover creates realized gains, because some turnover generates taxable losses; nonetheless, with the stock market having a long-term positive rate of return, turnover is generally a bad thing with respect to taxation—except for the option of tax-loss harvesting. Jeffrey and Arnott noted that the benefits of low turnover are nonlinear—not material unless very low turnover rates are reached.

Stein (2004a) likened tax deferral to an interest-free loan from the government. Although, superficially, this view is plausible, the source of value from tax deferral is actually something else. The fundamental issue is not the time value of money but, rather, participation in profits. The government is a silent risk-sharing partner in the investing but one that puts up no capital. The sharing mechanism is nearly identical to the carried interest in a private equity or venture capital partnership. The government has a claim on a share of all current income recognized, which includes interest and dividends, but the share of a capital gain is usually due only upon realization of the gain, the timing of which is mostly at the option of the investor. The way tax deferral adds value is through the differential compounding at a pretax rate of return versus at an after-tax rate of return. The longer the compounding goes untaxed, the greater the terminal wealth, subject to the single-period negative return of the final tax payment at the time of liquidation.[31] Jeffrey and Arnott suggested that the term "interest-free loan" as applied to tax deferral is unfortunate because it incorrectly implies that any future taxes are already assets of the Treasury and are simply due at the borrower's option.

For most investors and in most normal market conditions, somewhere in the vicinity of 10 years are needed to accumulate sufficient tax alpha from the differential in the compounding rates to make tax deferral an important factor for after-tax wealth. This finding is contrary to the assertions of those who believe relatively short-term tax deferral to be worthwhile. For holding periods longer than 8–12 years, the improvement in after-tax results starts to become material, and for very long holding periods, the potential for an enhanced effective after-tax rate of return is quite significant—on a par with the manager alpha alleged by many successful active managers.

TABLE 10.5   Wealth Accumulation for Investors with Various Strategies
($1,000 invested at 6% steady rate of return)

Years to Liquidation	No Tax	Tax Deferred	Annual Tax
5	$1,338.23	$1,287.49	$1,282.37
10	1,790.85	1,672.22	1,644.47
15	2,396.56	2,187.07	2,108.83
20	3,207.14	2,876.07	2,704.30
25	4,291.87	3,798.09	3,467.91
30	5,743.49	5,031.97	4,447.15

The power of long-term tax deferral is shown in Table 10.5, which compares returns for various holding periods for a tax-exempt investor, an investor deferring all capital gains recognition until final liquidations, and an investor who pays long-term capital gains tax on all gains annually.

Tax Deferral and the Estate Tax

For investors with long investment horizons, estate tax treatment can enhance the value of tax deferral. The estate tax is applied to the fair market value of assets held at death irrespective of the amount of unrealized profit. Even at the highest estate tax rates, voluntarily realizing capital gains during one's lifetime is never better than holding the estate unless an increase in future tax rates occurs and the unrecognized gain will not pass through one's estate untaxed. Consider the following:

- For investors for whom little or no estate tax will apply, the entire unrealized gain will completely escape taxation forever, and a step-up in cost basis to the fair market value at time of death will occur for the heirs.
- Investors who leave their estates to charity can avoid the estate tax.
- Assets above the exemption amount can be left to one's spouse without paying estate taxes, although no step-up in basis occurs and taxes may be due (above the spousal exemption amount) when the spouse dies.

As deferral times lengthen or the deferral puts the liquidation into the posture of an untaxed estate, the effective rate of return approaches the return for a tax-exempt investor.

In summary, tax deferral is valuable for investments that will be included in the investor's estate, is otherwise not important for U.S. individual investors other than for long holding periods, and can add value for long-term investors comparable to the alpha from successful active management.

Tax-Advantaged Savings and Retirement Accounts

Various forms of tax-deferred savings and retirement accounts add value in much the same way as the tax deferral described in the previous section, but a potential complication is that the tax rate on money coming out of these accounts may not be the same rate that would have applied at the time of the contribution.[32]

For very wealthy individuals, various offshore vehicles also allow the tax-free compounding of gains indefinitely. Upon repatriation of the profits, however, all the profits will be taxed as ordinary income. A {5 percent} nondeductible interest charge is also applied to the foreign income on which tax was not paid (to adjust for the time value of the deferred tax payments). Certain elections avoid the penalty but effectively negate the off-shore deferral advantage. For tax purposes, some states do not follow the federal rules but tax only profits earned in the calendar year of repatriation.

Certain types of offshore vehicles require special elections if income is not to be imputed as annual taxable income.[33]

Municipal Bonds

If markets were in perfect equilibrium and all taxable investors had the same tax rate, municipal bonds would trade with a yield correctly adjusted for their tax-exempt status; in other words, the advantages would be arbitraged away. But municipal bonds are not always priced to be equivalent to an instrument with equal credit, equal duration, and taxable yield; the difference is as much a factor of the investor's tax situation as of the market. The trading costs and the bid–ask spread for municipal bonds can greatly exceed those for comparable taxable bonds, and this factor should not be ignored. Particularly at the short end of the market, municipal bonds may sometimes be unattractive in yield if corporations in higher tax brackets are competing with individuals for yield.

Because municipal bonds are also exempt from state and local taxes if the issuer and the investor are of the same state, the breakeven yield has to take into account the net effect of state taxes, adjusted for their deduction against federal income. This analysis is not straightforward because of the various deduction limitations and the alternative minimum tax (AMT).

When the tax-exempt municipal bond yields are compared with the yields of U.S. Treasury securities (which are exempt from state and local taxes), the municipal bond advantage may be less than when the municipal bonds are compared with other taxable fixed-income instruments. For high-bracket investors taxable at the {35 percent} rate from the states with the highest income tax (e.g., California at {9.3 percent}), taxable yields may need to be as much as 1.7 times the tax-exempt yield to make the taxable bond worthwhile. Moreover, certain private-purpose bonds are seemingly tax exempt but are subject to the AMT, which creates a high effective marginal tax rate.

The fundamental question, then, is whether the tax-exempt yield is more or less than the taxable yield for an *equivalent* security. For this comparison, equivalency must take into account a number of factors in addition to yield, including

- the tax character of the accreted market discount,[34]
- transaction costs (which are higher for municipal bonds),
- liquidity (which is potentially lower for municipal bonds),
- mispricing (mispricing of the bonds and the bid–ask spread is more common in the municipal market),
- early redemption provisions (which allow issuers of municipal bonds to call, or prepay, the bond).

When the investor needs to trade bonds prior to maturity—for example, for portfolio rebalancing—these factors can become particularly important. Before advisors recommend that taxable investors buy *only* municipal bonds, advisors should also give proper consideration to the benefits of taxable bonds.

Alternative Minimum Tax

The AMT creates a quagmire of problems and issues for the taxable investor.[35] Although the taxable investor is generally better off with long-term capital gains at their lower tax rate than short-term gains, some degree of taxation from ordinary income may be desirable because of potential AMT issues. That is, if the investor is likely to be subject to the AMT, it may be wise to look for investments that produce high nominal returns subject to a higher tax rate because the effective marginal tax rate may make the net returns more attractive. Because of the complexity of the AMT, the advisor may need to model various investment scenarios to determine the likely optimal mix of ordinary income, short-term capital gains, and long-term capital gains. AMT rates are {26 percent} for up to {$175,000} of AMT-defined income and {28 percent} for greater income.

Capitalizing the Income Stream

Stocks have two components of return—price change and dividends. Bonds also have two components of return—price change and interest. For taxable bonds, the interest is ordinary income, generally taxed at a {35 percent} rate, whereas price appreciation, other than the accreted discount, is taxed at long-term capital gains rates if the bond is held longer than 12 months.

When interest rates have declined since the purchase of a bond, the investor may sometimes be able to improve after-tax investment returns by selling the appreciated bond, paying the capital gains tax on the sale, and reinvesting the net proceeds in a greater number of bonds bearing a lower coupon rate. This tactic is known as "capitalizing the income stream." The strategy presumes that the investor faces a capital gains tax rate that is lower than the tax rate applying to coupon interest (as is true in the United States for holding periods exceeding 12 months). In general, because the price changes of bonds that occur solely in response to interest rate changes adequately reflect pretax fair net present value, the unrealized capital appreciation is a close approximation to the pretax present value of the future income stream.[36] This strategy would not apply to holdings in tax-exempt bonds because an investor would not want to trade tax-exempt income for a capital gains tax liability. In practice, trading costs make this kind of bond-tax swapping most useful with very liquid bonds.

Portfolio Tilts

When dividend rates were higher than capital gains rates, some commentators argued that portfolios with low dividend yields were preferable for taxable investors. Stocks with low dividend yields may be growth stocks and efficiently using earnings for growth (capital appreciation) instead of paying out dividends. Much of the historic literature on the return from growth stocks versus the return from value stocks indicates that over long periods of time, value stocks outperform growth stocks. Whether this pattern continues or not, although portfolio tilts do change the risk and return characteristics of portfolios, with long-term capital gains rates identical to dividend tax rates, neither high nor low dividends offer any obvious advantage.

Tax Sheltering with Swaps and Other Derivatives

Tax-shelter swaps are another method of attempting to convert ordinary income to long-term capital gains. Swaps generally involve taking some difficult-to-quantify risk because of unclear and changing legal interpretations.

Changes in the "constructive ownership" rules eliminated the benefits of many types of swap transactions previously in use. Wall Street has nonetheless creatively developed other swap products in an attempt to get around the constructive ownership problem. The general form of these swaps involves some sort of counter-party (and thus some counterparty risk). The most common version is a total-return swap, in which the investor deposits money with a counterparty, who then invests in various investment funds, securities, or other assets. The counterparty agrees to pay an amount to the investor equal to the future value of the total return minus the costs of the swap and its administration.

To be successful, these swaps must adhere carefully to certain tax rules and must be considered with expert tax advice. Also, these tax swaps are unlikely to last a decade;[37] so, the tax-deferral component is not likely to be of much value, although the conversion of ordinary income to long-term capital gain, if successful, is valuable. The various legal issues involved with tax swaps are far beyond the scope of this chapter, but to the extent that the swaps pass legal muster, they add value primarily by converting what might be ordinary income or short-term capital gains into long-term capital gains. Certain types of transactions—for example, call options on hedge fund returns—give the investor the choice of taking losses as ordinary income or gains as long-term capital gains.

Insurance Wrappers

Investments held in a variable universal life insurance policy are particularly well tax advantaged. A sum of money is paid to the insurance company, up front or over a period of years, out of which life insurance premiums are paid and the balance is invested. The insured person need not be the same person as the owner, which creates the potential for transferring wealth without any transfer tax (gift or estate tax) because death benefits are tax free. Customized insurance products for large amounts have the advantages of lower negotiated fees and some flexibility and customization of the underlying investments.

Insurance products have been used to shelter (if held until death) or defer (if redeemed) returns from investments. Typically, payment is the cash surrender value if the policy is terminated before death or the greater of cash surrender value or death benefit if the policy pays off at the death of the insured person.

Analyzing the value of insurance is complicated. To take advantage of the tax-sheltering characteristics granted to the insurance industry, the investor must be willing to pay a number of fees and costs:

- mortality charges (the cost of the insurance protection based on actuarial projections),
- federal and state taxes on premiums,
- administrative charges,
- sales loads, and
- investment management fees.

Mortality charges are usually embedded in the whole life product but should be approximately equivalent to the term insurance costs of an equivalent death benefit. The expected return for most investors will be slightly negative, as would be anticipated because the insurance companies are in the business of making money from term insurance. The other costs are usually straightforward. Investment management fees are typically market rates or somewhat higher. Taken together, these fees are a significant drag on nominal returns and represent a significant hurdle to adding value or improving after-tax returns.[38]

Tax Asymmetries and Hedging

A topic too little explored in finance literature is the challenge for taxable investors of using derivatives to hedge. A simplified example will illustrate the types of problems that often go unrecognized. Suppose a dollar-based U.S. investor is purchasing $1,000 of an exchange traded fund (ETF) holding euro-denominated European stocks. The investor wants to hedge the euro currency exposure, and he uses $1,000 of euro futures to hedge the currency. Consider two possible scenarios:

1. In less than 12 months, the exchange rates change, causing the value of the ETF to go down $100 (from currency) and the value of the futures to go up $100. The futures have a short-term capital gain of $100, and the ETF has a short-term capital loss of $100—an exact offset. The investor is appropriately hedged on an after-tax basis.
2. In more than 12 months, the same thing happens, but now, the tax treatment is different. The futures are U.S. Internal Revenue Code Section 1256 contracts taxed at the end of each calendar year as marked-to-market sales with a rate of 60 percent long-term and 40 percent short-term gain/loss for a blended rate of {23 percent}. The ETF gain/loss is taxed as a long-term capital gain/loss at a {15 percent} rate. The investor liquidates both positions and has an $85 after-tax currency loss from the ETF but only $73 of after-tax profit from the futures. When large dollar amounts are involved, such a mismatch has a serious effect.

Complex hedging and swapping arrangements have to take into account tax treatment, as well as the more conventional factors, to ensure appropriate after-tax matching.

Portfolio Rebalancing

Portfolio rebalancing is an admirable goal, but it is not without cost, including tax consequences. The taxable investor needs to be cognizant of at least two important issues that do not affect tax-exempt investors.

First, the tax on unrecognized gains in the portfolio is effectively "owned" by the government, so in determining when an asset class is outside its target range, the *net* (of tax liability), not the gross, amount is the correct value to use in the calculation. Therefore, rebalancing will usually be somewhat less necessary or need to occur less often for taxable investors than they may realize. This factor is especially important in rebalancing multiple asset classes with different proportions of unrealized gain.

Second, the cost of rebalancing requires taking into account the loss of tax-deferral benefits as well as direct transaction costs. For short or medium time periods (e.g., less than about 10 years), the value of any tax deferral is not likely to be meaningful, but for longer periods, it can be significant. The analysis of rebalancing should account for the trade-off between the benefits of deferral and the benefits of risk–return management. (An example is given in the Appendix 10B.) The use of derivatives in rebalancing is fraught with the same issues mentioned in previous sections. A somewhat more detailed discussion of these issues is in Horvitz (2002).

Summary

Investment tax strategies fall into a few broad categories:

*   Convert the character of taxable return from high-tax ordinary income or short-term capital gains into low-tax long-term capital gains.

- Delay the recognition of gain or income for long periods of time.
- Hold off the recognition of gain or income until death so that only the estate tax, if any, applies.
- Create voluntary losses to offset current gains.
- Use government-sanctioned tax-sheltering vehicles (e.g., retirement accounts or insurance wrappers) to defer or eliminate taxation of investment returns.

Even when these various strategies have superficial appeal, however, the investor should be cautious to analyze the costs involved and should carefully weigh cost against the possible savings. Tax savings that may be only temporary may not be worth the up-front costs.

Although general rules of thumb are a good starting point (for example, municipal bonds are suitable for taxable investors), a complete understanding must include a detailed analysis of the investor's specific tax circumstances—now and *in the future*. This analysis must take into account *income and deductions from all sources* and an estimate of the *final disposition* of the investment assets. Investment advisors should also recognize that the tax rates and rules are constantly changing, so savings that depend on no changes in the status quo of the current tax rules may evaporate unpredictably in the future. Stein (2004a) provides an analysis of the impact of future tax increases.

PART III   ORGANIZING MANAGEMENT FOR PRIVATE CLIENTS

This part of the chapter concerns the needs of the professional money management organization as it tries to organize to best serve HNW clients. Even family offices focused on the needs of a single family may find the ideas helpful as the number of family members and interrelated but legally separate portfolios increases. The section on Institutional Money Management and the High-Net-Worth Investor revisits many of the issues noted in previous sections but from the specific viewpoint of the managing organization. It goes on to address organizationally useful procedures for eliciting investor goals and preferences and for measuring performance. The following section on Portfolio Management as a Manufacturing Process deals with the "manufacturing" approaches needed to deal with large numbers of HNW accounts while still providing effective customization.

INSTITUTIONAL MONEY MANAGEMENT AND THE HIGH-NET-WORTH INVESTOR

The common practices of investment management professionals who normally deal with large tax-exempt institutions require considerable change to be effective in dealing with a clientele of high-net-worth (HNW) individuals. For institutional investment firms, the key ingredient to success is the ability to understand and forecast the behavior of investment assets. In short, this kind of management is all about the markets. For investment professionals serving HNW clients, the complexity and heterogeneity of individuals require that efficient adaptations to the needs and preferences of specific investors be the centerpiece to which the bulk of intellectual effort and resources is devoted. This section explores recommended practices for serving an HNW investor. In doing so, the section reviews certain basic investment concepts and briefly notes numerous complex issues that are more fully developed elsewhere in this chapter.

Identifying the Private Investor's Objectives

The proper goal of the investment management process, whether for an institutional investor or an HNW individual, should be to produce investment results that best fulfill the investor's objectives. In the terminology of economics, the goal is to maximize the *utility* of the investor.

Three basic concepts of investor utility introduced by the mathematician Bernoulli in 1738 are still the basis of most methodologies in money management. The first concept is that investors prefer to earn more return on their investments rather than less. The second is that investors prefer less risk to more risk, although they may have difficulty describing exactly what risk is. The third is that investors exhibit decreasing marginal utility of wealth; that is, if someone is wealthy enough to own four different houses, gaining the wealth to buy house number five is less important than gaining the wealth to buy the first house. The sort of vast wealth increases that might allow an individual to fund extreme luxuries (e.g., buying a private island) are unlikely to arise from conventional investment portfolios, except over very long time horizons; so, such increases are usually given minimal attention in formulating investment policies.

A numerical way of conveniently expressing Bernoulli's ideas is to say that the investor's goal is to maximize the logarithm of his or her wealth. Levy and Markowitz (1979) showed that the log of wealth function can be closely approximated by a simple function of the mean and variance of periodic returns. Investor goals can be summarized as trying to maximize risk-adjusted returns—that is, the arithmetic average of the expected returns minus a penalty for the risk (i.e., variance of returns) that must be incurred to obtain the returns. The size of the risk penalty can be scaled to reflect the aggressiveness of the investor.

Refinements of Mean–Variance Optimization

A common criticism of the Markowitz approach is that it deals with only the mean and variance of return and does not consider higher moments, such as skewness or kurtosis. Cremers, Kritzman, and Page (2003) showed, however, that, with a few notable exceptions, the mean–variance method is fully sufficient to accurately express a wide range of utility functions for the purpose of allocating assets within an investor's portfolio.

Defining exactly what "risk-adjusted" means is not trivial in a practical context. If one makes the assumptions that the investor's only goal is to maximize expected wealth *in the distant future* and that the investor has all the information necessary to form the exact distribution for the expectations, then a risk adjustment that maximizes expected geometric mean return is appropriate. In the real world, however, investors care about what happens *in the interval* between now and the distant future and they must base their expectations only on their forecasts of an unknown future, not on exact foreknowledge about the distribution of future events. In other words, they not only don't know the future return, but they also don't actually know the probability distribution of future returns. Contrast this situation to roulette, where the players don't know which number will come up next, but they know exactly the odds of the game. Therefore, investors are, sensibly, more risk averse than required to merely maximize the geometric mean return.

An approach to describing investor behavior more usefully than simple frameworks for investor utility is Wilcox's concept of "discretionary" wealth (described in the section called

Theory and Practice in Private Investing). In this concept, investors seek to maximize the geometric mean return on the portion of their wealth they can afford to lose without unacceptable consequences. This mathematical construct can be used to define the right level of risk aversion to be applied in calculating risk-adjusted returns for the portfolio as a whole.

Finally, in extending this theoretical concept of risk-adjusted returns to the real world, keep in mind that investing is rarely costless. It entails fees to be paid to investment managers, transaction costs, and often taxes on the realized profits. The advisor can include these ideas in the framework by describing investor goals as trying to maximize *risk-adjusted returns, net of costs.*

The Individual's Utility Function

The process of describing the utility function of most institutional investors is relatively simple: For most pension funds, endowments, and insurance companies, the magnitude and timing of spending can usually be forecasted with reasonable precision. The goal is to maximize the risk-adjusted returns, net of costs, for the institutional investor's portfolio while maintaining sufficient liquid assets in the portfolio to fund the fulfillment of liabilities in a timely fashion.

The ultimate goal for most investors is to not merely accumulate wealth but to accumulate wealth so as to provide for the funding of consumption at a later date. In the case of individuals, the need to fund consumption during the person's own lifetime may be modest relative to the available wealth, so consumption is deferred to future generations or charitable organizations who receive bequests. Both the high uncertainty of demand for consumption by descendants and the lack of actuarially sufficient sample sizes make investment policy formation for wealthy individuals far more difficult than it is for institutional investors. The money management professional must respond to the potentially conflicting needs of the HNW investor with a great deal of planning and care. In addition, individuals may face tax liabilities that are large in magnitude and arcane in computation.

Consider a case in which an HNW client hires an investment manager with the instruction that a particular investment portfolio not generate more than $1 million in net capital gains during the upcoming tax year. The investment manager must research the likely impact of this constraint on investment success and inform the client if meaningfully better returns, and thus more wealth, could be obtained within a less restrictive constraint on gain recognition.

Unlike most institutions, individuals have finite lives. Their family circumstances and lifestyles evolve through time. These changes call for constant adjustment in the balance between returns obtained and risks taken. Unlike large institutional investors, which routinely employ actuaries and consultants to help form appropriate financial policies, many wealthy, even very wealthy, individuals have minimal professional advice in this regard. The investment management firm must thus assume the responsibility of educating their investment clients about appropriate financial policies.

The situation for HNW investors can be further complicated in a number of common ways. Individuals and families generally want to fund consumption (e.g., a new car) that is less predictable than the spending of typical institutions. Often, the investing goals of individuals are intertwined with the saving and consumption goals of other members of their families. Few wealthy families struggle with the dual need to save for retirement while funding expensive educations for their children. Finally, the HNW investor may have a variety of personal preferences that are entirely unrelated to financial matters. For example, individuals who are concerned about the environment or other important societal issues may direct that their investments be arranged in what they perceive to be a socially responsible fashion so as to avoid providing implicit financial support to companies or governments whose behavior they find objectionable.

With careful thought, most of the complexities associated with investing for HNW individuals can still be expressed through the basic concept of risk-adjusted return, net of costs. If conflicts among the various goals and preferences of the investor become too great, however, expressing the conflicting goals in tractable algebraic terms becomes difficult. In such cases, the investment professional must exercise judgment based on detailed communication with the investor. Ensuring consistency of qualitative policies can be difficult, however, for a large set of heterogeneous clients and in differing market conditions. Retail brokers are generally governed by regulations similar to the New York Stock Exchange's "know your customer" rule that requires brokers to have at least a specific set of facts about their clients' financial circumstances and investing experience. This information is often captured in a standardized questionnaire that can serve as the starting point for assessing the investor's financial needs. Bolster, Janjigian, and Trahan (1995) suggested procedures for converting an investor's answers to such questionnaires into explicit portfolio weights for asset allocation by using a technique called the "analytic hierarchy process." Related work by Detzler and Saraoglu (2002) extended the approach into mutual fund selection.

Taking Taxation into Account

Taxation of investments made by HNW individuals is quite different even from the taxation of institutions that do pay taxes on their portfolio gains, such as insurance companies, nuclear decommissioning trusts (in the United States), or pension funds in some countries (e.g., Australia). Taxes on investments generally occur at three points (at least) during an individual investor's lifetime.[39] First, taxes are sometimes due immediately on the income arising from an investment, such as bond interest or dividends from stocks. Second, the rise in value of investments may be subject to a capital gains tax when that investment is sold, irrespective of whether the proceeds will be used for consumption or reinvested in another asset. Third, the returns to tax-deferred vehicles, such as retirement plans [e.g., 401(k) plans in the United States], allow investments in the plans to realize income and capital gain without immediate taxation, but taxes are levied when the funds are withdrawn from the plan.[40] The tax includes both the accumulated investment profits and any original investment capital that was not taxed at the time it was originally earned. To the extent that an investor's portfolio would be subject to additional taxation from any of these sources if it were liquidated, the investor has a *contingent tax liability.*

A fourth point at which taxation may occur is upon the death of the investor. Many countries have some form of "death tax" based on the value of the estate that is passed upon death from one individual to heirs. The size of the estate, the nature of the assets, the need for liquidity, and the tax circumstances of the investor's portfolio during her or his lifetime—all can affect the magnitude of estate taxes. Depending on the individual's estate tax expectations, the investment policies likely to prove most beneficial for that particular investor can vary substantially. In addition, at the time this chapter is being written, some jurisdictions (such as the United States) are considering changing (minimizing or eliminating) estate taxes. Thus, the element of uncertainty surrounding the estate tax should also be incorporated when formulating expectations about estate taxes for a particular investor.

When Doing Well for the Client Appears Bad for Business

An obvious consideration for taxable investors is that *how much return your investments earn matters less than how much investment return you get to keep.* This important issue can easily get lost in the context of the relationship between an investor and a hired investment management provider. The disconnect arises because, to attract clients, the investment management firm has to demonstrate the effectiveness of its services. To the extent that HNW investors all come with investor-specific circumstances involving taxes, preexisting investment positions, and a variety of constraints and to the extent that the investment manager handles the account in accord with these circumstances, the performance of any one investment account can be judged only in its own context. That performance record is not helpful in demonstrating the manager's skill to others. In addition, the heterogeneity of taxable clients will naturally cause dispersion in the returns achieved by different investors. Although this dispersion can be affirmative evidence that an investment manager is actually doing a good job of customizing to each client's needs, many in the investment industry presume that the dispersion arises from poor quality control of the investment process across the many accounts managed by the firm. Therefore, many investment managers continue to focus their attention on obtaining pretax returns in excess of their benchmarks, even if this goal is not desirable for the investor.

Deferral of taxes is almost always a positive contributor to investor wealth. Consider a hypothetical investor in a 50 percent tax bracket. If that investor invests at 10 percent for 20 years on a tax-free basis, he will accumulate $6.73 for every $1 originally invested. If the investor earns the 10 percent gross return but pays taxes annually, the return falls to 5 percent after taxes and the accumulated wealth is only $2.65 for each $1 originally invested. If the investor earns 10 percent for 20 years but defers the payment of taxes to the end of the period, the taxes on the cumulative profit will be $2.86, leaving the investor with terminal wealth of $3.87, the equivalent of a 7 percent a year after-tax return.

The dramatic impact of taxes on investment returns has been amply demonstrated in the financial literature. Dickson and Shoven (1993) and Dickson, Shoven, and Sialm (2000) showed that performance rankings of mutual funds on a pretax and after-tax basis are nearly unrelated. KPMG (see Wolfson 2000) has distributed an extensive white paper detailing the dramatic effects of taxation on mutual fund investors.

Performance Measurement of Taxable Portfolios

Since 16 April 2001, the U.S. Securities and Exchange Commission (SEC) has required that all public mutual funds that accept capital from taxable investors report after-tax returns for 1, 5, and 10 calendar years in their advertisements (see SEC 2001). Two forms of the after-tax computation are required. The first assumes that the investor still holds his or her fund shares but has paid taxes due on any income or capital gain distributions during the measurement period. The second method assumes that the fund shares were sold at the end of the measurement period. Obviously, the tax rates assumed in these illustrative calculations may not be applicable to a specific investor.

The measure of gross investment returns is relevant to decision making only in the case of an investment that is truly tax free. For taxable or tax-deferred investments, appropriate estimates of after-tax rates of return should be used in making decisions about the attractiveness of particular investments or portfolios. In broad terms, forecasts of after-tax investment returns can be formulated in two ways. One approach formulates expected after-tax returns as a function of pretax returns and, given some anticipated level of portfolio turnover, the expected level of taxes. A more complex approach adjusts expected returns for taxes on the forecasted level of investment income (dividends and interest) but explicitly treats capital gains taxes as a form of expected transaction cost to be levied upon liquidation of each specific investment security.

Both the optimal asset allocation and the appropriate balance between active and passive strategies can be dramatically altered by the consideration of taxation. Many active strategies that appear attractive on a pretax basis do not offer the expectation of any after-tax excess returns.

An important issue in the relationship between professional money managers and their investor clients is how to judge the performance of the funds in comparison with appropriate benchmarks. Through both the Global Investment Performance Standards (GIPS®) and its predecessor version, the AIMR Performance Presentation Standards (AIMR-PPS®),[41] CFA Institute requires that "after-tax" return calculations be based on either the "anticipated tax rates" or the maximum federal (or federal/state/local/city) tax rate or rates applicable to each client.[42] It also requires that if any taxable accounts are included for the purposes of composite performance reporting, all taxable accounts managed according to a similar investment objective or style must be included. When such after-tax returns are compared with pretax returns for popular benchmark indices, the managed accounts obviously look like they are underperforming.

The simple answer is to create after-tax benchmark indices. As discussed in Stein (1998), however, such a task is much more complex than it seems. A benchmark could, seemingly, simply measure the taxes arising from a hypothetical index fund based on the particular index in question and then compute the after-tax return. The cost basis of the index fund would depend on when shares were purchased, however, and at what prices. Therefore, the after-tax return of the index fund for a given period would depend on the starting date of the index fund. The after-tax return for 1999 for a fund started in 1990 would be different from the performance of funds started in 1985 or 1995 because the cost basis of the positions would be different. Gulko (1998) proposed a time-weighting scheme to deal with this issue. In addition, cash inflows and outflows paralleling those of the investment account for which comparison is desired must be included in the simulation of the index fund for most precise comparison.

The most recent guidance published under the GIPS standards goes further than the earlier standards in addressing the matter of after-tax performance measurement. The current standards still require that realized taxes be included in return measurement simply as a cost. The standards now recommend that, in addition, the contingent tax liability (i.e., the taxes that would be payable if the investment account were liquidated immediately) be reported to investors as collateral information when investment returns are reported. Note that the use of the word "contingent" in this context does not imply optional; it is being used in a fashion consistent with accounting terminology. The liability is contingent (rather than absolute) because if the investments are held to a later date, they may fall in value to an extent that no gain has been made and, hence, no payment of taxes is due. Investors can thereby assess whether the contingent liability has grown or fallen during the reporting period and consider the implications for their wealth. Discussion continues as to whether a scheme similar to that adopted for mutual funds by the SEC should be incorporated into the CFA Institute standards.[43]

An important related issue is that of the contingent tax liability associated with purchasing public mutual funds in the United States. If an investor buys into a fund that has a preexisting liability for capital gains taxes, the investor may be taxed on fund profits that were actually received by other investors during prior time periods.

These taxes are then reflected as an adjustment to the cost basis of the mutual fund investment, so the situation really represents an acceleration of tax payments rather than an overpayment.

Concentrated Portfolios

HNW investors may have portfolios concentrated in a few holdings rather than in many diversified holdings. Frequently, such concentrated portfolios arise because of the belief that the realization of capital gains on a portfolio position with a low cost basis will create such a large tax liability that it outweighs the benefit of lower risk through portfolio diversification.

To the contrary, diversifying portfolios is often in the interest of investors, even if it means incurring significant taxes. A detailed mathematical analysis of the risk–tax trade-off is provided in Stein, Siegel, Narasimhan, and Appeadu (2000). They analyzed the problem by transforming it into a "tax-deferred equivalent" basis. The optimal decision is taken to maximize the net present value of the trade-off between paying taxes (reducing asset value today) and better diversification (lower risk, better long-term compounding).[44]

Relative and Absolute Return

Because explicitly defining investor goals and preferences is difficult, judging the performance of an investment manager in terms of whether the (often vaguely defined) goals have been achieved is difficult. Therefore, it has become customary in the investment industry to judge the performance of a manager on the basis of performance relative to a benchmark market index or a peer group of other managers rather than performance in meeting predefined objectives unique to the client. But consider a situation in which an investment manager achieved a return of -10 percent in a period when the benchmark index had a return of -15 percent. Is the manager a hero for outperforming the benchmark by 5 percentage points or a fool for having lost 10 percent of the investor's money? The answer may be either or both, depending on the investor's relative concerns about absolute return and risk in relation to benchmark-relative return and risk.

Almost all investors have two parallel concerns about the returns from their portfolios. They are concerned about the *absolute* returns from the portfolio and also about how the returns on the portfolio compare with the returns earned by other investors, proxied by the market.[45]

Institutional investors often put more emphasis on *relative* rather than absolute return and risk. For example, a corporate pension fund will be concerned that it have sufficiently good returns to meet its liabilities to pension beneficiaries, but it will also be concerned that the returns earned be competitive with the returns earned by the pension funds of companies against which the sponsoring company competes. If the pension fund earns less return than those of competing companies, the pension-related expenses of the sponsoring company will be greater, placing the company at a competitive disadvantage. Because of taxes, HNW investors tend to be more concerned with absolute return and risk. Taxes are generally levied on profits made from absolute investment returns, not market-relative returns. Note that taxes in most countries are levied on individual security transactions, not at the asset-class level. Therefore, the effect of taxation on the investor's preference for absolute risk and return cannot be adequately addressed through a change in asset allocation policy. Suppose an investor's portfolio is divided between a stock portfolio and a bond portfolio. Even if the asset allocation inputs are changed to reflect the expected after-tax returns and the after-tax volatilities of the two asset classes, the change will not reflect that the cross-sectional dispersion of returns in each portfolio is larger for a stock portfolio than for a bond portfolio. Therefore, the stock portfolio offers greater opportunity for tax-loss harvesting and may be somewhat more attractive (and worthy of greater allocation) than even an after-tax asset allocation would suggest.

The formulation of investment policy that simultaneously considers both the absolute and the market-relative context has been studied by Chow (1995). He found that the concept of "risk-adjusted returns, net of costs" still holds. Because investment returns add linearly, an increase in absolute return for an investment implies an equal increase in the market-relative return for the same period. The concept of risk-adjusted return needs to be extended, however, to include two separate penalties for risk—one for absolute risk and another for benchmark-relative risk. The risk-aversion scalars used in the two penalties will take on different values that convey the investor's relative concern about the two sources of risk. With two separate risk penalties, the familiar concept of the efficient frontier along two dimensions (return and risk) becomes a three-dimensional surface (return, absolute risk, and relative risk).

Luckily, one can frame the problem as having only two terms—return and risk—relative to a specially constructed benchmark. One can think of absolute risk as risk around a market index consisting of only cash. The portfolio can then be managed to a single benchmark that is a combination of the selected market index and cash. If an investor has twice as much concern about absolute risk as she has for relative risk, she could have a joint benchmark consisting of one-third the regular benchmark index and two-thirds cash. Once the investor and investment manager have agreed on such a joint benchmark, the manager's performance can be properly judged with respect to the investor's simultaneous concerns for both absolute and relative risk. HNW investors with sufficient wealth that the primary purpose of investing is to accumulate additional wealth for bequest to future generations do emphasize market-relative returns as a proxy for long-term purchasing power.

Investment policies are routinely formulated to express concerns about inflation, but some investors' needs to hedge inflation may be even greater than usually understood. The cause is the "wealth effect," as studied by Mehra (2001) and other economists, wherein individuals increase their discretionary spending as they feel wealthier.

Finally, it should be noted that tax payments truncate the distribution of absolute return outcomes. By sharing in an investor's profits, the government also shares in the risk to the extent that losses can be used to offset gains on other investments. Thus, the absolute risk tolerance of taxed investors should be higher than it is for otherwise comparable tax-exempt investors.

The wealth of private investors may also take the legal form of a trust, in which the income of capital and the growth of capital are payable to different beneficiaries. This characteristic may further complicate asset allocation by requiring some level of minimum income.

Summary

HNW investors, with needs that are both complex and far more heterogeneous than typical institutions, represent a great challenge to the investment professional. In an institutional investment process, the vast majority of intellectual effort is dedicated to forming advantageous expectations about the future return distributions of financial assets. Relatively little effort is expended on adapting the investment process to the needs and preferences of specific investors. Effective investment management for the HNW individual requires that the area of relative emphasis be reversed, giving precedence to the intelligent adaptation of the investment process to the needs of the individual.

Minimization of taxes must be considered a crucial element of performance together with pretax return and risk. What matters is not how much return investors make but how much they get to keep.

Absolute returns may be of equal or greater importance than market-relative returns for the HNW investor.

Convincing clients of what is really in their best interests (and thereby attracting and retaining clients) may not be easy. Therefore, as a business, investment management for HNW investors has particular challenges.

PORTFOLIO MANAGEMENT AS A MANUFACTURING PROCESS

The heterogeneity of high-net-worth (HNW) investors poses a special challenge to investment professionals. A large investment services firm may have thousands, even tens of thousands, of clients. The challenge of providing investment services that are simultaneously highly customized to the needs of individual investors and also having the research depth and analytical rigor commonly provided to institutional investor clients may seem insurmountable. This section describes a strengthening industry trend of bringing the operational disciplines of a "portfolio manufacturing" process into investment management practices. The section also provides a review of common practices in investment firms serving an HNW clientele.

"Mass Customization" of Portfolio Management

The clear goal of portfolio manufacturing is to allow mass customization of investment services but with a high degree of quality control. This approach is not greatly different from the efficient operation of industrial concerns, such as the auto industry, that have mass-produced goods to individual customer order for many years. In most traditionally organized investment services firms, the same individual investment officer may be responsible for maintaining the relationship with the investor client, participating in the firm's investment research process enough to reflect the firm's investment views in the client's portfolio, and maintaining routine supervision of the client's portfolio.

In the portfolio manufacturing paradigm, the investment process is separated into three distinct roles:

- maintaining client relationships to understand the needs and wants of the investor (like a car dealer),
- investment research and overall portfolio management (like auto engineers), and
- customizing the investment products offered by the firm to the specific needs of the individual client (running the factory floor to fill individual client orders).

As noted in the section on Theory and Practice in Private Investing, the bulk of customization for HNW clients involves tax issues, but many other factors can demand modifications of investment strategies.

The typical setup of the "assembly line" in portfolio manufacturing consists of a core of automated functions for analyzing each investor's portfolio on a regular and frequent basis (perhaps daily) and proposing transactions believed to be optimal in the current circumstances. The analyses are then reviewed by portfolio management personnel and approved or not. Every investor's portfolio is provided regular attention in a process of uniformly high quality. In the automation process, the core functions must be connected to the investment firm's accounting system so as to provide the managers with information about investor portfolios and a database of the investor preferences and constraints, and it must be connected to the firm's trading functions so that approved transactions can be implemented.

Investment accounts belonging to HNW investors are particularly labor intensive. Each account is different. Each has different tax circumstances arising from the different cost bases of investment securities held and the particular tax rates and regulations in the investor's state or country of domicile. In addition, investment accounts are commonly transferred to a new investment management firm in the form of preexisting positions, rather than as cash (the customary form of transfer with institutional investors). Finally, each account may be part of a group of accounts that, in aggregate, are the investment assets of a family or another interrelated group of individuals.

In a typical bank trust department, each investment officer oversees 200–300 individual accounts. According to a report from the consulting firm Cerulli Associates, some investment firms believe that with an automation platform, they can achieve productivity of up to 1,500 accounts per investment professional. Firms following the manufacturing approach have, essentially, completely automated many routine portfolio management functions (e.g., withdrawing cash from an account in a tax-sensitive fashion). Their investment professionals can thus spend their time on the subtle aspects of investment analysis and portfolio management that rightly require human judgment. Correctly implemented, the manufacturing approach improves investing results and saves money for the investment firm because it allows the most expensive resource, investment professionals, to be used in the most efficient fashion.

For the wealthiest investors, investment services have traditionally been highly customized. Their particular needs and preferences have been catered to by trust companies, specialized consultants, and family offices. Unfortunately, because of the complexities in the situations of HNW investors, many researchers have assumed that complicated investment methods cannot be applied to this group of investors. Therefore, the development of sophisticated investment methods applicable to HNW investors has lagged behind the rest of the investment industry. Only since about 2000 has a significant amount of rigorous research emerged on issues relating to HNW investors.

For investors with less investment capital than HNW investors, the opportunities for customization have been slim. Investment brokerage firms commonly offer "separately managed account" (SMA) programs to individual investors with sizable investment funds, but these programs provide no customization; rather, in these programs, investors own a legally separate copy of a model portfolio formulated by an external investment manager. Such an account does remove the conflict of interests inherent in a brokerage account for an individual investor.[46] SMAs may also allow large individual investors to diversify across several managers. Some programs, however, offer less customization for accounts under $100,000.

Unfortunately, SMA arrangements provide few benefits to investors not provided by a portfolio of mutual funds. Additionally, investment firms that offer no customization may run the risk that the U.S. Securities and Exchange Commission will view a large number of identical accounts as an unregistered (and hence illegal) mutual fund. Nevertheless, SMA programs are growing rapidly in popularity. In 2003, Cerulli Associates predicted that SMA assets in the United States will reach $2.6 trillion by 2008. Through the portfolio manufacturing approach, several investment firms have succeeded in bringing a high degree of customization to the SMA market.

Tax Management for the HNW Market

Taxation is of great importance to individual investors. Many active management strategies do not offer even the expectation of after-tax excess returns, as demonstrated by Jeffrey and Arnott (1993). Dickson and Shoven (1993) found little relationship between pretax and after-tax returns achieved by mutual funds. Peterson, Pietranico, Riepe, and Xu (2002), however, found time-series persistence in after-tax returns of mutual funds, suggesting that investors may be able to predict, at least partly, which funds are apt to offer better after-tax returns in the future. In addition, they found empirical evidence that investment style (e.g., pursuing "value" stocks, pursuing "growth" stocks, market timing) and portfolio risk level are important determinants of after-tax returns. Surprisingly, they found that turnover is not a statistically significant determinant of after-tax returns. The reason may be that mutual funds explicitly designed to be "tax aware" may try to defer capital gains by reducing portfolio turnover or by increasing turnover in specifically tax-related transactions (e.g., tax-loss harvesting). An alternative explanation of this result is that the turnover levels for almost all the funds were well above the low levels (5–10 percent a year) below which tax deferral starts to have an important impact.

A clear alternative to standard mutual funds that is attractive to tax-sensitive investors is the "tax-aware index fund." The advantages of such a fund were first described by Garland (1997). In some markets that are particularly efficient, the average actively managed fund underperforms passive index funds. Once the additional costs of active management and taxes are considered, passive funds are a natural way to produce competitive returns in these markets while minimizing turnover so as to defer realization of capital gains. Note that some market indices are more suitable than others for this purpose. Value-oriented and small-capitalization equity indices often drop a stock from the index when it has gone up too much by their metrics, leading to forced realizations of capital gains.

The vast majority of stock market indices are weighted by the company's market capitalization. Because economic equilibrium theories and models, such as the capital asset pricing model, assume that frictions such as transaction costs and taxes are nil, the market value–based portfolios may not be efficient in a world that includes taxable investors. Therefore, new forms of passive indices weighted by criteria other than capitalization may ultimately prove most beneficial for taxable investors (see Dammon 1988; Subrahmanyam 1998).

The simplistic answer to implementation of the desirable deferral of capital gains taxes is to never sell anything. For many family offices and trust companies, pseudopassive accounts have thus become the norm for accounts with low-cost-basis stock. By "pseudopassive," we mean that, unfortunately for investors, the accounts continue to be charged active management fees. The combination of effectively passive management and active fees dooms investors to consistently poor net returns.

For investors who prefer to allocate funds to actively managed strategies, investment managers must undertake to minimize the impact of taxation while continuing to pursue the active strategy for which they are being paid. Apelfeld, Granito, and Psarris (1996) showed that if asset managers have reasonable predictive skill (which they all purport to have), active strategies can be carried out in a tax-efficient fashion—through reducing turnover while intelligently realizing capital losses that can be used to offset realized capital gains.

Levels of Tax Awareness

Various levels of tax awareness and tax-aware strategies are discernible among investment management firms.

The most widespread practice with respect to taxes is to *ignore them altogether.* Most SMA programs use thousands of essentially identical accounts and require that incoming portfolios be liquidated (with large potential tax consequences) to fund the new portfolio. For investors in such portfolios, the only advantage of a separate account over a public mutual fund is the ability to use capital losses generated in the account to offset capital gains realized on other investments. This benefit is not trivial. Because U.S. mutual funds cannot distribute capital losses to their investors, a mutual fund investor would have to liquidate the holdings to realize a capital loss for tax purposes.

A slightly more tax-aware approach is for each individual account to copy a model portfolio that is managed with some degree of tax awareness, which can lead to effective deferral of capital gains taxes. This approach still requires liquidation of incoming security portfolios, creating the same potentially large tax consequences. And it is still suboptimal because investors will have different cost bases in their positions and other heterogeneities. No single investor will have the "average" tax circumstances purportedly represented by the model portfolio. The major advantage of such an account over a tax-aware mutual fund is that it allows tax losses to pass through to the investor without account liquidation.

A common practice among bank trust departments and family offices that routinely service HNW investors is to ignore taxes for the first 50 weeks of the tax year and, then, to do a manual year-end review of portfolio gains and losses. Selected positions with capital losses are sold at year-end to offset, at least partially, capital gains that may have been taken during the tax year as a result of routine portfolio transactions. Proceeds of year-end tax sales are then invested in new securities or "parked" in an exchange traded fund (ETF) during any applicable "wash sale" period and later reinvested in the same securities that had been subject to year-end sale.[47] At best, this process is a labor-intensive one that ignores the opportunities for tax-efficient investment transactions throughout the rest of the tax year.

A more sophisticated approach is to use a model account but use rule-based methods to prevent "tax dumb" transactions in individual accounts. For example, one could set a rule that a position with a short-term capital gain should never be sold. Rule-based methods can be applied to preexisting holdings when a new account is started, but to "migrate" preexisting accounts in a consistently rational fashion is difficult without considering explicit economic trade-offs (e.g., taxes) and risk–return expectations. In addition, rules must be customized to each manager's style (e.g., value versus growth, low turnover, high turnover, trading urgency, typical liquidity) or the rules can easily interfere with investment strategies.

Many firms are reluctant to use rule-based approaches because of the potential for client dissatisfaction when a rule prevents an investment manager from acting on a judgment that subsequently proves correct. For example, suppose an investment analyst covering Company XYZ stock believes the stock will fall substantially in value in the near future. The portfolio managers respond by selling XYZ stock out of tax-exempt accounts. If the firm has a rule against realizing short-term gains, XYZ will continue to be held in taxable accounts, however, where a sale would realize a short-term gain. If the stock does fall as predicted, clients that were forced by the rule to keep the position in XYZ may be unhappy. They may be hard to convince that the investment firm was prudent to hold XYZ to avoid realization of the capital gain.

Full exploitation of loss harvesting is becoming a popular technique. As described by Arnott, Berkin, and Ye (2001), tax-loss harvesting involves forming a rule that requires a security position to be sold when its price falls below the cost basis by a threshold percentage. To the extent that the returns of the securities in a portfolio have cross-sectional dispersion, the portfolio is apt to have some positions with losses, even when the portfolio has produced a positive return overall. The capital losses arising from loss harvesting can then be used to offset capital gains realized in the same portfolio, to offset capital gains realized in another portfolio held by the same investor, or to carry forward (with some limitations) to offset gains realized in future tax years (see Part II). The economic value of the tax deferral achieved through loss harvesting must always be weighed against the transaction costs needed to undertake loss-harvesting trades that would otherwise not be required for investment reasons. In addition, loss harvesting may not be compatible with some active management styles. For example, an active value manager may find stocks increasingly attractive as they fall in price. A loss-harvesting rule would force the sale of many securities at the precise moment they are considered most attractive by this manager.

The properties that would be desirable in any particular approach for large-scale tax-aware portfolio management would include the following:

- Explicit economic trade-offs among expectations of return, risk, taxes, and trading costs should be allowed.
- Beyond taxes, other forms of portfolio customization should be supported (e.g., different risk preferences and constraints).
- The ability to use tax lot–by–tax lot information to minimize taxes should be supported.
- The tax management process should inhibit the implementation of active management strategies as little as possible.
- The process should be algorithmic in nature so that it can be substantially automated. In this way, a large number of portfolios can be efficiently handled in a quality-controlled fashion.

Tax Overlays

An increasingly important aspect of portfolio manufacturing lies in choosing a middle ground between passive and active management for taxable investors. Such processes are often called "tax overlay" or "cloning." An overlay strategy works in a way that is similar to a tax-aware passive index fund. The index fund is managed so as to closely mirror the return and risk characteristics of a published index that is presumed to offer efficient return–risk trade-offs. Many index fund portfolios will not hold exactly the constituents of the index, but will concentrate the portfolio in a smaller number of liquid securities. The fund weights the positions to mirror the overall characteristics of the published index. Similarly, the tax-aware index fund may vary from the exact index constituents in an effort to defer net capital gains that may arise through changes in the membership of the index.

In a tax overlay, the procedure is essentially the same as in the tax-aware index fund but the portfolio tries to mirror something other than a published index. Many investment firms construct a model portfolio that, given the nature of their typical client, encompasses their beliefs about the best investment portfolio available. Tax optimization can then be used to customize the model portfolio to the tax circumstances of each particular investor.

The overlay process has a number of attractive qualities. First, the model portfolio need not be constructed by any quantitative process but can be built on any investment process that a particular firm uses. So, investment firms with strong fundamentals-based (rather than quantitative) approaches can continue to do what they believe they do well; the model portfolio embodies investment views without expressing those beliefs in a numerical form. Because the strategy involves overlays, it also allows investment firms to use historically successful funds—with audited and published track records—as models. This information gives investors an understanding of what they are investing in and its potential risks and returns.

In addition, use of a model portfolio can clarify the value of tax-deferral procedures because it creates a procedural distinction between active management and tax management. To highlight the value added by active management, the model portfolio (adjusted for assumed trading costs) can be measured against an appropriate published benchmark. The client's individual portfolio can be measured against the model portfolio on an after-tax basis to measure the value of tax awareness. Such a separation does not imply that a successful active portfolio combined with an efficient tax overlay will necessarily be better for investors than a tax-aware passive fund, but it allows a clearer investigation of the issue than the passive fund strategy allows.

Overlay procedures sidestep a frequent criticism of optimization techniques—namely, that errors in the return and risk estimates that are inputs to the optimization procedures can lead to portfolio weightings that are unintuitive—and sometimes irrational. The process provides the labor efficiency of automation but avoids this issue. To the extent that overlay procedures are themselves passive (they simply try to match the model portfolio), they do not require estimation of expected returns.[48]

Other Overlays

The overlay process can be used to handle a wide variety of heterogeneities in addition to taxes. For example, consider a firm that wishes to use a successful mutual fund as the model portfolio. Mutual funds may invest in hundreds of securities, which might be impractical for an HNW portfolio of a few million dollars. So, the firm might establish an overlay to the tax optimization procedure framed as follows: "Once a month, adjust Mr. X's portfolio to look as similar as possible to the model portfolio while minimizing taxes, subject to the condition of not having more than 50 stocks." Similarly, the overlay process can incorporate customized risk aversion for a conservative investor, an aggressive investor, or one who has different (from typical) attitudes about the relative importance of market-relative and absolute risk.

Even specific client constraints, such as "never buy stock in the company I work for" or "no utilities with nuclear power," can be easily accommodated in this framework. Not only can such an optimization process automatically handle such exclusions, but it can make substitutions of other securities as required to follow the model portfolio most efficiently.

Treating Taxes as a Transaction Cost

A key advance in the development of tax-aware portfolio management strategies was put forward by Apelfeld, Fowler, and Gordon (1996). Rather than try to estimate after-tax total returns on assets, they adjusted expected returns only for taxes on income. They explicitly modeled capital gains taxes as a form of transaction cost levied on position-closing trades—usually, sales. They modeled different tax lots of the same security as different securities so that different capital gains taxes could be applied to the different lots. The portfolio could then be subjected to the same sort of mean–variance portfolio optimization used by many quantitatively oriented managers for tax-exempt portfolios. The goal of this effort was to integrate the loss-harvesting strategy with an active or passive portfolio management process.

In this approach, capital losses are not harvested on the basis of a rule; the realization of tax losses and the potential offset against capital gains arises from the inputs of all the securities in the subject portfolio, including expected return, risk, and trading cost. For example, consider a situation in which the portfolio manager has a "sell" rating on a stock on which she will realize a large capital gain. The optimization procedure searches the portfolio for another stock with a potential capital loss and a "neutral" or "sell" rating. The manager sells both positions and thereby offsets the capital gain with the capital loss. The manager can then invest the proceeds of the two sales in new positions with "buy" ratings.

This simple example is easily understood, but what about a realistic HNW portfolio that contains 50–200 tax lots? Clearly, finding the set of the most desirable transactions among the millions of possible combinations of multiple trades requires significant computational power.

Since the late 1990s, a number of algorithms (and numerous refinements of them) based on the "taxes as trading costs" idea have been developed to mechanically balance risk, return, and tax expectations. The most important concept to emerge is that capital gains taxes need to be amortized over time to allow the proper tradeoffs among return, risk, and reduction or deferral of taxes. In the procedure, taxes on income are incorporated as adjustments to expected returns. For example, if the expected income yield on a particular stock in the portfolio is 3 percent and the expected income yield on the benchmark index is 2 percent, the tax on income will consume a larger portion of the expected return from that security. If we assume a 40 percent tax on income, the adjustment to benchmark relative expected return would be $(-40 \text{ percent} \times 1 \text{ percent}) = -0.4 \text{ percent}$.

Taxes on capital gains are treated as a trading cost but are amortized (i.e., converted to units of annualized return) over a long period that reflects the expected holding period of the security that will replace the one being sold, as well as other factors. Estimating the appropriate amortization rate for capital gains taxes can be complex. Among the potential considerations are the following:

- Although linear amortization is a sufficiently close approximation for small costs, such as trading commissions, estimates of a potentially large tax impact will not usually be accurate when linear approximations are used. The tax impact ought to be thought of *geometrically* because $(1 - 0.01) \times (1 + 0.01) = 0.999$, which is close to 1 whereas $(1 - 0.40) \times (1 + 0.40) = 0.84$, which is not close to 1. Trading a 1 percent cost today for a 1 percent improvement in return for one year will produce almost the same amount of wealth in a year. On the other hand, trading a 40 percent cost today for a 40 percent improvement in return for one year will result in significantly less wealth in a year.

- Deferring a transaction until a short-term gain becomes a long-term gain represents a true decrease in taxes. The *incremental* tax on short-term gain transactions should be amortized over the period from the present until that particular position would achieve long-term status.

- Because the compounding of returns allowed by tax deferral is important, long-term amortization rates should reflect the compounding benefit of tax deferral as well as the probability of escaping capital gains taxes at death.

- Limitations on tax-loss carryforwards may affect amortization rates. If the portfolio's value reflects the presence of a large number of unrealized losses that cannot be carried forward into future tax years, it may benefit the investor to change the amortization rate to encourage realizing some gains now rather than lose the economic value of the unrealized losses.

An important element of overlay procedures is recognition that model portfolios will not reflect any specific investor's concerns about market-relative and absolute risk. This weakness can be addressed by forming a modified model portfolio that includes an appropriate weight in cash.

Overlay procedures also introduce a form of "dual benchmark" problem. Suppose a firm's model portfolio is benchmarked to some published index (e.g., the Russell 1000 Index or the MSCI Europe/Australasia/Far East Index) and is likely to resemble that index to a large degree. The "cloned" portfolios are supposed to resemble the model portfolio, but after all the overlay changes, how does the manager ensure that actual investor portfolios also bear sufficient resemblance to the underlying published index? For example, the model portfolio may be tilted away from the published index toward a larger percentage of small-cap stocks. By virtue of tax optimization, however, an investor's individual portfolio might accidentally take an even larger tilt toward small-cap stocks, which might be viewed as excessive relative to the published index. Wang (1999) provides a detailed treatment of this issue.

Dealing with a Legacy Portfolio

Another frequent concern when managing the assets of HNW clients is how to deal with the preexisting (legacy) portfolio of a new client. Portfolio transition strategies can easily be illustrated in the overlay framework. At one extreme, the investor can simply keep the existing portfolio, which obviously creates no new net capital gains. At the other extreme, the investor can liquidate his or her current portfolio and purchase the firm's model portfolio, perhaps adapted for differences in risk aversion or other constraints. This approach is apt to lead to significant capital gains taxes. For intermediate cases, one can construct a "tax versus tracking error to the model" efficient frontier by running the optimization across a spectrum of various levels of risk aversion. For each value of risk aversion, a different optimal solution will result, with each solution placing a different emphasis in the trade-off between taxes and risk. By incorporating loss harvesting, the manager can often move an existing portfolio toward the model portfolio with no net capital gains—even perhaps with net capital losses. But this strategy is not without cost because, to the extent that losses harvested could have been used to offset involuntary gains, a dollar-for-dollar trade-off is forgone in tax savings.

Dealing with concentrated positions in a preexisting portfolio is another task that often arises in a large investment firm. One procedure that has been successfully implemented in the portfolio manufacturing context is the following:

1. Borrow against the concentrated holding to the extent allowable by margin requirements. Fund a "complementary" portfolio (see the section On Concentrated Risk) that hedges the concentrated holding with a broadly diversified portfolio of volatile stocks relative to a particular stock index (i.e., the S&P 500 Index).
2. Short index futures or ETFs (the choice will affect loss harvesting of short-term losses in the complementary portfolio) to put the exposure to market risk (but not exposure to other risk or return factors) back to the original level.
3. Carry out loss harvesting in the complementary portfolio. These losses can then offset gains realized by selling off pieces of the concentrated position. If the market falls, the

hedge position will gain value. (It may pay to harvest some short-term losses that can be carried forward to offset the realization of this possible eventual gain.)

4. Reinvest the proceeds from all sales of both the complementary portfolio and the concentrated position back into the complementary portfolio.

Over time, the portfolio will gradually transition out of the concentrated position at an accelerating rate while taxes are deferred in a controlled manner. Determining the appropriate balance between risk control and tax savings is discussed in detail in the section On Concentrated Risk and also in Stein, Siegel, Narasimhan, and Appeadu (2000).

Multiperiod Analysis

A few more issues need to be considered in setting the parameters of portfolio construction and trading in the portfolio manufacturing context. Mean–variance optimization operates as a single-period model. It assumes that the future is one period. Therefore, at any given moment, the usual optimization procedures assume that whatever views one now holds about expected returns and risk will be held forever. If transaction costs are zero, however, the lack of realism in this assumption is of little consequence because the manager can continuously adjust the portfolio as her or his beliefs change through time at no cost.

This attitude is clearly unrealistic in the context of taxable HNW portfolios. Broadie (1993), Chopra (1993), and Markowitz and Van Dijk (2003) have suggested that, given the potential for future changes in views, investors are indifferent to whether a portfolio is exactly optimal based on current views. Investors operate on the principle that a portfolio can be "close enough" to optimal. As long as a portfolio is "close enough," investors simply leave it alone.

Defining *how close* to optimal is close enough is mathematically complex for all but trivial cases, but such statistical techniques as resampling (a form of Monte Carlo simulation) can be used to numerically estimate the indifference region. This process not only leads to a reduction in unnecessary turnover but also adds an important benefit to the portfolio manufacturing process: Different portfolios do not all have to be traded at the same time. If a manager has 10,000 portfolios under management, he can use an automated procedure to check each one daily for its closeness to optimality, thereby ensuring that no portfolio that needs attention is neglected. At the same time, the preponderance of portfolios will be in the indifference region, meaning that they will not require any action. This factor will tend to spread the trading of client portfolios across time, reducing the market impact of aggregated trades and reducing the labor intensity of operations.

Accommodating Investment Styles

Investment style plays an important role in the ability of a portfolio manufacturing process to enhance investors' after-tax returns. Index funds obviously offer the least turnover and hence are the easiest investment style on which to defer realization of capital gains. Among active strategies, quantitative approaches often provide more flexibility than fundamentals-based approaches because quantitative approaches allow a nearly infinite number of combinations of different stocks to be constructed to provide a desired set of portfolio characteristics—for example, a portfolio that is tilted toward small-cap stocks (relative to the S&P 500) but has the same sector weights as the S&P 500. Even fundamentals-based approaches can be accommodated if tax losses are sensibly harvested to offset capital gains when realizing a gain becomes necessary because of a negative opinion on an appreciated security. Value strategies—for example, tilting toward stocks with low price-to-earnings ratios or low market value to book value—can be more difficult in terms of tax deferral because they naturally promote selling appreciated securities. Strategies driven by price momentum do the opposite.

The portfolio manufacturing concept can be extended to accommodate complex strategies involving multiple asset managers or multiple related accounts. Many HNW investors have chosen to diversify their portfolios among managers. Some financial services firms even offer preselected packages of several managers (known as "multiple disciplinary accounts," or MDAs), each specializing in a different part of the markets. Unfortunately, having multiple accounts among several active managers can lead to inefficient investing because the sum of the various subportfolios may be similar to the makeup of a passive index. The result is an index portfolio that suffers from both active management fees and unnecessary trading costs as different managers take offsetting actions. In addition, if the manager universes are not mutually exclusive, inadvertent wash sales are also possible because no manager is likely to be aware of what the others are doing.

A better way to include complex strategies is to have each of the multiple managers provide a model portfolio, each of which has its own benchmark. The selection universe for the model portfolios may or may not be overlapping, but the client's actual portfolio is traded as a *single*, central account. The individual manager portfolios are simply model portfolios, and no effort is made to make separate trades for "sleeves" (subaccounts). The goal in this situation is to perform a "global" optimization of the client's portfolio that is tax efficient across all of the managers and captures as much of the investment performance of the model portfolios as possible.

An even easier way to include complex strategies is to form a benchmark that combines the model portfolios, with each position weighted proportionally to the hypothetical fraction that each model portfolio constitutes of the entire benchmark portfolio. In this case, if Manager X is supposed to be 30 percent of the market value of the MDA and has a 4 percent position in IBM, the benchmark has a 1.2 percent (0.3×0.04) position in IBM. At this point, a simple "minimum variance" optimization of the existing positions against this benchmark will provide the tax optimization.

Unfortunately, this simple method is appropriate only when the multiple model accounts have mutually distinct universes of securities. Consider the following example of what happens when the positions overlap. An MDA has two managers, each with 50 percent of the investor's capital. Manager A thinks Exxon Mobil Corporation is a great stock and overweights it 3 percent. She has the market weighting for the airline sector. Manager B has a 5 percent overweight in airlines, which he considers undervalued, and he overweights Exxon 3 percent as a hedge against oil prices rising. If the MDA manager simply adds the positions together, the result will be 3 percent overweight in Exxon and a 2.5 percent overweight in airlines. But Manager B wanted to overweight Exxon as a hedge against his big airline bet. Because the airline sector is now overweighted only 2.5 percent, Manager B ought to want to overweight Exxon only 1.5 percent as a hedge (keep the same 5-to-3 ratio). So, the preferred overweight in Exxon ought to be 3 percent for Manager A and 1.5 percent for Manager B. Instead, a 2.25 percent, not 3 percent, overweight in Exxon becomes the correct "benchmark" (joint model portfolio) weight.[49]

A more sophisticated way to handle the MDA case is becoming increasingly popular among large *institutions* that use multiple managers. They follow the procedure outlined in diBartolomeo (1999) on running a central portfolio with multiple model portfolios as inputs. Essentially, this process involves each manager making inferences about the "implied" alpha for each stock. The central portfolio's manager can then weight the alpha values of the managers on the basis of their assigned weights in the central portfolio. Given the "consensus alphas," the central portfolio manager can optimize the portfolio in the conventional fashion. Numerous other advantages of the approach, enumerated in the original paper, can reduce costs and taxes and potentially improve the effectiveness of active management.

Why Shortcuts Won't Work

Portfolio manufacturing comes with some important caveats. The first is that it requires appropriate resources—in terms of investment professionals and analytical systems to undertake the key role of customizing the firm's investment products and beliefs to the needs and wants of each individual investor. Customization requires skills, tools, and experience that are quite distinct from the competent analysis of securities and financial markets.

The second caveat pertains to a dangerous issue in the manufacturing approach, which is the natural desire to oversimplify the complexities of managing investments for HNW individuals for the sake of extending operational efficiencies. The underlying economics of investing under taxation and a variety of other heterogeneous circumstances demand that investment professionals resist the temptation to take shortcuts. *Most prevalent among the ill-advised shortcuts is*: ignoring the actual economic circumstances of investors entirely and organizing "optimal" portfolio formation around simple sets of constraints.

For example, an investment firm might offer a product organized as follows: "Take a list of 50 stocks that our firm views favorably. Form a portfolio that includes as many of them as possible, subject to the conditions that no one stock be more than 4 percent of the portfolio and that there be at least 20 stocks in the portfolio. Limit turnover such that the portfolio does not generate net capital gains each year in excess of 10 percent of the portfolio value at the beginning of the calendar year." At first glance, such a plan does not seem unreasonable. The critical issue of balancing risk and taxes is handled in the crudest possible way, however, by simply ensuring some basic diversification and limiting tax realizations to an amount that might appear modest to investors. A detailed understanding of what portfolio specification actually makes the most sense for an individual investor is entirely missing.

A more subtle, but equally unsatisfactory, shortcut was exemplified by a certain successful institutional asset management firm that was quantitatively oriented. To get started managing for HNW investors, this otherwise sophisticated firm simply took its existing institutional equity portfolio and ran it through an optimization process designed to defer taxes. In simulations, the approach was successful in reducing the degree of net realized gains, at the cost of a modest decrease in active returns. The firm gave no thought, however, to the heterogeneous nature of the investors or to their different (as compared with tax-exempt institutions) preferences with respect to absolute and market-relative risks. Without a readiness to adjust its strategy to fit the varying needs of HNW investors, this firm found little acceptance among individual investors, and the entire effort was eventually abandoned. A "one size fits all" approach, even if derived from a sophisticated strategy that had been successful with institutional investors, is apt to fail.

Many individual investors do not understand what is in their own best interests. The portfolio manufacturing paradigm does not relieve investment professionals of the obligation to educate their clients sufficiently that the firm can make appropriate, well-thought-out choices about the parameterization of the portfolio management process. H.L. Mencken said, "For every complex problem, there is a solution that is simple, neat, and wrong."

Summary

"Portfolio manufacturing" is a concept dealing with how an investment firm should organize its activities so as to provide high-quality services appropriate to the heterogeneous needs of HNW investors in a cost-effective fashion. Many, although not all, of the differences among HNW investors revolve around taxes. Tax-aware investing considers

- balancing the need to sell appreciated securities for investment reasons (diversification, security selection) against the need to not sell them for tax reasons,
- balancing the need to sell at a loss for tax reasons against the need to not sell them for investment reasons, and
- harmonizing the purchases and sales within tax periods.

PART IV   SPECIAL TOPICS

How to locate stocks and bonds among tax-advantaged and ordinary portfolios has been a topic of controversy, so we provide separate treatment of it in the section on Individual Retirement Plans and Location. This topic is of considerable interest to those whose wealth is not many times larger than the amounts that can be set aside in individual retirement accounts, 401(k) plans, and so on. What to do with large proportions of wealth concentrated in a single asset with large unrealized capital gains is of potential interest to private investors *across* the wealth spectrum. This question is addressed in some detail in the section On Concentrated Risk. (Appendices 10A and 10B are included specifically for readers who want to gain a deeper understanding of the issues in those two sections through a hands-on quantitative exercise. Appendix 10A is needed to follow the later example in Appendix 10B.) Finally, the section titled Assessment and Benchmarking for Private Wealth includes a description—from the wealthy investor's viewpoint—of desirable features for any approach to benchmarking and assessing such an investor's investment management program.

INDIVIDUAL RETIREMENT PLANS AND LOCATION

One of the principal savings vehicles for individuals in the United States and many other countries is the individual retirement plan (IRP). These plans are often referred to as "defined-contribution" plans because the amount of money in the plan, which will be available (less taxes) to the participant, is based on a fixed contribution by the employee and/or plan sponsor, as increased by the investment returns in the fund. The investment performance risk is borne by the beneficiary.[50]

These kinds of plans are useful and valuable for high-net-worth (HNW) individuals in the lower ranks of wealth. For the very wealthy, the benefits may be worthwhile but are unlikely to make a material difference in overall wealth, so setting up and managing the plans may not be worth the effort. For sophisticated estate planning, these plans are even counterproductive in some circumstances. For example, transferring the economic value of IRPs out of one's estate can be very difficult. So, not everyone who qualifies for an IRP should use one.

IRPs (and some other tax-sheltering arrangements) create a new issue for asset management—namely, the *asset location* problem. HNW individuals will have assets located in tax-deferred vehicles and assets held (and taxed) directly in the name of the individual investor. Because the tax treatment of investments inside these plans is so different from the tax treatment of assets outside the plans, asset classes become functionally different on an after-tax basis.

Summary of U.S. Retirement Plans

In the United States, there are a number of IRP structures—known by a variety of designations. Each plan has different eligibility requirements for the individual and possibly the individual's employer. Each plan has different limitations on how much money can be contributed to the plan and on the extent to which those contributions will be tax advantaged. In most (not all) plans, both the monies contributed and the investment earnings are tax deferred until withdrawn. This characteristic is advantageous to the investor with respect to the compounding of investment returns on a pretax basis and has more potential benefits if the investor will be subject to lower marginal tax rates during their retirement years than their contribution years. Keep in mind that the very wealthy are unlikely to face a lower marginal tax rate in retirement.

The subsections that follow provide a brief overview of the U.S. plans as of the writing of this chapter.

Regular Individual Retirement Account

Almost every U.S. worker can, until approximately age 70 1/2, establish his or her own IRA plan. In this plan, an individual may contribute up to $4,000 a year.[51] People over age 50 can make small additional contributions. Depending on the individual's adjusted gross income, some or all of the monies earned to fund contributions is tax deferred for income tax purposes. Investment earnings within the plan are tax deferred. IRA planholders must begin to withdraw funds from their IRAs at age 70 1/2. Once withdrawals are under way, capital must be withdrawn according to a schedule of minimum annual rates. Monies withdrawn from IRA plans are subject to income tax at ordinary income rates. In addition, the plans impose a 10 percent penalty for withdrawals before age 59 1/2.

The income level of most HNW individuals severely limits tax-deferred contributions to regular IRAs. For HNW individuals, required withdrawal minimums may be counterproductive in estate planning.

Roth IRA

The Roth plan is similar to the regular IRA except that contributions are not tax deferred (i.e., not deductible in the contribution year). Withdrawals from Roth plans—whether arising from contributed funds or investment earnings—are free of federal income tax, however, if the plan owner is over age 59 1/2 and the account has been open for at least five years. Roth plans involve no mandatory withdrawals. The same 10 percent penalty exists as in regular IRAs for early withdrawals. Roth plans can be a good choice for individuals who believe they will be in a high marginal tax bracket during their retirement years. Therefore, these plans are usually appropriate for HNW individuals.

SIMPLE IRA

The SIMPLE IRA program helps small businesses (with fewer than 100 employees) offer a retirement plan with a minimum of paperwork. A regular IRA account is set up for each employee. Contributions to the account can be made in two ways. Either employers must match employee contributions up to 3 percent of employee compensation, or employers must make a contribution of at least 2 percent of compensation, even if the employee does not contribute.

SEP-IRA

This plan is designed for self-employed individuals and small businesses with a few employees. Employers can contribute up to 25 percent of an employee's compensation, up to a maximum of $42,000 per tax year, on a tax-deferred basis. Employees may contribute up to an additional $4,000, on a tax-deferred basis, if under age 59 1/2 or $4,500 if over age 59 1/2. Investment earnings of the plan are also tax deferred. Withdrawals made after age 59 1/2 are subject to normal income taxation. Withdrawals made before age 59 1/2 are subject to a 10 percent penalty, with certain exceptions. Withdrawals must begin by approximately age 70 1/2 and are subject to a schedule of annual minimum amounts.

Keogh Profit Sharing

This plan is designed for self-employed individuals and partnerships. Employers can contribute up to 25 percent of an employee's compensation up to a maximum of $42,000 per tax year on a tax-deferred basis. Investment earnings of the plan are tax deferred. Employee ownership of the value of the plan account may be subject to a vesting schedule defined by the employer. Employees may not contribute to a Keogh plan. Upon voluntary or involuntary termination of employment, employees may roll over the vested portion of a Keogh plan to a different plan under their personal control (i.e., an IRA). Withdrawals may begin at age 59 1/2 and must begin by 1 April of the year in which the participant became age 70 1/2. Distributions are subject to normal income taxation. The usual 10 percent penalty applies to withdrawals made before age 59 1/2.

401(k)

The 401(k) plan is the fastest growing type of defined-contribution plan. In a 401(k) plan, employees agree to defer part of their compensation, up to prescribed limits, to place in the plan. As of 2006, employees below age 50 may have up to $15,000 annually ($20,000 if over age 50) of their compensation directed into the plan on a tax-deferred basis. Investment earnings while capital is in the plan are tax deferred. Because monies directed into a 401(k) plan are considered a deferral of compensation, these monies are also free of the federal contributions required to the U.S. Social Security system and Medicare. Employers can also match employee contributions to 401(k) programs up to prescribed limits or choose to make nonelective contributions, even if the employee does not contribute. Contributions by employers are subject to "fairness rules" that limit the extent to which contributions for more highly compensated employees may be larger than the contributions to employees of lower compensation levels. Employers can also make provisions in the 401(k) plan to allow employees to borrow money from the 401(k) for certain purposes, such as purchasing a home. Withdrawals from 401(k) plans are subject to ordinary income taxes. Penalties may be levied on withdrawals before age 59 1/2. Distributions must begin by approximately age 70 1/2 and are subject to a schedule of minimum annual amounts. Effective 1 January 2006, investors may designate all or part of their 401(k) contributions to be treated in the Roth format, which allows many individuals to increase the amounts contributed under Roth status.

403(b)(7)

This plan is similar to the 401(k) salary-deferral plan but is targeted to nonprofit organizations, such as educational institutions, hospitals, and religious organizations. As of 2006, employees may have up to $15,000 (if the employee is under age 50) or $20,000 (if over age 50) of their compensation directed into the plan on a tax-deferred basis each year. These limits increase to $15,000 (under age 50) and to $20,000 (over age 50) in 2006. Investment earnings while capital is in the plan are tax deferred. Withdrawals may begin at the age of 59 1/2 under normal circumstances but may start at age 55 in the event of employment termination (voluntary or involuntary) or disability. Withdrawals must begin by approximately age 70 1/2 and are subject to a schedule of minimum annual distributions. Distributions are taxed at ordinary income rates. A 10 percent penalty is applied to early withdrawals before age 59 1/2 (with the exceptions for termination or disability).

Suitability of Plans for Various Wealth Levels

For very wealthy individual investors, individual retirement plans will form only a small part of overall investment assets and the plans are not typically required to support consumption during retirement years. A key issue for the plans of these HNW investors is estate planning. Obviously, if IRP assets can be passed to heirs as part of an estate, overall taxation will be lower for an IRP than if one were to distribute the funds from the retirement plan, pay taxes on the distributions, and then pass the previously taxed distributions to heirs as part of an estate. A variety of legislative proposals have been made to change the rules on mandatory minimum distributions so as to alleviate this problem in the future.

For investors for whom no estate tax will be due because they are below the exemption amount, retirement accounts can transmute high-yielding, highly taxed investments into tax-exempt investments because no tax is paid within the accounts and no tax is paid at the time of death. Beware, however, that mandatory distribution requirements affect this potential benefit.

For individuals with substantial income but little in accumulated investment capital, the need to fund consumption during retirement can be a major issue. As a rule of thumb, financial planning experts suggest that individuals will require a postretirement income of 75–80 percent of their preretirement income to maintain a comparable lifestyle. Although some portion of this required income is likely to come from government-funded pension schemes, such as Social Security, individuals of moderate net worth should make every effort to take maximum advantage of the tax deferral offered by individual retirement plans.

Asset Location

Whether to hold particular investment assets in a retirement account or not is a complex problem involving a host of variables that are difficult to estimate and, in the case of tax rates, subject to abrupt change.

Tax Aspects

The importance of retirement accounts is primarily to achieve tax deferral, the value of which is described throughout this chapter. *Whether a contribution to the account is made with after-tax money (and tax-free on withdrawal) or the contribution is made with pretax money (and taxed on withdrawal) is not key to the value of these accounts.* The reason is that the tax payment is mathematically identical to a single-period negative return and thus has the same effect on the geometric mean return whether it occurs at the beginning or at the end. But when the investor's estate will not be subject to tax (because it is less than the exemption amount), the ideal plan is one in which contributions are pretax, not after tax, because all taxes will be avoided—*now and in the future.*

In addition to the tax-deferral effect, investors are quite likely to be in a lower marginal income tax rate bracket when they are withdrawing funds from rather than depositing funds into their retirement accounts. Marginal income tax rates have fluctuated greatly since the establishment of the U.S. federal income tax, however, so there is no assurance that the future prevailing tax rates, even in lower income brackets, will be lower than the investor's tax rate at the time the funds are being placed in tax-deferred retirement accounts. In addition, many HNW investors will have sufficient income during their postretirement years that no decline in marginal tax rate ought to be expected.

Another important aspect arises when the total applicable tax rate is lower for investments held outside the retirement account than for those flowing through it. For example, long-term capital gains and dividends are taxed at a {15 percent} rate outside retirement plans, but although gains and dividends are not taxed while in the retirement plans, the money withdrawn will be taxed as ordinary income, which for most wealthy U.S. investors, means at the {35 percent} rate.[52] The correct analysis is not so simple, however, because with extremely long deferral times (e.g., multiple decades), the higher exit tax rate may be so diluted by the benefits of tax deferral that using an IRP is still economically advantageous. One cannot simply assume that a higher tax rate on withdrawal relative to the applicable tax rate on the same investment return held outside the IRP makes the IRP unattractive. It depends.

Losses in traditional IRAs can be used to offset gains only when all the individual's IRAs combined have been distributed—essentially in a complete liquidation of all the combined retirement account holdings—because the gains and losses are netted. Therefore, interim tax-loss harvesting is not possible. Although investors may wish to put some risky, highly volatile investments in their IRAs for nontax reasons (because these investments may constitute some part of any portfolio), doing so provides no tax advantage like the advantage that comes from accounts in which one can deduct a loss.

Nontax Aspects

Generally, the more tax inefficient the investment is relative to other investments the investor owns, the better off that tax-inefficient investment is in a retirement account. Keep in mind, however, that a key factor in asset location is the need for liquidity to deal with unexpected consumption expenditures. Other factors that can be relevant to the decision include the investor's life expectancy, existing portfolio holdings, embedded capital gains, and the available wealth levels in both the taxable and tax-deferred accounts.

Which Asset Classes to Hold in Retirement Accounts

A dynamic programming method for analyzing asset location was developed by Dammon, Spatt, and Zhang (2004). They came to the following important conclusions:

- The relative attractiveness of taxable and tax-exempt bonds is conditional on the availability of a tax-deferred vehicle for holding the bonds. In essence, asset location and asset allocation form a single joint decision.
- In the absence of other factors (e.g., asset allocation constraints), when the tax rate on dividends is lower than the tax rate on interest and is identical to the long-term capital gains tax rate, holding stocks in the retirement account is not worthwhile. (Presumably, this reasoning does not apply when substantial portions of the expected capital gains on stocks are short term and highly taxed.)

- For most investors, even relatively tax-inefficient stock investments (e.g., most mutual funds) should be kept outside the retirement account.
- Investors who hold bonds in their retirement account can benefit from holding a balanced portfolio of bonds and equities outside the tax-deferred accounts. Investors who hold a balanced portfolio inside their tax-deferred accounts can benefit from holding an all-equity portfolio outside the retirement accounts. The structure of holding equities and bonds in the tax-deferred retirement account *and* holding equities and bonds outside the tax-deferred account is generally unsuitable.
- Taxable bonds should almost always be held in retirement accounts. Only those investors seriously concerned about large, unanticipated "shocks" to their consumption (such as an enormous medical bill) that will require liquidity will find much advantage in holding taxable bonds outside the retirement account. HNW individuals typically have much higher consumption than the average investor, so the limits on the amount in a retirement account may make even this concern moot.

A study by Sialm and Shoven (2004) came to many similar conclusions. Their research also found that taxable bonds should be held in the tax-deferred retirement account. They argued that equities held outside the tax-deferred account should be selected to be tax efficient, such as index funds or "tax-aware" funds, whereas traditional actively managed funds should go inside the retirement account. Another extensive treatment of tax-advantaged savings vehicles can be found in Horan (2005).

Appendix 10A discusses a method for customizing location decisions and is necessary for the reader to understand the concentrated risk example in Appendix 10B.

Rebalancing

If stocks are held outside the retirement account and taxable bonds are held within the account, stocks are likely to outgrow the investor's target asset allocation. Therefore, some rebalancing will be necessary. When the rebalancing factor is considered, the conclusions about asset location may be somewhat contrary to the advice of the leading commentators cited in the last section.

Rebalancing usually requires selling stocks and buying bonds, which triggers taxable gains for stocks held directly and thereby increases the tax inefficiency of stocks, which can make it worth at least considering holding some stocks in a retirement account. But at {15 percent} for long-term capital gains, the tax rates are so favorable that selling the stocks may not be a material issue, especially when the tax is compared with the {35 percent} rate on bond interest. When the retirement account assets are small relative to the investor's total assets, as is common with very wealthy investors, the potential to bring about a material rebalancing in the retirement account may be small.

Summary

Retirement accounts, although nearly universally recommended by investment advisors, are not for everyone—especially very wealthy individuals. Whenever IRPs are considered, attention needs to be given to

- potential changes in future tax rates,
- trade-offs between low current tax rates and higher deferred withdrawal tax rates,
- the potential need for cash before withdrawals can be made without penalties,

- the likelihood of gain recognition even for low-tax-rate investments, and
- the relationship between the retirement account and the estate plan.

In summary, asset allocation and asset location for individual investors involve a holistic consideration of which assets are to be held inside and outside the retirement account in light of the likely tax consequences. The approach involves considering the timing of the person's needs for cash, the benefits of tax deferral, relative tax rates, and issues of rebalancing.

ON CONCENTRATED RISK

Wealthy investors are often vexed by the question of whether to diversify a large portion of their wealth that is concentrated in a single stock or business interest, especially when a substantial capital gains tax will need to be paid if they do. Investors may reasonably prefer to have the lower risk associated with a diversified portfolio but also prefer not to pay taxes. The challenge is how to decide how much to pay in tax to diversify.

Doing nothing accomplishes nothing with respect to lowering the risks of a portfolio that is concentrated in a small number of assets, nor does it provide the opportunity for consumption or reinvestment into more attractive opportunities. The tax code prohibits or severely limits how much in short sales against the box (shorting securities one owns), or closely related hedges, one can perform without triggering a capital gains tax event through a "constructive sale."[53] The result has been increasing complexity as investors find new approaches and the U.S. government passes new laws and regulations designed to close off the exceptions.

An approach to deciding how much of concentrated risk to alleviate through an outright sale is given in Appendix 10B. A better understanding of its mechanisms will result if the reader first masters the simpler example in Appendix 10A.

Proactive alternatives to reducing concentrated risk without triggering taxes use some combination of three principles: borrowing, "complementarity," and pooling. Hedging transactions—such as an offsetting short-sale or a tight "collar" combining a put and a call on the appreciated stock (and thus substantially removing both the possibility of loss and the opportunity for gain)—are considered constructive sales and do trigger taxes in the United States.

Borrowing

A common approach is to use borrowed funds. To avoid increasing overall risk, investors can use specially constructed transactions, such as short sales on related securities or on the market, "collars," or collar-containing "prepaid variable forwards" (PVFs). These techniques provide intermediate-term benefits but may involve long-term adverse tax treatment and high fees. The diversification benefits may be outweighed by additional hidden risks incurred through a combination of leverage and hedging positions. For example, because of the asymmetrical tax treatments of the instruments that make up a PVF collar, the minimum-risk hedge ratios derived from after-tax analysis are different from those derived on a pretax basis.

Leverage, Short Sales, and Tax-Loss Harvesting

When an investor's concentrated position is only a part of the investor's investment portfolio, the advisor can restructure the remainder of the portfolio to offset the risk of continuing to hold the concentrated position (see the "Complementarity" section). When the concentrated position is held at a large capital gain and is all, or nearly all of the investor's portfolio, however, more aggressive steps may be appropriate. One approach for these cases is to use a combination of leverage, short sales, and tax-loss harvesting. The investor borrows on margin against the concentrated stock position and offsets the leveraged market risk by taking a short-sale position, not on the specific security (which would constitute a constructive sale), but on either an exchange-traded fund or a market index futures contract. The net funds generated are invested in a diversified portfolio of stocks with high specific risk (above-average return volatility) and a below-average correlation with overall market returns.

This approach will increase the likelihood of effective tax-loss harvesting, irrespective of market direction, through a high degree of dispersion in the return cross-section. Because the risks of a concentrated position are largely asset specific by definition, this diverse portfolio will also have low correlation with the concentrated position. A program of tax-loss harvesting in this diversifying portfolio will produce tax losses that can then be used to offset taxable gains created by concurrent sales of the concentrated position. Proceeds from sales of the concentrated position can then be reinvested into the diversifying portfolio, accelerating the entire process.

Over time, the concentrated position will be gradually sold off, with reduced realization of taxable capital gains. In addition, the diversifying portfolio may produce short-term loss realizations that offset short-term gains of any profit on the hedge. This approach can be achieved with low initial costs. As the concentrated position is sold off, however, the tax-loss harvesting may not generate sufficient tax losses to cover hedging profits that could arise in a long-term market decline. The expected value of the net benefit depends on specific investor circumstances.

Collars

In a collar, rather than hold a short position on the market, the investor can reduce risk more directly by purchasing an out-of-the-money long-term put option on the concentrated security holding. The purchase is financed through the sale of an out-of-the-money call option. Because of its customized nature, such a transaction makes the most sense for large amounts. Once overall risk has been reduced, borrowing against the portfolio becomes safer.

What are the complications? The first is that the strategy can be expensive. Customized options incur large dealer spreads, and they must be renewed at intervals, each time with a fee. Also, out-of-the-money puts are generally priced higher than out-of-the-money calls, implying that the investor must give up more upside return than the downside protection obtained to make the transaction self-financing. Second, so-called straddles create tax asymmetries that can negate the tax benefits of trying to avoid realizing gains on the original security. In essence, if prices move outside the collar, the hedging gain is taxed at a high short-term gains rate. But if the process produces a hedging loss after two years, the tax write-off is at the long-term rate. And it cannot be taken until the transaction is completed at the end of the five-year (or similar) period or when the position is closed out. This asymmetry introduces an unintended volatility risk.

Prepaid Variable Forward

A forward contract avoids the limitation in the two previous approaches: government limits on margin borrowing. The investor contracts with a counterparty to deliver the concentrated stock shares at a forward date. This forward sale (carefully written as a sale rather than a loan, to avoid margin restrictions) generates cash. The ability of the investor to deliver the shares is reinforced by a collar—the purchase of an out-of-the-money put financed by the sale of an out-of-the-money call. To avoid having the forward transaction characterized as a constructive sale, the terms are contingent on a formula specified in such a way that the outcome has some risk, and the associated put and call strike prices must be materially different. No statutory "safe harbor" has established how far apart the prices must be, although some professionals advise 20 percent. This PVF approach has the same complications as the collar, which it includes, plus additional fees. Recently, the IRS has taken the position that transactions that also involve a share-lending component that allows the counterparty to dispose of the stock will be treated as a current sale.

Complementarity

Another technique is to construct a "complementary fund" in the form of a portfolio purposely diversified to offset the risks associated with the remaining concentrated position. Even without requiring leverage to fund new investment, the existing nonconcentrated portion of an investor's portfolio can be organized into a complementary fund.

Complementary funds are funds designed to maximally diversify security-specific risk rather than overall market risk. They can be built either elsewhere in the portfolio or through borrowed funds from one of the approaches that use leverage.

The "completion fund" is similar but does not go as far in reducing overall portfolio risk; it is designed to replicate the behavior of a market index by investing only in stocks that resemble the parts of the index not represented by the initial holdings. But a complementary fund, as defined here, is a different animal. Unlike a completion fund, it does not assume that the market index is the best available trade-off between risk and return. Also, unlike a completion fund, it is applicable even to cases where the concentrated risk position is too extreme to bring into harmony with an index without some form of leverage and hedging—and all the complications noted earlier.

Pooling

Other approaches involve loss of control of the original concentrated ownership position in exchange for the benefits of a diversified portfolio without triggering a capital gains tax.

Exchange Funds

The best example is an "exchange fund." A number of investors contribute their various concentrated positions to a partnership (typically a private limited partnership) or similar entity, and through this pooling, each investor increases diversification of his or her holdings. To qualify as a nontaxable event, the exchange fund is required to hold a material percentage of illiquid investments. This requirement has often been met through buying real estate by using additional borrowing, for which the stock portfolio is the collateral. The strategy may or may not entail a significant waiting period (a "lockup" period) before the investor can withdraw funds.

The consequent introduction of additional leverage and liquidity risk, albeit in a pooled investment, may increase risk, thereby frustrating the original risk-reduction intent.

Finally, exchange fund investments are specific to the contributions of a limited number of contributors in each fund and may be highly clustered in a few industries—therefore, not ideally diversified.

Charitable Remainder Trusts

If the investor is willing to give up both control and a significant part of the value of the concentrated stock, he or she may pool it by donating it to a charitable remainder trust, which may sell it tax free to obtain a different portfolio. The investor receives both a specified amount of future income and an immediate tax deduction for the portion that the IRS expects will become a charitable gift. With proper planning, much of this income can be realized from capital gains in the trust (or even from tax-exempt bonds). The remaining principal after death will pass to the benefit of the associated charity.

This approach, and its many variations, makes sense only for amounts of money that are large enough to justify the necessary legal assistance and only if the investor would have been a donor to the charity in any case. Community foundations and other charitable entities that routinely pool donations from many individuals often have packaged programs that can mitigate some of the legal expenses and include professional investment management of the ongoing portfolio.

Summary

The question of how to deal with concentrated positions carrying large unrealized capital gains is often troublesome because it requires both acumen in tax reduction and an objective approach to relinquishing assets to which the investor may be emotionally attached. For moderate risks and amounts, a targeted outright sale may be optimal. Otherwise, three broad practical approaches are possible:

- Borrowing can raise funds for diversification and dealing with the consequent risk management through some combination of short sales, option collars, or prepaid variable forwards; care must be taken that unanticipated tax or fee complications not spoil the long-term benefit.
- In complementary funds, the concentrated position is left in place but other parts of the balance sheet are revised to lower risks for the total portfolio.
- Pooling with other investors or donors can be effected through exchange funds or charitable remainder trusts.

ASSESSMENT AND BENCHMARKING FOR PRIVATE WEALTH

The section titled Institutional Money Management and the High-Net-Worth Investor presented the basics of performance measurement for taxable investors. This section represents a starting point for more comprehensive approaches to assessment and benchmarking. Its narrative is from the viewpoint of the informed wealthy investor.

A theme that has run throughout this chapter is the highly individualized nature of each investor's circumstances; not only do investors differ significantly from each other, but their circumstances are usually subject to significant changes over time. The usual benchmarking techniques based on risk-adjusted gross returns are worse than unsuitable—they can be seriously misleading.

An appropriate assessment method for private wealth must meet, at a minimum, the following criteria:

1. Risk and return measures must ultimately extend to the question of purchasing power.
2. The tax inputs in the calculations must be idiosyncratic to the specific investor; they cannot be general tax rates.
3. The advisor must have a clear, quantified understanding of at least the minimum wealth and spending levels that must be maintained at all times.

4. If the investor is responsible for other family members or charities, the analysis of the investment plan and its performance should take these people or organizations into account—their available assets, spending/saving, and taxation.

Measuring Return as Purchasing Power

The section on Lifestyle, Wealth Transfer, and Asset Classes introduced the four critical factors that have an impact on private wealth:

- investment expenses,
- taxes,
- inflation, and
- consumption.

These factors can be quantified as adjustments to the gross return measures typical of investment performance reporting. Measures of gross return are useful for comparing one manager with another as to ability (or luck). Typically, these benchmarks are either a universe of comparable managers or an index related to the style of the manager. Primarily, these kinds of measures assess security selection skills and, to a lesser extent, trading acumen and costs. These measures may have no relevance, however, for assessing the ability of a manager to meet the needs and objectives of a specific client.

For an illustration of the four-factor analysis, consider this simplified case of an investment account of $5 million consisting of 60 percent stocks and 40 percent bonds. The stock performance in the past year was 8 percent a year, consisting of 6 percent price appreciation and 2 percent dividends, and the bond performance (income only) was 4 percent a year. Turnover averaged 50 percent a year (which is low by most active standards), and a third of the price appreciation was short-term capital gains (2 percent of the 6 percent) and the rest was long-term capital gain (4 percent of the 6 percent). Investment management fees were 1 percent. Inflation was 3 percent. The tax rate for long-term capital gains and dividends was 15 percent, and the tax rate for interest and short-term capital gains was 35 percent.

Consider a comparison of this performance for a tax-exempt institutional investor with the same performance for a private, taxable investor. Both had a gross blended return of 6.4 percent and, less the management fees, a net-of-fees return of 5.4 percent.

The institutional investor has a real return (less inflation of 3 percent) of 2.4 percent. The real value of the assets will double in about 30 years.

For the taxable investor, the net-of-fees return is also 5.4 percent, but then taxes begin to change the picture. The tax components are shown in Table 10.6.[54] After subtracting inflation (3 percent) from the after-tax return shown in Table 10.6, the result is a net after-tax real

TABLE 10.6   After-Tax Return Components for the Taxable Investor

Tax Component	Computation	Result
Short-term gain	60% × 6% × 1/3 × (1 − 35%)	0.78%
Long-term gain	60% × 6% × 2/3 × (1 − 15%)	2.04
Dividends	60% × 2% × (1 − 15%)	1.02
Bond yield	40% × 4% × (1 − 35%)	1.04
Total after-tax blended return		4.88%

return for the individual investor of only about 1 percent, which will take about 70 years to double.

If spending out of the account is limited to the real after-tax return generated, the amount of real purchasing power available each year for the individual from this $5 million account will be only about $50,000. Such an outcome is probably not intuitively obvious to most private investors considering an investment firm marketing a track record of 8 percent for its stock fund and 4 percent for its bond fund; such returns would be viewed as providing a $320,000 gross return (at a blended 6.4 percent) on $5 million.

What return the manager is providing, as returns are conventionally reported, has little direct relationship to the numbers that matter for the taxable investor. No one can spend reported performance numbers. An adequate performance report must clearly disclose the details. By showing the impact of each element that affects net performance prior to consumption/savings, the manager gives the investor a simple but clear picture of the relevant factors.

As a start, a performance report might be constructed as follows:

1. gross return (net of transaction costs) of client portfolio,
2. return net of management fees,
3. return net of #2 and implied taxes, and
4. return net of #2, #3, and inflation.

What benchmark(s) can be used to measure these four line items? The first item can be benchmarked against an appropriate style index. The second item can be indexed against a passive (default) index fund with low or no fees. The third item can be indexed against standard tax rates or optimal achievable tax rates (e.g., a portfolio-weighted blend of long-term capital gains rates for price appreciation, dividend rates for dividends, and tax-exempt bond rates adjusted for the difference in average yield for top-credit/equivalent-duration taxable and tax-exempt bonds). The fourth item is simply the third item adjusted for inflation.

Measuring Long-Term Viability

The long-term sustainability of the investor's investment program is of critical concern—particularly for investors for whom investments generate important sources of cash for consumption. Because the time horizon is different for each investor, the sustainability of the investment program should be quantified.

One approach is to use the actuarially determined remaining life expectancy (remember that this life expectancy is conditioned upon already having reached age Y). A cushion factor may be added that consists of additional years but with an asymptotic maximum life span. Based on the investor's remaining actuarial life expectancy, the investment program can be modeled and stress-tested to estimate how long it can be sustained at various expected returns and tax rates (adjusted for inflation and, importantly, consumption). The investment assets can be modeled as an amortizing asset.

After the four factors have been taken into account, the results can be reported in relation to "years remaining" relative to a benchmark actuarial life expectancy. Any assessment report that does not take into account all four factors will be misleading—and potentially ruinous for the client in the long run.

If the investor anticipates supporting others (e.g., a spouse or children), those life expectancies also need to be accounted for in monitoring the long-term survival of the real investment assets.

For investors for whom substantially all of the investment return is being put toward savings, the focus should probably be on the *ultimate* use of the assets. For example, if some assets are intended for a charitable bequest, that target amount can be quantified and the assessment of whether the investment program is on a path to meet the target objectives is relatively simple. For investors who wish to leave money to their children, the analysis might be as follows:

> An investor has set aside $1 million in savings for investment in trusts for newly born twins. The investor would like to achieve at least $1 million in real (today's) purchasing power for each child when the twins are 35 years old. Meeting this goal will require a 2 percent compounded annual "quadruple-net" (net of the four factors) investment return.

The result of this approach is that the target cumulative rate can become the benchmark for the return performance of the investment program in the trusts. All four factors, including consumption, can be accounted for fairly easily, and the analysis of whether the program is on, above, or below the target compounding rate is straightforward. A compelling way to report this information is in the form of a graph with two lines—one for the cumulative target wealth as a function of time and one for the actual cumulative wealth.

Assessing Risk

Risk affects taxable investors in a number of forms. For example, in the benchmarking process, the advisor must consider risk in the form of interim volatility.[55] The lack of perfectly normal return distributions affects tax-exempt investors as well as taxable investors, but because of asymmetrical tax treatment, taxable investors face the more challenging calculations. Further complicating the advisor's job is that the tax posture of the investor is likely to change over time in ways unrelated to the drivers of return. Therefore, periodic updates are a necessity.

Modeling the value of losses (which can mitigate risk) requires understanding that they may be partly binary. That is, for some investors, large losses will have no offsetting gains and, therefore will have no value. The magnitude of downside risk will be essentially the same for such taxable investors as for tax-exempt investors, although the upside potential will not be.

Risk assessment can be approached through shortfall constraints—and their alter ego, discretionary wealth. By quantifying the minimum acceptable shortfall threshold for the investor, the manager or advisor can create reporting that shows the amount above or below the crucial minimum, which becomes a different kind of benchmark. This benchmark and its portfolio counterpart need to be adjusted for inflation, because the ultimate goal of all private wealth is purchasing power.

Although subject to well-identified problems, optimizers can also provide useful post hoc information on the portfolio. If the advisor uses gross risk and return inputs based on recent historical performance, the investor's actual portfolio can be compared with an efficient frontier composed of the accessible asset classes on both pre- and after-tax bases (with the use of standard tax table rates). Although far from exact (and subject to important caveats), such a depiction can help the advisor and the client see whether the portfolio is going wide of its intended mark in efficiently balancing risk and return. If the opportunity set of asset classes actually available to the investor has been used, anything showing extreme deviation from the standard tax rate–adjusted efficient frontier should trigger further analysis and inquiry.

The Life Cycle and Changes in the Risk–Return Trade-Off

Even if, hypothetically, the efficient frontier for investment portfolios could be known with some certainty, the investor would still have to decide her or his appropriate risk level and its associated return—that is, the correct location on the efficient frontier. This portfolio choice is driven by more than simply tax adjustments and available investment opportunities, and it is likely to change over time. Endowments may have relatively unchanging risk-and-return locations if they assume functionally infinite investment horizons. Other institutional investors, such as pension funds, may shift their risk–return locations based on changes in how assets and liabilities are matched (overfunding or underfunding). But individual investors are most likely to need a readjustment in their risk–return locations on the efficient frontier as they shift from asset accumulation to asset preservation and, finally, to asset dissipation. In the section on Theory and Practice in Private Investing, we introduced the concept of a *life-cycle balance sheet* for use in assessing an investor's discretionary wealth. This analysis can be effectively used to adjust the risk–return trade-offs during an investor's life. For investors who wish to take a less quantitative approach to this issue, we present generally appropriate practices here.

For individuals who have no heirs and no significant charitable goals, the appropriate risk level should decline significantly in old age. The target should be to have enough money to live on through the person' remaining years (using maximum life span, not actuarial life expectancy). For individuals with significant investment assets who have retired and who desire a more modest, perhaps simpler lifestyle, risk taking should also decline. Conceptually, this change can be thought of as a special case of an annuity, although it should be quantified on a worst-case basis so as not to run the risk of a shortfall in funds late in life. In this case, then, the appropriate benchmark will usually move to a lower risk and lower return level.

For investors who are accumulating additional wealth primarily for their heirs, as is common in multigenerational family wealthy management, or those with significant charitable goals, the appropriate strategy may look much like that of an endowment fund with functionally infinite life. That is, the allocation may not change in response to the investor's life cycle.

It is not the amount of wealth itself that dictates the appropriate location of investment assets on the efficient frontier; rather, it is the adequacy of the current assets relative to the future needs and goals of the individual. Because both current and future circumstances are likely to change over time, periodic reevaluation of location is necessary, although for most people, every few years is frequent enough.

The Whole Tax Picture

Affirmative confirmation that the total tax picture is being considered should be a hallmark of first-class private wealth investment practice. The discussion to this point has considered the assessment problem primarily from the perspective of a single investor—and even more narrowly, from the perspective of a single account handled by a manager or advisor. Rarely is life so simple. The two key parts of the next analysis are to identify, taking into account all the combined sources of taxable income, the actual tax posture of the investor and to look at what other persons or entities have assets related to the investor's goals that may properly be taken into consideration in crafting an optimal investment program.

The tax rates used in the previous simple examples are easily found in published tax tables, but rarely do they reflect the real-life complexities of actual investors. Ideally, the investment management process should involve a two-way flow of tax information between the investment manager and the client or the tax advisor. At least once a year, usually at the beginning of the fourth quarter of the calendar tax year, the client's advisor(s) should run a *pro forma* tax return incorporating year-to-date information and estimates for the balance of the year. This process should help establish the actual marginal tax rates for various classes of income and identify opportunities and risks for tax deferral, tax-loss harvesting, and so on. Marginal tax rates can be identified. For purposes of performance reporting, the functional tax rates for various types of income can be used in lieu of the standard tax table rates. Commonly used tax-preparation software is inexpensive and more than adequate for the type of *pro forma* modeling that allows the investment manager or advisor to stay on top of the actual tax posture of the investor.

When this modeling is routine, not the exception, it is likely to produce significant changes in asset classes from time to time, as when the investor is wasting deductions and subject to the alternative minimum tax (see Part II) whereas the investment manager is loading up on low-yielding municipal bonds for the taxable client.

Related Entities and Asset Location

Most of the time, the picture for the individual investor is not complete, even if the financial advisor has access to the individual's personal tax information. Wealthy investors often have other investment entities that need to be considered (e.g., trusts, retirement accounts, and businesses and real estate owned by the investor). These entities may not show up in tax information if they did not generate taxable events in a given year(s). A "consolidated balance sheet" approach may be useful in clarifying how related holdings and entities should be considered in a holistic approach, especially as to asset allocation.

Understanding of the entire picture of asset locations is critical before settling on an asset allocation strategy. Moreover, location and allocation cannot be fixed in a one-time exercise. They should be done annually to ensure that the right asset mixes are in the right pockets—particularly, that rebalancing is done with all the entities in mind. A performance report based on the four factors as applied to the consolidated balance sheet is a way to completely assess whether the investor's goals and needs are being met.

Inflation

Inflation is all too easy to overlook. Inflation can be the slow, unseen factor that erodes wealth irreplaceably. Using almost any measure of inflation is better than using none, but the broad standard measures (e.g., U.S. Consumer Price Index, U.S. Gross Income Deflator) are not likely to adequately represent the inflation changes that affect the wealthy. Instead, custom measures made up of the underlying components of the CPI but with more relevant weightings can be crafted to suit individual circumstances—or to suit at least a prototypical wealthy investor. Keep in mind that even though a custom inflation index may be good for a decade or more, its application needs to be at least annual with respect to performance measurement.

Summary

Approaches to assessing the performance measurement and benchmarking needs of wealthy individuals need to be comprehensive and need to recognize the highly individualized nature of each investor's circumstances:

- Investment returns should be reported net of investment expenses, taxes (realized and unrealized), and inflation.
- Taxes should be calculated on the basis of the actual circumstances in the tax year of the report and should take into account ex-portfolio tax factors.

- Measures of risk need to be adjusted for the actual tax circumstances of the investor and should be reported in the context of the specific shortfall constraints.
- To properly assess a portfolio's purchasing power, measures of wealth accumulation have to take into account inflation and consumption.
- Measures of the long-term adequacy of a plan have to take into account not only the investor's life horizon but also the horizons of relevant others.
- For accurately assessing whether the investor's goals are likely to be met by the plan, the advisor must use an integrated approach that considers *all* the entities holding the investor's monies.

REVIEW OF SECTION SUMMARIES

Introduction and Challenge

The professional investor who is used to managing institutional portfolios faces special challenges when serving private investors:

- the need for customization because of differences in investor situations,
- a huge increase in complexity caused by taxation rules and interlinked portfolios, and
- broader fiduciary responsibilities for private clients, who may be poorly informed and who may need more all-inclusive help than institutional clients.

Good practice in working with private clients requires an ethical standard that

- goes beyond choosing suitable securities to encompass specific attention to after-tax returns and absolute versus relative risk and
- proactively avoids misrepresentation by including investor education in the job—for example, by pointing out how difficult it is to project past performance rather than by merely providing an accurate performance record.

These requirements make private investors more expensive to service than institutional clients and encourage the development of cost-effective ways to meet private clients' needs.

Theory and Practice in Private Investing

Financial theory oversimplifies the problems of private investors. It provides a starting point, but to be useful, it must be adapted carefully and extensively. The main ideas and adaptations are as follows:

- Most ideas and data available to the public are already well priced, which makes picking stocks, timing markets, and picking good managers problematic for most investors. This situation increases the relative importance of risk and tax management. Investors face a trade-off between risk and return, but specifying it for private investors through utility theory, which is idealized and relates to a single period, is often impractical.
- Markowitz mean–variance optimization is the best tool we have for balancing risk and return efficiently, but its correct implementation requires careful study.

- Option valuation theory teaches us that the choice of when to realize a taxable gain or loss is valuable and is enhanced by dispersion in returns and ratios of market value to cost basis.
- Stochastic growth theory helps us understand how to correctly balance return and risk to achieve long-term goals without triggering shortfalls along the way.

Life-Cycle Investing

Combining stochastic growth theory with the notion of avoiding interim shortfalls leads us to a framework for

- managing discretionary wealth as the key to avoiding shortfalls and achieving long-term financial goals and
- expanding the investor's balance sheet to include implied liabilities, such as capitalized retirement, lifestyle maintenance, and taxes for unrealized capital gains, and to include implied assets, such as capitalized employment-related savings and unvested benefits.

The resulting framework for financial planning, which should be contingent on both age and financial outcomes, guides life-cycle investing, which involves

- summarizing current risk attitudes in the ratio of assets to discretionary wealth,
- subjecting plans to a disciplined review and revision as discretionary wealth and investment environment circumstances change, and
- clarifying the need to address flexibility, end-of-life risk reduction, and plans for excess wealth disposition.

Lifestyle, Wealth Transfer, and Asset Classes

The key points to check in evaluating the investment needs of the HNW investor are as follows:

- Ascertain the major components of expenditure liability and categorize them from necessity to highly discretionary.
- Ascertain how much in the way of expenditures is required and, of that amount, how much is consumption and how much is non-consumption spending.
- Ascertain the investment horizon, not of the investor alone but also of the others who may rely on or succeed in the ownership of the investment assets (e.g., family members, charities).
- Consider the entire family wealth picture in terms of the (current and long-term) intentions of the investor and the opportunity to locate assets in the most optimal way among family members.
- Consider charitable intentions carefully in terms of the high value for tax deferral.
- Carefully consider the interplay between taxation and inflation as they effect net investment returns relating to maintaining long-term purchasing power.
- Finally, when making allocations among asset classes, take into account fees and costs, taxes, inflation, and consumption—not simply optimization of gross returns.

Overview of Federal Taxation of Investments

The major points of this section can be summarized by considering the key questions related to taxes that the investor or investment advisor should ask when analyzing an investment.

First, what is the *character* of the components of expected return:

- ordinary income;
- dividends;
- long-term capital gain;
- short-term capital gain;
- asset class–specific tax rates—collectibles, real estate, recaptured depreciation, oil and gas depletion allowances, and so on;
- federal tax exemption;
- state/local tax exemption;
- foreign income subject to withholding?

Second, given the character of the income, the AMT, and the limitation on deductions, what will be the effective marginal tax rate for the nth dollar of return?

Third, what deductions, expenses, or offsets are available to reduce the tax on the investment return? Does this investment make the most efficient use of those potential benefits? Will the taxpayer be subject to the AMT, and if so, how will being subject to the AMT affect the net treatment of taxable income?

Fourth, especially for periods of fewer than 12 months, what is the anticipated holding period of the investment?

Fifth, how will potential future changes in tax rates affect the after-tax risk and return attractiveness of the investment?

Finally, how will the long-term attractiveness of the investment be affected by the application of the estate tax?

Techniques for Improving After-Tax Investment Performance

Investment tax strategies fall into a few broad categories:

- Convert the character of taxable return from high-tax ordinary income or short-term capital gains into low-tax long-term capital gains.
- Delay the recognition of gain or income for long periods of time.
- Hold off the recognition of gain or income until death so that only the estate tax, if any, applies.
- Create voluntary losses to offset current gains.
- Use government-sanctioned tax-sheltering vehicles (e.g., retirement accounts or insurance wrappers) to defer or eliminate taxation of investment returns.

Even when these various strategies have superficial appeal, however, the investor should be cautious to analyze the costs involved and should carefully weigh cost against the possible savings. Tax savings that may be only temporary may not be worth the up-front costs.

Although general rules of thumb are a good starting point (for example, municipal bonds are suitable for taxable investors), a complete understanding must include a detailed analysis of the investor's specific tax circumstances—now and *in the future*. This analysis must take into account *income and deductions from all sources* and an estimate of the *final disposition* of the investment assets. Investment advisors should also recognize that the tax rates and rules are constantly changing, so savings that depend on no changes in the status quo of the current tax rules may evaporate unpredictably in the future. Stein (2004a) provides an analysis of the impact of future tax increases.

Institutional Money Management and the High-Net-Worth Investor

HNW investors, with needs that are both complex and far more heterogeneous than typical institutions, represent a great challenge to the investment professional. In an institutional investment process, the vast majority of intellectual effort is dedicated to forming advantageous expectations about the future return distributions of financial assets. Relatively little effort is expended on adapting the investment process to the needs and preferences of specific investors. Effective investment management for the HNW individual requires that the area of relative emphasis be reversed, giving precedence to the intelligent adaptation of the investment process to the needs of the individual.

Minimization of taxes must be considered a crucial element of performance along with pre-tax return and risk. What matters is not how much return investors make but how much they get to keep.

Absolute returns may be of equal or greater importance than market-relative returns for the HNW investor.

Convincing clients as to what is really in their best interests (and thereby attracting and retaining clients) may not be easy. Therefore, as a business, investment management for HNW investors has particular challenges.

Portfolio Management as a Manufacturing Process

"Portfolio manufacturing" is a concept dealing with how an investment firm should organize its activities so as to provide high-quality services appropriate to the heterogeneous needs of HNW investors in a cost-effective fashion. Many, although not all, of the differences among HNW investors revolve around taxes. Tax-aware investing considers

- balancing the need to sell appreciated securities for investment reasons (diversification, security selection) against the need to not sell them for tax reasons;
- balancing the need to sell at a loss for tax reasons against the need to not sell them for investment reasons; and
- harmonizing the purchases and sales within tax periods.

Individual Retirement Plans and Location

Retirement accounts, although nearly universally recommended by investment advisors, are not for everyone—especially very wealthy individuals. Whenever IRPs are considered, attention needs to be given to

- potential changes in future tax rates,
- trade-offs between low current tax rates and higher deferred withdrawal tax rates,
- the potential need for cash before withdrawals can be made without penalties,
- the likelihood of gain recognition even for low-tax-rate investments, and
- the relationship between the retirement account and the estate plan.

In summary, asset allocation and asset location for individual investors involve a holistic consideration of which assets are to be held inside and outside the retirement account in light of the likely tax consequences. The approach involves considering the timing of the person's needs for cash, the benefits of tax deferral, relative tax rates, and issues of rebalancing.

On Concentrated Risk

The question of how to deal with concentrated positions carrying large unrealized capital gains is often troublesome because it requires both acumen in tax reduction and an objective approach to relinquishing assets to which the investor may be emotionally attached. For moderate risks and amounts, a targeted outright sale may be optimal. Otherwise, three broad practical approaches are possible:

- Borrowing can raise funds for diversification and dealing with the consequent risk management through some combination of short sales, option collars, or prepaid variable forwards; care must be taken that unanticipated tax or fee complications not spoil the long-term benefit.
- In complementary funds, the concentrated position is left in place but other parts of the balance sheet are revised to lower risks for the total portfolio.
- Pooling with other investors or donors can be effected through exchange funds or charitable remainder trusts.

Assessment and Benchmarking for Private Wealth

Approaches to assessing the performance measurement and benchmarking needs of wealthy individuals need to be comprehensive and need to recognize the highly individualized nature of each investor's circumstances:

- Investment returns should be reported net of investment expenses, taxes (realized and unrealized), and inflation.
- Taxes should be calculated on the basis of the actual circumstances in the tax year of the report and should take into account ex-portfolio tax factors.
- Measures of risk need to be adjusted for the actual tax circumstances of the investor and should be reported in the context of the specific shortfall constraints.
- To properly assess a portfolio's purchasing power, measures of wealth accumulation have to take into account inflation and consumption.
- Measures of the long-term adequacy of a plan have to take into account not only the investor's life horizon but also the horizons of relevant others.
- For accurately assessing whether the investor's goals are likely to be met by the plan, the advisor must use an integrated approach that considers *all* the entities holding the investor's monies.

APPENDIX 10A: MORE ON LOCATION

What if the assumptions behind the studies cited in the section on Individual Retirement Plans and Location should change? Can investment advisors derive good answers on asset location for themselves? Many readers who are only moderately quantitatively oriented will be able to do so. All one needs is a passing familiarity with matrix operations and an Excel spreadsheet program.[56]

Decisions on what kind of, and how much, investment assets to put in tax-advantaged vehicles can be made in many ways. At one extreme, decisions can be based entirely on rules of thumb. At the other, one might try to build tax implications, portfolio turnover, actuarial life, and return distributions into a large period-by-period simulation to optimize the total portfolio according to various measures of investor preference.

Mean–variance optimization is an intermediate approach. In this appendix, we show how location analysis through mean–variance optimization can be made practical for customized treatment of individual clients. The problem can be approximated as Markowitz mean–variance optimization by converting the tax effect of multiperiod tax payments to a nearly mathematically equivalent single-period rate.

Mean–variance optimization is often criticized as being overly sensitive to input estimation errors, but this weakness is a by-product of putting large amounts of assets into the problem without taking steps to minimize the impact of errors in estimation, which otherwise tend to increase as the square of the number of assets represented in a covariance matrix. To avoid dealing with this issue, in this appendix, we limit ourselves to five assets. The happy by-product is the possibility of illustrating a simple do-it-yourself solution in an Excel spreadsheet.

A strong advantage of our self-help approach is that it can be easily adjusted to specific circumstances, such as changed tax rates. It also allows one to jointly optimize asset location across taxable and tax-advantaged buckets, thereby optimizing the overall proportion of equities to bonds. The more typical approach of first deciding on the overall asset *allocation* (e.g., between stocks and bonds) and then deciding where to put them with respect to *location* is suboptimal.

To fit the location problem to the needs of the specific private investor, we precede conventional asset allocation with two additional steps. The first is that, rather than have the advisor ask the investor for a subjective risk preference, we use the discretionary wealth approach described at the end of the section on Theory and Practice in Private Investing and have the advisor ask for estimates of implied assets and liabilities. The *risk-aversion coefficient* for the mean–variance optimization will be half the ratio of assets to the resulting net discretionary wealth. Second, we transform the multiperiod taxes that would have to be paid into an effectively equivalent, "as if," tax rate for a single period.

For this second process, we need to translate the taxes paid on liquidation at posted rates to the equivalent effective single-period tax. To do so, we estimate the tax that, if paid annually, would produce the same final result.[57]

We can estimate an effective tax rate, T^*, such that

$$[1 + r(1 - T^*)]^n = (1 + r)^n(1 - T) + T, \qquad (10A.1)$$

where:

> r = expected compound price return of the asset class
> T = final posted tax rate
> n = number of years until liquidation

When dividends are included, we can use a weighted tax rate, T^{**}, which is derived from T^*, and the dividend tax rate, T_D. To calculate T^{**}, note that

$$(1 - T^{**})\text{Total return} = (1 - T_D)\text{Dividend yield} + (1 - T^*)\text{Price return}. \quad (10A.2)$$

As an example of how effective tax rates vary from the nominal rates, note from Equation A1 that if the expected compound growth rate of a bond portfolio in an individual retirement account (IRA) with interest reinvested is 6 percent but a 35 percent tax will be paid at its liquidation in 15 years, effective tax rate T^* is 26.7 percent. If the expected compound *total return* (because dividends are not taxed in the IRA) of a stock portfolio in an

IRA is 10 percent in the same circumstances, the effective tax rate will be approximately 22.5 percent.

We have simplified the estimation of the effective tax rate by taking out all the uncertainties. With the spreadsheet to be described, however, checking the sensitivity of final answers to variations in estimated effective tax rates is easy.

The example in Table 10A.1 illustrates holding hypothetical stocks and taxable bonds inside and outside an individual retirement account.[58] Given the hypothetical inputs in the shaded boxes in Table 10A.1, the ideal solution in terms of location weights is shown in the "Ideal weights" row below actual or input weights. How is this solution determined?

The example incorporates five asset classes for a mean–variance optimization: stocks in and out of tax-advantaged plans, bonds in and out of tax-advantaged plans, and the remainder of the portfolio. An aggregate balance sheet is used to calculate discretionary wealth and consequently to provide a default aversion to risk. The tax rates are purely hypothetical, illustrative "effective tax rates."[59] An additional constraint is included to prevent the sum of the

TABLE 10A.1   Location Problem Inputs and Ideal Solution

Problem Inputs		To find best location of assets in low-tax buckets: Change inputs in colored [shaded] boxes as desired.			
Financial assets	$462,000				
Implied assets	200,000		Press to optimize weights		
Financial liabilities	240,000		(except for fixed residual)		
Implied liabilities	$300,000				
	High-Tax Stocks	**Low-Tax Stocks**	**High-Tax Bonds**	**Low-Tax Bonds**	**Residual Assets**
Actual weights	10.0%	5.0%	15.0%	10.0%	60.0%
Ideal weights	21.3	0.0	0.0	18.7	60.0
Difference	11.3%	−5.0%	−15.0%	8.7%	0.0%
Mean pretax return	12.0%	12.0%	6.0%	6.0%	8.0%
Std. dev. pretax return	20.0%	20.0%	6.0%	6.0%	12.0%
Tax rate	15.00%	22.00%	35.00%	15.00%	20.00%
Return correlations					
High-tax stocks	1.00	1.00	−0.10	−0.10	0.50
Low-tax stocks	1.00	1.00	−0.10	−0.10	0.50
High-tax bonds	−0.10	−0.10	1.00	1.00	0.40
Low-tax bonds	−0.10	−0.10	1.00	1.00	0.40
Residual	0.50	0.50	0.40	0.40	1.00
Maximum weight	100.00%	20.00%	100.00%	20.00%	60.00%
Minimum weight	0.00	0.00%	0.00%	0.00%	60.00%
Maximum low-tax weight	20.00%				

TABLE 10A.2　Location Problem: Interim Calculations

Discretionary wealth fraction	**18.43%**			Low-tax total weight	**19.00%**
Appropriate risk aversion	**2.71**			Leverage	**5.43**
				Total weights	**100.00%**
After-tax rate	85.0%	78.0%	65.0%	85.0%	80.0%
After-tax mean	10.20	9.36	3.90	5.10	6.40
Mean contributions	2.1683%	0.0%	0.0%	0.9559%	3.8400%
After-tax risk	0.17	0.156	0.039	0.051	0.096
After-tax risk matrix	0.17	0.0	0.0	0.0	0.0
	0.0	0.156	0.0	0.0	0.0
	0.0	0.0	0.039	0.0	0.0
	0.0	0.0	0.0	0.051	0.0
	0.0	0.0	0.0	0.0	0.096
Covariance Matrix	0.0289	0.0265	−0.0007	−0.0009	0.0082
	0.0265	0.0243	−0.0006	−0.0008	0.0075
	−0.0007	−0.0006	0.0015	0.0020	0.0015
	−0.0009	−0.0008	0.0020	0.0026	0.0020
	0.0082	0.0075	0.0015	0.0020	0.0092

"low-tax" categories from exceeding the tax-advantaged plan capacity. Residual assets are, in this example, constrained to their initial values.

The ideal weights are estimated by maximizing the risk-adjusted after-tax portfolio return: the expected portfolio after-tax return less the product of risk aversion and portfolio after-tax return variance. The intermediate calculations are worked out in Table 10A.2. To follow the logic, the reader needs to know what is meant by "matrix multiplication" and "matrix transposition." Textbooks and online sites are sources of explanations, and these functions are implemented as built-in operators in Excel.

The contributions to portfolio mean return are the weighted after-tax mean returns (i.e., the products of the after-tax means and the weights for each asset).

Calculation of the after-tax covariance matrix begins with putting the after-tax standard deviations of return into a diagonal after-tax risk matrix. This square matrix has the standard deviations of return on the diagonal and zeros elsewhere. Matrix-multiply this diagonal after-tax risk matrix, the correlation matrix, and this diagonal after-tax risk matrix again to calculate the covariance matrix.

The weights, means, and covariance matrix, together with a default risk-aversion trade-off, are the ingredients of mean–variance optimization. Following the discretionary wealth approach, one uses half the leverage (the ratio of assets to discretionary wealth) as the risk-aversion parameter.

Finally, the optimized result and some interesting portfolio statistics are calculated in Table 10A.3.

The portfolio mean return is the sum of its individual contributions. The portfolio variance is more complicated. It is the sum of the entries in a weighted covariance matrix, which

TABLE 10A.3   Location Problem: Results

Portfolio mean return	0.0696	Mean Return	6.96%
Portfolio variance	0.0072	Portfolio Risk	8.47%
Markowitz objective	0.0502		
Expected growth rate of discretionary wealth			**27.24%**

is the matrix product of the weight vector, covariance matrix, and transposed weight vector. The Markowitz objective that was maximized is defined as the portfolio's mean return minus the product of the risk aversion and the portfolio variance.

Another concept to become familiar with is the *expected growth rate of discretionary wealth*; it is needed in Appendix 10B for solving the problem of deciding what to do with concentrated risk positions. The expected growth rate is approximated as the mean return on discretionary wealth minus half the variance of the return on discretionary wealth. Mean return on discretionary wealth is the mean return on assets times the leverage. Variance of the return on discretionary wealth is the portfolio variance times the squared leverage.

The ideal weights for each of the stock and bond asset classes in this example are initialized by using the actual weights; then, they are automatically varied by using Excel's Solver, which is set in motion by activating the button as indicated ("Press . . .") in Table 10A.1 until the resulting Markowitz objective can no longer be improved. In this case, because leverage is fixed, the maximum Markowitz objective also maximizes the expected growth rate of discretionary wealth.

In the example shown in the exhibits, all stocks are ideally put into the so-called high-tax location and all bonds are put into the low-tax location, just as one would expect, so the result is intuitive.

APPENDIX 10B: MORE ON CONCENTRATED RISK

Often an advisor wants to know in what circumstances selling part or all of a concentrated risk position would be worthwhile even if the investor would have to pay taxes on the results. This choice should be the first option checked before going to the expense of hiring assistance in pursuing the more complex alternatives that avoid outright sales discussed in the section On Concentrated Risk.

At one extreme in assessing outright sales, the advisor may rely on rules of thumb. At the other, the advisor might undertake period-by-period Monte Carlo simulations and stochastic dynamic programming models to find an answer. Mean–variance optimization offers a middle ground—but one that should be used with some care.

The description of the do-it-yourself spreadsheet solution we offer here depends on some terms defined in more detail in Appendix 10A, which addressed the simple problem of ongoing location of securities in taxable versus tax-advantaged buckets. We remind the reader that Appendix 10A and Appendix 10B require some familiarity with matrix operations, which will aid in following the logic. Access to an Excel spreadsheet incorporating the "Solver" add-in will be helpful in replicating the results.[60]

A Broad Objective Function

When significant changes in the investor's total discretionary wealth are involved, as when a large tax is paid, mean–variance optimization becomes part of a larger perspective that allows for changes in discretionary wealth affecting leverage and, consequently, appropriate risk aversion. It is not enough to simply maximize after-tax $E - LV/2$ (where L is leverage, E is expected single-period return, and V is variance). Such maximization assumes that leverage is constant, as in Markowitz mean–variance optimization. But in this case, because paying a large tax may change leverage materially, the advisor needs to consider the larger issue of maximizing after-tax $LE - L^2V/2$, which is approximately the expected growth rate in discretionary wealth.

In implementing this approach, the advisor can amortize the initial loss in discretionary wealth, because of the acceleration of the tax payment and all the transaction costs, as an adjustment to the expected discretionary wealth growth rate. The taxes and transaction costs must, like the security returns, be scaled up by leverage to reflect their impact on discretionary wealth.

This larger problem can be imagined in terms of Markowitz efficient frontiers only with difficulty because each change in leverage induces a change in the efficient frontier. That is, the variety of possible effects on discretionary wealth produces not one efficient frontier but a family of efficient frontiers, each with its own best tangent based on a different risk-aversion parameter. Learning to think in terms of effects on expected growth in discretionary wealth over a specified time horizon makes the problem far more tractable than imagining operations on a family of efficient frontiers.

Implementing the Spreadsheet

Table 10B.1 depicts a Microsoft Excel spreadsheet supported by the "Solver" add-in (here, selected by clicking a button). Table 10B.1 focuses on the inputs used to augment the spreadsheet used for location analysis in Table 10A.1. Appendix 10A describes how the inputs are used to form the expected portfolio return and the covariance matrix. Here, we focus on the new elements in the asset allocation problem.

TABLE 10B.1   Concentration Problem: Inputs and Solution

Basic Problem Inputs			Expanded Problem Inputs	
Concentrated stock	$1,000,000		Tax liability discount rate	6.00%
Residual assets	$1,000,000		Concentrated stock cost basis	$125,000
			Unrealized gain %	87.50%
Present value of tax liability	$ 103,962	Press to find best current plan for concentrated stock	Current gains tax	15.00
Other liabilities	1,500,000		Future gains tax	15.00%
Initial discretionary wealth	$ 396,038		Years to liquidation	4
Initial discretionary wealth %	19.80%		Future tax liability	$131,250

TABLE 10B.1   Concentration Problem: Inputs and Solution (Continued)

	Concentrated Stock	Replacement Stocks	Replacement Bonds	Residual Assets
Initial weights	50.0%	0.0%	0.0%	50.0%
Ideal weights	1.4	43.5	5.1	50.0
Difference	−48.6	43.5	5.1	0.0
Trading cost	0.80%	0.20%	0.10%	0.25%
Mean pretax return	15.0%	10.0%	5.0%	8.0%
Std. dev. pretax return	40.0%	15.0%	6.0%	12.0%
Effective tax rate	14.0%	14.0%	35.0%	25.0%
Return correlations				
Concentrated stock	1.00	0.60	0.00	0.50
Replacement stocks	0.60	1.00	0.00	0.60
Replacement bonds	0.00	0.00	1.00	0.40
Residual assets	0.50	0.60	0.40	1.00
Maximum weight	50.00%	50.00%	50.00%	50.00%
Minimum weight	0.00%	0.00%	0.00%	50.00%

The advisor needs only four assets—the concentrated stock, any replacement stocks, any replacement bonds (often overlooked as a possibility), and the residual portfolio. The replacement securities should begin with no weight or allocation.

Shaded cells represent the inputs the user can vary. In this case, the portfolio is assumed to be 50 percent invested in the concentrated position. The suggested new ideal allocation is shown (after the button "Press . . . " is clicked) in the row labeled "Ideal weights." In this case, the majority of the concentrated position is to be sold and, because the initial leverage on discretionary wealth is rather high, some of the proceeds are used to buy bonds. How was this solution determined?

The inputs to the expanded problem are given in the upper right of Table 10B.1. They allow calculation of the net present value of the product of the current unrealized gain and a future tax rate (which could be zero), a capital gains rate, or a higher estate tax. Table 10B.1 also has a place to enter the current capital gains tax, which might be at a different long-term capital gains rate or even at a higher short-term gains rate.

A new row for entering trading costs has been added. Note that, as in Appendix 10A, the effective tax rates to be compounded before the tax is paid may be lower than the posted rate. Finally, if the investor wants to constrain the result so that not all the position can be sold, that information is entered as the minimum weight for the concentrated stock asset.

Table 10B.2 shows interim calculations. The top half shows calculation of the modifications that must be made to discretionary wealth in light of the acceleration of tax payments and the trading costs consequent to changes in the weights. This information is used both in cost amortization and in determining a new appropriate aversion to risk. The bottom half determines expected mean and variance of return of the portfolio after reallocation, in the same way as in the Table 10A.2.

TABLE 10B.2   Concentration Problem: Intermediate Calculations

Concentrated stock	$ 27,376		Total weights	100.0%	
Total assets	$1,862,411				
Present value of tax			Discretionary		
liability	$ 2,650		wealth %	19.32%	
Other liabilities	1,500,000		Leverage	5.18	
Discretionary wealth	$ 359,761				
After-tax rate	86.0%	86.0%	65.0%	75.0%	
After-tax mean	12.90	8.60	3.25	6.00	
Mean contributions	0.18%	3.74%	0.17%	3.00%	
After-tax risk	34.40%	12.90%	3.90%	9.00%	
After-tax risk matrix	0.3440	0.0000	0.0000	0.0000	
	0.0000	0.1290	0.0000	0.0000	
	0.0000	0.0000	0.0390	0.0000	
	0.0000	0.0000	0.0000	0.0900	
Covariance matrix	0.118336	0.0266256	0.0	0.015480	
	0.0266256	0.016641	0.0	0.006966	
	0.0	0.0	0.001521	0.001404	
	0.01548	0.006966	0.001404	0.008100	

TABLE 10B.3   Concentration Problem: Results

Portfolio mean return	0.0709	**Portfolio mean return**	**7.09%**
Portfolio variance	0.0088	**Portfolio risk**	**9.40%**
Discretionary wealth mean	0.3668		
Discretionary wealth variance	0.2368		
Expected subsequent growth rate of discretionary wealth			**24.84%**
Current % loss of discretionary wealth			**9.16%**
Growth adjustment for initial loss			**−2.40%**
Expected growth rate of discretionary wealth			**22.44%**

Table 10B.3 shows the criterion to be maximized—namely, the total expected growth rate of discretionary wealth over the time horizon. It comes from, first, calculating the expected rate of growth of the discretionary wealth remaining after payment of taxes and transaction costs and, then, adjusting that growth rate for the known initial loss of discretionary wealth amortized over the time horizon. The adjustment is calculated as the natural log of the fraction of discretionary wealth remaining divided by the time horizon. The total asset portfolio's mean return and risk (as standard deviation) are also displayed.

Still More Complicated Situations

How would one use a spreadsheet that augments Markowitz mean–variance optimization in complicated situations? Here are two suggestions designed to produce pragmatic, effective results.

Question: What do I do if the concentrated wealth position is composed of several tax lots with different ratios of cost basis to current value?

Answer: To avoid mathematical complications, focus on the tax lot with the highest cost basis first and group the other tax lots with the residual assets; then, recalculate the first tax lot's mean, variance, and correlations. If that tax lot should be sold in its entirety, repeat the process with the next tax lots in descending order of cost basis.

Question: What do I do if future tax rates are uncertain, as is the case with the future U.S. estate tax?

Answer: Solve separately for several different scenarios and use your subjective probability of each scenario to construct a weighted-average allocation.

NOTES

1. The list of references in this chapter contains many more works that provide details on various specific topics.
2. Annuities and life insurance are central to the financial planning of many private investors not at the upper end of the wealth spectrum. In this chapter, however, we concentrate on those investment needs of individual investors that are not addressed through annuities or other insurance products.
3. Standards are from the CFA Institute Standards of Professional Conduct (www.cfainstitute. org).
4. This approach is developed further in the section on Life-Cycle Investing.
5. A CPPI strategy basically buys shares as they rise and sells shares as they fall based on a floor the investor sets below which the portfolio is not allowed to fall. The floor increases in value at the rate of return on cash. The difference between the assets and floor can be thought of as a cushion, so the CPPI decision rule is simply to keep the exposure to shares a constant multiple of the cushion. Usually, but not always, there is a constraint that the equity allocation not exceed 100 percent.
6. See the section on Lifestyle, Wealth Transfer, and Asset Classes for discussion of gradations in discretionary wealth.
7. We do not discuss in this chapter the present value of life insurance, but a market is developing for life insurance policies, from which the prices give some idea of the policies' present monetary value. That measure may not do justice, however, to the complementarity of life insurance to a family's employment assets, where life insurance functions in a way not dissimilar to a put option on continued employment consequences.
8. "Tax Stats at a Glance: Summary of Collections before Refunds by Type of Return, FY 2003." For these statistics and information on all federal taxes in this section, see www.irs.gov.
9. This has become true only recently in the United States; until 2003 when Congress lowered the tax on dividends to 15 percent, dividends were extremely tax inefficient.
10. As of fall 2005, the estate tax applies only to estates of more than $1,500,000, and this threshold is expected to rise.

11. For the mathematics, see Horvitz and Wilcox.

12. These results would be very different, and more attractive, if the analysis used today's tax rates, which are some of the lowest seen in the post–World War II era.

13. In one of the curiosities of the tax code, interest is a deductible expense for corporations but dividends are not. From a total-value point of view, combining the tax paid by the corporation with the tax paid by the investor, interest payments may actually be better if the equity can be characterized as debt. But rules concerning thinly capitalized corporations prohibit extreme abuses. Dividend-paying corporations with either tax-exempt or taxable shareholders have a higher cost of capital than otherwise identical interest-paying corporations and should be worth less, even to taxable investors.

14. A particular problem with the intermediary's management fee is that it is typically paid on total committed capital but the investor's money is deployed slowly and is outstanding for only a portion of the time the fees are paid. Consequently, the management fee as a percentage of average invested capital can be substantially higher than the stated fee rate.

15. A wrapper is a contract an insurance company provides in which the insurer maintains the principal and accumulated interest on an underlying portfolio at book value and guarantees the rate to be credited to current fund investors until the next rate reset. The costs include brokerage fees and commissions, various taxes, high asset management fees, policy fees, and an embedded actuarial-derived profit for the insurance company. One of the authors (Horvitz), in reviewing policies from five large insurance companies, found that only about half of the available tax savings from the most cost-effective (high-dollar, negotiated) insurance products was actually passed on to the policyholder, net of all costs.

16. Section 1256 contracts are regulated futures contracts, foreign currency contracts, nonequity (listed) options, dealer equity options, and dealer securities futures contracts. Straddles have special rules. The IRC can be found at www.fourmilab.ch/ustax/ustax.html.

17. For a more complete mathematical explanation, see Horvitz and Wilcox (2003).

18. The limitation on itemized deductions is scheduled to be rapidly phased out beginning in 2006, but the phase-out itself is currently subject to automatic repeal under a sunset provision in 2011. Normal itemized deductions include state and local taxes or, alternatively, sales tax; mortgage and interest (subject to various other limits); charitable contributions (subject to a maximum of {50 percent} of adjusted gross income, AGI); medical expenses (in excess of {7.5 percent} of AGI); casualty and theft losses in excess of {10 percent} of AGI; job and miscellaneous expenses, usually in excess of {2 percent} of AGI. AGI is defined by IRC Section 62 and generally consists of all taxable income—wages, interest, capital gains, retirement account distributions, and so on—subject to certain adjustments but before deductions and personal exemptions.

19. Currently, subject to the phase-out, the limit is the lesser of {3 percent} of income above the threshold or {80 percent} of itemized deductions.

20. We are indebted to Richard Dahab for this important insight.

21. For example, collectibles are taxed at {28 percent}. If the taxpayer has a net loss from collectibles carried forward to the next year and then has a long-term capital gain at the {15 percent} rate, the collectible loss carryforward must be used to offset long-term capital gains, thus "wasting" part of the tax value of the prior-year loss. Long-term capital losses, however, which otherwise are worth only {15 percent}, can be used to offset gains from collectibles at the {28 percent} rate.

22. When evaluating bonds and dividend payments from corporations, the investor should consider that, although bond interest is taxable to the investor, it is deductible to the corporation whereas dividends are paid from the corporation's after-tax earnings. When corporate and individual tax rates are similar, the net effect in terms of combined taxation is about a wash for interest payments but not for dividends. So, interest becomes the more tax efficient, even for taxable investors, when substituted for what would otherwise be a dividend-paying equity.

23. The rules for amortizing *discounts* and *premiums* for municipal bonds are different from the rules for taxable bonds.

24. The long-term capital gains rate for low-income taxpayers is only {5 percent}.

25. Some private equity funds have been attempting to recharacterize their management fees so as to get long-term capital gains treatment. Long-term versus short-term treatment makes no difference to the tax-exempt limited partner, of course, but short-term treatment significantly raises the cost to the taxable limited partner. Whether this technique will survive IRS challenges remains to be seen.

26. Under current law, the estate tax is to be repealed entirely in 2010 but only to be revived in 2011 at $1,000,000, the amount in the previous law. This nonsensical approach is almost certain to be replaced with some new estate tax law before it happens.

27. IRC Section 1014 is to be replaced by IRC Section 1022 after 2009, in the absence of further legislative changes, which will materially change the ways the step-up and carry-over tax basis are treated.

28. For example, Florida has no income tax but does have an "intangible" tax levied against the fair market value of publicly traded securities. Massachusetts has an income tax, which historically has differentiated interest and dividends from capital gains. In Massachusetts, rates for interest dividends and earned income have become the same as for long-term capital gains but short-term capital gains and profits from collectibles are taxed at more than double those rates {12 percent versus 5.3 percent}.

29. As of this writing, one can deduct either state income taxes or state sales taxes but not both.

30. Recall that tax rates and other statutory values in the tax code are shown in braces, { }.

31. The mathematics of tax deferral is fully described by Horvitz and Wilcox.

32. Tax-deferred accounts are discussed also in the Overview of Federal Taxation of Investments.

33. See the rules for passive foreign income corporations at www.irs.org.

34. Recall that when a bond is purchased in the secondary market, the difference between the purchase price and its stated redemption price at maturity is the market discount; the accreted (or accumulated) market discount is treated as ordinary interest income in the year the bond is sold, redeemed, or transferred. For tax-exempt bonds, the effective yield may be a blend of taxable and tax-exempt income and, therefore, may be less after tax than the same effective yield from a tax-exempt bond purchased at par.

35. See also the Overview of Federal Taxation of Investments.

36. Because the wash sale rules do not apply here, an investor can immediately repurchase the same security.

37. Wall Street firms are generally reluctant to create structured products for longer than five years.

38. In an unpublished analysis, Horvitz found that large privately negotiated variable life policies were generally not worthwhile without a lengthy holding period. The break-even point was at the 8-year to 12-year mark—similar to the point at which tax deferral

becomes material. Roughly half of the tax benefits (under 2005 and higher tax rates) were retained by the insurance companies in the form of fees and costs, and the other half accrued to the benefit of the policyholder.

39. See also Part II.

40. Keep in mind that the income used to make the investment in the first place is itself (in most cases) after-tax money.

41. Effective 1 January 2006, AIMR-PPS standards will converge with GIPS standards and the AIMR-PPS standards will be dissolved.

42. CFA Institute was formerly the Association for Investment Management and Research.

43. See www.cfainstitute.org/cfacentre/ips/pdf/Taxation_Provisions.pdf.

44. See also the example in Appendix 10B.

45. In aggregate, the average returns of other investors can be presumed to approximate the return on broad market indices because for someone to be above average in return, someone else must be below average in return.

46. The agency problem arises because the more the investor trades, the more money the broker makes.

47. See Part II for wash sale rules.

48. Numerous authors have found (e.g., Best and Grauer 1991; Chopra and Ziemba 1993) that the majority of suboptimal portfolio weights arise from errors in expected returns rather than errors in expected variances or correlations.

49. Similar distortions can occur even if the selection universes are mutually exclusive if one manager is much more aggressive than another.

50. A defined-benefit plan fixes the amount of the benefit to be paid to the beneficiary, so the plan sponsor must provide enough in contributions that, with the investment returns, enough money will be available to pay the benefits. The investment risk is borne by the plan sponsor.

51. Starting in 2008, the limit will be $5,000 plus an inflation adjustment.

52. Recall that tax rates and other statutory values in the tax code are shown in braces, { }.

53. For more information, see www.irs.gov.

54. Note that in this example, unrealized gains are treated as if liquidated because, as shown in Part II, the government "owns" this profit's interest. Although the government's holding is contingent, only the timing of the recognition is up to the taxpayer.

55. Standard volatility measures should be calculated on the basis of after-tax returns.

56. A working copy of the example used here may be available for download by e-mailing jarrod.wilcox@comcast.net.

57. Exactly the same consideration applies to capital gains taxes in fully taxed locations because the effective tax rate may be reduced through compounding long-term holdings; it may even be reduced to zero through a charitable contribution or a tax-exempt estate.

58. The example uses Microsoft Excel with the "Solver" add-in. It also incorporates a macro overlay that allows the optimization to be run by a single click, but that overlay is an unnecessary refinement.

59. The 22 percent tax rate for "low-tax" stocks is not an error; it is intended to illustrate the possibility that the effective tax rate on an IRA can be quite high because it is based on ordinary income tax rates. In this example, it makes the answer for ideal weights easy to guess.

60. A working copy of the example used here may be available for download by e-mailing jarrod.wilcox@comcast.net.

REFERENCES

Ait-Sahalia, Yasine, Jonathan A. Parker, and Motohiro Yogo. 2004. "Luxury Goods and the Equity Premium." *Journal of Finance*, vol. 59, no. 6 (December):2959–3004.

Apelfeld, Roberto, Gordon B. Fowler, Jr., and James P. Gordon, Jr. 1996. "Tax-Aware Equity Investing." *Journal of Portfolio Management*, vol. 22, no. 2 (Winter):18–28.

Apelfeld, Roberto, Michael Granito, and Akis Psarris. 1996. "Active Management of Taxable Assets: A Dynamic Analysis of Manager Alpha." *Journal of Financial Engineering*, vol. 5, no. 2 (June):117–146.

Arnott, Robert D., Andrew L. Berkin, and Jia Ye. 2001. "Loss Harvesting: What's It Worth to the Taxable Investor?" *Journal of Wealth Management*, vol. 3, no. 4 (Spring):10–18.

Bernoulli, Daniel. 1738. "Specimen Theorae Novae de Mensura Sortis (Exposition of a New Theory on the Measurement of Risk)." Translated from the Latin by Louise Sommer in *Econometrica*, vol. 22, no. 1 (January 1954):23–36.

Best, Michael J., and Robert R. Grauer. 1991. "On the Sensitivity of Mean–Variance-Efficient Portfolios to Changes in Asset Means: Some Analytical and Computational Results." *Review of Financial Studies*, vol. 4, no. 2:315–342.

Bolster, Paul J., Vahan Janjigian, and Emery A. Trahan. 1995. "Determining Investor Suitability Using the Analytic Hierarchy Process." *Financial Analysts Journal*, vol. 51, no. 4 (July/August):63–75.

Broadie, Mark. 1993. "Computing Efficient Frontiers Using Estimated Parameters." *Annals of Operations Research*, vol. 45, nos. 1–4 (December):21–58.

Brunel, Jean. 2002. *Integrated Wealth Management: The New Direction for Portfolio Managers*. London: Euromoney Books.

Chopra, Vijay K. 1993. "Near-Optimal Portfolios and Sensitivity to Input Variations." *Journal of Investing*, vol. 2, no. 3:51–59.

Chopra, Vijay K., and William T. Ziemba. 1993. "The Effect of Errors in Means, Variances, and Covariances on Optimal Portfolio Choice." *Journal of Portfolio Management*, vol. 19, no. 2 (Winter):6–11.

Chow, George. 1995. "Portfolio Selection Based on Return, Risk, and Relative Performance." *Financial Analysts Journal*, vol. 51, no. 2 (March/April):54–60.

Constantinides, George M. 1983. "Capital Market Equilibrium with Personal Tax." *Econometrica*, vol. 51, no. 3 (May):611–636.

Cremers, Jan-Hein, Mark Kritzman, and Séstien Page. 2003. "Portfolio Formation with Higher Moments and Plausible Utility." Revere Street Working Paper Series 272-12 (November).

Dammon, Robert M. 1988. "A Security Market and Capital Structure Equilibrium under Uncertainty with Progressive Personal Taxes." *Research in Finance*, vol. 7:53–74.

Dammon, Robert M., Chester S. Spatt, and Harold H. Zhang. 2004. "Optimal Asset Location and Allocation with Taxable and Tax-Deferred Investing." *Journal of Finance*, vol. 59, no. 3 (June):999–1038.

Detzler, Miranda Lam, and Hakan Saraoglu. 2002. "A Sensible Mutual Fund Selection Model." *Financial Analysts Journal*, vol. 58, no. 3 (May/June):60–73.

diBartolomeo, Dan. 1999. "A Radical Proposal for the Operation of Multi-Manager Investment Funds." Northfield Working Paper: www.northinfo.com/documents/61.pdf.

Dickson, Joel M., and John B. Shoven. 1993. "Ranking Mutual Funds on an After-Tax Basis." Working Paper 4393, National Bureau of Economic Research.

Dickson, Joel M., John B. Shoven, and Clemens Sialm. 2000. "Tax Externalities of Equity Mutual Funds."*National Tax Journal*, vol. 53, no. 3, part 2 (September): 607–628.

Fama, Eugene F. 1965. "The Behavior of Stock Market Prices."*Journal of Business*, vol. 38, (January):34–105.

Garland, James P. 1997. "The Advantage of Tax-Managed Index Funds."*Journal of Investing*, vol. 6, no. 1 (Spring):13–20.

Gordon, Robert N., and Jan M. Rosen. 2001. *Wall Street Secrets for Tax-Efficient Investing*. Princeton, NJ: Bloomberg Press.

Gulko, Les. 1998. "An After-Tax Equity Benchmark." General Re Working Paper.

Horan, Stephen M. 2005. *Tax-Advantaged Savings Accounts and Tax-Efficient Wealth Accumulation*. Charlottesville, VA: Research Foundation of CFA Institute.

Horvitz, Jeffrey E. 2002. "The Implications of Rebalancing the Investment Portfolio for the Taxable Investor." *Journal of Wealth Management* (Fall):49–53.

Horvitz, Jeffrey E., and Jarrod W. Wilcox. 2003. "Know When to Hold 'Em and When to Fold 'Em: The Value of Effective Taxable Investment Management." *Journal of Wealth Management*, vol. 6, no. 2 (Fall):35–59.

Ibbotson Associates. 2005. "Stocks, Bonds, after Taxes and Inflation 1925–2004." Ibbotson Associates (1 March).

Jeffrey, Robert H., and Robert D. Arnott. 1993. "Is Your Alpha Big Enough to Cover Its Taxes?" *Journal of Portfolio Management*, vol. 19, no. 3 (Spring):15–25.

Ledoit, Olivier. 1999. "Improved Estimation of the Covariance Matrix of Stock Returns with an Application to Portfolio Selection." Working Paper 3-99, UCLA Anderson School of Management.

Leibowitz, Martin L. 1992. "Asset Allocation under Shortfall Constraints."*Investing: The Collected Works of Martin L. Leibowitz*. Edited by Frank Fabozzi. Chicago, IL: Probus Publishing.

Levy, Haim, and Harry M. Markowitz. 1979. "Approximating Expected Utility by a Function of Mean and Variance."*American Economic Review*, vol. 69, no. 3: 308–317.

Markowitz, Harry M. 1959. *Portfolio Selection: Efficient Diversification of Investments*. New Haven, CT: Yale University Press.

Markowitz, Harry M., and Erik L. van Dijk. 2003. "Single-Period Mean–Variance Analysis in a Changing World."*Financial Analysts Journal*, vol. 59, no. 2 (March/April):30–44.

Mehra, Yash P. 2001. "The Wealth Effect in Empirical Life-Cycle Aggregate Consumption Equations." Federal Reserve Bank of Richmond, *Economic Quarterly*, vol. 87, no. 2 (Spring):45–68.

Messmore, Tom. 1995. "Variance Drain."*Journal of Portfolio Management*, vol. 21, no. 4 (Summer):104–110.

Michaud, Richard O. 2001. *Efficient Asset Management: A Practical Guide to Stock Portfolio Optimization and Asset Allocation*. Reprint. New York: Oxford University Press.

Montalto, Catherine P. 2001. "Households with High Levels of Net Assets." Report to the Consumer Federation of America and Providian Financial Corp.

Peterson, James D., Paul A. Pietranico, Mark W. Riepe, and Fran Xu. 2002. "Explaining After-Tax Mutual Fund Performance."*Financial Analysts Journal*, vol. 58, no. 1 (January/February):75–86.

Quadrini, Vincenzo, and Jose-Victor Rios-Rull. 1997. "Understanding the U.S. Distribution of Wealth."*Quarterly Review*, Federal Reserve Bank of Minneapolis, vol. 21, no. 2 (Spring):22–36.

Rubinstein, Mark. 1976. "The Strong Case for the Generalized Logarithmic Utility Model as the Premier Model of Financial Markets." *Journal of Finance*, vol. 31, no. 2 (May):551–571.

SEC. 2001. "Final Rule: Disclosure of Mutual Fund After-Tax Returns." U.S. Securities and Exchange Commission. 17 CFR Parts 230, 239, 270, and 274 (April).

Sharpe, William F. 1964. "Capital Asset Prices: A Theory of Market Equilibrium under Conditions of Risk." *Journal of Finance*, vol. 19, no. 3 (September):425–442.

Sialm, Clemens, and John B. Shoven. 2004. "Asset Location in Tax-Deferred and Conventional Savings Accounts." *Journal of Public Economics*, vol. 88, nos. 1–2 (January):23–38.

Stein, David M. 1998. "Measuring and Evaluating Portfolio Performance after Taxes." *Journal of Portfolio Management*, vol. 24, no. 2 (Winter):117–124.

———. 2004a. "Do You Anticipate an Increase in Tax-Rates? Deferring Capital Gains Is Not Always the Best Strategy." Commentary, Parametric Portfolio Associates (July).

———. 2004b. "Simulating Loss Harvesting Opportunities over Time." Research brief, Parametric Portfolio Associates.

Stein, David M., Andrew F. Siegel, Premkumar Narasimhan, and Charles E. Appeadu. 2000. "Diversification in the Presence of Taxes." *Journal of Portfolio Management*, vol. 27, no. 1 (Fall):61–71.

Subrahmanyam, Avanidhar. 1998. "Transaction Taxes and Financial Market Equilibrium." *Journal of Business*, vol. 71, no. 1 (January):81–118.

Veblen, Thorstein. 1994. *The Theory of the Leisure Class*. Reprint, first published 1899. Mineola, NY: Dover Publications.

Wang, Ming Yee. 1999. "Multiple-Benchmark and Multiple-Portfolio Optimization." *Financial Analysts Journal*, vol. 55, no. 1 (January/February):63–72.

Wilcox, Jarrod W. 2003. "Harry Markowitz and the Discretionary Wealth Hypothesis." *Journal of Portfolio Management*, vol. 29, no. 3 (Spring):58–65.

Wolfson, Neil. 2000. "Tax-Managed Mutual Funds and the Taxable Investor." KPMG Working Paper.

CHAPTER 11

CORE/SATELLITE STRATEGIES FOR THE HIGH-NET-WORTH INVESTOR

Clifford H. Quisenberry, CFA

Although a core/satellite structure makes a great deal of sense on a pretax basis, it makes even more sense on an after-tax basis. Implementing the strategy "optimally," however, is crucial to a positive outcome. Of note, the strategy must use a broad, tax-managed core portfolio. High-net-worth investors should consider adopting the core/satellite structure, but they must be aware of its limitations, such as high transition/tax costs and noisy inputs.

For the high-net-worth investor, a core/satellite strategy compares favorably with a traditional multimanager portfolio structure in terms of qualitative considerations as well as after-tax returns. In this presentation, I will review the traditional multimanager portfolio structure, describe the benefits of the core/satellite strategy, examine the multimanager structure in a taxable environment, and model the qualitative and quantitative relationships within the core/satellite structure.

TRADITIONAL APPROACH TO PORTFOLIO STRUCTURE

The traditional approach to a multimanager portfolio structure has been driven by theory and practice developed for the institutional investor. Modern portfolio theory and the capital asset pricing model, for example, indicate that returns are related to the major dimensions of

This presentation comes from the Wealth Management 2006 conference held in Tampa, Florida, on 27–28 April 2006.

Reprinted from *CFA Institute Conference Proceedings Quarterly* (December 2006):38–45.

risk and that a portfolio should be diversified in its sources of risk. Thus, the multimanager structure aims to meet both of these criteria through the creation of a basket of managers, each of which is pursuing a different strategy with a unique set of risk-adjusted return parameters. Theory also supports the concept that specialization improves performance and that segregation improves risk control.

The common approach to constructing traditional multimanager portfolios is to divide equity managers by size, style, and investment approach and evaluate their performance against a specific benchmark. In other words, large-cap value managers are compared with a large-cap value benchmark, small-cap value managers are compared with a small-cap value benchmark, and so forth. The resulting approach of segregating and hiring specialist managers is known as the "style box." This framework creates a portfolio decision model along the dimensions of size, style, geography, investment approach, or other similar categories.

The downside to this approach, however, is multifaceted. First, because the apparent goal is to diversify risk, the tendency is to include as many styles in the style box as possible. The thought process seems to be that if diversifying across styles is a good thing, then diversifying across managers within each style must be a really good thing. The evolution of this mindset has created an unwieldy portfolio structure that is overwhelmed by the administrative burdens associated with numerous managers. Administrative costs are high because sufficient professional staff must be on board to decide which managers to hire and fire. Consultants must also be hired to assist in the manager/style evaluation process.

Ironically, because all of these managers are evaluated against a benchmark, they tend to become closet indexers to avoid the risk of being fired. They begin buying stocks that they otherwise would not buy and end up diluting their alpha. At the end of the day, the client's portfolio as a whole looks a lot like the market portfolio. On the surface, the portfolio is diversified among many managers and in terms of size and style, but under the surface, the portfolio is just a broad-based index. To make matters worse, the costs associated with rebalancing and manager transitions can be quite large. In other words, to follow a traditional multimanager strategy means incurring alpha-type costs to receive beta.

CORE/SATELLITE STRATEGY

The core/satellite strategy originated because of the problems experienced in constructing and running traditional portfolios. Although the core/satellite strategy can be used for both tax-exempt and taxable clients, the taxable client reaps the greatest benefit. A typical core/ satellite strategy is composed of a passive broad-cap core portfolio complemented by satellite portfolios of active managers. These active managers are hired to run distinct strategies, such as mid-cap value, small-cap growth, and micro-cap investing, and should be taking true alpha bets to exploit areas of inefficiency in the market; they should not be closet indexing.

A major advantage of a core/satellite structure is fewer managers. By reducing the number of managers, the structure is easier to administer and the associated costs are lower, as are total manager fees. Lower fees come about for two reasons. First, the managers in the traditional structure, who had ultimately behaved as an unintended core portfolio, are replaced with a single, passive manager. Second, even though the satellite managers may charge higher fees because they deliver performance, the deadweight managers, or closet indexers, are eliminated from the arrangement. Thus, the portfolio's alpha can come from fewer satellite managers,

TABLE 11.1   Impact of Taxes on the Traditional Structure

Index	Pretax Return	After-Tax Return	Tax Impact
Russell 1000 Growth	7.40%	6.77%	−0.63%
Russell 1000 Value	12.03	10.91	−1.12
Russell 2000 Growth	5.16	4.97	−0.18
Russell 2000 Value	13.89	11.89	−2.00
Combined total	10.05%	9.11%	−0.94%
Russell 3000	10.05%	9.49%	−0.56%

Notes: Annualized 10-year returns ending 30 June 2005. After-tax returns estimated from historical pretax returns and turnover and by applying a 15 percent tax rate for long-term capital gains and qualified dividends and a 35 percent tax rate for short-term capital gains and nonqualified dividend income.

who theoretically are true specialists, producing higher alpha per dollar invested. In other words, with a core, the investor pays beta-type fees to get beta and only pays alpha-like fees to those managers who seek alpha and can provide it. And without fixed style boxes, the need to rebalance is reduced, which, in turn, drives down rebalancing costs.

When taxes are introduced, the balance shifts even more favorably toward the core/satellite approach. The theory that underpins the traditional portfolio approach and its practical implementation were developed for, and by, large institutions, not for the typical high-net-worth investor who is taxed at every turn in the road. Obviously, this disparity raises the practical point that the ideal portfolio for these two investor types should be constructed in different ways. Because the taxable investor's goal is to maximize not just pretax return but after-tax wealth, an approach is needed that adjusts pretax returns for taxes on realized gains and dividend income.

Table 11.1 illustrates the impact taxes have on the returns of various equity management styles that are typically used in the traditional portfolio structure. The table shows a mix of investment approaches proxied by four Russell style and size indices. Returns are for the last 10 years ending 30 June 2005. The pretax return for the four indices over this 10-year period was 10.05 percent, which was calculated by weighting each index with its subindex weight used in the calculation of the Russell 3000 Index.

The after-tax return paints a somewhat different picture. The after-tax return of these subindices, which is representative of the traditional style-box approach, was 9.11 percent for the period. But for the same period, the Russell 3000, which is representative of the core in a core/satellite approach, had an after-tax return of 9.49 percent. Hence, in a taxable environment, the advantage of a core/satellite strategy versus a traditional strategy is obvious. But what drives this 38 bp advantage?

The advantage arises because the core/satellite approach does not experience the turnover mandated by the style-box framework. Stocks are continually recategorized from one style box to another, triggering a sale within the traditional structure and consequently triggering a taxable event. For example, if a stock in the Russell 2000 Value Index performs well, it moves into the Russell 1000 Growth Index. Managers who are running a small-cap value allocation and are benchmarking against the Russell 2000 Value Index will be forced to sell the stock, and managers who are running a large-cap growth allocation and are benchmarking against the Russell 1000 Growth Index will be forced to buy the stock. In a core, proxied by the Russell 3000, having that same stock move from small-cap value to large-cap growth does not create a turnover event. In addition, good satellite managers, who by definition should be seeking alpha and not be tied to particular benchmarks, would not follow index constituent changes per se.

As shown in Table 11.1, the tax effect—the difference between pretax return and after-tax return for each style and size subindex—is greatest for the value indices. This result makes sense because the stocks in the value indices are moving up and out of the indices from a low price base, maybe even an undervalued position, so the gains realized are relatively large and the tax bite, relatively high. The 38 bp advantage is caused, therefore, by the broad-based index, or core portfolio, escaping the benchmark reconstitution effect.

Constructing the Core Portfolio

The core of the core/satellite portfolio should be a diversified portfolio with exposure to the broad market, encompassing large-cap, mid-cap, and small-cap stocks. As illustrated earlier, this index-type portfolio will be tax efficient because of low turnover and thus low gain realization. But the tax efficiency of the core can be improved if it is tax managed. A tax-managed core is an index, such as the Russell 3000, to which active tax management is applied. The active tax management in this case is tax-loss harvesting, or selling the specific tax lots in the portfolio that are "under water" at any given time. Loss harvesting must be done while maintaining tight risk control versus the benchmark. The goal is to hold the tracking error of the core portfolio to 1–2 percent.

Proceeds from loss-harvesting sales are reinvested in a basket of securities, which, based on a risk model and an optimizer, are selected to offset the risk of the underweights versus the benchmark caused by the loss-harvesting sales. And, of course, 30 days after a sale, at the expiration of the wash-sale period, the sold stock can be repurchased. Loss harvesting can produce a significant stream of losses equal to 5–6 percent of the core portfolio's market value for each year in the first five years after creation of the core/satellite structure. These losses, when used to offset realized gains from the satellite portfolios, can be worth 130–150 bps annually in additional after-tax return in the first 10 years of the portfolio.

Constructing the Satellite Portfolios

The primary goal in constructing the satellite portfolios is to improve efficiency pretax as well as after tax. Managers should be aggressive alpha seekers who target areas of inefficiency anywhere they find it. And they need to be independent of the broad benchmarks as well as the core portfolio. Independence from the benchmark and the core increases the total level of diversification in the strategy. Because of the aggressive stance of the managers, the satellite portfolios should have high turnover rates and realize substantial capital gains. These gains are absorbed by the loss stream generated by the tax-managed core, so the tax equation is effectively removed from the minds of satellite managers.

Core/Satellite Model

At Parametric Portfolio Associates, we built a model to learn more about the relationships, dynamics, and value added from the core/satellite strategy. We assumed an 8 percent annualized market return over a 10-year period. The tax-managed core was modeled using a Monte Carlo simulation of the loss-harvesting process and had a tracking error of 1.5 percent against the Russell 3000. The core had a standard deviation equal to that of the market (about 15 percent).

The loss stream from the core was used to offset the gains generated by the satellite managers. We also applied carryforward rules such that if in Year 1 the managers did not realize sufficient gains to offset the losses harvested from the core, the excess, unused loss became a loss carryforward that could be applied in the next period.

The satellite portfolios were modeled under the assumptions that the managers had pretax alpha of 3 percent, a turnover rate of 80 percent, tracking error against the benchmark of 3 percent, correlation with the core of 0.7 percent, and a standard deviation of 20 percent. With a pretax alpha of 3 percent and a tracking error of 3 percent, the managers' information ratio on a pretax basis equaled 1.

Model Results

Table 11.2 shows the results of the model base case compared with the benchmark, the Russell 3000. Over the 10-year period, the benchmark earned an annualized 8.00 percent pretax return and a 7.58 percent after-tax return. The difference between the two reflects a minimal tax bite that can be attributed to low turnover, maybe 4–5 percent a year, plus the income tax liability on the dividend stream.

The tax-managed core earned an annualized pretax return of 8 percent and obviously tracked closely the pretax return of the Russell 3000. The annualized after-tax return of 7.75 percent is actually a bit higher than the after-tax return of the index, which is a result of the tax-managed core generating losses that almost completely offset the gains realized by the benchmark's natural turnover of 4–5 percent. Because this analysis involved the core only, the excess realized loss was simply carried forward indefinitely and the added benefit of an offset to realized gains from other sources, such as the satellite portfolios, was never captured. When the satellite portfolios enter the picture, however, the excess loss from the core can be credited against realized gains in the satellites.

The satellite managers alone earned an annualized pretax return of 11.00 percent over the same period. This 11.00 percent return equals the 8.00 percent return of the benchmark plus alpha of 3.00 percent, which translates into an annualized after-tax return of 8.14 percent, representing a significant tax bite as a result of the high turnover associated with the active strategies. Although the 8.14 percent after-tax return is, in an absolute sense, higher than either the after-tax return of the benchmark or the after-tax return of the core, the relative tax bite is much larger.

When we combined the tax-managed core and satellite portfolios to create the core/satellite structure, the result was an annualized pretax return of 9.65 percent and an annualized after-tax return of 8.52 percent. In this case, the structure was 60 percent core/40 percent satellite. Pretax alpha dropped from 11 percent in the satellite-only scenario to 9.65 percent because the larger allocation to core dilutes the alpha of the satellite managers. Thus, although allocation to core definitely

TABLE 11.2   Model Results: Annualized Total Returns

Item	Pretax	After Tax
Benchmark (Russell 3000)	8.00%	7.58%
Tax-managed core only	8.00	7.75
Satellite managers only	11.00	8.14
Core (60%)/satellite (40%)	9.65	8.52

FIGURE 11.1   Optimal Core Allocation: Maximizing After-Tax Return

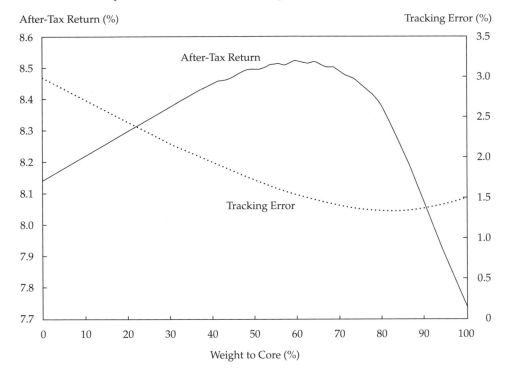

has a pretax cost, it is counterbalanced by the substantial after-tax benefit. The tax bite of the core/satellite structure is much lower than the tax bite of the satellite managers alone. The core/satellite combination added 38 bps a year in after-tax return over that of the satellite-only structure, even with the dilution of pretax alpha.

The dynamics shift as the weight of the core changes within the structure. Figure 11.1 graphs the changes in after-tax return and tracking error as the weight of the core moves from 0 to 100 percent. At a 0 percent weighting, the after-tax return of the core/satellite portfolio equals the after-tax return of the active managers only, which is 8.14 percent. With a 100 percent allocation to the core, the core/satellite portfolio yields a 7.75 percent after-tax return, which, not surprisingly, equals the after-tax return of the core-only portfolio.

In between the two extremes, however, is an interesting relationship. From a base of 0 percent, as more core portfolio is added to the satellite-only portfolio, after-tax return improves. The reason is that the marginal benefit of the core's absorption of the tax bite of the satellite managers outweighs the marginal cost of the core's dilution of the alpha of the satellite managers. At around a 60 percent core weighting, this benefit is maximized and begins to decline. After this point, giving a greater weight to the core simply generates losses that cannot be used because the increasingly smaller allocations to the active managers generate fewer and fewer gains for the whole portfolio. In other words, the marginal benefit is less than the marginal cost of alpha dilution. Note that this return-to-weight trade-off flattens at the top, so even though the optimal point appears to be 60 percent, the marginal improvement in after-tax return is only 7 bps between 40 and 70 percent. These allocation models are very helpful, but they are dealing with large amounts of noise in the inputs. Thus, a goal of pinpointing a precise weight for the core portfolio, such as 60 percent, is not necessarily achievable given that the marginal increase in return between a 40 percent and 60 percent weighting is minimal.

Figure 11.1 also shows the tracking error of the strategy as the core weight is increased. It declines from 3 percent at a 0 percent core weighting to 1.5 percent at a 100 percent core weighting. Note that tracking error reaches a minimum around 80 percent to core. This relationship of having a lower tracking error than even the 1.5 percent tracking error of the core is a result of the diversification benefit of combining the core's tracking error with the tracking error of the satellite managers. The tracking error of the satellite managers to the Russell 3000 is expected to be either uncorrelated or minimally correlated with the core's tracking error to the Russell 3000.

Optimal Core Allocation

The optimal core allocation ultimately depends on the variable that the investor wishes to maximize. The variable could be the after-tax return, after-tax information ratio (after-tax alpha/tracking error), or after-tax Sharpe ratio (after-tax return/standard deviation). The investor must match the metric to his or her investment goals. If relative risk is the main concern, the most appropriate variable to maximize is the after-tax alpha or the after-tax information ratio. If absolute risk is the main concern, the most appropriate variable to maximize is the after-tax Sharpe ratio. Thus, the metric selected is not as important as matching the metric to the client's goals.

Table 11.3 compares the optimal core allocations for the three metrics of after-tax return, after-tax information ratio, and after-tax Sharpe ratio. In the previous example, the after-tax return was maximized to determine an optimal core allocation of 60 percent. Using the same assumptions but maximizing the after-tax information ratio results in an optimal core allocation of 69 percent. At this allocation, the information ratio is 0.19 for satellite only and 0.65 for core/satellite. The higher optimal allocation when the after-tax information ratio is maximized is driven by the fact that tracking error is minimized around an 80 percent allocation to core weight, as shown in Figure 11.1. Because tracking error is the denominator in calculating the information ratio and the ratio becomes larger as tracking error declines (all other variables held constant), this minimum point effectively helps to draw the optimal core allocation further to the right toward it. The optimal core allocation when the after-tax Sharpe ratio is maximized is even higher at 76 percent to core, which translates to a Sharpe ratio of 0.56 for the core/satellite. The higher core allocation is a function of the higher standard deviations for the satellite managers versus the core portfolio.

TABLE 11.3   Optimal Core Allocations for Different After-Tax Metrics

Item	Return	Information Ratio	Sharpe Ratio
Optimal weight to core	60%	69%	76%
Value of maximized metric for the core/satellite	8.52%	0.65	0.56
Value of metric for satellite managers only	8.14%	0.19	0.41

In addition to the maximized variable, other critical variables influence the optimal core allocation. One of the most important factors is the return environment. Are expectations for a high-return, low-return, or flat-return environment? Also, if the satellite managers are generating large amounts of alpha, the opportunity cost to move to a higher core allocation is significant. Other factors that can influence the final decision include the comparative risk of the satellites versus the core and anticipated changes in tax rates. Clearly, if tax rates change, the entire picture changes.

These types of variables can be included in the allocation analysis by maximizing the primary variable, such as the after-tax information ratio, as a function of, for example, the expected market return. This type of analysis is illustrated in Table 11.4. Thus, when the market return is expected to be higher, the allocation to a tax-efficient core should be increased. In higher return environments, more gains are realized by the satellite managers and thus more losses are needed to offset them, requiring a larger allocation to the core portfolio. The table shows the allocation to the core increasing at a declining rate because as the return environment improves, the ability to take losses becomes more difficult. Although loss harvesting can be accomplished easily in stable, flat markets, it is a challenge in bull markets and can cause a drop in the efficiency of the loss-harvesting process, indicated by the increasing but decelerating allocation to core shown in Table 11.4.

Figure 11.2 shows a similar analysis. In this case, the core allocation is shown as a function of the maximized information ratio and expected alpha of the satellite managers. This comparison is a natural one to make because the expected alpha of the satellite managers is the opportunity cost of adding to the core in lieu of the satellites. Not surprisingly, the higher the expected information ratio or alpha, the lower the allocation to the core portfolio. The allocation model is not that sensitive to this variable, however, but rather is influenced much more heavily by tax costs.

To evaluate absolute risk-adjusted, after-tax return, the appropriate tool is the after-tax Sharpe ratio. Figure 11.3 illustrates the changes in the core allocation when the satellite's absolute risk, or standard deviation of returns, is varied. As the standard deviation increases, the core allocation very quickly approaches 100 percent. Obviously, adhering to such an allocation

TABLE 11.4   Allocation to Core Portfolio as a Function
of Market Return Expectations

Market Return	Allocation to Core Portfolio
0%	19%
2	42
3	59
6	67
8	69
10	75
12	81
14	85

FIGURE 11.2   Optimal Allocation to a Tax-Efficient Core as a Function of Satellite Manager Information Ratio

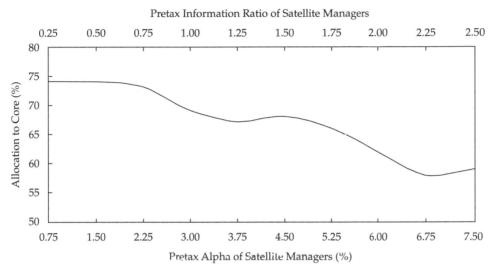

Note: Tracking error held constant at 3 percent.

FIGURE 11.3   Optimal Allocation to a Tax-Efficient Core as a Function of Satellite Standard Deviation

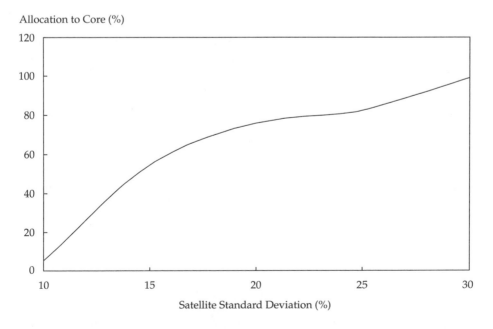

might not be practical, but this allocation is the one given by the model at high standard deviations, all other things being equal. In the real world, the manager's absolute return should conceivably also increase with risk.

Observations on the Core/Satellite Structure

Several observations can be made about the output of core/satellite allocation models. First, the higher the market return environment, the greater the need for the core portfolio's losses to offset higher realized gains. Second, the higher the satellite manager's information ratio, the lower the allocation to the core. Third, adding to the core, in general, helps reduce risk and helps boost the risk–reward ratio. And lastly, the solution offered by these models is extremely sensitive to the inputs.

The first step in implementing a core/satellite structure is to understand the investor's goal in pursuing such a strategy. Clearly, understanding the investor's objectives aids in selecting the most suitable metric to be maximized in the allocation process. If the wrong metric is chosen, the proposed allocation may not meet the investor's needs. Recall that the "optimal" allocation to the core portfolio can vary widely with even small changes in the metric. Another concern is finding "high-octane" satellite managers who can consistently produce alpha. Consistency in alpha production is critical because the allocation to the satellites, which is done in anticipation of a high alpha, means a smaller allocation to the core and smaller respective tax benefits than otherwise would occur if alpha turned out not to be as high as expected. Also, the initial tax costs associated with the transition to a core/satellite structure from a traditional structure may overcome the anticipated tax benefits of the core/satellite over the medium term and should be carefully evaluated. Thus, the decision to adopt a core/satellite strategy should be done on a case by case basis.

The big picture is that the core/satellite strategy can help an investor achieve a number of goals. For example, the strategy can encompass many different kinds of assets, not only the equity funds this presentation has focused on. Another advantage of the strategy is that it can ease the transition from a fired manager to a newly hired manager in that unrealized gains can be absorbed by the tax-managed core. Also, through the active risk-budgeting process inherent in the balancing act between the core and satellite allocations, tracking error can be controlled and minimized. Other advantages are that the gradual liquidation of a concentrated equity position can be facilitated within the core part of the structure quite easily, short-term gains from tax-inefficient hedge funds in the satellite portfolios can be sheltered, and the core can be used as the source from which to make gifts of low-basis stock to charitable remainder trusts or foundations. Finally, and obviously, the tax-managed core should improve overall cost control. Having satellite managers plus the index-like tax-managed core makes it possible, with coordination, to successfully achieve most of the investor's goals.

CONCLUSION

The core/satellite structure makes a great deal of sense on a pretax basis when both qualitative and quantitative factors are considered. And it makes imminently good sense on an after-tax basis for investors in a taxable environment. Implementing the strategy "optimally," however, is crucial to a positive outcome. Importantly, the strategy must use a broad, tax-managed core portfolio. High-net-worth investors should definitely consider adopting the core/satellite structure but must be aware of its limitations, such as high transition/tax costs and noisy inputs, which can influence the optimal allocation between the core and satellite portfolios.

QUESTION AND ANSWER SESSION

Question: How many names are in a typical diversified equity core portfolio?

Quisenberry: The number of stocks in a core portfolio varies based on the investor's concerns. If the investor is worried about absolute risk, then as few as 25–50 names can mitigate that concern. If the investor is worried about relative risk, then a much larger universe of stocks is needed in the core portfolio. For example, if the goal is to keep tracking error versus the Russell 3000 at 1.5 percent, the core portfolio should hold about 400–500 names.

Question: At what size does the core/satellite structure become cost efficient?

Quisenberry: Actually, an advantage of the core/satellite structure is that the core portfolio can be effectively managed at a size as small as $250,000.

Question: Would rising correlations between domestic and international markets alter the construction process of the core and satellite portfolios?

Quisenberry: I focus more on emerging markets than on developed markets, and for emerging markets, the 5-year correlations are actually lower than the 10-year correlations. Nevertheless, I would suspect that over time, correlations will probably increase, but I doubt the effect would be large enough to significantly alter the output of this type of model. Higher correlations could actually lower the risk reduction benefit of the core so that the allocation to the core is minimally decreased.

Question: Are 3 percent alpha and 3 percent tracking error realistic?

Quisenberry: They were not necessarily chosen to be realistic but, rather, to investigate the relationships among the critical variables in the model. But a tracking error of 3 percent would be consistent with a portfolio of about five satellite managers each having a tracking error of 6.5 percent. Thus, information ratios are below 0.5 and should be achievable. The combined portfolio of the five satellites benefits from the diversification effect so that the tracking error of the satellite group is reduced to about 3 percent, which gives the higher, overall information ratio of 1.

Question: What approach should be taken to construct the benchmark—a market-cap weighted, equal-weighted, or fundamental index approach?

Quisenberry: The two most suitable benchmarks are cap-weighted and fundamental indices. The benefit of a cap-weighted benchmark is low turnover in the core. An equal-weighted core is plagued by the need to rebalance to equal weights, which ramps up the tax costs. The distinction between the two approaches—cap weighted and equal weighted—is a function of the market environment because rebalancing in a stable market is not particularly onerous. But in a strong market environment, the realized gains from the rebalancing of an equal-weighted core are so high that typically all the core's losses, which were intended to offset the realized gains of the active satellite managers, are absorbed by the gains generated from the rebalancing. The fundamental indexing approach works well because turnover is generally in the 7–9 percent range, which is quite suitable for a core portfolio.

Question: Do the wash-sale rules create tracking error?

Quisenberry: The wash-sale rules are an issue in tracking error because the core portfolio is temporarily underweight the stock that was sold versus the benchmark during the 30-day wash-sale period. This exposure can be controlled quite well, however, through the creation of offsetting bets in, for example, size or style by using risk models and optimizers. The reality is that the core portfolio's tracking error can often be lowered to below 1.5 percent even while working around the wash-sale prohibition.

CHAPTER 12

THE HIGHER EQUITY RISK PREMIUM CREATED BY TAXATION

Martin L. Leibowitz

The literature on taxable investing appears to have overlooked the way in which different tax rates can lead to equity risk premiums that are actually greater than the original tax-free premiums. Moreover, this tax-based enhancement can occur in both a nominal and a real (after-inflation) framework. With the imminence of a new tax regime, it is high time to revisit the nature of this premium enhancement, especially in light of the striking implications of the enhancement for asset allocation.

Suppose the long-term risk-free rate is 5 percent, made up of a 3 percent real rate and a 2 percent inflation expectation—all pretax. Now consider the situation of a hypothetical investor who faces a tax rate of 40 percent on interest income (remember state taxes). Applying the 40 percent tax rate, as shown in Table 12.1, reduces the after-tax interest rate to 3.00 percent.

Now suppose the pretax risk premium is fixed at 3 percent so that with the interest rate at 5 percent, the pretax equity return is 8 percent, corresponding to 160 percent of the interest rate. Now, assume that all equity returns are taxed at 20 percent. (On the one hand, this assumption might be quite heroic for actively managed equity funds that generate short-term gains. On the other hand, the effective capital gains tax could be even further reduced by deferred realization, charitable contributions—or demise.[1]) On an after-tax basis, this 20 percent tax takes the 8 percent equity return down to 6.40 percent (see Table 12.1).

This 6.40 percent after-tax equity return represents 213 percent of the taxable risk-free rate of 3.00 percent (i.e., considerably higher than the 160 percent for the tax-free case). The 6.40 percent after-tax equity return can also be viewed as a 3.40 percent premium over the 3 percent after-tax fixed-income ratio (i.e., a 113 percent after-tax ratio compared with the pretax 60 percent ratio).

Modified from the *Financial Analysts Journal* (September/October 2003):28–31.

TABLE 12.1   Tax Effects

	Fixed Income (FI)	Equity	Equity to FI Ratio
Nominal interest rate	5.0%	5.0%	
Risk premium	—	3.0	60%
Pretax return	5.0%	8.0%	160%
Tax at 40%/20%	2.0	1.6	
After-tax return	3.0%	6.4%	213%
After-tax risk premium		3.4%	113%

Source: Morgan Stanley Research.

One of the key factors enhancing the after-tax premium is how equity's tax advantage is brought to bear on the underlying risk-free rate. The same 5 percent interest rate is taxed at 40 percent as a stand-alone fixed-income investment but at a favorable 20 percent rate when it is embedded in an equity investment. In essence, the equity structure projects its "tax shield" onto the fixed-income investment that forms the theoretical foundation beneath the equity risk premium. Because this tax advantage increases with higher interest rates, the somewhat surprising result is that the after-tax risk premium also rises with increases in the nominal pre-tax risk-free rate. Of course, if the equity return in an after-tax context is contrasted with a municipal risk-free rate, the shift in the risk premium will depend on the municipal-to-taxable yield ratio.

Now, what about the inflation effect? The 2 percent inflation rate reduces the 3.00 percent after-tax fixed rate to a real 1.00 percent and lowers the 6.40 percent after-tax equity return to a real 4.40 percent (see Table 12.2). The basic risk premium remains unaffected at 3.40 percent because the risk-free rate has already "absorbed" the inflation wedge. Thus, these after-tax premiums will always retain the same value on both a nominal and a real basis. However, this 3.40 percent real after-tax premium now represents a much larger 340 percent of the 1 percent inflation-reduced real after-tax interest rate.

TABLE 12.2   Tax and Inflation Effects

	Fixed Income (FI)	Equity	Equity to FI Ratio
Nominal interest rate	5.0%	5.0%	
Risk premium	—	3.0	60%
Nominal return	5.0%	8.0%	160%
Tax at 40%/20%	2.0	1.6	
After-tax return	3.0%	6.4%	213%
Inflation	2.0	2.0	
After-tax real return	1.0%	4.4%	440%
After-tax risk premium		3.4%	340%

Source: Morgan Stanley Research.

The taxable equity investment has another advantage over the tax-free investment: Its after-tax volatility may be lower. Because long-term gains are taxed and because losses can act as tax offsets, the taxable investor may experience a net after-tax price volatility that is only 80 percent of the literal market volatility. If so, the after-tax equity premium of 3.40 percent in the preceding example corresponds to lower equity volatility than in the pretax situation. Thus, with the risk premium viewed as compensation for volatility risk, the after-tax situation provides a higher risk premium for a lower level of volatility.

One simple way to achieve risk premium comparability in the two cases is to notionally lever up the equity position (or augment the equity allocation) so that the volatility risks are matched. The resulting enhanced after-tax risk premium could then be viewed as more "risk comparable" to the pretax premium. (This volatility-match argument also applies when municipals are taken for the risk-free rate in the taxable context.)

A 25 percent leveraging drives the total equity volatility from 80 percent up to 100 percent of the tax-free volatility. As shown in Table 12.3, with the after-tax volatility levered up by this 25 percent factor, the effective after-tax premium rises from 3.40 percent to 4.25 percent—1.25 percentage points greater than the original pretax premium of 3.00 percent.

Bringing all these results together, Table 12.4 shows that for the case of 2 percent inflation, the risk premium goes from 3.00 percent on a nominal pretax basis to 3.40 percent after taxes and then remains at 3.40 percent on a real after-tax basis (i.e., both before and after expected inflation). On a volatility-matched basis, the after-tax premium rises to 4.25 percent. In contrast, the interest rate declines from 5.00 percent pretax to 3.00 percent after tax and then to 1.00 percent on a real after-tax basis. As a percentage of the interest rate, the equity return rises from 160 percent on a nominal basis to 213 percent after tax, to 440 percent on a real after-tax basis, and finally to 525 percent after the volatility adjustment. Similarly, the equity risk premium as a percent of the fixed-income rate rises from 60 percent to 113 percent, to 340 percent, and finally to 425 percent on a volatility-adjusted real basis.

Table 12.5 displays the real after-tax returns for different inflation rates under the assumption that the real interest rate remains constant at 3.00 percent. At the more severe inflation level of 4 percent, a 7 percent nominal interest rate drops to 4.2 percent after tax and 0.20 percent on a real after-tax basis. The combination of taxes and higher inflation is seen to have a truly toxic effect on fixed-income returns. Moreover, these conditions create a particularly pernicious form of "money illusion," with inflation-driven higher nominal rates actually leading to much lower after-tax real returns.

TABLE 12.3 Volatility-Matched After-Tax Equity Returns

After-tax equity return (Table 12.1)	6.40%
After-tax interest rate (Table 12.1)	−3.00%
After-tax equity premium	3.40%
Higher equity exposure to match pretax volatility = 1/0.80 = 1.25	×1.25
Volatility-matched real after-tax equity premium	4.25%
After-tax interest rate	3.00%
Volatility-matched after-tax equity return	7.25%

Source: Morgan Stanley Research.

TABLE 12.4   Hierarchy of Returns under a 2 Percent Inflation Rate

	Fixed Income (FI)	Equity	Equity as % of FI	Equity Premium	Equity Premium as % of FI
Nominal pretax return	5.00%	8.00%	160%	3.00%	60%
After-tax return	3.00	6.40	213	3.40	113
After-tax real return	1.00	4.40	440	3.40	340
Volatility-adjusted after-tax real return	1.00	5.25	525	4.25	425

Source: Morgan Stanley Research.

TABLE 12.5   Returns Comparison under Varying Inflation Rates

Inflation rate	0%	2%	4%
Real interest rate	3.00	3.00	3.00
Fixed-income rates			
Nominal pretax	3.00%	5.00%	7.00%
After-tax at 40%	1.80	3.00	4.20
After-tax real	1.80	1.00	0.20
Equity returns			
Nominal pretax	6.00%	8.00%	10.00%
After-tax at 20%	4.80	6.40	8.00
After-tax real	4.80	4.40	4.00
Volatility-matched after-tax real	5.55	5.25	4.95
Volatility-matched after-tax real as % of after-tax real interest rate	308	525	—
Equity premiums			
Nominal pretax	3.00%	3.00%	3.00%
After-tax at 20%	3.00	3.40	3.80
After-tax real	3.00	3.40	3.80
Volatility-matched after-tax real	3.75	4.25	4.75
Volatility-matched after-tax real as % of after-tax real interest rate	208	425	—

Source: Morgan Stanley Research.

With the pretax risk premium kept constant at 3 percent, a 4 percent inflation rate would drive equity returns down from a pretax 10 percent to a volatility-matched after-tax real return of 4.95 percent (i.e., a risk premium of 4.75 percent over the corresponding 0.20 percent interest rate). This equity risk premium of 4.75 percent is considerably higher than the nominal pretax premium of 3.00 percent. It is also greater than the 3.75 premium under 0 percent inflation. At first, these results seem to argue that more inflation is better than less. However, it should be noted that while the risk premium (a relative measure) increases as inflation rises from 0 percent to 4 percent, the real after-tax equity return (an absolute measure) declines significantly from 5.55 percent to 4.95 percent.

What do these results imply for asset allocation? In essence, all that this work has done is to quantify the well-known tax advantage afforded to long-term capital gains (an advantage that recently has been enhanced and also extended to some dividends). In turn, this advantage means that the taxed investor can access a higher relative reward for accepting equity risk. If a given mean–variance allocation is derived in a tax-free framework (and if risk tolerances are comparable), then a somewhat higher equity allocation should be obtained in a taxable context than in the tax-free context.

This assumption of equal risk tolerances may be a stretch, however, especially given that taxed individuals typically have shorter time horizons and fewer standby resources than tax-free institutions. Another confounding issue is the downward shift in the overall pattern of absolute returns. Lower returns heighten the risk of triggering various shortfall conditions. The symmetrical character of a mean–variance optimization might not fully capture a taxed investor's aversion to such outcomes.

Although being taxed brings little joy, investors and investment managers should recognize the higher relative compensation for accepting long-term equity risk. This incremental risk premium may provide, in some circumstances, a small modicum of comfort.

ACKNOWLEDGMENTS

The author would like to express his deep gratitude to Brett Hammond and Anthony Bova for their help at many levels in the development of this chapter and to Peter L. Bernstein, Stanley Kogelman, David F. Swensen, and Jack L. Treynor for their valuable and insightful suggestions. This chapter focuses on basic concepts of financial theory and should not be construed as reflecting the official position of Morgan Stanley. The author is not a tax expert, and the information here should not be viewed as tax or legal advice. The computations shown are for illustrative purposes only and use tax rates intended to simplify calculations. Actual rates may vary.

NOTE

1. For an excellent discussion of the effective tax rates that can apply to various investments under various tax regimes, see Arnott, Berkin, and Ye (2000), Bodie and Crane (1997), Dybvig and Ross (1986), Scholes, Wolfson, Erickson, Maydew, and Shevlin (2002), and Shoven and Sialm (2000), among others.

REFERENCES

Arnott, R.D., A.L. Berkin, and J. Ye. 2000. "How Well Have Taxable Investors Been Served in the 1980s and 1990s?" *Journal of Portfolio Management*, vol. 26, no. 4 (Summer): 84–93.

Balcer, Y., and K.L. Judd. 1987. "Effects of Capital Gains Taxation on Life-Cycle Investment and Portfolio Management." *Journal of Finance*, vol. 42, no. 3 (July):743–758.

Bergstresser, D., and J. Poterba. 2000. "Do After-Tax Returns Affect Mutual Fund Inflows?" National Bureau of Economic Research Working Paper 7595.

Bodie, Z., and D.B. Crane. 1997. "Personal Investing: Advice, Theory, and Evidence." *Financial Analysts Journal*, vol. 53, no. 6 (November/December):13–23.

Dammon, R.M., and C.S. Spatt. 1996. "The Optimal Trading and Pricing of Securities with Asymmetric Capital Gains Taxes and Transaction Costs." *Review of Financial Studies*, vol. 9, no. 3 (Fall):921–952.

Dammon, R., C. Spatt, and H. Zhang. 2000. "Optimal Asset Location and Allocation with Taxable and Tax-Deferred Investing." Unpublished paper, Carnegie Mellon University.

Dybvig, P.H., and S.A. Ross. 1986. "Tax Clienteles and Asset Pricing." *Journal of Finance*, vol. 41, no. 3 (July):751–762.

Protopapadakis, A. 1983. "Some Direct Evidence on Effective Capital Gains Tax Rates." *Journal of Business*, vol. 56, no. 2 (April):127–138.

Scholes, M.S., M.A. Wolfson, M. Erickson, E.L. Maydew, and Terry Shevlin. 2002. *Taxes and Business Strategy.* 2nd ed. Upper Saddle River, NJ: Prentice Hall.

Shoven, J.B., and C. Sialm. 2000. "Asset Location for Retirement Savers," National Bureau of Economic Research Working Paper 7991 (November).

Tepper, I. 1981. "Taxation and Corporate Pension Policy." *Journal of Finance*, vol. 36, no. 1 (March):1–13.

CHAPTER 13

TAX DEFERRAL AND TAX-LOSS HARVESTING

Jeffrey E. Horvitz

By not realizing capital gains, equity investors can postpone or even fully avoid future tax payments to the government. The value of the tax deferral increases at an increasing rate as the holding period lengthens. For investors who actively trade, however, tax-loss harvesting can be used. Investors then maximize losses that can offset gains in other securities. For tax-loss harvesting to work, however, the present value of uncertain tax savings must more than offset higher transaction costs.

Equity investors who are subject to tax can realize substantial tax savings, but they must be disciplined and patient in order to reap these savings.[1] In this presentation, I will explain two basic but powerful strategies that investors and their advisors can follow. And although my focus is on equity investments, the principles apply to bond investments as well. I will also discuss the implications for the active versus passive management debate. I will not, however, discuss the myriad of tax shelters, such as insurance wrappers, offshore accounts, and retirement accounts.

The advice here is general rather than particular to an investor's unique tax circumstance, so the conclusions can be broadly applied. Keep in mind that my findings apply to U.S. investors, but the general conclusions apply to taxable investors in other jurisdictions.

The key insight about the taxation of investments, particularly stock investments, is as follows: Unlike what most people think, the U.S. federal tax code operates nearly identically to that of a carried interest in a private equity or venture capital partnership. That is, the federal government has an ongoing share of the profits in a portfolio of securities, *but the investor decides when the government will receive its share of taxes*. This situation can be thought of as an option owned by the investor. So, the investor should exercise the option when it is most suitable for him or her, rather than for the government. I will compare this carried interest analogy with conventional wisdom later.

Reprinted from *CFA Institute Conference Proceedings: Wealth Management* (October 2005):24–30.

SHORT-TERM VS. LONG-TERM CAPITAL GAINS TAXES

Why do active investment managers trade taxable accounts so often? Because they seek positive alpha for their clients. But the catch, from a tax perspective, is that frequent trades in mutual funds, private accounts, and broker-advised accounts can trigger recognized short-term gains—defined as those that occur within 12 months. This one-year horizon is of utmost importance because it means the difference between paying taxes at the same rate as ordinary income, which could be as high as 35 percent, versus paying the 15 percent long-term federal capital gains tax. With taxes, timing means everything; even one day can make a dramatic difference.

So, how much more return do investors need in order to justify paying the higher short-term capital gains tax? If one assumes that the short-term capital gains tax rate is 35 percent and the long-term capital gains tax rate is 15 percent, then the ratio of after-tax returns is $(1.0 - 0.15)/(1.0 - 0.35) = 0.85/0.65 = 1.31$. So, all else being equal, active investment managers who make only short-term trades need to earn a return that is 31 percent higher than that of managers who make only long-term trades.

This hurdle rate is staggering. I believe that few managers can break that hurdle in investment returns and certainly not with any consistency for their taxable clients. In addition, this hurdle rate makes no allowance for leakage caused by transaction costs, which would effectively increase the hurdle rate because managers who trade more often pay more in transaction costs.

And I have even more bad news: Short-term capital losses have to be used first to offset short-term capital gains, and then they can be used only to offset 15 percent long-term capital gains, and only then on up to $3,000 of ordinary income. So, apart from dividends, the worst possible form of income for most people is short-term capital gains. Yet, many investment managers generate lots of it.

The question then becomes whether investment managers are able to justify their trading activity. Table 13.1 is from an article by Robert Arnott, Andrew Berkin, and Jia Ye, who showed the percentage of mutual funds that beat the Vanguard S&P 500 Index Fund.[2] Even taking into account the costs associated with the Vanguard fund, one can see that it is not a big number. In fact, shockingly few managers can beat this benchmark.

To some extent, the amount of alpha, what Arnott et al. label as the "pure tax savings," looks puny here. And it is, but part of the reason for that small alpha is the turnover in the S&P 500, which itself triggers plenty of tax events. One could actually create passive portfolios that are much more tax efficient than the S&P 500. Another reason for the small "pure tax savings" is that the dividend component historically has been significant. Of course, dividends are paid periodically, and the size and timing of dividends are out of the control of investment managers.

TABLE 13.1   Percentage of Mutual Funds That Beat the Vanguard S&P 500 Index Fund

	10 Years 1989–1998	15 Years 1984–1998	20 Years 1979–1998
Before tax	14%	5%	22%
After tax including final liquidation	12	5	16
Pure tax savings over average fund	0.13	0.23	0.25

Source: Arnott, Berkin, and Ye (2000).

Aside from the anomaly of the 15-year period, which is probably a reflection of market conditions over that time, I believe that only about 15 percent of active managers can beat the Vanguard S&P 500 Index Fund on an after-tax basis, including all the tax at final liquidation. What is the likelihood of an investor picking one of those managers? What is the probability of picking three of those managers? It is low in both cases.

ALGEBRA OF DEFERRED TAXES

The longer investors can go without realizing gains, the more valuable the gains are to investors because the compounding works for the benefit of investors and not the U.S. Treasury. Investors themselves determine when to liquidate an unrealized gain. In this context, taxation can be thought of in the same way as the carried interest of a limited partnership (such as private equity or venture capital). That is, the investor and the government will earn their share of the gains and taxes on the gains, respectively, at the end of the holding period, allowing the gains to grow tax free during the holding period. This concept is essential for understanding the simple mathematical mechanism of how tax deferral adds value.

The following example will help explain how tax deferral works. Imagine a steady state rate of return, denoted by r. So, in each period, an investor's portfolio grows by $1 + r$. An investor's terminal wealth is the product of $1 + r$ for each compounding period times the investor's initial investment:

$$(1 + r_1) \times (1 + r_2) \times \cdots \times (1 + r_n).$$

First, consider the case where an investor recognizes gains annually and must pay the corresponding capital gains tax each year, denoted by τ. The preceding equation can be modified to recognize the investor's after-tax return:

$$[1 + r_1(1 - \tau)] \times [1 + r_2(1 - \tau)] \times \cdots \times [1 + r_n(1 - \tau)].$$

This equation, of course, assumes that the investor pays long-term capital gains tax at a constant rate over the entire holding period. Effectively, the investment is compounding at a lower rate.

Now, consider the extreme case of 100 percent tax deferral. (I refer only to capital gains tax deferral because dividends cannot be deferred; they are taxed when they are paid.) At the end of the investor's holding period is a final-period tax payment that can be thought of as a *negative* single-period return, denoted by r_{tax}:

$$(1 + r_1) \times (1 + r_2) \times \cdots \times (1 + r_{tax}).$$

It really does not matter where that negative return occurs from a purely mathematical perspective; but for this example, assume that it will always occur at the end of the holding period. A variant is a Roth IRA, where tax is paid only at the beginning. Remember that the government owns a profit interest in the returns, and the best that an investor can do is to defer the payment of taxes for as long as possible so that the compounding effect works to the investor's full advantage over the holding period. Therefore, the compounding effect can work to its full potential over the holding period and reduces the taxes payable to the government, as shown by the following equation:

$$(1 + r_1) \times (1 + r_2) \times \cdots \times (1 + r_n) \times (1 - \tau).$$

FIGURE 13.1   Terminal Wealth at Liquidation

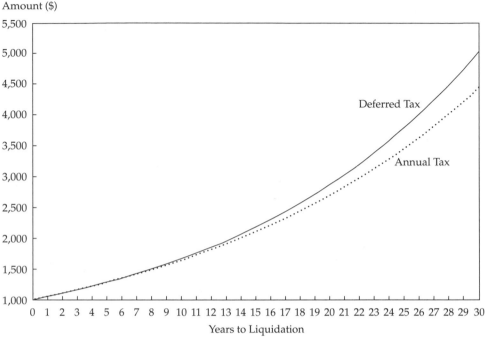

Notes: Price change only; dividends excluded. Annual rate of return of 6.0 percent, and capital gains tax of 15.0 percent.

I will now put these simple equations to work. Assume that investments grow at an annual rate of 6 percent and that the applicable tax rate is the long-term capital gains tax rate of 15 percent. Figure 13.1, which shows the growing divergence between terminal wealth when taxes are paid annually and terminal wealth under a buy-and-hold scenario where taxes are paid at liquidation, demonstrates the power of tax deferrals, particularly if liquidation can be deferred until at least 10 years. Before 10 years, the difference between the annual payment of taxes and deferral is not material. As the length of the holding period increases, however, the power of nonlinear compounding and deferred taxes becomes stronger, as can be seen by the spacing between the dotted line that denotes the annual tax payment and the solid line that denotes the tax deferral. Notice that the difference between the deferral and annual tax lines increases as the holding period lengthens. The spread illustrates the dilutive effect of stalling the government's share of investment gains for as long as possible. Horvitz and Wilcox demonstrated this effect in a recent article.[3] It is not something for which there are any exceptions, or at least important exceptions. This "carried interest" analogy will always work.

SHORT DEFERRAL PERIODS ARE NOT WORTHWHILE

Interestingly, many of those who have commented on tax deferral, those who sell tax-deferred accounts, and those who offer tax-deferred advice talk about tax deferrals over time periods shorter than 10 years. Figure 13.1 shows that material deferral benefits do not start until after

TABLE 13.2   Terminal Wealth as a Percentage of Tax-Exempt Investing

Years to Liquidation	No Tax	Tax Deferred	Annual Tax	Spread
5	100.0%	96.2%	95.8%	0.4%
10	100.0	93.4	91.8	1.5
15	100.0	91.3	88.0	3.3
20	100.0	89.7	84.3	5.4
25	100.0	88.5	80.8	7.7
30	100.0	87.6	77.4	10.2

Note: Price change only; rate of return = 6 percent.

10 years. So, when advisors are talking to clients about tax deferral, and if the clients are not prepared to have serious deferral, meaning somewhere around the 10-year mark and beyond, then it really is not worthwhile.

Table 13.2 examines the data from Figure 13.1 as a percentage of the tax-free terminal wealth. It uses the same return and tax assumptions and investigates, again, capital gains only, not dividends. Notice that at five years to liquidation, only a 40 bp difference exists between paying annual tax and deferring the tax. Think about how many products are being sold with a three- to five-year tax deferral for which clients are paying a material fee to earn a negligible benefit. (I assume that the deferral is complete and that the withdrawal occurs all at once.) These short-term tax deferrals are simply not worth doing.

The spread becomes material starting after 10 years. At the extreme in this illustration, the patient investor is rewarded with about 10.2 percent more wealth after 30 years. Incidentally, I have also investigated the spread assuming modest dividend payments and corresponding income tax each year, and the spreads are not overwhelmingly different. For 1.5 percent paid-in dividends each year, the corresponding taxes paid at the rate of ordinary income, a 9.2 percent spread still exists after 30 years.

Tax deferral over long holding periods is worthwhile, but the benefit over shorter periods greater than one year is negligible. So, if somehow investors believe in active management, or they believe they have the hot stock, or they believe they have an edge, they should not give that up just to get tax deferral *unless they can get the deferral for more than 10 years*. And this result also has a lot of bearing for clients who have highly concentrated portfolios. If the expectation is that their highly concentrated position, for one reason or another, will be sold and capital gains recognized, meaning for tax purposes in five years or just a few years longer, then they should not spend a whole lot of effort trying to defer that tax. It is just not worth it in that case.

MITIGATING ESTATE TAXES

Estate taxes are important, but not a lot is written about them. Table 13.3 shows proposed estate tax changes under current law. President Bush in 2001 signed into law the Economic Growth and Tax Relief Reconciliation Act of 2001, which gradually reduces the maximum tax rate and increases the annual exclusion amount (exemption) up until 2009.

TABLE 13.3   Estate Tax Changes, 2005–2011

Year	Maximum Rate	Exclusion Amount
2005	47%	$1,500,000
2006	46	2,000,000
2007	45	2,000,000
2008	45	2,000,000
2009	45	3,500,000
2010	(Estate tax repealed)	
2011	55	1,000,000

TABLE 13.4   Total Tax Paid

Gain Recognized before Death?	Exempt Estate	Nonexempt Estate
Yes	$75.00	$716.25
No	0	675.00

Interestingly, the act fully repeals any estate tax beginning on 1 January 2010. But absent any U.S. Congressional intervention, this repeal will "sunset" or expire on 1 January 2011, returning to the old tax system, which includes the 55 percent top tax rate. Of course, no one knows for sure what will happen beyond 2010. Not a single trust and estate attorney believes that the old tax system will be put back in place in 2011. And it would be unreasonable, I believe, to present clients with projections based on a reversion to a 55 percent maximum tax rate. At the same time, I would not be surprised to see the repeal expire with a new tax rate in place for 2011 and beyond or to see the estate tax schedule changed by Congress before 2010.

My axiom—deferring gain recognition until death is always better—holds true even if the estate is going to be subject to estate tax. Table 13.4 has some simple examples that illustrate the power of estate taxes. This simple matrix can be prepared for any client. In this instance, I assume the cost basis is $1,000, the future market value is $1,500, the long-term capital gains rate is 15 percent, and the estate tax rate is 45 percent.

If the estate is tax exempt and if the tax deferral lasts until death, then a taxable investor is converted into a tax-exempt investor with zero taxes payable. If the estate is tax exempt but the capital gain is recognized before death, then the investor pays $75 in capital gains tax [($1,500 − $1,000) × 0.15]. If the estate is not tax exempt but the capital gain is not recognized before death, then the investor pays $675 in estate tax [$1,500 × 0.45]. If the estate is not tax exempt and the capital gain is recognized before death, then the investor pays $75 in capital gains tax and $641.25 in estate tax [($1,500 − $75) × 0.45] for a total of $716.25.

Of course, the ultimate value of deferring taxes until death will depend on the status of the estate. Following are four possibilities: The estate is below the exemption, the estate is left to charity, the estate is subject to tax, and the estate is left to a spouse.

Estate Is Below the Exemption. When the estate is below the exemption, no tax is paid. There will be a step-up in basis, and the effect is to compound the deferrals just like for a tax-exempt investor. So, for older or ill clients who do not intend to spend all of their investment gains before they die, deferring the sale until after death is a way to make powerful changes in the residual estate, the amount of the estate that is left.

Estate Is Left to Charity. For an estate left to charity, the effect is the same as for the estate being below its exemption. For those investors who have charitable bequests in mind, tax deferral is quite valuable. Just think of the effects of long-term compounding on the value of the estate passed to the charity. The investor has been converted to tax-exempt status without ever having to consider a private foundation. For some reason, this bequeathing to charity is not typically recognized in the investment community.

Estate Is Subject to Tax. When the estate is subject to tax, there are large tax savings if an investor does not make *inter vivos* liquidations. The result is to reduce the effective long-term capital gains tax. The savings is equal to the long-term capital gains rate times the estate tax rate. So, if the estate tax rate is roughly 50 percent, then the investor cuts his or her effective long-term capital gains tax in half from 15 percent to roughly 7.5 percent.

Estate Is Left to a Spouse. If an investor leaves an estate to a spouse and the spouse takes the basis, then the investor can perpetuate the tax deferral. Think of it in terms of estimating the life span of this as a last-to-die insurance policy. The actuarial expectancy could be quite long and may provide a powerful way to elongate the long-term tax deferral. So, for a married couple (one not in divorce proceedings) where one spouse is expected to die before the other, which is almost certainly the case, taking advantage of the extension of tax deferral can be very beneficial.

TAX-LOSS HARVESTING

Some investors believe in active management's ability to create positive alpha. For these investors who recognize capital gains through trading, capital gains taxes can be mitigated.

Tax-loss harvesting means taking voluntary losses for the sole purpose of creating a current tax deduction to offset other gains. Of course, investors have other reasons to sell securities, but the sole motivation for tax-loss harvesting is to trigger tax savings through realized losses now to offset gains elsewhere in the portfolio.

For tax-loss harvesting to work, the present value of the tax deduction must meaningfully exceed the total transaction cost. This is the theory, but it is more difficult to quantify in practice. Furthermore, the amount of loss taken on each trade should be maximized. Other more complicated rules also apply—for example, in a highly volatile portfolio having multiple tax lots with multiple basis—but the basic principle holds. The investor needs to keep a record for gains as well as for losses. Without this disciplined accounting, the investor cannot be successful at tax-loss harvesting. Therefore, one of the essential tools that clients must have for tax-loss harvesting is adequate record keeping.[4]

Normally, the transaction costs are round-trip costs because, using my definition of tax-loss harvesting (i.e., for the sole purpose of creating realized losses), the investor is not really trying to dispose of the security. Rather, the investor is trying to keep the security. So, the investor somehow has to get it back.

Getting the security back would be easy except for the Internal Revenue Service's wash-sale rules. The wash-sale rules state that if an investor sells a security for a loss, the investor cannot buy the same security back within 30 days of the transaction or the loss will be disallowed for tax purposes. To further complicate matters, the investor also cannot have purchased the same security, or essentially the same security, for 30 days prior to the transaction. So, the investor has a 61-calendar-day window because the day of the trade itself is not counted. That is a long waiting period.

The problem with the purchase of the substitute security is that it is purchased at a lower tax basis due to the loss, and this lower basis could be recaptured through a higher realized capital gain in the future. This point is very important to understand because a lot of the products that engage in tax-loss harvesting ignore this gain, unless, of course, the investor can defer realized gains until after death, as I have already discussed.

The present value of the tax deduction is difficult to calculate. But the deduction effectively puts extra money in the investor's pocket, and so in this context only, tax-loss harvesting *is* like an interest-free loan from the government. (Do not confuse this with tax deferral, where the tax deferral is a future profits participation between the investor and the Treasury.) That is, investors can effectively spend the money derived from recognizing the tax loss and taking the tax deduction.

When this recapture occurs and how much it will be are hard to tell. There is no algorithm that yields an exact solution, but it can be modeled based on probability-adjusted recaptures that extend into the future. Then, the investor can apply a term structure of discount rates to each future recapture. This process gives a crude estimate of the present value of the recaptures. Going further, the investor can calculate the net present value (NPV) as the difference between the positive present value of the recaptures and today's transaction costs, which would include brokerage costs, commissions, and market impact, if the investor has a model for it. Transaction costs will be the most predictable in the NPV equation, but keep in mind that they can vary with investor size. That is, transaction costs are low for small traders and people who invest in mutual funds, they are really low for big institutions, and they are really high for everybody in the middle.

Before taking the tax-harvest loss, there should be a significant positive NPV because of the high uncertainty of the recapture. So, the investor does not want to just hit the breakeven point by a dollar. The calculated NPV must be large because its true value is not known. If the investor is wrong and the NPV is, in fact, negative, then the investor will lose money and he or she will never know it.

Thus, the operational problems of tax-loss harvesting are (1) how does the investor calculate the NPV of the tax deduction and the transaction costs when the recapture is uncertain and (2) how does the investor know when to trigger a loss recognition? That is, how does the investor know when the share is trading low enough? With perfect insight and hindsight, the investor would pick the bottom of the market for that particular stock, sell it, rebuy it, and then write it up. Of course, investors would do that anyway if they could, almost irrespective of the tax-loss harvesting. So, obviously, if it were that easy to do, everybody would be doing it for other reasons. Some people have suggested creating a rule of thumb, such as taking losses that are perhaps 30 percent of face value. And some researchers have simulated possible solutions, but I am interested in an algorithmic solution.

CONCLUSIONS

Investors subject to tax can realize substantial tax savings if they act and plan accordingly:

- *Avoid short-term capital gains.* Investors should wait for long-term capital gains. This should probably be the first rule of taxable investment management.

- *Federal taxation is like a carried interest in profits.* The investor and the government own the profits, and the share of the capital gains will be distributed to the investor and the government at the end of the holding period.
- *Tax deferral becomes more valuable as the holding period lengthens.* The deferral is not valuable for at least 8–12 years, under normal ranges of market performance. (Note that earlier I said that the minimum period was 10 years, but of course, that was based on my assumption of a 6 percent compounded return.)
- *The investor's estate tax situation is critical.* Tax deferral is particularly valuable when no estate tax will be due.
- *Tax-loss harvesting has to solve two key problems.* Tax-loss harvesting must address how to create a positive NPV out of the current tax savings when the potential future recapture is uncertain and how to maximize the loss for a given single transaction cost.

QUESTION AND ANSWER SESSION

Question: How does volatility affect the tax-loss harvesting strategy?

Horvitz: The more volatile the stocks, the more up and down you can get. So, you have more opportunity for tax-loss harvesting.

Question: What is the best way to measure an investor's after-tax performance?

Horvitz: If you want to know how well you are doing, create the unrecognized gains for purposes of performance measurement as if liquidated and taxed at whatever period you are looking at.

Question: What if tax rates are 70 percent when we withdraw? Shouldn't we give value to the "devil" we know versus deferring to unknown future tax rules?

Horvitz: Remember, it doesn't matter what the tax rate is, just as long as you can defer this all the way to a tax-exempt estate. Therefore, the problem of tax rates is irrelevant. In terms of the mathematics, we know that the deferral spreads will increase as the tax rate increases; it pays even more to defer as tax rates increase.

Tax rates right now are really about the lowest they have been since World War II. About 20 years ago, the long-term capital gains rates were either 20 percent or 28 percent, jumping more or less back and forth every few years. Today, the long-term capital gains tax rate is 15 percent. There are reasonable prospects that one day we will see higher rates.

Question: If an estate is left to the spouse, then half the amount is supposed to be updated with the date-of-death value. Then, there's a yes or no answer for this deferral to work. Shouldn't you gift all the assets to the second-to-die spouse while he or she is alive, if you can predict it?

Horvitz: To the extent that you have exemption left in the estate, then it is really an estate-planning question, which is pretty straightforward: Take the step-up in basis, and in all events, use up all of your exemption first. The remainder, then, goes to the spouse with the old basis, which you could also do directly or in a qualified terminal interest property trust. To the extent that there are grandchildren involved, you want to use up your complete generation-skipping transfer tax exemption.

The ideal estate-planning device is what's called a dynasty trust, in which you actually put the money in trust for all future generations. In the right jurisdictions, you can effectively defer taxes forever. There are enough jurisdictions to do this in, but the major drawback is the legal cost.

Question: Should tax-gain harvesting be used in the context of a tax-loss carryforward?

Horvitz: No, because normally there is a significant amount of gain that is involuntary. If you could control all your gains and losses, which you can't, the game would be quite different. Tax-loss harvesting is the voluntary loss recognition for purposes of offsetting gains. Do those gains have to occur right away? No, not particularly. I think it is more valuable to use the voluntary losses in most all cases to shelter the involuntary future gains.

Question: If you apply the taxdeferral advice to an investor who owns a concentrated position in IBM with a $2 cost basis, how do you deal with the trade-off of diversifying the investor's portfolio versus holding the deferral taxes as long as possible?

Horvitz: Irrespective of tax deferral, I would just sell the IBM stock. The amount of concentration risk is so extreme and the benefits of diversification so great that I can't imagine rationally maintaining this position.

In general, if you already own a well-diversified portfolio of stocks, then I don't think there is a trade-off. If you invest in a diversified index fund, then you can mitigate the risk of having too much concentration in any particular stock. To be somewhat cynical, an active manager has only a 15 percent chance of beating the S&P 500, which is even more compelling evidence to invest passively; you would avoid the diversification issue entirely.

NOTES

1. By "tax," I mean the U.S. federal capital gains tax, but I urge investors and advisors to take into consideration state and, in some instances, local taxes.
2. See Robert D. Arnott, Andrew L. Berkin, and Jia Ye, "How Well Have Taxable Investors Been Served in the 1980s and 1990s?" *Journal of Portfolio Management* (Summer 2000):84–93.
3. Jeffrey E. Horvitz and Jarrod W. Wilcox, "Tax Management of Stock Portfolios," *Journal of Investing* (Spring 2005):83–89.
4. Berkin and Ye discuss the highest in, first out (HIFO) method, whereby the shares with the highest cost basis are sold first. This approach minimizes the capital gains tax. See Andrew L. Berkin and Jia Ye, "Tax Management, Loss Harvesting, and HIFO Accounting," *Financial Analysts Journal* (July/August 2003):91–102.

CHAPTER 14

TAX MANAGEMENT, LOSS HARVESTING, AND HIFO ACCOUNTING

Andrew L. Berkin and Jia Ye

Virtually all companies and individuals are faced with the management of taxable assets. To manage these assets efficiently, investors need to be aware of the impact of taxes on investment returns. In the study we report in this chapter, we quantified the benefits of loss harvesting and highest in, first out (HIFO) accounting by using Monte Carlo simulations and investigated the robustness of these strategies in various markets and with various cash flows and tax rates. We concluded that a market with high stock-specific risk, low average return, and high dividend yield provides more opportunities to harvest losses. In addition, a steady stream of contributions refreshes a portfolio and allows the benefits of loss harvesting to remain strong over time. Conversely, withdrawals reduce the advantages of realizing losses. Our findings show that no matter what market environment occurs in the future, managing a portfolio in a tax-efficient manner gives substantially better after-tax performance than a simple index fund, both before and after liquidation of the portfolio.

All companies and individuals are faced with the management of taxable assets. In fact, a large portion of all investment capital is taxable. Apart from personal, high-net-worth assets and mutual funds, institutional examples include insurance reserves, voluntary employees' beneficiary association trusts, nuclear decommissioning trusts, and nonqualified pensions for senior managers. To manage taxable assets efficiently, investors need to be aware of the impact of taxes on investment returns. Until recently, however, after-tax performance information

Note: The authors would like to gratefully acknowledge the contributions of Robert D. Arnott to the chapter. The chapter was accepted for publication prior to Mr. Arnott's appointment as editor of the *Financial Analysts Journal*.

Reprinted from the *Financial Analysts Journal* (July/August 2003):91–102.

was not available to many investors; additionally, the cost of taxes was overshadowed by the long-lasting bull market and by investors' zealous quest for active alphas.

Most investment managers serving the taxable investing market are quite happy to trade off known (and often large) tax costs in the quest for stock selection alpha, which may or may not materialize. But the alpha for a taxable portfolio consists of a pretax alpha, which is highly uncertain, and a "tax alpha" (the tax consequences of active management), which can be managed with precision. The largest source of negative tax alpha is capital gains taxes, which are incurred on any profitable sale; the largest source of positive tax alpha is tax savings from realized losses—that is, the strategy that has become known as "loss harvesting."

We previously used Monte Carlo simulations to study the benefits of loss harvesting under standard market conditions (Arnott, Berkin, and Ye 2001b). This chapter expands on that work in several significant ways. First, in the study we report here, we systematically varied the market conditions to examine their effects on the rewards from loss harvesting. Second, we addressed the effects of portfolio considerations, such as cash flow, on the alpha obtainable through tax efficiency.

PAST STUDIES

Not until the past couple of years has the effect of taxes received the attention it deserves. Several studies have shown that active alphas are highly uncertain whereas the cost of taxes is very real (Jeffrey and Arnott 1993; Dickson and Shoven 1993; Arnott, Berkin, and Ye 2000). More and more investors realize that when they take profits after the market appreciates, taxes take a big bite out of their wealth. Furthermore, the recent increase in "new wealth" individuals (who have not used the family offices of "old wealth" families) that resulted from the boom years of the 1990s has created a new class of tax-conscious investor. A recent development is the increased focus on after-tax performance measurement (Stein 1998; Brunel 2000). In October 1999, the Vanguard Group announced that it would start publishing the after-tax performance of 47 of its mutual funds. On 16 April 2001, the U.S. SEC (2001) adopted a rule requiring mutual funds to disclose their after-tax returns, and AIMR (2001) proposed new standards for after-tax performance measurement. These new regulations and standards should enhance the tax consciousness of investors.

With the increasing attention devoted to tax-efficient investing, various ways have been proposed to improve after-tax returns (Dickson and Shoven 1994; Jeffrey and Arnott; Apelfeld, Fowler, and Gordon 1996; Stein and Narasimhan 1999; Arnott, Berkin, and Ye 2001a). Among them are loss harvesting (taxable investors should harvest losses to generate tax credits that can be used to offset capital gains), HIFO (highest in, first out) accounting procedures (taxable investors should use HIFO accounting whenever a security holding is sold), and yield management (whereas corporate taxable portfolios should tilt toward high-yield stocks to take advantage of the dividend exclusion, taxable investors should hold mostly low-yield assets to avoid income taxes on the yield). Although the rationale behind all these strategies is straightforward, the investment literature contains little documentation quantifying the benefit of each strategy in terms of tax savings, nor are the strategies widely used.

Dickson and Shoven (1994) were among the first to measure the benefits of loss harvesting and the HIFO accounting procedure. They constructed closed-end and open-end SURGE (strategies using realized gains elimination) funds that tracked the S&P 500 Index from August 1976 through December 1991. Not surprisingly, Dickson and Shoven found that the strategy of realizing large capital losses extracted greater tax benefit for the closed-end fund than for the open-end fund. (Because share prices typically rise over time, an open-end fund tends to have a higher cost basis from cash inflow than its closed-end counterpart. Therefore, an open-end fund is endogenously more tax efficient than a closed-end fund.) For the open-end fund, the tax benefit of HIFO accounting was 65–95 bps, with only 5–8 bps of value added by loss harvesting. The loss-harvesting strategy increased after-tax returns by 14–27 bps a year over the HIFO-only closed-end fund. In summary, this Dickson–Shoven study showed that both the open-end and closed-end SURGE strategies improve after-tax performance without harming before-tax returns.

The simulations in Dickson and Shoven (1994) were based on only one type of market environment (the U.S. market from 1976 through 1991, largely a bull market environment), so the applicability of their results in other market conditions is not clear. In this chapter, we use Monte Carlo simulations to examine the contributions from loss harvesting and HIFO accounting methods in various market environments.[1] We can thus show that the benefits of these techniques are not unique to a particular set of returns but consistently add value under a wide array of possible future market environments. In addition, we can quantify the value added.

LOSS HARVESTING AND HIFO

"Loss harvesting" refers to realizing losses by selling shares that have fallen below the original cost to generate tax credits. Tax credits can be used to offset capital gains either within or outside the portfolio. Because virtually all diversified portfolios have stocks that suffer losses, selling stocks that have fallen in value (or covering short positions in stocks that have rallied) is perhaps the easiest way to reduce taxes. Although the idea underlying this strategy is simple, its implementation requires diligence and discipline: To achieve the maximum tax savings, an investor should dispose of stocks with losses whenever a loss-harvesting opportunity is large enough to justify the trading costs. This discipline has been ignored by many investors, who tend to wait until year-end to realize losses.

In a world with nonzero transaction costs, one should harvest losses only to the extent that the tax credits they generate substantially outweigh the trading costs from loss realization.[2] Another constraint on loss harvesting is the "wash sale" rule, which prohibits the purchase of any securities that were sold at a loss during the previous 31 days. The wash sale rule introduces a source of risk to loss harvesting. An obvious way to minimize this risk is to simultaneously purchase stocks that share similar risk and return characteristics as the stocks that were sold at a loss. For active management, losses should be realized only when the tax benefit can overcome the cost of trading *and* the expected short-term gains of a stock. Given that the tax credit is a "bird in the hand" whereas short-term market prices are hard to predict, however, the wash sale rule should not have a significant effect on the trading strategies of a tax-efficient portfolio.

In HIFO accounting, whenever one must sell a security, one sells the shares with the highest cost basis first. The rationale is straightforward: The higher the cost basis, the lower the capital gains tax. This strategy minimizes capital gains taxes without any change in portfolio weights. It is, therefore, a Pareto optimal strategy from any perspective.

MONTE CARLO SIMULATIONS

In this section, we spell out the assumptions and results for the base case and then report robustness tests by (1) varying the market conditions (the assumptions) and rerunning the simulations and (2) varying the portfolio conditions and rerunning the simulations.

Base-Case Assumptions

As strategies, loss harvesting and HIFO accounting share a desirable feature—simplicity. Not only can investors implement these strategies easily, they can also measure the tax benefit with precision. We carried out this measurement in a series of Monte Carlo simulations.

Our model for asset returns is based on the standard capital asset pricing model (Sharpe 1964):

$$r_i = (1 - \beta_i)r_f + \beta_i r_M + \varepsilon_i,$$

where

r_i = expected return on stock i
β_i = risk exposure of stock i to the market
r_f = the risk-free rate
r_M = expected return on the market portfolio
ε_i = the residual

The risk-free rate in the base case was fixed at 0.54 percent a month, or 6.5 percent a year, which approximately matches the average of 1977–2002. We set the betas to be normally distributed, with a mean of 1 and standard deviation of 0.3, and capped them at −1 and 3.

We adapted historically typical values for the base-case scenario:

- an average monthly market return of 0.66 percent (8 percent a year, which represents a total return, or Price return + Dividend),
- average monthly market volatility of 4.3 percent (15 percent a year on a geometric basis), and
- dividend yield of 0.12 percent a month (1.44 percent a year based on current market yields).

We simulated a 300-month (25-year) performance history for a portfolio with 500 assets—in effect, a synthetic S&P 500. The monthly return on each asset was this market return plus a normally distributed random variable with 0 mean and 9 percent volatility. To simulate corporate actions and index rebalancing, we assumed that one existing company disappeared and one new company was added to the portfolio every month, which corresponds to an average of 2.4 percent annualized turnover in index composition.[3] For simplicity, we assumed the replacement stock was at the same index weight as the stock removed. The turnover of the portfolio each month and reinvestment of dividends led to tens of thousands of tax lots over the 25 years of the portfolio's life. We also assumed in the base case that no cash contributions or withdrawals occurred over time.

As for the tax rate, we noted that some investors pay nearly 50 percent marginal tax in combined federal, state, and local taxes whereas others, such as qualified nuclear decommissioning trusts (NDTs), pay as little as 20 percent.[4] In the simulations, we adopted a tax rate that is in the middle of the spectrum, 35 percent. This 35 percent assumption is exactly the federal rate that a corporate account would face. Individual investors are subject to differing long-term and short-term tax rates, and because of market appreciation, many of the losses will be at the more advantageous short-term rates. For simplicity, we did not explicitly consider different short-term and long-term tax rates, but this simplification should not have had a qualitative effect on our conclusions, although exact quantitative results would have varied. The interpretation of our results in light of the simplification is that the 50 percent taxpayer should care more about taxes than we suggest and the 20 percent taxpayer should care somewhat less.

To simulate the loss-harvesting strategy, we made three assumptions that minimized market friction and had marginal effects on the results.

- We assumed that transaction costs are zero and that the portfolio manager has no ability to discern which stocks are likely to perform well or badly. Under this assumption, we realized losses whenever the market price fell below the purchase price of a holding or exceeded the sale price of a short position. The impact of this assumption should not be large, because the turnover of a tax-advantaged portfolio is fairly low after the first few years. The effect of assuming zero transaction costs was that our turnover was larger than would actually be realized; a large number of trades were conducted for only slight loss realization. An actual managed tax-advantaged program would obviously sell only when the loss exceeded some threshold; selling at the first penny of loss is, to borrow a cliche, "penny wise and pound foolish."
- We assumed that we were not constrained by the wash sale rule. This assumption effectively took away the risk associated with loss harvesting; we could sell a stock at a loss and then buy it back immediately. Although the assumption might have produced a higher tax benefit from loss realization than in reality, the overstatement should be marginal because we could always purchase stocks that shared similar risk and return characteristics as the stocks we sold at a loss to achieve a similar effect.
- We assumed that the tax alpha created by harvesting losses could be treated as cash and reinvested in the portfolio. This assumption is reasonable because tax savings from loss harvesting provide a nearly immediate cash flow benefit. Whether dealing with corporate quarterly tax estimates or an individual investor's quarterly tax estimates, one can garner the benefit of tax savings from loss harvesting almost immediately. Consider, for example, a high-net-worth individual with assets in both a high-returning but tax-inefficient hedge fund and a tax-efficient S&P 500 fund similar to what we describe in this chapter. The losses realized from the S&P 500 portfolio translate directly into tax savings on the realized gains of the hedge fund, and this saved money can continue to remain invested.

One assumption we did not make is the presence of momentum (Jegadeesh and Titman 1993). A strategy that keeps winners and sells losers tends to acquire a momentum bias. Although the presence of short-term reversals would hurt such a strategy, longer-term gains from positive momentum should ultimately have a positive impact on performance—as long as the historical tendency for markets to exhibit momentum persists. For example, Chincarini and Kim (2001) found that momentum effects would have been beneficial to a tax-aware investor during the 1990s. We assumed this added value to be zero; our tax-efficient and naive portfolios have identical pretax returns.

In each simulation, we generated three portfolios.

- *Portfolio One* is a simple buy-and-hold portfolio with cost-averaging accounting, in which liquidations are presumed to have the average cost basis of the holding.
- *Portfolio Two* is a buy-and-hold portfolio with HIFO accounting.
- *Portfolio Three* is a tax-advantaged portfolio that incorporates both loss harvesting and HIFO accounting.

In each portfolio, for each month of each simulation, we tracked the three portfolio values in two ways: (1) gross value of the portfolio and (2) net value after subtracting the deferred taxes that remained unpaid. The latter measure is the net-of-tax liquidation value of the portfolio.

In the tax-advantaged portfolio, we swept through the portfolio each month to find all assets that had losses, sold those, and bought them back immediately (because we assumed away the wash sale rule). In the event of sales, we always sold the shares with the highest cost basis first, as the HIFO accounting strategy suggests. Once every quarter, we took any tax obligations from dividends and realized gains out of the portfolio and reinvested any tax savings from loss harvesting back into the portfolio. We repeated this exercise 500 times to generate a distribution of portfolio performance for the 25-year period.

Base-Case Results

The tax benefit of HIFO accounting alone is the difference between the market values of Portfolio Two and Portfolio One; the value added to the HIFO strategy by loss harvesting is the difference between the market value of Portfolio Three and Portfolio Two. The results of these base-case simulations reveal how much value these two strategies can add in normal market conditions.

Figure 14.1 and Figure 14.2 plot the 25th percentile, 50th percentile, and 75th percentile cumulative value added (before liquidation) of, respectively, the HIFO accounting strategy

FIGURE 14.1   Cumulative Alpha of HIFO Accounting Strategy

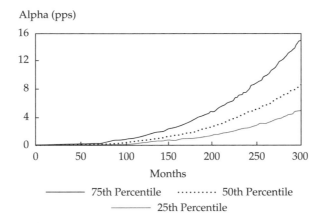

FIGURE 14.2   Cumulative Alpha of Loss Harvesting

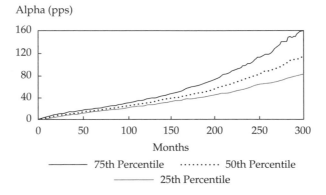

(Portfolio Two return minus Portfolio One return) and the loss-harvesting strategy (Portfolio Three return minus Portfolio Two return). As Figure 14.1 shows, the median cumulative tax benefit of HIFO accounting over the 25 years is a modest (but useful) 8.6 pps. Because of the limited selling that occurs with a buy-and-hold strategy, the accounting method has little impact in this base case (as the later analyses show, it has a much greater impact when cash flows are considered). The median cumulative benefit of the loss-harvesting strategy, shown in Figure 14.2, is a far more impressive 115 pps, much of which is from reinvestment and market appreciation over the years. The median cumulative value added by using both tax-efficient accounting and loss harvesting is 122 pps. If each loss-harvesting opportunity had been viewed as a chance to take out an interest-free loan (because most of these loans are taken out in the early years), then a tremendous amount of benefit would have accumulated after 25 years.

In our previous published articles (e.g., Arnott, Berkin, and Ye 2001b), we quoted a median 27 percent value added before liquidation for the tax-efficient portfolio versus a standard buy-and-hold strategy. This value is, of course, much lower than the 122 pps gain shown here, but the two results are equivalent. The difference lies in accounting. In the study reported in one of our previously published paper, we used a ratio of final portfolio values, which is 1.27. Here, we calculated the return of each portfolio for each time period as the final portfolio value for that time minus the cash flow during the period divided by the initial portfolio value. The returns for each portfolio were then accumulated geometrically, and the difference between the tax-advantaged portfolio's return and that of the standard portfolio is the value added.[5] In essence, in this chapter, we were comparing value added with the original portfolio amount by using cumulative return comparisons. Not only is this metric standard accounting, it is indispensable for considering cash flows, which we report later.

One concern investors may have about the loss-harvesting strategy is that the opportunity for loss realization could diminish as the portfolio ages (because the market goes up more often than down over the long run). Indeed, Figure 14.3 shows that a great deal of the benefit from loss harvesting is generated during the first few years. A typical alpha from loss harvesting can be as large as 7 pps in the first year of a program for a portfolio that is funded initially with cash. It quickly diminishes, however, falling to below 2 pps a year before three years are finished and to below 1 pp a year before five years are finished. Yet even after 25 years, the median tax alpha is still adding about 0.3 pp a year to portfolio wealth, an alpha that most active managers cannot add reliably before tax, let alone after tax.

FIGURE 14.3   Annualized Alpha of Loss Harvesting before Liquidation Taxes

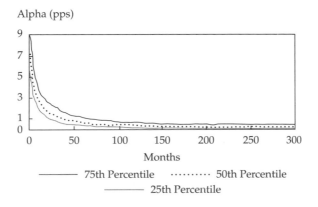

FIGURE 14.4   Annualized Alpha of Loss Harvesting after Liquidation Taxes

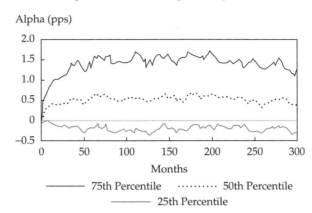

Alpha (pps)

FIGURE 14.5   Annualized Turnover of the Loss-Harvesting Strategy

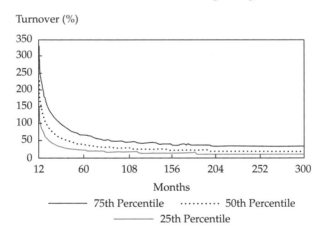

Turnover (%)

Another concern is that the realization of losses over time gradually reduces the cost basis of portfolio holdings, which may mean more tax obligation at the time of portfolio liquidation. To address this concern, we calculated the after-tax benefit of loss harvesting, net of all liquidation taxes, each month. The annualized results are presented in Figure 14.4. Here, we find a much more moderate early benefit (compared with Figure 14.3) from loss harvesting, indicating that the benefit of loss harvesting is almost exactly offset by a higher tax bill owed on liquidation. The "interest-free loan" of loss harvesting has not yet, in the early months, had time to accumulate returns. But the value added quickly stabilizes after three years to a median of 0.5 pps. When liquidating after 25 years, the cumulative value added is an impressive 58 pps.

Not surprisingly, the turnover generated by a loss-harvesting strategy is high at first, as shown in Figure 14.5, because the prices of almost half the stocks in the starting portfolio fall. As those assets fall in value and the losses are harvested, the proceeds are reinvested in new assets, almost half of which also fall, and so forth. This pattern has two implications. The first is that an assiduous effort to harvest losses is highly rewarding. The so-called tax-sensitive investment manager who engages in loss harvesting only once a year at the end of a fiscal year has probably seen numerous loss-harvesting opportunities appear and disappear during the course of that year. The second implication is that a "virtuous cycle" occurs in any sort of assiduous effort to harvest losses whenever they occur and whenever the tax alpha is large enough to justify the round-trip trading costs for the investor. The more careful one is to pounce on any meaningful loss-harvesting opportunity, the longer the opportunities linger into the future because of the new loss-harvesting opportunities created from the reinvestment of loss-harvesting proceeds. This pattern is illustrated in Figure 14.5, which shows substantial annualized turnover for the first year of a loss-harvesting program, with the turnover diminishing sharply over the next five years and then, remarkably, stabilizing over the next 20 years at a level higher than the level explained by corporate actions.

Varying Market Conditions

The Monte Carlo simulations presented in the previous section depended on the base-case assumptions. We used historically typical market conditions, which obviously may not persist into the future. In this section, we describe our explorations of the benefits of tax-efficient investing in a variety of market environments; for example:

- What if stock price volatility rises or falls?
- What if our assumption of returns is too aggressive or too conservative?
- What if the dividend yield changes?

We addressed these questions by running Monte Carlo simulations with varying assumptions. The simulations' results, of which we focus mainly on after-liquidation tax benefits, shed light on the robustness of the loss-harvesting and HIFO accounting strategies. In this section, we combine treatment of the loss-harvesting strategy and the HIFO accounting strategy, and the analysis deals with tax-advantaged portfolios that incorporate both. As noted previously, without cash flow, the benefits of HIFO accounting are modest, so not only does this approach simplify the presentation, but it also optimizes tax benefits. We also focus the discussion on the after-liquidation tax benefit, which is most appropriate for investors who will eventually liquidate; thus, we present a conservative view of how tax-efficient strategies can add value.

Risk

We first examined how the risk of stocks, either systematic or idiosyncratic, affects the performance of the tax-efficient strategy. We expected the tax-advantaged strategy to generate more value when stocks are more turbulent because more opportunities to harvest losses should appear when stock prices are volatile. In a similar vein, Brunel (1997) recommended that active managers take a positive volatility tilt, all else being equal, to increase loss-harvesting opportunities. In Panel A of Table 14.1, we show the average annualized alpha after liquidation for three levels of stock-specific volatility. We calculated the average alpha for three periods—the full 25 years, the first 5 years, and the last 5 years. Market volatility in this simulation was assumed to be uniform at 4.3 percent monthly. In Panel A, the stock-specific risk is varied down or up from the historical norm of 9 percent monthly residual volatility, given in the middle column.

We found that the average annual alpha, net of all liquidation taxes, over 25 years fell from 56 bps to 42 bps when we lowered the specific risk from 9 percent to 7 percent. If idiosyncratic (residual) risk was 2 pps higher than the historical norm, the alpha rose to 66 bps,

TABLE 14.1   Impact of Risk on Average Annualized Alpha after Liquidation Taxes

A. Impact of Idiosyncratic Risk

Period	7% Specific Risk	9% Specific Risk (base case)	11% Specific Risk
25 years	42 bps	56 bps	66 bps
First 5 years	30	42	49
Last 5 years	47	53	67

B. Impact of Systematic Risk

Period	3% Systematic Risk	4.3% Systematic Risk (base case)	5.6% Systematic Risk
25 years	54 bps	56 bps	52 bps
First 5 years	39	42	37
Last 5 years	55	53	59

on average, over 25 years. A comparison between the average alpha for the first five years and that for the last five years shows that the distribution of value added is not uniform over time. Not surprisingly, a long holding horizon is more tax efficient than a short horizon. These results are encouraging in light of the growing consensus that the quiet markets from the mid-1980s through the mid-1990s were anomalous and that increased volatility, particularly this sort of cross-sectional risk caused by the idiosyncratic variation of individual stocks, is here to stay.

Panel B of Table 14.1 shows the results for variation in marketwide volatility from the base case of 4.3 percent a month. In contrast to stock-specific risk, marketwide volatility has a mixed effect on the efficiency of the tax-advantaged portfolio; high systematic volatility does not necessarily lead to better opportunity in tax management. This result may come as a surprise, but it should not: The key source of loss-harvesting opportunities will be cross-sectional risk, not systematic market risk. Systematic risk drives the broad market return across time, whereas cross-sectional risk leads to loss-harvesting opportunities in every period. Because risk is symmetrical by our definition, for every month with low average market returns and ample loss-harvesting opportunities, there will be other months with large returns and minimal lots in which to harvest losses.

Market Returns

Our next investigation was the impact of the average market return. Recall that the base case had an average annual market return (or total return equal to price return plus dividend yield) of about 8 percent. Returns in the 1990s were, of course, much higher. Although few analysts expect such high returns to continue over the next 25 years, expectations vary greatly. Indeed, various articles suggest that expectations should be sharply reduced, relative to long-term past returns, because of the low dividend yield and earnings yield levels for the markets today (Arnott and Ryan 2001; Arnott and Bernstein 2002). We ran three sets of simulations (500 simulations in each set) under the assumption of average market returns of 5 percent (the expectation in the Arnott–Ryan and Arnott–Bernstein articles), 8 percent (the base case), and 11 percent (the base case used by William Sharpe's Financial Engines organization,

FIGURE 14.6   Impact of Market Returns: Median Cumulative Alpha after Liquidation Taxes

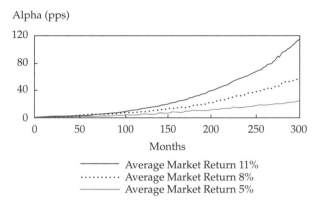

FIGURE 14.7   Impact of Market Returns: Median Annualized Alpha before Liquidation Taxes

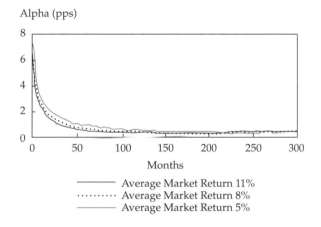

www.financial-engines.com). The median cumulative after-liquidation value added for each market-return scenario is plotted in Figure 14.6. The graphs in Figure 14.6 show that the more the market appreciates, the greater the cumulative tax benefit is. This result is not as surprising as it may seem; it is a consequence of a pure compounding effect, in that with a higher market appreciation rate, the tax benefit is compounded faster.

Of course, greater loss-harvesting *opportunity* should be expected when the market has lower returns, and indeed, this intuition is confirmed in Figure 14.7, where the median annualized value added of the tax-advantaged portfolios is plotted. Figure 14.7 shows that the benefit of the tax-efficient strategies is negatively related to the level of market appreciation during the first few years and then converges over time. More loss harvesting does indeed occur when market returns are lower; the median annualized benefit is up to 1 pp higher as the scenario varies from the lowest to the highest market return.

Dividend Rates

What happens to the returns from loss harvesting if the overall average total return remains fixed but dividends vary from the base case? This question is important because dividend yields of stocks marketwide have dropped sharply in the past 20 years—from more than 5 percent a

TABLE 14.2   Impact of Dividend Yield on Average Annualized Alpha after Liquidation Taxes

Period	0.08% a Month	0.12% a Month (base case)	0.16% a Month
25 years	50 bps	56 bps	55 bps
First 5 years	42	42	38
Last 5 years	54	53	58

year in 1982 to 1.5 percent in 2002. High dividend yields should have a mixed effect on the benefits of a tax-efficient strategy relative to a naive buy-and-hold strategy: On the one hand, the dividends paid are reinvested in new shares at a zero cost basis, which increases loss-harvesting possibilities in the future as some of those assets decline in value; on the other hand, dividends experience an immediate tax hit, which reduces the tax efficiency of all portfolios equally.

Table 14.2 is a report of the average annualized alpha after liquidation for dividend rates of 0.08 percent and 0.16 percent a month as well as the base case of 0.12 percent a month. Higher dividend rates in the simulations did increase opportunities for loss harvesting, but the greater tax drag accompanying the beneficial effects resulted in not much difference between the two higher-yield cases. Also note that, in reality, different stocks have different dividend yields and these yields are persistent. Consequently, tax-aware active managers can take an appropriate yield tilt. Individual investors, for example, will prefer to avoid high-yielding assets and their immediate short-term tax burden. Corporate investors, however, typically receive a dividend exclusion and hence may be better off with a high-yield tilt.

Varying Portfolio Conditions

We have so far explored various market conditions to see their impact on a tax-advantaged investment strategy compared with a standard buy-and-hold strategy. Tax-advantaged investing always produces significantly favorable returns, no matter the market scenario. This finding is comforting because although market conditions are not known in advance, taxable investors can know that they should always manage with loss harvesting and HIFO accounting. But the final outcome of tax-aware investing is also affected by factors that investors or managers may have some control over. For example:

- What if the turnover in the index is greater than we assumed because of more corporate actions or more active changes in the composition of the benchmark?
- What if additional cash is regularly contributed to the portfolio over time?
- How about withdrawals?
- What if tax rates are higher or lower?

Turnover

The composition of an index changes because of corporate actions (e.g., bankruptcies, mergers, and acquisitions). It may also change as a consequence of decisions made by the managers of the index itself. Standard & Poor's sometimes makes conscious decisions to delete small or less important companies to make room for new, large-capitalization, bellwether companies. The same happens on an even larger scale in the Russell indexes, where the composition varies annually with changes in market caps.

Our base case assumed that 1 out of the 500 stocks vanished every month, equivalent to an average 2.4 percent annual turnover associated with corporate actions in the hypothetical

TABLE 14.3   Impact of Index Changes on Average Annualized Alpha after Liquidation Taxes

Period	One a Month (base case)	Two a Month	Four a Month
25 years	56 bps	55 bps	54 bps
First 5 years	42	42	39
Last 5 years	53	62	57

S&P 500. This turnover was typical for the S&P 500 itself until the mid-1990s. Recent turnover in the actual S&P 500, however, has been notably higher than the base-case rate, typically 5–11 percent in names and 5–9 percent in market cap since the mid-1990s (Credit Suisse First Boston 2002). In this section, therefore, we consider two cases—one in which the effective "index turnover" is two times (4.8 percent) the pace of the base case and one in which it is four times (9.6 percent) the pace of the base case.

We assumed that the tax-aware portfolios had to match all index changes. As the index composition changes, a benchmark will be forced to liquidate holdings whether they are well above cost basis or not. Often, a tax-advantaged investor does not face such an onerous obligation. Active managers will not hold every stock in the index and also may choose to retain the shares of an acquiring company (e.g., keep Daimler after its acquisition of Chrysler). In the simulations we ran, however, we made a conservative assumption that liquidation was also mandatory for the tax-advantaged portfolios in the event of index rebalancing. This assumption obviously reduced the advantage of a tax-efficient portfolio because it had to liquidate the stock and incur the tax obligations sooner than intended. The simulation results for these scenarios with increased turnover costs, shown in Table 14.3, suggest that the tax benefit is slightly less when the index turns over more frequently, but the difference is modest enough to be erased with a more liberal assumption about the behavior of the managers of tax-efficient portfolios. We thus conclude that turnover in a broad market index such as the S&P 500 does not have a significant impact on the effectiveness of tax-advantaged strategies.

Some indexes are not tax efficient because they have far greater turnover than we have assumed, and high turnover is likely to lead to the realization of capital gains. For example, the Russell 2000 can have well more than 20 percent turnover in its annual reconstitution at the end of June, when the largest components are promoted to the Russell 1000. The turnover in the growth and value portions can exceed 40 percent from style reclassification. An investor who desires exposure to smaller-cap stocks, for example, would be better off using an index such as the Russell 3000.

Some taxable investors, however, may *want* a high-turnover index. For example, investors seeking a broad market exposure might be interested in only small-cap, low-cost-basis equities if they already have a great deal of money in large-cap stocks. In these cases, active tax management can nevertheless have large benefits. Loss harvesting can offset gains realized on stocks sold when they leave the index, and the purchase of new stocks entering the index increases the likelihood of further loss harvesting. Reinvested cash can be used to buy stocks likely to enter the index, and stocks likely to leave can be avoided. The sale of stocks leaving the index can be delayed if the sale will turn a short-term gain into a long-term one. And, of course, one can simply not sell the stocks when they leave the index. Ultimately, for an index with high turnover, the issue is the trade-off between tax efficiency and tracking error. This choice is up to the investor and not within the scope of this chapter.

The trade-off between tax efficiency and tracking error is part of the issue of portfolio lockup, which arises when gains are deferred and the increase in the market value of the portfolio becomes substantially larger than its cost basis. For passive investors, deferring gains comes at the expense of increased risk as the portfolio deviates from its benchmark, although having an appropriate benchmark minimizes this danger. For active investors, lockup involves the trade-off between tax efficiency and the quest for additional alpha. As we have noted (Arnott, Berkin, and Ye 2000), making the trade-off, given the high cost of taxes and the uncertainty of alpha, can be a difficult task. But the techniques outlined in this chapter can help offset the tax burden. Figures 14.4 and 14.5 show that even in passive portfolios, loss-harvesting opportunities persist well into the future. For active portfolios, greater turnover will lead to even more opportunities for tax management, because even the best managers have some stocks that will decline in value.

Cash Flows

The ultimate benefit of tax-efficient investing can be drastically affected by cash flows into and out of the portfolio, and in this case, unlike the case of market conditions, the investor may have a reasonable idea of what to expect. For example, NDTs may experience fairly steady inflows during the life of the nuclear plant, and some individual investors may regularly take cash out of a portfolio for living expenses. Mutual funds have both contributions and redemptions. Therefore, we turned our attention to exploring these effects through simulations.

The simulation results based on different levels of cash contributions before liquidation taxes are in Panel A of Table 14.4. In addition to the base case of no contributions, we also considered constant contributions of 0.5 percent and 1.0 percent of the benchmark portfolio value a month.[6] As is clearly shown, the value added before liquidation increases with the amount of cash contribution. Each time cash is infused, more shares are bought at a higher cost basis. This strategy creates many more opportunities for loss harvesting than in the zero-contribution case, where most of the shares were purchased in the first few periods at a low cost basis.

Interestingly, although the benefits of loss harvesting are enhanced by cash inflows prior to liquidation, the impact is reversed after liquidation, as Panel B of Table 14.4 shows. This result is not surprising because the cash contribution effectively raises the cost basis in a portfolio. The impact of the increased cost basis is clearly nonlinear. The benchmark portfolio, being less tax efficient than the tax-advantaged portfolio, benefits from the higher cost basis much more than the tax-efficient portfolio does.

TABLE 14.4   Impact of Cash Contributions on Average Annualized Alpha before and after Liquidation Taxes

Period	0% Contribution (base case)	0.5% Contribution	1% Contribution
A. Before Liquidation Taxes			
25 years	74 bps	121 bps	169 bps
First 5 years	210	241	270
Last 5 years	40	90	147
B. After Liquidation Taxes			
25 years	56 bps	51 bps	49 bps
First 5 years	42	37	38
Last 5 years	53	55	48

TABLE 14.5   Impact of Cash Withdrawal on Average Annualized Alpha before and after Liquidation Taxes

Period	0% Withdrawal (base case)	0.1% Withdrawal	0.25% Withdrawal
A. Before Liquidation Taxes			
25 years	74 bps	66 bps	54 bps
First 5 years	210	207	194
Last 5 years	40	30	26
B. After Liquidation Taxes			
25 years	56 bps	54 bps	54 bps
First 5 years	42	41	41
Last 5 years	53	57	58

We next considered the opposite situation, cash withdrawals. The results are shown in Table 14.5. Panel A clearly shows that cash outflows reduce the benefit of the tax-advantaged portfolios before liquidation. These results are intuitive because withdrawal forces the realization of capital gains. Given that the tax-advantaged strategy has a lower cost basis than the benchmark because of loss harvesting, the forced capital gain realization has a more negative impact on the tax-advantaged portfolio than on the benchmark portfolio. Furthermore, the withdrawals reduce the opportunity for loss harvesting later because some of the shares sold might have fluctuated below their purchase price in the future. This outcome is the exact opposite of the case with contributions.

The simulations with cash withdrawals also provide good evidence of the benefit of HIFO accounting. The tax-advantaged portfolios sold shares on a HIFO basis, realizing the least gains and allowing the largest possible portfolio value to continue to accrue market appreciation. In contrast, the benchmark portfolio used cost averaging, which led to a larger capital gains tax than in the HIFO accounting method. The value added of HIFO accounting is readily seen in Panel B of Table 14.5. The negative effect of cash withdrawal largely disappears after liquidation taxes have been subtracted, and the tax-advantaged cases with many securities sold on a HIFO basis all outperform their tax-naive counterparts no matter the amount of withdrawal.

We also ran simulations in which both cash inflows and outflows occurred. In these cases, each month, a random amount of cash was added or removed from the portfolios, with a mean of 0 and different variance for each set of simulations. Prior to liquidation, the average annual alpha increased as cash flows were increased, going from 74 bps to 85 bps and 98 bps over 25 years as the flows grew from 0 percent to 1 percent to 2 percent of the benchmark portfolio a month. Such figures are reasonable in light of our prior results. When cash comes in, it creates new loss-harvesting opportunities, and the subsequent benefit overrides the tax drag of forced liquidation when cash is withdrawn. After liquidation, the value added rose from 56 bps to 66 bps as cash flow variance went from 0 percent to 2 percent.

Tax Rates

Finally, we tested the impact of marginal tax rates on the benefits of tax-aware investing. As shown in Table 14.6, the *before-liquidation* tax advantage associated with our tax-efficient portfolios (Panel A) is roughly linearly related to tax rates. The marginal benefit of our strategies narrows

TABLE 14.6　Impact of Tax Rates on Average Annualized Alpha before and after Liquidation Taxes

Period	20% Tax Rate	35% Tax Rate	50% Tax Rate
A. Before Liquidation Taxes			
25 years	40 bps	73 bps	115 bps
First 5 years	116	209	304
Last 5 years	21	40	65
B. After Liquidation Taxes			
25 years	31 bps	56 bps	74 bps
First 5 years	26	42	48
Last 5 years	27	52	82

with the tax rate, however, on an *after-liquidation* basis (Panel B). For an investor in a 35 percent tax bracket, the tax-advantaged strategies yield an average annualized alpha of 73 bps over 25 years before liquidation and 56 bps after liquidation. This gain is impressive. For the investor in the 50 percent marginal tax bracket, the improvement leaps to, respectively, 115 bps and 74 bps.

Keep in mind that to achieve that 74 bp benefit with conventional active investing, one would have to earn a 148 bp alpha with no capital gains taxes on those trades, which most observers of active investing would consider nearly impossible. In "How Well Have Taxable Investors Been Served in the 1980s and 1990s?" (Arnott, Berkin, and Ye 2000), we found that only 5 percent of all funds outpaced the S&P 500 on an after-tax basis, with an average margin of victory of a scant 74 bps; so a 148 bp after-tax alpha is not a plausible target for most active managers—unless they place tax management at the very top of their asset management priorities. Surprisingly, even for the investor in a modest 20 percent tax bracket, Table 14.6 shows that the average annual alpha of loss harvesting and HIFO accounting over 25 years is still a lofty 40 bps before liquidation and 31 bps after liquidation.

CONCLUSION

We simulated monthly returns over 25 years for index portfolios, run both efficiently and naively with respect to taxes. The tax-efficient manager used HIFO accounting and harvested all losses, whereas the naive manager used cost averaging and simply held positions at a loss. We used standard market conditions for our base case and then varied those parameters to study their effects.

Our main finding is that no matter the environment, managing a portfolio in a tax-efficient manner provides substantially better after-tax performance than a simple index fund, both before and after liquidation of the portfolio. Active management would need to deliver a startlingly large alpha without triggering capital gains taxes merely to match a simple loss-harvesting strategy.

Taxes matter—a lot. But at least they are the one aspect of asset management known with certainty in advance, and therefore, portfolios can be managed effectively to minimize the tax impact.

NOTES

1. We do not consider the effects of yield management. Our approach is to consider portfolios that exactly replicate the index, which would not be possible with a dividend tilt. We note that in today's low-dividend environment, yield management is less important; in the subsection called "Varying Market Conditions," we show that the overall market dividend rate has little influence on the efficacy of tax-efficient investing.

2. One should take into account not only the round-trip trading costs but also the net present value of the extra tax that will have to be paid on eventual liquidation, because realizing a loss lowers the cost basis of the portfolio.

3. For a discussion of the tax effects on benchmark returns from corporate activity, see Minck (1998).

4. Most investors do not realize that with a top federal tax bracket of 38.6 percent, marginal rates can rise to almost 50 percent. It can happen as follows: Top-tax states range as high as 10 percent, and even with federal deductibility, 6.2 percent is added to the total tax bill, pushing marginal taxation to 44.8 percent. Itemized deduction phase-outs—at 3 percent for federal taxes, 6 percent in California, to cite one example—cost, respectively, 1.2 percent and 0.4 percent, which brings the total to 46.4 percent. For the self-employed, the Medicare portion of social security employer taxes, at 2.9 percent on uncapped gross earned income, pushes the total to 49.3 percent. For high-bracket corporate employees, this uncapped Social Security tax is still paid, but it is hidden from the employee's view as an "employer's share" of the tax bill.

5. Specifically, the median returns of the two portfolios are 472 percent for the tax-advantaged portfolio and 350 percent for the standard portfolio, for a difference of 122 pps. The ratio of final values would then be 5.72/4.50, or 1.27. Our previous papers used the more conservative "relative wealth" approach to measuring the value added from loss harvesting. In this chapter, we use the more aggressive, *but more widely accepted*, "cumulative return differences" approach, which would be the AIMR-compliant measure if these were live composite results rather than a simulation.

6. We could as easily have used a percentage of the tax-advantaged portfolio; the important point is that the same amount of money was added to both portfolios for a fair comparison.

REFERENCES

AIMR. 2001. "AIMR Performance Presentation Standards (AIMR-PPS®)," amended and restated as the AIMR-PPS® Standards, the U.S. and Canadian version of GIPS®: www.aimr.org/pdf/standards/aftertax_changes.pdf.

Apelfeld, Roberto, Gordon B. Fowler, Jr., and James P. Gordon, Jr. 1996. "Tax-Aware Equity Investing." *Journal of Portfolio Management*, vol. 22, no. 2 (Winter):18–28.

Arnott, Robert D., Andrew L. Berkin, and Jia Ye. 2000. "How Well Have Taxable Investors Been Served in the 1980s and 1990s?" *Journal of Portfolio Management*, vol. 26, no. 4 (Summer):84–94.

———. 2001a. "The Management and Mismanagement of Taxable Assets." *Journal of Investing*, vol. 10, no. 1 (Spring):15–21.

———. 2001b. "Loss Harvesting: What's It Worth to the Taxable Investor?" *Journal of Wealth Management*, vol. 3, no. 4 (Spring):10–18.

Arnott, Robert D., and Peter L. Bernstein. 2002. "What Risk Premium Is 'Normal'?" *Financial Analysts Journal*, vol. 58, no. 2 (March/April):64–85.

Arnott, Robert D., and Ronald Ryan. 2001. "The Death of the Risk Premium: Consequences of the 1990s." *Journal of Portfolio Management*, vol. 27, no. 3 (Spring):61–74.

Brunel, Jean. 1997. "The Upside-Down World of Tax-Aware Investing." *Trusts and Estates* (February):34–42.

———. 2000. "An Approach to After-Tax Performance Benchmarking." *Journal of Wealth Management*, vol. 3, no. 3 (Winter):61–67.

Chincarini, Ludwig, and Daehwan Kim. 2001. "The Advantages of Tax-Managed Investing." *Journal of Portfolio Management*, vol. 28, no. 1 (Fall):56–72.

Credit Suisse First Boston. 2002. "Index Watch" (14 January).

Dickson, Joel M., and John B. Shoven. 1993. "Ranking Mutual Funds on an After-Tax Basis." National Bureau of Economic Research (NBER) Working Paper No. 4393.

———. 1994. "A Stock Index Mutual Fund without Net Capital Gains Realizations." NBER working paper (April).

Jeffrey, Robert H., and Robert D. Arnott. 1993. "Is Your Alpha Big Enough to Cover Its Taxes?" *Journal of Portfolio Management*, vol. 19, no. 3 (Spring):15–25.

Jegadeesh, N., and S. Titman. 1993. "Returns to Buying Winners and Selling Losers: Implications for Stock Market Efficiency." *Journal of Finance*, vol. 48, no. 1 (March):65–91.

Minck, Jeffrey L. 1998. "Tax-Adjusted Equity Benchmarks." *Journal of Private Portfolio Management* (Summer):41–50.

Sharpe, William F. 1964. "Capital Asset Prices: A Theory of Market Equilibrium under Conditions of Risk." *Journal of Finance*, vol. 19, no. 3 (September):425–442.

Stein, David M. 1998. "Measuring and Evaluating Portfolio Performance after Taxes." *Journal of Portfolio Management*, vol. 25, no. 2 (Winter):117–124.

Stein, David M., and Premkumar Narasimhan. 1999. "Of Passive and Active Equity Portfolios in the Presence of Taxes." *Journal of Private Portfolio Management*, vol. 2, no. 2 (Fall):55–63.

U.S. SEC. 2001. "Disclosure of Mutual Fund After-Tax Returns," www.sec.gov/rules/final/33-7941.htm.

CHAPTER 15

INVESTING WITH A TAX-EFFICIENT EYE

Robert N. Gordon

Investors can gain exposure to a bond or stock in many ways—some of which are tax efficient and some of which are not. For instance, bond investors can realize long-term gains today and pay less tax overall tomorrow. And depending on the length of their investment horizon, equity investors can follow one of three tax-efficient strategies. Anomalies in the tax code also allow derivatives, especially options and swaps, to mitigate tax liability without altering investment returns. And finally, investors in collective investments, such as mutual funds and hedge funds, can use tax-efficient strategies as well.

In this presentation, I discuss a number of transactions, some of which may be unfamiliar. By including the unfamiliar, I hope to open advisors' minds to new ways of managing taxable clients' portfolios through the use of innovative transactions to improve after-tax performance. In my experience, portfolio managers tend to resist complex transactions, especially those involving derivatives and that require time and patience not only to explain to clients but also to properly construct. But I believe that advisors owe it to their clients to explore ways to improve the tax efficiency of their portfolios, whether their holdings are individual securities or collective investments, such as mutual funds and hedge funds. Fortunately, anomalies within the U.S. tax code enable savvy advisors to improve their clients' after-tax performance.

ACADEMIC FINDINGS

Groundbreaking research by Arnott, Berkin, and Ye found that investors should care about taxes and that they ought to have a disciplined approach to harvesting tax losses.[1] But do individual investors care about taxes? Two studies of tax efficiency of individual investors'

Reprinted from *CFA Institute Conference Proceedings: Wealth Management* (October 2005):31–40.

portfolios shed some light. Barber and Odean used data from 1994 and 1998 to investigate the tax awareness of individual investors.[2] For part of their study, they analyzed stock trades at a large discount brokerage house of tens of thousands of individual investors, many of whom had both taxable and tax-deferred accounts, such as individual retirement accounts and Keogh plans. They found that most individuals could improve their trading efficiency. For example, taxable investors took their gains more frequently than their losses. Interestingly, the researchers further observed that this behavior was almost double for married couples compared with the behavior of singles.

Ivković, Poterba, and Weisbenner studied whether tax incentives influence how investors realize capital gains and losses. They used the same trading data as Barber and Odean for a large discount brokerage house but for a six-year sample period from 1991 to 1996.[3] Ivković, Poterba, and Weisbenner compared the portfolio transactions made by the same person in two different accounts: the regular, taxable account and the tax-deferred account. They found stronger evidence than Barber and Odean did that investors care about tax. For example, they found a higher tendency for capital gains to be unrealized in taxable accounts than in tax-deferred accounts. This tendency was stronger for larger transactions and intensified as the investor's holding period lengthened. Individual investors were somewhat efficient in that tax-loss selling occurred throughout the year, although it was most pronounced in December, especially if an investor had realized capital gains earlier in the year. Collectively, this analysis of the same dataset implies that investors trade in ways that are tax efficient. Nonetheless, Ivković, Poterba, and Weisbenner were disappointed: At times, they found tax-exempt municipal bonds in the IRA account, meaning that asset allocation between taxable and tax-deferred accounts was suboptimal.

So, if these studies suggest that investors care about tax, then so should brokerage firms. In fact, given that clients could be trading in a suboptimal fashion, advisors perhaps have a duty to educate them. That is, advisors can find ways to implement tax-efficient trading strategies without distorting the investor's performance. Savvy practitioners on Wall Street have devised ways to replicate positions and synthesize investments. Pretax returns for the various positions and instruments may be the same, but the after-tax returns can be quite different. Thus, some investors ought to re-evaluate their positions and instruments to maximize their returns.

U.S. BOND STRATEGIES

Most brokerage firms, individual brokers, and investment advisors are well aware of bond swaps—the simultaneous sale of a bond with capital losses and purchase of another, similar bond. Near the end of the tax year, investors may hear: "Get out of your muni bond and switch into another bond and take the loss." Sometimes that transaction is genuinely in the client's best interest. But without being too cynical about the brokerage industry, of which I am a part, I would like to point out that getting out of one bond and into another provides a decent commission. Nevertheless, when interest rates are very low, investors should take their long-term gains on taxable bonds and then immediately repurchase those same bonds; there is no wash-sale rule for gains. Keep in mind that a brokerage house cannot charge an investor too much to sell a bond and to repurchase it immediately.

Although I am talking about trying to be tax efficient, advisors do not want to distort an investor's results. For example, say that several years ago an investor bought a U.S. Treasury note at par ($100) when interest rates were at 5 percent. Today, interest rates are at 2 percent and the note matures in one year. Theoretically, that bond will trade at $103.

If the investor does nothing, then in one year's time the $5 coupon will be taxed as ordinary investment income at rates as high as 35 percent. But if the investor sells the bond today at $103, and because it has been held for more than 12 months, the long-term capital gains tax of 15 percent applies to that $3. The wash-sale rules do not prevent an investor from realizing a capital gain. If an investor sells something and buys it back within the statutory 31 days and if the investor has a capital gain, the U.S. government is only too pleased to tax the investor on the gain. So, it is all right to sell the bond and buy it back a second later if the investor has a gain.[4]

When the investor repurchases this bond at $103, it trades at a premium because it will mature one year from today at $100. Under Section 171 of the IRS code, the federal government allows the investor to amortize the bond premium of $3. When the investor pays tax on investment income, the amount payable will be based on a gross 5 percent coupon, but the investor can deduct $3 of amortization against the $5. In essence, the investor is paying tax on only $2 of net interest rather than the full gross $5.

So, the investor faces two choices:

- Do nothing and pay a 35 percent ordinary investment income tax on $5, making the total tax payable $1.75, or
- Sell the bond and buy it back immediately, pay 15 percent long-term capital gains tax on $3, and pay a 35 percent tax on only $2, making the total tax payable $1.15.

Obviously, the investor is better off *voluntarily* paying the 15 percent long-term capital gains tax today in order to pay lower total tax in the future. Solely by selling and repurchasing this hypothetical government or corporate bond, this investor's tax bill is more than one-third lower than if he or she had done nothing. Clearly, this decision will influence the bond's after-tax performance.

If the bond in question were to mature 10 years from now, the investor could end up paying a large amount of tax today with the benefit spread out over the next 10 years. Therefore, the correct analysis would include the calculation of an internal rate of return (IRR) to derive the estimated benefit. Our analysis at Twenty-First Securities shows that if an investor lives in a high-tax state, such as New York (remember that the investor will pay state tax as well as federal tax), the after-tax IRR on a government bond due in 10 years is 11.72 percent.[5] This figure includes an eighth of a point for friction costs of getting in and out. If the bond were due in only one year, the after-tax IRR would become a breathtaking 74.96 percent—for doing nothing more than resetting the holding period.

The IRR analysis and sell/repurchase decision apply only to government bonds and corporate bonds, not to tax-free municipal bonds. One universal tax decision rule holds with respect to municipal bonds: *Do not engage in the sale and repurchase of the bond prior to maturity*.

Keep in mind an important caveat when analyzing a government bond: Effectively, the investor elects to pay a capital gains tax in the state where that interest income would have been tax-free later. Some nuances make the analysis more difficult than one might think.

S&P 500 INDEX STRATEGIES

A broad basket of large-cap equities, which can be proxied by the S&P 500 Index, is another basic building block that investors use in their portfolios. Please note that my discussion in this presentation is not about how to manage the individual securities in investors' portfolios more efficiently but, rather, how to choose the investment vehicles that are more efficient from a tax perspective.

Investors in recent years have embraced Standard & Poor's Depositary Receipts (SPDRs, or "Spiders"). SPDRs and the newer exchange-traded funds (ETFs), such as iShares, are a cost-effective way to quickly build a diversified portfolio. They are generally tax efficient *but only for long-term investors*. As Jeffrey Horvitz explained in his presentation, if an investor defers capital gains until death, then (as the tax laws read today) capital gains taxes can be forgiven upon the death of the investor.[6] So, if an investor can buy SPDRs or an ETF or even a mutual fund that minimizes distributions each year, then all the investor's unrecognized gains continue to grow and possibly can be forgiven at death.

It is estimated, however, that between 80 and 85 percent of all trading in SPDRs and iShares is done for fewer than 90 days. Therefore, profitable investors would be taxed at 35 percent, the rate for short-term capital gains. The implication is that investors are drawn to these popular vehicles not by the prospect of tax efficiency but, rather, by aggressive marketing campaigns. To get any tax efficiency, investors must commit to an investment horizon greater than one year. Indeed, at the extreme, the tax efficiency is maximized when an investor purchases a SPDR or ETF and holds it forever. Still, advisors can find tax-efficient vehicles for those taxable investors with short time horizons.

Time Horizon Impact on Strategies

Investors can own the S&P 500 in many ways, so at Twenty-First Securities, we determine the most tax-efficient investment vehicle by time horizon, as shown in Figure 15.1.

Horizon Less Than One Year

If an investor will be in and out of the S&P 500 in less than one year, then as I have explained, the SPDR will be taxed at 35 percent. But if the investor seeks exposure through

FIGURE 15.1   Effect of Time Horizon on Choice of Investment Vehicle

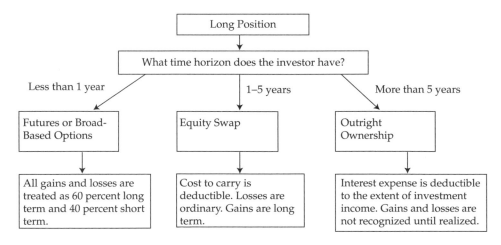

exchange-traded index options, realized gains will be taxed at a blended capital gains rate of only 23 percent.[7] So, if an investor will be invested for less than a year, index options make a lot of sense. Compared with a mutual fund, options do not distribute any gain, so even if a stock leaves the S&P 500, there will not be a recognized gain on an index option; a mutual fund will have some gains to pay as it removes that stock from its portfolio. The return of the S&P 500 can be replicated, more or less, with a deep in-the-money index option (options that are in the money behave more like the underlying than those that are out of the money). Although the pretax returns of a SPDR and an index option are the same, the after-tax returns will be different because of the quirkiness of U.S. federal tax law.

So, with index options, the investor chooses to be taxed at 23 percent if he or she makes money. If the investor loses money, however, he or she is burdened because only 40 percent of the capital loss will be calculated at the higher short-term tax rate of 35 percent and 60 percent of the loss will be calculated at the lower long-term tax rate of 15 percent, again yielding a blended tax rate of 23 percent.

My discussion so far has been on bullish sentiment—when one thinks the market will go higher. I will now discuss tax efficiency using options for bearish strategies. Investors consider short sales to be un-American (and so does the IRS). If an investor makes a short sale, no matter how long the holding period until a gain is realized, it will always be taxed as a short-term gain. When the investor owns a listed put from an exchange, the capital gains will be taxed at the now-familiar blended rate of 23 percent. But if the investor had bought a put from a dealer, then any short-term gains would have been taxed at 35 percent and the long-term gains would have been taxed at 15 percent, the only difference being the issuer of the contract.

Horizon between One and Five Years

Equity swaps are available only to investors with a high commitment, such as $1 million or more; they are not available to everybody. But the tax features of an equity swap are nonetheless interesting.

What is an equity swap? It is a private contractual agreement to exchange cash flows at intervals over a predefined period. A swap has two counter-parties, and each agrees to make the contractual payments to the other over the life of the swap. In this way, an equity swap, indeed all swaps, involves credit or counterparty risk. Every swap involves an unknown or floating payment. In an equity swap, that payment could be the total return (dividends and capital gains) on the S&P 500. In exchange for receiving the total return on the S&P 500, the other counterparty pays a fixed return.

In the eyes of the IRS, if an investor makes or takes contractual payments, the payments are taxed as ordinary income or loss. But if the investor terminates an equity swap before it expires, then the swap is taxed like a capital asset. So, the investor can decide how he or she would like to be taxed after knowing the outcome of the investment. For example, if an investor is two years into an equity swap and the market has declined, the investor should not terminate the swap early. He or she should continue to make the contractual payments because the losses will accrue as ordinary losses, rather than as capital losses constrained by the limit of $3,000 per tax year.

In contrast, if the investor had a profit over a holding period longer than 12 months, then he or she should terminate the swap sometime before its expiration. Again, it becomes a capital asset, and the investor recognizes a long-term gain.

I know of no other security for which investors can bank ordinary losses when they lose money, recognize a long-term capital gain when they make money, and have the luxury of deciding when to recognize each of these tax-mitigating strategies.

Horizon More Than Five Years

If the investor is going to hold an investment for more than, say, five years—maybe forever— then he or she should own the asset itself, not a derivative, because most derivative dealers will not write an equity swap for more than five years.

Other Rationales for Various Strategies

Table 15.1 summarizes the features of some of the alternatives I have been discussing. Notice from the table that economic reasons, as opposed to tax-efficiency reasons, might suggest the use of index options over ETFs. For example, ETFs have management and custodian fees built into them. And ETFs have a slight amount of tracking error against the index that they are designed to mimic; index options do not, provided they are held to expiration. Therefore, based on these reasons, using the listed or the unlisted index options is usually better than using ETFs.

An investor may trade an ETF anytime during the day, but the cost of that trade is the bid–ask spread associated with the cost of buying and selling, as well as a standard stock commission for a round-trip transaction. But if an investor purchases an open-end fund, it does not have that bid–ask spread; the open-end fund is bought and sold at the net asset value, and generally, an investor would not pay a commission. With options, investors will definitely pay a commission.

At a conference in 2002 at New York University, academic researchers demonstrated that low-cost open-end index funds outperformed SPDRs every year since their inception—both pretax and after tax.[8] I was surprised at the pretax performance, but keep in mind that open-end

TABLE 15.1   S&P 500 Investment Alternatives

Item	ETFs	Open-End Index Funds	Listed Index Options	Unlisted Index Options
Management fee	Yes	Yes	No	No
Tracking error	Yes	Yes	No	No
Commissions on purchase/sale	Yes	No	Yes	Yes
Short-term gains taxed at	35%	35%	23%	35%
Long-term gains taxed at	15%	15%	23%	15%
Marked to market at year-end	No	No	Yes	No
Distribution of gains	Yes	Yes	No	No
Possible mispricing	Yes	No	Yes	Yes
Trades intraday	Yes	No	Yes	Yes
Taxable dividends	Yes	Yes	No	No

funds can reinvest their dividends and SPDRs cannot. The after-tax outperformance also surprised me; open-end index funds did pay some distributions. Theoretically, SPDRs are more tax efficient than the open-end funds, but in this chapter, the distributions were just not big enough to make a difference.

Mutual Funds with Built-In Losses

Another strategy worth discussing was pointed out by Mark Hurley of JPMorgan Asset Management's Undiscovered Managers fund family. If a mutual fund takes capital gains, then these gains must be distributed by the end of the tax year, but if a mutual fund makes capital losses, then these losses can be carried for five years and do not flow through to investors. So, some funds could have a sizable bank of capital losses, which can shelter future gains. I certainly would not suggest screening Morningstar for funds that have the largest amount of losses because it also could suggest that the fund's manager is poor. But if an investor wanted to invest in an Internet fund, I would certainly suggest buying one that is seasoned with a bank of capital losses rather than a brand-new one without that benefit.

If an investor is going to buy an S&P 500 fund that contractually has to be invested in the constituents of the S&P 500, why would the investor not choose one that had built-in losses? Obviously, these accumulated losses swing from year to year, depending on whether the market is in a bull or bear phase. Purely in terms of tax efficiency, these funds and similar ones would be attractive to taxable investors because the gains would be tax free for quite some time. These opportunities can be explained by behavioral finance: Investors run into these funds at the high, and they run out at the low; the losses are realized, and they become a valuable bank of losses to offset future gains. Remember that a fund can carry forward the losses for only five years, just like any other corporation. So, take advantage of the window of opportunity while it remains open.

The Wash-Sale Rules

Earlier in the conference, Jeffrey Horvitz stated that he believes that no meaningfully statistical method exists for harvesting tax losses *without distorting investment returns*. But I disagree. I cite research conducted by David Schizer, dean of the Columbia Law School, who explains that it is possible to construct "perfect end runs." A perfect end run means that the economic position of the investment has changed but the investment return has not.[9]

No doubt, getting around the wash-sale rules is tricky. For example, if I own a stock, sell it for a loss, and then buy a call option, that series of transactions will trigger the wash-sale rules, which makes sense if the option is a replacement security. But note that if I bought a stock at $30 and it is down at $20 and I buy *any* call option, it triggers the wash-sale rules. If I bought a deep out-of-the-money call with a strike price of, say, $100, which certainly is not the same thing as stock ownership, it would trigger the wash-sale rules—just as if I had bought a deep in-the-money call with a strike price of, say, $1, which would be similar to owning the stock.

In contrast, if I have a short sale that I lost money on, I can cover my short and buy a put. Symmetry would indicate that this transaction should not be allowed under the wash-sale rules because selling a long and buying a call is no different from covering a short and buying a put. Yet again, this example demonstrates the anomalies within the

IRS tax code. So, until the law is changed, there are tax-efficient strategies that can be exploited.

Other ways do exist to work with the wash-sale rules. An obvious one is not to trigger it in the first place: Sell the stock and be out of it for 31 days. But if during those 31 days the share price skyrockets, the investor will probably regret being penny wise and pound foolish, and unlucky at speculative trading.

Some tax practitioners suggest doubling up. If an investor owned a thousand shares trading at a deep loss, the investor could buy another thousand shares of this loser stock and hold two thousand shares for 31 days. At the end of 31 days, the investor could sell a thousand of the older shares, not the ones purchased 31 days ago. This way, the investor can realize his or her loss within the wash-sale rules by owning twice as much of it. I believe that this is a scary position because of the overexposure for those 31 days, and the investment performance will certainly be distorted.

Nothing exists in the tax law, however, that says investors cannot totally remove the risk of owning that second lot of stock. If an investor buys a stock and then sells a call and buys a put *that has the same strike price as the call*, the investor can eliminate his or her performance risk. To illustrate, if you sell a call with a strike price of $30 and buy a put with a strike price of $30, then stocks trading above $30 at expiration will be taken away from you as the call writer. Alternatively, if the stock trades below $30 at expiration, you will put it to the put writer. Buying a stock, selling a call, and buying a put with the same strike price is called a forward conversion. It is a risk-free transaction that, in theory, should give a T-bill rate of return.[10]

The investor is still doubling up but without enduring the performance risk. And the investor earns an interest-like return on the forward conversion. At the end of the 31 days, one of the options will be exercised and the investor will deliver the highest basis shares against that option and thereby realize his or her loss. This strategy must be done before 28 November, however, if the investor wants the loss in the current tax year. Remember that the loss will not be realized until after 31 days and either one of the options has been exercised. Unfortunately, most investors harvest their losses in mid-December, which is too late for this strategy.

Interestingly, if investors miss the 28 November deadline, they can still come close to creating a perfect end run by voluntarily triggering the wash-sale rules. I will explain: The investor owns a stock bought at $50, and it has gone down to $20. The investor then sells the stock at $20 and buys a call option with a strike price of $30 for $1, purposely triggering the wash-sale rules. Why? The cost basis on that option will go from $1 up to $31. Immediately after buying the call, the investor repurchases the stock at $20. *Remember, the wash-sale rules can be triggered only once.* The timing here is crucial:

1. Sell stock.
2. Buy call.
3. Buy stock.

For some period of time, the investor will have more exposure to that stock because he or she also holds a call option. I recommend that investors hold that call option for a day or two. Obviously, this strategy is not a perfect end run because the investor is forced to own both the option and the stock for a few days. But if the investor delays recognizing losses until December, this approach is an alternative, although suboptimal, strategy.

In addition, because a significant 20 percentage point difference exists between what long-term losses are worth and what short-term losses are worth, the investor's holding period could be altered so that a long-term capital loss is transformed into a short-term capital loss, resulting in a larger bank of short-term losses that can offset short-term gains elsewhere in the portfolio. Here is how it works:

1. Sell the stock that has a long-term capital loss.
2. Buy a call on that stock.
3. Exercise the call.
4. Sell the stock acquired through the call exercise.

This exercise of the call started a new holding period, and investors must buy the call within 31 days after they have taken the long-term loss.

TAX INEFFICIENCIES OF HEDGE FUNDS

Hedge funds are tax inefficient: They recognize a lot of short-term capital gains, triggering taxable events. I recently wrote about another, more insidious tax problem with hedge funds.[11] When an investor receives his or her Schedule K-1 from a hedge fund, many times the accompanying cover letter assumes that the hedge fund is a *trader*. A trader is allowed to net its management fees against its gross profit; an investor is not. If the fees flow through (rather than being netted), they are treated as miscellaneous itemized deductions, which many high-net-worth investors cannot use.

Suppose that an investor owns a fund of funds, and a fund of funds clearly is not a trader. Assume that the fund of funds earned 11 percent in its underlying hedge fund portfolios and that it charged a 1 percent management fee and a 10 percent performance fee, leaving a net return of 9 percent. What actually goes on the investor's IRS Schedule K-1 (if completed properly) is that the investor is taxed on a *gross* rate of return of 11 percent, even though the investor earned a net return of only 9 percent. In other words, 11 percent is taxable income and 2 percent is miscellaneous itemized deductions that the investor probably cannot use, creating a tax on phantom income.

This issue is more important today than in the past because when investors were making 20 percent and 30 percent returns on their hedge funds, they really did not care much about taxes. Now that returns have come down, investors are more aware of what they can do around the edges to improve their returns. In addition, the IRS hedge fund audit manual prioritizes the challenging of trader status, and I believe that investors will have to amend their past tax filings to their disadvantage.

From a tax perspective, investors should invest in hedge funds so that they are taxed on a *net* basis, not a gross basis. One solution is to use offshore life insurance, in which investors pay on their profits only when they take the money out on a net basis. I am not enamored with these vehicles because no one knows the future tax rate that will apply when the money is taken out. (When I started working, tax rates on investment income were 70 percent and had just come down from 80 percent. We are now in a lull with rates at 35 percent. I am not sure that paying tax at 35 percent is so bad versus deferring into the future, when rates could be much higher than they are today.) But if the investor is going to leave the money offshore until he or she dies and then leave the money to his or her children, then the investor's estate will not pay any tax, provided that it is held as an insurance trust. But for shorter time periods, insurance does not make a lot of sense.

Another solution is to invest in an offshore hedge fund entity; this vehicle is typically used by tax-exempt investors and non-U.S. citizens. Of course, nothing is stopping a U.S. investor from entering into an offshore hedge fund entity. Because it is an off-shore corporation, it can be bought and sold at its net asset value. Therefore, investors pay tax only on the profits that are made on a net basis. But there is a downside. Because the entity is deemed a passive foreign investment company (PFIC), investors are allowed to defer and compound their taxable gains in that entity.[12] But when the money is repatriated, the IRS will tax the gains at the highest rate, which today is 35 percent, in addition to a 5 percent interest penalty per annum. Therefore, this tactic would be less effective for hedge funds that might realize income that would have been taxed at 15 percent.

Although the U.S. government enforces the PFIC rules, many states do not have PFIC rules. Interestingly, if an investor remains invested in a fund for seven years, only the profit made in the seventh year will be taxed in those states; the other six years will escape state taxation forever. Shrewd investors could stay in the fund for just one month into the seventh year and pay tax only on that one month's worth of profits; the other six years will escape state taxation.

Our analysis at Twenty-First Securities shows that investors in most high-tax states would be better off in an offshore fund than in an onshore fund. If an investor has a domestic-based hedge fund with a lot of long-term gains or qualifying dividend income, an offshore PFIC investment is not recommended because the gains in the U.S. hedge fund would be taxed at 15 percent, compared with 35 percent plus the 5 percent interest charge on the PFIC.

I am enthusiastic about mutual funds that engage in hedge fund strategies, of which there are roughly 61 long–short funds and 4 risk arbitrage funds. All these funds possess economic and tax advantages. Mutual funds typically do not engage in excessive leverage, and they are less inclined to suffer from the challenge of pricing illiquid securities. Both hedge funds and mutual funds have management fees, but mutual funds do not have any performance fees. Although these kinds of mutual funds are more expensive than the average fund, they are much cheaper than a hedge fund. From a tax perspective, investors in mutual funds pay tax only on net profits. Investors may not be excited about going to the next cocktail party and talking about their "mutual fund," but that may be the biggest impediment to investors realizing this golden opportunity.

Derivatives, such as equity swaps, are available on hedge funds. By itself, a derivative will not help investors get the long-term capital gains tax rate, but it will make sure that investors pay tax only on how much they make. The constructive ownership rule says that if an investor owns an equity swap on a hedge fund and it is held for more than a year and a day, that long-term gain reverts to ordinary income. But at Twenty-First Securities, we do not think that rule applies if an investor uses an equity swap on a *hedge fund index*. The law contains language about a derivative on a flow-through vehicle, like a limited partnership or a limited liability company, but it did not change the taxation of derivatives on an index. So, hedge fund indices now exist, such as the S&P Hedge Fund Index and the S&P Risk Arbitrage Index. Therefore, by investing in those indices through a derivative, investors will not pay tax until they want to, and then only at long-term capital gains tax rates.

TABLE 15.2   Fund-of-Funds Alpha Required for After-Tax Breakeven

Index Annual Return

	Tax Rate on Fund-of-Funds Income		
	28.00%	30.00%	35.00%
5.00%	1.06%	1.26%	1.83%
7.50%	2.07	2.39	3.30
10.00%	3.13	3.57	4.82
12.50%	4.24	4.81	6.39
15.00%	5.39	6.08	8.01

	Term of Investment (years)		
	5	6	7
5.00%	1.81%	1.82%	1.83%
7.50%	3.23	3.27	3.30
10.00%	4.70	4.76	4.82
12.50%	6.20	6.30	6.39
15.00%	7.74	7.88	8.01

	Fund-of-Funds Fees Deductible		
	No	Yes	Difference
5.00%	1.83%	0.80%	1.03%
7.50%	3.30	2.01	1.28
10.00%	4.82	3.28	1.54
12.50%	6.39	4.60	1.80
15.00%	8.01	5.96	2.06

A hypothetical comparison of the returns between a fund of funds and a hedge fund index-linked note is shown in Table 15.2. The assumed fund of funds has a management fee of 1 percent and a performance fee of 10 percent; the indices have a built-in management fee but no performance fee. A fund-of-funds manager may be able to outperform the index, but he or she would need a 14.82 percent return to equal the after-tax performance of a 10.00 percent return in the index. This 482 bps of alpha may be possible but quite a challenge. The source of the after-tax improvement can be decomposed into its constituents: extra fees, tax deferral and conversion to long-term gains, compounding, and deductibility of the fees, as shown in Table 15.3. For example, if the fees of the fund of funds are tax deductible to the investor, then the fund-of-funds manager needs to generate only 328 bps of alpha over an index—still a sizable amount—before the investor is indifferent between the two strategies.

TABLE 15.3 Return Analysis of a Hedge Fund Index-Linked Note and a Fund of Funds

Assumptions

Amount invested	$10,000,000
Term of investment (years)	7
Hedge fund index-linked note	
Annual index rate of return	10.00%
Annual management fee	1.75%
Final adjustment factor	88.37%
Tax rate on sale	15.00%
Fund of funds	
Annual rate of return	10.00%
Management fee	1.00%
Incentive fee	10.00%
Tax rate on income	35.00%
Fees deductible (yes/no)	No

Analysis

	Value after Seven Years	Cumulative Return	Annualized Return
Index-linked note net of fees and taxes	$16,138,468	61.38%	7.08%
Fund of funds net of fees and taxes	13,563,105	35.63	4.45
Fund-of-funds pretax return needed for after-tax breakeven			14.82
Less pretax index return			10.00
Fund-of-funds alpha required for after-tax breakeven			4.82%

CONSTRUCTIVE-SALE RULES

The Taxpayer Relief Act of 1997 forced investors to recognize capital gains on a constructive sale of a stock but not a debt instrument. So, if an investor has a bond with a big profit, the investor can lock in that profit by selling short the bonds that he or she already owns, known as a short against the box. In a short against the box, investors can get 99 percent of the money out of a bond and not pay the capital gains tax until they sell the long bonds.

But if an investor owns appreciated stocks, then he or she has to navigate around the constructive-sale rules. Any hedging strategy must contain a risk for further appreciation or losses; otherwise, the constructive sale could trigger a taxable event. One approach to protect gains is to create an options-based collar by simultaneously buying a put and selling a call; we believe investors need about a 15 percent band between the put and the call.

One of the problems is that this strategy could be a straddle, meaning any carrying costs are not deductible now at 35 percent but capitalized into the stock, thus causing a higher cost basis in the shares. And only if the investor actually disposes of the stock will he or she ever get the benefit of the deduction for those costs—and even then, it would be only at a 15 percent benefit. So, if the investor holds the stock until he or she dies, he or she will never get the benefit of the costs. Beware: A collar will usually destroy the holding period for the dividends, and then the investor will pay a 35 percent tax on them.

A nonrecourse loan is one way to avoid a straddle. Following is an example. If you want to purchase real estate worth $10 million, you could borrow $9 million with recourse only to the real estate itself and not against you as the borrower. And if the real estate appreciates, you can sell the real estate and pay off your loan, or roll over the loan. But if the value of the real estate goes down, you can walk away from the loan *and keep the $9 million*. In the eyes of the IRS, you have then, and only then, sold the real estate for $9 million. The benefit is that it does not create a straddle, and it does not affect the dividend holding period. Therefore, you would be taxed at only 15 percent on future dividends.

Now, imagine that you have owned an appreciated stock for 10 months and you want to eliminate it from your portfolio. You have a choice. First, you could sell it now and pay short-term capital gains tax at 35 percent. Second, you could wait for two months and a day, betting that the stock does not nose-dive in the meantime, and then have a long-term holding period. Or, you could borrow through a nonrecourse loan starting at 10 months, and your holding period will not reset. Therefore, you should borrow for 2 months and a day, taking you into the 12-month long-term tax rate, and if the stock is up, sell it for a long-term gain and pay off your loan. But if the stock is down, walk away from the loan; again, it is the day you walk away from a loan that you trigger a gain for tax purposes. Naturally, the higher the loan-to-value ratio, the higher the interest rate applicable to nonrecourse loans.

CONCLUSION

Investors ought to care about reducing their tax bills, and with various strategies, they can avoid paying the short-term capital gains tax of 35 percent to the federal government. Fortunately, the tax code contains anomalies, so ways exist to replicate an economic position without jeopardizing after-tax returns. And tax savings can be found almost everywhere: individual bonds and stocks, passive indices, mutual funds, and hedge funds. Many of the tax-efficient strategies include the use of derivatives, although the expenses and complications for some of them preclude their use for all but high-net-worth individuals. For those wealthy individuals, they have plenty of flexibility within the current tax code to make the payment of high taxes voluntary rather than statutory.

QUESTION AND ANSWER SESSION

Question: What size transaction do you need to make these transactions cost-effective? In other words, how big does the loss need to be?

Gordon: The loss has to be about 15 percent of the price of the stock for options and swap agreements obtained from a dealer, and you probably have to have $1 million of stock to get the dealer to transact with you. If the stock has listed options, then there is no minimum; a standard contract is for 100 shares. For positions of $1 million or 10,000 shares, whichever is less, you can use what are called flex options on the exchanges, which allow investors to pick their own expiration date and strike price just like with OTC options.

Question: What is the risk that the IRS will move quickly to stamp out some of these efficiency anomalies?

Gordon: This is always a risk with these structures, especially some of the more aggressive ones. But the United States has a tax code that makes prospective rather than retroactive changes. So, we should always have some time to figure out innovative ways to unwind unallowable positions into allowable ones. And as David Schizer explains, the wash-sale rules have many frailties so that wealthy investors can create those "perfect end runs."

Question: If I sell a stock to recognize a loss, can I re-buy it immediately in my IRA without violating the wash-sale rules?

Gordon: No. The tax law does not allow you to avoid the wash-sale rules by purchasing that stock for your IRA. In fact, this would apply to any related party—whether it is a business, a partnership, or a trust owned by a member of your family.

Question: What is the best investment approach for a tax-deferred IRA?

Gordon: Growth stocks are not optimal in an IRA because if you made money on a growth stock, it probably would have been a long-term gain taxed at 15 percent. If you lose money in a growth stock, then you have a capital loss that you can't use. I use growth stock as the substitute for a volatile asset, and I don't think a volatile asset belongs in an IRA. So, bonds are the most appropriate assets to hold in an IRA because they pay a dependable stream of income.

Question: Is the quality of managers available through mutual fund hedge funds equal to the quality of managers available through direct investing?

Gordon: Some mutual fund hedge funds employ the same managers who have hedge funds, so obviously, the quality will be the same because the managers are the same. Management quality issues are more relevant for indices because they will only give money to a hedge fund manager who allows total transparency in daily liquidity—not necessarily the manager with the best skill.

The Center for International Securities and Derivatives Markets (CISDM) has investigated skill differences between risk arbitrage and convertible arbitrage managers, and most of their returns are similar because they are all limited by the same subset of investments.[13] Only so many risk arbitrage deals are going on, and only so many convertible arbitrage opportunities are coming out of the new-issue calendar.

The performance of long–short managers is all over the place, as is that of macro managers.

Question: If you're going to use a derivatives strategy to get exposure to hedge funds, how do you deal with such issues as survivor-ship bias in the indices?

Gordon: Much of the academic work you are alluding to is by Malkiel, who investigated hedge fund indexes that went back about 20 years. He found that they excluded those managers who performed poorly and went out of business. So, overcoming survivor-ship bias there will be tough. The investable indices have been around for only two years, and everyone that was put into them is still there. So, they may not have the same distortions.

If we believe that a fund of funds must generate 482 bps of alpha to overcome tax inefficiencies, we certainly need to distinguish good managers from poor ones. But it is difficult to find managers who can make up the tax difference. Furthermore, that 482 bps won't be reached by those following convertible arbitrage or risk arbitrage strategies, where they're all stuck doing the same thing.

Question: With hedge funds originally being the province of private investors, why aren't they more tax efficient in the way they manage their assets?

Gordon: A lot of money is held in offshore funds, especially the stakes owned by the manager, which benefit from deferred compounding. So, why should they—and their advisors— bother with tax issues, especially because some of the onshore strategies are complex and expensive to enter into? They are not paid or incentivized to be tax friendly; it is only when investors start demanding it that tax efficiency will come to hedge funds.

NOTES

1. Robert D. Arnott, Andrew L. Berkin, and Jia Ye, "How Well Have Taxable Investors Been Served in the 1980s and 1990s?" *Journal of Portfolio Management* (Summer 2000):84–94. See also Jeffrey Horvitz's presentation in this proceedings, where this research is summarized.

2. Brad M. Barber and Terrance Odean, "Are Individual Investors Tax Savvy? Evidence from Retail and Discount Brokerage Accounts," *Journal of Public Economics* (January 2004):419–442.

3. Zoran Ivković, James Poterba, and Scott Weisbenner, "Tax-Motivated Trading by Individual Investors," NBER Working Paper No. 10275 (February 2004).

4. If the bond swap is done for tax purposes to realize a capital loss, the investor must avoid swapping into what the IRS deems to be the same security or the wash-sale rules will apply.

5. Our website has an online calculator that can be used to conduct a similar analysis: www.twenty-first.com/bond/index.htm.

6. See Jeffrey Horvitz's presentation in this proceedings.

7. For options that trade on an exchange, all gains or losses are considered 60 percent long term and 40 percent short term, which yields a blended 23 percent tax rate. The same OTC option purchased from a broker does not get this tax advantage.

8. Edwin J. Elton, Martin J. Gruber, et al. show this finding on a pretax basis in "Spiders: Where Are the Bugs?" and James M. Poterba and John B. Shoven draw after-tax conclusions in "Exchange Traded Funds: A New Investment Option for Taxable Investors." Links to these papers can be found at www.twentyfirst.com/newsletter/newsletter_ summer2002-4.htm.

9. David M. Schizer, "Scrubbing the Wash Sale Rules," *Taxes—The Tax Magazine*, vol. 82, no. 3 (March 2004).

10. Put–call parity on a European option (a put or a call that can be exercised only at expiry) says that, in theory, a risk-free investment can be created synthetically by selling a call, buying a put, and owning the underlying security. The risk-free investment will, naturally, earn the risk-free rate of return.

11. Robert N. Gordon, "Is Your Hedge Fund a Trader or an Investor?" *Journal of Wealth Management* (Summer 2005):54–57.

12. See Philip S. Gross, "Tax Planning for Offshore Hedge Funds: The Potential Benefits of Investing in a PFIC," *Journal of Taxation of Investments* (Winter 2004):187–195.

13. The CISDM website can be found at cisdm.som.umass.edu/.

CHAPTER 16

DIVERSIFYING CONCENTRATED HOLDINGS

Scott D. Welch

Meeting the special needs of clients who have concentrated equity holdings has become a productive way for investment managers to develop client relationships and stand out from the competition. Many hedging strategies for managing low-basis assets are available—from financial strategies using equity collars and variable prepaid forwards to charitable strategies and donor-advised funds. But the strategies are effective only when certain criteria are met, and the advantages and disadvantages of each must be carefully weighed in order to correctly structure the appropriate method for diversifying the risk of each particular client's position.

At CMS Financial Services, we specialize in working with high-net-worth clients. As a wealth management firm based in the middle of a high-technology economic region (northern Virginia), we constantly meet with a large number of clients who hold highly appreciated assets, in large part because of the high-technology boom, and whose overall portfolio contains far too high a concentration in one stock. These clients are typically entrepreneurs who successfully managed their companies and then sold them to a publicly traded company in exchange for stock in the acquiring company. They do not want to sell the stock and incur capital gains taxes, and quite frequently, they are still bullish on their shares.

An article in the July/August 2000 Bloomberg *Wealth Manager* said, "A new study finds that individual stock volatility has been rising, suggesting that investors must own more equities to maintain their grip on diversification."[1] In November 1999, the *CPA Journal*

Reprinted from *AIMR Conference Proceedings: Investment Counseling for Private Clients III* (August 2001):30–35.

reported "that volatility erodes any stock's compounding rate—the true measure of wealth accumulation."[2] Thus, because many individuals hold a majority of their wealth in one volatile stock position that is eroding their opportunity to accumulate future wealth, they need equity risk management services.

In this presentation, I will discuss several equity risk management products—among them tax-advantaged hedging and monetization strategies—that address the needs of private clients with concentrated equity holdings, and I will explain how to identify potentially good candidates for equity risk management transactions. Finally, I will compare the alternatives available in equity risk management for managing low-basis assets, which include not only collars and forwards but also other financial and charitable strategies.

EQUITY RISK MANAGEMENT

Equity risk management allows high-net-worth investors who hold concentrated positions in one stock or a basket of individual stocks to do four things. First, it allows them to protect the value of their shares at, or very close to, the current market price of the stock, which is a vital feature for many investors. Second, it allows investors to participate in a specified amount of the future growth of the stock. To be a tax-effective transaction, the investor must be at risk to a certain degree, and one way to do that is to allow the investor to keep some upside price potential on the stock. Third, it allows investors to generate immediate, tax-effective liquidity for reinvestment in a more diversified portfolio. And fourth, it allows investors to defer capital gains taxes—the key word being defer, not eliminate; every tax dollar not paid today has a tremendous impact in potential principal appreciation and compounding for clients. The tax bill will come due eventually, but its postponement is very valuable to the client in terms of additional wealth accumulation.

Equity risk management products offer investment advisors a great way to enhance the depth and profitability of existing and prospective client relationships. I have never met a client who was not at least willing to talk about these ideas, even if the client ultimately chose not to use them. These products also provide advisors tax-effective liquidity for reinvestment—a great way to increase the amount of assets under management. Finally, even in today's increasingly commoditized environment, these products offer a unique, high-value-added service to high-net-worth clients.

Concerns for Risk Management Clients

Most major financial institutions can provide risk management services to high-net-worth investors, but they typically do not provide *price discovery* as part of the process. Thus, a client can go to a broker or a private banker from Firm A or Bank X and get a bid on the concentrated stock holding, but the price received is not likely to be competitive, and in any event, the client has no assurance that the price is competitive. In addition, the client has no way to initiate *document discovery* (the process of negotiating or strengthening the document on behalf of the client without increasing the overall risk of the transaction). Typically, the document provisions on captive (i.e., noncompetitive) deals are not negotiated, even though the off-the-shelf documents governing these transactions that are used by most firms are not written for the benefit of the client.

Only a handful of firms that arrange hedging transactions act as objective, conflict-free intermediaries between the investment banking community and investors—sitting on the client's side of the table to negotiate on the client's behalf, putting every trade out for competitive bid, working with tax attorneys to negotiate the governing documents for the client to make them stronger from a tax perspective while making them more equitable in terms of flexibility, and so forth.

Characteristics of Investors

Several traits characterize the type of client who would be interested in a hedging or monetization transaction. Such clients must

- have a fairly high net worth and be financially sophisticated—traits mandated by the particular characteristics of these types of products, which are regulated by the U.S. SEC and bank regulatory authorities. That is, the investor must qualify as an "accredited investor" under SEC definitions (i.e., have a net worth in excess of $1 million and/or a current income in excess of $200,000 a year for the previous two years).
- still be bullish on the future of the concentrated stock holding. If a client believes that the stock is fairly valued or even overvalued (although I have never actually heard anyone say that), my recommendation will always be to sell. Such a decision is nonemotional, and many tax-effective ways of selling exist, such as through a charitable remainder trust (CRT).
- recognize the need for more diversification in their portfolios.
- want to defer capital gains taxes.
- believe that the continued growth in their concentrated stock holding plus the performance of their reinvestment portfolio will exceed the cost of funds (i.e., the financing cost) associated with the hedging transaction.
- qualify as "suitable" counterparties from a regulatory perspective.

The typical equity risk management client is an entrepreneur, partner, venture capital investor, or anyone who has sold out an ownership interest in his or her firm to a publicly traded company in a stock-for-stock merger. This description probably represents about 70 percent of my clients. Other candidates for risk management strategies include employees or affiliates who wish to diversify without selling their stock. In December 1999, the SEC issued a "no-action" letter that the markets have interpreted as opening the door for affiliate hedging transactions, which have been a big chunk of our business lately. Another potential candidate for a hedging or monetization strategy is the heir to a low-basis asset (where no step-up in basis was provided by the estate plan) who is seeking to diversify. Conversely, an elderly investor who wants to lock-in the value of an appreciated position for his or her heirs without selling the stock before his or her death is a candidate for an equity risk management strategy. Finally, additional candidates are retired employees who have built up large, concentrated positions through a stock compensation plan or private investors who now hold public shares following an initial public offering (IPO). The ability to hedge, however, for an investor with recent IPO stock is temporarily limited because the stock is subject to a six-month underwriter's lockup. During this period, the investor is unable to transact with the shares, and after the lockup, the ability to hedge will be dependent on the nature of the shares in question and how they are performing in the market.

Characteristics of Good Hedge Candidates

Some stocks can be hedged more easily than others. If a stock meets all of the characteristics listed below, I guarantee that a bank will provide a hedging price on multiple structures. The stock should

- be publicly traded;
- have a market cap in excess of $500 million;
- have good "borrowability" in the marketplace, which simply means that lots of institutional investors are willing to lend the stock;
- have an average daily trading volume greater than 75,000 shares; and
- have a stock price in excess of $20 a share.

Furthermore, in the ideal hedging position, the number of shares to be hedged should be less than 3–5 percent of the "market float" and the minimum trade size should be roughly $5 million. Trades can be smaller only if the investor has a net worth of at least $5 million.

Although I have devised risk management strategies for stock positions that violate two or three of these characteristics, once as many as four of these characteristics are missing, few banks are willing to quote a price on the stock, because at that point, a bank will have difficulty laying off in the marketplace the risk associated with the position.

THE IMPETUS FOR HEDGING

These hedging and monetizing strategies exist largely because of the Taxpayer Relief Act of 1997 (TRA '97). Before 1997, the preferred method of hedging a concentrated stock position and thus capturing its value without having to sell the stock was simply a *short against the box* (a short sale of securities when an identical long position is owned but will not be delivered until a later date). It was a great way to lock-in the price of the stock and generate a huge amount of liquidity from the position without having to sell the stock. This transaction was targeted explicitly by TRA '97 because of a deemed abuse by a specific family that was able to shield in excess of $100 million into perpetuity by an elegant and complex short-against-the-box transaction. TRA '97 defined several methods of hedging and monetization as *constructive sales* that are subject to capital gains tax *as if* the shares had been sold outright, even if no physical sale of the securities took place. These are

- short-against-the-box transactions,
- total return equity swaps,
- forward or futures contracts that deliver a "substantially fixed amount" of the appreciated asset for a "substantially fixed price," and
- any other similar transaction proscribed in IRS regulations.

The two phrases in quotes in the third bullet point are important. The minute that a regulation is put into writing, the smart folks in the banking, legal, and accounting communities start to find ways around it. These experts interpreted the phrases in the third bullet point to say that as long as they do not set a substantially fixed price for the asset or, conversely, set a substantially fixed number of shares to be sold, then they have not created a constructive sale. This, in fact, is the impetus behind the two strategies that I will discuss in the next section. These strategies introduce into the hedging transaction enough uncertainty in the outcome, either in the form of the sale price or the number of shares to be delivered, to avoid being a constructive sale. This is not something that is even gray in terms of the tax code; it is rather clear-cut.

COMMONLY USED STRATEGIES

The two most frequently used hedging strategies—not currently defined as constructive sales—are equity collars and variable prepaid forwards. These instruments tend to be (but are not exclusively) OTC options as opposed to exchange-traded options.

Equity Collars

The equity collar begins with a long-dated put option. The maturities I work with range between two and seven years, with three to five years being the maturities for the majority of the transactions. The long-dated put option provides the price protection sought by the client on the concentrated stock holding. The put option gives the investor the right to sell the stock at a certain price. The investor pays for that protection by selling a call option at a higher strike price, thus producing (typically) a "zero-premium" structure with no out-of-pocket costs to the investor at the time the transaction is initiated. Or the investor can initiate an income-producing collar where the price of the call sold exceeds the price of the put purchased. Regardless of the structure, the idea behind the collar is to create a defined range of potential value for the hedged stock position over the life of the collar. These are European-style options, so at least on the OTC side, they cannot be exercised prior to maturity, although the client has the ability to terminate the trade early at his or her discretion.

Suppose a client has a concentrated stock position, XYZ, which is trading at $100, and wants to establish a price floor under the stock. The client wants to keep some growth potential in the stock, but the client also wants to defer the capital gains taxes that would be incurred if the stock were sold and to create a more diversified investment portfolio. Once the equity collar is created that effectively sets a minimum value for the underlying equity position, then the protected equity position can be used as collateral to *monetize* (take cash out of) the underlying position without physically selling the shares. The bank will lend money against the underlying stock position at an attractive rate of interest, and that money can be used to create a more diversified investment portfolio.

The amount an investor can borrow depends on the hedging structure chosen. With the combination of a collar and a loan, the margin-lending regulations (U.S. Federal Reserve Regulations U and T) apply, even though the investor should never be subjected to a margin call because the bank knows that the stock has a guaranteed minimum value at maturity. Thus, the investor must represent to the bank his or her intent for borrowing. If the intent is to reinvest in a more diversified equity portfolio (i.e., the investor seeks a "purpose" loan), then the bank is restricted to lending a maximum of 50 cents on the dollar against the stock position. On the other hand, if the investor wants to buy a ranch, take a world cruise, buy insurance, update his wardrobe, or do anything other than invest in equities (i.e., the intent is a "nonpurpose" loan), then the bank is typically willing to lend up to 90 percent of the put strike value. Therefore, the investor who wants to borrow to invest in a blue chip equity portfolio can borrow 50 cents on the dollar, but the investor who wants to borrow to buy a ranch in Texas can potentially borrow 81 cents on the dollar. I would argue that such a situation runs counter to the intent of the regulations. Nonetheless, that is the way the regulations are written.

Variable Prepaid Forwards (VPFs)

If the investor is seeking to maximize the amount of money that can be borrowed without any restrictions on its reinvestment, a strategy other than the combination of the collar and the loan is needed. In such a case, many clients prefer the variable prepaid forward. A VPF is essentially a forward sale of a contingent number of shares of an investor's stock, with an agreed future delivery date, in exchange for a cash advance today. It is not a constructive sale because of the "contingent number of shares" aspect to the trade (i.e., the number of shares that will actually be delivered at maturity depends on the underlying stock's price at maturity).

In this transaction, the investor enters into a contract with a bank to sell his or her shares at some point in the future, but the number of shares that will be sold is contingent on the stock's price at the maturity of the contract. In exchange for that agreement, the bank advances a discounted current market value of the stock to the investor today. If this trade is properly documented and structured, it is neither a constructive sale nor subject to the margin-lending restrictions. Thus, the investor can invest the proceeds however he or she pleases, unlike with the collar and loan strategy.

That is, suppose the investor creates a zero-premium collar in which the band is 90 percent on the downside and 175 percent on the upside over a three-year period. If the investor documents that transaction as a collar and a loan on a traditional basis and wants to reinvest in equities, the most that could be borrowed is 50 cents on the dollar. But if the same structure and range of value—the 90 percent on the downside and the 175 percent on the upside—is documented as a variable forward over a three-year period, the amount borrowed could be as high as about 75 percent of the current market value of the stock, with no restrictions on reinvestment. The decision as to which strategy is appropriate depends primarily on what the client is trying to accomplish with the reinvestment portfolio. Obviously, a VPF is a better choice than a collar when the investor wants to borrow the maximum amount possible to reinvest in equities.

Using VPFs is also preferable when the investor is an affiliate of the company that has issued the underlying stock. As I mentioned earlier, in December 1999, the SEC issued a no-action letter at the request of Goldman, Sachs & Company that the markets have interpreted as effectively laying out a road map for how affiliate shareholders can hedge their stock using the VPF. The risk prior to the issuance of the no-action letter was whether entering into a hedging transaction (typically a collar) would put the investor at increased risk of tripping the short-swing profit disgorgement rules, one of the SEC Section 16 rules. The market interpreted the no-action letter as specifying that from a *regulatory* perspective, the date of sale of the stock is the date that the transaction is entered into, which is helpful when trying to manage Section 16 risk. At the same time, the date of sale for *tax* purposes is deemed to be the maturity date of the transaction. So, the date of sale for regulatory reasons is Day 1, and the date of sale for tax purposes is the maturity date. At the same time, if done correctly, the bank can take the restricted shares, clean them up, and have the restrictive legends removed (i.e., turn the shares into fully registered, freely tradable shares), which gives the investor increased flexibility.

The variable forward is the appropriate hedging transaction for equity investors who would like to maximize the amount of up-front liquidity from a position or, conversely, would like to sell but want to defer capital gains taxes.

COMPARING ALTERNATIVE STRATEGIES

Several risk management strategies are available for low-basis assets, and they can be divided roughly into either financial strategies or charitable strategies. The three most common financial strategies are hedges (using one of the collars or variable forward transactions), exchange funds, and completion funds. The charitable strategies that are typically used are CRTs and donor-advised funds.

Collars and VPFs

The ideal collar or variable forward (both of which I have described earlier) is a hedging transaction that protects the value of underlying low-basis shares and allows the investor to participate in the future growth of the stock, to generate liquidity out of the position for reinvestment without selling, and to defer the taxes that would otherwise be incurred if the stock was sold. Such a hedging strategy offers many advantages to the investor. It offers great flexibility in terms of the maturity of the transaction and the structure of the trade—including the amount of upside versus downside protection and the amount of money the investor is trying to get out of the transaction. An investor can terminate the trade early, restructure it, and maintain control of the assets. In fact, being able to maintain control of and retain some risk in the assets is critical to the viability of the tax argument—the ability to defer the tax bill. The investor retains ownership, achieves tax deferral, and gets the diversification sought in the asset allocation model.

Several other issues, however, are intrinsic to the hedging transaction and should be considered carefully by the investor. One issue is the leverage incurred by the investor, whether the investor takes a cash advance against the forward sale or borrows with a straight collar and loan strategy. I would suggest that it is protected leverage because of the put option, but nonetheless, the investor is borrowing money to create a diversified portfolio. Another consideration is counterparty risk, because the investor is dealing with a counterparty on the other side of the trade. The investor needs to be comfortable with what will happen at maturity and be familiar with the alternatives that are available to settle the transaction in terms of physical settlement versus cash settlement and the differences between the two. I personally do not find the consideration of tax complexity to be overly burdensome, but because these tax issues are new to most investors and are not symmetrical, investors should be aware of them—and should retain independent tax counsel to advise them. The final issue is that both of these strategies (collars and VPFs) in their typical forms are considered to be *straddles* for tax purposes (under IRS Section 1092), which affects the tax treatment of the interest expense that is incurred. Also, if a short-term stock (i.e., stock that has not seasoned for 12 months) is hedged, the holding period is lost. So, if I hedge stock that is three or four months old in a three-year collar or variable forward, at the end of three years, my stock will be one day old for tax purposes.

Exchange Funds

In an exchange fund, an investor takes an individual holding and contributes it to a partnership of like-minded investors who have also contributed their individual stocks to the partnership. In exchange for the contribution, the investor receives a *pro rata* ownership position in that pool of assets, which is considered a tax-free exchange, at least under current tax law. So, the investor takes his or her stock and, in essence, exchanges it for a portfolio of other stocks in a tax-free exchange.

Exchange funds have several advantages. First, the investor can achieve a tax deferral. Also, some diversification is gained, but because the diversification is limited to a specific pool of assets, it is not true diversification as defined by modern portfolio theory. For example, the investor might achieve diversification in large-cap or tech stocks but not broadly across the market, as defined in a true asset allocation model. Another advantage of the exchange fund is that no leverage is involved because the investor is simply exchanging his or her shares for a *pro rata* position in a larger pool of shares.

Exchange funds, however, also have several drawbacks. In my opinion, for what they deliver, they have very high costs and annual fees. There is typically a seven-year lockup on the fund to achieve the desired tax-deferred status. That is, if the investor pulls out of the fund within seven years, he or she will receive a *pro rata* number, based on the current market value of the overall portfolio, of the original shares contributed with the original basis intact, which defeats the purpose of engaging in the exchange fund strategy in the first place. Plus, the investor has little control over the assets once they are pledged to the pool. Another consideration is that an exchange fund is effectively a passively managed portfolio, for which the providers charge an actively managed fee. Finally, the rules require the portfolio to have least 20 percent of its assets in illiquid investments, typically real estate investment trusts, which may not fit an investor's personal investment criteria.

Completion Funds

The completion fund is a simple concept. This strategy involves selling the low-basis stock gradually over time and using the proceeds of the sale to create a more diversified portfolio. Thus, an advantage of a completion fund is the achievement of diversification within a given time frame. Other advantages include retaining control of the underlying asset, participating in the price appreciation of the asset, managing the timing of the sale, implementing the strategy with ease, and avoiding the costs and limitations involved with borrowing that other strategies require.

The drawbacks of a completion fund include the lack of immediate liquidity and the amount of time needed to implement the strategy. And in the time it takes to liquidate the entire stock position, the investor has no price protection on the stock. Moreover, the completion fund strategy may or may not be tax efficient if the periodic sales generate a high taxable gain for the investor. And because the market value of both the stock and the surrounding portfolio changes over time, periodic rebalancing is required to keep the rest of the portfolio in line with the overall investment strategy.

Charitable Strategies

A charitable strategy provides a tax-effective way to liquidate low-basis stock. The investor gains some tax deduction, but the amount of the deduction depends on the strategy used. Thus, a charitable strategy not only provides tax deferral but also some degree of tax relief. Diversification is also achievable when a CRT is used. And leverage is not involved with these strategies.

One drawback of charitable strategies is that they are somewhat inflexible. Charitable strategies also require high maintenance compared with other alternatives. Another consideration is that using a charitable strategy means that the asset is effectively removed from the investor's portfolio and the investor can no longer participate in any potential price appreciation. Investors should realize that the charity, as the beneficiary of the CRT, may be the primary

TABLE 16.1   Comparison of Equity Risk Management Products

Feature	Collars/ VPFs	Donor- Advised Funds	Exchange Funds	Completion Funds	CRTs
Maintain control of asset	Yes	No	No	Yes	No
Protect value of stock	Yes	No	No	No	No
Generate liquidity for reinvestment	Yes	No	No	Yes, over time	Yes
Participate in growth of stock	Yes	No	Yes, to a degree	Yes	No
Philanthropic result	No	Yes	No	No	Yes
Charitable tax deduction	No	Yes	No	No	Yes
Financing cost	Yes	No	No	No	No
Management fee	Yes	Yes	Yes	Yes	Yes
Flexible	Yes	Yes	No	Yes	No
Revocable	Yes	No	No	Yes	No

winner in the transaction if the stock and subsequent reinvestment portfolio significantly appreciate in value. If that situation does not fit the investor's personal goals, then the investor should consider other alternatives to diversify the concentrated holding.

Table 16.1 summarizes the trade-offs between these different risk management techniques for low-basis assets.

CONCLUSION

By helping investors manage the risks inherent in concentrated stock positions and leverage the return prospects for these positions, equity risk management products can be valuable tools for clients with low-basis stock. In general, investors benefit by using these strategies in that they are able to protect the value of their shares at or very close to today's price, participate in the future growth of the stock, generate immediate liquidity for diversification, and achieve tax deferral that would not be possible if the shares were sold. The benefits for the investment advisor include creating liquidity for reinvestment, distinguishing the advisor from the competition, and enhancing client relationships.

QUESTION AND ANSWER SESSION

Question: What are the typical transaction costs related to diversification strategies? How much profit do the banks make on these strategies?

Welch: The banks play it close to the chest with the exact profit they make on these trades. But I typically assume, and I have been told by my contacts at the banks that it is not unreasonable to assume, that they are pricing a 1.5–2 percent "anticipated" trading profit into the transaction—anticipated being the critical word because the banks have to manage the risk of this position for the life of the transaction to actually realize the profit.

With respect to transaction costs, at least in our case, our fee is priced into the structure in the form of either a slightly lower call strike price or a slightly lower cash advance on the forward, and it is paid to us by the counterparty bank on the other side of the transaction and fully disclosed to the client.

With respect to legal costs, we always recommend that every client have his or her trades reviewed by outside independent tax counsel. Again, the legal cost depends on the transaction, but for a typical, not particularly complex, trade, the legal cost is probably going to be $5,000–$10,000.

Question: Please briefly describe completion funds.

Welch: I think of a completion fund as diversification over time out of a concentrated stock position. Again, I will use my example: You have $10 million worth of AOL Time Warner, and your goal is to lower your exposure. You do not want to dump all the stock today because you do not want to pay the taxes. The investment consultant should create the ideal allocation around that position and then begin to liquidate the position over time. So, you sell 10 percent of the stock today, pay your taxes, and use the proceeds to buy some uncorrelated assets with AOL Time Warner. Six months later, or whatever the time frame is, you sell another 10 percent of your stock; and so over time, you are liquidating your position in AOL Time Warner and creating a diversified portfolio. With each sale you are rebalancing to make sure that the inclusion of AOL Time Warner is being factored into the overall expected return and risk of the portfolio. The idea behind the completion fund is that it is a straightforward, disciplined liquidation over time of a concentrated stock position that redeploys the after-tax proceeds into an allocated portfolio.

Question: What happens when options in collars expire after three years?

Welch: There will most likely be a taxable event, which will vary depending on whether the trade is cash settled or physically settled or rolled over into a new trade. As a general comment, if the trade is physically settled—that is, the investor delivers stock to settle the trade—the day the shares are delivered is the date of sale for tax purposes, and the investor will face a long-term capital gains tax on the difference between the sales price and the basis (assuming the stock was already long term when hedged). If the trade is cash settled or rolled over, the investor will face a short-term capital gain (if the bank owes the investor money) or a long-term deferred loss (if the investor owes the bank money)—a loss the investor cannot realize until the shares are actually sold. Investors should always retain professional tax counsel to walk them through the tax treatment of these trades before entering into them.

Question: Can you hedge stock held in a GRAT (grantor retained annuity trust)?

Welch: I believe stock can be hedged in a GRAT. The counterparty bank will want to see a copy of the trust agreement to make sure the trust is authorized to engage in this type of transaction, and the bank may require an opinion letter to this effect from the attorney who drafted the agreement.

Question: What is the cost basis at the end of a forward contract when delivering cash or shares?

Welch: With collars, your cost basis is your original basis plus the interest expense you paid on any borrowing you may have taken against the collared stock (i.e., the interest on the loan cannot be deducted against current investment income but, rather, is capitalized into your basis). So, you get some relief for the interest you pay, but it is deferred until you sell the stock, and you only achieve a capital, rather than an ordinary, offset.

With forwards, the implied financing cost is not added to your basis, but it is taken off the sales price for the shares when you physically settle at maturity. The net result is similar—no current deduction on the implied financing cost but some capital relief realized when you ultimately sell the shares.

Question: Can you discuss the tax implications of the rehypothecation of securities pledged as collateral in connection with the hedge/monetized transaction?

Welch: Because rehypothecating the shares lowers the cost and risk of hedging the trade for the bank, the investor will receive better pricing on the trade. Remember, however, that one of the main points of any of these trades is to remain the beneficial owner of the shares for tax purposes; that is why these trades do not trigger the constructive sale rules. If you allow the bank to rehypothecate (i.e., borrow and then sell short) your shares, some tax attorneys feel you have weakened your argument that you remain the beneficial owner of those shares. The investor should be made aware of the trade-off associated with rehypothecation (i.e., better pricing versus possible increased tax risk), and the trade documents should specify explicitly whether the bank has the right to rehypothecate. But the ultimate decision lies with the investor, based on input from a retained tax professional.

Question: How bullish must a client be on his or her individual stock for these strategies to make sense? Does the expected rate of appreciation need to exceed that of the market to make these strategies worthwhile?

Welch: We assume that the portfolio the client reinvests in will be the same whether or not the shares are sold or hedged and borrowed against, so what really matters at the end of the day is how the hedged stock performs over the life of the trade. Hedging is certainly a tax-deferral technique, so in that sense, it doesn't matter what happens to the stock after you hedge. But our clients are typically comparing hedging the stock today with selling the stock today. So, if the stock price falls or stays flat after you hedge, you would have been better off selling (because of the financing cost associated with hedging and borrowing). How much the stock price needs to rise before hedging puts more money in your pocket than selling does depends on the structure and the stock, but my experience is that if the stock increases by more than approximately 4–5 percent a year, then hedging adds value compared with selling.

Question: Doesn't the "least expensive" method (i.e., little upside) expose one to the capital gains tax (i.e., stock called away), making it a very expensive method (vis-à-vis the "more expensive," more upside method)?

Welch: The contracts we work with are European-style options, so the stock can never be called away prior to maturity, and the client always has the right to cash settle if he or she does not want to deliver stock.

Question: Regarding purpose and nonpurpose loans from a collar, is it safe to assume that money used to pay down margin debt would be considered a "purpose" loan? Is it better to do a variable prepaid forward?

Welch: We always use a prepaid forward to repay margin debt because (1) it fixes the interest rate for the life of the trade, and (2) forwards are not subject to Reg T or Reg U, so the issue of purpose does not come into play.

Question: What are the costs and other considerations when liquidating part or all of the underlying stock prior to maturity of a collar or forward?

Welch: The banks typically are not trying to realize any more profit on an early termination than was already priced into the trade. So, aside from a bid–offer spread, you should get a fair market valuation from the bank when you terminate early.

That said, the valuation you receive will depend on the market conditions at the time of the early termination—how much time is left in the original trade, interest rates, volatility, and so on. From my perspective, there are only two situations in which you should unwind early: (1) you expect the stock to skyrocket from that point forward (and thus increase in value by more than enough to pay for the time value you have to pay to unwind early), and (2) the stock has, in your mind, peaked prior to maturity, and you fear that it may fall before the trade matures by more than what it will cost you to terminate it early.

NOTES

1. James Picerno, "Quantity Control," Bloomberg *Wealth Manager* (July/August 2000).
2. Alan R. Feld, "High Exposure to Low-Basis Stock: Too Much of a Good Thing?" *CPA Journal* (November 1999); www.nysscpa.org/cpajournal/d601199a.html.

CHAPTER 17

HEDGING LOW-COST-BASIS STOCK

Robert N. Gordon

After the Taxpayer Relief Act of 1997 added a few twists to tax law regarding constructive sales, the hedging of low-cost-basis stock positions has become rather complicated. Using options to diversify concentrated holdings can trigger the constructive sale rules, depending on how the transaction is structured. Before a manager can recommend a hedging strategy to one of his or her clients, the manager must begin by identifying the client's reasons for wanting to hedge. Only then can the manager devise a strategy that avoids unnecessarily large tax bills and achieves the client's goals. A customized decision tree can help clients find the appropriate strategy for hedging low-cost-basis stock.

Many strategies exist for hedging low-cost-basis stock, but tax laws, as well as the proliferation of analytical tools available in the market, make the entire procedure fiendishly complex. Before the Taxpayer Relief Act of 1997, our recommendation at Twenty-First Securities Corporation would have been a short sale against the box (selling securities short that the client owns and creating a sale position that remains open for an indefinite period of time). Once the law changed, however, managers had to begin questioning investors about their goals related to their low-cost-basis stock in order to decide which strategy could best achieve the investors' objectives. As a result, at Twenty-First Securities, we created an interactive decision tree survey on our Web site (www.twenty-first.com) called "Hedging Low-Basis Stock: An Interactive Guide." Based on client responses, the survey builds a model suited to the client's investment needs. The first question the survey asks is:

> Does the client hold a substantial position in a stock that was acquired for little or no cost?

(Screen 1)

Reprinted from *AIMR Conference Proceedings: Investment Counseling for Private Clients III* (August 2001):36–43.

The investor must answer "yes" to proceed with the survey; otherwise, there is no need to continue with the exercise. My presentation will go through the subsequent steps of our Web site survey and explain the reasons behind asking the questions. Although I will not cover all the possible branches of the decision tree, I will discuss the main points. Note that the Web site itself offers many opportunities for further explanation on relevant topics to taxable investors, such as links to definitions of key terms and articles of interest.

HEDGE OR MONETIZE

At Twenty-First Securities, we see two categories of investors who are interested in hedging low-cost-basis stock. One group wants to monetize its stockholdings for greater diversification. A person in this group is not willing to liquidate his or her position, however, because of the tax burden associated with that strategy. That is, this client would sell if taxes did not exist. The second group seeks to hedge unrealized capital gains. This type of client loves the stock he or she owns and wants simply to put a floor under the stock's price—and lock-in a profit if the stock's price begins to fall. These two reasons for hedging require different hedging strategies, and the differences in these hedging strategies create two different economic payoff patterns.

The survey thus asks:

> Does the client want to protect gains and let profits run? or Does the client want to get the money out of the position without triggering a tax?
>
> (Screen 2)

If the client answers "yes" to the first question, then the Hedge button is selected. If the client answers "yes" to the second question, then the Monetize button is selected.

Choosing to Monetize

At this point, assume the client chooses to monetize. The survey then asks:

> Is the client's tax basis less than ½ the current market price?
>
> (Screen 3)

This question is important because when an investor monetizes—a two-step process that involves hedging the asset while being mindful of the constructive sale rules and simultaneously borrowing money to invest in another security—the investor incurs an ongoing carrying cost to keep the monetizing strategy in place.[1] To make the strategy worthwhile, the expected gain from the strategy must exceed the carrying cost of the strategy; in other words, the potential tax savings must outweigh the carrying costs incurred to avoid the tax.

For example, if an investor paid 50 cents for a security that is now worth $1, the capital gains tax on that 50 cents of profit would be 10 cents (at a 20 percent long-term capital gains tax rate) if the position is liquidated. If, alternatively, the investor chooses to monetize the low-cost-basis stock rather than liquidate the position, the carrying cost of a monetizing strategy would be about half of a percent. That is, suppose for an investment with a market value of $100 the investor earns 5 percent ($5) in an income-producing collar.[2] By borrowing $90 (the put strike price in the collar and thus the maximum the lender will lend) at 6 percent and paying $5.40, the investor has a 40 basis point negative carry, roughly a net cost of 0.5 percent to undertake the strategy. Thus, if an investor has to pay 0.5 percent a year for the benefit of the use of the money that would otherwise be paid in capital gains tax, the investor must earn a return of 5 percent (50 cent carrying cost divided by the extra $10 of capital available for investment) on the borrowed funds to cover carrying costs and to create a cost-effective strategy.

This bogey of 5 percent is relatively easy to beat. But if the security has not at least doubled in value (which is the reason behind the tax-basis question in Screen 3), the return bogey on the borrowed funds is larger than 5 percent. If, however, the unrealized gain on the low-cost-basis stock is larger than 50 percent of the market value of the position (i.e., the tax basis is less than half of the market value of the position), then the carrying-cost bogey associated with maintaining the monetizing strategy will be less difficult to overcome. In addition, the benefits of the strategy increase as the tax basis approaches zero because the client is avoiding an ever larger capital gains tax. For an investment with a $100 market value and a zero cost basis, the investor would only have to earn a 2.5 percent (50 cent carrying cost divided by $20 capital gains tax) return on the borrowed funds to breakeven. Compare this 2.5 percent with the 5 percent return needed to breakeven when the tax basis equaled 50 percent of market value.

Therefore, if the investor's stock has not at least doubled in value (the investor answers "no" to Screen 3), then we recommend an outright sale of the stock. If the client replies positively to Screen 3, the investor continues down the decision tree to the following screen:

> In choosing "monetize," you indicated a desire to pull money out of the position. The "option combination" strategies are meant to create income. The most income comes with the least potential for profit on the stock.
>
> Do you prefer the least expensive monetization method accompanied by the least economic exposure? or A higher annual cost with more continued upside?
>
> (Screen 4)

We tell clients up front that the option combination strategies are meant to create income and that the most income is associated with the least potential for profit on the stock.

Least Expensive

Suppose the investor chooses the least expensive method to monetize the low-cost-basis stock position. The investor is then taken to a screen that discusses the income-producing collar.

On the "monetize" side of the tree, we are trying to generate cash to lower the net cost of the borrowing so that the objective—to defer the capital gains tax if the low-cost-basis stock is sold—is worthwhile. To accomplish this goal, we use an income-producing collar. Suppose a client's stock is valued at $100. To create an income-producing collar, the client buys a put with a strike price of $90 (90 percent of the value of the underlying stock), which would cost $14. Then the client sells a call that gives away most of the upside without triggering the constructive sale rules. (In this case, suppose it is the $105 call.) The client must sell a call with a strike price close enough to the current price of the stock so that the call will be priced higher than the put (i.e., the cash inflow from the sale of the call will exceed the cash outflow from the purchase of the put). Thus, net–net, the two concurrent transactions create an income-producing collar.

For example, the client may sell a call for $30. When the $14 paid for the put is deducted from the $30 received for the call, the client nets a profit of $16. No tax is due in the current period because the collar is considered an "open" transaction for tax purposes. With a three-year option, the client would earn about 5.2 percent a year in income, or the $16 excess premium spread over the three-year option period divided by the current stock

FIGURE 17.1   Illustration of the Profit/Loss Scenario of an Income-Producing Collar

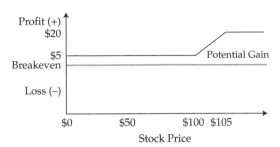

price of $100, which equals 5.2 percent. This 5.2 percent a year offsets the 6 percent a year the client pays in interest expense on the borrowed funds that monetize the stock position. As a result, the client's net cost is only 80 basis points annually to monetize and avoid paying the capital gains tax associated with liquidation of the stock position.

Graphically, this income-producing collar is shown in Figure 17.1. Remember that this collar is composed of a long put at $90, a short out-of-the-money call at $105 (a 15 percent band around the current stock price of $100), and a three-year option; the client is long the stock. The starting point of the potential profit/loss line is a profit of approximately $5. If the stock price is lower at the expiration of the three-year option term and the put is exercised, the collar is guaranteed to leave the client with a $5–$6 profit—the net $16 call premium when the strategy was put in place less the $10 ($100 market value less $90 put price) of lost market value in the stock. On the other hand, if the stock price is stable, the collar will generate roughly a $16 profit. And if the stock price rises, the maximum profit generated by the collar will be $20 with the added appreciation in the stock's price of $5 (the difference between $100 market value and $105 call price) plus the roughly $16 of net call premium. At this point, the stock position has not yet been monetized. The first step, which I have just described, is hedging the position by creating a collar (the income-producing collar) that affords the client the ability to monetize.

The constructive sale rules effectively control the tightness of the bands on the put and the call around the stock's price. When these rules became effective in 1997, the U.S. government said that options would not trigger the constructive sale rules if the option position was not abusive. The government has yet to define an abusive option position. Consequently, we are relying on the "Blue Book," a general explanation of tax laws published by the Joint Committee on Taxation. The 1997 Blue Book provides an example of a nonabusive option— a collar with a put at 95 percent of the stock price and a call at 110 percent of the stock price, or a 15 percent band. Thus, hiding behind the skirts of the government's own words, we never go narrower than a 15 percent band because it would be difficult for the government to claim that an option that conforms to its own example is abusive.

More Upside

If back at Screen 4 the client had chosen the strategy that presented more upside profit potential, the client would have been taken to the following screen:

> There are several strategies that increase the potential upside in the position. In considering the different approaches, you should be aware that there is a trade-off between income and potential profit. You should also understand that your choices are limited

by the constructive sale rules. These rules state that the investor must retain some ability to win or lose after hedging; otherwise, the trade may trigger a capital gains tax.

Here are several possibilities utilizing 3-year options. Please select one:

5¾% income with a maximum 5% profit.

4% income with a maximum 20% profit.

0% income with a maximum 50% profit.

(Screen 5)

If the client chooses the first option, the screen describing the income-producing collar appears. If the client chooses the second option, the client is asked whether he or she wants to proceed with a customized analysis. If the client chooses the third option, the client is taken to a screen describing a cashless collar, or zero-cost collar, which will be discussed in the next section.

Choosing to Hedge

If instead of choosing to monetize the low-cost-basis stock position at Screen 2 the client had chosen to "protect gains and let profits run," the client would have been opting to hedge. The following screen in the decision tree would have appeared:

The client can purchase insurance in the form of a put option. As an example, the put option could be structured to create a floor at today's stock price. These options typically cost 10–12% annually. If this is an acceptable cost, please press the continue button.

There are alternative strategies that will lower the cost of insurance by giving away some of the stock's upside potential. If this is of interest, please press the alternatives button.

(Screen 6)

Therefore, the hedging strategies available to the client include buying insurance in the form of a put option with a cost of 10–12 percent a year or using an alternative strategy that would lower the cost of acquiring the "insurance" by limiting the stock's upside potential. Notice that no concern is raised about the tax basis in the stock position, whether or not the tax basis is at least 50 percent of the market value of the stock. This lack of concern about the tax basis occurs because these put strategies have nothing to do with improving diversification; they merely truncate the opportunity for loss in a particular stock position.

Many alternatives to the long put strategy exist, the possibilities of which are limited only by the constructive sale rules. Clicking on the Alternatives button takes the client to a screen that says:

There are many hedges that cost less than 10% per year. In fact, some hedges even create income. Higher income is associated with the least potential for profit on the stock.

The possibilities are only limited by the constructive sale rules outlined in IRC Section 1259. These rules state that the investor must retain some ability to win or lose after hedging, otherwise the trade may trigger a capital gains tax.

Here are several possibilities utilizing 3-year options. Please select one.

6% hedging cost with a maximum 80% profit.

0% hedging cost with a maximum 50% profit.

4% income with a maximum 20% profit.

(Screen 7)

FIGURE 17.2   Illustration of the Profit/Loss Scenario of a Cashless Collar with a 100 Percent Put

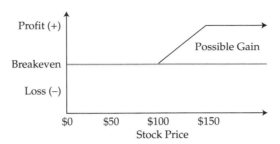

Thus, as an alternative to the long put option, which has a significant cost but unlimited upside potential, the client can choose one of the three preceding strategies with varying combinations of a cost/profit relationship.

The middle strategy, zero cost with potential profit of 50 percent, is a cashless collar, or a zero-cost collar. The collar is created by buying an out-of-the-money put and simultaneously selling an out-of-the-money call, with the strike price of the call set so that the call premium is exactly enough to pay for the cost of the put. Figure 17.2 illustrates the profit/loss scenario for a cashless collar. Assume the client owns a stock that trades at $100. The client buys a put with a strike price equal to 100 percent of the market value of the stock (an out-of-the money put). To pay for the put, the client sells an out-of-the-money call. For illustrative purposes, I will use a $150 call. Thus, the client has established, for zero cost, a floor equal to the stock's current price, but the client has a maximum profit potential of 50 percent of the current price of the stock.

CUSTOMIZED ANALYSIS

When a client gets to the point in the decision tree where a customized analysis is requested, he or she is asked to supply information on the name of the stock, the number of shares in the position, and what percentage of the market value of the stock he or she wants to borrow. After the client enters this initial information, from which the decision tree creates the client's basic investment scenario, the survey then generates strategy specifics. If the client chooses to proceed with the suggested strategy, the client must answer a few more questions. The client is asked if he or she is an affiliate or a control person, if the client's stock is restricted, if the client's stock is subject to a "lock up" agreement (many lock up agreements today do not allow hedging), if the client's stock was acquired after 1984 (which I will discuss in more detail later in this presentation), if the client's stock is involved in a stock-for-stock merger, and if the client wants to borrow more than 50 percent of the current market value of the stock.

Merger-Related Stock

We ask if the client's stock is involved in a stock-for-stock merger because if the client owned, for example, True North Communications and was going to get Interpublic stock in the merger, we would suggest that the client short the Interpublic stock before the deal closes (before the client actually owns the new stock) while there is still deal risk. When the deal closes, the client will be short against the box in Interpublic, which will be fine because the tax law measures what a person does when he or she does it, not what the transaction becomes later. This is a good short against the box that is totally grandfathered, has a step-up in basis, and is everything that the client could have received previously.

For that matter, the short-against-the-box strategy still lives. A manager can still use short-against-the-box positions for clients who do distress debt investing. If an investor paid $30 for a bond that is now worth $80, this investor should go short against the box on the bond. The constructive sale rules apply only to equities; they do not apply to debt. So, there are many ways that the short against the box can still be used.

Pre- or Post-1984

One of the most important questions we ask the client is whether the client purchased the stock before or after 1984. If the stock was bought after 1984, the straddle rules apply to the transaction, which affects the hedge construction.[3] If the client does not have to worry about dancing around the straddle rules, then setting up the hedge is much easier. If the stock was acquired after 1984, the straddle rules prohibit an investor from taking any losses until the entire position is closed but do not give equal treatment to gains; taxes must be paid on gains as they occur. Also, any interest expense must be capitalized.

Zero-Cost Collar

If the client owns stock bought after 1984 and wants to hedge, a collar (say, a zero-cost collar) would be the recommended strategy. For example, the client owns stock valued at $100 and wants to establish a $90/$175 collar. The client buys a put with a strike price of $90 for $14 and sells the call with a strike price of $175 for $14. Three years later, the stock is somewhere between $90 and $175; the stock has neither gone below the 90 percent threshold nor above the 175 percent threshold. What happens? The options expire worthless, right? But what happens with taxes? The $14 the client received from selling the call is a short-term gain on which the client must pay tax. The $14 the client paid for buying the put is not deductible until disposition of the entire position, including the stock. Depending on the particular circumstances, the client may never be able to use the deduction. Therefore, the client may pay the short-term capital gains tax, $5.60, before any profits are realized and without the corresponding benefit of a tax loss deduction. This unfortunate phenomenon is a by-product of a hedge construction using two separate options.

Wall Street offers many products that, for lack of a better technical term, meld the put and the call together, which corrects the mismatch in treatment of gains and losses. The client could do a one-contract option incorporating both the put and the call, which would effectively be a zero-cost collar with a put at $90 and a call at $175. The price of the contract would be zero. When the contract expires worthless, no tax would be imposed.

Prepaid Variable Forward

The client could also use a prepaid variable forward to mitigate the problem caused by the straddle rules. The prepaid variable forward, however, is the worst choice of all the available strategy alternatives and should be used only as a last option for those who purchased their shares pre-1984. Let me explain why. A client can borrow against an income-producing collar using either a margin loan or a prepaid variable forward. A prepaid variable forward is a type of forward sale contract with an embedded collar in which the investor receives an up-front payment in exchange for a commitment to deliver securities in the future, with the number of shares to be delivered varying with the underlying share price.

The leverage available with the prepaid variable forward is equal to the leverage available with a margin loan. The U.S. Federal Reserve, in Regulation T, imposes an initial margin requirement of 50 percent of the value of the underlying security if the purpose of the margin loan is to purchase stock. In addition, an investor can also borrow up to 50 percent of the market value of the securities purchased with the margin loan. Thus, the investor ends up with a dollar's worth of debt for every two dollars of portfolio value—50 cents against the collared position (the initial stockholding) and 50 cents against the diversified position (bought with the borrowed funds). So, a regular margin loan provides one-for-one leverage, and the prepaid variable forward cannot improve on this leverageability. Furthermore, who would not prefer to have $1 of deductible interest expense today rather than a capital loss when the stock in the forward is sold at the expiration date? Because the margin interest is deductible, every $1 of interest expense is transformed into an after-tax cost of only 60 cents, making the margin loan preferable to a prepaid variable forward.

A prepaid variable forward can be illustrated by the following example. Suppose the investor buys a cashless collar executed through a variable forward with a $100 put/$150 call priced at $85. Carrying costs are $15. If at expiration the stock is worth less than $100, the investor sells the stock at $85 and realizes $15 less in long-term capital gains than would otherwise have been the case. These gains would have been taxed at 20 cents on the dollar, so the true cost is $12 after tax. Thus, at the end of the three years, at expiration, the client who has chosen the prepaid forward gets a deduction of 20 cents on the dollar. If, instead, the collar had been combined with a margin loan, the interest expense deduction would have been 40 cents on the dollar in the first year. Who would want a deduction of 20 cents three years from now instead of a deduction of 40 cents today? So, the $15 cost of the prepaid variable forward on an after-tax basis is $12 versus the interest expense of a margin loan on an after-tax basis of only $9. Thus, a 33 percent higher cost is borne by the client simply as a result of choosing the wrong hedging tool.

So, when is it appropriate to use a prepaid variable forward? If the client cannot sign the purpose letter required when an amount greater than 50 percent of the underlying stock is borrowed on margin, then a prepaid variable forward makes sense. The purpose letter states that the client does not plan to use the borrowed funds as the original margin to buy new stock. And we believe, and most of the broker/dealers that we clear through believe, that if the client wants to use the borrowed funds to invest in a hedge fund, then the client cannot sign the purpose letter. In a case such as this, a prepaid variable forward would be appropriate. And the only reason that clients are in this position is because they are paying off margin debt.

The Federal Reserve does not let an investor use a nonpurpose loan to pay off margin debt and will not let an investor borrow more than 50 percent of the market value of the collateral to invest in equities. Equities that are not marginable are the only ones that cause a problem. If a client wanted to borrow and buy private equity, that would be okay, but if the client wanted to buy public equity, the client would have to do it with 50 cents of debt against the hedge position and 50 cents against the new portfolio. If this client wanted to invest in a hedge fund that was invested in stocks, the broker/dealer might tell him or her that it is not a valid purpose under the purpose test, and then he or she would have to use a variable forward.

Swaps

U.S. Vice President Dick Cheney recently faced a similar situation regarding his Halliburton Company employee stock options. It was suggested that he use prepaid variable forwards to hedge his profits; however, I would not recommend this strategy. Halliburton stock is at $60, and Cheney's options are nonqualifying options; they shed ordinary income. So, if his hedge is at $60 and the stock goes up to $80, he has $20 more of ordinary income on each employee option and $20 of capital losses on the hedge. But capital losses are not deductible; they are only offsetable against realized gains. So, Halliburton's price can skyrocket, but Cheney will not make any money. He will, however, have a giant tax bill because he has $20 of ordinary income for every share he owns and $20 of capital losses he cannot use.

I would have recommended another hedging tool—a swap with an embedded collar—for which cash payments paid or received are treated as ordinary losses and ordinary income. Thus, a swap is the better hedging tool to hedge employee options because any income or gain from the movement in the stock price is completely offset in character as well as in dollars.

CONCLUSION

Hedging low-cost-basis stock is not a simple process, particularly after the tax laws changed in 1997. Central to the process is the identification of the investor's reason for wanting to hedge and potentially monetize low-cost-basis stock as well as the knowledge of when the shares were originally purchased and their cost basis. This information is important to the choice and success of the strategy adopted, which can range from income-producing collars to zero-cost collars and prepaid variable forwards.

QUESTION AND ANSWER SESSION

Question: What are the typical transaction costs related to diversification strategies? How much profit do the banks make on these strategies?

Gordon: In terms of short selling, the dealer is shorting the stock and taking the risk of the hedge strategy. Whether money will be made on the trade is debatable. Actually, the crash of 1987 was dynamic hedging gone awry. Yet none of the banks took that event as a lesson, and most banks are still doing exactly what they were doing before: They are dynamically hedging their positions. Dynamic hedging starts with the assumption that you can always sell at the right price without driving the price down, and that is exactly what happened to LOR (Leland O'Brien Rubinstein Associates) in the crash of 1987. I think the profit the banks actually make on these strategies is debatable.

Question: Regarding straddles, if a private company has been in existence for many years and is acquired by a publicly traded company for equity after 1984, does the straddle rule apply?

Gordon: The first question is easier to answer than the second one. Whether you owned stock in a public company or a private company that was taken over in a stock-for-stock deal after 1984 does not matter. The legal advisors we work with believe the pre-1984 situation applies, and the straddle rules would not be invoked. We have had only three or four clients get legal opinions on such a situation, but all have been positive. The sale and repurchase may be ignored for the purpose of the reorganization but might not be ignored in deciding whether it triggers gain. Most of the advisors believe it is ignored for both purposes.

Question: Has recent tax law hindered the benefit of equity flex options?

Gordon: Equity flex options as they stand now are very useful because they have the same characteristics in the listed market that they have in the OTC market. The option can be European style, or the investor can pick the strike price. With flex options, you always have the AAA rating of the Options Clearing Corporation. If you want to get out early, you can, rather than having to buy your way out from a derivative dealer. So, equity flex options have many advantages.

Some proposed regulations were released in the beginning of January 2001, but they have not yet been finalized. The proposed regulations provide some give and take. These regulations implicitly encourage investors that own stock acquired after 1984 to use listed options, because the regulations provide that if you write a call that is out of the money and listed, it is not a straddle—even if you bought the stock after 1984. That situation created fantastic opportunities.

Take the case of someone who has just exercised an incentive stock option. Within the one-year period, if she buys a put, it will stop her holding period, but she still could sell the call if it is a qualified covered call under these rules. But it has to be listed. Although the proposed rules would broaden this ability and allow OTC options to be qualified covered calls, none of the options can be longer than a year. To be in a stock that you purchased after 1984 and to roll over those calls and get whipsawed every 11½ months is not worth the strategy required for *not* being a straddle. If these regulations are passed, I do not see any great advantage to flex options and qualified covered calls. Until recently, however, there was a clear benefit to both.

Question: What happens when options in collars expire after three years?

Gordon: There can be negative tax consequences to "rolling over" the hedge. This is even more of a problem for those open to the straddle rules. Some hedges can be constructed that mitigate the problems associated with "rolling" the hedge.

Question: What is the cost basis at the end of a forward contract when delivering cash or shares?

Gordon: If you deliver shares, your original basis is the cost basis. If you cash settle the forward, then a gain or loss will be measured from your cash flow on termination, not referenced to the stock you held. Beware of the straddle rules as to whether the loss can be currently deducted.

Question: Can you discuss the tax implications of the rehypothecation of securities pledged as collateral in connection with the hedge/monetized transaction?

Gordon: IRC Section 1058 discusses the requirements for loaning securities without triggering a gain. Section 1058 provides a safe harbor if you loaned the shares in a way that did not also transfer risk. Because risk may be limited by lending the security, you may be out of the safe harbor and thus open to questions. We think this strategy is acceptable in the eyes of the IRS, but the client should be informed of the risks. In 2006, the IRS released TAM 200604033 that takes the position that a share loan and a prepaid variable forward together trigger a gain.

Question: How bullish must a client be on his or her individual stock for these strategies to make sense? Does the expected rate of appreciation need to exceed that of the market to make these strategies worthwhile?

Gordon: A client doesn't need to be bullish, but the client must have a need to lock-in profits without triggering gains. We believe the basis should be 50 percent or less of the current market price, or an outright sale to liquidate the position should be made.

Question: Doesn't the "least expensive" method (i.e., little upside) expose one to the capital gains tax (i.e., stock called away), making it a very expensive method (vis-à-vis the "more expensive," more upside method)?

Gordon: No, options can be cash settled. There is *never* a need to deliver shares even if the options are physically settled; other shares can be purchased to deliver against the option.

Question: How do taxes affect the income-producing collar?

Gordon: All option proceeds are without tax at inception and receipt but taxable at their conclusion after gain or loss can be established in a "closing transaction."

Question: Regarding purpose and nonpurpose loans from a collar, is it safe to assume that money used to pay down margin debt would be considered a "purpose" loan? Is it better to do a variable prepaid forward?

Gordon: Paying off a margin loan is *not* a permitted purpose; it is not allowed. We use prepaid forwards when the intent is to repay a margin loan.

NOTES

1. Section 1259 of the U.S. Internal Revenue Code (IRC) states that investors must retain some potential profit or loss when constructing a hedging strategy or they will trigger a taxable event. That is, investors cannot hedge away too much of the potential loss or gain or they will be seen as having sold an "appreciated financial position," which is a taxable event.
2. See the discussion of Figure 17.1 in this presentation for an explanation of how and why the income-producing collar earns 5 percent.
3. Straddle rules are governed by U.S. Internal Revenue Code Section 1092. These rules affect stock positions purchased after December 31, 1983, and govern when gains and losses can be taken on the two legs of the straddle.

PART III

TAX-EFFICIENT WEALTH ACCUMULATION

CHAPTER 18

TAX-ADVANTAGED SAVINGS ACCOUNTS AND TAX-EFFICIENT WEALTH ACCUMULATION

Stephen M. Horan, CFA

FOREWORD

Academics and practitioner researchers have developed a large body of impressive research for determining optimal investment strategies and valuation models, yet much of this research abstracts from real-world complexities, such as transaction costs, liquidity constraints, limitations on access to credit, and of particular importance, taxes. Indeed, the standard by which many scholars evaluate research is neither relevance nor reality but, rather, mathematical elegance. This attitude is jokingly summarized by the aphorism, *the real world is an uninteresting, special case of my model.* Thankfully, Stephen M. Horan, CFA, is well grounded in the real world as evidenced by this outstanding chapter, *Tax-Advantaged Savings Accounts and Tax-Efficient Wealth Accumulation.*

As corporations shift from defined-benefit pension plans to 401(k) plans and the government offers a wider menu of tax-deferred accounts, individual investors and their financial advisors are faced with a more complex set of investment choices. How they direct the flow of their savings and where they locate their assets is now a first-order consideration for wealth accumulation. Horan artfully disentangles this new and more complex reality with a fine balance of mathematical precision, accessibility, and pragmatism.

The time value of money serves as the foundation of Horan's analysis, which focuses mainly on retirement savings. Horan uses this familiar methodology to evaluate a variety of investment choices including, for example, alternative investment vehicles, front-end versus back-end tax benefits, employer-matching contributions, investment in nondeductible IRAs versus taxable investments, and early withdrawal penalties. Of necessity in a piece of this size, he abstracts from tax minutiae and concentrates on the important issues. He uses clear examples to demonstrate the advantage of one approach versus another, and he provides numerous

---

Reprinted from The Research Foundation of CFA Institute (June 2005).

tables to illustrate and generalize his points. For those unwilling to engage in mathematical detail, Horan summarizes many of these topics with clearly and concisely stated guidelines. And for those who demand more mathematical detail, he includes of variety of technical appendices.

The essential concepts and tools of investment management were developed primarily in the sterile world of tax-exempt investing, and perhaps justifiably so given the dominance of institutional investors, such as pension funds and eleemosynary institutions. But that is not the world we live in today. Individual investors control vast sums of wealth, and they demand tax-efficient investment strategies. The Research Foundation is especially pleased to contribute this excellent chapter to the cause of developing a more robust framework for tax-efficient investing.

Mark Kritzman, CFA
Research Director
The Research Foundation of CFA Institute

PREFACE

Taxing investment returns is largely a 20th century phenomenon. The first temporary federal income tax in U.S. history was passed in the early 1860s to subsidize the Civil War and included a tax on interest and dividends paid to investors of insurance companies and banks.[1] Originally accepted as an emergency wartime measure, the 3 percent tax on income of more than $800 was allowed to expire in 1872. After a series of conflicting U.S. Supreme Court decisions and tax acts, the income tax regained its foothold in U.S. fiscal policy in 1913 with the passage of the Sixteenth Amendment, which serves as the basis for a permanent, progressive income tax. Modest as the income tax may have been initially (1–2 percent on income of more than $3,000), World War I transformed it into the centerpiece of federal finance, raising the top rate to 6 percent. By 1919, the top rate had risen to 77 percent, and in 1921, Congress passed a preferential tax rate for capital gains.

Despite a long history of high tax rates for investment returns, most modern portfolio theory is grounded in a pretax framework. Only recently have researchers investigated the impact of taxes and tax-preferred savings accounts on risk and return characteristics of a portfolio and wealth accumulation. Nonetheless, a fundamental issue facing investors, particularly those investing for retirement, is how to invest funds in a tax-efficient manner. Using tax incentives, the U.S. federal government encourages retirement savings through many different tax-advantaged savings programs. The proliferation of traditional individual retirement accounts (IRAs), defined-contribution plans, 401(k) plans, 403(b) plans, Keogh plans, Roth IRAs, and other tax-preferred savings accounts expands opportunities for efficient wealth accumulation but also adds complexity to the investor's decision. These programs offer tax-deferred accumulation of savings and allow the taxpayer to either contribute to or withdraw from the account on a tax-exempt basis.

Often called tax-deferred accounts, or TDAs, these investment vehicles are quite popular. According to the U.S. Department of Labor, almost half of all full-time U.S. workers in 2003 used payroll deductions to make contributions to defined-contribution plans.[2] The assets held in defined-benefit and defined-contribution plans totaled $4.2 trillion in 2003, most of which was held in defined-contribution plans controlled, at least to some extent, by the employee.[3] Another $3 trillion was invested in IRAs, which are becoming more popular than employer-sponsored plans. Contributions to IRAs in 2003, for example, were three times larger than contributions to defined-benefit and defined-contribution plans combined.[4] Another indication of the IRA's popularity is that net contributions to employer-sponsored plans have fallen by more than half in the past 10 years, whereas the amount in IRAs has more than doubled over the same time period.[5] These trends reflect the growing responsibility borne by individual investors and their financial advisors to invest tax efficiently. They also emphasize the need for developing methods that can be used to evaluate various tax-advantaged investment alternatives.

The problem of tax-efficient investing is aggravated by the complexity and instability of the tax code. Since 1997 alone, investors in the United States have experienced three major tax reforms that significantly affect an investor's optimal decision making regarding the use of tax-deferred savings accounts: the Taxpayer Relief Act (TRA) of 1997, the Economic Growth Tax Relief Reconciliation Act (EGTRRA) of 2001, and the Jobs and Growth Tax Relief Reconciliation Act (JGTRRA) of 2003. The TRA of 1997 created the Roth IRA, which has been the forerunner of many different types of back-end-loaded, tax-advantaged savings accounts. The EGTRRA of 2001 lowered marginal tax rates and lowered the tax rate on realized capital gains to 20 percent. The JGTRRA of 2003 accelerated the implementation of marginal tax rate reductions and further eroded the double taxation of equity returns by reducing the tax rate on realized capital gains, as well as dividends, to 15 percent. All of these measures affect an investor's decisions regarding tax-efficient wealth accumulation.

The issue of tax-efficient investing is not unique to U.S. investors. Most industrialized and developing countries have tax incentives to encourage retirement savings. An international survey of 24 industrialized and developing countries commissioned by the American Council for Capital Formation (ACCF) indicates that tax-advantaged savings accounts are offered to taxpayers by two-thirds of the countries surveyed, including Australia, Canada, Germany, Italy, the Netherlands, and the United Kingdom.[6] All but one of these countries permits tax-deductible contributions. In addition, a related survey commissioned by the ACCF indicates that many countries have tax investment income much like the United States, albeit at a generally lower level.[7] For example, all but two countries surveyed have different tax rates for interest income and capital gains. Therefore, the analysis developed herein has international applicability.

Until recently, the issue of tax-efficient investing has been largely overlooked by the mainstream literature. And simple heuristics to guide investors and their advisors are not always as obvious as they might initially seem. The pages that follow provide a compendium of the recent advances in this area, as well as some updates and extensions. The ultimate aim is to lay a foundation that yields practical rules of thumb that can be used as a basis for analyzing a series of investment decisions in an individual's unique circumstance.

This chapter explores central issues surrounding the use of tax-deferred investment accounts as a means of accumulating wealth. Most of the chapter focuses on retirement savings. As the reader will discover, however, it also examines nonretirement savings issues, including using tax-deferred retirement accounts for nonretirement purposes and using education savings accounts for noneducational purposes. Much of the literature analyzing the tax implications of tax-efficient investment strategies involves sophisticated methods. My aim is to present a useful framework, grounded in basic time-value-of-money concepts, that can be readily implemented by investment professionals. Using basic algebra, I dissect and package the model into intuitive components, emphasize important relationships, and derive practical rules of thumb. Another practical feature of this framework is its flexibility. Because the model is based on general time-value-of-money and tax principles, it can be adapted easily to different tax environments. Therefore, non-U.S. investors will find the framework equally applicable in their home countries. The framework will also remain relevant to investors over time as they respond to endless changes in the tax code.

The initial sections of this chapter lay the analytical foundations for examining a series of common financial decisions that are explored in later sections. The Introduction presents different types of investment vehicles and reviews their salient characteristics. The following section lays the foundation for evaluating tax-advantaged investment decisions. By introducing a framework for calculating future values in different tax environments, this fundamental section addresses the question of choosing between TDAs with front-end tax benefits, such as traditional IRAs, and those with back-end tax benefits, such as Roth IRAs. Armed with these basic tools, I examine other TDA investment decisions in the following sections: Employer Matching and Converting a Traditional IRA to a Roth IRA, Choosing between Nondeductible IRAs and Taxable Investments, Valuing Tax-Sheltered Assets on an After-Tax Basis, and Early Withdrawal Penalties and Breakeven Time Horizons. The section called Employer Matching and Converting a Traditional IRA to a Roth IRA examines the implications of employer-matching arrangements that are often found as part of 401(k) plans or other defined-contribution plans. The results show that it is rarely optimal for an investor to forgo the benefits of employer matching. The section on Choosing between Nondeductible IRAs and Taxable Investments applies a similar analysis to the choice between nondeductible IRA investments and taxable investments. Perhaps surprisingly, taxable investments are preferred to nondeductible IRA investments in many instances. The section called Valuing Tax-Sheltered Assets on an After-Tax Basis uses basic technology to determine the after-tax value of assets held in tax-sheltered accounts. Depending on the circumstance, the after-tax value of a dollar held in a TDA may be more or less than $1.00. I then examine the notion of early withdrawal penalties in the section called Early Withdrawal Penalties and Breakeven Time Horizons. The analysis helps determine when an investor might rationally use a TDA and knowingly incur an early withdrawal penalty rather than use a taxable account.

In the segment on Asset Location between Taxable and Tax-Deferred Savings Accounts, I move beyond the investment analysis among and within TDAs to take a somewhat broader view, examining the interaction between asset allocation and asset location. Asset allocation, of course, refers to how an investor allocates his or her investment portfolio among different asset classes. Asset location refers to how assets are distributed among taxable accounts and TDAs. A strictly formal analysis of this issue is prohibitively complicated, but I review the recent research and provide intuitive and sometimes counterintuitive rules of thumb. I conclude in the final section on Implications for Financial Analysts with some general guidance for financial professionals seeking to make investment decisions that are informed by an understanding of the tax implications of wealth accumulation in tax-advantaged savings accounts.

The reader should note that this chapter does not include an exhaustive treatment of all the nuances in the U.S. tax code associated with tax-advantaged savings accounts. Such publications already exist and do not lend themselves to economic analysis and practical application. Instead, I focus on salient features of TDA investing and incorporate them into the analysis. Consequently, I abstract from some of the seemingly infinite loopholes and tax minutiae. This chapter also does not contain a macroeconomic analysis of the impact of tax incentives on aggregate savings, the pension system, or tax receipts. These questions have fiscal policy implications more than investment decision-making implications. I present useful tools that financial analysts can readily apply to the investment decision-making process.

I am grateful to the many people who have directly and indirectly helped make this chapter a reality. I am indebted to my wife, Connie, who has been a constant source of encouragement, enduring endless hours of my absence and contributing her editing prowess. I am also grateful to those who have encouraged and sharpened my thinking on many of these issues over the years, including Robert McLeod, Jeffrey Peterson, Karen Eilers Lahey, Conrad Ciccotello, and William Jennings. The Research Foundation of CFA Institute deserves special recognition as well. In supporting this endeavor, it has demonstrated leadership and courage in helping to set a research agenda that has only begun to find its way into mainstream financial literature.

S.M.H.

St. Bonaventure, New York

April 2005

INTRODUCTION

The United States has a long history of encouraging retirement savings by providing tax incentives for investors.[8] Although individual retirement accounts (IRAs) were first introduced in 1974 for employees without pension plans, fewer than 3 percent of taxpayers contributed to such plans that year. The Economic Recovery Tax Act of 1981 increased contribution limits and expanded eligibility requirements for IRAs, allowing almost all working taxpayers to contribute. As a result, contributions to IRA accounts increased substantially until the Tax Reform Act of 1986 excluded higher-income taxpayers with employer-provided pension plans from making tax-deductible contributions. The 401(k) savings program, which also became popular in the early 1980s, permits tax-deductible contributions and tax deferral on accumulated earnings until funds are withdrawn, much like the traditional IRA. And like the IRA, withdrawals from 401(k) plans prior to age 59½ are subject to a 10 percent early withdrawal penalty.[9] In addition, the investor is generally required to make minimum withdrawals starting at age 70½. But unlike IRAs, 401(k) plans are sponsored by an employer, have much higher contribution limits, and permit employers to make additional contributions to supplement employees' contributions. Traditional IRA, 401(k), 403(b), 457, and Keogh plans are sometimes said to have front-end-loaded tax benefits because the initial contribution is tax deductible in many cases and the withdrawal is taxed as ordinary income.[10]

The Taxpayer Relief Act (TRA) of 1997 introduced a variation on this theme—the Roth IRA. Named after the Delaware senator William Roth, who sponsored the bill, Roth IRAs are sometimes said to have back-end-loaded tax benefits because, although the investor enjoys no tax deduction for the initial contribution, accumulated earnings and withdrawals are free from tax. This new type of IRA reignited investor interest in IRAs, as evidenced by annual contributions nearly doubling over the 1996–2003 period.[11] The U.S. Congress, as well, must have liked the idea of encouraging savings with back-end-loaded tax benefits. And why not? Legislators forgo no tax revenue for the initial contribution and leave it to future Congresses to handle the forgone tax revenue created by tax-exempt withdrawals. As a result, taxpayers are witnessing the introduction and proposal of similar targeted savings accounts, including Section 529 College Savings plans, new Roth 401(k) plans, health care savings accounts, and lifetime savings accounts (LSAs). Introduced in 2001, Section 529 plans are designed to encourage higher education saving and are nearly equivalent to the Roth IRA from a tax perspective: Withdrawals for noneducational purposes are subject to a 10 percent withdrawal penalty. Congress created the Roth 401(k) in the Economic Growth Tax Relief Reconciliation Act (EGTRRA) of 2001. Although the Roth 401(k) is scheduled to take effect

TABLE 18.1   Tax Treatment of Different Savings Accounts

Item	Traditional IRA, 401(k), 403(b), 457, and Keogh Plans	Roth IRA, 529, and Roth 401(k) Plans and LSAs	Nondeductible IRA	Taxable Account
Initial contribution	Tax deductible	Not deductible	Not deductible	Not deductible
Accumulated earnings	Tax deferred	Tax exempt	Tax deferred	Taxable as ordinary income, dividend, or capital gain as realized
Withdrawal	Taxable as ordinary income	Tax exempt	Accumulated earnings taxable as ordinary income	Previously unrealized gains taxed as capital gain

1 January 2006, as of this writing, the Bush administration has proposed accelerating its availability a year and renaming it Roth Employee Retirement Savings Accounts (ERSAs). The same budget proposal includes a provision for LSAs that would be nearly identical to Roth IRAs but would have more liberal contribution and withdrawal policies.

Tax law is ever changing; contribution limits, eligibility requirements, and withdrawal policies vary from plan to plan. But the basic theme is that all accounts offer the opportunity to accumulate earnings in a tax-deferred manner. Some accounts allow tax-free contributions, and others permit tax-free withdrawals. The salient tax features of the most popular TDAs and taxable accounts are summarized in Table 18.1, which separates the investment horizon of a savings account into three phases: the initial contribution, the accumulation phase, and withdrawal. The taxable account is taxed in all three phases. During the accumulation and withdrawal phases, the timing of taxable events and the associated tax rate for the taxable account depend on the proportion of return that is ordinary income dividend, realized capital gain, or unrealized capital gain. Withdrawals from traditional IRAs are taxed as ordinary income, whereas contributions to Roth IRAs are taxed as ordinary income. One could say that the nominal taxes paid upon withdrawal for a traditional IRA will be greater than those paid upon contribution for a Roth IRA. But properly discounting these future taxes at the opportunity cost of capital exactly offsets their nominal growth. So, the present value of the traditional IRA tax liability upon withdrawal is exactly equal to the additional tax paid on a Roth IRA contribution, depending on how tax rates change over time. This assumption is pivotal, and I examine it in detail in the pages that follow.

Taxpayers who do not qualify for tax-deductible IRA contributions may be allowed to make nondeductible IRA contributions. These funds enjoy the same taxdeferral status for earnings as other IRAs and are taxed as ordinary income upon withdrawal. The initial contribution, however, does not lower the investor's tax bill. In some circumstances, an investor may optimally forgo a nondeductible IRA investment in favor of a taxable investment that might have some inherent tax advantages of its own, such as tax deferral through unrealized capital gain and lower tax rates on realized capital gains. Unlike a nondeductible IRA, a taxable investment is not taxed as ordinary income upon withdrawal and may receive preferential tax treatment in the form of capital gains and dividends. The trade-off between the tax advantages of these two strategies is examined in the section on Choosing between Nondeductible IRAs and Taxable Investments.

Table 18.2 highlights some other features of tax-advantaged savings accounts. The EGTRRA of 2001 increased the contribution limits on these accounts and set a schedule for future increases. Prior to its passage, the contribution limit for IRAs stood at $2,000 for many years. This legislation also created "catch up" contributions for taxpayers 50 years of age or older. Table 18.2 also shows that employer-sponsored plans have much higher contribution limits than IRA accounts. Income limitations for the traditional IRA are much lower than those for the Roth IRA or employer-sponsored plans, which can be somewhat complicated. Because the income limits for married couples are less than twice the limits for single filers, some may say a "marriage penalty" exists in this part of the tax code. Withdrawals before age 59½ are generally subject to a 10 percent penalty unless an exemption applies, such as disability, medical expenses, or a first-time home purchase. Early withdrawals from 401(k)s are a bit more restrictive, but investors can often borrow funds from their account or use their account as collateral for a loan, which is not allowed for IRA accounts. In any case, investors are required to make mandatory withdrawals starting at age 70½.

The next section abstracts a bit from these details and lays the foundation for analyzing the best choice among different tax-advantaged savings plans. This framework considers the salient features outlined in Tables 18.1 and 18.2 and is based on fundamental concepts of time value of money, which are familiar to all investment professionals.

CHOOSING BETWEEN TRADITIONAL IRAs AND ROTH IRAs: THE BASICS

Motivated by the passage of the TRA of 1997, Crain and Austin (1997) modeled the choice between a traditional IRA and a Roth IRA. Their analysis, and most of the following analysis in this chapter, should be interpreted with the understanding that the term "traditional IRA" generically represents all TDAs with front-loaded tax benefits, including 401(k), 403(b), 457, and Keogh plans. Likewise, the term "Roth IRA" can most often be understood as omnibus vernacular representing TDAs with back-loaded tax benefits, such as Section 529, Roth 401(k), and LSA plans. This section focuses on the choice between TDA accounts having front-end tax benefits and those having back-end tax benefits. The analysis, therefore, has much broader applicability than merely IRA accounts, despite the fact that I proceed using the IRA nomenclature for simplicity.

Another point of taxonomy is in order. One might think of this section's central issue as an "asset location" question. This term, however, is generally understood to mean something different. It relates to where an investor might optimally hold stocks or bonds (or some other asset class) when both taxable and TDA accounts are used for investing. This section, in contrast, focuses on the investor's choice between different types of TDA accounts for a given investment. For the sake of clarity, I avoid using the term "asset location" until the section called Asset Location between Taxable and Tax-Deferred Savings Accounts, which addresses it directly.

This section establishes that comparing traditional IRA and Roth IRA investments by equalizing the pretax investment is equivalent to equalizing the after-tax investment as long as one is consistent in making assumptions about how tax savings are invested. Using this insight

TABLE 18.2   Contribution, Eligibility, and Withdrawal Policies of Tax-Advantaged Savings Accounts

Item	Traditional IRA	Roth IRA	401(k) and 403(b)
A. Contribution limits			
2004	$3,000[a]	$3,000[a]	$13,000[b]
2005	$4,000[a]	$4,000[a]	$14,000[b]
2006	$4,000[a]	$4,000[a]	$15,000[b]
2007	$4,000[a]	$4,000[a]	Indexed[c]
2008	$5,000[a]	$5,000[a]	
2009	Indexed[c]	Indexed[c]	
B. Income limitations for 2005			
Single			
Full contribution	$50,000[d]	$95,000[e]	$90,000[f]
Partial contribution	$60,000[d]	$110,000[e]	
Married filing joint			
Full contribution	$70,000[d]	$150,000[e]	$90,000[f]
Partial contribution	$80,000[d]	$160,000[e]	
C. Withdrawal policies			
Minimum age	59½	59½	59½
Mandatory age	70½	None	70½
Early withdrawal penalty	10% of withdrawal	10% of earnings	10% of withdrawal
Penalty exemptions	Disability, death, medical expenses, first-time home purchase, higher education expenses	Disability, death, medical expenses, first-time home purchase, higher education expenses	Disability, death, medical expenses, separation of service after age 55

[a]Taxpayers 50 years of age or older can contribute an additional $500 through 2005 and an additional $1,000 through 2008.

[b]Taxpayers 50 years of age or older can contribute an additional $3,000 in 2004, $4,000 in 2005, and $5,000 in 2006. These "catch up" contributions will be indexed for inflation in $500 increments.

[c]Indexed for inflation in $500 increments.

[d]Income limitations for the traditional IRA relate to the tax deductibility of the contribution and do not apply if a taxpayer does not participate in a qualified employer-sponsored retirement plan.

[e]Income limitations for the Roth IRA relate to contribution eligibility.

[f]An income limitation applies only if the percentage of income that highly compensated employees defer into the plan is more than 2 percentage points higher than non-highly compensated employees. A highly compensated employee owns more than 5 percent of the business or earned more than $90,000 the previous year.

to establish a general framework, this section shows that traditional IRAs become relatively more attractive than Roth IRAs when an investor's withdrawal tax rate declines. The intuition is simple: The tax shelter of the traditional IRA is greatest when contribution tax rates are high, and the tax shelter of the Roth IRA is greatest when withdrawal tax rates are high.

When an investor maximizes the pretax contribution, however, part of the traditional IRA strategy must include a taxable investment, which hampers its performance compared with the Roth IRA. In this case, if the investor drops two tax brackets during retirement, the traditional IRA is almost always preferred to the Roth IRA because the benefit of the low-withdrawal tax rate outweighs the disadvantage of the taxable investment associated with the traditional IRA strategy. When the same investor drops only one tax bracket, the traditional IRA is optimal only for short time horizons or for investments with low rates of return.

Equalizing the Investment

Crain and Austin compared the after-tax accumulations of traditional IRAs and Roth IRAs for various returns and investment horizons. For a meaningful comparison, they held the pretax investment constant for the two investment choices and implicitly assumed that it was less than the after-tax contribution limit.[12] Under the premise that investors are better advised to make investment decisions net of taxes, other authors have standardized the after-tax investment.[13] As it turns out, Horan (2003) showed that the two seemingly contrasting approaches are reconcilable and can be combined into one cohesive framework. The issue is best understood by way of example.

Consider an investor currently in the 25 percent tax bracket (denoted as T_o) who wishes to make a $3,000 investment *before taxes* (I_{BT}). The contribution limit (L) for both traditional and Roth IRAs in the 2004 tax year is $3,000. The entire $3,000 may be invested in the traditional IRA and escape taxation; withdrawals from this account will be taxed as ordinary income. For the Roth IRA, only $2,250 [i.e., $3,000(1 − 0.25)$] can be invested because contributions are taxable. Although the after-tax investment is lower for the Roth IRA than the traditional IRA, withdrawals from the Roth IRA are not taxed. Panel A of Table 18.3 displays the instance in which the pretax contribution is less than the contribution limit (i.e., $I_{BT} \leq L$).

One can equivalently view the scenario in Panel A as a standardized $2,250 after-tax investment. Doing so, however, requires one to make an assumption about how tax savings are to be invested. Contributing $2,250 to the traditional IRA generates an initial tax savings of $562.50 (i.e., $2,250 \times 0.25$). Because the IRA contribution limit is $3,000 and has not yet been reached, these tax savings can be reinvested in the traditional IRA, which creates more tax savings. The total amount of tax savings that can be reinvested in the traditional IRA is $750 [i.e., $562.50/(1 − 0.25)$], yielding a total investment for the traditional IRA of $3,000, which is identical to the standardized pretax investment scenario. This equivalency between the two approaches holds for any pretax investment up to and including the IRA contribution limit ($I_{BT} \leq L$).[14] Therefore, a standardized pretax investment less than or equal to the IRA contribution limit is equivalent to a standardized after-tax investment in which tax savings are assumed to be reinvested in the deductible IRA.

A similar equivalence exists when one maximizes the pretax contribution. This hypothetical investor can contribute up to $4,000 pretax into the traditional IRA [i.e., $3,000/(1 − 0.25)$]. In this case, a non-IRA investment in some kind of taxable investment is required for the $1,000 above the contribution limit. The exact type of taxable investment is considered below, but in any case, it is initially taxed as ordinary income, leaving $750 after taxes [i.e., $1,000(1 − 0.25)$]

TABLE 18.3   Example of Standardized Pretax Investments in a Traditional IRA and
Roth IRA

Item	Traditional IRA	Roth IRA
A. $I_{BT} \leq L$		
Pretax investment (I_{BT})	$3,000	$3,000
After-tax investment		
IRA investment	3,000	2,250
Non-IRA investment	0	—
Total after-tax investment	$3,000	$2,250
B. $I_{BT} = L/(1 - T_o)$		
Pretax investment (I_{BT})	$4,000	$4,000
After-tax investment		
IRA investment	3,000	3,000
Non-IRA investment $[(I_{BT} - L)/(1 - T_o)]$	750	—
Total after-tax investment	$3,750	$3,000
C. $L < I_{BT} < L/(1 - T_o)$		
Pretax investment (I_{BT})	$3,500	$3,500
After-tax investment		
IRA investment	3,000	2,625
Non-IRA investment $[(I_{BT} - L)/(1 - T_o)]$	375	—
Total after-tax investment	$3,375	$2,625

Note: The investor faces a 25 percent tax bracket (T_o) and a $3,000 after-tax contribution
limit (L).
Source: Horan (2003).

to be invested in a non-IRA vehicle. As Panel B illustrates, the $4,000 pretax traditional IRA
investment comprises a $3,000 tax-sheltered investment, a $750 taxable investment, and $250 in
taxes. For the Roth IRA alternative, the $4,000 pretax investment comprises the $3,000 contribution and $1,000 of taxes.

One can equivalently view the scenario in Panel B as a standardized after-tax investment
of $3,000. An investor contributing $3,000 after-tax dollars into a traditional IRA will
generate $750 of tax savings that can be invested in some kind of taxable investment. In a
standardized after-tax framework, the $750 is the tax savings from the IRA strategy. In a pretax
framework, it is the after-tax investment in excess of the IRA contribution limit. The main
point is that a standardized pretax investment equal to the maximum allowable pretax allocation to an IRA is equivalent to a standardized after-tax investment equal to the IRA contribution limit in which the tax savings are invested in some kind of taxable account.

A similar equivalence holds when the pretax investment is greater than the contribution
limit but less than the maximum pretax Roth IRA investment, such as the $3,500 pretax
contribution illustrated in Panel C of Table 18.3. In this case, $2,625 [i.e., $3,500(1 − 0.25)]
is invested in the Roth IRA. Because the contribution limit is $3,000, only a portion of the

$3,500 pretax investment can be allocated to the traditional IRA, leaving $500 pretax for a taxable investment. The result is a $375 [i.e., $500(1 − 0.25)] non-IRA investment. Any marginal pretax investment greater than $4,000 is treated identically under both the traditional IRA and Roth IRA alternatives in that it must be invested in a taxable investment and does not, therefore, affect the decision between the traditional and Roth IRA.

Notice that the total after-tax investment for the traditional IRA strategy is always $750 greater than that for a Roth IRA. The difference between the three cases rests in how the $750 is invested. In the first case, the entire $750 can be reinvested in the traditional IRA. In the second case, the $750 is invested in a taxable, non-IRA account. In this last case, a portion can be allocated to the traditional IRA ($375) and the remainder ($375) invested in a non-IRA vehicle. This last scenario represents a hybrid of the first two scenarios. A proof of this equivalency for all scenarios is located in Appendix 18A. The main point, however, is that whether the pretax investment is held constant or the after-tax investment is held constant, one must make an assumption about how the tax savings are invested in the pretax framework or how the pretax investment in excess of the contribution limit is invested in the after-tax framework. The two approaches are equivalent as long as their respective assumptions are consistent.

With this foundation, the next section presents a flexible model that considers all the scenarios just presented. It is also general enough to accommodate different tax structures for the non-IRA investment. For instance, the taxable return could be fully taxed each year as ordinary income (e.g., fixed-income investments), tax deferred until withdrawal as a capital gain (e.g., non-dividend-paying stocks), or taxed as some combination of ordinary income, dividend, unrealized capital gain, and realized capital gain (e.g., mutual funds). It is important to recognize that the typical mutual fund has inherent tax-deferral characteristics in this regard, making it a relatively tax-efficient investment in many cases. (The precise impact of these tax-deferral characteristics will be discussed later in this chapter.) In addition to capturing salient features of the tax code, the following framework permits variation in tax rates over time, which allows one to assess the effect of increasing or decreasing tax rates.

The Basic Framework

For a given pretax investment (I_{BT}), the after-tax investment for a Roth IRA is $I_{BT}(1 - T_o)$, where T_o is the initial marginal tax rate on ordinary income at the time of the contribution. The standard future value formula shows that the after-tax future value of a Roth IRA after n years is

$$\text{FV}_{Roth} = I_{BT}(1 - T_o)(1 + r)^n, \tag{18.1}$$

where r is the expected annual pretax return on the investment. Now, consider the future value of a traditional IRA when the after-tax contribution is less than or equal to the contribution limit. Because an investor does not pay tax on the contribution, the entire pretax investment will accumulate earnings. The investor pays tax when withdrawing funds at the then-prevailing tax rate, T_n. Therefore,

$$\text{FV}_{Trad^*} = I_{BT}(1 + r)^n(1 - T_n). \tag{18.2}$$

The asterisk on the subscript "Trad" denotes this as a special case where the after-tax contribution is less than the contribution limit. A more general approach follows. In any case, a straightforward comparison of Equation 18.1 and Equation 18.2 reveals that the only difference between the future values of the Roth IRA and the traditional IRA is the tax rate, which yields the following rule of thumb: If the prevailing tax rate when funds are withdrawn is less than the tax rate when funds are invested, then the traditional IRA will accumulate more after-tax wealth. Otherwise, the Roth IRA is a better investment.

This fundamental result carries two important caveats. First, this analysis is limited to situations in which the pretax contribution is less than or equal to the contribution limit. The previous example only applied to pretax contributions up to $3,000. The hypothetical investor, however, can contribute up to $4,000 pretax, and investors in higher tax brackets can contribute even more. So, the analysis is incomplete. The second caveat is that the tax rate ultimately prevailing when the investor withdraws funds from a traditional IRA is uncertain. Nonetheless, one can say something about an investor's marginal tax rate during retirement at least in relation to his or her preretirement tax rate. On average, retirement income is about 64 percent of preretirement income, suggesting that marginal tax rates for retirees are likely to fall over their investment horizon.[15] For example, according to the 2004 tax code, a married couple filing jointly with an adjusted gross income of $180,000 has a marginal tax rate of 33 percent. At a 64 percent average replacement rate, retirement income would be $115,000 and the marginal tax rate becomes 25 percent, or a drop of two tax brackets. Although it may be more likely for retirees to drop one tax bracket rather than two, tax rates probably decline as most investors enter retirement. I will discuss more about the uncertainty of the withdrawal tax rate later.

Despite these limitations, both of which I will address in turn, this analysis produces an important heuristic result that permeates this section: *Traditional IRAs become relatively more attractive as future tax rates decline, and Roth IRAs become more attractive as future tax rates increase.*

A More General Foundation

As demonstrated earlier, an investment in a traditional IRA strategy potentially has two components: an IRA contribution up to the contribution limit (L) and a non-IRA contribution for any pretax investment in excess of the limit. These two components of the after-tax traditional IRA investment can be expressed as

$$I_{AT,Trad} = \min(I_{BT}, L) + \max[0, (I_{BT} - L)(1 - T_o)]. \qquad (18.3)$$

At first glance, this equation looks a bit onerous, but the first term is simply the after-tax investment in the traditional IRA up to the contribution limit, L. The second term represents the after-tax investment, if any, applied to a non-IRA taxable account when the pretax contribution exceeds the contribution limit. If the pretax investment is less than the contribution limit, the second term drops out leaving just I_{BT}.

If, however, the pretax contribution is greater than the contribution limit, then one must choose how the excess (i.e., the second term) will be invested. To draw a reliable comparison between the traditional IRA strategy and the Roth IRA, both strategies must have similar investment risk so that the tax structure differences between the two can be isolated as determining factors. Therefore, any taxable investment of tax savings associated with the traditional IRA strategy must be similar to the investment of the IRAs.[16] Under the current tax code, the return on a taxable investment, such as a mutual fund or equity portfolio, can be taxed using three ways. First, interest and short-term capital gains are taxed annually as ordinary income. Second, for a mutual fund or equity portfolio, a significant portion of earnings is typically unrealized capital gains that are not taxed until the fund sells the appreciated securities or until shareholders sell their fund shares. As a result, mutual funds have an inherent, albeit partial, tax-deferral feature. Third, according to the Jobs and Growth Tax Relief Reconciliation Act (JGTRRA) of 2003, the portion of earnings distributed as realized capital gains or dividends is typically taxed at 15 percent, which is substantially lower than the marginal tax rate on ordinary income.[17] As a result, mutual funds have significant tax advantages over investments having returns that are taxed each year as ordinary income.

If the taxable portion of the traditional IRA investment strategy is invested instead in a mutual fund, then a portion of the annual return is distributed to shareholders as ordinary income (p_{oi}) and taxed at t_{oi}. Another portion is distributed to shareholders as capital gains (p_{cg}) and taxed at t_{cg}. Using this notion, I can express the future value of an after-tax dollar in a taxable investment earning a return with these different taxable components as

$$\text{FVIF}_{TX} = (1 + r^*)^n(1 - T^*) + T^*, \tag{18.4}$$

where $r^* = r - rp_{oi}t_{oi} - rp_{cg}t_{cg} = r(1 - p_{oi}t_{oi} - p_{cg}t_{cg})$, or the effective annual after-tax return, and $T^* = t_{cg}(1 - p_{oi} - p_{cg})/(1 - p_{oi}t_{oi} - p_{cg}t_{cg})$, which is the effective capital gains tax rate after adjusting the basis for previously paid taxes on ordinary income and realized capital gain. It is worth taking a moment to understand this expression because it serves as the bedrock for much that follows.

The effective annual after-tax return (r^*) reflects the tax erosion caused by a portion of the return being taxed as ordinary income and another portion being taxed as realized capital gain or dividend. The form of the effective capital gains tax rate (T^*) is less intuitive, but it incorporates the notion that only price appreciation is taxed as a capital gain and that the gain is calculated against an adjusted basis. An investor who automatically reinvests returns and sells mutual fund shares beyond an 18-month holding period does not typically pay tax on the entire appreciation of the mutual fund's net asset value because a portion of that appreciation was already taxed as either ordinary income or capital gain in a prior tax year. Therefore, the adjusted basis used for calculating the capital gain is stepped up by the taxes previously paid on ordinary income or capital gain, and T^* reflects this stepped-up basis. Appendix 18A contains a derivation. The important realization is that this expression is essentially a future value interest factor like those used in introductory finance courses, except it is adapted for a broad range of taxable environments.[18]

Another way to understand Equation 18.4 is to consider the future value of an investment that is taxed entirely as capital gain at the end of the investment horizon, n. In this case, the after-tax future value is $(1 + r)^n - t_{cg}[(1 + r)^n - 1]$. The first term is the pretax accumulation. The second term is the capital gains tax rate times the capital gain. Rearranging terms simplifies this expression to $(1 + r)^n(1 - t_{cg}) + t_{cg}$, which is analogous to Equation 18.4. In fact, Equation 18.4 reduces to this expression when none of the investment return is distributed as ordinary income or capital gain until the end of the investment period, at which time it is taxed entirely as capital gain (see Appendix 18A for a proof). Therefore, T^* can be thought of as an effective deferred capital gains tax rate after an adjustment for taxes paid on returns previously distributed as ordinary income or realized capital gains.

Appendix 18A also shows that if the entire return is taxed annually as ordinary income, then the future value expression reduces to $[1 + r(1 - t_{oi})]^n$, which is the familiar future value expression when one substitutes an after-tax rate of return for the pretax rate of return. The more general expression in Equation 18.4, although less familiar, accommodates more typical and complex taxing schemes, as well as their more simple counterparts. It is used frequently in the pages that follow.

This taxable future value interest factor allows one to calculate the after-tax accumulation of the traditional IRA investment strategy when the pretax contribution exceeds the contribution limit by applying the future value operators in Equations 18.2 and 18.4 to the investment in Equation 18.3. I have already considered contributions below the limit and discovered that the optimal choice involves a simple comparison of the contribution and withdrawal tax rates. For pretax investments above the contribution limit, the future value of a traditional IRA investment is

$$\text{FV}_{Trad} = L(1 + r)^n(1 - T_n) + (I_{BT} - L)(1 - T_o)(\text{FVIF}_{TX}). \qquad (18.5)$$

The first term is the future value of the maximized IRA contribution. The second term is the future value of the taxable investment in excess of the contribution limit. T_n and t_{oi} are similar to each other in that they are both ordinary income tax rates. They are different in that t_{oi} applies over the term of the investment and T_n is the prevailing tax rate upon withdrawal. Consequently, the model permits some variation in the tax rate over time. This expression requires one to know the proportion of return that is taxed as ordinary income, dividend, realized capital gain, and unrealized capital gain. For equity mutual funds, these proportions depend in part on the investment style and whether the fund is passively managed or actively managed. As I will show, the tax structure of the non-IRA investment is important when choosing between a traditional IRA and Roth IRA.

Table 18.4 displays the proportion of distributed ordinary income and capital gains for typical equity mutual funds. Distribution practices vary widely. In Panel A, average distribution rates for ordinary income range from 5 percent of the total pretax return to about 38 percent, and distribution rates for realized capital gains range from about 30 percent to more than 60 percent of the total pretax return. Growth funds tend to distribute less return as ordinary income probably because of a tendency for growth stocks to be low-dividend-yielding stocks. Balanced funds, of course, tend to distribute more ordinary income. In Panel B, actively managed funds tend to make more taxable distributions; index funds tend to make less. Although index funds tend to be tax efficient and distribute little realized capital gain, they are almost always weighted by market

TABLE 18.4   Proportion of Return Distributed as Ordinary Income and Capital Gain for Equity Mutual Funds

Fund Style	Ordinary Income (p_{oi})	Realized Capital Gain (p_{cg})	Unrealized Capital Gain
A. Mean of 10 randomly selected mutual funds[a]			
Aggressive growth	5.2%	63.5%	31.3%
Growth	7.0	44.2	48.8
Growth and income	20.5	45.4	34.2
Balanced	37.9	30.7	31.4
B. Large mutual funds[b]			
Actively managed	27.3%	50.9%	21.8%
Vanguard Index 500	21.4	11.1	67.5

[a]Mean from 10 randomly selected active and passive funds for 1992–96 reported in Crain and Austin (1997). Short-term capital gains are included as realized capital gains.
[b]Median distribution rates from the five largest actively managed funds with the greatest total assets beginning in 1979, as reported by Shoven and Sialm (2003). Short-term capital gains and dividends are included as ordinary income distributions because of their tax treatment during the sample period. The distribution rates are the average rates for each fund for 1979–98.

capitalization, which increases their exposure to stocks that tend to have higher dividend yields than small stocks. Therefore, index funds distribute a fair amount of their return as ordinary income. In the illustrative examples that follow, I use a 20 percent distribution rate for ordinary income and a 45 percent distribution rate for realized capital gains.

Two salient features of the JGTRRA of 2003 are revised lower tax brackets for ordinary income and lower taxes on dividends and capital gains. The new tax rates for ordinary income are 10, 15, 25, 28, 33, and 35 percent. In addition, tax rates on dividends and capital gains have been reduced to 15 percent for taxpayers in all but the two lowest tax brackets. The tax reduction on equity returns decreases the double taxation of equity and increases the tax efficiency of equity investment so that potentially all distributions from equity mutual funds are taxed at 15 percent. It is worth noting that the distribution rates in Table 18.4 treat dividends as ordinary income because the then-prevailing tax law did so. Today, dividends might be better grouped with capital gains because JGTRRA of 2003 taxes them similarly. As a result, the distribution rates for ordinary income in Table 18.4 might be overstated, and the distribution rates for capital gains might be understated. Nonetheless, with these figures as inputs, Table 18.5 displays the relative values of a traditional IRA and a Roth IRA for investors in the 28 percent tax bracket seeking to maximize their pretax contribution. It uses the average distribution rates of mutual funds for ordinary income and capital gains reported by Crain and Austin and Shoven and Sialm (2004) and marginal tax rates established by the JGTRRA of 2003 passed by Congress in May 2003. Values greater (less) than 1 indicate that the traditional IRA (Roth IRA) is more attractive. Investors are indifferent between the two accounts when the ratio is 1. The algebraic expression for this ratio and its derivation are found in Appendix 18A.

According to Panel A of Table 18.5, investors maximizing their pretax contribution and staying in the same tax bracket are always better off using a Roth IRA account rather than a traditional IRA. For example, an investor expecting a 10 percent return over a 20-year time horizon would accumulate 94.3 percent as much wealth using a traditional IRA and investing funds in excess of the contribution limit in a typical mutual fund as he or she would using a Roth IRA. Regardless of their initial tax brackets, investors remaining in the same tax bracket will be better off with the Roth IRA because the traditional IRA strategy is disadvantaged by a portion of the pretax investment (i.e., the amount in excess of the contribution limit) being invested in a taxable account. According to Bernheim, Skinner, and Weinberg (2001), however, retirement income is about 64 percent of preretirement income. So, investors are likely to drop into lower tax brackets when they withdraw funds during retirement. Panel B displays value ratios for investors dropping into the 25 percent tax bracket and shows that, although the traditional IRA strategy becomes relatively more attractive, it is more advantageous than the Roth IRA only for relatively short time horizons or low rates of return. But when investors drop to the 15 percent tax bracket, they will almost always favor the traditional IRA strategy (Panel C). Therefore, the traditional IRA becomes relatively more attractive as the withdrawal tax rate decreases.

Notice that the Roth IRA becomes relatively more attractive as the investment horizon increases and as the investment return increases. The taxable investment portion of the traditional IRA strategy creates this trend. For long time horizons and high returns, the taxable investment becomes a larger drag on the traditional IRA strategy, and the more complete tax shelter of the Roth IRA becomes more valuable.

Table 18.6 presents value ratios for taxpayers in the 33 percent tax bracket. The ratios in Panel A are nearly identical to the ratios for taxpayers in the 28 percent tax bracket when the withdrawal tax rate stays constant. Dropping down one tax bracket for the 33 percent tax bracket investor, however, more strongly favors the traditional IRA strategy. In Panel B, the

TABLE 18.5 After-Tax Future Value Ratios of a Traditional IRA and Roth IRA for an Investor in the 28 Percent Tax Bracket

r	Investment Horizon in Years (n)							
	5	10	15	20	25	30	35	40
A. 28 percent withdrawal tax rate								
2%	0.996	0.992	0.988	0.985	0.981	0.978	0.975	0.972
4%	0.992	0.985	0.978	0.972	0.966	0.961	0.955	0.950
6%	0.989	0.979	0.970	0.961	0.953	0.946	0.939	0.933
8%	0.985	0.973	0.962	0.952	0.942	0.934	0.926	0.918
10%	0.982	0.968	0.955	0.943	0.933	0.923	0.914	0.905
12%	0.979	0.963	0.948	0.935	0.924	0.913	0.903	0.893
14%	0.977	0.958	0.942	0.928	0.916	0.904	0.893	0.883
16%	0.974	0.954	0.937	0.922	0.908	0.896	0.884	0.873
18%	0.972	0.950	0.932	0.916	0.902	0.888	0.876	0.865
B. 25 percent withdrawal tax rate								
2%	1.026	1.022	1.018	1.015	1.011	**1.008**	**1.005**	**1.002**
4%	1.022	1.015	1.008	**1.002**	**0.996**	0.991	0.985	0.980
6%	1.019	1.009	**1.000**	0.991	0.983	0.976	0.969	0.963
8%	1.015	1.003	0.992	0.982	0.972	0.964	0.956	0.948
10%	1.012	**0.998**	0.985	0.973	0.963	0.953	0.944	0.935
12%	1.009	0.993	0.978	0.965	0.954	0.943	0.933	0.923
14%	1.007	0.988	0.972	0.958	0.946	0.934	0.923	0.913
16%	1.004	0.984	0.967	0.952	0.938	0.926	0.914	0.903
18%	**1.002**	0.980	0.962	0.946	0.932	0.918	0.906	0.895
C. 15 percent withdrawal tax rate								
2%	1.126	1.122	1.118	1.115	1.111	1.108	1.105	1.102
4%	1.122	1.115	1.108	1.102	1.096	1.091	1.085	1.080
6%	1.119	1.109	1.100	1.091	1.083	1.076	1.069	1.063
8%	1.115	1.103	1.092	1.082	1.072	1.064	1.056	1.048
10%	1.112	1.098	1.085	1.073	1.063	1.053	1.044	1.035
12%	1.109	1.093	1.078	1.065	1.054	1.043	1.033	1.023
14%	1.107	1.088	1.072	1.058	1.046	1.034	1.023	1.013
16%	1.104	1.084	1.067	1.052	1.038	1.026	1.014	**1.003**
18%	1.102	1.080	1.062	1.046	1.032	1.018	**1.006**	0.995

Notes: In this example, the investor makes the maximum allowable pretax contribution; non-IRA investments are invested in a typical taxable mutual fund; and dividends and capital gains are taxed at 15 percent through the accumulation phase. Bold numbers indicate approximate indifference points between the traditional IRA and the Roth IRA.

TABLE 18.6   After-Tax Future Value Ratios of a Traditional IRA and Roth IRA for an Investor in the 33 Percent Tax Bracket

r	Investment Horizon in Years (*n*)							
	5	10	15	20	25	30	35	40
A. 33 percent withdrawal tax rate								
2%	0.995	0.991	0.986	0.982	0.978	0.974	0.970	0.967
4%	0.991	0.982	0.974	0.967	0.960	0.954	0.947	0.941
6%	0.987	0.975	0.964	0.954	0.945	0.937	0.929	0.921
8%	0.983	0.968	0.955	0.943	0.932	0.922	0.912	0.903
10%	0.979	0.962	0.947	0.933	0.921	0.909	0.898	0.888
12%	0.976	0.956	0.939	0.924	0.910	0.897	0.886	0.874
14%	0.973	0.951	0.932	0.916	0.901	0.887	0.874	0.862
16%	0.970	0.946	0.926	0.908	0.892	0.877	0.864	0.851
18%	0.967	0.941	0.920	0.901	0.884	0.868	0.854	0.841
B. 28 percent withdrawal tax rate								
2%	1.045	1.041	1.036	1.032	1.028	1.024	1.020	**1.017**
4%	1.041	1.032	1.024	1.017	1.010	**1.004**	**0.997**	0.991
6%	1.037	1.025	1.014	**1.004**	**0.995**	0.987	0.979	0.971
8%	1.033	1.018	1.005	0.993	0.982	0.972	0.962	0.953
10%	1.029	1.012	**0.997**	0.983	0.971	0.959	0.948	0.938
12%	1.026	1.006	0.989	0.974	0.960	0.947	0.936	0.924
14%	1.023	**1.001**	0.982	0.966	0.951	0.937	0.924	0.912
16%	1.020	0.996	0.976	0.958	0.942	0.927	0.914	0.901
18%	1.017	0.991	0.970	0.951	0.934	0.918	0.904	0.891
C. 25 percent withdrawal tax rate								
2%	1.075	1.071	1.066	1.062	1.058	1.054	1.050	1.047
4%	1.071	1.062	1.054	1.047	1.040	1.034	1.027	1.021
6%	1.067	1.055	1.044	1.034	1.025	1.017	1.009	**1.001**
8%	1.063	1.048	1.035	1.023	1.012	**1.002**	**0.992**	0.983
10%	1.059	1.042	1.027	1.013	**1.001**	0.989	0.978	0.968
12%	1.056	1.036	1.019	1.004	0.990	0.977	0.966	0.954
14%	1.053	1.031	1.012	**0.996**	0.981	0.967	0.954	0.942
16%	1.050	1.026	1.006	0.988	0.972	0.957	0.944	0.931
18%	1.047	1.021	**1.000**	0.981	0.964	0.948	0.934	0.921

Notes: In this example, the investor makes the maximum allowable pretax contribution; non-IRA investments are invested in a typical taxable mutual fund; and dividends and capital gains are taxed at 15 percent through the accumulation phase. Bold numbers indicate approximate indifference points between the traditional IRA and the Roth IRA.

indifference points (i.e., points at which the ratio is equal to 1) shift to the lower right compared with the same panel for the 28 percent taxpayer because dropping down one tax bracket represents a 5 percentage point drop in tax rate rather than a 3 percentage point drop. For a 6–10 percent return, indifference time horizons extend about 5–10 years. For a 15-year time horizon, the indifference return increases about 4 percent. Therefore, the traditional IRA is optimal in a wider range of circumstances for the 33 percent taxpayer compared with the 28 percent taxpayer. Reverse logic explains why the indifference points in Panel C of Table 18.6 shift to the upper left somewhat compared with those in Panel C of Table 18.5. Even so, the traditional IRA remains attractive in most situations when an investor drops two tax brackets upon withdrawing funds.

Unreported results indicate that when the non-IRA portion of the IRA strategy is fully taxed as ordinary income, indifference points are about five years shorter than those reported in Table 18.5. The IRA is penalized in these scenarios because the pretax contribution exceeding the contribution limit has a heavier tax burden. The next section provides a sense of this effect. Not maximizing the pretax contribution significantly improves the attractiveness of the traditional IRA. For example, recall that for pretax contributions less than or equal to the contribution limit, investors are indifferent when the tax rate remains the same and prefer the traditional IRA whenever tax rates decrease. These tables are not intended to exhaust all possible scenarios. They are intended to provide a heuristic sense of important factors in choosing between IRA accounts. The financial analyst may use the formulas directly and change the inputs to match an investor's specific circumstances.

A note about an investor's investment horizon is in order. The investment horizon is often deceptively long. It is not necessarily the time until withdrawals from a retirement account begin. Rather, it is conceptually equal to the length of time until the marginal withdrawal created by the proposed investment. For example, consider a 50-year-old investor with $100,000 invested in a Roth IRA with an expected return of 10 percent. She plans to begin making withdrawals 15 years from now at age 65 when the Roth IRA is expected to be worth $417,715 [i.e., $100,000(1.10)^{15}$]. Because she wishes to make annual after-tax withdrawals of about $68,000 at the end of each year, her nest egg can support about 10 years of withdrawals, that is, until age 75.[19]

She may have three different motivations for making an additional $3,000 contribution to a TDA. First, she may intend for the proposed investment to extend past age 75, the time period over which she makes her $68,000 annuitized withdrawals. At age 75, her investment could support almost six months of marginal withdrawals.[20] Second, she may wish to maintain her 10-year retirement period but increase the annual $68,000 withdrawal. This strategy would permit withdrawals of more than $70,000 from the Roth IRA. Third, she may wish to accelerate retirement, commencing withdrawals at, say, age 64.

Each of these scenarios has a different investment horizon. In the first case, the marginal withdrawal created by the investment will occur 25 years hence, which would be the appropriate investment horizon. In the second case, the marginal withdrawal begins in 15 years and is annuitized over 10 years. Research indicates that withdrawal patterns from TDAs affect their after-tax present values, an issue explored in more detail in the section on Early Withdrawal Penalties and Breakeven Time Horizons.[21] One may thus infer that the withdrawal pattern would affect the time horizon used in choosing between IRA accounts. But as I will show, the withdrawal pattern affects the value of traditional IRAs and Roth IRAs in identical ways, entering the analysis as a constant that would be multiplied on both the numerator and the denominator of the ratios in Tables 18.5 and 18.6. As such, the relative values of the traditional IRA and Roth are unchanged, leaving the investor's choice between the two unchanged. For the third case in which the investor hopes to commence withdrawals at age 64, the appropriate investment horizon is 14 years. This example shows that an investment's expected effect on an investor's withdrawal pattern determines his or her investment horizon for purposes of this analysis.

Breakeven Withdrawal Tax Rates

Tables 18.5 and 18.6 illustrate the effect of changing tax rates on the relative attractiveness of traditional and Roth IRAs. Another way to view the importance of the withdrawal tax rate and the impact of the tax structure for the non-IRA investment is to solve for the withdrawal tax rate below which an investor would prefer the traditional IRA strategy.[22] The algebraic solution for this breakeven withdrawal tax can be found in Appendix 18A, but Figure 18.1 presents breakeven tax rates that maximize the pretax contribution for investors in the 28 percent tax bracket. This examination allows one to investigate the impact of the taxing scheme for the non-IRA portion (i.e., the portion exceeding the contribution limit) of the traditional IRA strategy on the choice between accounts.

Panel A in Figure 18.1 is based on the assumption that the non-IRA investment in excess of the contribution limit is fully taxed each year as ordinary income at 28 percent.[23] This assumption might be appropriate for fixed-income investors or equity traders that exhibit high turnover that results in mostly short-term capital gains. The curved lines across the surface area represent tax rates in 5 percent increments. The breakeven withdrawal tax rates here are quite low, dipping to 5 percent for investors with very long investment horizons and high returns. If an investor expects to withdraw funds at a tax rate below the breakeven point, the traditional IRA will accumulate more wealth. Therefore, low breakeven tax rates, like those in Panel A, favor the Roth IRA. For example, an investor in the 28 percent tax bracket facing a five-year time horizon and expected return of 9 percent has a 25 percent breakeven tax rate, or a drop of one tax bracket. A withdrawal tax rate below (above) 25 percent indicates that the traditional (Roth) IRA is better. The steepness of the surface area indicates that the choice between IRA accounts is sensitive to the investment horizon and investment return.

Panel B repeats these calculations with the assumption that the non-IRA portion of the traditional IRA strategy is invested in a typical mutual fund.[24] This tax structure might also be appropriate for an active equity investor with modest turnover that generates mostly long-term capital gains. In this case, the breakeven withdrawal tax rates increase substantially, indicating that the traditional IRA becomes much more attractive. Breakeven tax rates fall below 20 percent only for investments with very long time horizons and high returns. In the extreme (Panel C), all the taxable return might be long-term capital gain realized upon withdrawal.[25] This tax structure might be applicable to a passive equity investor with a buy-and-hold investment strategy for non-dividend-paying stocks. In this case, the breakeven withdrawal tax rates barely dip below 24 percent, making the traditional IRA strategy much more attractive. The flatness of the surface area in Panel C indicates that the ideal choice between IRA accounts is insensitive to the investment horizon and investment return when the non-IRA investment is taxed as unrealized capital gain.

Naturally, breakeven tax rates for investors in the 33 percent tax bracket, shown in Figure 18.2, are higher. But the traditional IRA can be relatively more attractive for these taxpayers because the tax rate in the next lower tax bracket is 5 percentage points lower, rather than 2 or 3 percentage points lower as is the case for investors in the 35 percent and 28 percent tax brackets, respectively. The same basic trends from Figure 18.1 hold here. But a single tax bracket drop takes the investor a bit farther down the surface because of the larger increment. Therefore, the traditional IRA may be optimal in a broader range of circumstances. These figures become useful again in the next section.

FIGURE 18.1   Breakeven Withdrawal Tax Rates for a 28 Percent Tax Bracket Investor:
Non-IRA Investment

A. Fully Taxed as Ordinary Income (trader)

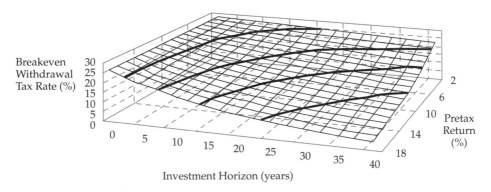

B. Taxed as a Typical Equity Mutual Fund (active investor)

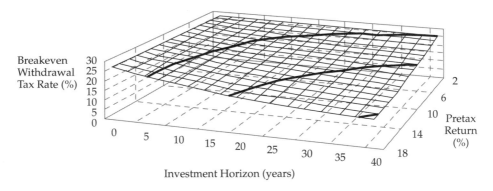

C. Taxed Entirely as Deferred Capital Gain (passive investor)

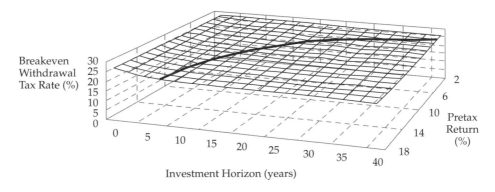

The traditional IRA becomes significantly more attractive as well when an investor does
not make pretax investments in excess of the contribution limit. In this case, no taxable
investing is necessary with the traditional IRA strategy, which increases its relative attractiveness. It is not possible to review the nearly infinite number of possible scenarios, but this
framework allows the analyst to calculate the breakeven withdrawal tax rate for any particular

FIGURE 18.2   Breakeven Withdrawal Tax Rates for a 33 Percent Tax Bracket Investor: Non-IRA Investment

A. Fully Taxed as Ordinary Income (trader)

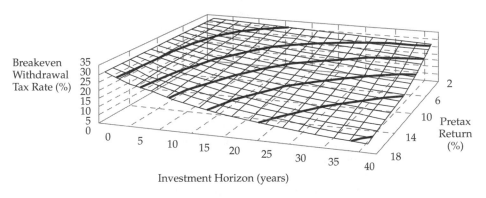

B. Taxed as a Typical Equity Mutual Fund (active investor)

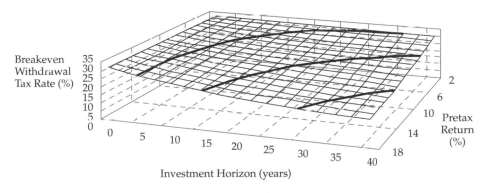

C. Taxed Entirely as Deferred Capital Gain (passive investor)

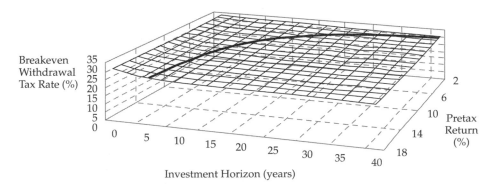

circumstance. These figures also show that the tax structure of the non-IRA investment is important in choosing between TDAs.

As one can see, the optimal choice between a traditional IRA and a Roth IRA depends largely on the tax rate prevailing when the funds are withdrawn from the traditional IRA. Although scenario analyses provide some heuristic sense of the impact of uncertain future tax rates, what more can be said? One argument is that uncertainty about future tax rates cannot favor either type of IRA "because tax rates are just as likely to go up as they are to go down."[26] But as I have shown, retirees are likely to be in lower tax brackets when withdrawing retirement funds because retirement income tends to be 64 percent of preretirement income. Future tax rates may also be more likely to decrease (or vice versa) depending on the current and expected political climate. For example, the passage of the EGTRRA of 2001 and JFTRRA of 2003 reflects a secular conservative trend of declining tax rates and portends lower withdrawal tax rates for many investors if it can be sustained. Other pundits see current and future budget deficits as signs of increasing tax rates. In any case, a fair discussion about future fiscal policy and political trends is far beyond the scope of this chapter.

An alternative argument focuses on the effect of uncertainty on the rate used to discount future cash outflows, like taxes. A higher discount rate on a negative future cash flow yields a less-negative present value and is, therefore, a smaller liability than a negative cash flow with a lower discount rate. By this logic, a taxpayer prefers uncertainty about future tax rates because it lowers the present value of his or her tax liability. Disagreement exists about whether this paradoxical analysis is appropriate, but an alternative approach provides similar intuition. Uncertain cash outflows, like taxes on investment returns, essentially have negative systematic risk, which hedges the positive systematic risk of investment inflows. If one views an uncertain after-tax future value of a traditional IRA as a combination of positive cash flows (i.e., pretax accumulation) and negative cash flows (i.e., taxes), the risk (and, hence, discount rate) of the combined cash flows is less than the risk of the pretax value alone and thereby increases the present value.[27] In other words, by taxing investment returns, the government shares in the risk as well as the return of taxable investments.[28] Consequently, the uncertainty surrounding future tax rates can be thought of as a hedge that tends to favor the traditional IRA.

Finally, it is important to recognize that uncertain future tax rates increase the importance of having the option to choose the type of account from which to make withdrawals upon retirement. For example, an investor with only traditional IRAs or only Roth IRAs at retirement is forced to make withdrawals from only one type of account. But an investor with both types of accounts may choose the account from which withdrawals are made prior to the mandatory withdrawal age of 70½ years. This choice has value because in low-tax-rate regimes, investors can withdraw from the traditional IRA. In high-tax-rate regimes, the Roth IRA can produce tax-free retirement income. Even if an investor is required to make withdrawals from the traditional IRA, the choice can still have value if voluntary withdrawals exceed the mandatory minimums. Having both types of accounts available when making withdrawals creates tax diversification and valuable flexibility for retirees akin to a real option in a capital budgeting context. To my knowledge, this seemingly valuable flexibility has yet to be analyzed in the literature.

Alternative Minimum Tax

Established in 1970 to ensure that high-income taxpayers pay some minimum amount of tax, the alternative minimum tax (AMT) has historically affected only a small number of individuals. Over time, an increasing number of taxpayers are covered by the AMT because it is not indexed for inflation. Ironically, recent tax cuts have also increased coverage because they have not been accompanied by similar cuts in the AMT. Under the current law, 95 percent of taxpayers earning between $100,000 and $500,000 will be subject to the AMT (see Burman, Gale, Rohaly, Harris 2002). It, therefore, makes sense to discuss its impact on the choice between TDAs and the related decisions I discuss hereafter.

A detailed analysis of the AMT is beyond the scope of this chapter, but some of its main features have a bearing on this analysis. Basically, the AMT is a parallel tax system that allows fewer deductions than the standard tax system and has marginal tax rates of 26 percent and 28 percent. Taxpayers calculate their tax liability under both systems and pay the greater of the two tax liabilities. Although the AMT marginal tax rates may be lower than many tax brackets, it often results in a higher tax liability because it disallows certain deductions, such as state tax, property tax, personal exemptions, and dependent exemptions. The first implication of the AMT on this analysis is that the standard tax brackets made permanent by the JGTRRA of 2003 may not be an investor's true marginal tax rate. Rather, marginal tax rates for the AMT taxpayer may be 26 percent or 28 percent. If the AMT reduces an investor's marginal tax rate (even if it increases the overall tax liability), then the Roth IRA becomes relatively more attractive when one holds the withdrawal tax rate constant. Other nuances of the AMT, however, make this implication less straightforward than it initially appears.

The AMT includes initial exemptions that reduce taxable income. The JGTRRA of 2003 increased these exemptions to $40,250 for single taxpayers and $58,000 for those who are married and filing jointly. These exemptions are phased out, however, if income exceeds an established base level. For example, a couple filing jointly has their exemption phased out at a rate of 25 cents for every dollar of income above $150,000. This phase-out effectively increases the marginal tax rate. Each dollar of income above $150,000 for a married couple filing jointly has two tax effects. On that dollar, the AMT-taxpaying couple pays 26 cents of tax and has 25 cents of their exemption phased out and subject to tax, creating an additional 6½ cents of tax (i.e., 0.26×0.25). In this case, the marginal tax rate is 32½ percent, not 26 percent.[29] So, an investor's marginal tax rate can be quite high and a bit illusive under AMT. It is this potentially illusive tax rate that should be used as the initial tax rate, T_o, in the model. Marginal tax rates this high tend to favor the traditional IRA over the Roth IRA.

The exemption phase-out can also impact the effective tax rate on capital gains. Ostensibly, the tax rate on long-term capital gains is 15 percent under both tax systems. But in some circumstances, a capital gain can reduce or even eliminate the AMT exemption, which effectively increases the tax rate on capital gains. For example, suppose the aforementioned couple has $150,000 of income before recognizing a long-term capital gain of $100,000 on a piece of investment property. Under the standard tax system, recognizing this gain would create a capital gains tax of $15,000. But the $100,000 gain reduces their AMT exemption by $25,000, exposing that much income to a 26 percent tax, or an extra $6,500 tax liability. In other words, the $100,000 long-term capital gain created a $21,500 (or 21.5 percent) tax liability. The model discussed here can accommodate this situation by setting t_{cg} equal to 21.5 percent, which decreases the value of taxable investments and will disadvantage the traditional IRA strategy in some cases.[30]

The AMT can affect the choice between TDAs in other ways as well. Contributions to TDAs with front-end tax benefits decrease a taxpayer's adjusted gross income (AGI), which decreases the potential of being covered by the AMT tax and/or reduces the amount of AMT exemption that would otherwise be phased out. Contributions to TDAs with back-end tax benefits, such as Roth IRAs and 529 plans, do not decrease AGI or reduce AMT coverage. Therefore, the threat of AMT coverage can favor the traditional IRA over the Roth IRA. Because taxpayers can contribute up to $14,000 to 401(k) plans and 403(b) plans in 2005, these plans can be significant tools in reducing either AMT coverage or the AMT exemption phase-out.

Summary

Standardizing the pretax investment is equivalent to standardizing the after-tax investment as long as one makes assumptions about investing either the tax savings or the pretax contribution in excess of the contribution limit. The fundamental result is that traditional IRAs become relatively more attractive than Roth IRAs when an investor's withdrawal tax rate declines because the tax shelter of the traditional IRA is greatest when contribution tax rates are high, whereas the tax shelter of the Roth IRA is greatest when withdrawal tax rates are high. If the pretax contribution falls below the contribution limit, the choice between the two is dictated by a simple comparison of the contribution and withdrawal tax rates.

When an investor maximizes the pretax contribution, however, part of the traditional IRA strategy includes a taxable investment, which creates a tax drag. If the investor drops two tax brackets during retirement, the traditional IRA is nonetheless optimal because the benefit of the low withdrawal tax rate outweighs the disadvantage of the taxable investment associated with the traditional IRA strategy. When the same investor drops only one tax bracket, the traditional IRA is optimal only for short time horizons or for investments with low rates of return.

EMPLOYER MATCHING AND CONVERTING A TRADITIONAL IRA TO A ROTH IRA

An additional circumstance that investors may face when investing with TDAs is choosing between a Roth IRA and a 401(k) plan in which the employer matches contributions. The methodology from the previous section suggests that an investor facing constant or increasing tax rates during the withdrawal phase of a TDA investment is better off using a TDA with a back-end tax benefit, such as a Roth IRA, than one with a front-end tax benefit. But if the investor's employer matches some or all of the contributions to a 401(k) plan, forgoing employer-matching opportunities may be too costly. This section analyzes this trade-off and shows that the answer depends on how tax savings from the 401(k) investment are invested. If tax savings are reinvested into the 401(k) or another tax-deductible account without employer matching, then the choice between the 401(k) and the Roth IRA reduces to a simple comparison of contribution and withdrawal tax rates. With only modest employer matching, the 401(k) is generally optimal even if tax rates increase and even if tax savings are invested in a taxable account. In other words, the employer matching is almost always more valuable than the marginal tax benefits of a Roth IRA.

This section also explores the decision to convert a traditional IRA to a Roth IRA. Taxpayers are permitted to make this conversion but are required to pay tax on the converted amount. This situation helps determine when it is worthwhile to convert and how best to satisfy the tax liability. Conversion is more attractive if the tax liability is paid from funds in a highly taxed account rather than a tax-sheltered account, such as the IRA itself. If the tax liability is paid from IRA balances, conversion is generally not optimal unless the investor's tax rate increases by about 11 percent to compensate for the resulting earlier withdrawal penalty. If taxable assets are tapped to pay the conversion tax, then investors facing constant or increasing tax rates benefit from conversion. Regardless, conversion becomes more valuable as the investment horizon and expected return increase because the value of the tax shelter increases as well.

Employer Matching

Choosing between a 401(k) investment and a traditional IRA investment is straightforward. Because they are taxed similarly, the 401(k) is the better location for an investment as long as the employer matches any of the employee's contributions.[31] The choice between an employer-matched 401(k) investment and a Roth IRA is more complicated because it requires an assumption about how tax savings are invested.

Recall from Table 18.2 that the contribution limits for 401(k) plans (e.g., $13,000 for 2004) are far greater than contribution limits for Roth IRAs ($3,000 for 2004). This difference changes the options available to the investor when he or she is choosing how to invest the tax savings associated with the 401(k) contribution. For example, consider from the previous section the hypothetical investor in the 25 percent tax bracket facing a $3,000 contribution limit on a Roth IRA. I will ignore employer matching for the moment. He or she could contribute up to $4,000 pretax. The entire $4,000 may be invested in the 401(k) plan on an *after-tax* basis because the contribution limit is $13,000. In essence, the tax savings from a $3,000 after-tax investment have been invested in a fully deductible TDA. The Roth IRA permits a $3,000 after-tax investment. The other $1,000 is paid in tax.

Reinvesting Tax Savings into the 401(k)

Using the logic presented in the previous section, this scenario can be viewed as a $3,000 after-tax investment in a Roth IRA. An equivalent investment in the 401(k) generates $1,000 worth of tax savings [i.e., ($3,000 × 0.25)/(1 − 0.25)] that can either be reinvested in the 401(k) or put in a taxable account. If tax savings are reinvested into the 401(k), whereby the individual investor simply increases his or her 401(k) contribution in anticipation of a reduced tax liability, then the problem reduces to a scenario in which the pretax investment is less than the contribution limit and the simple rule applies.[32] In this case, the Roth IRA is preferred if the withdrawal tax rate is greater than the contribution tax rate (the accumulations are equivalent if the tax rates are the same) and the 401(k) is preferred otherwise. Remember, I have temporarily assumed away employer matching.

Obviously, the 401(k) becomes more attractive when employers match contributions, thus changing the previously mentioned math. In this case, the 401(k) will accumulate more wealth even when contribution and withdrawal tax rates are the same but especially when tax rates decline. The question is whether the Roth IRA can be optimal in the unlikely circumstance that tax rates increase when the investor retires. The ratio of accumulations for the employer-matched 401(k) to the Roth IRA in this case has a simple expression. The after-tax accumulation of a pretax 401(k) investment in which the employer matches π percent of the employee's investment and the tax savings are reinvested in the 401(k) is

$$\text{FV}_{401(k)^*} = (1 + \pi)I_{BT}(1 + r)^n(1 - T_n). \tag{18.6}$$

The asterisk denotes the case where tax savings are reinvested in the 401(k). This expression is simply the future value of a traditional IRA in which the pretax contribution is less than or equal to the contribution limit from Equation 18.2 grossed up by the employer's contribution. I can then take the ratio of this expression to the future accumulation of the Roth IRA given in Equation 18.1. After canceling terms, I have a straightforward relationship:

$$\frac{\text{FV}_{401(k)}}{\text{FV}_{Roth}} = \frac{(1 + \pi)(1 - T_n)}{(1 - T_o)}. \tag{18.7}$$

TABLE 18.7   After-Tax Future Value Ratios of a 401(k) and Roth IRA When Tax Rates Increase and Tax Savings Are Reinvested in the 401(k)

Employer Match (π)	Contribution Tax Rate (T_o)					
	25 Percent			28 Percent		33 Percent
	Withdrawal Tax Rate (T_n)					
	28%	33%	35%	33%	35%	35%
5%	**1.008**	0.938	0.910	0.977	0.948	1.019
10%	1.056	**0.983**	0.953	**1.024**	**0.993**	1.067
15%	1.104	1.027	**0.997**	1.070	1.038	1.116
20%	1.152	1.072	1.040	1.117	1.083	1.164
25%	1.200	1.117	1.083	1.163	1.128	1.213
30%	1.248	1.161	1.127	1.210	1.174	1.261
35%	1.296	1.206	1.170	1.256	1.219	1.310
40%	1.344	1.251	1.213	1.303	1.264	1.358
45%	1.392	1.295	1.257	1.349	1.309	1.407
50%	1.440	1.340	1.300	1.396	1.354	1.455
55%	1.488	1.385	1.343	1.442	1.399	1.504
60%	1.536	1.429	1.387	1.489	1.444	1.552
65%	1.584	1.474	1.430	1.535	1.490	1.601
70%	1.632	1.519	1.473	1.582	1.535	1.649
75%	1.680	1.563	1.517	1.628	1.580	1.698
80%	1.728	1.608	1.560	1.675	1.625	1.746
85%	1.776	1.653	1.603	1.722	1.670	1.795
90%	1.824	1.697	1.647	1.768	1.715	1.843
95%	1.872	1.742	1.690	1.815	1.760	1.892
100%	1.920	1.787	1.733	1.861	1.806	1.940

Note: Bold numbers indicate approximate indifference points between the 401(k) and the Roth IRA.

In other words, when $(1 + \pi)(1 - T_n) > (1 - T_o)$, the 401(k) will accumulate greater after-tax wealth. When $(1 + \pi)(1 - T_n) < (1 - T_o)$, the Roth IRA is better, which can only occur if the withdrawal tax rate is greater than the contribution tax rate. The investor is indifferent otherwise. Table 18.7 examines the case for different levels of employer contribution for some common tax brackets in the current U.S. tax code.

It is clear that only modest levels of employer matching are needed to make the 401(k) a better investment than the Roth IRA even when withdrawal tax rates increase. Table 18.7 provides a valuable rule of thumb: If an investor reinvests 401(k) contribution tax savings into the 401(k) or some other tax-deductible TDA, then the 401(k) accumulates more wealth than the Roth IRA with only modest levels of employer matching. The 401(k) dominates even when withdrawal tax rates increase.

Some employers match a certain percentage of contributions (as I have explicitly assumed), and others match contributions up to a specific dollar amount. Table 18.7 can be used for the latter arrangement, as well, by separating the choice into two decisions. Say, for example, an employer matches contributions up to $5,000. According to Table 18.7, the employee should clearly forgo the Roth IRA in favor of the 100 percent matching contribution up to $5,000. Additional contributions that receive no matching should be evaluated using the framework presented in the previous section for choosing between TDAs with front-end-loaded and back-end-loaded tax benefits.

Reinvesting Tax Savings into a Taxable Account

The preceding analysis assumed that tax savings from 401(k) contributions were invested in a deductible TDA, such as the 401(k) itself. If one alternatively assumes that expected 401(k) contribution tax savings are invested in a typical taxable mutual fund, the analysis is less clear. Consider an after-tax Roth IRA investment of $I_{BT}(1 - T_o)$. Investing an equal sum into a 401(k) generates tax savings of $I_{BT}T_o$, which I assume will be invested in a taxable account.[33] The after-tax accumulation of a 401(k) in which the employer matches π percent of the employee's investment and the tax savings are invested in a mutual fund is

$$\text{FV}_{401(k)} = (1 + \pi)I_{BI}(1 - T_o)(1 + r)^n(1 - T_n) + I_{BT}T_o[\text{FVIF}_{TX}]. \qquad (18.8)$$

The first term is the future accumulation of the 401(k) portion of the investment strategy with the employer matching. The second term is the future value of the tax savings using the taxable future value interest factor from Equation 18.4.[34]

Table 18.8 examines the ratio of the 401(k) accumulation to the Roth IRA accumulation for various levels of employer matching under the assumption that the tax savings are invested in a typical mutual fund. For an investor in the 28 percent tax bracket, it is always better to take advantage of employer matching rather than invest in a Roth IRA even if tax savings are invested in a taxable mutual fund. Unreported results show that neither the tax bracket nor the return affects this conclusion. In fact, this rule of thumb remains intact when the investor's withdrawal tax rate increases as I show next.

Even in the unusual circumstance in which an investor has a higher tax rate when withdrawing funds than when making the contribution, the 401(k) is generally the better investment. A concise way of demonstrating this result is to calculate the breakeven withdrawal tax rate for different tax brackets and taxing schemes. A derivation of these breakeven withdrawal tax rates is found in Appendix 18B. Figure 18.3 displays them for an investor in the 28 percent tax bracket who would receive a match on 25 percent of the contributions to the 401(k). Withdrawal tax rates below the breakeven tax rate indicate that the employer-matched 401(k) dominates the Roth IRA. In general, the breakeven withdrawal tax rates are quite high (above 28 percent in almost every instance), which indicates that the 401(k) with a modest 25 percent employer matching is a better investment than the Roth IRA. If the taxpayer invests the tax savings in a fully taxable vehicle, such as a fixed-income security, Panel A shows that the investment horizon needs to be quite long and the return quite high for the Roth IRA to be worth forgoing the employer matching of the 401(k) because the breakeven withdrawal tax rates are high. Because fixed-income instruments are fully taxed as ordinary income and tend to have relatively low returns, the Roth IRA is not likely to be more attractive than the 401(k) for fixed-income instruments. An active equity trader with high turnover could have a similar tax structure, however,

TABLE 18.8   After-Tax Future Value Ratios of a 401(k) and Roth IRA When Tax Savings Are Invested in a Typical Equity Mutual Fund

Employer Match (π)	Investment Horizon in Years (n)							
	5	10	15	20	25	30	35	40
5%	1.120	1.100	1.082	1.066	1.051	1.038	1.025	1.013
10%	1.156	1.136	1.118	1.102	1.087	1.074	1.061	1.049
15%	1.192	1.172	1.154	1.138	1.123	1.110	1.097	1.085
20%	1.228	1.208	1.190	1.174	1.159	1.146	1.133	1.121
25%	1.264	1.244	1.226	1.210	1.195	1.182	1.169	1.157
30%	1.300	1.280	1.262	1.246	1.231	1.218	1.205	1.193
35%	1.336	1.316	1.298	1.282	1.267	1.254	1.241	1.229
40%	1.372	1.352	1.334	1.318	1.303	1.290	1.277	1.265
45%	1.408	1.388	1.370	1.354	1.339	1.326	1.313	1.301
50%	1.444	1.424	1.406	1.390	1.375	1.362	1.349	1.337
55%	1.480	1.460	1.442	1.426	1.411	1.398	1.385	1.373
60%	1.516	1.496	1.478	1.462	1.447	1.434	1.421	1.409
65%	1.552	1.532	1.514	1.498	1.483	1.470	1.457	1.445
70%	1.588	1.568	1.550	1.534	1.519	1.506	1.493	1.481
75%	1.624	1.604	1.586	1.570	1.555	1.542	1.529	1.517
80%	1.660	1.640	1.622	1.606	1.591	1.578	1.565	1.553
85%	1.696	1.676	1.658	1.642	1.627	1.614	1.601	1.589
90%	1.732	1.712	1.694	1.678	1.663	1.650	1.637	1.625
95%	1.768	1.748	1.730	1.714	1.699	1.686	1.673	1.661
100%	1.804	1.784	1.766	1.750	1.735	1.722	1.709	1.697

Notes: The investor is in the 28 percent tax bracket during the contribution and withdrawal phase and earns a 10 percent return. The mutual fund distributes 20 percent of its return as dividends and 45 percent as long-term capital gain. Dividends and capital gains are taxed at 15 percent.

accompanied by a higher investment return. Even so, the return needs to be quite high for the breakeven withdrawal tax rates to favor the Roth IRA in Panel A.

The Roth IRA becomes even less attractive when the non-401(k) investment of the tax savings is taxed as a typical mutual fund, as in Panel B. In this case, the breakeven withdrawal tax rates are all greater than the highest tax bracket, indicating that forgoing the employer matching associated with the 401(k) would never be optimal. Panel C presents similar findings when the tax savings are invested in a non-401(k) investment that is taxed entirely as deferred capital gain. The following rule of thumb then provides general guidance in most circumstances: *An investor is better off accepting even modest matching of 401(k) contributions than investing in either a traditional IRA or Roth IRA, even if the withdrawal tax rate increases.*

FIGURE 18.3   Breakeven Withdrawal Tax Rates between a 401(k) with 25 Percent Employer Matching and a Roth IRA for a 28 Percent Taxpayer: Non-401(k) Investment

A. Fully Taxed as Ordinary Income (trader)

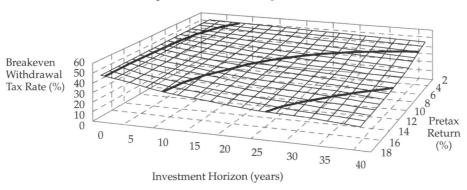

B. Taxed as a Typical Equity Mutual Fund (active investor)

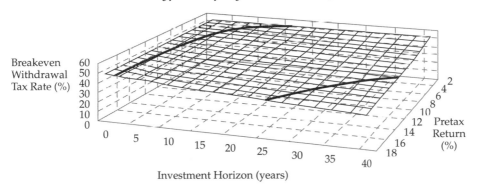

C. Taxed as Deferred Capital Gain (passive investor)

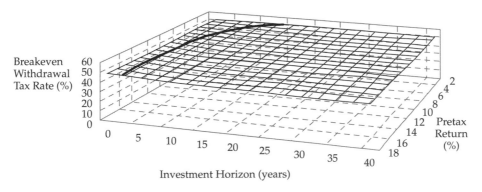

Converting a Traditional IRA to a Roth IRA

Investors with adjusted gross incomes of no more than $100,000 may convert existing traditional IRAs to Roth IRAs. One potential advantage of doing so is that Roth IRAs have no mandatory distribution rule at age 70½, so investors can potentially enjoy the benefits of tax deferral for an extended period of time. A disadvantage of conversion is that all withdrawals of deductible contributions and earnings from the traditional IRA that are rolled over to the

Roth IRA are subject to income tax. Generally, funds that are rolled over in a timely manner are not subject to the 10 percent early withdrawal penalty. But if an investor elects to use funds from the traditional IRA to pay the conversion tax, then these funds are not rolled over and are subject to a 10 percent early withdrawal penalty if the conversion occurs before age 59½. So, conversion is generally a bad idea unless the investor can pay the conversion tax from a taxable savings account. The following analysis illustrates this point.

Using IRA Assets to Pay the Conversion Tax

Assume an investor in the 25 percent tax bracket has a $10,000 traditional IRA and wishes to pay the conversion tax and any early withdrawal penalty from the traditional IRA balance. The investor will withhold $2,500 from rolling over into the Roth IRA to pay the conversion tax. This holdback, however, is subject to a 10 percent early withdrawal penalty of $250. If this amount is also held back from being rolled over to pay the penalty, it too will be subject to an early withdrawal penalty. The total amount to be withheld from the conversion to pay the penalty is about $278 [i.e., $250/(1 − 10%)] in addition to the $2,500 for the conversion tax, leaving $7,222 to be rolled over into the Roth IRA and accumulate earnings tax free. Paying the tax liability out of the assets being converted decreases the principal in the new Roth IRA, of course. More generally, if an investor uses IRA funds to pay the conversion tax and penalties, each dollar in the traditional IRA can be converted to $1 − T_o/(1 − \phi)$ dollars in a Roth IRA, where ϕ is the early withdrawal penalty, which is 10 percent. A proof is in Appendix 18B. So, the future value of this converted amount is

$$\mathrm{FV}_{RothConv^*} = \left(1 - \frac{T_o}{1 - \phi}\right)(1 + r)^n. \tag{18.9}$$

The asterisk in the subscript denotes the special case in which the conversion tax and penalty are paid from IRA assets. Taking the ratio of this future value to the future value of each dollar in a traditional IRA and solving for a breakeven tax rate yield a simple expression and rule of thumb: The breakeven withdrawal tax rate under these assumptions is $T_n = T_o/(1 - \phi)$. For a 10 percent early withdrawal penalty, the breakeven tax rate is about 11 percent (i.e., $1/0.9$) higher than the current tax rate. In other words, *an investor wishing to pay the conversion tax and penalties from IRA balances is generally better off staying with his or her traditional IRA unless the withdrawal tax rate is 11 percent higher than his or her current tax rate.*[35] Because most retirees have less income in retirement than in their preretirement years, this would be a somewhat unusual circumstance. This analysis assumes that minimum distribution requirements for the traditional IRA are not binding. That is, an investor plans withdrawals beyond the age of 70½ at least as large as those required by the IRS.

Using Taxable Assets to Pay the Conversion Tax

Conversion opportunities become more attractive when the conversion tax is paid from a taxable account, thus avoiding any early withdrawal penalty and preserving more of the IRA tax shelter. Paying the tax liability from IRA assets is suboptimal if the conversion tax can be paid with dollars that do not qualify for tax-deferred or tax-exempt earnings accumulation. If the tax liability can be paid from assets that would not qualify for tax-deferred status, the principal in the new Roth IRA is unchanged from the traditional IRA. This technique has the effect of lowering the opportunity cost associated with paying the conversion tax. In this case, the future value of a converted IRA dollar is equal to the future value of the new Roth IRA dollar less the after-tax future value of conversion tax, $T_o[\text{FVIF}_{TX}]$, or

$$\text{FV}_{RothConv} = (1 + r)^n - T_o[\text{FVIF}_{TX}]. \qquad (18.10)$$

The first term represents the future value of a dollar in the new Roth IRA. The second term represents the lost future value of T_o dollars used to pay the conversion tax that would have otherwise accumulated earnings in a taxable account.[36] As usual, one needs to have a sense of the expected return and tax structure of the taxable account from which the funds are taken to pay the conversion tax. By examining the ratio of the traditional IRA to the converted Roth IRA, one can determine whether conversion is worthwhile. A value ratio less than 1 indicates conversion is worthwhile. Panel A and Panel B of Table 18.9 indicate that investors facing constant or increasing tax rates benefit from converting a traditional IRA to a Roth IRA.

The more common scenario, however, is that tax rates fall when withdrawing funds. In this case, Panel C shows that conversion is optimal only for higher returns or moderately long time horizons. For example, an investor dropping into the 25 percent tax bracket and earning a 10 percent return needs an investment horizon of 10 years to make conversion worthwhile. These tables show that the value ratios decrease as the investment horizon and return increase, demonstrating that conversion is more beneficial for investors with longer investment horizons and higher expected returns.

Breakeven Withdrawal Tax Rate

Another approach for understanding the conversion issue is to examine the breakeven withdrawal tax rate. Perhaps not surprisingly, breakeven withdrawal tax rates for Roth IRA conversions (when the conversion tax is paid from a taxable account) are identical to breakeven withdrawal tax rates for the choice between a traditional IRA and Roth IRA when the pretax contribution is maximized. Appendix 18B contains the derivation of the breakeven withdrawal tax rate and its equivalence to the traditional Roth IRA breakeven withdrawal tax rate. So, Figures 18.1 and 18.2 from the previous section apply equally well to the conversion decision as they do to the initial investment decision except that the titles should be modified to replace "Non-IRA Investment" with "Conversion Tax Investment." When the conversion tax is taken from an investment that is fully taxed annually as ordinary income, as in Panel A of Figure 18.2, breakeven withdrawal tax rates decrease quickly as the time horizon and return increase. Low breakeven withdrawal tax rates indicate conversion is attractive. For example, an investor in the 33 percent tax bracket expecting a 9 percent return over a 10-year investment horizon has a 25 percent breakeven withdrawal tax rate. In other words, as long as the investor's withdrawal tax is above 25 percent (a drop of two tax brackets), conversion is optimal. If the account from which the conversion tax is paid is taxed as a typical mutual fund (Panel B), the breakeven withdrawal tax rate increases to about 30 percent. So, if the investor were to drop one tax bracket to 28 percent, she would find that *not* converting would result in a higher after-tax accumulation. Breakeven tax rates never fall below 28 percent if the conversion tax comes from an investment that would have been entirely taxed as deferred capital gain (Panel C), in which case conversion is optimal only if the investor's withdrawal tax bracket stays the same or increases.

Although the indifference points and breakeven withdrawal tax rates are identical to those in the previous section, the conversion value ratios presented earlier are not. The reason why breakeven tax rates are the same but value ratios are not is that paying the conversion tax

TABLE 18.9   After-Tax Future Value Ratios of a Traditional IRA to a Converted Roth IRA for an Investor in the 28 Percent Tax Bracket

r	Investment Horizon in Years (n)							
	5	10	15	20	25	30	35	40
A. 33 percent withdrawal tax rate								
2%	0.925	0.920	0.916	0.911	0.907	0.903	0.899	0.895
4%	0.921	0.912	0.903	0.896	0.889	0.882	0.876	0.870
6%	0.916	0.904	0.893	0.883	0.874	0.866	0.858	0.851
8%	0.912	0.897	0.884	0.872	0.862	0.852	0.844	0.836
10%	0.908	0.890	0.875	0.862	0.851	0.840	0.831	0.822
12%	0.905	0.885	0.868	0.854	0.841	0.830	0.820	0.811
14%	0.901	0.879	0.862	0.846	0.833	0.821	0.810	0.800
16%	0.898	0.875	0.856	0.840	0.826	0.813	0.802	0.791
18%	0.895	0.870	0.850	0.833	0.819	0.806	0.794	0.783
B. 28 percent withdrawal tax rate								
2%	0.994	0.989	0.984	0.979	0.975	0.970	0.966	0.962
4%	0.989	0.980	0.971	0.963	0.955	0.948	0.942	0.935
6%	0.985	0.971	0.959	0.949	0.939	0.930	0.922	0.915
8%	0.980	0.964	0.949	0.937	0.926	0.916	0.906	0.898
10%	0.976	0.957	0.941	0.927	0.914	0.903	0.893	0.884
12%	0.972	0.951	0.933	0.918	0.904	0.892	0.881	0.871
14%	0.969	0.945	0.926	0.910	0.895	0.882	0.871	0.860
16%	0.965	0.940	0.920	0.902	0.887	0.874	0.862	0.851
18%	0.962	0.935	0.914	0.896	0.880	0.866	0.853	0.842
C. 25 percent withdrawal tax rate								
2%	1.036	1.030	1.025	1.020	1.015	**1.011**	**1.006**	**1.002**
4%	1.030	1.020	1.011	**1.003**	**0.995**	0.988	0.981	0.974
6%	1.026	1.012	**0.999**	0.988	0.978	0.969	0.961	0.953
8%	1.021	1.004	0.989	0.976	0.964	0.954	0.944	0.935
10%	1.017	**0.997**	0.980	0.965	0.952	0.941	0.930	0.920
12%	1.013	0.990	0.972	0.956	0.942	0.929	0.918	0.907
14%	1.009	0.984	0.965	0.947	0.933	0.919	0.907	0.896
16%	1.006	0.979	0.958	0.940	0.924	0.910	0.897	0.886
18%	**1.002**	0.974	0.952	0.933	0.916	0.902	0.889	0.877

Notes: The conversion tax is assumed to be paid from a taxable account that is invested in a typical equity mutual fund that distributes 20 percent of its return as dividends and 45 percent as long-term capital gain. Dividends and capital gains are taxed at 15 percent. Bold numbers indicate approximate indifference points between the traditional IRA and the converted Roth IRA.

from a taxable account is akin to making an additional investment in a TDA account. In effect, a converting investor is committing more after-tax dollars to a tax-preferred investment strategy, thereby amplifying the effects of conversion when it is worthwhile and when it is not. An example will illustrate this point.

Consider the hypothetical investor in the 25 percent tax bracket deciding between an initial contribution between a traditional IRA and a Roth IRA. He or she maximizes the pretax investment, which is $4,000, and chooses the traditional IRA. In the previous section, I showed that the traditional IRA strategy includes a $3,000 IRA investment and a $750 non-IRA investment in a taxable account. Now, suppose for the time being that the investor immediately converts the traditional IRA to a Roth IRA. The $3,000 conversion will generate a conversion tax of $750 [i.e., $3,000 × 0.25], which can be taken from the taxable, non-IRA investment, and the investor is in exactly the same situation had the Roth IRA been chosen in the first place. In the previous section, the future value of the $750 was added to the numerator. In this analysis, it is subtracted from the denominator, which changes the ratio.

Now, suppose the investor does not convert immediately but waits five years instead. After five years of earning, say, a 10 percent pretax return, the traditional IRA will be worth $4,832. If one assumes that the non-IRA investment is fully taxable as ordinary income, the $750 non-IRA investment will grow to $1,077 over the same time period. Converting to a Roth IRA at this point triggers a conversion tax of $1,208 [i.e., $4,832 × 25%]. Notice that the non-IRA investment is not sufficient to pay the conversion tax because the tax drag prevents it from growing at the same rate as the IRA. The investor must make an additional $131 investment in conversion tax to roll over the traditional IRA into a Roth IRA. Therefore, the conversion decision effectively involves making an additional after-tax investment in a Roth IRA.

In any case, the following guidance may help investors considering a conversion from a traditional IRA to a Roth IRA: *If the conversion tax is paid from a taxable account, not the traditional IRA, then investors facing increasing or constant tax rates during withdrawal periods will generally benefit from converting. Investors facing decreasing tax rates will not benefit from conversion. As long as the tax is paid from an account with a relatively heavy tax burden, conversion becomes more attractive as the return and time horizon increase.*

CHOOSING BETWEEN NONDEDUCTIBLE IRAS AND TAXABLE INVESTMENTS

Income limitations prevent some investors from making deductible contributions to a traditional IRA or 401(k) account or after-tax contributions to a Roth IRA (see Table 18.2). Because the income limitations are higher for the Roth IRA than the traditional IRA, some investors may qualify for Roth IRA contributions but not deductible IRA contributions. In this instance, the Roth IRA is at least as good as nondeductible contributions to a traditional IRA, even in the extreme case of a zero tax rate upon withdrawal. Some taxpayers in the 28 percent and higher tax brackets may be precluded from making either a deductible contribution to a traditional IRA account or an after-tax contribution to a Roth IRA. These investors can still choose between a nondeductible IRA contribution (which is not tax deductible but accumulates earnings tax deferred) or a taxable investment.[37]

The choice, not surprisingly, depends on the tax structure for the taxable investment.[38] A different choice dominates in each of the extreme taxing schemes that I have examined thus far—a return taxed entirely as ordinary income or a return taxed entirely as deferred capital gain. If returns are fully taxed as ordinary income, the nondeductible IRA is optimal because it has tax-deferral benefits whereas the taxable investment does not. If returns are taxed entirely as deferred capital gains, the taxable account is optimal because the capital gain tax shelter is more valuable than the tax deferral associated with the nondeductible IRA. Although the choice is less clear when the taxable return has a hybrid taxing scheme, as most mutual funds do, the nondeductible IRA is often the best alternative for investors with very long investment horizons and high returns because the marginal benefit of deferring taxes increases at an increasing rate as time passes.

Analysis

If the investment under question is a bond, its return (assuming no capital appreciation or depreciation) is fully taxed annually as ordinary income if it is held in a taxable account. The same is true for a trader who exhibits high turnover and realizes return as short-term capital gains. In a nondeductible IRA, tax is deferred until funds are withdrawn. Because the tax deferral is valuable, the nondeductible IRA is better than a taxable account for investments with returns that are taxed entirely as ordinary income.

In contrast, if the return is composed entirely of deferred capital gain (e.g., a buy-and-hold strategy of non-dividend-paying stocks), the entire return is tax deferred until it is liquidated. In a taxable account, the accumulated appreciation receives preferential tax treatment as a capital gain. But a withdrawal from a nondeductible IRA is subject to the higher tax rate on ordinary income. Therefore, the taxable account is better than the nondeductible IRA for investments with returns composed entirely of capital appreciation.

Although the analysis is less clear when the investment has a return with different taxable components, it follows the same basic approach I have developed thus far. The after-tax investment, $I_{BT}(1 - T_o)$, is identical for both the nondeductible IRA and the taxable investment. It can, therefore, be ignored. According to Equation 18.4, the future after-tax accumulation of each dollar in a taxable account is

$$\text{FV}_{TX} = (1 + r^*)^n(1 - T^*) + T^*. \tag{18.11}$$

Although the initial contribution to a nondeductible IRA is taxable, earnings accumulate tax deferred until funds are withdrawn, at which point they are taxed as ordinary income. Therefore, the after-tax accumulation of a dollar invested in a nondeductible IRA is equal to the pretax accumulation less the tax paid on the accumulation, or

$$\text{FV}_{NonDedIRA} = (1 + r)^n - T_n[(1 + r)^n - 1]$$
$$= (1 + r)^n(1 - T_n) + T_n. \tag{18.12}$$

I can then take the ratio of the after-tax accumulations of the taxable account and the nondeductible IRA for different pretax returns and investment horizons to determine under which circumstances one or the other is preferred. Panel A of Table 18.10 shows that the 28 percent taxpayer facing a constant tax rate is generally better off with a taxable investment. For these investors, the benefit of the lower tax rate on dividends and capital gains outweighs the tax deferral offered by the nondeductible IRA account. Interestingly, the relative value of the nondeductible IRA increases as the time horizon and return increase but then begins to decrease. For shorter time horizons and lower returns, the marginal benefit of the preferred capital gains tax outweighs the benefit of deferring taxes until withdrawal. But as the time

TABLE 18.10   After-Tax Future Value Ratios of a Taxable Account and a Nondeductible IRA for an Investor in the 28 Percent Tax Bracket

	Investment Horizon in Years (n)							
r	5	10	15	20	25	30	35	40
A. 28 percent withdrawal tax rate								
2%	1.012	1.023	1.033	1.041	1.048	1.054	1.058	1.061
4%	1.023	1.041	1.054	1.062	1.066	1.066	1.063	1.057
6%	1.033	1.054	1.065	1.067	1.062	1.051	1.036	**1.018**
8%	1.041	1.063	1.068	1.060	1.044	1.021	**0.994**	0.965
10%	1.048	1.068	1.065	1.046	1.018	**0.984**	0.948	0.910
12%	1.054	1.070	1.057	1.027	**0.988**	0.945	0.901	0.857
14%	1.060	1.069	1.046	**1.005**	0.957	0.906	0.856	0.807
16%	1.064	1.067	1.033	0.982	0.926	0.868	0.813	0.761
18%	1.068	1.063	**1.018**	0.959	0.895	0.833	0.774	0.718
B. 25 percent withdrawal tax rate								
2%	1.009	1.017	1.024	1.030	1.034	1.038	1.040	1.041
4%	1.017	1.030	1.038	1.042	1.042	1.039	1.033	1.026
6%	1.024	1.038	1.043	1.040	1.031	1.018	**1.001**	0.982
8%	1.030	1.043	1.041	1.029	**1.010**	0.985	0.958	0.929
10%	1.035	1.044	1.035	1.012	0.982	0.984	0.912	0.875
12%	1.039	1.044	1.025	**0.992**	0.952	0.909	0.866	0.823
14%	1.042	1.041	1.012	0.969	0.921	0.871	0.822	0.775
16%	1.045	1.036	**0.997**	0.946	0.890	0.834	0.781	0.730
18%	1.047	**1.030**	0.982	0.922	0.860	0.800	0.743	0.689
C. 15 percent withdrawal tax rate								
2%	**1.000**	0.999	0.997	0.994	0.991	0.988	0.984	0.979
4%	0.999	0.995	0.988	0.980	0.970	0.959	0.947	0.933
6%	0.997	0.989	0.976	0.960	0.942	0.922	0.901	0.880
8%	0.996	0.982	0.962	0.938	0.911	0.883	0.854	0.826
10%	0.993	0.974	0.946	0.914	0.879	0.844	0.809	0.775
12%	0.991	0.965	0.929	0.889	0.847	0.806	0.766	0.727
14%	0.988	0.955	0.912	0.865	0.817	0.771	0.726	0.684
16%	0.985	0.945	0.895	0.841	0.788	0.737	0.690	0.645
18%	0.982	0.935	0.878	0.818	0.761	0.706	0.656	0.608

Notes: In this example, non-IRA investments are invested in a typical taxable mutual fund, and dividends and capital gains are taxed at 15 percent through the accumulation phase. Bold numbers indicate approximate indifference points between the taxable account and the nondeductible IRA.

horizon and return increase, the marginal value of deferring taxes increases at an increasing rate.[39]

If the taxpayer drops into the 25 percent tax bracket, as in Panel B, the nondeductible IRA becomes a bit more attractive, but not dramatically. The same trends of increasing then decreasing relative values are present. But if the withdrawal tax rate is 15 percent tax, the nondeductible IRA is always better because the withdrawal tax rate and capital gains tax rate are equal. So, the deferral associated with the nondeductible IRA dominates the taxable investment. This table also shows that for very long time horizons and high returns, the difference in relative values are quite large, indicating that the proper choice between a taxable account and a nondeductible IRA has significant wealth implications.

Table 18.11 displays after-tax value ratios for a taxpayer in the 33 percent tax bracket. The taxable account is relatively more valuable to these investors compared with the investors paying 28 percent because the indifference points have longer time horizons and higher returns in Panel A and Panel B. The taxable account is more attractive to investors in the 33 percent tax bracket because they derive a comparatively larger benefit from the 15 percent tax rate on dividends and capital gains than investors in the 28 percent tax bracket. The same trend of increasing then decreasing relative values with respect to the time horizon and return are also evident. When the 33 percent taxpayer drops two tax brackets to the 25 percent tax bracket (Panel C), the nondeductible IRA becomes attractive for long investment horizons and high returns. In these cases, the preferred tax rate on capital gains is relatively less valuable and the benefit of deferring taxes grows.

Breakeven withdrawal tax rates offer another perspective on the choice between a nondeductible IRA and a taxable account. Appendix 18C contains an expression for the breakeven withdrawal tax rate, but an important characteristic is that it is independent of the investor's current tax rate because the after-tax investments for the two types of accounts are the same. Appendix 18C also presents the breakeven tax rate for partially deductible IRAs. Figure 18.4 presents breakeven withdrawal tax rates under three different assumptions about how ordinary income distributions from mutual fund returns are taxed. A withdrawal tax rate below the breakeven rate indicates that the nondeductible IRA accumulates more wealth than the taxable account. So, high breakeven withdrawal tax rates favor nondeductible IRAs. Panel A assumes that a mutual fund distributes income in the form of dividends, which are taxed at 15 percent. The breakeven withdrawal tax rates are relatively low, indicating that the taxable account is attractive in many circumstances. Moreover, the breakeven withdrawal tax rate is quite sensitive to the investment horizon and expected return. Nondeductible IRAs become much more attractive than taxable accounts as the investment horizon and investment return increase. So, investors should estimate these factors carefully when choosing between the two types of accounts.

Panel B and Panel C show how the breakeven tax rate changes if the income generated by the mutual fund is taxed as ordinary income rather than taxed as a dividend at 15 percent. This situation is particularly relevant for high-tax-bracket investors who are likely to be subject to the AMT. The AMT affects a small but growing number of taxpayers. Originally targeted to prevent a small number of high-income households from paying no taxes, the AMT is a parallel tax system that functions much like a flat tax of 26 percent or 28 percent on income exceeding a specific amount. Long-term capital gains receive the same preferential tax treatment under the AMT as they do under the ordinary income tax. Large gains, however, may reduce or eliminate the amount of income one can exempt from the AMT. So, indirectly, capital gains can create a marginal tax liability in excess of the 15 percent preferred rate. A detailed analysis of the AMT is far beyond the scope of this chapter, but its potential impact can be incorporated into the discussion.

TABLE 18.11   After-Tax Future Value Ratios of a Taxable Account and a Nondeductible IRA for an Investor in the 33 Percent Tax Bracket

r	Investment Horizon in Years (n)							
	5	10	15	20	25	30	35	40
A. 33 percent withdrawal tax rate								
2%	1.017	1.033	1.047	1.060	1.071	1.081	1.090	1.097
4%	1.033	1.060	1.081	1.097	1.108	1.114	1.115	1.113
6%	1.047	1.081	1.103	1.114	1.116	1.111	1.099	1.083
8%	1.060	1.097	1.115	1.117	1.106	1.086	1.016	1.032
10%	1.071	1.109	1.119	1.108	1.084	1.052	**1.015**	**0.976**
12%	1.081	1.116	1.116	1.093	1.056	**1.012**	0.966	0.920
14%	1.090	1.121	1.109	1.073	1.024	0.972	0.918	0.866
16%	1.098	1.122	1.098	1.050	**0.992**	0.932	0.873	0.817
18%	1.104	1.121	1.085	1.026	0.960	0.894	0.831	0.772
B. 28 percent withdrawal tax rate								
2%	1.012	1.023	1.033	1.041	1.048	1.054	1.058	1.061
4%	1.023	1.041	1.054	1.062	1.066	1.066	1.063	1.057
6%	1.033	1.054	1.065	1.067	1.062	1.051	1.036	**1.018**
8%	1.041	1.063	1.068	1.060	1.044	**1.021**	0.994	0.965
10%	1.048	1.068	1.065	1.046	1.018	0.984	0.948	0.910
12%	1.054	1.070	1.057	1.027	**0.988**	0.945	0.901	0.857
14%	1.060	1.069	1.046	**1.005**	0.957	0.906	0.856	0.807
16%	1.064	1.067	1.033	0.982	0.926	0.868	0.813	0.761
18%	1.068	1.063	**1.018**	0.959	0.895	0.833	0.774	0.718
C. 25 percent withdrawal tax rate								
2%	1.009	1.017	1.024	1.030	1.034	1.038	1.040	1.041
4%	1.017	1.030	1.038	1.042	1.042	1.039	1.033	1.026
6%	1.024	1.038	1.043	1.040	1.031	1.018	**1.001**	**0.982**
8%	1.030	1.043	1.041	1.029	**1.010**	**0.985**	0.958	0.929
10%	1.035	1.044	1.035	1.012	0.982	0.948	0.912	0.875
12%	1.039	1.044	1.025	**0.992**	0.952	0.909	0.866	0.823
14%	1.042	1.041	1.012	0.969	0.921	0.871	0.822	0.775
16%	1.045	1.036	**0.997**	0.946	0.890	0.834	0.781	0.730
18%	1.047	1.030	0.982	0.922	0.860	0.800	0.743	0.689

Notes: In this example, non-IRA investments are invested in a typical taxable mutual fund, and dividends and capital gains are taxed at 15 percent through the accumulation phase. Bold numbers indicate approximate indifference points between the taxable account and the nondeductible IRA.

FIGURE 18.4   Breakeven Withdrawal Tax Rates between a Taxable Account and a Nondeductible IRA

A. Distributions Taxed as Dividends at 15 Percent

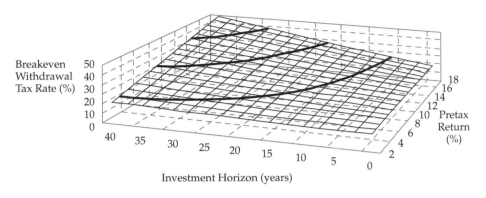

B. Distributions Taxed as Ordinary Income at 28 Percent

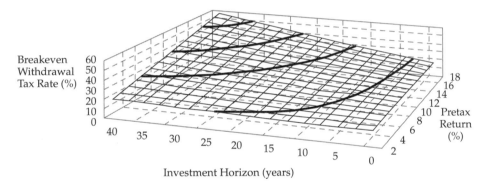

C. Distributions Taxed as Ordinary Income at 33 Percent

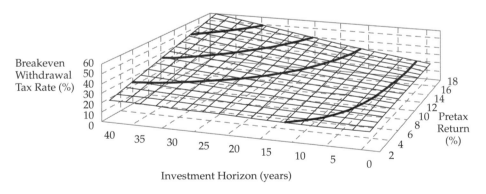

The breakeven tax rates for ordinary income taxed at 28 percent (Panel B) are 3–7 percentage points higher than in Panel A, in which income is assumed to be taxed at 15 percent. Therefore, the nondeductible IRA becomes attractive in more situations when the preferential tax treatment of dividends associated with the taxable investment is reduced or lost. Breakeven tax rates increase another percentage point or two in Panel C, which assumes ordinary income is taxed at 33 percent. Nonetheless, the taxable account remains a viable investment alternative in many situations.

Summary

Investors with income limitations on deductible IRA contributions may face the decision of whether to invest using a nondeductible IRA or a taxable account. The following rule of thumb may be useful to investors choosing between a taxable account and a nondeductible IRA: If returns are fully taxed as ordinary income, the nondeductible IRA is optimal because it has tax-shelter benefits. If returns are taxed entirely as deferred capital gains, the taxable account is optimal because the capital gain tax shelter is more valuable than the tax deferral associated with the nondeductible IRA. The nondeductible IRA is often the best alternative especially for investors with very long investment horizons and high expected returns. For taxpayers subject to the AMT, the nondeductible IRA alternative becomes increasingly attractive.

VALUING TAX-SHELTERED ASSETS ON A TAXABLE EQUIVALENT

The proliferation of TDAs (such as pension funds, traditional IRAs, 401(k)s, and Roth IRAs) has increased their significance in investors' portfolios. It has also increased the importance of valuing assets held in TDAs on a taxable equivalent basis. The idea of valuing financial assets held in TDAs can sound a bit confusing to an economist who understands these assets to be denominated in dollars and priced by the marketplace. The marketplace certainly can and does price the assets within a TDA, but the value of a dollar depends on how it is taxed when it is used for consumption purposes. For example, a dollar in a traditional IRA is subject to withdrawal taxes, which decreases the amount of goods and services an investor can buy, whereas a dollar in a Roth IRA is not subject to taxes, barring any unqualified withdrawals. So, in general, a dollar in a Roth IRA is worth more than a dollar held in a traditional IRA. As the reader will see, the taxable equivalent value of a dollar in a TDA is not an objective market value. It is contingent on the particular circumstances and financial plans (e.g., tax profile, investment return, withdrawal patterns) faced by a given investor and, therefore, varies from one investor to the next.

The notion of valuing assets in a TDA on a taxable equivalent basis is based on determining the amount of taxable assets that would produce the same after-tax cash flow as the TDA. For both traditional IRAs and partially deductible IRAs, the taxable equivalent value can be either greater than or less than the pretax accumulation depending on the investment return and time horizon. As the return and investment horizon increase, the taxable equivalent value of the TDA increases because the effect of its tax shelter increases. For Roth IRAs, the taxable equivalent value is always greater than the pretax accumulation as well as the traditional IRA after-tax values because withdrawals from Roth IRAs are free from tax. Although annuitized withdrawal patterns generate higher after-tax values than lump-sum withdrawals at the beginning of the annuity period, the difference is more modest than previous research suggests and can be safely ignored in most cases.

But why would one care about valuing assets held in TDAs on a taxable equivalent basis? Researchers have investigated how the introduction of TDAs has affected savings rates and investors' taxable savings habits.[40] Most often, however, they treat a dollar in a TDA as equivalent to a dollar in a taxable account when, in fact, they might be quite different based on the type of TDA, the taxing scheme of the taxable account, and the withdrawal pattern. Several authors have recognized the need to consider the after-tax value of assets in a TDA arguing that retirees and investors make consumption decisions using after-tax dollars. Retirees and investors, therefore, should make their asset allocation and investment decisions using after-tax dollars.[41] Researchers have recently developed models of varying sophistication to address this issue so that financial assets within TDAs can be compared on an equal footing with assets in taxable accounts.[42]

Reichenstein (1998), for example, made a first approximation by simply multiplying the pretax value of TDA assets by 1 minus the tax rate. This approach, however, assumes that funds are immediately withdrawn from the TDA in their entirety and, therefore, subject to taxation. Sibley (2002) proposed a more sophisticated framework by deriving a taxable equivalent—that is, the amount of taxable assets that would produce the same after-tax cash flow as a withdrawal from the tax-sheltered account at some future date. This approach is useful because it accounts for the value of assets earning tax-deferred or tax-free returns before they are withdrawn. His approach is limited, however, because it focuses on single withdrawals and assumes that returns on the taxable equivalent are fully taxed annually at a single, constant tax rate. Following Horan (2002), I can apply the methods developed in earlier sections to value assets held in TDAs on an after-tax basis.

Sibley introduced the idea of valuing tax-sheltered accounts by discounting future after-tax withdrawals from the account at an after-tax cost of capital, thereby deriving a taxable equivalent. The taxable equivalent is the amount of taxable assets that would be required to produce the same after-tax cash flows that the TDA produces.[43] I follow a similar approach but use a model with discount factors based on a typical mutual fund taxing scheme outlined in the section called Choosing between Traditional IRAs and Roth IRAs: The Basics, whereby a portion of the return is taxed each year as distributed ordinary income, a portion is taxed as distributed dividend or capital gain, and the remainder is taxed as capital gain when the investment is sold. The result is an opportunity cost of capital associated with a typical mutual fund investment, which is appropriate to use if the investor uses a mutual fund or some other taxable portfolio to invest the taxable equivalent in lieu of the tax-sheltered vehicle.

It should be noted that the concept of taxable equivalent values is related to, but distinct from, the notion of after-tax values introduced by Reichenstein (1998) and others. That distinction, however, is beyond the scope of this section.

Taxable Equivalent Value for a Traditional IRA with a Lump-Sum Withdrawal

The previous section showed that the future after-tax withdrawal after n years of investment return for each dollar in a fully deductible traditional IRA is

$$\text{FV}_{TradIRA} = (1 + r)^n (1 - T_n), \qquad (18.13)$$

where T_n is the applicable tax rate upon withdrawal. Using this accumulation, I can determine the taxable equivalent—the amount of money invested today in a taxable account that will produce that same after-tax accumulation as the traditional IRA—by taking the present value of this figure. The present value calculation requires a taxable present value interest factor (i.e., PVIF_{TX}) that appropriately accommodates the different taxable components of an investment's return: ordinary income, realized capital gains and dividends, and unrealized capital gains. The taxable equivalent present value interest factor is simply the reciprocal of the after-tax future value interest factor introduced in the section called Choosing between Traditional IRAs and Roth IRAs: The Basics, or

$$\text{PVIF}_{TX} = \frac{1}{\text{FVIF}_{TX}}$$

$$= \frac{1}{(1 + r^*)^n (1 - T^*) + T^*}. \qquad (18.14)$$

Therefore, the taxable equivalent in today's dollars of each dollar invested in a traditional IRA is equal to the product of Equation 18.13 and Equation 18.14, or

$$PV_{TradIRA} = \frac{(1 + r)^n(1 - T_n)}{(1 + r^*)^n(1 - T^*) + T^*}$$

$$= (1 + r)^n(1 - T_n)[PVIF_{TX}].$$

(18.15)

Equation 18.15 is essentially the ratio of the after-tax future value of a traditional IRA to the after-tax future value of a taxable account. So, the process of valuing TDAs on a taxable equivalent basis boils down to comparing the after-tax accumulation of the TDA with that of the taxable account.

If an investor has the taxable equivalent in lieu of the tax-sheltered account, the proceeds might be invested in an investment fully taxed each year as ordinary income, such as a fixed-income instrument or a high turnover portfolio that realizes short-term capital gains. Alternatively, the taxable equivalent might be an investment with a return entirely deferred as unrealized capital gain, such as a passively managed portfolio of non-dividend-paying stocks. The taxable equivalent might more likely be a portfolio of investments with a blended taxing scheme that includes taxable components of ordinary income, realized capital gain, and unrealized capital gain, such as an actively managed portfolio or a mutual fund. Regardless, the inputs of Equation 18.15 can be adjusted to reflect these different taxation schemes. The denominator in Equation 18.15 will generally be smaller for fully taxable investments, which will increase the after-tax value of the traditional IRA because the tax-sheltering benefits of a TDA increase if the alternative investment has a heavy tax burden. By reverse logic, the after-tax value of the TDA becomes less valuable if the taxable equivalent is invested in a vehicle with a light tax burden because the TDA tax advantages are relatively less valuable.

Table 18.12 displays taxable equivalent valuations for a traditional IRA under various scenarios for an investor in the 28 percent tax bracket during the contribution and withdrawal phase. Panel A shows that the taxable equivalent value increases as the time horizon and return increase and that the value is quite sensitive as these factors change. For example, the value of each dollar in a traditional IRA for an investor with a five-year investment horizon expecting a 6 percent return is 78 cents. Therefore, the taxable equivalent value of a $200,000 traditional IRA would be $156,000. By contrast, the value of a traditional IRA for an investor with a 40-year investment horizon expecting a 12 percent return is 2.44 times the pretax value of the account. In other words, the taxable equivalent value of the same $200,000 traditional IRA would then be $488,000.

The reason for these dramatic differences is that the value of tax deferral increases as the pretax return increases. The higher the return and time horizon, the greater the tax deferral benefits, especially for a taxable equivalent that is fully taxed as ordinary income. It is interesting to note that the taxable equivalent value of a traditional IRA can be either greater than or less than its pretax value. It depends on the return and when the withdrawal is made. It stands to reason that the value depends on how the withdrawal is made as well. I will address the impact of annuity withdrawal patterns below.

A comparison of the values across the three panels shows that the taxable equivalent values are greatest when the taxable equivalent has a return that is fully taxed as ordinary income. And the difference is quite large for high returns and long investment horizons because the value of the TDA's tax shelter grows under these conditions.

Panel B of Table 18.12 displays taxable equivalent values for a typical equity mutual fund in which a portion of the return is taxed as dividend, realized capital gain, and short-term capital gain. The same basic trends hold, but the taxable equivalent values are lower,

TABLE 18.12　Taxable Equivalent Value of a Traditional IRA Withdrawn as a Lump Sum for an Investor in the 28 Percent Bracket

	Investment Horizon in Years (n)							
r	5	10	15	20	25	30	35	40
A. Fully taxable discount rate (trader)								
2%	0.740	0.761	0.782	0.804	0.826	0.849	0.873	0.897
4%	0.760	0.802	0.847	0.894	**0.944**	**0.996**	**1.052**	1.110
6%	0.780	0.845	0.915	**0.991**	1.073	1.163	1.259	1.364
8%	0.800	0.888	**0.986**	1.095	1.216	1.350	1.499	1.665
10%	0.819	0.932	1.060	1.206	1.372	1.561	1.775	2.020
12%	0.838	0.976	1.137	1.324	1.542	1.795	2.091	2.435
14%	0.858	**1.022**	1.217	1.450	1.727	2.057	2.450	2.919
16%	0.877	1.068	1.300	1.583	1.927	2.347	2.858	3.480
18%	0.896	1.114	1.386	1.724	2.144	2.667	3.318	4.127
B. Typical equity mutual fund discount rate (active investor)								
2%	0.731	0.741	0.751	0.761	0.771	0.781	0.791	0.801
4%	0.741	0.761	0.780	0.800	0.819	0.838	0.857	0.875
6%	0.750	0.780	0.808	0.836	0.864	0.891	0.919	0.947
8%	0.760	0.797	0.834	0.870	0.907	0.943	**0.980**	**1.018**
10%	0.768	0.814	0.859	0.904	0.948	**0.994**	1.041	1.089
12%	0.777	0.831	0.883	0.936	**0.989**	1.045	1.102	1.162
14%	0.785	0.846	0.906	0.967	1.030	1.095	1.164	1.237
16%	0.793	0.861	0.929	**0.998**	1.070	1.146	1.227	1.314
18%	0.801	0.876	0.951	1.028	1.110	1.198	1.291	1.392
C. Completely deferred capital gains discount rate (passive investor)								
2%	0.730	0.740	0.749	0.757	0.765	0.772	0.778	0.784
4%	0.740	0.757	0.771	0.784	0.794	0.803	0.811	0.817
6%	0.748	0.771	0.789	0.803	0.814	0.822	0.828	0.833
8%	0.756	0.783	0.802	0.816	0.826	0.832	0.837	0.840
10%	0.763	0.793	0.813	0.825	0.833	0.839	0.842	0.844
12%	0.770	0.802	0.821	0.832	0.838	0.842	0.844	0.845
14%	0.776	0.809	0.827	0.836	0.841	0.844	0.846	0.846
16%	0.781	0.814	0.831	0.839	0.843	0.845	0.846	0.847
18%	0.786	0.819	0.835	0.842	0.845	0.846	0.847	0.847

Notes: The investor maintains the same marginal tax rate throughout the investment horizon. The mutual fund distributes 20 percent of its return as dividends and 45 percent as long-term capital gain. Dividends and capital gains are taxed at 15 percent. Bold numbers correspond approximately to break-even pretax and after-tax values.

especially for long time horizons and high returns. For example, a 20-year investor expecting a 12 percent return has an after-tax value of about 94 percent of pretax asset value if the taxable equivalent is a typical equity mutual fund. If the taxable equivalent is fully taxable as in Panel A, the taxable equivalent value increases to 132 percent.

In the extreme case in which the return for the taxable equivalent is entirely deferred as a capital gain until the end of the investment period (Panel C), the taxable equivalent value of a traditional IRA is always less than its pretax value. The intuition is simple. Both the traditional IRA and the taxable equivalent are taxed at the end of the investment period. The former is taxed as ordinary income, and the latter is taxed at the lower capital gains tax rate. In this case, the TDA will always produce a lower after-tax cash flow than the taxable equivalent.

The taxable equivalent values for investors in the 33 percent tax bracket are reported in Table 18.13. The indifference points at which the pretax value equals the taxable equivalent value in Panel A are about the same as those for the 28 percent taxpayer. But the variance of taxable equivalent values is higher. That is, compared with the 28 percent taxpayer, low after-tax values are lower for the 33 percent taxpayer and high after-tax values are higher. The variance is higher because the TDA's positive tax benefits are relatively more valuable for long time horizons and high returns. For short time horizons and low returns, the tax burden on the taxable equivalent is not terribly onerous, which makes the relative value of the traditional IRA low.

In Panel B of Table 18.13, the indifference points are about 5–10 years longer and the after tax values are about 5–10 percent less than those reported for the 28 percent taxpayer. The intuition here is that dividends and realized capital gains are still being taxed at 15 percent for the equity mutual fund in the taxable equivalent. All that is changing is the withdrawal tax rate, which has increased to 33 percent. The higher withdrawal tax rate decreases the taxable equivalent value.

Table 18.14 shows that a decreasing tax rate when funds are withdrawn increases the after-tax value of a traditional IRA, which comes as no surprise. The effect is modest for low returns and short time horizons because the accumulation in these scenarios is modest. Decreasing withdrawal tax rates has a more pronounced effect for high returns and long investment horizons. For example, the taxable equivalent value of a traditional IRA for a taxpayer expecting a 12 percent return over a 40-year time horizon is more than three times the pretax value if the investor drops from the 33 percent tax bracket to the 28 percent tax bracket. When the marginal tax rate on ordinary income stays constant, the number is 2.828 times. When the investor drops two tax brackets to 25 percent, the after-tax value is 3.17 times the pretax value. Notice that the values in Panel C for Tables 18.12 and Table 18.13 are identical. This is true because all that matters when returns are fully taxed as a deferred capital gain is the withdrawal tax rate, which is 28 percent in both cases.

This analysis indicates that the withdrawal tax rate affects the taxable equivalent value of a traditional IRA. But the return, time horizon, and taxing scheme of the taxable equivalent seem to be more important determinants of the taxable equivalent value for traditional IRAs.

Taxable Equivalent Value for a Roth IRA with a Lump-Sum Withdrawal

I can follow similar logic to find the taxable equivalent value of a lump-sum withdrawal from a Roth IRA. Because withdrawals from Roth IRAs are free from tax and earnings accumulate tax free, the future value of each dollar in a Roth IRA after n years is

$$\mathrm{FV}_{RothIRA} = (1 + r)^n. \qquad (18.16)$$

TABLE 18.13   Taxable Equivalent Value of a Traditional IRA Withdrawn as a Lump Sum for an Investor in the 33 Percent Tax Bracket

	Investment Horizon in Years (n)							
r	5	10	15	20	25	30	35	40
A. Fully taxable discount rate (trader)								
2%	0.692	0.715	0.739	0.763	0.788	0.814	0.841	0.869
4%	0.714	0.761	0.811	0.865	0.922	**0.983**	**1.048**	1.117
6%	0.736	0.809	0.889	**0.977**	**1.073**	1.180	1.296	1.424
8%	0.758	0.858	**0.971**	1.099	1.244	1.408	1.593	1.803
10%	0.780	0.909	1.058	1.232	1.435	1.671	1.946	2.266
12%	0.802	0.960	1.150	1.376	1.648	1.973	2.362	2.828
14%	0.824	**1.013**	1.246	1.533	1.885	2.318	2.850	3.506
16%	0.846	1.068	1.348	1.701	2.147	2.710	3.421	4.319
18%	0.867	1.123	1.454	1.882	2.437	3.155	4.085	5.288
B. Typical equity mutual fund discount rate (active investor)								
2%	0.680	0.690	0.699	0.709	0.718	0.727	0.736	0.745
4%	0.689	0.708	0.726	0.744	0.762	0.780	0.797	0.815
6%	0.698	0.725	0.752	0.778	0.804	0.829	0.855	0.881
8%	0.707	0.742	0.776	0.810	0.844	0.877	0.912	0.947
10%	0.715	0.758	0.800	0.841	0.882	0.925	0.969	**1.014**
12%	0.723	0.773	0.822	0.871	0.921	0.972	**1.026**	1.082
14%	0.731	0.788	0.844	0.900	0.958	**1.019**	1.083	1.151
16%	0.738	0.802	0.865	0.929	**0.996**	1.067	1.142	1.222
18%	0.745	0.815	0.885	0.957	1.033	1.114	1.202	1.295
C. Completely deferred capital gains discount rate (passive investor)								
2%	0.680	0.689	0.697	0.705	0.712	0.718	0.724	0.730
4%	0.688	0.704	0.718	0.729	0.739	0.748	0.754	0.760
6%	0.696	0.718	0.734	0.747	0.757	0.765	0.771	0.775
8%	0.704	0.729	0.747	0.759	0.768	0.775	0.779	0.782
10%	0.710	0.738	0.756	0.768	0.776	0.780	0.783	0.785
12%	0.716	0.746	0.764	0.774	0.780	0.784	0.786	0.787
14%	0.722	0.752	0.769	0.778	0.783	0.786	0.787	0.787
16%	0.727	0.758	0.774	0.781	0.785	0.787	0.787	0.788
18%	0.732	0.763	0.777	0.783	0.786	0.787	0.788	0.788

Notes: The investor maintains the same marginal tax rate throughout the investment horizon. The mutual fund distributes 20 percent of its return as dividends and 45 percent as long-term capital gain. Dividends and capital gains are taxed at 15 percent. Bold numbers correspond approximately to breakeven pretax and after-tax values.

TABLE 18.14   Taxable Equivalent Value of a Traditional IRA Withdrawn as a Lump Sum for an Investor in the 33 Percent Tax Bracket Who Drops One Tax Bracket

r	Investment Horizon in Years (n)							
	5	10	15	20	25	30	35	40
A. Fully taxable discount rate (trader)								
2%	0.744	0.768	0.794	0.820	0.847	0.875	0.904	0.933
4%	0.767	0.818	0.872	0.930	0.991	**1.056**	1.126	1.200
6%	0.791	0.869	0.955	**1.050**	1.154	1.268	1.393	1.531
8%	0.815	0.922	**1.044**	1.181	1.337	1.513	1.712	1.938
10%	0.838	**0.976**	1.137	1.324	1.542	1.795	2.091	2.435
12%	0.862	1.032	1.235	1.479	1.771	2.120	2.538	3.039
14%	0.885	1.089	1.339	1.647	2.025	2.491	3.063	3.767
16%	0.909	1.147	1.448	1.828	2.307	2.913	3.677	4.641
18%	0.932	1.207	1.562	2.023	2.619	3.391	4.390	5.683
B. Typical equity mutual fund discount rate (active investor)								
2%	0.733	0.746	0.759	0.772	0.785	0.798	0.811	0.824
4%	0.746	0.772	0.797	0.823	0.848	0.874	0.900	0.926
6%	0.758	0.796	0.834	0.872	0.910	0.949	**0.989**	**1.029**
8%	0.770	0.819	0.869	0.919	0.971	**1.024**	1.079	1.136
10%	0.781	0.842	0.904	0.967	1.032	1.100	1.171	1.246
12%	0.793	0.864	0.938	**1.013**	1.093	1.177	1.266	1.362
14%	0.803	0.886	0.971	1.060	1.154	1.256	1.365	1.484
16%	0.814	0.907	**1.004**	1.106	1.217	1.337	1.468	1.611
18%	0.824	0.927	1.036	1.153	1.280	1.420	1.574	1.745
C. Completely deferred capital gains discount rate (passive investor)								
2%	0.730	0.740	0.749	0.757	0.765	0.772	0.778	0.784
4%	0.740	0.757	0.771	0.784	0.794	0.803	0.811	0.817
6%	0.748	0.771	0.789	0.803	0.814	0.822	0.828	0.833
8%	0.756	0.783	0.802	0.816	0.826	0.832	0.837	0.840
10%	0.763	0.793	0.813	0.825	0.833	0.839	0.842	0.844
12%	0.770	0.802	0.821	0.832	0.838	0.842	0.844	0.845
14%	0.776	0.809	0.827	0.836	0.841	0.844	0.846	0.846
16%	0.781	0.814	0.831	0.839	0.843	0.845	0.846	0.847
18%	0.786	0.819	0.835	0.842	0.845	0.846	0.847	0.847

Notes: The investor drops into the next lower tax bracket upon withdrawing funds from the traditional IRA account. The mutual fund distributes 20 percent of its return as dividends and 45 percent as long-term capital gain. Dividends and capital gains are taxed at 15 percent. Bold numbers correspond approximately to breakeven pretax and after-tax values.

The taxable equivalent value of the lump-sum withdrawal is the present value of this amount. The taxable equivalent present value interest factor shows that the Roth IRA value is

$$PV_{RothIRA} = \frac{(1 + r)^n}{(1 + r^*)^n(1 - T^*) + T^*}$$

$$= (1 + r)^n[PVIF_{TX}].$$

(18.17)

Notice that this expression is simply the taxable equivalent value of the traditional IRA in Equation 18.15 divided by $(1 - T_n)$, creating a predicatable effect. Taxable equivalent values for Roth IRAs will be greater than those for traditional IRAs, and the difference will be more pronounced for higher values. Furthermore, taxable equivalent values for Roth IRAs will always be greater than 1 because the numerator of Equation 18.17 is always larger than the denominator for positive values of n and r.

Table 18.15 displays taxable equivalent values of a dollar invested in a Roth IRA. These values are independent of the contribution and withdrawal tax rates. But they do depend on the rate at which returns on the taxable equivalent are taxed and how those returns are taxed. So, Table 18.15 displays values when the taxable equivalent is fully taxed as ordinary income at 25 percent and at 33 percent. It also contains values for taxable equivalents that are taxed as a typical equity mutual fund. As predicted previously, all the values are greater than 1 and are larger than those for traditional IRAs. The difference is magnified for large values. Values are highest for a taxable equivalent fully taxed as ordinary income at 33 percent because the value of the Roth IRA tax shelter is greater when tax rates are high. The relative value is more than four times the pretax value for an investor with a 40-year time horizon and 12 percent expected return.

Values decrease substantially but remain large for taxpayers in the 25 percent tax bracket (Panel B). The tax burden is lightest, however, for a typical equity mutual fund that has a return that is only partially taxed at a preferential rate (Panel C). Nonetheless, the values remain greater than 1, indicating that a dollar in a Roth IRA is always worth more than a dollar in a taxable account.

Because taxable equivalent values of Roth IRAs are greater than traditional IRAs, one might be tempted to infer that contributions to a Roth IRA are always more beneficial, despite the analysis in the section on Choosing between Traditional IRAs and Roth IRAs: The Basics. This thinking overlooks the fact that each dollar contributed to a Roth IRA requires a larger after-tax investment than a contribution to a traditional IRA, which affords an investor the opportunity to invest the tax savings associated with a traditional IRA contribution. That taxable portion of the traditional IRA investment strategy is not considered in the valuation of traditional IRA assets. As a result, one should avoid confusing the valuation of TDA assets with the analysis for choosing between different types of TDAs.

Taxable Equivalent Value for a Partially Deductible IRA with a Lump-Sum Withdrawal

Income limitations preclude some investors from making fully deductible contributions to a traditional IRA. If investors make contributions to a tax-sheltered account in excess of the allowable deductible limits, they might make partially deductible or nondeductible contributions to an IRA account. The nondeductible portion of an IRA contribution earns returns on a tax-deferred basis until the funds are withdrawn, just like deductible contributions. When nondeductible IRA investments are withdrawn, the funds can be identified as either earnings

TABLE 18.15   Taxable Equivalent Value of a Roth IRA Withdrawn as a Lump Sum

	Investment Horizon in Years (n)							
r	5	10	15	20	25	30	35	40
A. Fully taxable discount rate for 33 percent tax bracket								
2%	1.033	1.067	1.102	1.139	1.176	1.215	1.255	1.296
4%	1.066	1.136	1.211	1.291	1.376	1.467	1.564	1.667
6%	1.099	1.208	1.327	1.458	1.602	1.761	1.935	2.126
8%	1.132	1.281	1.450	1.640	1.857	2.101	2.378	2.691
10%	1.165	1.356	1.579	1.839	2.141	2.494	2.904	3.382
12%	1.197	1.433	1.716	2.054	2.459	2.944	3.525	4.220
14%	1.230	1.512	1.860	2.287	2.813	3.459	4.254	5.232
16%	1.262	1.593	2.011	2.539	3.205	4.045	5.106	6.446
18%	1.295	1.676	2.170	2.809	3.637	4.709	6.097	7.893
B. Fully taxable discount rate for 25 percent tax bracket								
2%	1.025	1.050	1.076	1.103	1.131	1.159	1.188	1.217
4%	1.049	1.101	1.156	1.213	1.273	1.336	1.402	1.472
6%	1.074	1.153	1.238	1.330	1.428	1.534	1.647	1.768
8%	1.098	1.206	1.324	1.453	1.596	1.752	1.924	2.112
10%	1.122	1.258	1.412	1.584	1.777	1.993	2.236	2.508
12%	1.145	1.312	1.503	1.721	1.971	2.258	2.586	2.963
14%	1.169	1.366	1.596	1.866	2.181	2.548	2.978	3.481
16%	1.192	1.420	1.693	2.017	2.404	2.865	3.415	4.070
18%	1.215	1.475	1.792	2.176	2.643	3.211	3.900	4.736
C. Typical equity mutual fund discount rate								
2%	1.015	1.029	1.043	1.058	1.071	1.085	1.099	1.113
4%	1.029	1.057	1.084	1.111	1.137	1.164	1.190	1.216
6%	1.042	1.083	1.122	1.161	1.199	1.238	1.276	1.315
8%	1.055	1.108	1.159	1.209	1.259	1.310	1.361	1.414
10%	1.067	1.131	1.193	1.255	1.317	1.380	1.446	1.513
12%	1.079	1.154	1.227	1.300	1.374	1.451	1.531	1.614
14%	1.091	1.176	1.259	1.343	1.430	1.521	1.617	1.718
16%	1.101	1.197	1.290	1.386	1.486	1.592	1.704	1.824
18%	1.112	1.217	1.321	1.428	1.542	1.663	1.793	1.933

Notes: The mutual fund distributes 20 percent of its return as dividends and 45 percent as long-term capital gain. Dividends and capital gains are taxed at 15 percent.

or the original contribution. The earnings associated with nondeductible contributions are taxed as ordinary income when withdrawn. The original contribution, however, may be withdrawn free of tax. The future value of a dollar, a portion of which represents a nondeductible contribution, in a traditional IRA and withdrawn as a single cash flow can be expressed as

$$\text{FV}_{PartDedIRA} = (1 + r)^n(1 - T_n) + aT_n, \tag{18.18}$$

where a is the nondeductible portion of the contribution. If all the contributions to the IRA account are nondeductible, a is equal to 1 and the expression reduces to the future value of a nondeductible IRA in Equation 18.12. The first term is simply the future value of a traditional IRA with fully deductible contributions. The second term represents the basic tax adjustment associated with the nondeductible portion of the contribution when the funds are withdrawn. Once again, I can calculate the present value of this future sum using the taxable equivalent present value interest factor, giving

$$\begin{aligned}\text{PV}_{PartDedIRA} &= \frac{(1 + r)^n(1 - T_n) + aT_n}{(1 + r^*)^n(1 - T^*) + T^*} \\ &= [(1 + r)^n(1 - T_n) + aT_n][\text{PVIF}_{TX}]. \end{aligned} \tag{18.19}$$

A comparison of Equation 18.19 and Equation 18.15 shows that the taxable equivalent value of nondeductible IRAs is greater than taxable equivalent values of deductible IRAs because a portion of the tax was already paid when the contribution was made. The value differential, however, is only appreciable for short investment horizons and low returns because the tax relief from the extra term on the numerator, aT_n, is fixed and does not grow with the account's value over time. As the account value grows, the relative value of the original nondeductible contribution becomes smaller compared with the overall account value. Table 18.16 demonstrates this relationship for an investor in the 33 percent tax bracket who has made contributions that are completely nondeductible. For example, in Panel A, taxable equivalent values for the nondeductible IRA are more than 30 percent larger than taxable equivalent values for the deductible IRA for an investor expecting a 4 percent return over a 10-year investment horizon. But for investors expecting a 12 percent return over a 35-year or 40-year investment horizon, the values are nearly identical. The relationship between these relative values is basically unchanged for the other taxing schemes in Panel B and Panel C. Again, the intuition for this result is that as the nominal value of the account grows over time, the size of the nondeductible contribution (which is exempt from withdrawal tax) decreases in relation to the nominal value of the account.

Taxable Equivalent Value for a Traditional IRA Withdrawn as an Annuity

The preceding analysis derives taxable equivalent values of tax-sheltered accounts for a single withdrawal. Typically, however, investors draw on their retirement assets more evenly over time. One would expect values to increase if withdrawals are extended over a period of time rather than taken as a lump sum at the *beginning* of the withdrawal period because the remaining assets are sheltered from taxes for a longer period of time. By contrast, values for annuitized withdrawals should be less than lump-sum withdrawals at the *end* of the annuity period. The analysis can be modified to accommodate annuity-style withdrawal patterns that more closely resemble typical retirement behavior. One approach is to calculate the after-tax value for a series of single payments. But this procedure is cumbersome and time consuming. A model that specifically accommodates annuitized withdrawal patterns would yield more expedient results and heuristic guidance for investors and their advisors.

TABLE 18.16   Taxable Equivalent Value of a Nondeductible IRA Withdrawn as a Lump Sum for an Investor in the 33 Percent Tax Bracket

	Investment Horizon in Years (*n*)							
r	5	10	15	20	25	30	35	40
A. Fully taxable discount rate (trader)								
2%	1.001	1.004	1.009	1.016	1.025	1.035	1.048	1.062
4%	1.003	1.015	1.033	1.059	1.092	1.132	1.178	1.231
6%	1.007	1.032	1.072	1.127	1.197	1.281	1.379	1.493
8%	1.012	1.054	1.122	1.215	1.333	1.477	1.646	1.844
10%	1.019	1.081	1.183	1.322	1.500	1.718	1.980	2.290
12%	1.026	1.113	1.253	1.447	1.696	2.005	2.384	2.843
14%	1.035	1.148	1.332	1.587	1.920	2.340	2.865	3.515
16%	1.044	1.187	1.419	1.744	2.173	2.726	3.431	4.324
18%	1.054	1.229	1.514	1.916	2.456	3.166	4.091	5.292
B. Typical equity mutual fund discount rate (active investor)								
2%	0.983	0.968	0.955	0.943	0.933	0.925	0.918	0.912
4%	0.968	0.944	0.925	0.912	0.903	0.898	0.897	0.898
6%	0.955	0.925	0.906	0.897	0.896	0.900	0.910	0.923
8%	0.944	0.911	0.897	0.896	0.904	0.920	0.942	0.969
10%	0.934	0.902	0.894	0.902	0.923	0.951	**0.986**	**1.025**
12%	0.925	0.896	0.896	0.915	0.947	**0.988**	1.035	1.087
14%	0.918	0.892	0.902	0.932	0.976	1.029	1.089	1.154
16%	0.911	0.891	0.910	0.952	**1.008**	1.073	1.145	1.224
18%	0.905	0.892	0.921	0.974	1.041	1.118	1.203	1.296
C. Completely deferred capital gains discount rate (passive investor)								
2%	0.983	0.967	0.952	0.938	0.925	0.914	0.903	0.893
4%	0.967	0.939	0.914	0.893	0.876	0.861	0.849	0.838
6%	0.953	0.915	0.885	0.862	0.844	0.830	0.820	0.812
8%	0.940	0.895	0.863	0.840	0.824	0.813	0.805	0.800
10%	0.928	0.878	0.845	0.824	0.811	0.802	0.797	0.794
12%	0.917	0.864	0.832	0.814	0.803	0.797	0.793	0.791
14%	0.907	0.852	0.822	0.806	0.798	0.793	0.791	0.790
16%	0.898	0.843	0.815	0.801	0.794	0.791	0.790	0.789
18%	0.889	0.834	0.809	0.797	0.792	0.790	0.789	0.789

Notes: The investor maintains the same marginal tax rate throughout the investment horizon. The mutual fund distributes 20 percent of its return as dividends and 45 percent as long-term capital gain. Dividends and capital gains are taxed at 15 percent. Bold numbers correspond approximately to break-even pretax and after-tax values.

One way to view withdrawing funds as an annuity instead of as a single cash flow is to consider the duration of the cash flow stream. Duration is the weighted-average timing of the payments using present values as weights. In the case of the single withdrawal, the duration of the cash flow stream is simply the time when the withdrawal occurs. The duration of an annuity having the same time horizon is significantly less than half the time period over which an annuity withdrawal occurs, particularly for long time horizons. Because the weights are larger for nearer term payments, the duration of an annuity is much shorter than the duration of a single cash flow at the end of the annuity period. Therefore, taxable equivalent values of tax-sheltered accounts for annuitized withdrawals should be much less than values for single cash flows at the end of the same period.

The first step to valuing an annuitized pattern of withdrawals from a tax-sheltered account is to find the annuity payment that can be sustained by the current value of the traditional IRA over m years while earning a pretax return of r. The annuity payment is calculated using the standard time-value-of-money techniques involving the present value interest factor of an annuity (PVIFA).

Specifically, the before-tax annuity payment supported by a dollar in a fully deductible IRA over m years is

$$
\begin{aligned}
\text{PMT} &= \frac{1}{(1/r) - 1/[r(1 + r)^m]} \\
&= \frac{1}{\text{PVIFA}_{r,m}},
\end{aligned} \tag{18.20}
$$

where the denominator is the well-known present value interest factor for an annuity for return r over m years. This annuity withdrawal is fully taxable as ordinary income at the rate prevailing during retirement or whenever withdrawals are made starting at time n. The after-tax annuity payment is determined by multiplying the value in Equation 18.20 by $(1 - T_n)$. Knowing the after-tax annuity payment, I can determine the amount of money (held in a taxable account) that would be required to generate the same after-tax payments over m years. This value is the taxable equivalent. An example may help illustrate this point.

Consider a 60-year old investor with $1,000,000 invested in a traditional IRA with an expected return of 10 percent. Her goal is to withdraw funds evenly in the form of an annuity from age 71 to age 90, a 20-year period. Through age 70, the traditional IRA will grow in value to $2,593,742, which will sustain pretax withdrawals of $304,660 over the next 20 years until age 90.[44] If she is in the 33 percent tax bracket, the after-tax withdrawals will be $204,122. One approach to determining the taxable equivalent (which becomes algebraically necessary with the complex tax structure of a mutual fund or diversified equity portfolio) is to calculate the future value of the after-tax withdrawals as of age 90 using an after-tax future value interest factor of an annuity for a taxable investment over 20 years ($\text{FVIFA}_{TX,r,m}$). Appendix 18D shows that the future value interest factor of an annuity of a taxable investment at r percent over m years is

$$
\text{FVIFA}_{TX,r,m} = \frac{(1 + r^*)^m - 1}{r^*}(1 - T^*) + mT^*. \tag{18.21}
$$

Discounting this value back to age 60 using the taxable equivalent present value interest factor for a taxable investment for 30 years ($\text{PVIF}_{TX,r,n+m}$) from Equation 18.14 produces the taxable equivalent. Figure 18.5 illustrates this example using a summarized four-step process.

FIGURE 18.5   Example of Four-Step After-Tax Valuation Method for an Annuity Withdrawal Pattern

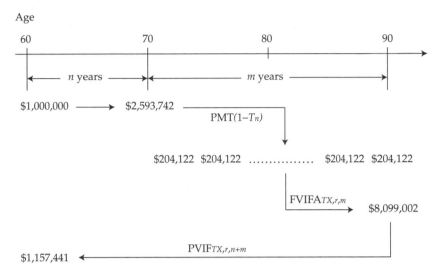

Step 1: Calculate the pretax account value at the beginning of the annuity withdrawal period at time *n*. The $1,000,000 corpus for the 60-year-old investor will grow to $2,593,742 by age 70.

Step 2: Calculate the after-tax annuity payment that supports the pretax account value from Step 1 by multiplying Equation 18.20 by $(1 - T_n)$. Her $2,593,742 account supports after-tax withdrawals of $204,122 from age 71 until age 90.

Step 3: Calculate the future value of these withdrawals had they been invested in a taxable account for *m* years using the $\text{FVIFA}_{TX,r,m}$ from Equation 18.21. The investor's after-tax withdrawals have a future value of $8,099,002 as of age 90.

Step 4: Calculate the present value over $n + m$ years using the after-tax present value interest factor that accommodates different taxable components of an investment's return ($\text{PVIF}_{TX,r,n+m}$) from Equation 18.14. If the investor had $1,157,441 in a taxable account at age 60, she could replicate the same after-tax cash flows as the $1,000,000 she currently holds in her traditional IRA.

This four-step process can be condensed into a single equation that yields the after-tax value of a traditional IRA if one assumes withdrawals are made as an annuity for *m* years beginning $n + 1$ years from now:

$$\text{PV}_{TradeIRAAnn} = (1 + r)^n \left[\frac{1 - T_n}{(1/r) - 1/[r(1 + r)^m]} \right] \left[\frac{\frac{(1 + r^*)^m - 1}{r^*}(1 - T^*) + mT^*}{(1 + r^*)^{n+m}(1 - T^*) + T^*} \right]$$

$$= (1 + r)^n \left[\frac{1 - T_n}{\text{PVIFA}_{r,m}} \right] [\text{PVIFA}_{TX,r,m,n}]. \qquad (18.22)$$

This equation looks quite onerous, but its individual parts are simply the four steps from the forgoing analysis. The first term is the future value of each dollar in the traditional IRA as of the beginning of the annuity withdrawal period in n years as in Step 1. The second term is the annuity payment after-withdrawal taxes that can be generated from each dollar in a traditional IRA starting in $n + 1$ years and lasting for m years from Step 2. The numerator of the third term is the future value interest factor of the m-year annuity for a taxable investment (FVIFA$_{TX,r,m}$) from Step 3. The denominator of the third term brings this value back to the present over $n + m$ years, according to Step 4. Taken as a whole, the third term incorporates Step 3 and Step 4. It can, therefore, be interpreted as the present value interest factor of an m-year annuity drawn from a taxable investment beginning in $n + 1$ years, or

$$PVIFA_{TX,r,m,n}$$

Table 18.17 presents some examples of taxable equivalent values of a traditional IRA for a typical equity mutual fund investor in the 28 percent tax bracket. Several observations can be made from this table. First, the taxable equivalent values can be either greater than or less than their pretax accumulations. Second, the taxable equivalent values seem to be relatively insensitive to the withdrawal horizon, m. For a 10-year withdrawal period, taxable equivalent values in Panel A range from about 74 percent of the pretax accumulation for short investment horizons and low returns to 144 percent of the pretax accumulation for long investment horizons and high returns. The corresponding values for a 20-year withdrawal period in Panel B range from 75 percent to 145 percent, respectively. As expected, the taxable equivalent value increases as the withdrawal period lengthens, but the difference is quite modest because the duration of the annuity increases at a decreasing rate as the withdrawal period increases. Third, the taxable equivalent values are quite similar to those for lump-sum distributions. Comparing the after-tax values in Table 18.17 with the after-tax values for a lump-sum withdrawal in Panel B of Table 18.12, one sees that the values are quite similar. Therefore, the taxable equivalent value of traditional IRAs appears to be insensitive to the withdrawal pattern.

This result appears inconsistent with prior literature showing that annuitized withdrawals significantly decrease the taxable equivalent value of tax-sheltered accounts compared with single withdrawals over the same time period (e.g., Horan 2002). The different conclusions stem from differences in the model. The model presented here is more flexible in that it allows the investment horizon, n, to differ from the withdrawal period, m. The previous research constrained the investment horizon to be equal to the withdrawal period (i.e., $n = m$). It indicated that if an investor has a 20-year investment horizon and commences withdrawals in the first year of the 20-year period, the after-tax value is far less than if the investor withdrew the entire accumulation at the end of 20 years. The results here are different. They show that if assets remain invested in the traditional IRA for 20 years, the taxable equivalent value is insensitive to whether the entire accumulation is withdrawn as a lump sum at the end of 20 years or whether it is withdrawn as an annuity over the following 10 years. When the opportunity cost of capital is fully taxed as ordinary income, taxable equivalent values remain insensitive to the withdrawal pattern, although the effect of withdrawal patterns is somewhat more pronounced.

Taxable Equivalent Value for a Roth IRA Withdrawn as an Annuity

The taxable equivalent value of a Roth IRA if one assumes annuitized withdrawals follows the same logic used with the traditional IRA with only a slight modification. The pretax annuity payment over m years supported by a Roth IRA account is the same as that for the traditional IRA expressed by Equation 18.20. But because withdrawals from Roth IRAs are

TABLE 18.17 Taxable Equivalent Value of a Traditional IRA Withdrawn as an Annuity for an Equity Mutual Fund Investor in the 28 Percent Tax Bracket

	Investment Horizon in Years (n)							
r	5	10	15	20	25	30	35	40
A. 10-year withdrawal horizon (m = 10)								
2%	0.741	0.751	0.761	0.771	0.781	0.790	0.800	0.810
4%	0.760	0.779	0.797	0.816	0.834	0.852	0.870	0.889
6%	0.776	0.803	0.830	0.856	0.883	0.909	0.937	**0.964**
8%	0.791	0.825	0.859	0.894	0.929	0.965	**1.001**	1.039
10%	0.804	0.845	0.887	0.930	0.974	**1.019**	1.066	1.115
12%	0.815	0.864	0.913	0.964	**1.018**	1.073	1.132	1.193
14%	0.826	0.882	0.939	**0.998**	1.061	1.128	1.198	1.272
16%	0.836	0.898	0.963	1.032	1.104	1.182	1.265	1.354
18%	0.845	0.914	**0.987**	1.064	1.148	1.237	1.333	1.437
B. 20-year withdrawal horizon (m − 20)								
2%	0.750	0.759	0.769	0.778	0.788	0.797	0.807	0.816
4%	0.773	0.791	0.808	0.826	0.844	0.861	0.879	0.897
6%	0.791	0.817	0.842	0.868	0.893	0.920	0.947	**0.974**
8%	0.807	0.839	0.872	0.905	0.940	**0.975**	**1.012**	1.050
10%	0.819	0.859	0.899	0.941	**0.985**	1.030	1.077	1.126
12%	0.830	0.877	0.925	0.975	1.028	1.084	1.143	1.204
14%	0.840	0.893	0.949	**1.009**	1.072	1.138	1.209	1.284
16%	0.848	0.909	0.973	1.041	1.114	1.192	1.276	1.365
18%	0.856	0.923	**0.996**	1.073	1.157	1.247	1.344	1.448

Notes: The investor maintains the same marginal tax rate throughout the investment horizon. The mutual fund distributes 20 percent of its return as dividends and 45 percent as long-term capital gain. Dividends and capital gains are taxed at 15 percent. Bold numbers correspond approximately to break-even pretax and after-tax values.

not taxed, this value is the after-tax withdrawal as well. Calculating the future value of this annuity over m years and discounting it back $n + m$ years yield

$$PV_{RothIRAAnn} = \left[\frac{(1 + r)^n}{PVIFA_{r,m}}\right][PVIFA_{TX,r,m,n}]. \qquad (18.23)$$

This expression is quite similar to Equation 18.22. The value is larger, however, because the numerator is not multiplied by $1 - T_n$. This difference reflects the fact that withdrawals from traditional IRAs are taxable whereas withdrawals from Roth IRAs are not. Therefore, the taxable equivalent values of Roth IRAs and traditional IRAs differ only by the constant $1 - T_n$. Because Roth IRA withdrawals are not taxed, the after-tax value of a dollar in a Roth IRA is always greater than 1. The other inferences made previously for traditional IRAs, however, hold

TABLE 18.18   Taxable Equivalent Value of a Roth IRA Withdrawn as an Annuity for an Equity
Mutual Fund Investor in the 28 Percent Tax Bracket

r	Investment Horizon in Years (n)							
	5	10	15	20	25	30	35	40
A. 10-year withdrawal horizon (m = 10)								
2%	1.029	1.043	1.057	1.071	1.084	1.098	1.111	1.124
4%	1.055	1.081	1.107	1.133	1.158	1.183	1.209	1.234
6%	1.078	1.115	1.152	1.189	1.226	1.263	1.301	1.339
8%	1.098	1.146	1.193	1.241	1.290	1.340	1.391	1.443
10%	1.116	1.174	1.232	1.291	1.352	1.415	1.481	1.549
12%	1.133	1.200	1.269	1.340	1.413	1.491	1.572	1.657
14%	1.148	1.224	1.304	1.387	1.474	1.566	1.664	1.767
16%	1.161	1.248	1.338	1.433	1.534	1.642	1.757	1.880
18%	1.174	1.270	1.371	1.478	1.594	1.718	1.852	1.996
B. 20-year withdrawal horizon (m = 20)								
2%	1.041	1.055	1.068	1.081	1.094	1.107	1.120	1.133
4%	1.073	1.098	1.123	1.147	1.172	1.196	1.221	1.246
6%	1.099	1.134	1.169	1.205	1.241	1.277	1.315	1.353
8%	1.120	1.165	1.211	1.258	1.305	1.355	1.405	1.458
10%	1.138	1.193	1.249	1.307	1.368	1.431	1.496	1.564
12%	1.153	1.218	1.285	1.355	1.428	1.506	1.587	1.673
14%	1.166	1.240	1.319	1.401	1.488	1.581	1.679	1.783
16%	1.178	1.262	1.351	1.446	1.548	1.656	1.772	1.896
18%	1.189	1.282	1.383	1.491	1.607	1.732	1.866	2.012

Notes: The investor maintains the same marginal tax rate throughout the investment horizon. The
mutual fund distributes 20 percent of its return as dividends and 45 percent as long-term capital gain.
Dividends and capital gains are taxed at 15 percent.

for Roth IRAs as well. That is, the length of the withdrawal period does not have a significant
effect on the after-tax value of a Roth IRA account as can be seen in Table 18.18. Consequently,
the taxable equivalent values for the Roth IRA withdrawn as an annuity are quite similar to
those in Table 18.15, Panel C, which assumes a lump-sum withdrawal.

Taxable Equivalent Value for a Partially Deductible
IRA Withdrawn as an Annuity

A similar process yields the taxable equivalent value of a partially deductible IRA withdrawal
in annuity form. The difference is that a portion of the annuitized withdrawals is taxable and
a portion is not. The nondeductible portion, *a*, of the initial contribution is not taxed upon

withdrawal. If one assumes that the taxable and nontaxable portion of the withdrawals are applied on a pro rata basis to each payment over the life of the annuity, the after-tax value of a partially deductible IRA is

$$\text{PV}_{PartIRAAnn} = \left[\frac{(1 + r)^n(1 - T_n) + aT_n}{\text{PVIFA}_{r,m}}\right][\text{PVIFA}_{TX,r,m,n}]. \tag{18.24}$$

The drawback of this formulation is that investors will realistically withdraw the nondeductible contribution first because it is tax free. Investors would typically commence taxable withdrawals only after the tax-free withdrawals have been exhausted. For long time horizons, however, the nondeductible portion of the initial contribution is typically quite small relative to the future accumulation as I discussed earlier in this section. Therefore, Equation 18.24 is quite accurate even if actual withdrawals are not taxed on a pro rata basis.

Summary

Pretax and taxable equivalent values of assets held in tax-deferred accounts can differ substantially. For both traditional IRAs and partially deductible IRAs, the taxable equivalent value can be either greater than or less than the pretax accumulation. For Roth IRAs, the taxable equivalent value is always greater than the pretax accumulation and the traditional IRA taxable equivalent values because withdrawals from Roth IRAs are not taxed. In any case, taxable equivalent values increase with the pretax return and the investment horizon because both these factors increase the value of the tax shield offered by TDAs.

Previous research indicates that withdrawal patterns affect taxable equivalent values significantly. But the more flexible model presented here suggests otherwise. If withdrawals are taken as an annuity over a period of time rather than as a lump sum at the beginning of the withdrawal period, the value of the tax shelter increases. The differential is modest, however, and can be safely ignored in most cases. Valuing tax-sheltered assets on a taxable equivalent basis can be an important factor in appropriately calculating an investor's asset allocation, determining credit limits for loans secured by tax-sheltered assets, and valuing assets for litigious purposes.[45] I will explore this notion more thoroughly in the section on Asset Location between Taxable and Tax-Deferred Savings Accounts.

EARLY WITHDRAWAL PENALTIES AND BREAKEVEN TIME HORIZONS

The U.S. federal government uses tax-advantaged savings accounts to encourage saving for specific purposes. The different IRA accounts are, of course, designed to encourage retirement savings. More recently, Section 529 plans have been developed as TDAs that encourage saving for education, and President Bush has proposed health care savings accounts to encourage saving for medical expenses. These accounts impose a penalty (typically 10 percent) on nonqualified withdrawals—that is, withdrawals for purposes other than that intended by the specific account. Withdrawals from IRA accounts before age 59½, for example, are subject to a 10 percent withdrawal penalty.[46] Although an early withdrawal penalty encourages an investor to keep funds in a retirement account once they have been invested, it may also discourage an investor from saving in the first place.

An important question then for taxpayers considering a tax-advantaged account is: How long must funds be invested in a retirement account for the tax advantages to outweigh the 10 percent penalty should funds need to be withdrawn early? The answer is called the breakeven time horizon or the breakeven holding period. All else being equal, savers facing short breakeven time horizons should be more inclined to commit money to a tax-advantaged savings account, and those with longer breakeven time horizons should be more circumspect about saving via a potentially restrictive investment account. In fact, investors with short breakeven holding periods may even choose to use an IRA purposefully for nonretirement investment goals, knowing they would face an early withdrawal penalty. Similarly, they might choose to use a Section 529 plan for noneducational investment goals.

The breakeven holding period depends in part on the tax structure of the taxable alternative. If the taxable investment option is heavily taxed, then the breakeven point is relatively short because the TDA's tax-sheltering properties become relatively more valuable even in the presence of the early withdrawal penalty. But if the taxable alternative has some inherent tax-sheltering properties (such as an index mutual fund), the breakeven time horizon can be prohibitively long. If tax rates decrease, however, when the funds would be withdrawn from the TDA, breakeven points can be as short as a few years. Because early withdrawals from Roth IRAs can be taxed as ordinary income in addition to being penalized, their breakeven time horizons are quite long.

Many researchers have investigated the breakeven holding period over the past 25 years.[47] Early research assumed simplified tax structures.[48] More recently, authors have noted the need to incorporate more realistic sophistication into the model to capture important complexities of the tax code.[49] This section, as those that preceded it, allows portions of the investment return to be taxed separately and closely follows the development set forth in Horan (2004).

Breakeven Investment Horizon for a Traditional IRA

An investor is indifferent between a taxable investment and a traditional IRA investment with an early withdrawal penalty when the accumulation in the taxable investment equals that for the traditional IRA less an early withdrawal penalty of, say, ϕ. Recall from the section called Choosing between Traditional IRAs and Roth IRAs: The Basics that the future accumulation of a traditional IRA depends in part on whether the pretax contribution is less than or greater than the contribution limit, L. I begin by examining the scenario in which the pretax contribution is less than or equal to the contribution limit (i.e., $I_{BT} \le L$). In this case, setting the future value of a taxable investment equal to the future value of a traditional IRA less an early withdrawal penalty of ϕ yields

$$\text{FV}_{TX} = \text{FV}_{TradIRAPen}$$

$$(1 - T_o)[(1 + r^*)^n(1 - T^*) + T^*] = (1 + r)^n(1 - T_n - \phi).$$

(18.25)

Interestingly, the scenario in which the pretax contribution is maximized, namely $I_{BT} = L/(1 - T_o)$, yields the same condition because any investment in excess of the contribution limit is assumed to be invested in a taxable instrument, which is treated in the same manner as the taxable investment option. Treating them differently would not produce a meaningful comparison. Therefore, the size of the contribution does not affect the breakeven time horizon.

Simplified Ordinary Income Tax Structure

Solving for the breakeven time horizon in Equation 18.25 requires an iterative process of trial and error. But when the tax structure is simplified such that the investment returns in the taxable account are fully taxed each year as ordinary income, Equation 18.25 permits a direct solution.

If the taxable account is fully taxed, then $pj = 1$, $p_{cg} = 0$, $T^* = 0$, and $r^* = r(1 - t_{oi})$, in which case the breakeven time horizon can be expressed as

$$n^* = \ln\left[\frac{(1 - T_n - \phi)}{1 - T_o}\right] \bigg/ \ln\left[\frac{1 + r(1 - t_{oi})}{1 + r}\right]. \tag{18.26}$$

See Appendix 18E for a derivation. This more straightforward expression offers the opportunity for intuitive insight. A withdrawal after time n^* results in a higher after-tax accumulation for a traditional IRA with the early withdrawal penalty than for the taxable investment. When the term in brackets in the numerator is equal to 1, then the breakeven time horizon is zero. In other words, when $(1 - T_n - \phi) = (1 - T_o)$, an investor should use a tax-advantaged account even if funds are withdrawn immediately, thereby incurring a penalty. The same is true when $(1 - T_n - \phi) > (1 - T_o)$. In this case, the breakeven time horizon is negative. (Note that for any positive tax rate, t_{oi}, the fraction in brackets in the denominator is less than 1, making its natural log negative.) The numerator is positive when the fraction in its brackets is greater than 1. When the numerator is positive and the denominator is negative, the breakeven time horizon is negative and an investor should use a tax-advantaged account even if funds are withdrawn immediately, thereby incurring a penalty. The breakeven time horizon is positive when $(1 - T_n - \phi) < (1 - T_o)$.

Another way to interpret this relationship is that the breakeven point depends on the contribution tax rate compared with the withdrawal tax rate. As the withdrawal tax rate decreases, the breakeven point decreases, making the traditional IRA more attractive to investors despite an early withdrawal penalty. This result is reasonable because the traditional IRA allows a taxpayer to avoid taxes now in exchange for paying them later. A declining tax rate works to the taxpayer's advantage in this case. Put differently, when the withdrawal tax rate plus the early withdrawal penalty is less than or equal to the current tax rate (i.e., $T_n + \phi \leq T_o$), the TDA is always a better investment. When $T_n + \phi > T_o$ some positive holding period is required to outweigh the early withdrawal penalty.

Another interesting relationship is that as t_{oi} approaches zero, the absolute value of the denominator becomes infinitesimally small and the breakeven holding period becomes infinitely large. This relationship suggests two things. First, the traditional IRA becomes less attractive at low tax rates because its tax advantages become relatively less valuable. Second, for low tax rates, a small change in the tax rate will produce large changes in the breakeven time horizon.

Simplified Capital Gain Tax Structure

A direct solution is also possible when the entire investment return is in the form of capital gain that is realized and taxed at the end of the period. In this case, $p_{oi} = p_{cg} = 0$, which makes $r^* = r$ and $T^* = t_{cg}$. Substituting these values into the breakeven condition in Equation 18.25 and solving for n yields a breakeven time horizon of

$$n^* = \ln\left[\frac{t_{cg}(1 - T_o)}{(1 - T_n - \phi) - (1 - T_o)(1 - t_{cg})}\right] \bigg/ \ln(1 + r). \tag{18.27}$$

A derivation is found in Appendix 18E. This expression produces longer breakeven points than those that assume that investment returns are fully taxed as ordinary income because deferring capital gains tax until the end of the investment period achieves some of the same tax-shelter benefits of the traditional IRA, thereby decreasing some of its comparative advantage.

Table 18.19 displays the breakeven time horizons for a traditional IRA investment with a 10 percent early withdrawal penalty for various tax rates and annual returns. Tax rates are

TABLE 18.19   Breakeven Time Horizon for a Traditional IRA with Early Withdrawal Penalty for Constant Tax Rates

$T_o = T_n$	Annual Return (r)						
	4%	6%	8%	10%	12%	14%	16%
A. Return fully taxed as ordinary income at $t_{oi} = T_o$ (trader)							
15%[a]	65.0	44.2	33.7	27.5	23.3	20.3	18.1
25%	14.8	10.0	7.7	6.2	5.3	4.6	4.1
28%	13.8	9.4	7.1	5.8	4.9	4.3	3.8
33%	12.7	8.6	6.5	5.3	4.5	3.9	3.5
35%	12.3	8.3	6.4	5.2	4.4	3.8	3.4
B. Tax structure for a typical growth mutual fund (active investor)							
15%[a]	86.0	58.4	44.6	36.3	30.8	26.9	23.9
25%	28.1	19.1	14.5	11.8	10.0	8.7	7.7
28%	29.6	20.0	15.3	12.4	10.5	9.1	8.1
33%	32.3	21.9	16.7	13.6	11.5	10.0	8.9
35%	33.5	22.7	17.3	14.1	11.9	14.0	9.2
C. Return fully taxed as deferred capital gain (passive investor)							
15%[a,b]	—	—	—	—	—	—	—
25%	56.0	37.7	28.5	23.1	19.4	16.8	14.8
28%	66.4	44.7	33.8	27.3	23.0	19.9	17.5
33%	135.2	91.0	68.9	55.6	46.8	40.5	35.7
35%[b]	—	—	—	—	—	—	—

Source: This table follows the model and design of Horan (2004).

Notes: The investor maintains the same marginal tax rate throughout the investment horizon. The mutual fund distributes 20 percent of its return as dividends and 45 percent as long-term capital gain. Dividends and capital gains are taxed at 15 percent.

[a]For taxpayers in the 10 percent and 15 percent tax brackets, the JGTRRA of 2003 reduces the tax rate on dividends and capital gains to 5 percent.

[b]Breakeven time horizons in this row are undefined because the natural log of a negative number is undefined.

assumed to be constant over the investment period from contribution to withdrawal. It uses average distribution rates of mutual funds for ordinary income and capital gains reported by Crain and Austin (1997) and Shoven and Sialm (2003) and marginal tax rates established by the JGTRRA of 2003 passed by Congress in May 2003. Several trends are apparent. According to Panel A, which assumes the taxable return is fully taxed as ordinary income, the breakeven time horizon is quite sensitive to the annual return and decreases at a decreasing rate as the investment return increases. The reasoning is that the value of the tax deferral associated with an IRA is greater as the pretax return increases. This panel is appropriate for individuals investing in fixed-income securities or equity portfolios with high turnover that create short-term capital gains. Another trend evident in Panel A is that breakeven time horizons are much shorter for investors in high tax brackets. It decreases rapidly as the investor's initial tax rate increases because the initial tax deduction of the traditional IRA is more valuable for high-tax-bracket investors.

Similar trends exist in Panel B, which assumes the taxable return is taxed as a typical mutual fund, which might be appropriate for active investors. The breakeven points are substantially higher than those in Panel A, doubling and tripling in some scenarios, suggesting that the breakeven time horizon is quite sensitive to the taxing scheme. The breakeven points are longer because the relative advantage of the IRA tax shelter is greater when the investment is fully taxed as ordinary income as compared with a mutual fund investment that has some inherent tax advantages. It should be noted that if an investor stays in the 10 percent or 15 percent tax brackets, dividends and capital gains are taxed at only 5 percent.

It is also important to note that IRA withdrawals after the age of 59½ are penalty free. Consequently, very high breakeven holding periods in Table 18.19 have no practical significance because the early withdrawal penalty disappears at age 59½. In such cases, the IRA account without the penalty dominates the taxable investment, but the taxable investment dominates if IRA funds are withdrawn early. One may be surprised to find that the breakeven time horizons in Panel B increase slightly for investors in the 35 percent tax bracket. The reason is that for investors facing high tax rates, mutual funds offer relatively effective tax shields, which decrease the relative advantage of the traditional IRA.

When returns are taxed only as capital gain at the end of the investment period, as in Panel C, the breakeven points become even longer and, in some cases, approach infinity because the tax deferral characteristics of the traditional IRA are replicated somewhat by the tax deferral of the unrealized capital gain in the taxable investment. Passive investors implementing a buy-and-hold strategy of non-dividend-paying stocks would find themselves in this situation. In any case, the breakeven points are sensitive to the assumed tax structure.

By comparing the breakeven holding periods in Table 18.20 with those in Table 18.19, one can see the impact that declining tax rates have on breakeven time horizons. Table 18.20 presents breakeven time horizons when investors drop into the next lower tax bracket when withdrawing funds and illustrates that the impact of declining tax rates is quite substantial. According to Panel A, the breakeven holding periods can be short when the taxable investment is fully taxed as ordinary income at the investor's initial tax rate, T_o, which is the case for interest income on fixed-income investments. For investors in high tax brackets facing a 10 percent expected return, the tax shelter of the IRA is relatively valuable and the breakeven time horizons decrease substantially to four years or less. For investors in the 25 percent tax bracket dropping to the 15 percent tax bracket, a traditional IRA with an early withdrawal penalty is a superior investment vehicle for any time horizon as indicated by the zero breakeven time horizon.[50] The zero breakeven points for taxpayers in the 25 percent tax bracket indicate that such an investor is always better off using a traditional IRA and paying an early withdrawal penalty.

The reader may notice that breakeven points in Table 18.20 do not monotonically decrease as the initial tax rate increases as in the previous table. Rather, they "jump around" as one peruses down each column. The reason is that the value of the traditional IRA and its ability to overcome the cost of the early withdrawal penalty is driven more by the *change* in the tax rate than the level of the tax rate. For example, an investor initially in the 35 percent tax bracket dropping to the 33 percent tax bracket (the last row of Panel A) has breakeven time horizons that are about 60 percent longer than an investor initially in the 33 percent tax bracket dropping to the 28 percent tax bracket (the second to last row of Panel A). The difference becomes

TABLE 18.20   Breakeven Time Horizon for a Traditional IRA with Early Withdrawal Penalty for an Investor Dropping One Tax Bracket

T_o	Annual Return (r)						
	4%	6%	8%	10%	12%	14%	16%
A. Return fully taxed as ordinary income at $t_{oi} = T_o$ (trader)							
15%[a]	31.5	21.4	16.3	13.3	11.3	9.8	8.8
25%	0.0	0.0	0.0	0.0	0.0	0.0	0.0
28%	9.4	6.4	4.9	4.0	3.4	2.9	2.6
33%	6.1	4.1	3.1	2.5	2.2	1.9	1.7
35%	9.7	6.6	5.0	4.1	3.4	3.0	2.7
B. Tax structure for a typical growth mutual fund (active investor)							
15%[a]	37.4	25.4	19.4	15.8	13.4	11.6	10.4
25%	0.0	0.0	0.0	0.0	0.0	0.0	0.0
28%	19.4	13.1	10.0	8.1	6.9	6.0	5.3
33%	14.4	9.7	7.4	6.0	5.1	4.4	3.9
35%	25.6	17.3	13.2	10.7	9.1	7.9	7.0
C. Return fully taxed as deferred capital gain (passive investor)							
15%[a,b]	—	—	—	—	—	—	—
25%	0.0	0.0	0.0	0.0	0.0	0.0	0.0
28%	26.6	17.9	13.6	11.0	9.2	8.0	7.0
33%	17.5	11.8	8.9	7.2	6.1	5.3	4.6
35%	43.8	29.5	22.3	18.0	15.2	13.1	11.6

Source: This table follows the model and design of Horan (2004).

Notes: The investor drops one tax bracket when funds are withdrawn. The mutual fund distributes 20 percent of its return as dividends and 45 percent as long-term capital gain. Dividends and capital gains are taxed at 15 percent.

[a]For taxpayers in the 10 percent and 15 percent tax brackets, the JGTRRA of 2003 reduces the tax rate on dividends and capital gains to 5 percent.

[b]Breakeven time horizons in this row are undefined because the natural log of a negative number is undefined.

more pronounced for the other taxing schemes in the following two panels. It stems from the fact that the former investor experiences a 2 percentage point decrease in the tax rate, and the latter investor experiences a 5 percentage point decrease in the tax rate, demonstrating that the change in the tax rate is more important than the level of the tax rate.

Panel B contains the results under the assumption the investment is a mutual fund with average distribution rates for ordinary income and capital gains. Again, breakeven points in this panel are longer than those in Panel A, suggesting that the tax structure of the non-IRA investment is important in determining the breakeven point. They are, however, about half the length, assuming that tax rates remain constant. The breakeven investment horizons for investors in the 15 percent tax bracket are much longer because dividends and capital gains are taxed at only 5 percent for these investors, substantially decreasing the value of the tax deferral associated with the traditional IRA. Breakeven time horizons when the investment return is fully taxed as a capital gain at the end of the investment period are displayed in Panel C. They are slightly longer than those in Panel B because the taxable investment in this case offers significant tax-deferral characteristics. The differences are not large, however. Panel A and Panel C represent different extremes for the taxable investment. For most investors, the actual taxing scheme would fall somewhere between these two extremes. These tables indicate that two important factors in the breakeven investment horizon are the taxing scheme for the taxable alternative and the relationship between the prevailing tax rates upon contribution and withdrawal.

Breakeven Investment Horizon for a Roth IRA

When examining the breakeven time horizon for Roth IRA investments with an early withdrawal penalty, one must recognize that the early withdrawal penalty for the Roth IRA applies only to earnings, not the initial contribution. Therefore, if the early withdrawal is less than the initial contribution, no early withdrawal penalty applies and the breakeven time horizon is effectively zero. But withdrawals in excess of the initial contribution are subject not only to the 10 percent early withdrawal penalty but also ordinary income tax. This nonqualified distribution tax creates a double tax when earnings are withdrawn early—once when funds are contributed and again when they are withdrawn—and can create long breakeven points when withdrawals exceed the initial contribution.

For a Roth IRA, the after-tax accumulation after paying ordinary income tax and a penalty for early withdrawal on earnings is

$$
\begin{aligned}
\text{FV}_{RothP} &= I_{BT}(1 - T_o)\{[(1 + r)^n - 1](1 - T_n - \phi) + 1\} \\
&= I_{BT}(1 - T_o)[(1 + r)^n(1 - T_n - \phi) + T_n + \phi].
\end{aligned}
\tag{18.28}
$$

Setting this expression equal to the future value of a taxable investment and solving for n yields the breakeven condition, which can be rearranged as

$$
\left[\frac{1 + r^*}{1 + r}\right]^n = \frac{1 - T_n - \phi}{1 - T^*} + \frac{\phi + T_n - T^*}{(1 + r)^n(1 - T^*)}.
\tag{18.29}
$$

A proof is in Appendix 18E. This analysis is similar in spirit to Terry and Goolsby (2003), who analyze the usefulness of Section 529 plans for retirement savings. The tax structures of Section 529 plans and Roth IRAs are nearly equivalent, and Section 529 withdrawals for purposes other than education are subject to a similar penalty and income tax as are early withdrawals from a Roth IRA.

If one assumes a simplified tax structure for the Roth IRA in which investment returns are taxed each year as ordinary income, it does not yield a closed-form solution for n. But if one assumes the returns are taxed as capital gains at the end of the period, it does. In this circumstance, $p_{oi} = p_{cg} = 0$, which makes $r^* = r$ and $T^* = t_{cg}$. Substituting these values into Equation 18.29 and solving for n yields a breakeven time horizon of zero in all cases. In other words, an investor is always better off with an investment taxed entirely as tax-deferred capital gains rather than a Roth IRA with a withdrawal penalty if all funds in the Roth IRA are withdrawn early. Recall that withdrawals of initial contributions are neither penalized nor taxed as a nonqualified distribution, making the breakeven time horizon for early withdrawals of only initial contributions effectively zero. But there are many similarities when comparing a complete early withdrawal from a Roth IRA with a taxable investment taxed as deferred capital gain. The initial investment of both alternatives is initially taxed. Both alternatives offer tax deferral during the accumulation phase. And both are taxed at the end of the investment period. The only difference is the early withdrawal penalty on earnings associated with the Roth IRA, making the Roth IRA less desirable than the taxable investment. Therefore, when the taxable alternative is taxed entirely as deferred capital gain, a taxable account is always better than making a complete withdrawal from a Roth IRA that would be subject to the early withdrawal penalty.

The breakeven point is less obvious with other taxing schemes. One relationship to note is that the breakeven time horizon for a Roth IRA does not depend on the investor's initial tax rate because the investment in both the taxable investment and the Roth IRA is taxed identically. Table 18.21 displays breakeven holding periods for a Roth IRA if one assumes a complete early withdrawal of contribution and earnings. The table assumes that early withdrawals less than the initial contribution are not penalized or taxed but that earnings are subject to the 10 percent early withdrawal penalty as well as income tax as a nonqualified distribution. In Panel A, returns are assumed to be fully taxed as ordinary income at a rate of T_n during the accumulation phase. The breakeven time horizons are significantly longer than

TABLE 18.21 Breakeven Time Horizon for a Roth IRA with Early Withdrawal Penalty for Constant Tax Rates

T_n	Annual Return (r)						
	4%	6%	8%	10%	12%	14%	16%
A. Return fully taxed as ordinary income at $t_{oi} = T_n$ (trader)							
10%[a]	48.3	33.0	25.3	20.7	17.6	15.4	13.8
15%[a]	36.5	24.9	19.2	15.7	13.4	11.8	10.5
25%	26.6	18.3	14.1	11.6	9.9	8.7	7.9
28%	25.1	17.3	13.3	11.0	9.4	8.3	7.4
33%	23.4	16.1	12.4	10.2	8.8	7.7	7.0
35%	22.9	15.7	12.2	10.0	8.6	7.6	6.8
B. Tax structure for a typical growth mutual fund (active investor)							
10%[a]	124.1	84.3	64.4	52.5	44.5	38.8	34.6
15%[a]	132.3	89.8	68.6	55.9	47.4	41.4	36.8
25%	95.9	65.2	49.8	40.6	34.5	30.1	26.8
28%	109.4	74.3	56.8	46.3	39.2	34.2	30.5
33%	132.7	90.1	68.8	56.1	47.5	41.5	36.9
35%	142.5	96.7	73.9	60.2	51.0	44.5	39.6

Source: This table follows the model and design of Horan (2004).

Notes: The investor maintains the same marginal tax rate throughout the investment horizon. The mutual fund distributes 20 percent of its return as dividends and 45 percent as long-term capital gain. Dividends and capital gains are taxed at 15 percent.

[a]For taxpayers in the 10 percent and 15 percent tax brackets, the JGTRRA of 2003 reduces the tax rate on dividends and capital gains to 5 percent.

those associated with traditional IRAs because earnings associated with early withdrawals from Roth IRAs are taxed as ordinary income in addition to being penalized, whereas qualified withdrawals are neither taxed nor penalized.

Panel B presents some very long breakeven points for returns taxed as typical growth mutual fund returns, especially for investors in high tax brackets. Recall that IRA withdrawals after the age of 59½ are penalty free. Consequently, very high breakeven holding periods in Table 18.21 have no practical significance. The breakeven points are significantly longer than in Panel A because the benefits of tax deferral associated with the Roth IRA are relatively less valuable when compared with a mutual fund investment. The breakeven points increase with the withdrawal tax rate because the early withdrawal of earnings from a Roth IRA is taxed as ordinary income. Although not displayed in this table, one could use different tax rates for the accumulation and withdrawal phases.

Taken at face value, these results suggest that, in most instances, using Roth IRAs exclusively for nonretirement investment goals is not advantageous. But the early withdrawal penalty and the nonqualified distribution income tax only apply to withdrawals greater than the initial contribution. The previous analysis assumes a total withdrawal rather than a partial withdrawal. For a partial withdrawal not exceeding total contributions, the breakeven period for a Roth IRA is essentially zero. In contrast, withdrawals that exceed the initial contribution have longer breakeven points. If withdrawals are made over time, whereby early withdrawals are less than the initial contributions, then the early withdrawal penalty may disappear for laterwithdrawals of earnings if they occur after age 59½. Therefore, an optimal ordering exists of withdrawals from Roth IRAs. Nontaxable contributions should be withdrawn first. Contributions from converted traditional IRA contributions are treated a bit differently and should come next. Finally, earnings should be withdrawn last.

Summary

This section shows that the breakeven holding period is sensitive to the annual return and decreases at a decreasing rate as the return increases. Moreover, the tax structure for the non-IRA investment greatly influences the attractiveness of using an IRA for nonretirement purposes. For example, breakeven points are substantially longer when a significant proportion of the return on the taxable investment is in the form of either realized or unrealized capital gains, as is the case with many equity mutual funds.

For the traditional IRA, the breakeven point is also sensitive to whether tax rates increase or decrease from the time of contribution to withdrawal. Breakeven points can be short (a few years) when investors drop into the next lower tax bracket and returns are high. In contrast, the breakeven investment horizons for the Roth IRA are not dependent on the initial tax rate. They are substantially higher than traditional IRA breakeven points, however, because earnings associated with early withdrawals are taxed as nonqualified distributions in addition to being subject to an early withdrawal penalty.

ASSET LOCATION BETWEEN TAXABLE AND TAX-DEFERRED SAVINGS ACCOUNTS

The previous section examined conditions under which an investor accumulates more after-tax wealth by using a tax-advantaged account with an early withdrawal penalty than by using a taxable account. And the section called Choosing between Nondeductible IRAs and Taxable

Investments analyzed the choice between nondeductible IRAs and taxable accounts. These sections investigated whether an investor should use a taxable account *or* a tax-deferred account. But what if an investor has a portfolio of stocks and bonds that are to be located in taxable *and* tax-deferred accounts? In which account—the tax deferred or the taxable—should the investor locate the stocks, and where should the investor locate the bonds? This choice is called the *asset location* decision and is distinct from the *asset allocation* decision, which determines the mix of stocks and bonds in the aggregate portfolio. Moreover, does the location of assets affect the investor's overall asset allocation? If so, how? This section examines the asset location decision and how it interacts with the asset allocation decision.

The asset location decision has recently attracted the attention of researchers who have examined the issue theoretically and empirically.[51] Although some of the theoretical models overlook many tax code nuances that were considered in previous sections, they are nonetheless quite sophisticated and do not lend themselves to easy application. Incorporating additional complexities of the tax code is not likely to ameliorate that problem. Fortunately, one can extract valuable intuition and heuristic guidance from the literature.

Much of the intuition is based on an arbitrage argument developed for corporate pension fund policy by Black (1980) and Tepper (1981). For a company, contributions to a pension plan are tax deductible and the returns on pension assets are exempt from tax, much like a traditional IRA for an individual investor. The basic idea behind the arbitrage argument is that a company should place what would otherwise be highly taxed assets (e.g., fixed-income securities) within the tax shelter of the pension fund and locate securities with less tax burden in the form of, say, deferred capital gains (e.g., equities) outside the pension fund. A fair question might be: How would this policy be implemented if the ideal asset allocation does not call for high-taxed assets, such as bonds, in the absence of taxes? Black and Tepper prescribed that borrowing outside the pension fund can offset any excessive fixed-income investment in the pension fund. The proceeds from borrowing can then be invested in equities. In this way, lending in the pension fund offsets borrowing outside the pension fund, leaving the company with only equity exposure on net. The exact amount of borrowing required to offset the fixed-income investment in the pension depends on the tax rate and how assets are taxed, but the concept remains the same.

Since then many authors have applied this logic to individual investors and the tax-advantaged retirement accounts available to them.[52] That is, investors should place fixed-income securities in their tax-deferred accounts and any equities in their taxable accounts. If filling the tax-deferred account with bonds overweights the asset allocation too heavily toward fixed income, investors can borrow money to offset the lending in the tax-deferred account and use the proceeds to purchase additional equity in the taxable account.

Several considerations can complicate this basic arbitrage argument. First, when considering an individual's asset allocation, Reichenstein (2001) argued that the traditional approach fails to distinguish between pretax and after-tax values. In the section called Valuing Tax-Sheltered Assets on a Taxable Equivalent, I discussed methods for valuing tax-sheltered assets on an after-tax basis, showing that a TDA's pretax value can differ substantially from its after-tax value. Because goods and services are purchased with after-tax dollars, a more accurate treatment of asset allocation would rely on after-tax values rather than pretax values. Recall that the after-tax value of a dollar in a TDA can be either greater than or less than a dollar, depending on the type of account, return, time horizon, and withdrawal pattern from the account. Therefore, the leverage in the taxable account needed to offset lending in the tax-deferred account can be either greater than or less than its bond investment. Furthermore, an investor's trading behavior affects the effective tax burden of some investments. Active investors with high turnover realize more short-term capital gains, which are taxed as ordinary income, than passive buy-and-hold investors, who defer realizing capital gains, which are taxed at a lower rate.

Second, including municipal bonds, which are exempt from state and local taxes, in the set of possible investment opportunities may make shifting stock to a TDA optimal. Although stock tends to be more tax efficient than corporate and government bonds, municipal bonds are more tax efficient than both. A third complication to the basic arbitrage argument for asset location is that investors may be constrained from borrowing or face other portfolio constraints that make executing the arbitrage strategy costly or impossible. Finally, investors may face liquidity constraints that make the arbitrage strategy costly. For example, if the equity in a taxable account suffers a substantial decline in value, an investor may be forced to liquidate assets in the tax-deferred account to finance consumption, which may trigger an early withdrawal penalty for some investors. I will address each of these issues in turn.

It is important to remember that the asset location decision involves a series of trade-offs. On the one hand, the higher expected return associated with equity investments increases the value of deferring taxes on their return (as opposed to bond returns), as I have shown in previous sections, suggesting stocks might be optimally located in tax-deferred accounts. On the other hand, the effective tax rate on equities is lower than on fixed-income instruments, suggesting stocks might be optimally located in taxable accounts. The asset location decision should balance these considerations.

A complicating factor in this trade-off, however, is the effect of asset location on portfolio risk. Holding stock in a taxable account produces less after-tax portfolio risk than holding stock in a tax-deferred account because the government shares in some of the risk (not just the return) of the equities when they are held in a taxable account. Although lending or borrowing can be adjusted to offset this change in risk associated with the asset location decision, this asset allocation change can, in turn, affect asset location, which creates a recursive process that does not lend itself to a direct solution. Therefore, the two decisions affect each and, in a technical sense, must be solved jointly.

Taxable Equivalent Asset Allocation

Conventional methods of examining asset allocation use pretax values. That is, a dollar held in a taxable account is treated in the same way as a dollar held in a TDA. I showed in the section on Valuing Tax-Sheltered Assets on an After-Tax Basis, however, that the taxable equivalent value of a tax-sheltered dollar can be either greater than or less than the value of a dollar held in a taxable account, depending on the type of tax-sheltered account (e.g., traditional IRA versus Roth IRA), the type of asset in which the dollar is invested (e.g., stocks versus bonds), how those assets are turned over, the length of time the money is held in the tax-deferred account, and how the funds are withdrawn. Because consumption is based on after-tax dollars, an asset allocation measure that uses taxable equivalent values would be more accurate.

Consider a hypothetical investor who is retired, 50 years old, in the 28 percent tax bracket, and planning withdrawals over 30 years. This investor has just purchased $100,000 of a mutual fund in a taxable account. In addition, he has $200,000 invested in an equity mutual fund located in a traditional IRA and $300,000 invested in fixed income in a Roth IRA. These pretax values are displayed in Table 18.22, Panel A. Stocks and bonds are expected to return 12 percent and 6 percent, respectively. On a pretax basis, asset allocation is one-half stock and one-half bonds. Using the taxable equivalent valuation tables in the Valuing Tax-Sheltered Assets on an After-Tax Basis section, I can convert these pretax values to taxable equivalent values, which vary dramatically. If funds are withdrawn from the TDAs

TABLE 18.22   Taxable Equivalent Asset Allocation for an Investor in the 33 Percent Tax Bracket with a 30-Year Horizon

Item	Taxable Equivalent Value	Dollar Value	Proportion	Stock Proportion
A. Pretax values				
Taxable mutual fund (stock)		$100,000	16.7%	50.0%
Fully deductible IRA (stock)		200,000	33.3	
Roth IRA (bond)		300,000	50.0	
Total		$600,000		
B. After-tax values (lump-sum withdrawal)				
Taxable mutual fund (stock)	1	$100,000	12.2%	35.8%
Fully deductible IRA (stock)	0.972	194,400	23.6	
Roth IRA (bond)	1.761	528,300	64.2	
Total		$822,700		
C. After-tax values (annuity withdrawal)				
Taxable mutual fund (stock)	1	$100,000	14.5%	38.1%
Fully deductible IRA (stock)	0.816	163,200	23.6	
Roth IRA (bond)	1.428	428,400	61.9	
Total		$691,600		
D. Post-arbitrage after-tax values (annuity withdrawal)				
Taxable mutual fund (stock)	1	$273,933	38.1%	38.1%
Taxable borrowing (short bond)	1	(173,933)	(24.2)	
Fully deductible IRA (bond)	0.957	191,400	26.6	
Roth IRA (bond)	1.428	428,400	59.5	
Total		$719,800		

as a lump sum in 30 years, the taxable equivalent value of the equity in the traditional IRA is $194,400 (shown in Panel B). This value comes from multiplying the $200,000 pretax value by 0.972, which is the taxable equivalent value factor from Table 18.13, Panel B, for a 12 percent investment and a 30-year investment horizon. The taxable equivalent value of the Roth IRA is calculated using the taxable equivalent value factor from Table 18.15, Panel A, for a 6 percent return over 30 years. Using these taxable equivalent values changes the equity exposure from 50 percent to 35.8 percent.

If funds are withdrawn from the TDAs as an annuity over 20 years beginning 10 years hence (as shown in Panel C), the change is less dramatic but still substantial. The taxable equivalent value factors are not reported in this chapter, but the factors for the traditional IRA and the Roth IRA are 0.816 and 1.428, respectively. In this case, after-tax equity exposure is 38.1 percent. Reichenstein (2001) and others have argued that properly assessing portfolio risk requires the use of after-tax values because by taxing returns or withdrawals, the government shares in investment risk as well as return. Therefore, an investor substituting bonds for stock in a traditional IRA needs to use after-tax values to determine the appropriate amount of borrowing used to finance an offsetting equity purchase in the taxable account to keep portfolio risk constant. As mentioned in the Valuing Tax-Sheltered Assets on an After-Tax Basis section, taxable equivalent values are related to but distinct from after-tax values. The concepts illustrated in this section apply equally with both.

For example, suppose the current investor sells the $200,000 of stock mutual funds in the traditional IRA and purchases bonds in the same account with the proceeds. With an annuitized withdrawal pattern, the taxable equivalent value of the stock sold is $163,200 and the taxable equivalent value of the bonds purchased is $191,400.[53] The difference of $28,200 represents the value gain from the asset location shift. To maintain the same 38.1 percent equity exposure, the investor must borrow $173,933 in a taxable account at 6 percent and use the proceeds to purchase additional shares of the stock mutual fund for a total of $273,933 of equity in the taxable account.[54] As Table 18.22, Panel D, indicates, this shift maintains the same taxable equivalent asset allocation and hence the same level of risk. Notice, however, that the taxable equivalent value of the portfolio increased to $719,800 without affecting taxable equivalent asset allocation. This example illustrates the potential importance of asset location on the taxable equivalent value of a portfolio of tax-advantaged savings account. It suggests that investors should place bonds, which have a heavy tax burden, in TDAs and use taxable accounts to gain equity exposure and to borrow or lend to adjust the risk of the overall portfolio. This basic advice seems to hold even in relatively more complex environments as described in the following section.

The literature on the asset location decision is still developing. As yet, I am unaware of asset location research that distinguishes between TDAs with front-end tax benefits and TDAs with back-end tax benefits. Nor has the literature on asset location recognized that an investor's investment horizon and withdrawal pattern affect the taxable equivalent value of tax-sheltered assets and thus taxable equivalent asset allocation. By affecting taxable equivalent asset allocation, these factors can affect the asset location decision as well.

Borrowing Constraints

The preceding tax arbitrage example is illustrative, but for many investors, implementing it is not practical because they face restrictions on the amount and form of borrowing. For instance, the tax arbitrage argument assumes that investors can borrow and lend at the same rate in whatever amounts they wish. In reality, such is not the case. Investors using margin accounts for their investment borrowing typically pay the broker call rate or a premium above it, which is undoubtedly greater than the yield on a bond of similar risk. Some or all of the tax gains from the arbitrage are, therefore, consumed by this rate differential. Furthermore, investors are typically restricted from initially borrowing more than 50 percent of the value of their equity portfolio, potentially limiting the extent to which one might be able to carry out this strategy.

Some defined-contribution plans permit participants to borrow against a portion of their accumulations. The amount of borrowing is typically restricted, however, and the collateralized assets must oftentimes be held in a low-risk investment vehicle with a low yield, far less than the interest rate on the loan. Therefore, many researchers have investigated the asset location decision with the assumption that investors are unable to borrow. I will proceed from here using that assumption as well. The tax arbitrage argument with borrowing constraints dictates that, to the extent possible, bonds should be held in TDAs subject to the investor's after-tax asset allocation dictated by his or her risk tolerances.

TABLE 18.23   Taxable Equivalent Value Factors for an Investor in the 28 Percent Tax Bracket

Item	$r = 10\%$ Equity Mutual Fund	$r = 6\%$ Bonds	Gain from Stocks to Bonds
A. 10-year investment horizon and 20-year withdrawal horizon			
Traditional IRA	0.859	0.973	$0.114
Roth IRA	1.193	1.352	$0.159
B. 30-year investment horizon and 30-year withdrawal horizon			
Traditional IRA	1.036	1.406	$0.370
Roth IRA	1.439	1.952	$0.523

One may then ask which type of TDA—a traditional IRA or Roth IRA—is best suited to carry the bonds should the investor's taxable equivalent asset allocation accommodate equity and bonds in TDAs? The answer depends, of course, on many factors, but the Roth IRA is best in many instances because the taxable equivalent value factor for heavy tax burden investments is typically greater for Roth IRAs than for traditional IRAs.

Consider, for example, an investor with a 28 percent tax rate through the investment and withdrawal phases with 10 years to retirement ($n = 10$), at which time she will commence 20 years of annuitized withdrawals ($m = 20$). Table 18.23, Panel A, displays the taxable equivalent value factors for stocks and bonds in a traditional IRA and a Roth IRA, under the assumption stocks have a 10 percent return and bonds a 6 percent return. For each dollar shifted from stocks to bonds in the traditional IRA, the after-tax value increases by 11 cents. The same shift in the Roth IRA produces a 16 cent increase, suggesting that this investor might best place bonds in the Roth IRA first. If the desired after-tax asset allocation calls for more bonds, they should then be placed in the traditional IRA. A more pronounced effect is noticed for investors with longer investment horizons. Panel B shows that the same investor with a 30-year investment horizon and withdrawal horizon can realize a greater increase in taxable equivalent value by locating bonds in the Roth IRA rather than the traditional IRA.

It must be noted that, for simplicity, I have ignored in this simple exercise how the after-tax asset allocation is affected by this change in asset location. Nonetheless, it provides heuristic guidance. More research is needed to incorporate an investor's utility function and risk aversion into the analysis.

Municipal Bonds

The basic tax arbitrage example introduced earlier considers only taxable bonds and equity as possible asset classes. The interest on municipal bonds, however, is exempt from state and federal taxes. Because investors are willing to accept a lower yield to have this benefit, the pretax return on municipal bonds is typically lower than that on taxable bonds such that $r_m = r_b(1 - t_m)$, where r_m is the return on a tax-exempt municipal bond, r_b is the return on a taxable bond of similar risk, and t_m is the implied tax rate of municipal bonds. Using data from bond mutual funds, Shoven and Sialm (2003) reported that the *ex post* implied tax rate from 1979 to 1998 was 26 percent, which is smaller than the tax rate on ordinary income for many investors. In addition, the municipal bond funds seem to be considerably more risky than the corporate bond funds. Shoven and Sialm also examined the asset location decision when municipal bonds were part of the investment opportunity set.

When investors are constrained from borrowing or short selling and cannot hold more than 50 percent of their wealth in a TDA, Shoven and Sialm (2003) showed that high-income investors in the 40 percent tax bracket generally are better off holding stock in taxable accounts and taxable bonds in TDAs if the mutual fund tax burden is relatively light. As the stock fund becomes more tax inefficient (i.e., distributes more of its return as dividends or capital gains), the investor should increase his or her stock holdings in the TDA, thereby increasing the investor's pretax exposure to equities. The intuition for increasing the pretax stock allocation as the tax burden increases is that the government shares in the risk and return of the equity investment as its tax burden increases, thereby decreasing the investor's after-tax exposure to that asset class. To hold the after-tax asset allocation constant, the investor increases his or her pretax equity exposure.

At some point, however, if the tax inefficiency of equities becomes sufficiently onerous such that 68.6 percent or more of the annual returns are distributed, the investor is better off shifting the equities from the taxable account to the TDA and buying municipal bonds in the taxable account. Interestingly, this break point is close to the mean total distribution rates reported in Table 18.4. For a medium-income individual in the 30 percent tax bracket, the optimal asset location is similar. When distribution rates of the stock fund are low, investors should hold stock in the taxable account and favor bonds in the TDA. But as the stock fund distributes more than 88.5 percent of its return (i.e., is highly tax inefficient), stocks are better placed in the TDA and the taxable account should hold municipal bonds.

In this context, the usefulness of tax-exempt bonds comes with several caveats. First, the Shoven and Sialm study incorporated a preferred tax rate of 20 percent on long-term capital gains. It did not, however, incorporate the new tax realities of the JGTRRA of 2003, which lowers the capital gains tax rate to 15 percent and lowers the tax rate on dividends from the ordinary income tax rate to 15 percent. The new tax law increases the tax efficiency of stock mutual funds and decreases the relative attractiveness of holding municipal bonds in a taxable account for an investor's equity exposure. Second, actively managed equity funds tend to be less tax efficient than passively managed index funds. In addition, index funds tend to have higher risk-adjusted returns, on average, than actively managed funds. Investors using index funds benefit from their higher risk-adjusted return and improved tax efficiency, which together mitigate the usefulness of locating stock in a TDA and tax-exempt bonds in a taxable account.

Therefore, the opportunity to use municipal bonds to optimize asset location is limited to investors using actively managed equity. In fact, Dammon, Spatt, and Zhang (2004) found that the opportunity to invest in tax-exempt bonds did not alter the general advice of locating bonds, to the extent possible, in TDAs and stock in taxable accounts provided that equity can be held in a relatively tax-efficient form, such as an index fund.

Trading Behavior

The tax burden for many asset classes, such as equities, depends on an investor's trading behavior or that of the mutual fund held by the investor. Therefore, gains from optimal asset location and perhaps the optimal asset location itself will depend on the trading behavior of an individual investor. Reichenstein (2001) considered three types of investors. In his model, all gains for a *trader* are short term and taxed as ordinary income each year. For an *active investor,* all gains are realized annually as long-term gains and taxed at the capital gains tax rate, which at the time of his writing was 20 percent. The *passive investor* buys and holds stock, never paying capital gains tax via charitable contributions or the step-up in cost basis at the owner's death or the death of his or her spouse.[55]

For the trader, stock and bonds are taxed similarly. In Reichenstein's model, stocks can be located in either the TDA or the taxable account. The optimal asset allocation in each case, however, calls for a relatively large pretax exposure to the asset held in the taxable account because the after-tax value of each dollar in the taxable account is typically less than the after-tax value of a dollar in the TDA in his model.[56] Therefore, the after-tax asset allocation to the asset in the taxable account is too low unless more is allocated to that asset. For the active investor, bonds should be located, to the degree possible, in TDAs, but the improvement in the investors' utility is modest. For the passive investor, not locating bonds in TDAs can have a much larger effect on utility. But Reichenstein found that a proper investment management strategy remains more important than the proper asset location strategy. That is, avoiding mutual funds that are tax inefficient and that produce negative pretax alpha has a greater impact on investor utility than optimally locating assets in TDAs and taxable accounts.

On average, active managers have difficulty matching the risk-adjusted returns of passively managed index funds on a pretax basis. The additional tax liabilities created through active management create an even higher hurdle for managers. Reichenstein (2001) found that even if active managers produce identical risk-adjusted pretax returns as index funds, investors stand to gain more from pursuing a passive investment strategy with a low tax drag than optimally locating assets among TDAs and taxable accounts.

Liquidity Constraints

The strategy of locating bonds in TDAs, to the extent that borrowing constraints allow, may maximize a portfolio's tax efficiency, but it also increases the risk of the taxable portion of the portfolio because the taxable account will have a disproportionately large allocation of equity relative to the TDA. The added risk in the taxable account can be important to investors in the presence of borrowing constraints because it increases the risk that an investor's taxable investments fall short of providing the investor's minimum level of consumption. If a large shock to consumption were to arise whereby consumption exceeded the value of the assets held in the taxable account, it could become necessary to withdraw funds from a TDA prior to age 59½ thereby imposing an early withdrawal penalty on the investor.

Dammon, Spatt, and Zhang (2004) analyzed this situation and found that the impact of liquidity constraints on the optimal asset location decision depends on the magnitude and likelihood of consumption shocks and their correlation with equity returns. Deviating from the traditional admonition to locate bonds in TDAs requires a large likelihood of a large consumption shock that would have to be strongly negatively correlated with equity returns. Therefore, liquidity constraints associated with holding equity in taxable accounts do not appear to have a significant effect on the asset location decision.

Up to this point, the general advice for investors seems to be to hold heavily taxed assets, such as bonds, in TDAs and favor equities in taxable accounts. Amromin (2002) argued that the asset location decision can be affected not only by tax efficiency considerations but also by precautionary liquidity considerations. He posited that households that are more likely to suffer a catastrophic shortfall in labor income are more likely to abandon tax-efficient investing in favor of having less risk in their taxable account. He posited further that households with less accumulated wealth or a high share of their wealth in TDAs are likely to behave similarly to avoid the costs associated with accessing funds in TDAs early. In addition, investors facing greater restrictions on accessing TDA assets should hold less equity in their taxable accounts, all else being equal.

Empirical Evidence of Investor Behavior

I demonstrated in the section on Valuing Tax-Sheltered Assets on an After-Tax Basis that the after-tax value of tax-preferred savings accounts is an increasing function of the marginal tax rate an investor pays on returns in an otherwise taxable account. Intuitively, this result is sensible because tax shelters would be worthless in the absence of taxes. Auerbach and King (1983) predicted that under certain conditions, portfolio cienteles will form such that investors will hold assets that have a lower tax burden for them. By extension, location cienteles should form as investors hold highly taxed assets in TDAs, to the extent possible, and more lightly taxed assets in taxable accounts.

Evidence suggests that investors deviate from this predicted behavior. Generally, the prescriptions described previously indicate that investors should locate their taxable bonds in TDAs subject to their desired after-tax asset allocation. In the presence of borrowing constraints, if taxable bonds are held in taxable accounts, the investor should have filled the TDA entirely with taxable bonds and should want to hold more. Therefore, investors with taxable bonds in taxable accounts should not be holding equity in TDAs. Poterba and Samwick (2003) reported, however, that 56.9 percent of investors who hold taxable bonds in taxable accounts also hold equity in tax-deferred accounts. Similarly, investors holding equity in TDAs should be doing so because they have already satisfied their bond holdings in TDAs and should not, therefore, be holding taxable bonds in taxable accounts. Poterba and Samwick reported that 35.1 percent of investors holding tax-deferred equity also hold taxable bonds in taxable accounts.

As discussed previously, Shoven and Sialm showed that municipal bonds can play a useful role in the asset location decision for certain highly taxed investors so long as the distribution rates on equity investments are sufficiently high. Their model suggests that investors holding municipal bonds (in taxable accounts, of course) should generally not be holding equity in taxable accounts but rather in TDAs. But 53.9 percent of investors holding tax-exempt bonds also hold equity in taxable accounts. It could be, of course, that investors hold a variety of equity vehicles with different tax burdens. They could be holding tax-efficient equity in taxable accounts and more heavily taxed equity in TDAs. Amromin reported similar findings but suggested that this apparent deviation from optimal asset location behavior is the result of the early withdrawal penalty and other TDA-accessibility restrictions that might prove costly to an investor who experiences an unexpectedly large shock to consumption or shortfall in income. Investors may, therefore, choose to sacrifice tax efficiency in favor of greater liquidity in their taxable account.

Summary

In making the asset allocation decision, it is important to use asset allocation proportions that are based on after-tax values and to consider the effect that the location decision has on these after-tax proportions. Differences between pretax and after-tax asset allocations can be substantial. In a world characterized by unlimited borrowing and equal borrowing and lending rates, investors should hold taxable bonds in TDAs. Their taxable accounts should be used to hold more lightly taxed equity and to borrow or lend to adjust their after-tax asset allocation to match their risk tolerances. In the presence of borrowing constraints, the general advice of holding highly taxed assets, such as fixed income, in TDAs to the extent possible is robust in many circumstances. As of now, there seems to be two caveats to this directive.

First, highly taxed investors holding heavily taxed equity may benefit from getting their bond exposure from municipal bonds held in taxable accounts. If so, then equity might optimally be held in TDAs. But holding more tax-efficient equity in a taxable account would obviate the need to do this and tends to make the investor better off. Because one's trading behavior affects the tax drag of equity, a way to lighten the tax burden of equity may be to pursue a passive buy-and-hold strategy rather than a high-turnover, active short-term trading strategy. Another deviation from the general rule can result from investors wishing to maintain lower investment risk levels in their taxable accounts to preserve their liquidity. When it is costly to access funds held in the TDA, investors wishing to insulate themselves from unexpectedly high consumption needs or unexpected shortfalls in labor income may rationally forgo tax efficiency in favor of greater liquidity. It is fair to say, however, that investors and researchers have more to learn regarding the optimal asset location.

IMPLICATIONS FOR FINANCIAL ANALYSTS

Most modern portfolio theory that financial analysts rely on is grounded in a pretax framework. Recently, researchers have advanced the understanding of the impact of tax structure, the value of tax-timing options, and how the effect of taxes interacts with trading behavior.[57] They have developed models to help investors make optimal decisions in a taxable environment characterized by somewhat complex tax structures in which taxation depends on the type of asset and the account in which it is held. Many of these advances have yet to find their way into mainstream financial analysis, in part because of their complexity. This chapter is designed to package salient tax considerations into a tractable framework that requires of the analyst only a basic understanding of algebra and time-value-of-money concepts. The purpose of this approach is to provide analysts with tools that they can reasonably incorporate into their analyses. Although this compendium focuses largely on how investors might optimally use tax-advantaged savings accounts, the fundamental framework has broader applications. It has significant implications that permeate the entire portfolio management process and the approach that analysts use in developing portfolio optimization techniques.

Portfolio Management and Investment Objectives

Many financial institutions market their services by offering to help prospective clients navigate the many TDA options available to investors. These efforts create an onus for the financial advisor to be aware of the salient characteristics of TDAs and perhaps more importantly to use them effectively to a client's advantage in the portfolio management process. Knowing how TDAs might be used to accumulate wealth in a tax-efficient manner can have an impact on the financial analyst's approach in establishing return objectives and risk tolerances for clients. When a financial analyst synthesizes a client's particular circumstances and investment goals into a set of return objectives, the objectives are typically expressed in pretax terms and often without regard for the tax structure of the account(s) in which the portfolio is held. Moreover, the notion that the risk of a security or a portfolio from an investor's perspective is greater when held in a tax-sheltered account versus a taxable account (because the government shares more fully in the risk of the latter) has yet to find its way into the collective consciousness of the financial analyst profession. Yet, this understanding can affect a financial advisor's assessment of an investor's return requirements, risk tolerances, and investment constraints.

For example, suppose Mrs. Klondike, a 60-year-old widow with a $2 million portfolio, wishes to draw out $50,000 annually on a pretax basis indefinitely. She hopes further that her withdrawals grow by the rate of inflation, which is expected to be 3 percent indefinitely, so that she maintains her purchasing power. Mrs. Klondike also wishes to protect and grow the corpus of her portfolio so that it might be bequeathed to the local YWCA upon her death. A typical advisor would determine her spending rate to be 2½ percent per year and her return requirement to be 5½ percent per year. If her portfolio consists of taxable bonds yielding 5½ percent held in a taxable account, she will meet her spending needs in the near term. But over time, she will be unable to meet her spending needs and grow the corpus of her portfolio. Why? Suppose the portfolio's entire return will be taxed at 30 percent. In the near term, the portfolio will generate more than enough income to meet her needs. But the portfolio's after-tax return is 3.85 percent [i.e., $0.055 \times (1 - 0.30)$], which over time will be insufficient to maintain the purchasing power of Mrs. Klondike's withdrawals and to grow the corpus of the portfolio.

If, however, the portfolio of bonds is held in a traditional IRA, all of Mrs. Klondike's investment goals will be met. Her $50,000 pretax withdrawals will still grow by the rate of inflation because only her withdrawals will be taxed.[58] The remaining portion of the annual return will be compounded on a tax-deferred basis. Furthermore, the assets may pass to the charitable organization free of tax if the account and estate are properly structured. The picture looks even better if the assets are held in a Roth IRA. In this case, none of Mrs. Klondike's withdrawals are taxed, decreasing her spending rate from 2½ percent to 1¾ percent [i.e., $50,000 \times (1 - 0.30)/\$2,000,000$]. All of her withdrawals and earnings will accrue free of tax, allowing her corpus to grow.

As this simplified example illustrates, the tax structure of an account can affect an investor's pretax return objectives, which serve as the foundation for properly constructing portfolios that meet investors' needs. Because different asset classes have different tax structures (e.g., fixed-income instruments are taxed more heavily than equity when held in a taxable account), proper asset allocation must also consider the accounts in which different asset classes are held and how they are taxed.

This example also helps illustrate the notion that Mrs. Klondike's risk exposure is not identical for the three scenarios. Her risk exposure in the Roth IRA account is greatest because she is the residual claimant on all of the investment gains and losses. The government shares in a portion of her investment risk when the portfolio is held in a traditional IRA because withdrawals from the account are taxed. The government may share in an even greater proportion of portfolio risk if the portfolio is held in a taxable account, depending on the tax structure of the assets. This insight is important because if the financial advisor recognizes that the taxable account will not satisfy Mrs. Klondike's long-term financial goals, he may increase the risk of the portfolio by introducing equities, knowing that the government will share in some of the risk. Conceptually, he could add equity until the after-tax portfolio risk is equal to that of the all-bond portfolio if it were held in a Roth IRA.

This example also highlights the importance of viewing asset allocation on an after-tax basis. The section called Valuing Tax-Sheltered Assets on an After-Tax Basis showed that a dollar in a TDA does not necessarily have the same value as a dollar in a taxable account. As a result, if an investor's aggregate portfolio is held in a series of taxable and TDA accounts, pretax asset allocation measures can be misleading, as I demonstrated in the previous section. Measuring a portfolio's exposure to different asset classes on an after-tax basis provides a more accurate picture of an investor's asset allocation. Yet, financial advisors routinely ignore this approach and risk creating portfolios that do not match the return requirements and risk tolerances of their clients.

To this point, the discussion has taken the type of investment account as a given in the portfolio management process. And I have argued that analysts may not be adequately considering this factor in their work. Financial analysts and financial advisors should include the choice of investment account (e.g., traditional IRA, Roth IRA, 401(k), taxable account) as a decision variable in the portfolio management process. That is, investors should be advised on whether to use TDAs in their investment strategy and which TDAs might be best given their current and expected tax situation. Unlike trusts, TDAs are relatively straightforward and do not require an extensive understanding of tax and estate law. It is reasonable then to expect financial advisors to be well versed in their proper use. For example, a financial advisor should be able to recommend whether it is beneficial to use a TDA in meeting investment objectives, to choose between TDAs with front-end tax benefits and back-end tax benefits, to convert or refrain from converting a traditional IRA to a Roth IRA, and to hold bonds in either TDAs or taxable accounts. That is, the financial advisor should provide guidance regarding asset location as well as asset allocation.

Portfolio Management and Investment Constraints

In addition to affecting the development of investment objectives (i.e., return requirements and risk tolerances), a focus on tax-efficient wealth accumulation also affects an investor's investment constraints. Investment constraints are commonly thought to consist of tax considerations, time horizon, liquidity requirements, legal and regulatory factors, and unique circumstances. A common example of how tax considerations might affect asset allocation is that tax-exempt investors should avoid municipal bonds, which have lower yields because of their tax-favored status but from which tax-exempt organizations do not benefit. A more holistic view of tax-efficient wealth accumulation recognizes that tax considerations interact with the other investment constraints, the investment objectives, and even the portfolio management strategy.

For example, the tax status of an investor's account might affect the investor's time horizon. An investor with a greater proportion of assets held in TDAs may be able to reach her retirement goals more quickly than one with a greater percentage of assets held in taxable accounts. Interestingly, the time horizon may also affect tax considerations. As the section on Early Withdrawal Penalties and Breakeven Time Horizons investigated, investors with sufficiently long preretirement investment horizons may find it beneficial to use TDAs and incur an early withdrawal penalty rather than use a taxable account. The same holds true for using 529 plans for noneducational investment purposes. Often, the breakeven time horizon is quite short, in which case a TDA may be an efficient investment tool in spite of the early withdrawal penalty. If so, this decision will affect the return requirements, risk tolerances, and asset allocation as described previously.

Tax considerations may also affect liquidity requirements and vice versa. The possibility of early withdrawal penalties can place a liquidity constraint on the portfolio. Conversely, as the previous section showed, liquidity requirements may discourage investors from placing more volatile assets, such as equity with a relatively light tax burden, in taxable accounts where they might otherwise be optimally placed from a tax perspective. Because a precipitous decline in the value of equity in a taxable account may necessitate withdrawing assets from a TDA, which may be subject to an early withdrawal penalty, holding bonds (perhaps municipal bonds) in a taxable account may be advisable. In this way, liquidity requirements may affect tax considerations, which may, in turn, affect asset allocation.

A deeper understanding of the tax considerations and investment constraints can also affect asset allocation strategy, portfolio rebalancing, and trading behavior. A buy-and-hold investment strategy is a passive asset allocation strategy in which the initial mix of asset classes is allowed to drift with price movements. Because it entails no rebalancing, and hence no turnover, it is efficient from a tax perspective and may be well suited for assets held in taxable accounts. In contrast, constant mix and constant proportion portfolio insurance strategies require rebalancing to maintain the proper proportion of assets among asset classes, depending on whether there is a minimum floor value below which the value of the portfolio should not drop. Rebalancing generally creates a heavier tax burden than a buy-and-hold strategy and may, therefore, be more attractive in TDAs that negate the tax consequences of frequent rebalancing. Of course, the tax implications for a rebalancing strategy will depend heavily on the parameters that dictate how often rebalancing is required.

Similarly, tax considerations can affect equity investment strategy. Active portfolio management for the equity portion of a portfolio requires some degree of turnover. Some strategies entail higher trading levels than others. Active investment strategies with high turnover are generally less tax efficient than passive strategies with little or no turnover. Therefore, all else being equal, high-turnover active management investment strategies might best be pursued in TDAs, and low-turnover passive equity strategies might best be pursued in taxable accounts. The interaction of asset allocation strategy, equity investment strategy, and the tax status of different accounts has not been fully investigated. But this chapter provides some heuristic guidance and highlights the importance of tax-efficient wealth accumulation on the portfolio management process.

Portfolio Optimization

Beyond the portfolio management process, this research has implications for portfolio optimization. Traditional portfolio optimization techniques create an efficient set of portfolios that have different levels of expected return and risk. But the expected returns and covariance matrix used in this process are almost always based on pretax returns. This chapter shows that tax structure and trading behavior can dramatically affect terminal wealth accumulations, which by implication suggests that pretax efficient frontiers may not be reasonable proxies for after-tax efficient frontiers. A seemingly simple solution is to substitute after-tax returns for pretax returns as inputs into the optimization process. The problem with this approach, however, is that determining an annual after-tax return for an investment that has a large taxable event when it is liquidated or withdrawn from an account is difficult. Most likely, the analyst knows neither the timing nor the size of that tax liability. So, translating this information into annual after-tax returns for individual assets or asset classes for use as input in a portfolio optimization process is not straightforward. One alternative is to redefine the objective function to maximize expected terminal wealth (rather than expected annual return) subject to various risk constraints. This approach forces the analyst to think about wealth accumulation rather than annual return and may be useful only if the investor can identify a specific investment horizon.

Another approach is to use simulation techniques that incorporate after-tax account values. Simulations might incorporate variability in an investor's tax rate and investment return over time. In any case, the significance of taxes in the investing environment creates an impetus for the financial analyst to focus on after-tax wealth accumulation and incorporate tax considerations into the portfolio optimization process.

Many of the implications for portfolio management and portfolio optimization deserve more research before they can be properly incorporated into financial analysts' common body of knowledge. And this chapter falls short of doing that. But it hopefully introduces important concepts, provides useful techniques that can help guide analysts and investors, and creates an impetus for analysts to focus on tax-efficient wealth accumulation in the disposition of their duties.

APPENDIX 18A: PROOF OF EQUIVALENCY FOR STANDARDIZED PRETAX AND AFTER-TAX INVESTMENTS

To compare the future accumulations of a traditional IRA and a Roth IRA, one must hold the investment constant. The analysis is unaffected whether the pretax investment for the two accounts is standardized or the after-tax investment is standardized. Consider a standardized pretax investment of I_{BT} and an after-tax investment of $I_{BT}(1 - T_o)$. In either case, the amount of money invested in the Roth IRA is $I_{BT}(1 - T_o)$.

The investment in the traditional IRA requires some explanation. Consider first pretax investments (I_{BT}) less than the contribution limit (L). If one standardizes the pretax investment (I_{BT}) for both accounts, the amount invested in the traditional IRA is simply I_{BT} because the investment is tax deductible. If one standardizes the after-tax investment at $I_{BT}(1 - T_o)$ for both accounts, the traditional IRA investment of $I_{BT}(1 - T_o)$ generates tax savings of $I_{BT}T_o$ if tax savings are invested in the traditional IRA. Adding these two values yields I_{BT}, which is the same investment in the pretax scenario.

Now consider pretax investments greater than the after-tax contribution limit but less that the maximum pretax Roth IRA investment, such that $L < I_{BT} < L/(1 - T_o)$. The Roth IRA is still $I_{BT}(1 - T_o)$ whether the pretax or after-tax investment is held constant. The allocation for the traditional IRA strategy has two components, however: the IRA contribution up to the contribution limit (L) and a non-IRA contribution for any investment in excess of the limit. This total can be expressed as

$$I_{Trad} = \min(I_{BT}, L) + \max[0(I_{BT} - L)(1 - T_o)]. \qquad (18A.1)$$

The first term of Equation 18A.1 represents the after-tax investment in the deductible IRA up to the IRA contribution limit, L. The second term represents the amount, if any, applied in a non-IRA, nondeductible investment. When $I_{BT} > L$, standardizing the pretax investment at I_{BT} yields $L + (I_{BT} - L)(1 - T_o)$. If the after-tax investment is standardized at $I_{BT}(1 - T_o)$, only the portion up to L can be invested in the traditional IRA. This portion, however, will generate tax savings of LT_o. Rearranging terms shows that the sum of these two values, $I_{BT}(1 - T_o) + LT_o$, equals the standardize pretax investment, $L + (I_{BT} - L)(1 - T_o)$. Therefore, the investment in both accounts is unaffected by the choice of standardizing the pretax investment or standardizing the after-tax investment.

Development of the Future Value of a Taxable Investment

Crain and Austin (1997) showed that for a taxable mutual fund investment, a dollar invested for n years has a before-withdrawal tax future value of

$$FV_{TXb} = (1 + r - rp_{oi}t_{oi} - rp_{cg}t_{cg})^n, \qquad (18A.2)$$

where $r - rp_{oi}t_{oi} - rp_{cg}t_{cg}$ is the annual after-tax return. Although the investor pays tax annually on the portion of the annual return that is distributed as ordinary income or capital gain, he or she must also recognize a capital gain when the mutual fund shares are sold at time n and pay capital gain tax. The capital gain is equal to the value in Equation 18A.2 less the adjusted basis, which is composed of the initial investment plus ordinary income and capital gain distributions (on which tax has already been paid) less the income tax on those distributions. The adjusted basis can be expressed as

$$\text{Adjusted basis} = 1 + rp_{oi}(1 - t_{oi})\frac{(1 + r - rp_{oi}t_{oi} - rp_{cg}t_{cg})^n - 1}{(r - rp_{oi}t_{oi} - rp_{cg}t_{cg})}$$

$$+ rp_{cg}(1 - t_{cg})\frac{(1 + r - rp_{oi}t_{oi} - rp_{cg}t_{cg})^n - 1}{(r - rp_{oi}t_{oi} - rp_{cg}t_{cg})}. \tag{18A.3}$$

The first term of this expression is the original \$1.00 investment. The second term is the accumulated ordinary income distributions over the life of the investment and has two parts. The first part is the after-tax portion of the return distributed as ordinary income. The second part of the second term is an after-tax future value factor that determines the accumulated value of the after-tax ordinary income distributions. The third term is analogous to the second except that it pertains to the capital gain distributions.

Taking the before-tax accumulation in Equation 18A.2 and subtracting capital gains tax on the adjusted basis in Equation 18A.3 yields

$$\text{FVIF}_{TX} = (1 + r - rp_{oi}t_{oi} - rp_{cg}t_{cg})^n - t_{cg}\bigg[(1 + r - rp_{oi}t_{oi} - rp_{cg}t_{cg})^n - 1$$

$$- rp_{oi}(1 - t_{oi})\frac{(1 + r - rp_{oi}t_{oi} - rp_{cg}t_{cg})^n - 1}{(r - rp_{oi}t_{oi} - rp_{cg}t_{cg})} \tag{18A.4}$$

$$- rp_{cg}(1 - t_{cg})\frac{(1 + r - rp_{oi}t_{oi} - rp_{cg}t_{cg})^n - 1}{(r - rp_{oi}t_{oi} - rp_{cg}t_{cg})}\bigg].$$

This unwieldy equation can be simplified by setting $r^* = r - rp_{oi}t_{oi} - rp_{cg}t_{cg}$ and $T^* = t_{cg}(1 - p_{oi} - p_{cg})/(1 - p_{oi}t_{oi} - p_{cg}t_{cg})$. Rearranging terms produces

$$\text{FVIF}_{TX} = (1 + r^*)^n(1 - T^*) + T^*. \tag{18A.5}$$

When the investment is taxed entirely as capital gain at the end of the investment period, $p_{oi} = p_{cg} = 0$. Substituting these values reduces to $r^* = r$ and $T^* = t_{cg}$. Equation 18A.5 then simplifies to $(1 + r)^n(1 - t_{cg}) + t_{cg}$. When the investment is taxed entirely as ordinary income each year, then $p_{oi} = 1$ and $p_{cg} = 0$. Substituting these values makes $r^* = r(1 - t_{oi})$ and $T^* = 0$. Equation 18A.5 then simplifies to $[1 + r(1 - t_{oi})]n$, which is a familiar after-tax future value formula.

Derivation of Relative Values of Traditional IRAs and Roth IRAs

The relative future value of the traditional IRA and the Roth IRA is the ratio of Equation 18.5 to Equation 18.1, or

$$\frac{\text{FV}_{Trad}}{\text{FV}_{Roth}} = \frac{L(1 + r)^n(1 - T_n) + (I_{BT} - L)(1 - T_o)[(1 + r^*)^n(1 - T^*) + T^*]}{I_{BT}(1 - T_o)(1 + r)^n} \tag{18A.6}$$

Dividing the first term of the numerator through by $(1 + r)^n$, distributing $(1 - T_o)$ in the second term of the numerator, and dividing through by $(1 - T_o)$ yields

$$\frac{\text{FV}_{Trad}}{\text{FV}_{Roth}} = \frac{L(1 - T_n)}{I_{BT}(1 - T_o)} + \frac{I_{BT}[(1 + r^*)^n(1 - T^*) + T^*]}{I_{BT}(1 + r)^n}$$
$$- \frac{L[(1 + r^*)^n(1 - T^*) + T^*]}{I_{BT}(1 + r)^n}.$$

(18A.7)

Dividing to unity and collecting terms yields

$$\frac{\text{FV}_{Trad}}{\text{FV}_{Roth}} = \frac{L(1 - T_n)}{I_{BT}(1 - T_o)}$$
$$+ \left(1 - \frac{L}{I_{BT}}\right)\frac{(1 + r^*)^n(1 - T^*) + T^*}{(1 + r)^n}.$$

(18A.8)

Derivation of the Breakeven Withdrawal Tax Rate

The breakeven withdrawal tax rate is found by setting Equation 18A.8 to 1 and solving for T_n. Doing so and subtracting 1 from both sides gives

$$0 = \frac{L(1 - T_n)}{I_{BT}(1 - T_o)}$$
$$- 1 + \left(1 - \frac{L}{I_{BT}}\right)\frac{(1 + r^*)^n(1 - T^*) + T^*}{(1 + r)^n}.$$

(18A.9)

Dividing through by L, multiplying through by $I_{BT}(1 - T_o)$, and distributing I_{BT}/L through the third term results in

$$0 = (1 - T_n) - \frac{I_{BT}(1 - T_o)}{L}$$
$$+ (1 - T_o)\left(\frac{I_{BT}}{L} - 1\right)\frac{(1 + r^*)^n(1 - T^*) + T^*}{(1 + r)^n}.$$

(18A.10)

Adding T_n to both sides and canceling T_o on the right-hand side produces

$$T_n = T_o + (1 - T_o) - \frac{I_{BT}(1 - T_o)}{L}$$
$$+ (1 - T_o)\left(\frac{I_{BT}}{L} - 1\right)\frac{(1 + r^*)^n(1 - T^*) + T^*}{(1 + r)^n}.$$

(18A.11)

Finally, collecting terms around $-(1 - T_o)$ and $(I_{BT}/L - 1)$ yields Equation 18A.12:

$$T_n = T_o - (1 - T_o)\left(\frac{I_{BT}}{L} - 1\right)$$
$$\times \left[1 - \frac{(1 + r^*)^n(1 - T^*) + T^*}{(1 + r)^n}\right].$$

(18A.12)

APPENDIX 18B: SIMPLIFICATION WHEN TAX SAVINGS ARE REINVESTED IN 401(k)

The after-tax accumulation of a 401(k) in which the employer matches π percent of the employee's investment and the tax savings are invested in a mutual fund is

$$\text{FV}_{401(k)} = (1 + \pi)I_{BT}(1 - T_o)(1 + r)^n(1 - T_n) + I_{BT}T_o[\text{FVIF}_{TX}]. \qquad (18\text{B}.1)$$

If the tax savings in the second term are reinvested in the 401(k), then FVIF_{TX} reduces to $(1 + r)^n$ and the investment is grossed up to $(1 + \pi)$ by the employer's contribution. Therefore, the expression becomes

$$\text{FV}_{401(k)^*} = (1 + \pi)I_{BT}(1 - T_o)(1 + r)^n(1 - T_n) + (1 + \pi)I_{BT}T_o(1 + r)^n. \qquad (18\text{B}.2)$$

Collecting terms around $(1 + \pi)I_{BT}(1 + r)^n$ produces

$$\text{FV}_{401(k)^*} = (1 + \pi)I_{BT}(1 + r)^n(1 - T_n). \qquad (18\text{B}.3)$$

Breakeven Withdrawal Tax Rate Between a 401(k) and a Roth IRA

Setting the future accumulation of an employer-matched 401(k) to that of a Roth IRA and solving for T_n determines the breakeven withdrawal tax rate between the two types of accounts. Therefore, setting Equation 18B.1 to Equation 18.1 yields

$$\text{FV}_{Roth} = \text{FV}_{401(k)} \qquad (18\text{B}.4)$$

$$I_{BT}(1 - T_o)(1 + r)^n = (1 + \pi)I_{BT}(1 - T_o)(1 + r)^n(1 - T_n) + I_{BT}T_o[\text{FVIF}_{TX}].$$

Dividing through by I_{BT}, subtracting $I_{BT}T_o[\text{FVIF}_{TX}]$ from both sides, dividing both sides by $(1 + \pi)I_{BT}(1 - T_o)(1 + r)^n$, subtracting 1 from both sides, and multiplying through by -1 yields

$$T_n = 1 - \frac{(1 - T_o)(1 + r)^n - T_o[\text{FVIF}_{TX}]}{(1 + \pi)(1 - T_o)(1 + r)^n}. \qquad (18\text{B}.5)$$

Substituting for FVIF_{TX}, separating terms, canceling terms, and factoring out $-1/(1 + \pi)$ yields

$$T_n = 1 - \frac{1}{1 + \pi}\left[1 - \frac{T_o[(1 + r^*)^n(1 - T^*) + T^*]]}{(1 + \pi)(1 - T_o)(1 + r)^n}\right]. \qquad (18\text{B}.6)$$

Future Value of Roth IRA Conversion

An investor converting a traditional IRA to a Roth IRA must pay a withdrawal (or conversion) tax on funds coming from the traditional IRA. An investor wishing to pay this conversion tax from IRA assets must pay an early withdrawal penalty as well on the amount not rolled over into the Roth IRA. Under this scenario, for each dollar rolled over from the traditional IRA, $(1 - T_o)$ dollars get rolled over into the Roth IRA because T_o dollars are held back to pay the conversion tax. Each of the T_o dollars held back and not rolled over is subject to an early withdrawal penalty of $T_o\phi$ dollars, where ϕ is the percentage early withdrawal penalty. To hold back enough funds from the traditional IRA to cover the withdrawal tax and early withdrawal penalty, the investor must withhold a total of $T_o\phi/(1 - \phi)$ dollars from the Roth IRA for each dollar rolled over from the traditional IRA. Therefore, the future value of each dollar rolled over from a traditional IRA into a Roth IRA is

$$\text{FV}_{RothConv^*} = \left[1 - T_o - \frac{T_o\phi}{1 - \phi}\right](1 + r)^n. \tag{18B.7}$$

The first term in the brackets represents each dollar withdrawn from the traditional IRA to be converted into the Roth IRA. The second term in the brackets is the tax withheld on each dollar rolled over from the traditional IRA. The third term in the brackets is the additional amount withheld to pay the conversion tax. Multiplying the numerator and the denominator of the second term by $1 - \phi$ and canceling terms yields

$$\text{FV}_{RothConv^*} = \left[1 - \frac{T_o}{1 - \phi}\right](1 + r)^n. \tag{18B.8}$$

Breakeven Withdrawal Tax Rate for a Roth IRA Conversion

The future value of each dollar held in a traditional IRA is $(1 + r)^n(1 - T_n)$. By setting this value equal to Equation 18.5, the future value of a dollar converted to a Roth IRA becomes

$$(1 + r)^n(1 - T_n) = (1 + r)^n - T_o[\text{FVIF}_{TX}]. \tag{18B.9}$$

Distributing $(1 + r)^n$ on the left-hand side, subtracting $(1 + r)^n$ from both sides, and manipulating yields

$$T_n = T_o \frac{\text{FVIF}_{TX}}{(1 + r)^n}. \tag{18B.10}$$

Equivalence to Breakeven Withdrawal Tax Rate for Initial Investment

The breakeven withdrawal tax rate previously mentioned is equal to that for the choice between a traditional IRA and a Roth IRA when the investment decision is initially made as long as the pretax investment is maximized. In this case, $I_{BT}(1 - T_o) = L$. Substituting this expression into the breakeven Equation 18A.12 produces

$$T_n = T_o - (1 - T_o)\left(\frac{I_{BT}}{I_{BT}(1 - T_o)} - 1\right)\left\{1 - \frac{(1 + r^*)^n(1 - T^*) + T^*}{(1 + r)^n}\right\}. \tag{18B.11}$$

Setting 1 in the large parentheses equal to $I_{BT}(1 - T_o)/I_{BT}(1 - T_o)$, distributing terms, and canceling terms yields Equation 18B.10. Therefore, the breakeven withdrawal tax rates are equal.

APPENDIX 18C: DERIVATION OF BREAKEVEN WITHDRAWAL TAX RATE FOR NONDEDUCTIBLE IRA

The withdrawal tax rate at which an investor is indifferent between a taxable account and a nondeductible IRA satisfies the condition that Equation 18.11 equals Equation 18.12. Setting them equal to each other yields

$$\text{FV}_{TX} = \text{FV}_{NonDedIRA}$$
$$(1 + r^*)^n(1 - T^*) + T^* = (1 + r)^n(1 - T_n) + T_n. \tag{18C.1}$$

Rearranging and solving yields

$$T_n = \frac{(1 + r)^n - (1 + r^*)^n(1 - T^*) - T^*}{(1 + r)^n - 1}.$$

(18C.2)

When a portion of the IRA contribution is deductible and another portion is nondeductible, the future value of a dollar withdrawn as a single cash flow can be expressed as

$$FV_{PartDedIRA} = (1 + r)^n(1 - T_n) + aT_n,$$

(18C.3)

where a is the nondeductible portion of the contribution. If all the contributions to the IRA account are nondeductible, a is equal to 1. Following the identical logic as previously mentioned, the breakeven withdrawal tax rate for a partially deductible IRA is

$$T_n = \frac{(1 + r)^n - (1 + r^*)^n(1 - T^*) - T^*}{(1 + r)^n - a}.$$

(18C.4)

APPENDIX 18D: DERIVATION OF FUTURE VALUE INTEREST FACTOR OF A TAXABLE ANNUITY

Consider an annuity investment in which an after-tax dollar is invested each year for m years into a taxable investment. In this case, the future value of this accumulation can be expressed as the sum of the future values of each annual investment, or

$$FVIFA_{TX,r,m} = \sum_{t=0}^{m-1}[(1 + r^*)^t(1 - T^*) + T^*].$$

(18D.1)

Distributing the summation operator and factoring out $(1 - T^*)$ yields

$$FVIFA_{TX,r,m} = (1 - T^*)\sum_{t=0}^{m-1}(1 + r^*)^t + \sum_{t=0}^{m-1}T^*.$$

(18D.2)

Substituting the well-known expression for the future value of an annuity yields

$$FVIFA_{TX,r,m} = (1 - T^*)\frac{(1 + r^*)^m - 1}{r^*} + mT^*.$$

(18D.3)

APPENDIX 18E: BREAKEVEN INVESTMENT HORIZON FOR A TRADITIONAL IRA AND A ROTH IRA

Beginning with Equation 18.25 as a breakeven condition, I can divide both sides by $(1 + r)^n$ and $(1 - T_o)$, distribute the terms, and divide through by $(1 - T^*)$, yielding

$$\left[\frac{1 + r^*}{1 + r}\right]^n = \frac{(1 - T_n - \phi)}{(1 - T_o)(1 - T^*)} - \frac{T^*}{(1 + r)^n(1 - T^*)}.$$

(18E.1)

Because n is an exponent on both sides, no closed-form solution exists and solving for n requires an iterative process of trial and error. If the investment return is fully taxed as ordinary income, the simplified tax structure sets $p_{oi} = 1$ and $p_{cg} = 0$. In this case, $T^* = 0$ and $r^* = r(1 - t_{oi})$ and the previous equation simplifies the breakeven condition to

$$\left[\frac{1 + r(1 - t_{oi})}{1 + r}\right]^n = \frac{(1 - T_n - \phi)}{(1 - T_o)}.$$

(18E.2)

Taking the natural log of both sides and solving for n produces

$$n = \ln\left[\frac{(1 - T_n - \phi)}{(1 - T_o)}\right] \bigg/ \ln\left[\frac{1 + r(1 - t_{oi})}{1 + r}\right]. \qquad (18E.3)$$

If the investment is taxed entirely as capital gain, then $p_{oi} = p_{cg} = 0$, which makes $r^* = r$ and $T^* = t_{cg}$. The breakeven condition in Equation 18.25 then reduces to

$$(1 - T_o)[(1 + r)^n(1 - t_{cg}) + t_{cg}] = (1 + r)^n(1 - T_n - \phi). \qquad (18E.4)$$

Distributing $(1 - T_o)$ and factoring out $(1 + r)^n$ yields

$$(1 + r)^n = \frac{t_{cg}(1 - T_o)}{(1 - T_n - \phi) - (1 - T_o)(1 - t_{cg})}. \qquad (18E.5)$$

Taking the natural log of both sides and solving for n produces

$$n = \ln\left[\frac{t_{cg}(1 - T_o)}{(1 - T_n - \phi) - (1 - T_o)(1 - t_{cg})}\right] \bigg/ \ln(1 + r). \qquad (18E.6)$$

To solve for the breakeven investment horizon for a Roth IRA, set the after-tax and after-penalty future value of a Roth IRA in Equation 18.28 to the future value of a taxable investment yields

$$(1 - T_o)[(1 + r^*)^n(1 - T^*) + T^*] = (1 - T_o)[(1 + r)^n(1 - T_n - \phi) + T_n + \phi]. \qquad (18E.7)$$

I can divide both sides by $(1 - T_o)$ and rearrange terms to produce

$$(1 + r^*)^n(1 - T^*) = (1 + r)^n(1 - T_n - \phi) + T_n + \phi - T^*. \qquad (18E.8)$$

Dividing both sides by $(1 - T^*)$ and by $(1 + r)^n$ yields

$$\left[\frac{1 + r^*}{1 + r}\right]^n = \frac{1 - T_n - \phi}{1 - T^*} + \frac{\phi + T_n - T^*}{(1 + r)^n(1 - T^*)}. \qquad (18E.9)$$

NOTES

1. Historical tax information can be accessed online from the Tax History Project at www.tax.org/Museum.
2. Bureau of Labor Statistics, "National Compensation Survey: Employee Benefits in Private Industry in the United States, 2002–2003," Table 1, p. 5. This survey can be accessed online at www.bls.gov/ncs/ebs/sp/ebbl0020.pdf.
3. Federal Reserve Board, "Flow of Funds Accounts of the United States, First Quarter 2004" (10 June 2004), Tables L.119.b and L.119.c, p. 113. This study can be accessed online at www.federalreserve.gov/releases/z1/20040610/z1.pdf.
4. Federal Reserve Board, "Flow of Funds Accounts of the United States, First Quarter 2004" (10 June 2004), Table L.225.i., p. 113. This study can be accessed online at www.federalreserve.gov/releases/z1/20040610/z1.pdf.
5. Ibid.
6. American Council for Capital Formation, "An International Comparison of Incentives for Retirement Saving and Insurance" (June 1999). This study can be accessed online at www.accf.org/publications/reports/sr-intcompretirement1999.html.
7. American Council for Capital Formation, "Small Saver Incentives: An International Comparison of the Taxation of Interest, Dividends, and Capital Gains" (October 1998). This

study can be accessed online at www.accf.org/publications/reports/sr-smallsaver-oct1998. html.

8. Hubbard and Skinner (1996) and Crain and Austin (1997) have good reviews, from which some of this section is drawn, of legislative developments designed to encourage retirement savings.

9. 401(k) plans and IRAs are somewhat distinct from each other in their access to savings before age 59½.

10. 403(b) plans, which Congress introduced in 1958, are similar to 401(k) plans but are designed for certain employees of public schools, employees of certain tax-exempt organizations, and certain ministers. Keogh plans allow self-employed workers opportunities for tax-deferred retirement savings and have significantly higher contribution limits than IRAs, 401(k) plans, or 403(b) plans. Similar to 401(k) and 403(b) plans, Section 457 plans offer government employees and employees of non-church-controlled tax-exempt organizations opportunities for retirement savings with front-end-loaded tax benefits.

11. Federal Reserve Board, "Flow of Funds Accounts of the United States, First Quarter 2004" (10 June 2004), Table F.225.i, p. 112. This study can be accessed online at www. federalreserve.gov/releases/z1/20040610/z1.pdf.

12. Horan, Peterson, and McLeod (1997) took a similar approach in their analysis. Stout and Barker (1998) also held the pretax investment constant but allowed the pretax contribution to exceed the after-tax contribution limit, which required them to make an assumption about how the pretax investment in excess of the after-tax contribution was invested.

13. Examples include Krishnan and Lawrence (2001) and Horan and Peterson (2001).

14. See Appendix 18A for a proof.

15. See Bernheim, Skinner, and Weinberg (2001) for a discussion of a panel study of income dynamics.

16. I note in the section called Asset Location between Taxable and Tax-Deferred Savings Accounts, as does Reichenstein (2001), that an identical investment has different risk–return characteristics to the investor depending on whether it is held in a taxable or tax-deferred account. Because the government taxes these accounts differently, it also shares in their risk and return differently. The residual risk for the investor is, therefore, affected. I abstract from that notion here to retain the tractability of the analysis.

17. For taxpayers in the 10 percent and 15 percent tax brackets, the JGTRRA of 2003 reduces the tax rate on dividends and capital gains to 5 percent.

18. This after-tax future value interest factor can be easily adapted to accommodate returns partitioned into even more taxable components simply by adding terms to r^* and T^*. It also reduces to more simple forms when the tax structure is less complex. For example, when the return is fully taxed as ordinary income, then $p_{oi} = 100\%$ and $p_{cg} = 0$, in which case r^* reduces to $r(1 - t_{oi})$ and T^* reduces to zero. See Appendix 18A for a more complete discussion.

19. $417,725 = PMT(\text{PVIFA}_{n,r}) \approx \$68,000\{1/0.10 - 1/[0.10(1.10)^{10}]\}$.

20. $3,000(1.10)^{25} = \$32,504$.

21. See, for example, Sibley (2002) and Horan (2002).

22. Several authors have followed this approach, including Krishnan and Lawrence (2001), Horan and Peterson (2001), and Horan (2003).

23. The appropriate model inputs in this case are $p_{oi} = 100$ percent, $p_{cg} = 0$ percent, and $t_{oi} = 28$ percent.

24. The model inputs in this case are p_{oi} = 20 percent, p_{cg} = 45 percent, and t_{oi} = t_{cg} = 15 percent.

25. The appropriate model inputs in this case are p_{oi} = p_{cg} = 0.

26. Krishnan and Lawrence (2001, p. 82)

27. Lewellen (1977) proffers a more complete version of this argument.

28. I expand on the notion of the government's sharing investment risk in the section on Asset Location between Taxable and Tax-Deferred Savings Accounts.

29. Income in excess of the base level (e.g., $175,000 for a couple filing jointly) is taxed at 28 percent. Therefore, the effective marginal rate on income in the next AMT tax bracket is 35 percent (i.e., $0.28 + 0.28 \times 0.25$).

30. Technically, it is a bit higher because a gain of this size will push the taxpayer into the next AMT tax bracket.

31. Taxpayers participating in 401(k) plans were once excluded from making deductible contributions to a traditional IRA. Now, an investor may contribute to both, but there are income limitations on the deductibility of the IRA contribution. Single taxpayers who participate in a qualified employer-sponsored pension plan, such as a 401(k), and who earn less than $50,000 in 2005 can deduct a $4,000 annual IRA contribution. Married joint filers must have a combined income of less than $70,000 in 2005. Partial deductions on the IRA contribution in 2005 are available to single filers earning between $50,000 and $60,000 and to married joint filers with combined income between $70,000 and $80,000. Employees not participating in an available 401(k) plan are not subject to income requirements. This information is summarized in Table 18.2.

32. The algebraic expression for this after-tax accumulation is given by Equation 18.6.

33. The tax savings are based on the pretax investment, not the after-tax investment. For example, a $750 after-tax investment for a 25 percent tax bracket investor is associated with a $1,000 pretax investment. The tax savings of $250 is equal to 25 percent times $1,000.

34. Horan and Peterson (2001) present a similar model in an after-tax investment framework. Appendix 18B shows how Equation 18.8 reduces to Equation 18.6 when the tax savings are reinvested in the 401(k).

35. Note that an 11 percent increase does not mean an 11 percentage point increase.

36. Equation 18.10 reduces to Equation 18.9 when funds to pay the conversion tax are taken from a front-end-loaded TDA.

37. Randolph (1994) was among the first to address this question. Crain and Austin (1997) extended his work, allowing for different tax rates on ordinary and capital gains.

38. Gokhale and Kotlikoff (2003) noted that some investors may be better off with taxable accounts rather than a TDA account if applicable tax rates when assets are withdrawn are higher than when funds are contributed.

39. A standard comparative statics analysis can identify the maximum points, but it offers little insight to the practicing analyst.

40. See, for example, Engen and Gale (2000), Engen, Gale, and Scholz (1996), and Poterba, Venti, and Wise (1996).

41. Reichenstein (1998) and Reichenstein and Jennings (2003), for example.

42. See Sibley (2002), Horan (2002), and Poterba (2004) for examples.

43. Poterba (2004) also followed a similar approach except that his framework used continuous compounding.

44. FV_{10} = $1,000,000(1.10)^{10}$ = $2,593,742. Using this figure as the present value of an annuity and solving for the payment, $2,593,742 = PMT[PVIFA_{20,10\%}]$ = PMT[8.5136]; PMT = $304,660.

45. Reichenstein (2001) and Horan (2002) provided different methods of calculating an investor's after-tax asset allocation and showed how the asset allocation picture can be dramatically affected by ignoring after-tax values.

46. Exceptions do exist. For example, withdrawals for a first-time home purchase or to pay for an education can be exempt from the penalty. See Table 18.2 for more information.

47. Burgess and Madeo (1980), Bogan and Bogan (1982), and O'Neil, Saftner, and Dillaway (1983) are among the first to address the breakeven time horizon in the presence of an early withdrawal penalty.

48. For example, Bogan and Bogan (1982), Mano and Burr (1984), and Doyle (1984).

49. Prakash and Smyser (2003) followed an approach identical to Bogan and Bogan (1982). But Benvin (2003) and Kitces (2003) pointed out that the investment return in their model was taxed entirely as ordinary income and could provide misleading results.

50. The algebraic reason for these zero breakeven points is that the first coefficient in Equation 18.26 becomes zero in this instance.

51. Some of the more comprehensive examples include Shoven and Sialm (2003), Dammon, Spatt, and Zhang (2004), and Huang (2000).

52. For example, Auerbach and King (1983), Huang (2003), Shoven and Sialm (2003), and Dammon, Spatt, and Zhang (2004).

53. The after-tax value factor in this case is 0.957.

54. The amount of borrowing that is used to purchase additional equity is equal to the after-tax value of the stock sold in the traditional IRA plus the preshift equity exposure times the value gain. In other words, $173,933 = $163,200 + 0.381($28,200).

55. Although Reichensten (2001) used similar terminology as that in previous sections of this chapter, his definitions differ slightly from mine. They are, however, conceptually similar.

56. The after-tax value tables in the section called Valuing Tax-Sheltered Assets on an After-Tax Basis demonstrate that this is not always the case. Reichenstein (2001) focuses on returns rather than after-tax accumulations and therefore ignores the withdrawal tax for the TDA. Therefore, his model works for Roth IRAs but not for traditional IRAs.

57. Dammon and Spatt (1996) and Dammon, Spatt, and Zhang (2001) have examined optimal trading, security pricing, consumption, and portfolio decisions in the context of capital gains tax but outside the context of tax-deferred savings accounts.

58. For expositional ease, I am assuming away mandatory distribution requirements.

REFERENCES

Amromin, Gene. 2002. "Portfolio Allocation Choices in Taxable and Tax-Deferred Accounts: An Empirical Analysis of Tax Efficiency." Unpublished manuscript, Board of Governors of the Federal Reserve System.

Auerbach, Alan. J., and Mervyn A. King. 1983. "Taxation, Portfolio Choice, and Debt-Equity Ratios: A General Equilibrium Model." *Quarterly Journal of Economics*, vol. 98, no. 4 (November):587–610.

Benvin, Anthony B. 2003. "On 'The Break-Even Frontier for Early Withdrawal from a Tax Deferred Account.'" *Journal of Financial Planning*, vol. 16, no. 11 (November):20.

Bernheim, B. Douglas., Jonathan S. Skinner, and Steven Weinberg. 2001. "What Accounts for the Variation in Retirement Wealth among U.S. Households?" *American Economic Review*, vol. 91, no. 4 (September):832–857.

Black, Fischer. 1980. "The Tax Consequences of Long-Run Pension Policy." *Financial Analysts Journal*, vol. 36, no. 4 (July/August):21–28.

Bogan, Elizabeth C., and Thomas R. Bogan. 1982. "Individual Retirement Accounts and Preretirement Savings Goals." *Financial Analysts Journal*, vol. 38, no. 6 (November/December):45–47.

Burgess, Richard D., and Silvia A. Madeo. 1980. "A Simulation Study of Tax Sheltered Retirement Plans." *Journal of the American Taxation Association*, vol. 1, no. 2:34–41.

Burman, Leonard E., William G. Gale, Jeffrey Rohaly, and Benjamin Harris. 2002. "The Individual AMT: Problems and Potential Solutions." *National Tax Journal*, vol. 55, no. 3 (September):555–596.

Crain, Terry L., and Jeffrey R. Austin. 1997. "An Analysis of the Trade off between Tax Deferred Earnings in IRAs and Preferential Capital Gains." *Financial Services Review*, no. 6, vol. 4 (Winter):227–242.

Dammon, Robert M., and Chester S. Spatt. 1996. "The Optimal Pricing of Securities with Asymmetric Capital Gains Taxes and Transaction Costs." *Review of Financial Studies*, vol. 9, no. 3 (Fall):921–952.

Dammon, Robert M., Chester S. Spatt, and Harold H. Zhang. 2001. "Optimal Consumption and Investment with Capital Gains Taxes." *Review of Financial Studies*, vol. 14, no. 3 (Fall):583–616.

———. 2004. "Optimal Asset Location and Allocation with Taxable and Tax-Deferred Investing." *Journal of Finance*, vol. 59, no. 3 (June):999–1037.

Doyle, Robert J. 1984. "IRAs and the Capital-Gains Tax Effect." *Financial Analysts Journal*, no. 40, vol. 3 (May/June):60–65.

Engen, Eric, and William Gale. 2000. "The Effect of 401(k) Plans on Household Wealth: Differences across Earnings Groups." Working Paper 8032, National Bureau of Economic Research.

Engen, Eric, William Gale, and J. Karl Scholz. 1996. "The Illusory Effects of Saving Incentives on Saving." *Journal of Economic Perspectives*, vol. 10., no. 4 (Fall):113–138.

Gokhale, Jagadeesh, and Laurence Kotlikoff. 2003. "Who Gets Paid to Save?" In *Tax Policy and the Economy*, vol. 17 (September). Edited by James Poterba. Cambridge, MA: MIT Press.

Horan, Stephen M. 2002. "After-Tax Valuation of Tax-Sheltered Assets." *Financial Services Review*, vol. 11, no. 3 (Fall):253–276.

———. 2003. "Choosing between Tax-Advantaged Savings Accounts: A Reconciliation of Standardized Pretax and After-Tax Frameworks." *Financial Services Review*, vol. 12, no. 4 (Winter):339–357.

———. 2004. "Breakeven Holding Periods for Tax Advantaged Savings Accounts with Early Withdrawal Penalties." *Financial Services Review*, vol. 13, no. 3 (Fall):233–247.

Horan, Stephen M., and Jeffrey H. Peterson. 2001. "A Reexamination of Tax-Deductible IRAs, Roth IRAs, and 401(k) Investments." *Financial Services Review*, vol. 10, no. 1 (Spring):87–100.

Horan, Stephen M., Jeffrey H. Peterson, and Robert McLeod. 1997. "An Analysis of Non-Deductible IRA Contributions and Roth IRA Conversions." *Financial Services Review*, vol. 6, no. 4 (Winter):243–256.

Huang, Jennifer. 2000. "Taxable or Tax-Deferred Account? Portfolio Decisions with Multiple Investment Goals." Unpublished manuscript, Massachusetts Institute of Technology, Cambridge, MA.

————. 2003. "Portfolio Decisions with Taxable and Tax-Deferred Accounts: A Tax-Arbitrage Approach." Unpublished manuscript, Massachusetts Institute of Technology, Cambridge, MA.

Hubbard, Glenn R., and Jonathan S. Skinner. 1996. "Assessing the Effectiveness of Saving Incentives." *Journal of Economic Perspectives*, vol. 10, no. 4 (Fall):73–90.

Kitces, Michael E. 2003. "More on Early Withdrawals and the Breakeven Frontier." *Journal of Financial Planning*, vol. 16, no. 11 (May):20–21.

Krishnan, V. Sivarama, and Shari Lawrence. 2001. "Analysis of Investment Choices for Retirement: A New Approach and Perspective." *Financial Services Review*, vol. 10, no. 1 (Spring):75–86.

Lewellen, Wilbur G. 1977. "Some Observations on Risk-Adjusted Discount Rates." *Journal of Finance*, vol. 31, no. 4 (September):1331–37.

Mano, Ronald M., and Ted Burr. 1984. "IRAs versus Nonsheltered Alternatives for Retirement Savings Goals." *Financial Analysts Journal*, vol. 40, no. 3 (May/June):67–75.

O'Neil, Cherie J., Donald V. Saftner, and Peter M. Dillaway. 1983. "Premature Withdrawals from Retirement Accounts: A Break-Even Analysis." *Journal of the American Taxation Association*, vol. 4, no. 2 (Spring):35–43.

Poterba, James M. 2004. "Valuing Assets in Retirement Accounts." Working Paper CRR WP 2004–11, Center for Retirement Research at Boston College (March).

Poterba, James M., and James A. Samwick. 2003. "Taxation and Household Portfolio Composition: US Evidence from the 1980s and 1990s." *Journal of Public Economics*, vol. 87, no. 1 (January):5–38.

Poterba, James M., Steven F. Venti, and David A. Wise. 1996. "How Retirement Saving Programs Increase Saving." *Journal of Economic Perspectives*, vol. 10, no. 4 (Fall):91–112.

Prakash, Arun. J., and Michael W. Smyser. 2003. "The Break-Even Frontier for Early Withdrawal from a Tax Deferred Account." *Journal of Financial Planning*, vol. 16, no. 8 (November):56–61.

Randolph, William L. 1994. "The Impact of Mutual Fund Distributions on After-Tax Returns." *Financial Services Review*, vol. 3, no. 2 (Summer):127–141.

Reichenstein, William. 1998. "Calculating a Family's Asset Mix." *Financial Services Review*, vol. 7, no. 3 (Fall):195–206.

————. 2001. "Asset Allocation and Asset Location Decisions Revisited." *Journal of Wealth Management*, vol. 4, no. 1 (Summer):16–26.

Reichenstein, William, and William Jennings. 2003. *Integrating Investments and the Tax Code*. Hoboken, NJ: John Wiley & Sons.

Shoven, John B., and Clemens Sialm. 2003. "Asset Location in Tax-Deferred and Conventional Savings Accounts." *Journal of Public Economics*, vol. 88, no. 1/2 (January):23–38.

Sibley, Michael. 2002. "On the Valuation of Tax-Advantaged Retirement Accounts." *Financial Services Review*, vol. 11, no. 3 (Fall):233–251.

Stout, Gary R., and Robert L. Barker. 1998. "Roth IRA Planning." *Journal of Accountancy*, vol. 186, no. 2 (August):59–69.

Tepper, Irwin. 1981. "Taxation and Corporate Pension Policy." *Journal of Finance*, vol. 34, no. 1 (March):1–13.

Terry, Andy, and William C. Goolsby. 2003. "Section 529 Plans as Retirement Accounts." *Financial Services Review*, vol. 12, no. 4 (Winter):309–318.

CHAPTER 19

AFTER-TAX ASSET ALLOCATION

William Reichenstein, CFA

Several studies have found fundamental flaws in the traditional approach to managing individual investors' portfolios, including a failure to distinguish between $1 of pretax funds in a 401(k) and $1 of after-tax funds in either a taxable account or Roth IRA. This chapter recommends that an individual's asset values be converted to after-tax values and the asset allocation be based on the after-tax values. In general, within the target asset allocation, individuals should hold bonds and other assets subject to ordinary income tax rates in retirement accounts and hold stocks, especially passively managed stocks, in taxable accounts.

In the asset management world, agreement is widespread that an investor's most important decision is asset allocation. Based on this consensus, you might think that there is wide agreement about how an individual's asset allocation should be calculated. If you thought this, you would be wrong!

Several studies have concluded that we have been mismanaging individual investors' asset allocations in two ways. First, the asset allocation should distinguish between pretax funds in a tax-deferred account, such as a 401(k), and generally after-tax funds in other savings vehicles. For example, the traditional approach to calculating asset allocation inappropriately implies that $1 of *pretax* funds in a 401(k) is the same size as $1 of *after-tax* funds in a taxable account. Yet, if withdrawn in retirement today by someone in the 33 percent tax bracket, the $1 in the 401(k) would buy $0.67 of goods and services whereas the $1 in the taxable account would buy $1 of goods and services. According to these studies, an individual's asset allocation should be based on assets' after-tax values.[1]

Second, when considering whether someone is prepared for retirement, financial advisers routinely consider income from all resources—Social Security, defined-benefit plans, and the individual's financial portfolio. When considering someone's asset allocations, however, advisers may look only at the financial portfolio. Several studies have concluded that financial

---

Reprinted from the *Financial Analysts Journal* (July/August 2006):14–19.

advisers should manage an individual's extended portfolio, which goes beyond the traditional financial portfolio to include the values of all sources of retirement income.[2]

Not surprisingly, Nobel Laureate Harry M. Markowitz was one of the first to recognize the implications of the "clear differences in the central features of investing for institutions and investing for individuals" (1991, p. 1). To note one key difference, institutional funds are usually tax deferred or tax exempt but individual funds are often taxable. Markowitz stated that the family is clearly concerned with after-tax returns. He discussed the impact of taxes on the calculation of an individual's asset allocation and related issues. Concerning the concept of an individual's extended portfolio, Markowitz proposed studying individual portfolio management as a "game of life" that includes "such things as IRAs, Keogh plans, social security payments, [and] pension plans" (p. 4). The game-of-life model requires the financial adviser to manage the individual's extended portfolio.

A lot of research has been conducted since Markowitz's paper on the differences between managing institutional and individual portfolios. In this chapter, I concentrate on the importance of distinguishing between pretax funds and after-tax funds when calculating asset allocation. I explain why assets' after-tax values should be used in calculating an individual's asset allocation. In addition, I present models that indicate how the choice of savings vehicles affects the percentage of principal effectively owned by, returns received by, and risk borne by the individual investor. Finally, I refer to some of the investment implications of this after-tax asset allocation framework.

LOGIC OF AFTER-TAX ASSET ALLOCATION

This section builds on previous research concluding that the traditional approach to calculating an individual's asset allocation is wrong because it fails to distinguish between pretax and after-tax funds. An individual's asset allocation should be based on each asset's after-tax value. In addition, I explain here how pretax funds should be converted to after-tax funds.

Table 19.1 presents the savings vehicles of Dan and Danielle, a married couple in their mid-50s. They are in the 33 percent ordinary income tax bracket before retirement and expect to remain in this bracket during retirement. Dan invests $1,000 today in a 401(k) or any other tax-deferred account (TDA). The contribution reduces his taxable income by $1,000, which reduces taxes by $330. So, this contribution reduces this year's spending by $670. We can think of the $1,000 contribution as consisting of $330 of tax savings plus $670 of Dan's after-tax funds. Danielle invests $670 today in a Roth IRA. Both Danielle's $670 contribution to the Roth and Dan's $1,000 contribution to the 401(k) represent contributions of $670 of after-tax funds, and they both reduce this year's spending by $670.

Each invests in the same mutual fund for the same length of time. It could be a money market fund, a bond fund, or a stock fund. For simplicity, assume it's a stock fund and the monies are withdrawn during retirement after the account values have doubled. The Roth IRA is worth $1,340 after taxes (assuming the Roth was established at least 5 years earlier and Danielle is at least 59 1/2 years old). The 401(k) is worth $2,000 pretax, which translates to $1,340 after taxes. So, both Dan and Danielle invested $670 of after-tax funds and they are both worth $1,340 after taxes at withdrawal.

Suppose the 401(k) and Roth are Dan and Danielle's only two financial assets. Their market values are $2,000 and $1,340 at retirement, and Danielle transfers her Roth IRA to a bond fund. What is their allocation?

TABLE 19.1   Pretax Funds in 401(k) vs. After-Tax Funds in
Roth IRA

Savings Vehicle	Original Investment	Ending Wealth
Dan—401(k)		
Pretax	$1,000	$2,000
Tax savings	330	660
After tax	$670	$1,340
Danielle—Roth IRA		
After tax	$670	$1,340

According to the traditional approach to calculating their asset allocation, the $2,000 in the 401(k) is 49 percent larger than the $1,340 in the Roth IRA. So, they have a 60 percent stock/40 percent bond asset allocation.

According to the after-tax approach, we should first convert the accounts' market values to after-tax values and then calculate the asset allocation on the basis of these after-tax values. The after-tax approach converts the $2,000 of pretax funds in the 401(k) to $1,340 of after-tax funds. This approach says their asset allocation is 50 percent stocks (Dan's $1,340 after taxes) and 50 percent bonds (Danielle's $1,340 after taxes).

If the traditional approach is wrong, then the profession has been miscalculating individual investors' asset allocations and thus mismanaging their portfolios. Furthermore, the traditional approach's miscalculation—overstating the stock allocation by 10 percent in this example—can be substantial.

This example illustrates three points. First, when calculating asset allocation, the $2,000 of pretax funds in Dan's 401(k) is the same size as the $1,340 of after-tax funds in Danielle's Roth IRA because they both buy the same amount of goods and services. The asset allocation calculation should be based on assets' after-tax values because goods and services are purchased with after-tax funds. Stated differently, the asset allocation calculation should be based on assets' after-tax values because this approach equates after-tax dollars to after-tax dollars. In contrast, the traditional approach equates $1 of *pretax* funds in TDAs to $1 of *after-tax* funds.

Second, when the tax rate in the contribution year equals the tax rate in the withdrawal year, the after-tax value of funds in TDAs grows effectively tax exempt.

Third, we can convert pretax funds in TDAs to after-tax funds by multiplying by $(1 - t_r)$, where t_r is the expected tax rate during retirement. Dan's $1,000 original deposit and the $2,000 at withdrawal should be viewed as worth $670 and $1,340 after taxes. Some individuals may say they do not know what their marginal tax rate will be during retirement. However, because the traditional approach views the $2,000 in the 401(k) as being worth 49 percent more than the $1,340 in the Roth IRA, it implicitly assumes that the expected tax rate during retirement will be zero. Although an individual's tax rate during retirement may be uncertain, an adviser can easily improve upon an implicit assumption of zero.

A second example will illustrate that, even if the tax rates in the contribution year and withdrawal year are not the same, the proper way to convert pretax values in TDAs to after-tax values is to multiply by $(1 - t_r)$. Jake and Janet are similar to Dan and Danielle in that they are in their mid-50s and in the 33 percent tax bracket before retirement, but they expect to be in the 28 percent bracket during retirement. Jake contributes $1,000 to a 401(k) and expects to withdraw the funds during retirement. What is the after-tax value of this investment immediately after the contribution? Although the $1,000 contribution reduces this year's spending only by $670, after the contribution, they should view its after-tax value as $720 or $1,000(1 − t_r). Because Jake expects to withdraw the funds during retirement, the pretax value of his TDA should be converted to after-tax funds by multiplying by (1 − t_r). The after-tax value grows from $1,000(1 − t_r) today to $1,000(1 + r)^n(1 − t_r) in n years, where r is the asset's pretax rate of return. *The after-tax value of tax-deferred accounts grows effectively tax exempt.*

Adjusting Taxable Accounts for Embedded Gains and Losses

Sometimes, an asset in a taxable account has embedded but unrealized capital gains or losses. In this case, the appropriate approach may be to reduce the asset's market value for the embedded tax liability or increase the market value for the tax savings from the embedded tax loss. Unfortunately, as Markowitz noted, "it is not always clear . . . how to treat unrealized capital gains" (1991, p. 9).

Suppose a stock has a market value of $10,000 and a cost basis of $6,000 and the individual is in the 15 percent capital gains tax bracket and 33 percent ordinary income tax bracket. If the stock is sold today as a short-term gain, taxes are $1,320 on the $4,000 gain and the after-tax value is $8,680. If the stock is sold today as a long-term gain, the after-tax value is $9,400. In Reichenstein and Jennings (2003), we argued that the $9,400 after-tax valuation is probably reasonable for individuals who plan to sell the stock within a few years. In two scenarios, however, there will be no taxes on the unrealized gain. If the individual (1) awaits the step-up in basis at death or (2) uses the appreciated asset to finance a charitable donation, the gain is tax free. In these scenarios, the stock's after-tax value will be the same as the market value. In short, there is not one way that is always the "right" way to handle the tax consequences of the unrealized gain. A financial adviser can add value to clients' accounts, however, by helping them understand the tax consequences of their stock management strategies.

Calculating the After-Tax Asset Allocation

To calculate the after-tax asset allocation, we must first convert all asset values to after-tax values and then calculate the asset allocation based on these after-tax values. From my experience, the major adjustment for most individuals is the conversion of pretax funds in their TDAs to after-tax values. In other words, for most individuals, there is relatively little difference between pretax values and after-tax values of assets held in taxable accounts.

SHARING OF PRINCIPAL, RETURNS, AND RISK

Models can indicate how the choice of savings vehicles (e.g., Roth IRA, TDA, or taxable account) affects the individual investor's ownership of principal, returns, and risks. Table 19.2 presents after-tax ending wealth models per $1 currently in a Roth IRA, a TDA, and a taxable account. For assets held in a taxable account, the assumption is that the assets' cost bases equal their market values. The underlying asset can be a bond or stock. The pretax rate of return is r. For simplicity, assume the stock returns are all in the form of capital gains. (The major conclusions do not change, however, as long as any portion of stock returns is taxed at a rate lower than the

TABLE 19.2   After-Tax Ending Wealth Models for Bonds and
Stocks in Various Savings Vehicles

Savings Vehicle	Bonds	Stocks
Roth IRA	$(1 + r)^n$	$(1 + r)^n$
TDA	$(1 + r)^n(1 - t_r)$	$(1 + r)^n(1 - t_r)$
Taxable account		
Bonds	$[1 + r(1 - t)]^n$	
Day trader		$[1 + r(1 - t)]^n$
Active investor		$[1 + r(1 - t_c)]^n$
Passive investor		$(1 + r)^n(1 - t_c) + t_c$
Exempt investor		$(1 + r)^n$

Note: Assumptions are that the individual is at least 59-$\frac{1}{2}$ years old
before withdrawing funds from the Roth and TDA and that the
Roth has been in existence for at least 5 years.

ordinary income tax rate.) Each model presents the after-tax ending wealth after n years per $1 currently in the savings vehicle. The ordinary income tax rate is t for all years before withdrawal and t_r in the withdrawal year. The long-term capital gains tax rate is t_c, and t_c is lower than the ordinary income tax rates (i.e., $t_c < t$ and $t_c < t_r$).

For bonds and stocks held in a Roth IRA, the after-tax ending wealth model is $(1 + r)^n$. The account begins with $1 of after-tax funds and is worth $(1 + r)^n$ after taxes n years hence.

For bonds and stocks held in a TDA, the account begins with $1 of pretax funds. It is worth $(1 + r)^n$ pretax and $(1 + r)^n(1 - t_r)$ after taxes n years hence.

For assets held in taxable accounts, bonds have one model but stocks have a separate model for each management style. For bonds, the model states that $1 of after-tax funds earns r percent pretax annually and grows at the $r(1 - t)$ after-tax rate of return.

Among the stock management styles, the day trader realizes all gains within a year and pays taxes on all returns at the ordinary income tax rate. The active investor realizes all gains as soon as they are eligible for the capital gains tax rate (i.e., at one year and one day) and pays taxes at the long-term capital gains rate, t_c. The investor either actively manages individual stocks or invests in an active stock fund that is managed in this style. According to the model, $1 of after-tax funds earns r pretax annually and grows at the $r(1 - t_c)$ after-tax rate of return.

The passive investor buys and holds stocks for n years and realizes the gain at the end of n years. This investor either passively manages individual stocks or buys and holds passively managed stock funds. The model is $(1 + r)^n(1 - t_c) + t_c$ or, equivalently, $(1 + r)^n - t_c[(1 + r)^n - 1]$. The second version may be easier to explain. The $1 of after-tax money grows tax deferred at the rate of r for n years. Its pretax value immediately before withdrawal is $(1 + r)^n$. Upon withdrawal, the deferred returns—that is, $[(1 + r)^n - 1]$—are taxed at t_c, the capital gains tax rate; the original $1 was already after taxes and can be withdrawn tax free.

As the name implies, exempt investors never pay taxes on capital gains. They either donate the appreciated stock to a qualified charity or await the step-up in basis at death. If they donate the stock, they can deduct the market value, $(1 + r)^n$, and the charity, because of its tax-exempt status, can avoid taxes. If investors await the step-up in basis, then at their

TABLE 19.3 Principal Owned, Return Received, and Risk Borne by Individual Investors in Various Savings Vehicles

Savings Vehicle	Principal	Return	Risk
Roth IRA (bonds and stocks)	100%	100%	100%
TDA (bonds and stocks)	$(1 - t_r)$	100	100
Taxable account			
Bonds	100	$(1 - t)$	$(1 - t)$
Stocks, day trader	100	$(1 - t)$	$(1 - t)$
Stocks, active investor	100	$(1 - t_c)$	$(1 - t_c)$
Stocks, passive investor	100	$> (1 - t_c)$	$> (1 - t_c)$
Stocks, exempt investor	100	100	100

death, their beneficiaries' cost basis is stepped up to $(1 + r)^n$, the market value at death. No one pays taxes on the n years of unrealized capital gains.

These stock models illustrate specific advantages of being a progressively more passive investor. Compared with the day trader, the active investor benefits from the preferential capital gains tax rate. Compared with the active investor, the passive investor defers taxes until the end of the investment horizon. Compared with the passive investor, the exempt investor never pays taxes.

Table 19.3 indicates the percentages of principal effectively owned by, return received by, and risk borne by individual investors in each savings vehicle. As shown, in contrast to bonds and stocks held in a Roth IRA, for bonds and stocks held in a TDA, the investor effectively owns $(1 - t_r)$ of the principal but receives 100 percent of returns and bears 100 percent of risks.

The example of Jake and Janet illustrated this insight. Jake had $1,000 of pretax funds in a TDA and expected to withdraw the funds in retirement, at which time, he would be in the 28 percent tax bracket. When calculating his asset allocation, the adviser should consider today's $1,000 of pretax funds to be $720 of after-tax funds. Jake's after-tax value grows from $1,000(1 - 0.28)$ today to $1,000(1 - 0.28)(1 + r)^n$ in retirement; the after-tax value grows at the pretax rate of return; thus, it grows effectively tax exempt. When bonds are held in taxable accounts (with cost bases equal to market values), the investor owns 100 percent of the principal but receives about $(1 - t)$ of the pretax return and bears about $(1 - t)$ of the pretax risk. The government takes the remaining return and bears the remaining risk.

To illustrate the risk and return sharing of bonds held in taxable accounts, we assume bonds have a 4 percent expected return and 8 percent standard deviation and that the investor is in the 25 percent tax bracket. Suppose bonds earn pretax returns of −4 percent, 4 percent, and 12 percent in three years; that is, they earn the mean return and 1 standard deviation below and above the mean. The standard deviation of these returns is 8 percent. Assuming the 4 percent loss is used to offset that year's taxable income, the investor's after-tax returns are −3 percent, 3 percent, and 9 percent, for a standard deviation of 6 percent. In this case, the investor receives $(1 - t)$ of pretax returns and bears $(1 - t)$ of pretax risk. If the loss is used to offset long-term capital gains that would have been taxed at 15 percent, then the 4 percent pretax loss produces a 3.4 percent after-tax loss; in this case, the investor receives approximately $(1 - t)$ of returns and bears approximately $(1 - t)$ of risk. Although only approximate, Table 19.3 assumes the individual receives $(1 - t)$ of the bond returns and bears $(1 - t)$ of their risk.

When stocks are held in taxable accounts (with cost bases equal to market values), the investor owns 100 percent of the principal but the portion of returns the investor receives and the risk borne depend on the stock management style. For the passive investor, for example, the portion is about $(1 - t_c)$ when the investment horizon is one year, but the effective tax rate decreases as the horizon lengthens. For instance, if the underlying asset earns 8 percent a year for 20 years, then for a $1 original investment, the after-tax ending wealth is

$$(1.08)^{20} (1 - 0.15) + 0.15 = \$4.11.$$

This amount is a 7.33 percent after-tax rate of return:

$$4.11^{(1/20)} - 1 = 0.0733, \text{ or } 7.33\%,$$

which is an effective annual tax rate of

$$\frac{0.08 - 0.0733}{0.08} = 0.084, \text{ or } 8.4\%.$$

To illustrate risk and return sharing, we assume stocks have an 8 percent expected return and 12 percent standard deviation. Stocks earn pretax returns of -4 percent, 8 percent, and 20 percent in three years—that is, the mean return and 1 standard deviation below and above the mean. The standard deviation of -4 percent, 8 percent, and 20 percent is 12 percent. If the 4 percent loss is used that year to offset long-term capital gains, the active investor's after-tax returns are -3.4 percent, 6.8 percent, and 17 percent for a standard deviation of 10.2 percent. In this case, the investor receives $(1 - t_c)$ of pretax returns and bears $(1 - t_c)$ of pretax risk. If the 4 percent loss is used to offset that year's taxable income or a later year's capital gain, the active investor receives about $(1 - t_c)$ of returns and bears about $(1 - t_c)$ of risk, as assumed in Table 19.3.

Table 19.3 provides several lessons:

- First, the adviser should think of the individual investor with a TDA as owning $(1 - t_r)$ of its principal.
- Second, the choice of savings vehicle affects the portion of return received by and risk borne by the individual investor. Individuals effectively receive all returns and bear all risks on assets held in a TDA or Roth IRA, but they generally receive only a portion of returns and bear only a portion of risks on assets held in taxable accounts.
- Third, the same underlying asset can be effectively a different asset when held in a different savings vehicle. For example, consider a bond with a pretax expected return of 4 percent and pretax risk of 8 percent. For an individual in a 25 percent tax bracket, the bond's after-tax return and after-tax risk are 4 percent and 8 percent when the bond is held in a TDA or Roth IRA, whereas after-tax return and risk are about 3 percent and 6 percent when held in a taxable account. Therefore, in a mean–variance optimization, a bond held in a Roth IRA or TDA is effectively a different asset from the same bond held in a taxable account.

The assumption that the cost bases of assets held in taxable accounts equal their market values can be relaxed. When a capital gain is built in, the individual may effectively own less than 100 percent of the principal. But the choice of savings vehicle still affects the portion of returns received by and risk borne by the individual investor.

ASSET LOCATION IN AN AFTER-TAX FRAMEWORK

This framework has implications for the determination of an individual's optimal asset location as well as optimal asset allocation. *Asset location* refers to the decision to locate bonds in retirement accounts and stocks in taxable accounts, or vice versa, while the target asset allocation is retained. Until recently, scholars recommended that these decisions be made sequentially: First, determine the optimal asset allocation, and then, determine the optimal asset location (see Shoven and Sialm 1998; Shoven 1999). Today, we recognize that these decisions must be made jointly.

One of the conclusions we can draw from the after-tax framework is that, except for the extreme case of a day trader, individuals should locate bonds in retirement accounts and stocks, especially passively managed stocks, in taxable accounts. The benefit of this asset location increases with the spread between the ordinary income tax rate and the effective tax rate paid on stocks held in taxable accounts. So, the asset location decision should be most important to high-income individuals who passively manage stocks held in taxable accounts. Reichenstein (2001a) and Dammon, Spatt, and Zhang (2004) examined the implications of stock management style for individuals; Brunel (2001, 2004) expanded asset location issues to include assets held in trusts and other savings vehicles.

CONCLUSION

Taxes matter! Financial advisers who use the traditional approach to calculate individuals' asset allocations are miscalculating their true allocations. This approach fails to distinguish pretax funds from after-tax funds. Furthermore, the measurement errors can be substantial. Obviously, proper management of individuals' portfolios requires proper measurement of their asset allocations. This chapter advocates the calculation of an individual's after-tax asset allocation. This approach compares after-tax funds with after-tax funds, so it corrects the major deficiency in the traditional approach.

Taxes also matter for the choice of savings vehicles. The difference in taxation of assets held in Roth IRAs, TDAs, and taxable accounts affects the portions of principal effectively owned by, returns received by, and risk borne by individual investors. In a Roth IRA, the individual investor effectively owns all principal, receives all returns, and bears all risk. In a TDA, the individual effectively owns $(1 - t_r)$ of principal, receives all returns, and bears all risk. In taxable accounts (with cost bases equal to market values), the individual effectively owns all principal but generally receives only a portion of returns and bears a portion of risk.

Therefore, the after-tax approach has implications for asset location. In general, bonds and other assets whose returns are taxed at ordinary income tax rates should be held in retirement accounts, whereas stocks, especially passively managed stocks, should be held in taxable accounts.

NOTES

1. Reichenstein (1998, 2000, 2001b); Reichenstein and Jennings (2003); Jennings and Reichenstein (2004); Dammon, Spatt, and Zhang (2004).
2. For more discussion of this second issue, see Reichenstein (1998, 2000, 2001b), Reichenstein and Jennings (2003), and Jennings and Reichenstein (2004).

REFERENCES

Brunel, Jean. 2001. "Asset Location—The Critical Variable: A Case Study." *Journal of Wealth Management*, vol. 4, no. 1 (Summer):27–43.

———. 2004. "The Tax Efficient Portfolio." In *The Investment Think Tank*. Edited by Harold Evensky and Deena Katz. Princeton, NJ: Bloomberg Press.

Dammon, Robert M., Chester S. Spatt, and Harold H. Zhang. 2004. "Optimal Asset Location and Allocation with Taxable and Tax-Deferred Investing." *Journal of Finance*, vol. 59, no. 3 (June):999–1037.

Jennings, William, and William Reichenstein. 2004. "A Holistic Approach to Asset Allocation." In *The Investment Think Tank*. Edited by Harold Evensky and Deena Katz. Princeton, NJ: Bloomberg Press.

Markowitz, Harry M. 1991. "Individual versus Institutional Investing." *Financial Services Review*, vol. 1, no. 1:1–8.

Reichenstein, William. 1998. "Calculating a Family's Asset Mix." *Financial Services Review*, vol. 7, no. 3:195–206.

———. 2000. "Calculating the Asset Allocation." *Journal of Wealth Management*, vol. 3, no. 2 (Fall):20–25.

———. 2001a. "Asset Allocation and Asset Location Decisions Revisited." *Journal of Wealth Management*, vol. 4, no. 1 (Summer):16–26.

———. 2001b. "Rethinking the Family's Asset Allocation." *Journal of Financial Planning*, vol. 14, no. 5 (May):102–109.

Reichenstein, William, and William W. Jennings. 2003. *Integrating Investments and the Tax Code*. New York: John Wiley & Sons.

Shoven, John B. 1999. "The Location and Allocation of Assets in Pensions and Conventional Savings Accounts." Working Paper 7007, National Bureau of Economic Research (March).

Shoven, John B., and Clemens Sialm. 1998. "Long Run Asset Allocation for Retirement Savings." *Journal of Wealth Management*, vol. 1, no. 2 (Summer):13–26.

CHAPTER 20

WITHDRAWAL LOCATION WITH PROGRESSIVE TAX RATES

Stephen M. Horan, CFA

Optimal withdrawal strategies are developed for retirees with multiple types of tax-advantaged savings accounts. In an environment of progressive tax rates, the ability to convert pretax funds in traditional IRAs at low tax rates substantially increases investors' residual accumulations and withdrawal sustainability. Specifically, informed withdrawal-location strategies, in which traditional IRA distributions can be applied against exemptions, deductions, and lightly taxed tax brackets, can increase residual accumulations by more than $1 million. In these strategies, the optimal tax bracket through which an investor should take distributions is directly related to the investor's wealth level.

As a growing percentage of the population enters retirement, increasing numbers of investors are facing critical decisions about withdrawing funds from tax-advantaged savings accounts, sometimes referred to as tax-deferred savings accounts (TDAs). Moreover, as defined-contribution plans become increasingly popular, retirees and those planning for retirement are forced to make decisions that past generations did not have to make. The introduction of various tax-advantaged savings accounts [e.g., Roth IRAs, Section 529 plans, and Roth 401(k) plans] complicates matters and increases the decisions retirees face.

Fortunately, researchers have recognized these trends and developed models to help guide financial planners and investors. Most advances thus far, however, have focused on tax-efficient *investment* decisions. That is, research has examined the optimal choice among various TDAs (e.g., those with front-end tax benefits versus those with back-end tax benefits), Roth IRA conversion decisions, and early-withdrawal penalties.[1] In *Tax-Advantaged Savings Accounts and Tax-Efficient Wealth Accumulation* (Horan 2005b), my intention was to provide a review and synthesis of the literature on tax-efficient investing and extend or advance previous technologies in a cohesive theoretical framework.

Reprinted from the *Financial Analysts Journal* (November/December 2006):77–87.

Tax-efficient withdrawal, the focus of this chapter, has attracted less attention. Retirees with multiple types of tax-advantaged accounts from which to withdraw, however, would benefit from guidance regarding optimal withdrawal policies. For example, should traditional IRA or Roth IRA balances be drawn down first? Should a retiree use some combination of withdrawals from both accounts?

The term "withdrawal location" derives from the literature on asset location, which analyzes the types of accounts (taxable or tax advantaged) in which investors should hold bonds and equity.[2] In the 1980s, Black (1980) and Tepper (1981) proffered an arbitrage argument for corporate pension funds that can be extended to individual investors to suggest that they should place highly taxed assets, such as bonds, in tax-sheltered accounts and place tax-preferenced securities, such as equity, in taxable accounts. To the extent that bonds are undesirable to the investor from an asset allocation perspective, he or she should offset lending in the tax-sheltered account with borrowing in the taxable account. Other authors have extended this basic premise to consider such factors as borrowing constraints, the use of municipal bonds, trading behavior, and liquidity constraints.[3]

Several authors have investigated the sustainability of retirement withdrawals, but few have focused on tax-efficient withdrawal policies.[4] An exception is work by Ragsdale, Seila, and Little (1993, 1994), who approached the issue from the perspective of tax codes. They developed a mathematical programming model that incorporated a myriad of then-prevailing tax regulations governing retirement distributions, including early-withdrawal penalties, minimum distribution taxes, excess distribution taxes, and estate taxes. Since the publication of their work, the Taxpayer Relief Act of 1997 (TRA) has repealed excess distribution taxes and introduced the Roth IRA, changing the calculus and balance of considerations. Also, in an unpublished manuscript (Horan 2005a), I showed heuristically that if tax rates vary over time, retirees with multiple types of TDAs can benefit from taking traditional IRA distributions when tax rates are low and taking Roth IRA distributions when tax rates are high. I developed that work in a deterministic framework, however, that lacks the insights that Monte Carlo analysis would provide.

In this chapter, in contrast to those works, I develop a model that focuses on the salient features of a tax code with multiple marginal tax rates and abstracts from the code's seemingly infinite loopholes and minutiae. Specifically, the model recognizes that withdrawals from some types of accounts are taxed as ordinary income and withdrawals from other accounts are not taxed. Therefore, the ability to choose the type of account from which to make withdrawals is valuable and the model is designed to highlight opportunities for tax-efficient withdrawal locations created by a progressive tax rate system.

The analysis considers a progressive tax rate structure characterized by exemptions and deductions. This approach is meaningful for investors for whom retirement account withdrawals represent the totality of taxable income. In that case, withdrawals are subject to a series of progressively higher tax rates. This chapter also has implications for the literature addressing after-tax valuation of assets held in TDAs.[5] Although the models vary in their degree of sophistication, none recognizes that a portion of traditional IRA distributions may be tax exempt or subject to a series of marginal tax rates. Therefore, this chapter may help advance our understanding of after-tax valuation of TDAs.

THE MODEL

The withdrawal model is designed for the presence of a progressive tax rate scheme with six tax brackets that allow exemptions and deductions. Withdrawals from a tax-advantaged account with front end–loaded tax benefits, such as a traditional IRA, are taxed as ordinary income.

In contrast, withdrawals from tax-advantaged accounts, such as a Roth IRA, are not taxed.[6] It applies to investors who have little to no exogenous taxable income that might otherwise deplete the exemptions, deductions, or tax brackets with modest rates—that is, in cases where retirement withdrawals represent the totality of taxable income.[7] And the model is designed to analyze the impact of various withdrawal algorithms on residual accumulations and withdrawal sustainability.

Consider a retiree with balances in both a traditional IRA and a Roth IRA, the pretax balance in each account at any time t is represented by, respectively, $V_{Trad,t}$ and $V_{Roth,t}$. The portfolios are similarly invested to generate a pretax expected return, r, over some withdrawal horizon, n. The retiree intends to make after-tax withdrawals initially equal to w percent of the combined pretax value of the two accounts at the beginning of the year. The retiree increases this initial after-tax withdrawal annually by g to maintain purchasing power. Therefore,

$$W_t \equiv w(V_{Trad,0} + V_{Roth,0})(1 + g)^{t-1}$$

represents the retiree's after-tax withdrawal requirement for period t.

The retiree can implement one of eight withdrawal strategies: two naive strategies and six informed strategies. The first naive strategy satisfies the retiree's after tax withdrawal requirement by making withdrawals from the traditional IRA each year until its balance is depleted, at which time, withdrawals from the Roth IRA commence. The second naive strategy reverses this sequence by satisfying the retiree's after-tax withdrawal requirement from the Roth IRA until its balance is depleted and then from the traditional IRA.

The six informed distribution strategies withdraw from the traditional IRA balance, if available, either up to the exemption and deduction limit or up to a specified tax bracket. The available exemptions and deductions and the level of tax brackets grow by the rate of inflation, π, over time.[8] Any additional funds required to satisfy the after-tax withdrawal requirement are distributed from the Roth IRA.

For example, consider a retiree with a $50,000 after-tax withdrawal requirement and with exemptions and deductions totaling $16,400. In the tax regime, taxable income up to $14,600 is taxed at 10 percent. Based on the first of the informed withdrawal strategies, the retiree would take $16,400 from the traditional IRA and the remaining $33,600 from the Roth IRA, in which case the investor would pay no tax on distributions. In the second informed withdrawal strategy, the retiree would take $31,000 from the traditional IRA. Of this amount, $16,400 would escape taxation and $14,600 would be taxed modestly at 10 percent, generating a total after-tax distribution of $29,540. The remaining $20,460 after-tax required distribution would be withdrawn from the Roth IRA. The remaining informed withdrawal strategies would be similarly constructed except that each withdrawal from the traditional IRA would increase taxable distributions to the next tax bracket. Appendix 20A contains mathematical algorithms for these withdrawal strategies.

RESIDUAL ACCUMULATIONS AND WITHDRAWAL SUSTAINABILITY

Scenario analysis can help decipher the effects of withdrawal strategies on residual accumulations and withdrawal sustainability. The base case is a retiree with $1,000,000 in pretax funds in a traditional IRA and $666,667 in a Roth IRA. These balances are comparable on a taxable-equivalent basis because distributions from these two accounts are taxed differently.[9] The base case also assumes that a retiree has a 6 percent after-tax withdrawal requirement, so the initial after-tax distribution is \$100,000 [that is, 0.06 × (\$1,000,000 + \$666,667)], and this distribution grows by 3 percent annually (i.e., $g = 3$ percent) over a 25-year withdrawal horizon.[10] For a meaningful comparison of residual accumulations of traditional and Roth IRAs at the end of this time period, I compare them on a taxable-equivalent basis, similar to the view of the initial balances.[11] For example, the "traditional, then Roth" withdrawal strategy might leave \$80,000 remaining in the Roth IRA at the end of 25 years. At an 8 percent return, this sum would produce annual after-tax withdrawals of \$11,922 for 10 years. The residual accumulation would then be converted to a "taxable equivalent"—that is, a sum held in a taxable account that would produce the same after-tax 10-year annuity produced by the Roth IRA. I apply a similar procedure, assuming a 28 percent tax rate on distributions, to residual balances in the traditional IRA.[12] In any case, the reported results are insensitive to these conditions.

The analysis begins with the personal exemptions, standard deduction, and tax brackets for a married couple filing jointly in 2005, as displayed in Table 20.1. Of course, individual circumstances vary, but the analysis can be modified accordingly.[13] The levels of the exemptions and tax brackets generally increase over time by the rate of inflation. The base case assumes that these values increase at the 2.5 percent inflation rate. A pretax return of 8 percent is also assumed.

Panel A of Table 20.2 displays residual accumulations 25 years hence and withdrawal sustainability under various after-tax withdrawal rates for each of the six strategies: the two naive strategies (withdrawing from either the traditional IRA or Roth IRA until the balance is depleted, then withdrawing from the other) and the six informed strategies (taking distributions from the traditional IRA up to the available exemptions and deductions or up to the top of a specified tax bracket and satisfying the remainder of the withdrawal requirement from the Roth IRA). According to Panel A, withdrawing from the

TABLE 20.1   Data for a Married Couple Filing Jointly in 2005

Adjusted Gross Income		Taxed at Rate
From	To	
\$ 0	\$ 16,400[a]	0%
16,400	31,000[b]	10
31,000	75,800	15
75,800	136,350	25
136,350	199,200	28
199,200	342,850	33
342,850	Greater	35

[a]This amount represents personal exemptions plus the standard deduction. Taxpayers over the age of 65 are entitled to an additional standard deduction of \$1,000 per spouse.
[b]This amount represents the top of the 15 percent tax bracket plus the personal exemptions and deductions, or \$14,600 plus \$16,400. The remaining amounts in this column should be interpreted analogously.

TABLE 20.2 Residual Accumulations and Withdrawal Sustainability for Various Strategies and Withdrawal Rates

				Withdrawal Rate, w					
Strategy	4.0%	4.5%	5.0%	5.5%	6.0%	6.5%	7.0%	7.5%	8.0%
A. Residual accumulations and withdrawal sustainability									
Naive 1: Trad., then Roth	4,612,749	3,648,393	2,704,153	1,772,786	869,832	[24]	[21]	[19]	[17]
Naive 2: Roth, then trad.	3,735,164	3,000,054	2,250,068	1,491,069	722,091	[24]	[21]	[18]	[16]
Withdrawal from trad.									
Up to exemption	3,878,717	3,142,400	2,389,500	1,622,084	846,444	61,375	[21]	[19]	[17]
Up to 10% bracket	4,087,292	3,237,748	2,468,517	1,697,960	921,667	131,395	[22]	[19]	[17]
Up to 15% bracket	4,649,409	3,799,865	2,950,321	2,130,777	1,251,233	401,689	[23]	[20]	[18]
Up to 25% bracket	4,612,749	3,648,393	2,704,153	1,772,786	869,832	[24]	[21]	[19]	[17]
Up to 28% bracket	4,612,749	3,648,393	2,704,153	1,772,786	869,832	[24]	[21]	[19]	[17]
Up to 33% bracket	4,612,749	3,648,393	2,704,153	1,772,786	869,832	[24]	[21]	[19]	[17]
B. Incremental residual accumulations and withdrawal sustainability over Naive 1									
Naive 2: Roth, then trad.	−877,585	−648,339	−454,085	−281,717	−147,741	[0]	[0]	[1]	[1]
Withdrawal from trad.									
Up to exemption	−734,033	−505,993	−314,653	−150,702	−23,388	nmf	[0]	[0]	[0]
Up to 10% bracket	−525,457	−410,644	−235,635	−74,826	51,835	nmf	[1]	[0]	[0]
Up to 15% bracket	36,660	151,472	246,168	327,991	381,400	nmf	[2]	[1]	[1]
Up to 25% bracket	0	0	0	0	0	[0]	[0]	[0]	[0]
Up to 28% bracket	0	0	0	0	0	[0]	[0]	[0]	[0]
Up to 33% bracket	0	0	0	0	0	[0]	[0]	[0]	[0]

Notes: For an investor with $1 million in a traditional IRA and $666,667 in a Roth IRA. The amounts in brackets represent the number of years over which withdrawals are fully sustained.

nmf = not a meaningful figure.

489

traditional IRA until funds are exhausted before withdrawing from the Roth IRA (Naive 1) is the better of the two naive strategies. Taking initial distributions from the traditional IRA rather than the Roth IRA is preferable because a portion of the distribution is applied to exemptions and deductions and a portion is taxed very lightly—at 10 percent or 15 percent. In fact, distributions up to $75,800 are taxed at 15 percent or less. This modest tax burden decreases the pretax distribution required to generate the after-tax withdrawal requirement, leaving more after-tax assets in tax-sheltered accounts. Panel B shows that incremental residual accumulations from Naive 1 over Naive 2 range from about $150,000 to about $900,000.

The traditional, then Roth IRA strategy (Naive 1) performs far better than the reverse strategy because Naive 2 wastes chances in early retirement years to take traditional IRA distributions that are shielded from tax. Although the Naive 2 strategy avoids taxes in the initial years of retirement, it misses opportunities to convert pretax funds in traditional IRAs to after-tax funds at "low" rates (as the reader will see, "low" is a relative term). Note that neither of the naive withdrawal strategies sustains withdrawal rates greater than 6 percent for the 25-year horizon.

The performance of the informed strategies in comparison with Naive 1 is presented in Panel B of Table 20.2. The informed withdrawal strategies take distributions from the traditional IRA equal to the allowable exemptions and deductions or up to the top of a specific tax bracket. The remainder of the withdrawal requirement is satisfied from the Roth IRA. According to Panel B, only one informed strategy performs substantially better than Naive 1. Taking distributions from the traditional IRA through the 15 percent tax bracket with any additional withdrawal requirement met from Roth IRA distributions is optimal. This strategy can produce residual accumulations almost $400,000, or more than 40 percent, greater than Naive 1. And the difference tends to increase, although not monotonically, with the withdrawal rate. At high withdrawal rates, the optimal withdrawal strategy produces an extra year or two of sustainability. Making traditional IRA withdrawals through the 25 percent or higher tax brackets produces identical results to the Naive 1 strategy because it yields identical withdrawal patterns; that is, distributions are taken from the traditional IRA until funds are depleted. As the reader will see, the optimal withdrawal strategy for wealthier investors is to make withdrawals through higher tax brackets.

Note that, despite the assumption of stable returns, no informed strategy can sustain growing withdrawals greater than 6.5 percent of the initial pretax values beyond 25 years. Part of the reason is that the base case assumes that the nominal value of the withdrawal is growing at a higher rate than the value of the tax brackets. Furthermore, sustainable withdrawal rates in a dynamic environment in which returns are a random variable that varies from one year to the next are usually lower than they are in a stable, deterministic environment (see Milevsky and Robinson 2005).

Among the sources of uncertainty in this analysis is the long-term rate of inflation. Therefore, it is useful to know whether inflation rates, which drive the nominal growth in tax brackets, affect the relative value of the various withdrawal strategies. Table 20.3 presents outcomes of the strategies for various long-term inflation rates and tells a consistent story. Table 20.3 assumes the base-case withdrawal rate of 6 percent and assumes that this withdrawal grows at a nominal rate of 3 percent regardless of the rate of inflation. Although withdrawing from the traditional IRA first (Naive 1) is the better naive strategy, making withdrawals through the 15 percent tax bracket produces the best outcomes, regardless of the inflation rate. Other informed strategies also perform better than Naive 1

TABLE 20.3 Residual Accumulations and Withdrawal Sustainability for Various Withdrawal Strategies by Inflation Rate

	Inflation Rate, n								
Strategy	1.0%	1.5%	2.0%	2.5%	3.0%	3.5%	4.0%	4.5%	5.0%
A. Residual accumulations and withdrawal sustainability									
Naive 1	819,581	837,613	853,836	869,832	886,292	903,228	920,655	938,588	957,042
Naive 2	589,019	633,216	679,324	722,091	760,729	802,432	847,449	896,050	944,147
Withdrawal from trad.									
Up to exemption	720,025	761,250	805,280	846,444	883,378	923,271	965,795	1,011,133	1,055,811
Up to 10% bracket	795,754	833,140	877,461	921,667	959,914	995,232	1,033,484	1,081,723	1,119,973
Up to 15% bracket	1,098,153	1,147,432	1,199,995	1,251,233	1,251,643	1,253,376	1,250,943	1,252,000	1,251,194
Up to 25% bracket	830,620	840,199	853,836	869,832	886,292	903,228	920,655	938,588	957,042
Up to 28% bracket	819,581	837,613	853,836	869,832	886,292	903,228	920,655	938,588	957,042
Up to 33% bracket	819,581	837,613	853,836	869,832	886,292	903,228	920,655	938,588	957,042
B. Incremental residual accumulations and withdrawal sustainability over Naive 1									
Naive 2	−230,562	−204,397	−174,512	−147,741	−125,563	−100,796	−73,206	−42,538	−12,895
Withdrawal from trad.									
Up to exemption	−99,556	−76,363	−48,556	−23,388	−2,914	20,042	45,139	72,545	98,770
Up to 10% bracket	−23,827	−4,473	23,625	51,835	73,622	92,004	112,828	143,135	162,931
Up to 15% bracket	278,571	309,819	346,159	381,400	365,351	350,148	330,288	313,412	294,152
Up to 25% bracket	11,039	2,586	0	0	0	0	0	0	0
Up to 28% bracket	0	0	0	0	0	0	0	0	0
Up to 33% bracket	0	0	0	0	0	0	0	0	0

Notes: For an investor with $1 million in a traditional IRA and $666,667 in a Roth IRA. Withdrawal rate = 6 percent; withdrawal growth rate = nominal 3 percent.

491

TABLE 20.4   Incremental Accumulations and Withdrawal Sustainability of Best Informed Strategy vs. Naive Strategies

Pretax Return, r	Withdrawal Rate, w								
	4.0%	5.0%	6.0%	7.0%	8.0%	9.0%	10.0%	11.0%	12.0%
A. Best informed strategy compared with Naive 1									
4.0%	11,007	13,120	19,359	25,860	36,660	−9,801	−10,651	−11,590	−12,629
5.0%	[1]	[1]	154,942	196,209	246,168	186,960	75,441	−63,952	−132,543
6.0%	[1]	[1]	[1]	nmf	381,400	350,836	290,313	209,975	76,204
7.0%	[0]	[1]	[1]	[1]	[2]	492,904	461,616	427,419	367,318
8.0%	[0]	[0]	[0]	[1]	[1]	[1]	[2]	658,583	581,295
9.0%	[1]	[0]	[0]	[0]	[0]	[1]	[1]	[2]	842,716
10.0%	[0]	[1]	[0]	[0]	[0]	[0]	[1]	[1]	[1]
B. Best informed strategy compared with Naive 2									
4.0%	93,007	217,295	391,243	616,064	914,245	1,166,237	1,472,935	1,854,903	2,276,311
5.0%	[1]	[1]	246,447	442,633	700,253	901,968	1,151,434	1,463,537	1,856,915
6.0%	[1]	[1]	[1]	134,353	529,142	711,215	899,745	1,165,882	1,497,068
7.0%	[0]	[1]	[1]	[1]	[2]	549,371	725,433	951,426	1,207,116
8.0%	[0]	[0]	[0]	[1]	[2]	[1]	[2]	806,279	1,030,683
9.0%	[1]	[0]	[0]	[1]	[0]	[1]	[1]	[2]	930,775
10.0%	[0]	[1]	[0]	[0]	[0]	[0]	[1]	[2]	[1]

Notes: For an investor with $1 million in a traditional IRA and $666,667 in a Roth IRA. The "best informed strategy" is defined as making withdrawals from the traditional IRA through the 15 percent tax bracket. Figures in brackets represent the incremental number of years over which withdrawals are fully sustained.

nmf = not a meaningful figure.

in some situations. Specifically, at low inflation rates, making withdrawals through the top of the 25 percent tax bracket performs better than Naive 1. Making withdrawals through the 15 percent tax bracket, however, is still optimal. At high inflation rates, making withdrawals through the 10 percent bracket performs better than Naive 1. Again, differences approach $400,000.

Panel A of Table 20.4 displays the incremental outcomes of the best informed strategy (making withdrawals from the traditional IRA through the 15 percent tax bracket) over Naive 1 for various withdrawal tax rates and pretax returns. The advantage of the informed strategy generally increases with the pretax return and the withdrawal rate. Specifically, the incremental value of the informed strategy is greatest for high returns and high withdrawal rates, with incremental accumulations exceeding $500,000 in many cases. This result indicates that following an informed strategy is particularly important for retirees with aggressive investment and withdrawal strategies. Panel B indicates that the outperformance of the best informed strategy over the worst naive strategy, Naive 2, is enormous—with incremental residual accumulations of approximately $2 million in some cases.

Consider now an investor who is twice as wealthy as the one in this base case; that is, this higher-net-worth (HNW) investor has $2 million in a traditional IRA and $1.33 million in a Roth IRA. For this investor, Panel A of Table 20.5 shows that the optimal strategy is to take taxable withdrawals from the traditional IRA through the 25 percent tax bracket—an informed strategy that more than doubles the residual accumulation of either naive strategy. Panel B indicates that the incremental accumulations can be almost $800,000 more than those of Naive 1. As previously, informed withdrawal-location strategies can add an additional year or two to withdrawal sustainability. Panel C examines for the HNW investor the incremental accumulation for various pretax rates of return. At high rates of return and aggressive withdrawal rates, incremental residual accumulation over Naive 1 approaches $1.5 million. Comparing these results with those in Table 20.4 shows that these differences can be two to three times as large as the differences for the more moderately endowed investor. In unreported results, I found that incremental residual accumulations can exceed $2 million.

Table 20.6 displays incremental accumulations for an investor endowed with $3 million of traditional IRA assets and $2 million of Roth IRA assets (a HNW+ investor). Panel A indicates that the optimal strategy for this investor is to take taxable distributions from the traditional IRA up through the top of the 28 percent tax bracket, in which case residual accumulations can be about $1.2 million greater than Naive 1 provides. Alternatively, the investor can sustain withdrawals for an additional year or two. At higher rates of withdrawal and pretax return, the investor's residual accumulations may be more than $2 million greater than Naive 1 provides (see Panel B).

In unreported results, I found that taking taxable distributions from the traditional IRA up to the top of the 28 percent tax bracket is also optimal for investors with $4 million in traditional IRA assets. For investors with a $6 million balance in a traditional IRA, this informed strategy remains optimal in many situations, but taking taxable distributions from the traditional IRA up through the top of the 33 percent tax bracket may be preferable for higher withdrawal rates. Part of the reason that taking taxable distributions from the traditional IRA up through the 28 percent tax bracket remains optimal in many situations is that the increment to the next tax bracket represents 5 percentage points (33 percent minus 28 percent) rather than 3 percentage points (28 percent minus 25 percent).

TABLE 20.5 Residual Accumulations and Withdrawal Sustainability for the HNW Investor

A. Residual accumulations and withdrawal sustainability

					Withdrawal Rate, w				
Strategy	4.0%	4.5%	5.0%	5.5%	6.0%	6.5%	7.0%	7.5%	8.0%
Naive 1	8,053,069	6,192,727	4,332,948	2,468,964	626,853	[22]	[19]	[17]	[15]
Naive 2	7,172,878	5,576,834	3,919,076	2,241,291	535,219	[22]	[19]	[17]	[15]
Withdrawal from trad.									
Up to exemption	7,398,864	5,789,938	4,123,259	2,432,715	718,471	[22]	[19]	[17]	[15]
Up to 10% bracket	7,535,905	5,917,392	4,242,863	2,542,995	833,386	[23]	[20]	[17]	[16]
Up to 15% bracket	8,038,681	6,339,593	4,643,161	2,922,385	1,180,053	[23]	[20]	[18]	[16]
Up to 25% bracket	8,215,521	6,516,433	4,817,345	3,118,257	1,419,169	[24]	[20]	[18]	[16]
Up to 28% bracket	8,053,069	6,198,733	4,488,889	2,789,801	1,090,713	[23]	[20]	[18]	[16]
Up to 33% bracket	8,053,069	6,192,727	4,332,948	2,468,964	626,853	[22]	[19]	[17]	[15]

B. Incremental residual accumulations and withdrawal sustainability over Naive 1

					Withdrawal Rate, w				
Strategy	4.0%	4.5%	5.0%	5.5%	6.0%	6.5%	7.0%	7.5%	8.0%
Naive 2	−880,191	−615,892	−413,872	−227,673	−91,635	[0]	[0]	[0]	[0]
Withdrawal from trad.									
Up to exemption	−654,205	−402,789	−209,689	−36,249	91,618	[0]	[0]	[0]	[0]
Up to 10% bracket	−517,164	−275,334	−90,084	74,031	206,533	[1]	[1]	[0]	[1]
Up to 15% bracket	−14,388	146,866	310,213	453,421	553,200	[1]	[1]	[1]	[1]
Up to 25% bracket	162,453	323,707	484,397	649,293	792,316	[2]	[1]	[1]	[1]
Up to 28% bracket	0	6,006	155,942	320,837	463,860	[1]	[1]	[1]	[1]
Up to 33% bracket	0	0	0	0	0	[0]	[0]	[0]	[0]

C. Best informed strategy compared with Naive 1 strategy

Withdrawal Rate, w

Pretax return, r	4.0%	5.0%	6.0%	7.0%	8.0%	9.0%	10.0%	11.0%	12.0%
4.0%	111,358	139,499	198,438	236,182	162,453	59,832	0	0	0
5.0%	[1]	[1]	397,233	492,688	484,397	468,184	415,752	352,797	249,674
6.0%	[0]	[1]	[1]	[1]	792,316	853,783	890,125	936,720	1,000,058
7.0%	[0]	[1]	[1]	[1]	[1]	[1]	1,174,363	1,343,135	1,474,675
8.0%	[0]	[0]	[0]	[1]	[1]	[1]	[1]	nmf	1,664,095
9.0%	[0]	[1]	[0]	[0]	[0]	[1]	[0]	[1]	[2]
10.0%	[0]	[0]	[0]	[1]	[0]	[0]	[0]	[1]	[1]

Notes: For an investor with $2 million in a traditional IRA and $1.33 million in a Roth IRA. The "best informed strategy" is defined as making withdrawals from the traditional IRA through the 25 percent tax bracket. Figures in brackets represent the number of years over which withdrawals are fully sustained. nmf = not a meaningful figure.

TABLE 20.6 Incremental Accumulations and Withdrawal Sustainability for the HNW + Investor

A. Incremental residual accumulations and withdrawal sustainability over Naive 1

	Withdrawal Rate, w								
Strategy	4.0%	4.5%	5.0%	5.5%	6.0%	6.5%	7.0%	7.5%	8.0%
Roth then Trad.	−619,178	−381,985	−243,143	−109,156	−90,339	[0]	[0]	[0]	[0]
Trad. to exemption	−336,603	−117,865	3,820	106,523	95,455	[0]	[1]	[1]	[0]
Trad. to 10% bracket	−157,137	30,193	162,344	233,105	261,719	[0]	[1]	[1]	[0]
Trad. to 15% bracket	351,061	532,091	608,983	681,158	647,166	[1]	[1]	[1]	[0]
Trad. to 25% bracket	527,902	747,442	927,666	994,119	941,822	[1]	[1]	[1]	[0]
Trad. to 28% bracket	527,902	747,442	927,666	1,142,672	1,235,763	[2]	[2]	[1]	[1]
Trad. to 33% bracket	0	0	13,529	227,463	362,451	[1]	[1]	[1]	[0]

B. Best informed strategy compared with Naive 1 strategy

	Withdrawal Rate, w								
Pretax Return, r	4.0%	5.0%	6.0%	7.0%	8.0%	9.0%	10.0%	11.0%	12.0%
4.0%	262,441	336,910	439,532	532,912	527,902	500,983	479,161	560,472	645,717
5.0%	[0]	[1]	nmf	842,905	927,666	1,026,338	1,162,437	1,264,916	1,396,507
6.0%	[1]	[0]	[1]	[1]	1,235,763	1,491,103	1,718,239	1,958,873	2,268,839
7.0%	[0]	[0]	[1]	[1]	[2]	[2]	nmf	2,396,025	2,868,060
8.0%	[0]	[1]	[1]	[1]	[1]	[1]	[1]	323,389	2,622,180
9.0%	[1]	[0]	[0]	[1]	[1]	[1]	[1]	[1]	[2]
10.0%	[1]	[0]	[1]	[0]	[0]	[1]	[1]	[0]	[1]

Notes: For an investor endowed with $3 million of traditional IRA assets and $2 million of Roth IRA assets. The "best informed strategy" is defined as making withdrawals from the traditional IRA through the 28 percent tax bracket. Figures in brackets represent the number of years over which withdrawals are fully sustained. nmf = not a meaningful figure.

CONCLUSION

This chapter investigated the effects of various withdrawal patterns on residual accumulations and withdrawal sustainability for retirees having two types of tax-advantaged savings accounts from which to make withdrawals in a progressive tax rate regime. Because distributions from traditional IRAs are taxable and those from Roth IRAs are not, making withdrawals from traditional IRAs is advantageous when the tax burden is light and making withdrawals from Roth IRAs is advantageous when the tax burden would otherwise be heavy. When taxable distributions can be applied against personal exemptions and deductions or against tax brackets with relatively low tax rates, a naive strategy of withdrawing from the traditional IRA first was found to perform substantially better than the naive strategy of withdrawing from the Roth IRA first. However, an informed strategy of taking traditional IRA distributions up to the top of a "low" tax bracket and satisfying the remainder of the withdrawal requirement from the Roth IRA yields residual accumulations that are substantially greater than the better naive strategy.

Of course, minimum distribution requirements from traditional IRAs dictate to some extent required withdrawals from traditional IRAs after age 70-$\frac{1}{2}$. To the extent retirees have discretion over accounts from which they make withdrawals, however, they can manage their tax obligations and dramatically affect their residual accumulations and withdrawal sustainability.

Light and heavy tax burdens mean different things to different investors. The definition of a "low" tax bracket is directly related to an investor's wealth. I found that for retirees with initial balances in traditional and Roth IRAs of, respectively, $1 million and $667,000, the optimal strategy is to take taxable distributions through the top of the 15 percent tax bracket. Residual accumulations may be $400,000, or 40 percent, greater than the better naive strategy (Naive 1). For initial balances in traditional and Roth IRAs of, respectively, $2 million and $1.33 million, the optimal strategy was found to be making taxable withdrawals through the top of the 25 percent tax bracket. Residual balances in this case could be $800,000 to $1.5 million for investors with high-return portfolios and aggressive withdrawal strategies. When initial traditional and Roth IRAs balances are, respectively, $3 million and $2 million, I found that the optimal strategy is to make withdrawals through the top of the 28 percent tax bracket. Incremental accumulations were found to exceed $1 million and could exceed $2.5 million for investors with high-return portfolios and aggressive withdrawal strategies.

In general, the value of an informed strategy increases as the aggressiveness of both the retiree's investment strategy and withdrawal requirements increases. As a result, retirees can significantly improve the sustainability of their retirement portfolios by embarking on an optimal withdrawal program that exploits opportunities to take traditional IRA distributions at low tax rates.

This theme generalizes well to other tax rate structures. For example, distributions from traditional IRAs may not be subject to multiple marginal tax rates but to a single, uniform marginal tax rate because other taxable income exhausts the opportunity to use exemptions, deductions, and tax brackets with low tax rates. Nonetheless, if tax rates vary over time (because of changes in political regimes, fiscal policy, or the investor's tax status), the overriding lesson remains: Withdraw funds from traditional IRAs when funds will be taxed at low rates.

Several avenues for future research are suggested by this chapter. First, mandatory distribution requirements from traditional IRAs could be incorporated into the withdrawal models.

Second, this chapter suggests valuable withdrawal strategies to the extent that minimum distribution requirements allow. This constraint may not be binding in many circumstances because the optimal naive strategy calls for the retiree to deplete the traditional IRA before making Roth IRA withdrawals. Furthermore, the optimal informed strategy calls for significant withdrawals from the traditional IRA anyway. In either case, the retiree is making substantial traditional IRA distributions. Therefore, future research might formally incorporate the effect of traditional IRA distributions on the taxation of Social Security benefits or implement similar withdrawal models that assume a different return structure. Third, future research might integrate the impact on withdrawal location of taxable accounts outside traditional and Roth IRA plans.

Finally, on a fundamental level, this chapter highlights the notion that investors derive option value from having more than one type of account from which to make retirement withdrawals. Therefore, a contingent-claims analysis assuming a stochastic marginal tax rate based on Monte Carlo simulations would help estimate the value to investors of having withdrawal flexibility. The insights from this analysis would then have implications for an investor's initial asset-location decision. Alternatively, one could apply a Monte Carlo analysis to different tax rate regimes by using simulated returns based on historical time series of various asset classes, based on an assumed distribution with parameters derived from historical experience, or based on a factor model.

At any rate, the results contained in this chapter provide valuable lessons to retirees and their advisers. In particular, withdrawal strategies should capitalize on opportunities to convert pretax funds in traditional IRAs to after-tax funds at low tax rates.

APPENDIX 20A: ALGORITHMS FOR WITHDRAWAL STRATEGIES

To model the withdrawal strategies, the first step is to establish a function that defines the pretax distribution that would be required to generate a particular after-tax cash flow, X, in a progressive tax rate structure characterized by exemptions and deductions at low income levels and six tax brackets. Such a function, P, can be expressed as

$$P(X) = \min(X, A_{0,t}) + \sum_{j=1}^{6} \frac{\max[0, \min(X, A_{j,t}) - A_{j-1,t}]}{1 - T_{bj}}, \qquad (20A.1)$$

where $A_{j,t}$ is the top of the jth tax bracket in period t and T_{bj} is the applicable tax rate for bracket j. In this formulation, $A_{0,t}$ represents exemptions and deductions available in period t. So, $A_{1,t}$ is the sum of $A_{0,t}$ and the amount of income that could be taxed at T_{b1}.

Note that the tax brackets in Equation 20A.1, $A_{j,t}$, are expressed on an after-tax basis. For example, for the retiree discussed in the text with a $50,000 after-tax withdrawal requirement and with exemptions and deductions totaling $16,400, A_1 is not $31,000, or $16,400 plus $14,600. Rather, A_1 is $29,540, the after-tax income resulting from $31,000 of taxable income.

The inverse of this function, the after-tax proceeds of a pretax withdrawal, Y, can be expressed as

$$F(Y) = \min(Y, B_{0,t}) + \sum_{j=1}^{6} \max[0, \min(Y, B_{j,t}) - B_{j-1,t}](1 - T_{bj}), \qquad (20A.2)$$

where $B_{j,t}$ is the top of the jth tax bracket expressed on a pretax basis in period t. For instance, B_0 would be $16,400 and B_1 would be $31,000 in the example.

Naive Withdrawal Strategies

For either IRA account type i, let the value of the account at time t be

$$V_{i,t} = V_{i,t-1}(1 + r), \tag{20A.3}$$

which reflects the effect of the tax-sheltered investment earnings on asset growth. Therefore, the traditional IRA distribution for the first naive strategy, in which the retiree draws from the traditional IRA until funds are depleted, can be expressed as

$$D_{1,Trad,t} = \min[P(W_t), V_{Trad,t}]. \tag{20A.4}$$

The first value inside the minimum operator, $P(W_t)$, is the pretax withdrawal from the traditional IRA necessary to generate the after-tax withdrawal requirement, W_t. It recognizes that portions of the pretax withdrawal are taxed at potentially six different rates. The second value inside the minimum operator, $V_{Trad,t}$, is the remaining traditional IRA balance if it is insufficient to satisfy the after-tax withdrawal requirement.

The Roth IRA distribution is then

$$D_{1,Roth,t} = \max\{0, \min[W_t - F(D_{Trad,t}), V_{Roth,t}]\}, \tag{20A.5}$$

which implies that withdrawals from the Roth IRA should commence once the balance in the traditional IRA becomes insufficient to meet the after-tax withdrawal requirement. These withdrawals are constrained to not exceed the available Roth IRA balance. Notice that the pretax distribution function in Equation 20A.1 is not applied to W_t because withdrawals from Roth IRAs are not taxed, whereas traditional IRA distributions are considered on an after-tax basis.

The residual balance in either type of IRA at withdrawal horizon n can now be expressed as the future value of the initial balance less the future value of any distributions:

$$V_{i,n} = V_0(1 + r)^n - \sum_{t=1}^{n} D_{i,t}(1 + r)^{n-t}. \tag{20A.6}$$

The second naive withdrawal strategy directs the retiree to make withdrawals from the Roth IRA as long as funds are available, followed by withdrawals from the traditional IRA. In this case, the Roth IRA withdrawal algorithm is

$$D_{2,Roth,t} = \min[W_t, V_{Roth,t}]. \tag{20A.7}$$

The traditional IRA withdrawal is similar to Equation 20A.4, but the desired after-tax income from the traditional IRA is not W_t. It is the difference between the after-tax withdrawal requirement and the Roth IRA distribution, if positive. Substituting $\max(0, W_t - D_{Roth,t})$ for W_t in Equation 20A.4 yields

$$D_{2,Trad,t} = \min\{P[\max(0, W_t - D_{Roth,t})], V_{Trad,t}\}. \tag{20A.8}$$

Informed Withdrawal Strategies

Each of the six informed withdrawal strategies specifies withdrawals from the traditional IRA up to some exemption or tax bracket limit, $B_{j,t}$, to the extent that funds are available and to the extent that the withdrawal requirement demands the withdrawals. The first informed withdrawal strategy makes traditional IRA withdrawals up to allowable exemptions and deductions, $B_{0,t}$. The second informed withdrawal strategy makes traditional IRA withdrawals up to the first tax bracket, $B_{1,t}$, and so on. The remaining withdrawal requirement, if any, would be distributed from the Roth IRA. Each of these strategies for tax bracket j can be expressed with the following algorithms,

$$D_{j,Trad,t} = \max\{\min[B_{j,t}, V_{Trad,t}, P(W_t)], \min[P(W_t - V_{Roth,t}), V_{Trad,t}]\} \quad (20A.9)$$

and

$$D_{j,Roth,t} = \min(W_t - D_{Trad,t}, V_{Roth,t}). \quad (20A.10)$$

The first algorithm, Equation 20A.9, stipulates a traditional IRA withdrawal up to the top of the jth tax bracket in period t, $B_{j,t}$, subject to fund availability and the size of the withdrawal requirement. The second algorithm, Equation 20A.10, indicates that the remaining withdrawal requirement will be distributed from the Roth IRA to the extent that funds are available. If the Roth IRA contains insufficient funds for the remainder of the withdrawal, the traditional IRA is tapped for the additional withdrawal, which is represented in the second value in the braces of Equation 20A.9. One advantage of these strategies is that they relax, at least to some degree, the constraints imposed by traditional IRA minimum distribution requirements, which are not explicitly incorporated into the models. That is, minimum distribution requirements mandate traditional IRA withdrawals that these informed strategies call for anyway, potentially making the minimum distribution constraint nonbinding.

NOTES

1. For example, Burgess and Madeo (1980); Bogan and Bogan (1982); O'Neil, Saftner, and Dillaway (1983); Mano and Burr (1984); Doyle (1984); Randolph (1994); Crain and Austin (1997); Horan, Peterson, and McLeod (1997); Krishnan and Lawrence (2001); Horan and Peterson (2001); Horan (2003, 2004); Gokhale and Kotlikoff (2003); Prakash and Smyser (2003); Benvin (2003); Kitces (2003).
2. I thank an anonymous referee for suggesting the use of the term "withdrawal location."
3. Authors who have examined asset location include Auerbach and King (1983), Reichenstein (2001), Shoven and Sialm (2003), Huang (2003), and Dammon, Spatt, and Zhang (2004). A proper treatment of asset location requires an understanding of the after-tax value of tax-sheltered assets. Reichenstein (1998), Sibley (2002), Horan (2002), Reichenstein and Jennings (2003), and Poterba (2004) are among those who have addressed the issue of valuing tax-sheltered assets on an after-tax basis.
4. Papers focusing on the sustainability of withdrawals include Cooley, Hubbard, and Walz (1998, 1999, 2001, 2003a, 2003b), Tezel (2004), Ervin, Filer, and Smolira (2005), and Milevsky and Robinson (2005). Sabelhaus (2000) analyzed aggregate accumulations and withdrawals for the United States.
5. For example, Reichenstein and Jennings (2003); Poterba (2004); Horan (2002, 2005b).
6. For succinctness, I use the term "traditional IRA" to represent generically all tax-deferred accounts with front-loaded tax benefits, including 401(k), 403(b), 457, and Keogh plans. Similarly, the term "Roth IRA" is understood as generally representing TDAs with back-loaded tax benefits, such as Section 529, Roth 401(k), and lifetime savings accounts. Therefore, the applicability of the model developed in the chapter is broader than the terminology I use might suggest.

7. Alternatively, an investor might have exogenous income that subjects retirement distributions to a single marginal tax rate. I investigated this setting in Horan (2005a).

8. Inflation rate π, by which tax brackets are assumed to grow over time, is distinct from g, the nominal growth rate of the retiree's withdrawal amount. The simulations assume that π is 2.5 percent and g is 3.0 percent, so the growth rate of the retiree's withdrawal does more than preserve purchasing power; that is, withdrawals grow slightly in real terms over time.

9. Sibley (2002) and Horan (2002) showed that the taxable equivalent of a traditional IRA equals $(1 - T_n)$ of a Roth IRA with the same pretax balance. Others have advocated after-tax approaches (e.g., Reichenstein 1998; Reichenstein and Jennings 2003), but the distinction is irrelevant in this case.

10. Keep in mind that growth in nominal distributions is distinct from the general rate of inflation.

11. Because a portion of Social Security benefits may, depending on the retiree's total income and marital status, be taxable, a retiree's marginal tax rate can be a bit elusive. Traditional IRA withdrawals are treated as income, so these distributions can make some Social Security benefits subject to tax, thereby increasing the effective marginal tax rate.

12. I supply details of this conversion procedure in Horan (2005b). An alternate and more straightforward approach is to evaluate residual balances on an after-tax basis.

13. In addition to the additional standard deduction of $1,000 for a spouse that taxpayers over the age of 65 are entitled to, taxpayers may have itemized deductions that would shield additional distributions from taxation.

REFERENCES

Auerbach, Alan J., and Mervyn A. King. 1983. "Taxation, Portfolio Choice, and Debt–Equity Ratios: A General Equilibrium Model." *Quarterly Journal of Economics*, vol. 98, no. 4 (November):587–610.

Benvin, Anthony B. 2003. "On 'The Break-Even Frontier for Early Withdrawal from a Tax Deferred Account.'" *Journal of Financial Planning*, vol. 16, no. 11 (November):20.

Black, Fischer. 1980. "The Tax Consequences of Long-Run Pension Policy." *Financial Analysts Journal*, vol. 38, no. 4 (July/ August):31–38.

Bogan, Elizabeth C., and Thomas R. Bogan. 1982. "Individual Retirement Accounts and Preretirement Savings Goals." *Financial Analysts Journal*, vol. 38, no. 6 (November/ December):45–47.

Burgess, Richard D., and Silvia A. Madeo. 1980. "A Simulation Study of Tax Sheltered Retirement Plans." *Journal of the American Taxation Association*, vol. 1, no. 2 (Winter):34–41.

Cooley, Philip L., Carl M. Hubbard, and Daniel T. Walz. 1998. "Retirement Savings: Choosing a Withdrawal Rate That Is Sustainable." *AAII Journal*, vol. 10, no. 3 (February):16–21.

———. 1999. "Sustainable Withdrawals from Your Retirement Portfolio." *Financial Counseling and Planning*, vol. 10, no. 1 (September):39–47.

———. 2001. "Withdrawing Money from Your Retirement Portfolio without Going Broke." *Journal of Retirement Planning*, vol. 4, no. 4 (September/October):35–42.

———. 2003a. "A Comparative Analysis of Retirement Portfolio Success Rates: Simulation versus Overlapping Periods." *Financial Services Review*, vol. 12, no. 2 (Summer):115–138.

———. 2003b. "Does International Diversification Increase the Sustainable Withdrawal Rates from Retirement Portfolios?" *Journal of Financial Planning*, vol. 16, no. 1 (January): 74–80.

Crain, Terry L., and Jeffrey R. Austin. 1997. "An Analysis of the Tradeoff between Tax Deferred Earnings in IRAs and Preferential Capital Gains." *Financial Services Review*, vol. 4, no. 6 (Winter):227–242.

Dammon, Robert M., Chester S. Spatt, and Harold H. Zhang. 2004. "Optimal Asset Location and Allocation with Taxable and Tax-Deferred Investing." *Journal of Finance*, vol. 59, no. 3 (June):999–1037.

Doyle, Robert J. 1984. "IRAs and the Capital-Gains Tax Effect." *Financial Analysts Journal*, vol. 40, no. 3 (May/June):60–65.

Ervin, Danny M., Larry H. Filer, and Joseph C. Smolira. 2005. "International Diversification and Retirement Withdrawals." *Mid-American Journal of Business*, vol. 20, no. 1 (Spring):55–63.

Gokhale, Jagadeesh, and Laurence Kotlikoff. 2003. "Who Gets Paid to Save?" In *Tax Policy and the Economy*. Edited by James Poterba. Cambridge: MIT Press.

Horan, Stephen M. 2002. "After-Tax Valuation of Tax Sheltered Assets." *Financial Services Review*, vol. 11, no. 3 (Fall):253–276.

———. 2003. "Choosing between Tax-Advantaged Savings Accounts: A Reconciliation of Standardized Pre-Tax and After-Tax Frameworks." *Financial Services Review*, vol. 12, no. 4 (Winter):339–357.

———. 2004. "Breakeven Holding Periods for Tax Advantaged Savings Accounts with Early Withdrawal Penalties." *Financial Services Review*, vol. 13, no. 3 (Fall):233–247.

———. 2005a. "Optimal Withdrawal Strategies for Retirees with Multiple Savings Accounts." Unpublished manuscript, St. Bonaventure University.

———. 2005b. *Tax-Advantaged Savings Accounts and Tax-Efficient Wealth Accumulation*. Charlottesville, VA: Research Foundation of CFA Institute.

Horan, Stephen M., and Jeffrey H. Peterson. 2001. "A Reexamination of Tax-Deductible IRAs, Roth IRAs, and 401(k) Investments." *Financial Services Review*, vol. 10, no. 1 (Spring):87–100.

Horan, Stephen M., Jeffrey H. Peterson, and Robert McLeod. 1997. "An Analysis of Non-Deductible IRA Contributions and Roth IRA Conversions." *Financial Services Review*, vol. 6, no. 4 (Winter):243–256.

Huang, Jennifer. 2003. "Portfolio Decisions with Taxable and Tax-Deferred Accounts: A Tax-Arbitrage Approach." Unpublished manuscript, Massachusetts Institute of Technology.

Kitces, Michael E. 2003. "More on Early Withdrawals and the Breakeven Frontier." *Journal of Financial Planning*, vol. 16, no. 11 (May):20–21.

Krishnan, V. Sivarama, and Shari Lawrence. 2001. "Analysis of Investment Choices for Retirement: A New Approach and Perspective." *Financial Services Review*, vol. 10, no. 1 (Spring):75–86.

Mano, Ronald M., and Ted Burr. 1984. "IRAs versus Nonsheltered Alternatives for Retirement Savings Goals." *Financial Analysts Journal*, vol. 40, no. 3 (May/June):67–75.

Milevsky, Moshe A., and Chris Robinson. 2005. "A Sustainable Spending Rate with Simulation." *Financial Analysts Journal*, vol. 61, no. 6 (November/December):89–100.

O'Neil, Cherie J., Donald V. Saftner, and Peter M. Dillaway. 1983. "Premature Withdrawals from Retirement Accounts: A Break-Even Analysis." *Journal of the American Taxation Association*, vol. 4, no. 2 (Spring):35–43.

Poterba, James M. 2004. "Valuing Assets in Retirement Accounts." *National Tax Journal*, vol. 57, no. 2 (June):489–512.

Prakash, Arun J., and Michael W. Smyser. 2003. "The Break-Even Frontier for Early Withdrawal from a Tax Deferred Account." *Journal of Financial Planning*, vol. 16, no. 8 (November):56–61.

Ragsdale, Cliff T., Andrew F. Seila, and Philip L. Little. 1993. "Optimizing Distributions from Tax-Deferred Retirement Accounts." *Personal Financial Planning*, vol. 5, no. 3:20–28.

————. 1994. "An Optimization Model for Scheduling Withdrawals from Tax-Deferred Retirement Accounts." *Financial Services Review*, vol. 3, no. 2 (Summer):93–108.

Randolph, William L. 1994. "The Impact of Mutual Fund Distributions on After-Tax Returns." *Financial Services Review*, vol. 3, no. 2 (Summer):127–141.

Reichenstein, William. 1998. "Calculating a Family's Asset Mix."*Financial Services Review*, vol. 7, no. 3 (Fall):195–206.

————. 2001. "Asset Allocation and Asset Location Decisions Revisited." *Journal of Wealth Management*, vol. 4, no. 1 (Summer):16–26.

Reichenstein, William, and William Jennings. 2003. *Integrating Investments and the Tax Code*. Hoboken, NJ: John Wiley and Sons.

Sabelhaus, John. 2000. "Modeling IRA Accumulation and Withdrawals."*National Tax Journal*, vol. 53, no. 4 (December):865–875.

Shoven, John B., and Clemens Sialm. 2003. "Asset Location in Tax-Deferred and Conventional Savings Accounts." *Journal of Public Economics*, vol. 88, nos. 1–2 (January):23–38.

Sibley, Michael. 2002. "On the Valuation of Tax-Advantaged Retirement Accounts."*Financial Services Review*, vol. 11, no. 3 (Fall):233–251.

Tepper, Irwin. 1981. "Taxation and Corporate Pension Policy." *Journal of Finance*, vol. 34, no. 1 (March):1–13.

Tezel, Ahmet. 2004. "Sustainable Retirement Withdrawals." *Journal of Financial Planning*, vol. 17, no. 7 (July):52–57.

PART IV

AFTER-TAX PERFORMANCE MEASUREMENT

CHAPTER 21

AFTER-TAX PERFORMANCE EVALUATION

James M. Poterba

Focusing on after-tax returns is a great way to add value and gain competitive advantage in the investment management business. Managers need to understand the factors that affect tax efficiency, to realize that a "one size fits all" performance measure and tax strategy will not work, and to integrate portfolio management with income tax and estate tax planning. Algorithms, such as the "accrual equivalent" tax rate, can help managers educate clients about the various implications of taxes for their portfolios.

The after-tax return associated with a given pretax return may vary considerably among individual tax-paying clients. Portfolio returns from the perspective of pretax reporting or performance management for tax-exempt clients can look very different from returns from the perspective of tax-paying individual investors.

This presentation focuses on the general issue of measuring after-tax performance—how taxes interact with performance management. This focus includes the AIMR Performance Presentation Standards (AIMR-PPS™ standards) and, more generally, the design of broad-based performance evaluation standards. This presentation examines whether an algorithm can be designed and used to tell a particular client the likely after-tax consequences of various portfolio strategies and to compare the after-tax performance of various managers. The presentation also provides an overview of the U.S. income tax environment for high-net-worth households, with particular emphasis on capital gains tax issues. Finally, the presentation reviews three important estate-planning tools that individuals can use to effectively manage estate taxes.

Reprinted from *AIMR Conference Proceedings: Investment Counseling for Private Clients II* (August 2000): 58–67.

WHY THE AFTER-TAX FOCUS

A focus on after-tax returns is worthwhile for several reasons. One is that most managers who work with individual clients know that increasingly sophisticated individual investors are demanding analysis of how their taxes are influenced by manager behavior, portfolio selection, and asset allocation. Therefore, managers need to report results in a way that puts taxes into the broader picture.

Another reason is that reducing the tax drag on a portfolio may be an easier way of increasing after-tax returns than searching for additional pretax risk-adjusted returns (alpha). For example, when a manager is liquidating a position, selling highest-cost-basis shares rather than shares with an acquisition price close to the average basis is straightforward and enhances after-tax returns. A manager does not need to be a rocket scientist or need to accurately predict future earnings to follow that strategy. Therefore, a focus on after-tax returns allows recognition that there is some "low-hanging fruit" that many managers can harvest.

Finally, being able to make a coherent presentation on the tax consequences of various investment strategies and management styles can gain a manager an advantage in the competition for client money.

FACTORS AFFECTING TAX EFFICIENCY

Certain key factors influence any portfolio's tax efficiency—that is, the difference between the portfolio's pretax return and its after-tax return for a taxable investor:

- *Portfolio turnover.* Portfolio turnover is clearly one of the key factors affecting tax efficiency, but the notion that high turnover equals bad tax efficiency is a myth. Turnover is like cholesterol: There is good, and there is bad. Good turnover is the harvesting of losses and the early realization of positions that have losses. Bad turnover is the selling of gains and the early triggering of capital gains tax liability. Tax-efficient portfolios should have more of the good and less of the bad turnover.
- *Inflows versus withdrawals.* A second key factor affecting tax efficiency is the pattern of asset inflows and withdrawals. The importance of this factor is particularly clear when examining the after-tax return performance of mutual funds. Consider two funds that are holding identical portfolios at the beginning of a year, and assume that these portfolios have substantial embedded, unrealized capital gains. One of the funds experiences large redemptions; the other experiences inflows during the year. The redeeming fund will have, on average, a higher tax burden for the year. A central issue that the AIMR-PPS Implementation Committee has wrestled with is the extent to which the manager is burdened with the taxes that are realized as a result of withdrawals that are beyond his or her control.
- *Dividend yield versus capital gains.* This factor, as most managers of taxable assets know, is critical. Because dividends are taxed more heavily than realized capital gains for most taxable investors and because unrealized capital gains are taxed even more favorably, a portfolio that generates a high fraction of its returns in the form of dividends will face a higher tax burden than a fund that generates primarily capital gains.

The factors driving tax efficiency are fairly simple, so clients might expect most managers to behave in a tax-efficient manner. But many managers do not. Several hypothetical examples will show how these factors can increase the difference between pretax and after-tax returns.

Mutual Fund Example

Suppose a hypothetical portfolio has the following characteristics:

Beginning-of-period market value	$10.00
Realized long-term capital gains	1.75
Realized short-term capital gains	0.25
Dividend income	0.50
Unrealized capital gains	0.50
Total pretax earnings	3.00

Pretax returns for this portfolio are an impressive 30 percent for the period. Unfortunately, after-tax returns are significantly less. After-tax returns on this fund, for an individual investor in the top U.S. federal marginal income tax bracket, can be calculated as follows:

$$\frac{\$1.75(1.00 - 0.20) + (\$0.25 + \$0.50)(1.00 - 0.396) + \$0.50}{\$10.00} = 23.5\%.$$

The terms $(1.00 - 0.20)$ and $(1.00 - 0.396)$ correspond, respectively, to the *after-tax* value of one dollar of realized long-term capital gains (taxed at 20 percent) and one dollar of realized short-term gains and dividend income, which is taxed at the federal marginal tax rate of 39.6 percent. Published estimates of pretax and after-tax returns on various mutual funds, such as those reported each year in *BusinessWeek*, show just how much of the pretax return can be consumed by taxes. There is typically enormous variation among mutual fund managers in the amount of taxable income they generate for a given amount of pretax return. This variation reflects differences in each of the portfolio attributes described previously in this section.

Given the range of effective tax burdens among mutual funds and the diversity of effective tax rates among private clients, taxable investors should consider after-tax returns when selecting mutual funds.

Client Portfolio with Cash Withdrawals

Cash inflows and withdrawals also influence after-tax portfolio returns. The following example illustrates the measurement of after-tax performance for a client portfolio that has cash withdrawals:

Initial portfolio value	$1,000
Initial unrealized gains	500
Final prewithdrawal portfolio value	1,150
Final postwithdrawal portfolio value	1,100
Total capital appreciation	150
Client cash withdrawal	50
Realized long-term gains	140
Final unrealized gains	510
Cash dividends (distributed)	30

The pretax return on this portfolio is given by

$$\text{Pretax return} = \frac{\text{Dividends} + \text{Change in portfolio value} + \text{Cash withdrawal}}{\text{Initial value}}.$$

In this example, the pretax return is 18 percent. Suppose the general AIMR-PPS algorithm for after-tax performance measurement is used to measure the after-tax returns. This algorithm is as follows:

$$
\text{After-tax return} = \frac{
\begin{array}{l}
\text{Realized long-term gains } (1 - t_{CG}) \\
+ \text{ (Realized short-term gains} \\
+ \text{ Dividends) } (1 - t_{DIV}) \\
+ \text{ Unrealized gains} + \text{Tax-free income} \\
+ \text{ Client withdrawal adjustment factor}
\end{array}
}{\text{Starting asset value}},
$$

where t_{CG} stands for the marginal tax rate on long-term capital gains realizations and t_{DIV} stands for the ordinary income tax rate that applies to dividend income. These tax rates are set at 20 percent and 39.6 percent, respectively.

In this algorithm, the client withdrawal adjustment factor is

$$
\frac{t_{CG}(\text{Net withdrawal})(\text{Realized} + \text{Unrealized gains})}{(\text{Final portfolio value} + \text{Net withdrawal})}.
$$

When the AIMR-PPS algorithm is used, the after-tax return is significantly less—14.58 percent—than the pretax return of 18 percent. The client withdrawal factor *raises* the reported after-tax return by 6 basis points.

MEASURING AFTER-TAX PERFORMANCE

Differences in investors' income tax rates, and the interplay between investor characteristics and decisions about realizing capital gains, represent major challenges to measuring and evaluating after-tax performance. Therefore, managers need to understand how each investor's federal tax rates and potential estate taxes interact to influence portfolio management decisions. A good starting point for this analysis is the AIMR-PPS algorithm for measuring after-tax performance.

AIMR-PPS Algorithm

According to the AIMRPPS standards, managers are to use the maximum federal statutory rate for each type of client. So, a manager would use 20 percent as the statutory long-term capital gains rate. But the tax rates clients face actually can vary, even among high-net-worth clients. Therefore, managers may want to customize this rate in the calculation of after-tax return. An investor with large capital loss carryforwards from a failed past investment may face a lower effective capital gains tax rate than someone without such a loss carryforward.

The AIMR-PPS standards also tell managers to exclude state and local taxes. The argument for doing so is that people live in different states. Everyone lives in some state, however, and for people who live in high-tax-burden states—in California (where the top income tax rate is 11 percent), New York (where the rate is 7–8 percent at the state level and more for New York City), and Massachusetts (which used to have a 12 percent tax rate on interest and dividend income)—managers should include the state tax rate in the algorithm so they can report what those taxes do to their clients' returns. Few investors would try to compare the returns on taxable and tax-exempt bond portfolios without recognizing the role of federal and state taxes. Similarly, a manager needs to recognize the role of state and local taxes in after-tax equity portfolio performance.

Individual Federal Tax Rates

Individual investors' federal tax rates vary for several reasons.

Dependence of Taxes on Income, Not Wealth

Some investors have substantial accumulated net worth, but their incomes do not put them in the top end of the income distribution. Managers can get a more systematic handle on this information than from anecdotal client interviews from a database that is collected every three years by the U.S. Federal Reserve Board, which is summarized in the Survey of Consumer Finances. This survey is the best publicly available nonproprietary information on the highest-net-worth part of the U.S. population. In collecting these data, the Fed focuses on households in wealthy communities. The result is a database that includes a nontrivial number of respondents from the segment of the U.S. population with the highest net worth.

The data show that only about a fifth of the households that were in the top 1 percent of the income distribution in 1995 were also in the top 1 percent of the net-worth distribution. In 1995, a family needed an income of about $225,000 to be in the top 1 percent of the income distribution. To be in the top 1 percent of the net-worth group, a family needed about $3 million in total household assets, including retirement accounts.

Whether investment managers' clients have high net worth or high income or both may not be clear. Part of the reason is that many individuals in high-net-worth households are past their prime earning years; they may be retirees whose income is primarily capital income. At the same time, some high-earning younger households may not yet have had time to accumulate substantial assets.

Variation in Income and Asset Values

Taxes also vary because different assets generate different income profiles. People with substantial net worth in real estate or municipal bonds, for example, may have low taxable income relative to others in their net-worth category. Therefore, their tax status may be different from that of others with similar net worth.

Special Circumstances

Finally, individuals' taxes vary because of "specialized tax circumstances." The importance of particular tax conditions, such as tax-planning problems generated by low-cost-basis stock, the alternative minimum tax (AMT), or loss carryforwards, is hard to identify. Nevertheless, such factors generate substantial scope for variations in tax rates.

These issues argue against using a one-size-fits-all performance measure. Managers need to think about a particular client's circumstances. The differences can be accounted for in simple computer programs that allow one to plug in various marginal tax rates as well as underlying information about the realization of gains and the income components of a given pretax return. Once the manager understands the person's marginal federal and state tax rates and other tax complications, the manager can tailor the presentation to those conditions.

Marginal Income Tax Rates

The notion of the "effective marginal tax rate" rather than the "average tax burden" should drive both managers' and clients' behavior. In 1998, the top federal marginal tax rates on interest and dividends were 39.6 percent starting at $271,050 of taxable income, 36 percent starting at $151,750, and 31 percent starting at $99,600. In addition, phase-out rules on deductions can propel top-bracket taxpayers into a tax bracket with a marginal tax rate as high as 41 percent. Managers can get a handle on how the rules on deductions affect a client's marginal tax rate by asking the client to add another $200 of interest income to his or her reported taxable income and then to recompute the taxes. In many cases, this additional income will not change the taxes by 39.6 percent times $200. It will change the taxes by more in some (most!) cases and by less in others. This exercise will give managers an idea of the true marginal tax rate the client faces.

The actual dividend tax rate faced by households with different characteristics is revealing. Table 21.1 is based on a data set that the U.S. Internal Revenue Service (IRS) has released for researchers that includes actual (but anonymous) tax returns for tax year 1994. Note that for households that reported at least $50,000 of dividend and interest income, only about 40 percent were facing tax rates higher than 37 percent. Many people who reported that much in dividend and interest income fell in the 28 percent bracket. In other words, a significant number of households with substantial liquid assets face a marginal tax rate that is lower than the top rate. In the category of households receiving dividends and interest of more than $200,000, about 70 percent faced tax rates of more than 37 percent, whereas nearly 95 percent of those who have high wage and salary income are in the 37–41 percent tax range. There is more variation in the taxes on capital income than on earned income.

Capital Gains Taxes

Taxes on interest and dividends are not a very exciting part of the after-tax portfolio problem. Capital gains are where the action is. Most managers know the tax rules on short-term versus long-term capital gains. The tax rate on short-term capital gains—gains on securities held for less than one year—can go as high as 39.6 percent. Today, the top rate on long-term capital gains is 20 percent; starting in 2005, that rate will come down to 18 percent on assets that have been held for at least five years. The difference between the rates on short-term and long-term gains will be even larger in the future than it is today. The tax-efficient strategy, therefore, when all other aspects of a portfolio are the same, is to realize losses and hold gains until they become long term.

TABLE 21.1   Percentage of Households Paying Various Marginal Federal Tax Rates

Marginal Tax Rate	Dividends + Interest > $50,000	Dividends + Interest > $200,000	Wages + Salaries > $500,000
< 16 percent	10.0%	10.5	1.0
16–29 percent	28.4	13.8	3.5
29–37 percent	22.7	4.1	0.3
37–41 percent	37.7	70.2	94.7
> 41 percent	1.3	1.6	0.6
Number of taxpayers	402,800	51,000	76,300

Source: Calculations made using National Bureau of Economic Research TAXSIM model.

TABLE 21.2   Top Federal Marginal Tax Rate over Time

Category	1996	1998	2005 (estimate)
Dividends and interest	~41%	~41%	41%
Long-term capital gains	28	20	18

The advantages of generating long-term capital gains relative to other kinds of portfolio income are larger today than they have been in the past. Table 21.2 shows how the Taxpayer Relief Act of 1997 increased the advantages of tax-efficient investing. As recently as 1989, the top marginal tax rate on the highest dividend income and interest income recipients was 28 percent, which was also the top tax rate on capital gains. During the past decade, a zero tax rate differential has widened to a 20 percentage point differential. In the future, the difference between taxes on capital income and long-term capital gains could be as large as 23 percentage points.

This tax environment explains the benefits of tax-efficient portfolio management, but it also raises the issue of tax code risk. The tax system can shift in ways that destroy the advantages of previous tax-efficient behavior. Should investors and managers try to hedge bets on the tax system? Should taxpayers hold some qualified money in a Roth Individual Retirement Account and some in a traditional IRA? The tax treatment of these accounts is different, and one (the Roth) is not affected by future changes in marginal income tax rates. The answer is probably yes, although deciding how to model tax code risk is an unexplored problem.

Unrealized Capital Gains

One of the most difficult problems in measuring after-tax portfolio performance concerns handling unrealized capital gains. The AIMR-PPS standards recommend ignoring potential future taxes on unrealized capital gains. I believe that some positive tax burden should be applied to unrealized gains because they are not untaxed but, rather, carry a contingent future tax liability.

The precise tax burden on unrealized gains depends on client circumstances. First, is the client likely to face substantial "forced realizations"? Such realizations may result from a transaction that sells them out involuntarily from a position in a low-cost-basis stock or from a substantial consumption demand on the client's part—demand for a new house, a new yacht, or so on. Second, is the client someone who, perhaps because of age, is in a position, from the standpoint of dynastic wealth accumulation, to take advantage of basis step-up at death? Third, is the client going to carry out a gifting strategy that will transfer asset basis to the next generation? If so, the manager should consider carryover basis rather than basis step-up as the likely scenario for assets received by the next generation. These issues can be explored with clients to determine what capital gains tax circumstances apply. They need to be covered in the client's investment plan, not left to the tax planners.

One way to describe the capital gains burden on unrealized gains is with the "accrual equivalent" capital gains tax rate. This concept finds the accrual tax system that gives the client the same total after-tax portfolio value at the end of the "realization period" as the current realization-based system, assuming asset sale at the end of the realization period. The approach is similar to asking what tax rate in New Zealand (which uses an accrual system on capital gains) would give you the same wealth after tax at the end of a given number of years as the 20 percent realization-based tax rate in the United States. The concept is useful to managers in explaining that deferring taxes is not the same as never paying them. It is a way of quantifying the interest-free loan a client is getting from the IRS when the client defers realizing capital gains on a position.

For example, suppose a client buys an asset in Year 0 for $100 and it generates capital gains at 10 percent a year. The asset pays no dividends. If the gains were realized each year and taxed as short-term gains (that is, every 364 days, the manager realized the gains on the position), then the after-tax return each year would be

$$10(1.00 - 0.396) = 6.04\%$$

because the short-term capital gains tax rate is 39.6 percent. After 10 years, no additional taxes would be due and the value would be

$$\$100.00(1.064)^{10} = \$185.96.$$

The value of the portfolio would be greater if the asset were held for 10 years and then the capital gains were realized. Assuming that the asset grew at 10 percent a year for 10 years and that 20 percent of the gains were taxed away in Year 10, the asset's after-tax value in 10 years would be

$$(1.00 - 0.20)[\$100.00(1.10)^{10} - \$100.00] + \$100.00 = \$227.50.$$

The accrual equivalent tax rate depends on the rate of return the asset manager would have had to earn on an after-tax basis year after year to get to the value of $227.50 in 10 years. To find this key bit of information, simply solve the following expression for R, the rate of return:

$$\$100.00(1.00 + R)^{10} = \$227.50.$$

The answer is $R = 8.57\%$. Thus, the accrual equivalent tax rate is

$$\frac{10.00\% - 8.57\%}{10.00\%} = 0.143, \text{ or } 14.30\%.$$

Using the accrual equivalent rate is like comparing the accumulated assets in an IRA with assets that are invested in a taxable account. How can one compare the values of those two investments? One way would be to find the internal rate of return on assets in the IRA that provides the same return as that available, after tax, outside the IRA. The accrual equivalent tax rate is the tax rate that if it were charged to your account every year on the accruing gains, would give you the same after-tax portfolio value at the end of the planning horizon that you would have had if you had been working under the realization-based system in which you pay taxes only at the end. The 14.3 percent accrual equivalent tax rate can be compared with the other tax rates applicable to the client. Because clients are accustomed to thinking in terms of 39.6 percent as an interest tax burden and 20 percent as the statutory tax burden on long-term realized gains, the 14.3 percent is a comparable measure. It describes what the rate would have to be if every year the assets with unrealized gains were marked to market and taxed on their gains.

The accrual equivalent tax rate provides a flexible tool for analyzing future tax burdens. If the client's tax rate is likely to change in the future, the manager can build that change into the calculation of an accrual equivalent tax rate. It can also be used to illustrate the value of deferring capital gains realizations over different horizon lengths.

Table 21.3 shows how the accrual equivalent tax rate changes as the holding period increases. If capital gains were realized after one year, the after-tax return would be 8 percent,

TABLE 21.3   Accrual Equivalent Return by Holding Period

Holding Period	Return
1 year	8.00%
5 years	8.28
10 years	8.57
20 years	8.98
Until death	10.00

which implies a 20 percent effective tax burden relative to the pretax 10 percent return. By 20 years, the tax burden is down to about 10 percent. The best outcome, as far as taxes go, is if the asset is held until death because then the tax liability is extinguished. If this asset generates only capital gains, the accrual equivalent return moves up to the 10 percent pretax return because of basis step-up at death.

The tax return data the IRS receives indicate that in the mid-1990s, the average holding period for corporate stock on which gains were subject to long-term capital gains tax treatment was about 6.5 years. Managers may be able to persuade their clients to hold assets longer by using a similar analysis to that of Table 21.3. This table can also illustrate the important benefits of a low-realization tax-management strategy.

Estate Tax Issues

Table 21.3 shows the potentially substantial tax savings that can flow from holding appreciated assets until death. Is the scenario realistic? Managers need to make some assumptions about the future tax circumstances of clients and about their estate-planning advice to evaluate the chance of basis step-up.

Life expectancy is one factor that applies in judging the likelihood of holding an asset until death. Table 21.4 shows that life expectancy in the United States is quite long, even

TABLE 21.4   Life Expectancy at Various Ages, 1994

Age/Sex	Years Expectancy
65-year-old	
Man	16.1
Woman	20.0
75-year-old	
Man	9.8
Woman	12.8
85-year-old	
Man	5.3
Woman	6.9

Source: U.S. Social Security Administration, unpublished tables used in preparing the 1995 Social Security Administration Trustee's Report.

TABLE 21.5   Age Distribution of 1992 Taxable Decedents

Age at Death (years)	Percentage of Tax Returns	Percentage of Estate Value
< 50	1.9%	3.1%
50–60	3.1	6.2
60–70	9.9	16.0
70–80	23.4	26.7
> 80	61.7	47.9

Source: Martha B. Eller, "Federal Taxation of Wealth Transfers, 1992–1995," *Statistics of Income Bulletin* (Winter 1996–97):8–63.

for people already at advanced ages. These data are based on the entire U.S. population, and the wealthy clients with whom managers deal are likely to live longer than these averages. The exact cause of wealth-related differences in mortality experience is not known, but there is a stark disparity between the mortality rates faced by those in the bottom 20 percent of household income or wealth distribution and those at the top. In short, even if the client is an 85-year-old woman, the client's life expectancy may be 7 years, so whether a basis step-up is just around the corner is hard to judge. Managers, therefore, need to be mindful that the planning horizon, even for older clients, could be substantial.

Most decedents with substantial estates die at quite advanced ages. Table 21.5 shows that in 1992, nearly two-thirds of taxable decedents were in their 80s when they died and more than three-quarters of the value of the estates reported were for decedents who were older than 70.

The estate tax is a large and important tax in relation to other taxes for the small set of taxpayers who are likely to face it. The estate tax will change in the future as a result of a sliding scale of tax thresholds that will phase in between now and 2006. At the moment, an estate must be more than $625,000 to incur federal estate taxes; by 2006, the threshold will be $1 million. Today, marginal estate tax rates start at 37 percent at that $625,000 level and go as high as 60 percent. For a client who is thinking about keeping the assets that he or she has built for the next generation, the estate tax is thus an important part of the tax environment.

Traditional Bequests

Assets can be passed from the wealth accumulator to the next generation in three ways, and the three methods have different tax consequences. The first method, and the one that receives the most attention, is traditional bequests. Assets are held until the accumulator, or the spouse of the accumulator, dies, and then the assets pass as a bequest to the next generation. Such assets are subject to the estate tax. They receive a basis step-up on any accrued unrealized capital gains, but the heirs face a variety of costs at the time of death, which may involve probate, valuation, and other issues. The costs are likely to be lower for publicly traded securities than for interests in privately held businesses or other, less liquid, assets.

Tax-Free Inter Vivos Gifts

The second way to transfer assets is by carrying out a gifting strategy during the lifetime of the accumulator generation. The allowed annual gifts of $10,000 per recipient per donor avoid the estate tax but do not participate in any step-up in basis, so the capital gains tax liability

TABLE 21.6   Households Making Gifts of at Least $10,000 a Year, 1995

Household Head's Age (years)	Net Worth $1.2 Million to $2.4 Million	Net Worth Greater than $2.4 Million
55–64	12%	29%
65–74	20	30
75+	26	22

Source: Federal Reserve Board, the Survey of Consumer Finances.

is not extinguished. In general, high-net-worth clients can have either capital gains tax relief or estate tax relief but not both. So, for taxpayers who could shift a substantial share of the wealth to the next generation in the form of *inter vivos* gifts, the tax gains from basis step-up are not as great as the simple analysis suggests. Capital gains taxes may be reduced at the cost of higher estate taxes.

For anyone who focuses on tax planning, the data on participation in gifting is remarkable. Table 21.6 shows the percentage of households with householders 55 years old or older that gave assets of $10,000 in support of other households by net worth and by age. (The $10,000 is not $10,000 per child; it is simply giving $10,000 total.) The Survey of Consumer Finances, from which these data are drawn, asks donors about their gifts. It also asks the potential recipients, younger households typically, about the *inter vivos* gift amounts that they received. It turns out that the amount of *inter vivos* giving reported is about twice the amount of *inter vivos* receiving that is reported. No one understands why, but keep it in mind when analyzing these numbers. Table 21.6 indicates that only about a fifth of the households that are headed by somebody over the age of 75 with a net worth of more than $2.5 million are making these kinds of gifts. Whatever the reason, the high-net-worth band is leaving unnecessary tax burdens to their heirs by underusing the *inter vivos* giving option.

Taxable Gifts

The third possibility, which is attractive only for very high-net-worth clients, is to make taxable gifts of more than the untaxed $10,000 per recipient a year. On an after-tax basis, pursuing a taxable gifting strategy is attractive for two reasons. The first is that the effective tax burden on a taxable gift is lower than the effective tax burden on a bequest. Estates and gifts are taxed ostensibly under the same tax rules because we have a unified estate and gift tax in the United States. However, gifts are taxed on a net-of-tax basis, whereas bequests are taxed on a gross basis. The result is that if the estate tax rate facing a potential decedent is T, the tax rate on the gifts is $T/(1 + T)$ instead of T. With a 50 percent statutory tax rate, the tax rate on the gifts (0.5/1.5) effectively becomes a 33 percent rate instead of a 50 percent rate. This consideration is very important, and it is widely underappreciated.

Taxable gifting is greatly preferable to leaving assets to pass through a taxable estate. This is true because of the tax rate difference and because paying the gift tax avoids the later estate and gift tax liability on whatever subsequent appreciation occurs on the assets given away. Appreciation on the assets and income on the assets will accrue to the next generation instead of to the donor generation. The gifting strategy raises, once again, the income tax versus estate tax trade-off. Taxable gifts reduce estate tax burdens, but they preclude taking advantage of capital gains basis step-up at death.

Only a tax lawyer can advise on the trade-offs among estate, gift, and capital gains taxes, but a starting point is that estate and gift tax rates tend to be much higher than the long-term capital gains rate. Estate and gift taxes start at 37 percent and can go as high as 60 percent. So, avoiding the estate tax and paying the capital gains tax at a rate of 18–20 percent along the way is often the preferable strategy.

This issue crystallizes the importance of understanding client-specific circumstances in measuring after-tax results. For example, the trade-off between capital gains and estate/gift taxes is moot for those who are perfectly happy to leave their assets to a charitable foundation; they have a different strategy for reducing estate taxes, a strategy in which the capital gains tax liability is not important. For clients who wish to leave their assets to their children, however, reducing the combination of capital gains taxes and estate taxes is important.

CONCLUSION

Measurement of after-tax portfolio performance is a crucial undertaking for any manager with private clients, and the AIMR-PPS standards are an important systematic effort to bring the industry up to speed in presenting returns on an after-tax basis.

Taxes are complicated, however, for high-net-worth clients. Managers may find that the AIMR-PPS standards are too broad for reporting performance for particular clients. Managers may need to customize the algorithm by client or client group to recognize particular tax circumstances. This customization may involve building in specific tax rates, future tax liabilities, and even intergenerational plans in terms of wealth accumulation and wealth transfers. Tools such as the accrual equivalent tax rate provide managers a straightforward way to explain to clients how important and how valuable deferring capital gains can be. Managers need to think about modeling the client's after-tax returns for various portfolios.

Managers also need to consider the implications of gifting behavior. Apparently, most high-net-worth couples are likely to pass along some assets at the death of the second-to-die spouse, and the estate tax is likely to affect their intergenerational transfers. This practice raises the probability that some assets will face a zero capital gains tax rate (through the basis step-up) and underscores the need to integrate the investment manager into the tax-planning and tax-management picture. In some cases, wealth accumulation must be viewed from the family rather than the individual perspective. Gift giving complicates the problem of measuring marginal tax rates for after-death performance evaluation.

A common misconception is that taxes and investments can be managed separately. But investment managers cannot expect to achieve the best possible after-tax returns if they handle only the portfolio side of a client's affairs and turn over other aspects to tax managers, accountants, or tax planners. These aspects are intertwined. Accountants cannot try to minimize taxes when they are given a pretax return stream as the outcome of what the portfolio manager has done. Two-way communication is necessary if the strategy is to leave the client the largest after-tax wealth possible.

QUESTION AND ANSWER SESSION

Question: How do you benchmark after-tax returns when the accrual equivalent tax rate is used?

Poterba: You have all the mechanics in the basic formula, where a zero tax rate is being applied to the unrealized component of capital gains. The only question is whether to use a positive tax rate. If you want to work with the accrual tax rate, the modification is to put in a 1 minus 10 percent or 1 minus 12 percent tax burden on the unrealized capital gains term. Operationally, after you've run through the calculation for a client and identified the holding period as 20 years, that calculation tells you that the effective accrual capital gains rate on a gain that accrues today is on the order of 10 percentage points. You would assign that rate when you calculated after-tax returns.

Question: Is it reasonable to assume that a client who withdraws 10 percent a year from the assets will have different after-tax performance from a client who adds 10 percent a year to the assets?

Poterba: Yes, the situation is similar to the cost basis of a mutual fund that is getting positive cash flows versus one with negative cash flows. The one with positive flows doesn't have to realize as many gains. A fund with a 10 percent negative cash flow will have to realize gains and will have lower after-tax returns. That outcome is as true for a separately managed account as it is for a mutual fund.

I would use effective accrual rates to cast light on the effect of withdrawals versus infusions. For example, consider a client who plans to withdraw 10 percent of the portfolio each year. That information tells you that the time horizon or the effective duration for which the money is going to be under management is significantly shorter than for someone who plans to contribute 10 percent of the portfolio value each year until he or she dies. What's driving the difference is that the person who is adding money year after year is getting much longer average interest-free loans on the unrealized capital gains. You would expect to see a substantial difference in the after-tax return performance of those two portfolios.

Of course, the portfolio manager would be wise to recognize that the strategies and the investments that are optimal for someone who plans to add 10 percent a year will not be the same as the strategies that are optimal for someone who is planning to withdraw 10 percent a year. The trade-offs between the tax savings for low-dividend securities generating capital gains and the potential risks or other costs that arise from tilting the portfolio in that direction will be very different for those two clients.

Question: Is after-tax performance useful or not, then, in measuring manager value?

Poterba: What's the alternative? Is it best to ignore the fact that there were tax consequences associated with realizations and not try to make corrections? Some sort of measurement of after-tax performance makes sense; AIMR introduced the adjustment factor to account for such differences in strategies, but comparability is still not perfect. If you are trying to make comparisons of after-tax performance among managers, what you'd really like to see is the kinds of accounts a manager is running that have withdrawal characteristics like the account you're bringing to the table. The ability to dissect a manager's accounts by client objectives is the sort of information that could be useful, but that sort of detailed performance analysis is virtually impossible.

Question: How does one deal with realized losses that must be carried forward to a future tax year? Are any adjustments made?

Poterba: One thing you can do, in the spirit of the effective accrual tax rate, if a client has a very simple portfolio position with a limited number of managers working with the client and the client realizes a loss that is too large to use up this year (so the losses carry forward) is to ask: What is the discounted present value today of being able to reduce taxable income by $3,000 a year this year, next year, and all along the way until the loss is used up? If the tax rate at which you're deducting those losses is 39.6 percent today and you have $6,000 worth of losses, then you're getting 39.6 percent on the first $3,000 and 39.6 discounted for one period; so, it may be effectively 36 percent on next year's losses in today's dollars.

   Simple analysis, however, omits the fact that managers can also modify their behavior with respect to future gain realizations so as to accelerate the use of the loss as a device for sheltering other gains. Therefore, the real issue is how valuable it is to have losses on the books today, given that the client can use these losses to realize some gains tax free and thereby rebalance the portfolio.

Question: What do you do about taking over a portfolio that has large embedded gains when you have been hired to diversify the portfolio (so, the after-tax returns are going to be biased downward)?

Poterba: You need to make some sort of correction in reporting portfolio performance, perhaps group client portfolios that start from similar positions. The issue is reminiscent of the debate that sometimes goes on in the popular press about mutual funds with different amounts of embedded capital gains: If you started tracking two funds today—one a new fund and the other an old fund with substantial embedded capital gains—you would expect the fund with the embedded capital gains to generate more taxable realizations going forward. Comparing the managers would be unfair because they start from different positions.

Question: At what net worth should you suggest to someone that they gift? For example, is $1.2 million enough assets for a 70-year-old couple that may face nursing home costs?

Poterba: The most likely explanation for the low level of taxable gifting, at least among those with net worth below, say, $3 million, is the fear of substantial expenses sometime before the end of their lives. Nursing homes probably loom largest in those anxieties. In most case, those expenses do not, however, make a substantial dent in high-net-worth household assets. Something like 20 percent of 70-year-olds will go into a nursing home at some point before death—the percentage is higher for women than for men. Most stays in nursing homes are relatively short, although most of the dollars spent on nursing home care are spent for the small subset of very long-term stays. Most of these households retain substantial assets at the time of death of the surviving spouse. The reason I focused on the $2.5 million net-worth category is that in that range, potential nursing home bills will not draw down most of the accumulated assets.

   One could probably build a simple Monte Carlo simulation to get a handle on the risk of nursing home need versus tax savings. For example, you could find out the rough odds of various expenditures and then point out the tradeoff between, say, a 5 percent chance of needing to pay an expense and the saving of 40 percent in terms of the difference between the estate tax and the capital gains tax.

CHAPTER 22

TAXABLE BENCHMARKS: THE COMPLEXITY INCREASES

Lee N. Price, CFA

After-tax benchmarks must adhere to standard benchmark rules while incorporating tax-related concerns (such as income tax rates), but a big hurdle in establishing appropriate benchmarks is choosing which tax rate to use. An after-tax benchmark can best be constructed by using a combination of three levels of approximation as well as a shadow portfolio that allows for adjustments in cash flows and calculations of portfolio-specific cost bases.

Of those who manage taxable portfolios or represent taxable clients, only a small percentage report after-tax returns. One of the reasons managers give for not calculating after-tax returns is the lack of generally available after-tax benchmarks. After addressing the issue of benchmarks in general, I will explain how to calculate after-tax returns according to AIMR-PPS™ standards; the same rules apply to calculating after-tax benchmarks. I will then discuss three levels of approximation for the calculation of after-tax benchmark returns and potential combinations of these approaches.

STANDARD BENCHMARK RULES

A number of well-established principles exist for creating benchmarks. A benchmark should be (1) appropriate to the manager's asset class and investment strategy, (2) unambiguous, (3) specified in advance, (4) investable, and (5) measurable. When constructing an after-tax benchmark, a sixth rule is also applicable: (6) subject to the same (or similar) tax considerations as those of the clients whose portfolios are being evaluated against the benchmark.

Reprinted from *AIMR Conference Proceedings: Investment Counseling for Private Clients III* (August 2001): 54–64.

Obviously, an after-tax benchmark must have the same or similar tax considerations as those of the accounts that are being managed, but that does not mean that the benchmark should not also be unambiguous and specified in advance and, most important, appropriate to the manager's investment strategy.

The problem with after-tax benchmarks is that no single after-tax performance number is applicable to all users of the benchmark. One size does not fit all. Whereas pretax benchmark users can expect to have a single number for benchmark performance, after-tax benchmark users should never expect a single value. The S&P 500 Index's pretax return in 1999 was 21.04 percent, according to Ibbotson Associates. But managers who want to compare their results with an after-tax benchmark must recognize the complications involved. The benchmark has to take into account not only the different tax rates of clients but also the variation in capital gain taxes depending on the client's starting cost basis.

A nuclear decommissioning trust with a 20 percent flat tax rate on capital gains should have a different after-tax benchmark from that of an individual with a 46 percent total state and federal tax rate. Equally important is the fact that the after-tax benchmark return depends on the inception date of the portfolio. If the account began in 1998, the 1999 after-tax return will reflect only a minimal amount of capital gains. If the account began in 1989, however, then the 1999 after-tax benchmark return will have a much larger capital gains component generated by every stock sold. The account will reflect 10 years of compounded gains built into the portfolio return, and when the manager sells the stocks, the manager will realize a much larger capital gain than that of the account that had been open for only one year. Consequently, after-tax benchmark returns for any given year tend to be smaller than those for longer holding periods.

AIMR AFTER-TAX STANDARDS

The initial task of the Taxable Portfolios Subcommittee of the AIMR Performance Presentation Standards Implementation Committee, which I chaired when it was formed in 1994, was to evaluate the various ways of computing after-tax returns. We considered everything from cash basis (using only custodian-computed, tax-related cash flows) to full liquidation, partial liquidation, and a present value methodology that would account for the potential tax liability of future portfolio liquidation in current dollars. The committee decided that the realized-basis method was the only acceptable way to report after-tax performance.

Advantages of Realized Basis

In the committee's view, the most important advantage of reporting after-tax returns using realized-basis accounting (which the U.S. SEC now calls "preliquidation") is that implied taxes are linked directly, and in the same period, to the taxable event giving rise to them. Regardless of when taxes are actually paid, the realized-basis method forces the manager to be aware of the tax impact of portfolio trading and security selection. This is true of both taxes on dividend and interest income and of capital gain taxes on security sales. A second important advantage is that after-tax performance computed in this manner will be completely in sync with pretax performance calculated according to the AIMR-PPS standards. All of the same rules regarding interest and dividend income accrual apply in the after-tax arena as well.

Disadvantages of Realized Basis

The biggest disadvantage of using the realized-basis methodology is that it requires complicated accounting—accurate tax lots, calculation of accrued interest, and accretion of OID discounts/

premiums—and a great deal of precision. Many investment managers lack the necessary capabilities in their computer systems, even though some software vendors have been working hard to solve that problem.

Another disadvantage of this approach is that it slightly understates performance for all assets by charging taxes before they are actually due.

AIMR-PPS Standards

For before-tax performance, calculations are generally done according to a balance-sheet approach. The balance-sheet approach means that the manager uses the asset values at the end and the beginning of the period and adjusts for both the income received and the cash flows (positive and negative) during the period; the calculation is basically the difference between ending and beginning asset values divided by the average asset value for the period:

$$\text{Pretax performance} = \frac{\text{Ending market value} - \text{Cash flows} - \text{Beginning market value}}{\text{Beginning market value} + \text{Weighted cash flows}}. \quad (22.1)$$

This method works well for pretax performance calculations but not for the analysis of tax implications.

A completely analogous method, using exactly the same numbers, is an approach based on investment flows. The manager looks at the flow activity during the period rather than focusing on the ending and beginning asset values. The manager can divide the return, in terms of flow, among the various sources of return to the portfolio—realized gains, unrealized gains, and income—and then apply the appropriate tax rate to each type of flow. The denominator is the same as in the pretax calculation—the average assets for the period:

$$\text{After-tax performance} = \frac{\text{Unrealized gains} + \text{Realized gains} (1 - t) + \text{Income} (1 - t)}{\text{Beginning market value} + \text{Weighted cash flows}}. \quad (22.2)$$

With this methodology, the after-tax implication is clearer because no taxes are incurred on the unrealized gains during the period. This equation is a simplification because realized gains and income are taxed at different rates depending on holding period and type of income, but it is useful for conceptualizing the process. An easier way to calculate the same result is: After-tax performance equals pretax performance minus the tax burden, where the tax burden is as follows:

$$\text{Tax burden} = \frac{(\text{Realized gains} \times \text{Capital gains rate}) + (\text{Income} \times \text{Income tax rate})}{\text{Beginning market value} + \text{Weighted cash flows}}. \quad (22.3)$$

IMPORTANCE OF THE CAPITAL GAIN REALIZATION RATE

The realization of capital gains plays a vital role in after-tax performance. The driving force behind the impact of taxes on a portfolio is the relative size of realized capital gains and the frequency with which they are realized. Table 22.1 shows the long-term return for a growth portfolio. I assume that the annual capital gain from price appreciation is 7.5 percent, the percentage of gain realized each year is 40.0 percent, the capital gain tax rate is 28.0 percent, the percentage average dividend yield is 2.3 percent, and the client's income tax rate is 39.6 percent with no dividend exclusion. The long-term pretax return based on these assumptions is 9.8 percent (7.5 percent + 2.3 percent), and the after-tax return is 6.8 percent.

Table 22.1 shows that in the beginning, taxes have only a minor impact on the portfolio, but as the performance period lengthens, the after-tax return decreases because the

TABLE 22.1   Implications of Varying the Rate of Realization of Capital Gains

Item	Year 0	Year 1	Year 4	Year 8
Price index (untaxed)	100.0%	107.5%	133.5%	178.3%
Cost basis	100.0	100.0	111.5	141.6
Pretax gain this year	0.0	7.5	9.3	12.1
Pretax value	100.0	107.5	133.6	173.7
Unrealized gain (cumulative)	0.0	7.5	22.1	32.1
Realized gain	0.0	3.0	8.8	12.8
Tax	0.0	0.8	2.5	3.6
After-tax value[a]	100.0	108.0	132.9	172.3
Compound after-tax return		8.0	7.4	7.0

Note: Assume all capital gains taxes paid and dividends received at year-end.

[a]Including dividends after tax.

amount of imbedded gains increases. After a holding period of about 20 years, the after-tax return drops to about 6.8 percent and remains constant. So, according to this particular set of assumptions, a 9.8 percent pretax return converts to 6.8 percent after-tax return. When looking at after-tax performance (particularly long-term after-tax performance), the capital gain realization rate (CGRR) is an important concept. The CGRR is not necessarily the turnover rate. The Taxable Portfolios Subcommittee concluded that the measure of the CGRR should be the net gains or losses realized during the period divided by the average of the available gains during the period. The average stock of available capital gains during the period is

$$\frac{1}{2} \text{ (Stock of unrealized gains at start + Realized gains + Stock of unrealized gains at end).} \quad (22.4)$$

Although turnover alone is not the measure that defines CGRR, keep in mind that portfolio turnover is not necessarily bad. For example, turnover may include the selling, or turnover, of cash equivalents. This type of turnover does not affect taxes at all because the tax basis is always 100 percent of the market value. Or the manager may have intentionally harvested losses, which increases turnover but reduces the portfolio's net capital gain realization.

The effect of the CGRR on after-tax returns is rather dramatic. Table 22.2 shows the after-tax returns calculated with this same model under slightly different assumptions to illustrate the two things an investment manager can control: the CGRR—at the left of the table—and the investment style (namely, dividend yield)—at the top of the table. A manager cannot control the direction or the volatility of the market, but he or she can control the amount of turnover—a proxy for CGRR—in the portfolio. And the manager can control his or her investment style, whether the manager invests in high-dividend-yield stocks or low-dividend-yield stocks, growth versus value, and so on. Table 22.2 uses exactly the same assumptions presented in Table 22.1, with one exception: The portfolio's rate of total pretax return is 10 percent (rather than 9.8 percent) a year for the next 20 years, regardless of how the portfolio is structured. So, based on a completely hypothetical efficient market assumption, the after-tax returns range from about 9 percent for a portfolio with low turnover and a low dividend yield to 5.5 percent for a portfolio with high turnover and a high dividend yield.

TABLE 22.2   Effect of CGRR on After-Tax Return for Various Combinations of Appreciation and Dividend Yield

CGRR[a]	Appreciation/Dividend Yield (%)					
	4.0/6.0	5.0/5.0	6.0/4.0	7.5/2.5	8.0/2.0	9.8/0.2
5%	6.9%	7.3%	7.6%	8.2%	8.4%	9.0%
10	6.5	6.8	7.2	7.7	7.9	8.5
20	6.1	6.4	6.7	7.2	7.4	7.9
40	5.7	6.0	6.3	6.8	6.9	7.4
60	5.6	5.9	6.2	6.6	6.7	7.2
80	5.5	5.8	6.1	6.5	6.6	7.1

Note: Assumes a 28 percent tax rate.

[a]Percent of gains realized each year.

CONVERTING A STANDARD PRETAX BENCHMARK

One approach to constructing an after-tax benchmark is to convert a standard pretax benchmark to an after-tax one. Roughly 50–100 pretax benchmarks are used by managers, with 10–15 used widely. The after-tax benchmarks can be converted using various tax rates and investment periods (different inception dates). As I mentioned earlier, even if one adopts the AIMR-PPS standard realized-basis method, there are three levels of approximation in converting a pretax benchmark to an after-tax benchmark, and I will describe those three levels in this section. At the end of this section, I will cover some of the special problems associated with converting a standard pretax benchmark to an after-tax benchmark.

First Level of Approximation

To convert a pretax benchmark into an after-tax benchmark, at the first level of approximation, the manager must begin by splitting the pretax return between the sources of return: for example, dividend income and appreciation—realized and unrealized. (I will use the S&P 500 as an example, and fortunately, Ibbotson has already split the returns for the S&P 500.) For this first level of approximation, the manager must also assume that the pretax benchmark has a fairly constant CGRR. (I will assume that the CGRR is 5.5 percent for the S&P 500.)

Keep in mind that the CGRR can vary widely depending on the index chosen and the number of years used to construct the data. The CGRR could be 25 percent for the Russell 2000 Index or even 50–70 percent for some of the value indexes. And although the S&P's CGRR has averaged 5.5 percent for the past 12 years, the average depends on which years are used to calculate the measure. The manager must also assume a capital gains tax rate (28 percent) and an income tax rate (39.6 percent) for dividends. Finally, the manager must apply the CGRR to the assumed portfolio appreciation and compound the remaining unrealized gains.

The equations for creating an after-tax benchmark for the S&P 500 are as follows:

$$\text{Price} = \text{Price}(-1) \times (1 + \text{Appreciation}) \qquad (22.5)$$

$$\text{Realized gain} = \text{CGRR} \times [\text{Price} - \text{Cost}(-1)] \qquad (22.6)$$

$$\text{Cost} = \text{Cost}(-1) + \text{Realized gain } (1 - \text{Capital gains tax})$$
$$+ \text{Dividends } (1 - \text{Dividend tax}) \qquad (22.7)$$

$$\text{Tax} = \text{Realized gain} \times \text{Capital gains tax} + \text{Dividends} \times \text{Dividend tax} \quad (22.8)$$
$$\text{After-tax value} = \text{After-tax value} (-1) \times (1 + \text{Appreciation} + \text{Dividends} - \text{Tax}) \quad (22.9)$$
$$\text{After-tax return} = \text{After-tax value}/\text{After-tax value} (-1) - 1. \quad (22.10)$$

Note that the realized gains and dividends are both calculated as a percentage of Price(-1).

To start the calculation, the manager must have a beginning price, and then he or she increments that beginning price by 1 plus the portfolio appreciation. Next, the manager calculates the potential realized gain, which is the difference between the price at the end of the period and the cost basis. The cost footnoted minus 1 is for the previous period (which is rolled forward each period). The manager multiplies the potential amount of realized gains by the CGRR, and the cost is incremented to reflect the reinvestment of proceeds, but only arithmetically. The U.S. IRS does not allow managers to compound the cost basis, so the manager calculates the cost using the cost of the previous period plus the realized gains from security sales in the current period times the quantity (1 minus the capital gains tax paid) plus the dividends received in the current period times the quantity (1 minus the income tax paid on the dividends). And then finally, the manager can calculate an after-tax return, which is computed on a running basis divided by the previous period's value. The methodology is straightforward and, most importantly, is sensitive to the manager's assumed CGRR and assumed tax rates.

Table 22.3 shows the results of calculating after-tax performance according to the above methodology. For this example, I used the performance of the S&P 500 for the past 10 years. The table shows the pretax return for the S&P 500 for each of the years for 1990 to 1999 and the after-tax performance for each of the same years. Beginning in 1991, more than one after-tax performance number exists for each year because the starting year for the calculation (for the cost) varies. For example, if the portfolio's inception date was 1989 and the market was down 3.2 percent (pretax) in 1990, the after-tax return was a negative 4.4 percent, which may seem odd. Even though the portfolio was just started in 1989 and should not have realized many gains on average in 1990, thus creating only a minimal capital gain tax liability, the average dividend earned on the S&P 500 in 1990 was high. Thus, the income tax liability

TABLE 22.3   S&P 500 After-Tax Return for 1990–99 as a Function of Starting Year

Item	1990	1991	1992	1993	1994	1995	1996	1997	1998	1999
Pretax[a]	−3.17%	30.55%	7.67%	9.99%	1.31%	37.43%	23.07%	33.36%	28.58%	21.04%
Starting year for after-tax return										
1989	−4.43	28.35	6.05	8.46	−0.07	35.13	20.96	31.14	26.43	19.08
1990		28.21	5.94	8.36	−0.17	35.04	20.89	31.08	26.38	19.04
1991			6.22	8.62	0.08	35.28	21.08	31.24	26.51	19.14
1992				8.66	0.11	35.32	21.11	31.27	26.52	19.16
1993					0.19	35.39	21.16	31.31	26.56	19.19
1994						35.34	21.13	31.28	26.54	19.17
1995							21.48	31.58	26.76	19.35
1996								31.81	26.94	19.49
1997									27.27	19.75
1998										20.05

[a]S&P 500 pretax return.

TABLE 22.4   S&P 500 Example: Difference between Pretax and After-Tax Returns

Year	1990	1991	1992	1993	1994	1995	1996	1997	1998	1999
1989	1.26%	2.20%	1.62%	1.53%	1.38%	2.30%	2.11%	2.22%	2.15%	1.96%
1990		2.34	1.73	1.63	1.48	2.39	2.18	2.28	2.20	2.00
1991			1.45	1.37	1.23	2.15	1.99	2.12	2.07	1.90
1992				1.33	1.20	2.11	1.96	2.09	2.06	1.88
1993					1.12	2.04	1.91	2.05	2.02	1.85
1994						2.09	1.94	2.08	2.04	1.87
1995							1.59	1.78	1.82	1.69
1996								1.55	1.64	1.55
1997									1.31	1.29
1998										0.99

alone would have had a significant tax impact on the portfolio. Because of the high dividend tax rate assumed in this analysis, the income taxes paid exceeded the net effect of realizing losses, assuming a 5.5 percent portfolio turnover rate. As the holding period increases, the after-tax numbers are always lower than the pretax numbers, and they get lower and lower the longer the investor holds the portfolio, even with a relatively low 5.5 percent CGRR.

This effect is most noticeable in Table 22.3 for the 1999 period. For a portfolio started in 1998, the after-tax return was down about 1 percent—20.05 percent versus the pretax return of 21.04 percent. But if that portfolio had been started in 1989, the after-tax return would have been 19.08 percent.

Table 22.4 highlights the difference between the pretax and after-tax returns for the S&P 500. The one-year difference between pretax and after-tax returns is roughly between 1.0 percent and 2.3 percent, with a 1.75 percent average reduction across the 10 sample years (1990–1999). But for portfolios with a holding period of three years, the difference in the pretax and after-tax return is roughly 1.25–2.1 percent, and by six years, the range is 1.9–2.3 percent. By the time the investor has had the portfolio nine years, the difference is consistently above 2 percent.

The significant cumulative effect of taxes on portfolio returns explains the reason for the SEC's proposal that mutual funds be required to report after-tax returns to their clients. Table 22.5 shows some of the cumulative differences (for portfolios with holding periods of up to 10 years) in pretax and after-tax returns for the years 1995–1999. Again, the difference is negligible in the first year, just 1–2 percent. But at 5 years, the difference accumulates to 19 percent on average, and at 10 years, the cumulative difference is about 77 percent. In other words, the cumulative 10-year pretax return for the S&P 500 in 1999 was about 300 percent, whereas the cumulative after-tax return was about 225 percent, for an approximate difference of 75 percent, which is a fairly striking number. This large cumulative difference is obviously why the SEC is concerned about taxable investors investing in mutual funds to provide for their retirement years. Their realized return will be much lower than what is reported to them on a pretax basis.

Second Level of Approximation

The second level of approximation entails the same general concept as in the first level, but rather than make the assumption that the CGRR is constant every year, the manager must go

TABLE 22.5   S&P 500 Example: Cumulative Difference between Pretax and
After-Tax Returns

Starting Date	1995	1996	1997	1998	1999
1989	17.92%	26.07	39.87%	57.77%	77.43%
1990	16.84	25.04	38.85	56.87	76.78
1991	8.66	13.77	22.37	33.91	47.01
1992	5.93	10.19	17.32	27.09	38.37
1993	3.59	7.00	12.70	20.69	30.11
1994	2.09	5.20	10.34	17.69	26.51
1995		1.59	4.28	8.41	13.60
1996			1.55	4.16	7.63
1997				1.31	3.22
1998					0.99

further and determine the actual CGRR of the index for each period. Historically, companies were dropped from the S&P 500 if their market capitalization shrank or if they declared bankruptcy, events that were usually not likely to create large capital gains. But recently, companies are being dropped because they have been acquired. This heightened merger and acquisition activity has had a noticeable effect on indexes such as the Russell 2000. In addition, the best performers, the ones that rise to the top, often no longer meet the capitalization requirements and are pushed out of the index. Huge capital gains are associated with that kind of turnover.

Looking at the CGRR in detail, not on an average basis but analyzing it year by year, can add a lot of value to the after-tax benchmarking process. The manager has to determine for each year which companies left the index (because of bankruptcies, buyouts, or mergers) and whether the event was taxable. If it was a merger for stock, for example, and the company being dropped from the index was merged in a tax-free exchange with a company already in the same index, then no capital gain tax would be incurred. That kind of turnover does not affect after-tax returns. But if the company being dropped was bought out by a company that was not in the index (perhaps a non-U.S. company), then a manager benchmarked against that index would have to sell that stock and take the capital gain. That is, the manager would have to calculate capital gains based on the actual capital gains realized each period as a function of the tax rate and starting cost basis.

The question then arises as to what happens to after-tax returns as a function of CGRRs. Table 22.6 shows the differential between pretax and after-tax returns for various CGRRs and holding periods. The return differential in Year 1 does not vary greatly as the CGRR varies, but by Year 10, the difference between a CGRR of 5.50 percent (return differential of 1.96 percent) and a CGRR of 30 percent (return differential of 6.54 percent) is substantial. Therefore, calculating an after-tax benchmark using the second level of approximation creates a valuable tool. If the manager assumes a constant CGRR (as in the first level of approximation) when calculating the after-tax returns of the benchmark, the result will be better than not accounting for the tax implications at all, even though it will not be an accurate reflection of what really occurred in the index. If, in fact, the manager's benchmarked index is changing with time (which it is), by incorporating the true CGRR in the after-tax return calculations, the benchmark's after-tax performance numbers will differ from those calculated using the first level of approximation and will more accurately portray reality.

TABLE 22.6   Average Annual Difference in Pretax and After-Tax Returns as a Function of the CGRR: S&P 500 Index

CGRR	Year 1	Year 2	Year 3	Year 4	Year 5	Year 6	Year 7	Year 8	Year 9	Year 10
5.50%	1.50%	1.69%	1.74%	1.84%	1.96%	2.10%	2.08%	2.10%	2.08%	1.96%
10.00	1.71	2.04	2.20	2.39	2.61	2.86	2.92	3.03	3.05	2.93
20.00	2.16	2.79	3.13	3.50	3.90	4.39	4.59	4.88	5.00	4.86
30.00	2.61	3.49	3.96	4.47	5.02	5.73	6.04	6.49	6.70	6.54

Third Level of Approximation

The third level of approximation involves tracking the actual dividend reinvestment income and reinvesting at the then-current (i.e., at the time of the reinvestment) prices. The manager also rebalances the benchmark portfolio whenever capital action occurs and tracks the new cost basis.

Special Problems

The Dow Jones Industrial Average is probably the most commonly used index by taxable investors. The Dow is price weighted rather than market-cap weighted, which means that every time a corporate action occurs—a stock dividend, a stock split, and so on—the index must be adjusted. For example, if IBM splits two for one, a manager benchmarking against the Dow has to sell half of the IBM shares in the portfolio, regardless of the investment implications. As a result, the manager's portfolio will realize a capital gain, pay capital gain taxes, and reinvest the proceeds in the other 29 stocks in the index. So, an entirely new class of events become taxable events for the price-weighted Dow that would not be considered taxable events for the S&P 500 or most of the other indexes that are constructed according to a market-cap weighting.

Style indexes also have some unique problems, such as when a stock falls in value and drops out of the Russell 1000 Index (a large-cap index) and goes into the Russell 2000 Index (a small-cap index). A manager who is benchmarking against the Russell 1000 would consequently have to sell that stock and realize the gain. In this case, the gain realized may not be large because the stock has dropped in value, but the process applies in the other direction as well. That is, when a stock moves from a small-cap index into a midcap or large-cap index, huge gains might be realized if that stock has to be sold from a small-cap manager's benchmark portfolio.

Fixed-income indexes pose even greater problems for adjustment to an after-tax basis because index providers frequently do not list the securities in the index. Fixed-income indexes tend to be created by percentages of exposure to sectors—a certain percentage of Treasuries, mortgage-backed collateralized bond obligations, corporates, and so on. Thus, managers typically do not know which specific bonds (issuers, coupons, and maturities) are actually in the index. Figuring out this index composition can be difficult, if not impossible. Most fixed-income performance, however, comes from income rather than appreciation, so fixed-income indexes do not usually have the problem of accumulating unrealized capital gains, unless there has been a long period of declining interest rates.

SHADOW PORTFOLIOS

Converting a standard pretax benchmark is one way to construct an after-tax benchmark. A more precise methodology, however, is to create a shadow portfolio that varies according to the client. In other words, the shadow portfolio pays the same *pro rata* capital gain taxes for

TABLE 22.7   S&P 500 Example Shadow Portfolio

| Date | Inflow | | | | Tax Rates | | Benchmark Rates | | | Returns | |
	Value	Cost Basis	Outflow	Dividends	Capital Gains	Pretax Return Price	Pretax Return Income	Capital Gains Realization	Pretax	After Tax
12/98	100	100		39.60%	28.00%	5.64%	0.12%	0.46%	5.76%	5.71%
01/99				39.60	28.00	4.10	0.08	0.46	4.18	4.14
02/99				39.60	28.00	−3.23	0.12	0.46	−3.11	−3.17
03/99				39.60	28.00	3.88	0.12	0.46	4.00	3.94
04/99				39.60	28.00	3.79	0.08	0.46	3.87	3.82
05/99				39.60	28.00	−2.50	0.14	0.46	−2.36	−2.43
06/99				39.60	28.00	5.44	0.11	0.46	5.55	5.49
07/99				39.60	28.00	−3.20	0.08	0.46	−3.12	−3.17
08/99				39.60	28.00	−0.63	0.13	0.46	−0.50	−0.57
09/99				39.60	28.00	−2.86	0.11	0.46	−2.75	−2.81
10/99				39.60	28.00	6.25	0.07	0.46	6.32	6.28
11/99				39.60	28.00	1.91	0.13	0.46	2.04	1.97
12/99			50	39.60	28.00	5.78	0.11	0.46	5.89	1.90
Total									21.02	15.75

Note: Model from David Stein, Parametric Portfolio Associates.

withdrawals as the actual portfolio. And every time the client gives the manager more money, the shadow portfolio brings that money in at the cost basis at that time.

Clients have different cash flows, and the shadow portfolios (i.e., the benchmarks) will be different for each client. Table 22.7 shows a shadow portfolio of the S&P 500 for a single year. The starting point at the end of 1998 is 100, and then the various monthly returns are shown. Table 22.7 shows a single withdrawal (half of the initial value, which is admittedly an extreme example) by the client at the end of 1999. This withdrawal causes the pretax return (21.02 percent) to drop significantly (to 15.75 percent) as a result of the capital gains tax paid on the capital gains realized from the security sales—security sales that were needed to generate the proceeds for the distribution requirement (withdrawal).

Table 22.8 shows the impact on the after-tax return for the period (1999) if the withdrawal had been made in each month of the year—January, February, and so on. The return for the "No cash flows" row is the same, 20.20 percent, as in the standard benchmark conversion approach. The benchmark return using a shadow portfolio and a 50 percent withdrawal in January, however, is 16.7 percent. So, this withdrawal makes a big difference in the after-tax return, but the impact of the withdrawal varies by month. If the withdrawal had been made in February, the return would have been 18.4 percent; if it had been made in May, 17.3 percent. Because the index price varies, the benchmark, which is the S&P 500 in this case, also varies as a function of when the withdrawal is made.

TABLE 22.8   S&P 500 Example for 1999 with 50 Percent
Withdrawal in Various Months

No cash flows	20.20%
January	16.73
February	18.36
March	17.53
April	16.87
May	17.32
June	16.47
July	17.01
August	17.12
September	17.71
October	16.66
November	16.38
December	15.75

CONCLUSION

Constructing after-tax benchmarks is not easy, which is why I have been involved in the AIMR-sponsored effort to create a standardized methodology. Perhaps the most important aspect of constructing an after-tax benchmark is starting with the correct pretax index. The next step is to carry out the first level of approximation—splitting the appreciation and income return sources because of different tax rates and then applying a constant CGRR. The second level of approximation—calculating the after-tax returns with the appropriate CGRR each year—yields an even more accurate view. And finally, a combination of these approximations, plus adjusting for significant cash flows through a shadow portfolio to calculate a portfolio-specific cost basis, produces the most detailed and accurate after-tax benchmark.

QUESTION AND ANSWER SESSION

Question: How would limits on the deductibility of capital losses factor into after-tax benchmarks and portfolio returns?

Price: That question was raised when the Taxable Portfolios Subcommittee first met. Our conclusion then, which has been reiterated in the revised AIMR-PPS standards that will be coming out soon,[1] was that most investors have more than one basket of investments. As a result, we assumed that all losses could be used, although we knew that would not be true in every situation.

These after-tax performance numbers are not a substitute for reported accounting records. We were not trying to create 1099s or any number that would be going to the government. What we were trying to do was look at the investment manager's added value after taxes to see whether the manager was taking his or her losses, which is generally a good thing to do.

For example, if you added a new client in January 2000 and took losses during the year, your after-tax performance was probably higher than your pretax performance for 2000, based on the performance of the S&P 500. If that same account was started in 1995, however, this would not be the case. The huge run up in the S&P 500 would have been reflected in your client's account; even though you took losses in 2000 and benefited from them, you probably also incurred a fair amount of taxable capital gains in the account.

Question: Can exchange-traded funds (ETFs) serve as a proxy for after-tax benchmarks?

Price: Various types of after-tax benchmarks have been proposed. For some mutual funds, such as those based on the S&P 500, you can determine the dividend and appreciation proportions and use that data to construct an after-tax benchmark. In fact, you can get an actual 1099 if you happen to own that mutual fund and appropriately allocate the short-term and long-term gains and so on. Other methodologies, such as using ETFs or options, also exist. These methods are not wrong; their approximations are just different from the ones suggested here.

A big problem with creating after-tax benchmarks for mutual funds or ETFs is the timing issue, or the percentage of unrealized gains in the benchmark or portfolio. Suppose you were marketing to private clients and wanted an after-tax performance composite. The Taxable Portfolios Subcommittee brought up the point that when creating groups of after-tax portfolios, putting all 50 of your taxable clients together wouldn't necessarily make sense, because some might have started with you last year and others 20 years ago. As a result, the percentage of unrealized, or embedded, capital gains in the portfolios would differ dramatically. But that is what a mutual fund in effect is doing when it reports after-tax performance. Its numbers will also be dramatically affected by net cash inflows or outflows, which may reduce or increase the realization of capital gains.

One solution for managers of individual accounts is to calculate after-tax returns by starting year (those from 20 years ago, those from 15 years ago, etc.), but the result might be only one or two portfolios for each composite, which doesn't make sense and is not helpful to prospective clients. Another way to group those accounts is by percentage of unrealized gains in the portfolios. That same methodology applies to benchmarks. Grouping several different starting years for the S&P 500 and then developing benchmarks that are presented as a percentage of book to value would be easier than having separate benchmarks for every month of every year going back *ad nauseam*.

Question: If a benchmark should be created for each starting year, should you also calculate a separate benchmark for each client?

Price: Back in 1995 (roughly), the Subcommittee recommended that managers create separate composites not for each client but for each type of client. Qualified nuclear decommissioning trusts, for example, have a flat 20 percent tax rate. You can combine all such accounts in one composite and not include those of individual portfolios or property and casualty insurance companies, which have different tax regimes. If you look at types of clients as opposed to specific tax rates, few types probably exist. You may end up with four or five different types, and for that reason, you may end up with four or five different after-tax benchmark returns by tax rate in addition to the by-year distinction. In order to be consistent with the AIMR-PPS standards, the goal should clearly be to create composites of similar portfolios rather than to benchmark separately for each client. But as noted in my presentation, individual shadow portfolios can also be helpful in the case of significant cash flows, even if only for purposes of communication with a particular client.

Question: Can these approaches be used to create after-tax benchmarks for hedge funds?

Price: Conceptually, these same approaches could be applied to hedge funds, but such leveraged portfolios have the more pressing problem of calculating true pretax performance. A hedge fund may have a long–short strategy and be truly market neutral, but what is the divisor? What are the assets at risk? To say that hedge funds don't have any risk and then divide by zero doesn't make sense. And if the hedge fund is truly market neutral, the definition of assets at risk is unclear. The same problem arises even if the fund is only partially hedged. A subcommittee of AIMR's Investment Performance Council (IPC) is studying this issue and hopes to make recommendations soon.

Question: How do you account for state taxes?

Price: The current AIMR-PPS after-tax reporting standards do not factor in state taxes because the subcommittee wanted to get as close as possible to an "apples-to-apples" comparison between managers. Some members thought including state taxes would just muddy the waters. Instead, the suggestion was made that managers use the maximum federal tax rate appropriate for the type of client under management.

Nevertheless, since that standard was adopted, managers have found that some clients want to factor in their state taxes. But if managers include state taxes for individual clients, they must create two presentations: one that ignores state taxes to comply with the AIMR-PPS standards and one that includes state taxes to meet client needs (the second would be shown as supplemental information). Managers have also found that clients want their actual anticipated federal tax rate to be used, not simply the maximum applicable to their type of investor category.

The new standards, I suspect, will allow managers to report based on whichever tax rates they actually use in making investment decisions for clients. The standards will encourage managers to talk to clients about all applicable tax rates, not just federal and state but local as well. If you happen to live in New York or New Jersey and the local tax rates apply to investment income, for example, then those could also be included. Managers would need to create composites of all the accounts that share roughly the same tax rates and would have to disclose what the tax rates were (the weighted average for their composite), but they could then use the same client calculations for their composites.

I still have mixed feelings on this issue. Something in the area of comparability is lost when different managers use different rates, yet I understand why we were getting the complaints and the practical reasons for the new standards.

Question: Are managers required to report after-tax performance?

Price: Remember that all of the AIMR standards regarding performance, including the AIMR-PPS standards, are optional. Nobody has to be in compliance. Even if you feel that the marketplace, your consultants, or your clients require you to be in compliance with AIMR-PPS standards, you do not have to be compliant with the after-tax standards. They are purely optional; the AIMR-PPS standards merely state that if you intend to claim compliance and show after-tax performance, then you must do so according to the after-tax standards.

The same is not true for mutual funds. In January 2001, the U.S. SEC issued its final decision about a proposal that had been floating around for almost a year.

Effective April, 16, 2001, mutual funds must report their after-tax performance. Then, starting October 2001, after-tax performance will have to be included in fund advertisements and sales material; in February 2002, mutual fund prospectuses will also provide the information. For mutual funds, the taxable event is when the fund actually declares the dividend, which happens about once or twice a year. So, calculating after-tax performance for mutual funds will be much less complicated than for separately managed portfolios.

Requiring managers to report after-tax numbers helps make them aware of the tax impact on their portfolios and also helps clients reduce their expectations of what their returns will be for the long term. If clients consider after-tax performance, they will realize that no matter whether they have an index fund, an IRA, or an actively managed portfolio, the actual after-tax returns will be lower than the pretax returns.

Question: Do the after-tax return computations ignore the present value of taxes accrued currently and payable in the future?

Price: The realized basis method does ignore the present value of taxes on capital gains that have not yet been realized. Some managers use alternative methodologies to estimate such taxes, based on assumptions of when stocks may be sold and what the discount rate would be between now and then.

Although I understand such concepts, particularly for use by nuclear decommissioning trusts (which may have fairly well-defined termination dates), the committee recommended against such methodologies because of the huge variability introduced by the timing and discount rate assumptions. We did not feel comfortable in mandating specific numbers, but without such a standard, two different managers with identical after-tax performance on a realized basis could show widely different present value performance.

Question: Isn't the issue of after-tax returns more about forcing the manager to take losses versus just having the losses affect the portfolio market value?

Price: This is certainly one of the issues, and it makes sense to take losses, unless you are worried about a wash sale or immediate stock bounce. But after-tax performance covers a lot more than just taking losses; it is about being tax aware when taking gains and selecting a bias toward growth stocks rather than higher-taxed dividend income stocks.

Question: As an international manager with clients around the world who are subject to different tax rates, what information am I providing to prospects when I create an after-tax composite rate of return?

Price: AIMR recognizes that both the current and expected newly revised after-tax guidelines are U.S.-centric, which is why they have been developed by the Performance Presentation Standards Committee, the North American representative to the IPC, rather than by the global group itself. Other countries have already expressed interest in doing something similar—Canada and Australia in particular—but because tax rates and methodologies vary tremendously around the world, creating a worldwide standard for reporting after-tax performance is unlikely.

NOTE

1. This presentation was given before the redrafted AIMR-PPS standards were approved and released in final form.

CHAPTER 23

EXPLAINING AFTER-TAX MUTUAL FUND PERFORMANCE

James D. Peterson; Paul A. Pietranico, CFA;
Mark W. Riepe, CFA; and Fran Xu, CFA

Published research on the topic of mutual fund performance focuses almost exclusively on pretax returns. For U.S. mutual fund investors holding positions in taxable accounts, however, what matters is the after-tax performance of their portfolios. We analyzed after-tax returns on a large sample of diversified U.S. equity mutual funds for the 1981–98 period. We found the variables that determined after-tax performance for this period to be past pretax performance, expenses, risk, style, past tax efficiency, and the recent occurrence of large net redemptions.

For U.S. investors in high tax brackets, after-tax mutual fund returns may differ greatly from pretax returns. For example, U.S. equity fund investors in high tax brackets lost an average of about 2.2 percentage points (pps) annually to taxes in the 1981–98 period. Despite the important impact of taxes on investor returns, we are not aware of any studies, however, about the determinants of after-tax mutual fund performance. We sought to fill that void with this chapter of the 1981–98 period. Our goal was to identify a concise set of publicly available variables that, together, were useful for explaining subsequent after-tax U.S. equity fund performance. For purposes of comparison, we also studied the effects of fund characteristics on pretax performance and on tax efficiency. Both comparisons help to highlight the unique role that certain characteristics play in determining after-tax returns.

In our analysis, we build on research into the determinants of pretax mutual fund performance (e.g., Carhart 1997; Peterson, Pietranico, Riepe, and Xu 2001). Although the results of various prior studies differ in some respects, the common wisdom is that risk, investment style, past pretax performance, turnover, and fund expenses are important determinants of

Reprinted from the *Financial Analysts Journal* (January/February 2002):75–86.

pretax equity fund returns.[1] Therefore, we hypothesized that these characteristics would also be important determinants of after-tax returns.[2] Because our objective was to explain specifically after-tax returns, we also considered the effects of past tax efficiency, net cash flow, and manager turnover on future after-tax returns.[3]

DATA

We sought to identify the determinants of after-tax performance, pretax performance, and tax efficiency over the 1981–98 period by using a sample of 1,170 diversified U.S. equity funds. The mutual fund data source is the December 1998 Center for Research in Security Prices (CRSP) Survivor-Bias Free US Mutual Fund database. Although mutual fund data were available as early as December 1961, our chapter begins in 1981 because of data limitations described later.

Measuring After-Tax Returns

Mutual funds typically do not distribute capital gains more often than once a year. This practice limited our choice of measurement intervals for after-tax returns to periods of one year or longer. A fairly long time period is important for measuring after-tax returns. To understand why, consider the example of a tax-inefficient fund that does not distribute capital gains in a particular year because of some random event, such as abnormally poor performance. If such a fund's after-tax return is measured over a one-year period, the fund will appear to be tax efficient (i.e., its after-tax return will be roughly the same as its pretax return). Moreover, a fund can manage the realization of capital gains and, therefore, taxable distributions and after-tax returns in the short run. Thus, lengthening the measurement period improves the estimate of after-tax return and provides a better chance of rejecting hypotheses about the effect of certain fund characteristics on after-tax returns. Fund managers and investment styles change over time, however, so using a measurement period that is too long is also probably not a good idea. For these reasons, we report results for after-tax returns measured over a three-year horizon.[4]

CRSP does not report after-tax returns, so we explain in Appendix 23A the procedure we used to calculate after-tax returns.

Fund Characteristics

An important task in this chapter was to identify fund characteristics that might be significant determinants of after-tax mutual fund returns. Common wisdom suggested that risk, investment style, past pretax performance, expenses, and turnover are important determinants of pretax mutual fund performance. So, these characteristics, among others, are also likely to be important determinants of after-tax fund returns. Therefore, we included these five factors as explanatory variables in our model. A key feature of our analysis is that the characteristics we hypothesized to be important determinants of after-tax performance could actually have been observed by investors prior to investors making their fund selections.

Past pretax performance, risk, and style were estimated via a three-factor asset-pricing model similar in spirit to that of Fama and French (1993). Specifically, for each fund included in the sample for a particular three-year period, the following ordinary least-squares (OLS) regression was estimated over the 36-month period prior to the beginning of that three-year period:

$$r_{i,t} - r_{f,t} = \alpha_i + \beta_i(r_{m,t} - r_{f,t}) + s_i SML_t + v_i VMG_t + e_{i,p} \qquad (23.1)$$

where

$r_{i,t}$	= pretax return to individual fund i in period t
$r_{f,t}$	= risk-free rate
α_i	= historical risk- and style-adjusted pretax performance of the fund (we included the annualized value of the estimate of α_i in our tests)
β_i	= risk parameter to be estimated
s_i	= size parameter to be estimated
v_i	= value–growth style parameter to be estimated
$r_{m,t} - r_{f,t}$	= the market risk premium
SML_t	= return to small-cap stocks minus return to large-cap stocks
VMG_t	= return to value stocks minus return to growth stocks
$e_{i,t}$	= regression error term

Fama and French constructed their market capitalization and value–growth factors by using CRSP and Compustat data. We constructed our series by using data from Ibbotson Associates. (We use slightly different notation from that of Fama–French to help distinguish these series.) Table 23.1 contains these variables and the relevant Ibbotson Associates data series. Because we required three years of historical data to estimate Equation 23.1 and the value–growth series became available to us only beginning in 1978, our analysis of fund returns begins in 1981.

The time-series regression equation (Equation 23.1) was estimated once for each three-year return observation in the sample. For example, consider a fund's after-tax return observed for the three-year period 1981–1983. In this case, Equation 23.1 was estimated from 36 months of fund pretax return data beginning in January 1978 and ending in December 1980. The annualized estimate of α_i obtained from estimating Equation 23.1 for this period is an estimate of the fund's historical risk- and style-adjusted pretax performance, and it is associated with the after-tax return observed for the 1981–83 period. The estimates of β_i, s_i, and v_i represent estimates of the risk and style variables associated with this return.

Keep in mind that after-tax returns may be related to the beta measure of risk for reasons other than compensation for bearing systematic risk. Financial theory dictates that securities with high systematic risk should have high pretax returns. For this reason, studies of pretax returns typically include a measure of systematic risk, such as beta, as an explanatory variable. The argument is that investors are not rewarded for bearing unsystematic risk because this type of risk can be diversified away. Total risk, or variance, which is a measure of systematic

TABLE 23.1   Time-Series Data for Risk and Style Estimates

Variable	Ibbotson Associates Series
r_f	U.S. 30-day T-bill total return
$r_m - r_f$	U.S. equity risk premium
SML	U.S. small-stock premium
VMG	[(Wilshire large-cap value − Wilshire large-cap growth) + (Wilshire small-cap value − Wilshire small-cap growth)]/2

plus unsystematic risk, may affect after-tax mutual fund returns because high-variance funds are more likely than low-variance funds to have capital losses to offset capital gains. Because mutual funds tend to be well diversified, however, beta and variance/standard deviation are highly correlated.[5]

Two factors remain that have been identified as important for pretax returns and may be important for after-tax returns: turnover in the fund's stock holdings and fund expenses. Turnover, which is computed by taking the lesser of purchases or sales and dividing by average monthly net assets, is a measure of the fund's trading activities. Expenses are measured by the fund's reported expense ratio, which is the percentage of fund assets paid for operating expenses and management fees, excluding brokerage costs.

In addition to these factors, we needed measurements of three factors that may have particular effects on after-tax returns—tax efficiency, cash flows (inflows and outflows), and manager turnover.

Tax efficiency may be affected by a fund's turnover in stock holdings or vice versa. Some analysts have argued that high-turnover funds are tax inefficient because selling a security that has appreciated in value causes the fund to realize a capital gain. Tax-efficient funds may have the higher turnover, however, because their managers seek to offset such gains with capital losses. Therefore, turnover may not be a good proxy for tax efficiency. As an alternative to turnover, we considered the fund's "return lost to taxes" (RLT), which we measured as follows:

$$RLT_t = \left| \frac{(1 + r_i^{aftertax})}{(1 + r_i^{pretax})} - 1 \right|,$$ (23.2)

where $|\cdot|$ denotes absolute value and r_i^{pretax} and $r_i^{aftertax}$ are the annualized pretax and after-tax returns on fund i measured over the 36-month period ending just prior to the period for which the returns being studied were measured. The hypothesis we tested is that funds that were tax efficient (inefficient) in the past subsequently had higher (lower) after-tax returns.

Note that the RLT measure is similar to Morningstar's tax-efficiency measure. Morningstar computes tax efficiency as $r_i^{aftertax}/r_i^{pretax}$. This measure of tax efficiency is applicable, however, only when both pretax and after-tax returns are positive. If pretax returns are negative, the tax-efficiency ratio is greater than or equal to 1, but a tax-efficiency ratio greater than 1 implies that after-tax returns are bigger than pretax returns. This cannot be the case for a mutual fund, however, because mutual fund losses cannot be passed through to the investor to reduce the investor's income. Therefore, a tax-efficiency ratio is not reported unless it is between 0 and 1. In an extended down market, the tax-efficiency ratio is not likely to fall in this range. Yet, tax efficiency is an important consideration even when pretax returns are negative, because after-tax returns may be even more negative. Our calculation of RLT in Equation 23.2 is applicable for either positive or negative values for both pre- and after-tax returns.

After-tax performance may also be affected by cash flows into or out of a fund. Managers faced with large cash redemptions may be forced to sell appreciated shares, which results in a capital gains distribution. Managers faced with large net cash inflows may add higher-cost-basis shares to existing positions. For those funds that specifically identify the shares they sell for tax purposes, selling the high-cost-basis shares first can minimize taxable distributions.

Net cash flow is defined as follows:

$$NCF_{i,t} = \frac{NA_{i,t} - NA_{i,t-1}(1 + r_{i,t-1}^{Preetax})}{NA_{i,t-1}},$$ (23.3)

where $NA_{i,t}$ is the net assets of fund i at time t. Fund managers can usually accommodate small net redemptions and small net inflows without any tax ramifications. Thus, to consider large net cash flows only, we constructed two dummy variables: *LgnegNCF* was set to 1 if the fund's cash flow was in the bottom 25 percent in terms of net cash flow for all funds with *NCF* less than 0 in the year prior to the period in which the returns being studied were measured and set to 0 otherwise; *LgposNCF* took on a value of 1 if the fund's cash flow was in the top 25 percent in terms of net cash flow for all funds with *NCF* greater than or equal to 0 in the prior year and took on the value of 0 otherwise.[6] If funds with large net redemptions incur more taxes than funds with small net redemptions, then funds with large negative net cash flows should subsequently underper-form comparable funds on an after-tax basis. Conversely, if large net inflows lead to lower taxes, then funds with large positive net cash flows should subsequently outperform comparable funds on an after-tax basis.

Large net cash flows may have implications for future fund returns that are not entirely tax related. For example, many analysts argue that large net inflows lead to lower performance, particularly for small-cap funds. Therefore, multiple cash flow effects may neutralize each other in after-tax returns.

Recent manager turnover may also have implications for subsequent after-tax fund returns. New managers may trade extensively to implement their own investment plans, potentially triggering large capital gains distributions. To include this consideration, we used the date the manager took control of the fund (as identified in the CRSP database) and set a variable *Mgrturn* to 1 if the current manager took control within the previous year and to 0 otherwise. If manager turnover leads to higher taxes, then funds with recent manager turnover should subsequently underperform comparable funds on an after-tax basis.[7]

Using a sample of 492 managers, Chevalier and Ellison (1999) found, among other things, that manager age was an important determinant of mutual fund returns in the 1988–94 period. We do not have data on manager age, but our manager turnover variable could be related to manager age (i.e., a manager with short tenure is more likely to be young). To further control for a manager age/tenure effect, we established the variable *Tenure*, which was set to 1 if the fund's manager had responsibility for managing the fund for at least five years and 0 otherwise.

Therefore, funds with *Tenure* = 1 are funds whose managers have had a long tenure; funds with *Mgrturn* = 1 are funds whose managers have had a short tenure. We conducted the tests involving manager tenure information for a shorter time period (1992–1998) than for other tests because the CRSP database does not report the date the current manager took control of the fund prior to 1992.

Finally, investment style is an important determinant of pretax returns, and therefore, style is almost surely an important determinant of after-tax returns for reasons that have nothing to do with taxes. In addition, fund style may have unique implications for after-tax returns. For example, value funds may be less tax efficient than growth funds because of the former's tendency to hold higher-dividend-paying stocks. Small-cap funds may sell high-performing stocks to avoid style drift, which could force a capital gains distribution. The stocks held in small-cap funds tend to exhibit more overall risk, however, than those held in large-cap funds. So, small-cap managers are much more likely to have capital losses to offset capital gains, which promotes tax efficiency.

METHODOLOGY

Our primary objective was to measure the marginal effects of the characteristics identified in the previous section on after-tax mutual fund performance; other objectives were to measure the effects of the characteristics on pretax performance and on tax efficiency. To fully investigate the importance of investment style to after-tax returns, we also extended the analysis of the characteristics' effects to four subsamples of the full sample based on size and value orientation versus growth orientation.

A common approach to estimating the marginal effects of variables on return is the two-step estimation technique developed by Fama and MacBeth (1973).[8] In the first step of the Fama–MacBeth technique, a cross-sectional regression is estimated for each period (typically monthly) in the sample. In studies of mutual fund returns, the dependent variable in this regression is a measure of fund return for a particular period and the independent variables are the fund characteristics potentially associated with that return. In the second step, the time-series averages of the regression coefficient estimates obtained from the first-step regressions are computed. The average associated with a particular characteristic is interpreted as an estimate of the average premium in fund returns associated with that characteristic.

A large number of time-series observations are required in the second step of the Fama–MacBeth method to obtain precise estimates of the average premiums. For this reason, most applications of the Fama–MacBeth technique use monthly data. For reasons discussed in the previous section, we measured after-tax returns over long holding periods—in particular, six consecutive three-year holding periods beginning in 1981 and ending in 1998. Unfortunately, six time-series observations are not enough to draw reliable inferences from the data. Therefore, we used a slightly different technique.

The estimation technique we used has features that are similar to the Fama–MacBeth approach. The Fama–MacBeth technique accommodates time variation in estimates of the premiums in returns. The premium in returns associated with a specific mutual fund characteristic may or may not be expected to vary over time. For example, the fact that stock market investments are risky implies that the stock market risk premium will vary with changing economic conditions (i.e., in some years, investors will be rewarded for taking on stock market risk; in other years, taking on risk will be costly). Similar arguments suggest that investment-style premiums might also vary over time. Therefore, like the Fama–MacBeth approach, the estimation technique we used had to accommodate variation in estimates of risk and style premiums.

There is no reason to expect that the "true" premiums associated with non-risk-related and non-style-related characteristics, such as the expense ratio, will vary over time. Therefore, pooling the cross-sectional and time-series data for such traits so that a single regression is estimated, instead of one regression for each period in the sample, is beneficial.[9] Pooling the data potentially increases the precision of the regression coefficient estimates for those coefficients that are not expected to vary over time. Because the estimated premiums on some of the characteristics in our analysis are expected to vary over time and some are not, our approach was to pool the time-series and cross-sectional data and to model time-series variation in the estimated premiums when doing so was appropriate. Specifically, the average premiums in after-tax returns were estimated via the following pooled time-series and cross-sectional OLS regression:

$$
\begin{aligned}
r_{i,t} - r_{f,t} = \mu_o + \sum_{m=2}^{T}\lambda_m D_m + \sum_{j=1}^{J}\delta_j x_{i,j,t-1} \\
+ \sum_{j=1}^{J}\sum_{m=2}^{T}w_{j,m}x_{i,j,t-1}D_m + \sum_{k=1}^{K}\gamma_k x_{i,J+k,t-1} + \epsilon_{i,t},
\end{aligned}
\tag{23.4}
$$

where

μ_o = regression intercept

D_m = (for $m = 2, \ldots, T$) indicator, or dummy, variables that take on the value of 1 if $m = t$ and 0 otherwise

λ_m = (for $m = 2, \ldots, T$) regression parameters associated with the intercept dummy variables

δ_j = (for $j = 1, \ldots, J$) regression parameters associated with the J risk and style variables

$x_{i,c,t-1}$ = value of characteristic c for fund i observed *prior* to period t (e.g., if characteristic c is a fund's expense ratio, then $x_{i,c,t-1}$ is the actual value of the expense ratio for fund i observed prior to period t)

$\omega_{j,m}$ = (for $j = 1, \ldots, J$, $m = 2, \ldots, T$) regression parameters associated with the slope dummy variables on the risk and style variables

γ_k = (for $k = 1, \ldots, K$) regression parameters associated with the K variables that are not risk or style related

$\epsilon_{i,t}$ = regression error term

The first summation term in Equation 23.4 is for the $T-1$ dummy variables included to allow the intercept estimate to vary over each period t, $t = 1, \ldots, T$, in the sample. The results we present are for the case in which t is three years long. In this case, μ_0 represents the regression intercept for the first three-year period in the sample, 1981–83. The intercepts for each of the five remaining three-year periods in the 1981–98 sample are given by $\mu_0 + \lambda_m$, for $m = 2, \ldots, 6$.

The second summation term in Equation 4 is for the J risk and style variables in the regression (i.e., β, s, and v). The next (double) summation term is for the $J(T-1)$ terms included to allow the estimated premiums on the risk and style variables to vary by period. When t is three years long, δ_j represents the premium associated with risk or style variable j for the first three-year period in the sample, 1981–1983. The premiums for each of the five remaining three-year periods in the 1981–98 sample are given by $\delta_j + \omega_{j,m}$, for $m = 2, \ldots, 6$. The average of the six estimated premiums for variable j represents the average premium for that variable over the sample period.[10]

The final summation term is for the remaining K fund characteristics—those that are neither risk nor style related (i.e., past performance, expenses, turnover, past tax efficiency, large net redemptions, large net inflows, tenure, and manager turnover). The estimated premiums on these variables were not allowed to vary over time. We consider a variable a determinant of returns if the estimated average premium associated with that variable is (statistically) significantly different from zero.

For purposes of comparison, we also estimated Equation 23.4 with pretax returns (less the risk-free rate) as the dependent variable. The results from this exercise serve as a benchmark for comparison with results for after-tax returns. In addition, we compared our results with those obtained from a similar analysis of return lost to taxes, our measure of tax efficiency. Both comparisons help to highlight the unique role that certain characteristics play in determining after-tax returns.

RESULTS

As Table 23.2 indicates, correlations between the explanatory variables are near zero. Thus, the regression results do not suffer from a multicollinearity problem.

Full Sample of Funds

The estimated average annualized premiums in pretax returns, after-tax returns, and return lost to taxes associated with the fund characteristics discussed previously are in Table 23.3.

TABLE 23.2   Correlation Matrix of Explanatory Variables

	RLT	Turnover	Tenure	Mgrturn	LgnegNCF	LgposNCF	Expense Ratio	α	β	v	s
RLT	1.00										
Turnover	0.14	1.00									
Tenure	0.07	0.14	1.00								
Mgrturn	0.08	0.14	-0.30	1.00							
LgnegNCF	0.02	0.04	-0.03	0.06	1.00						
LgposNCF	-0.13	0.03	-0.04	-0.02	-0.11	1.00					
Expense ratio	-0.26	0.12	-0.02	0.00	0.04	0.07	1.00				
α	0.12	-0.02	0.09	-0.07	-0.19	0.26	-0.22	1.00			
β	-0.09	0.00	-0.05	0.00	-0.02	0.00	-0.05	-0.14	1.00		
v	0.17	-0.11	0.02	0.02	-0.03	-0.07	-0.07	-0.24	-0.08	1.00	
s	-0.08	0.09	0.05	-0.02	0.02	0.13	0.21	0.01	0.30	-0.16	1.00

Note: Correlations were estimated for the 1981–98 period with the exception of correlations involving manager tenure and manager turnover, which were estimated for the 1992–98 period.

TABLE 23.3   Determinants of Fund Performance (except where otherwise noted, parentheses indicate *t*-statistics)

| | Annualized Average Premium Estimates (percent) | | | | | |
| | 1981–98 | | | 1992–98 | | |
Explanatory Variable	Pretax Return	After-Tax Return	Return Lost to Taxes	Pretax Return	After-Tax Return	Return Lost to Taxes
Expense ratio	−1.60* (−8.96)	−1.38* (−7.81)	−0.18* (−4.85)	−1.71* (−6.75)	−1.46* (−5.72)	−0.20* (−3.81)
α	0.11* (4.28)	0.10* (4.03)	0.01 (1.22)	−0.01 (−0.16)	0.04 (0.92)	−0.04* (−4.31)
β	4.40* ($F = 43.83$)	4.10* ($F = 38.50$)	0.16 ($F = 1.44$)	10.38* ($F = 177.41$)	10.56* ($F = 179.50$)	−0.36* ($F = 5.04$)
v	0.98* ($F = 7.90$)	0.78* ($F = 5.24$)	0.15 ($F = 3.75$)	−0.69 ($F = 1.74$)	−0.45 ($F = 0.40$)	−0.19 ($F = 3.19$)
s	−2.83* ($F = 31.37$)	−2.41* ($F = 23.03$)	−0.35* ($F = 11.01$)	−6.12* ($F = 86.19$)	−6.17* ($F = 85.40$)	0.15 ($F = 1.19$)
Turnover[a]	0.04 (0.26)	−0.01 (−0.07)	0.03 (1.04)	−0.38 (−1.79)	−0.45* (−2.06)	0.05 (1.06)
RLT	−0.01 (−0.11)	−0.41* (−4.39)	0.35* (17.77)	0.09 (0.59)	−0.39* (−2.44)	0.40* (12.68)
LgnegNCF	−0.50 (−1.51)	−0.72* (−2.20)	0.19* (2.87)	−0.56 (−1.12)	−0.79 (−1.57)	0.22* (2.12)
LgposNCF	−0.55 (−1.52)	0.01 (0.02)	−0.48* (−6.37)	−0.20 (−0.42)	0.19 (0.41)	−0.35* (−3.63)
Tenure	NA	NA	NA	−0.71* (−2.39)	−0.85* (−2.85)	0.13* (2.17)
Mgrturn	NA	NA	NA	0.79 (1.61)	0.59 (1.20)	0.14 (1.37)
R^2	49	50	30	40	39	17

NA = not available.

[a]The average premium numbers displayed in the table for the turnover variable are the actual values multiplied by 10^{-2}.

*Significantly different from zero at the 5 percent level.

Results for the entire 1981–98 period do not include average premium estimates for manager turnover and tenure, which are given for the shorter, 1992–98, time period.

Determinants of Pretax Returns

Table 23.3 shows that, as expected, the estimated premium on fund expenses in pretax returns is negative and statistically significant. The estimated value of −1.60 percent implies that for the 1981–98 period, funds with expense ratios that were 1 pp higher than comparable funds had pretax returns that were on average 1.6 pps lower than comparable funds on an annualized basis.

The estimated α premium (historical risk- and style-adjusted pretax performance) of 0.11 percent is also statistically significant. This result suggests that for the 1981–98 sample period, funds with superior risk-adjusted and style-adjusted performance in one period of 36 months, as measured by α in Equation 23.1 performed better, on average, in the next 36 months.[11]

The estimated average premium associated with β risk in future pretax returns in our time period (4.4 percent a year) is also statistically significant, which implies that mutual fund investors received a positive premium for bearing market risk. The estimated average premium associated with the value–growth variable, v, of 0.98 percent a year indicates that, on average, value funds outperformed growth funds in the 1981–98 period. Moreover, the estimated average premium associated with the market capitalization variable, s, of −2.83 percent suggests that, on average, large-cap funds outperformed small-cap funds in this time period.

Unreported regression results revealed that the estimated risk, value–growth, and market-cap premiums varied dramatically from period to period. For example, in the first nine years of the sample, the value–growth premium was positive, but in the last nine years, it was negative. The propensity for these premiums to switch back and forth between positive and negative values over time highlights the importance of diversifying among investment styles.

Although the argument is often made that high turnover reduces pretax returns, we found that the average premium associated with turnover in subsequent pretax returns was not significantly different from zero over this sample period.[12]

Not surprisingly, the average premiums on the variables introduced to capture tax effects were not statistically significant when regressed against pretax returns. In addition to finding no significant premium associated with turnover in subsequent pretax returns, we found that the average premium on past tax efficiency, as defined by RLT, in the 1981–98 period was near zero. The signs of the average premiums on large negative and large positive cash flow are negative, but neither is statistically significant.

In the 1992–98 period (studied separately because tenure and manager turnover could be measured only for this period), the estimated average premium in pretax returns associated with the *Tenure* variable, −0.71 percent, is statistically significant, which implies that managers having at least five years of experience with their funds underperformed managers with less experience by an estimated 0.71 pps a year over the 1992–98 period. This result suggests that newer, and possibly younger, managers outperform their more seasoned counterparts and is reminiscent of Chevalier and Ellison's finding that young managers outperform older managers. The estimated average premium associated with the manager turnover variable, *Mgrturn*, is positive (i.e., funds that have recently changed managers do better in the future on a pretax basis) but not statistically significant.

Determinants of After-Tax Returns

Consistent with the full-period pretax results reported in Table 23.3, fund expenses, style, past risk- and style-adjusted performance, and beta were important determinants of future after-tax returns. The estimated premiums in after-tax returns associated with these variables are similar to those reported for pretax returns.

We found no evidence of a relationship between turnover and future after-tax returns for the 1981–98 time frame. Our results suggest that *RLT* was a better proxy for future after-tax returns than turnover was during the full period. When we excluded *RLT* from the regressions entirely (results not shown), we still found no relationship between turnover and future after-tax returns.

The relationship between *RLT* and future after-tax performance is negative and, unlike the relationship for pretax returns, statistically significant. The estimated premium of −0.41 percent implies that an annualized *RLT* of 1 percent over the prior 36-month period was associated with an annualized 41 bp reduction in after-tax return over the next 36-month period during the full sample period. This result suggests that past tax efficiency as measured by *RLT* is a useful indicator of future after-tax returns.

We also found no evidence of a relationship between large net cash inflows and future after-tax returns over the 1981–98 time period, but large net redemptions were associated with lower subsequent after-tax returns over this period. The estimated premium of −0.72 percent on *LgnegNCF* implies that funds in the bottom quartile in terms of net redemptions in the prior year subsequently underperformed comparable funds by 0.72 pps on an annualized basis in the 1981–98 period. Further analysis (results not shown) revealed that small net redemptions and small net inflows had no effect on future after-tax performance.

Consistent with the results for pretax returns over the 1992–98 period, the average premium in after-tax returns associated with the *Tenure* variable is negative and statistically significant. This result suggests that managers who have at least five years of experience with their funds underper-formed managers with less experience in terms of both pretax and after-tax returns.

Investigation of the hypothesis that manager turnover hurts future after-tax performance was hindered by the short sample period we could use. For a period as short as 1992–1998, finding statistically significant results is unlikely because of the statistical noise inherent in the estimated premiums. The fact that the estimated average premium on *LgnegNCF* is more negative than it was for the full period but is no longer statistically significant is evidence of the estimates' inherent imprecision. If manager turnover causes future taxable distributions, then the estimated premium on *Mgrturn* should be negative. Yet, the estimated premium is positive, although not statistically significant. Thus, we provide no evidence supporting a systematic manager turnover effect in after-tax returns.

Determinants of Tax Efficiency

We now turn to an analysis specifically of tax efficiency—the "Return Lost to Taxes" columns in Table 23.3. To understand why this analysis is useful, recall that a characteristic can affect pretax returns and tax efficiency in opposing ways. Therefore, some variables may affect tax efficiency in one way but have an opposite or neutral effect on after-tax returns.

Given the after-tax return results reported in Table 23.3 for the 1981–98 period, it is not surprising that past tax efficiency, as measured by *RLT*, and past large net redemptions, as measured by *LgnegNCF*, were important descriptors of future tax efficiency. More interesting is that large cash inflows, *LgposNCF*, were associated with lower return lost to taxes (i.e., higher tax efficiency) in this period. This result provides support for the claim that large cash inflows promote tax efficiency, but it does not imply that taxable investors should concentrate their investments in funds with large cash inflows. To understand why, note that the estimated large-cash-inflow premium in pretax returns shown in Table 23.3 is –0.55 percent, implying that funds with large net inflows subsequently underperformed on a pretax basis (although this effect is not statistically significant). The estimated large-cash-flow premium in return lost to taxes is –0.48 pps, implying that large net inflows were associated with less return lost to taxes (greater tax efficiency). In after-tax returns, these two effects neutralize each other. This result highlights the dangers of focusing strictly on tax efficiency. Investors who do so may minimize return lost to taxes, but they would be better off focusing on maximizing after-tax returns (for their chosen risk tolerance).

When other variables were controlled for, results for the s variable show that small-cap funds were more tax efficient over the full sample time period. This result is consistent with the hypothesis that managers of small-cap funds are likely to have more opportunities to offset capital gains with capital losses than are their large-cap counterparts. This tax efficiency is an extremely small part of the overall effect, however, that market cap has on after-tax returns.

High-expense funds also appear to have been more tax efficient in the 1981–98 period. A possible reason is that expenses are deducted from portfolio income, so a high-expense fund has a smaller income distribution. Of course, the data could result from random error, or the expense ratio may proxy for measurement error in one or more of the other explanatory variables; for example, high-expense funds are more likely to be small cap and the s variable may be measured with error. Another possibility is that expenses proxy for some variable important for determining return lost to taxes that we did not include in our analysis.

For the 1992–98 period, Table 23.3 shows an estimated premium on *Tenure* that is positive and statistically significant, which indicates that the funds of managers with more than five years of tenure are less tax efficient than the funds of less-tenured managers. But the estimated premium of 0.13 pps is economically small. The results shown in Table 23.3 for the 1992–98 period indicate that manager turnover also is positively related to return lost to taxes, but the effect is not statistically significant.

Results by Investment Style

In this section, we contrast the results for the sample broken into four subsamples—large-cap value, large-cap growth, small-cap value, and small-cap growth—to results for the full sample. To categorize a fund by style at a specific point in time, we first used the prior 36 months of return data to compute the correlation of the fund's returns with the returns on the relevant Wilshire index. We then categorized each fund's style as the style of the Wilshire index exhibiting the highest correlation with the fund's returns.

Table 23.4 provides the results from the analysis of after-tax returns and return lost to taxes for the full 1981–98 period.[13] Although the estimated α premiums in after-tax returns are positive for all four style subsamples, they are not statistically significant in the two value categories. This result suggests that performance persistence was limited to growth funds in the 1981–98 period. (Our analysis of pretax returns, not shown, yielded the same conclusion.) Carhart found that momentum investing largely accounts for performance persistence in pretax mutual fund returns. Therefore, a plausible explanation for this result is that the investing strategies of growth fund managers are more consistent with momentum strategies than are the strategies of value fund managers.

TABLE 23.4 Results by Investment Style (except where otherwise noted, parentheses indicate *t*-statistics)

| | Annualized Average Premium Estimates (percent) | | | | | | | |
| | Large-Cap Growth | | Large-Cap Value | | Small-Cap Growth | | Small-Cap Value | |
Explanatory Variable	After-Tax Returns	Return Lost to Taxes	After-Tax Return	Return Lost to Taxes	After-Tax Return	Return Lost to Taxes	After-Tax Return	Return Lost to Taxes
Expense ratio	−1.44* (−6.67)	−0.05 (−0.88)	−1.14* (−2.87)	−0.12 (−1.15)	−1.22* (−3.87)	−0.25* (−4.30)	−1.15 (−1.78)	−0.07 (−0.60)
α	0.25* (6.58)	0.00 (0.42)	0.03 (0.30)	−0.02 (−0.85)	0.15* (3.59)	0.01 (1.45)	0.10 (1.03)	0.01 (0.71)
β	3.83* ($F = 18.75$)	0.42 ($F = 2.82$)	3.07 ($F = 2.36$)	0.57 ($F = 1.25$)	4.28* ($F = 11.48$)	0.16 ($F = 0.49$)	4.45 ($F = 2.54$)	−0.84 ($F = 2.77$)
ν	0.61 ($F = 1.00$)	−0.06 ($F = 0.11$)	4.84 ($F = 2.51$)	−2.21 ($F = 7.89$)	1.41* ($F = 4.58$)	0.29* ($F = 5.87$)	−1.60 ($F = 0.14$)	1.77* ($F = 5.35$)
s	2.18 ($F = 2.94$)	0.06 ($F = 0.02$)	−10.64* ($F = 17.82$)	0.95 ($F = 2.18$)	−4.09* ($F = 14.16$)	−0.56* ($F = 7.95$)	2.69 ($F = 0.77$)	−0.94 ($F = 2.89$)
Turnover[a]	0.01 (0.03)	0.06 (1.23)	−0.06 (−0.17)	0.25* (2.37)	−0.00 (−0.00)	−0.00 (−0.09)	−0.01* (−2.00)	0.04 (0.47)
RLT	−0.65* (−5.79)	0.42* (12.93)	−0.97* (−4.49)	0.65* (11.87)	−0.10* (−0.62)	0.23* (7.38)	−0.10 (−0.24)	0.32* (4.74)
LgnegNCF	−0.18 (−0.51)	0.12 (1.22)	−1.80* (−2.76)	0.66* (3.96)	−0.29 (−0.47)	0.19 (1.73)	1.43 (0.98)	0.05 (0.21)
LgposNCF	0.19 (−0.51)	−0.33* (−3.16)	−0.16 (−0.26)	−0.08 (−0.50)	−0.54 (−0.93)	−0.62* (−5.84)	−2.29 (−1.86)	0.02 (0.07)
R^2	74	34	67	50	37	24	40	53

[a]The average premium numbers displayed in the table for the turnover variable are the actual values multiplied by 10^{-2}.
*Significantly different from zero at the 5 percent level.

547

Note that the relationship between past tax efficiency, as measured by *RLT*, and future after-tax returns is negative for all four style subsamples, but it is not statistically significant for the two small-cap categories. *RLT* is significantly positively related to future tax efficiency, however, for all four style subsamples.

Table 23.4 indicates that a relationship between large cash outflows and future returns is restricted to large-cap value stocks. A possible explanation may lie in the empirical observation that value funds, particularly large-cap value funds, tend to turn over their investments less frequently than other funds. For example, the average turnover during the 1981–98 sample period for the large-cap value funds in our sample was 56 percent, whereas the average turnover for large-cap growth, small-cap growth, and small-cap value was, respectively, 65 percent, 82 percent, and 74 percent. (The differences between the average turnover for large-cap value funds and the average turnover for each of the other three categories are statistically significant.) To satisfy requests for large redemptions, a manager of a fund with low turnover may have to sell lower-cost-basis shares than would a manager of a fund with higher turnover, which would result in higher capital gains distributions and lower after-tax returns for the low-turnover fund.

CONCLUSIONS AND IMPLICATIONS

The main findings from our analysis of after-tax returns for the 1981–98 period are as follows: After we controlled for other factors,

- funds that were historically tax efficient outperformed comparable funds on an after-tax basis,
- funds that experienced large net redemptions, particularly large-cap value funds, subsequently underperformed comparable funds on an after-tax basis,
- risk, investment style, past pretax performance, and expenses were important determinants of after-tax and pretax returns, and
- turnover did not appear to be related to future after-tax returns.

When we analyzed mutual fund tax efficiency in the 1981–98 period, we found, after controlling for other factors, that funds that did not experience recent large cash redemptions, did experience recent large cash inflows, were historically tax efficient, were classified as small capitalization, or had high expense ratios tended subsequently to be more tax efficient. But although funds with large cash inflows, high expense ratios, or an emphasis on small-cap stocks tended to be more tax efficient in the sample period, they also tended to have lower pretax returns. In fact, for all three variables, the negative influence on pretax return was at least as great as the positive influence on tax efficiency—implying a neutral or negative net effect on after-tax returns.

These results suggest that taxable investors should not make investment decisions with tax efficiency as their sole focus. Instead, they should emphasize maximizing after-tax returns (for their chosen risk tolerance). Moreover, U.S. equity investors should diversify across investment styles (large–small, value–growth). When choosing equity funds for a taxable account, investors should focus on funds with good past pretax performance, low expenses, and high past tax efficiency (i.e., low return lost to taxes) that have not recently experienced large net redemptions. Our results suggest that the benefits of being a tax-aware investor are substantial.

ACKNOWLEDGMENTS

The authors wish to thank Terry Banet, Kimberly LaPointe, Mark Sheridan, and Gordon Fowler for helpful comments and suggestions. Remaining errors are our responsibility.

APPENDIX 23A: CONSTRUCTION OF TAX-ADJUSTED RETURNS

CRSP reports key data for each distribution—capital gain, income, or split—over the life of each fund in its database. We used this information, together with information on short- and long-term tax rates (to be discussed), to construct a monthly after-tax return series for each fund in the CRSP database. We obtained after-tax returns for longer frequencies by compounding the monthly return data.

For each month t, we identified the total number of distributions N that occurred in that month for a fund. Assuming an arbitrary \$1 investment in the fund at the closing net asset value (NAV) from the prior month, the number of shares invested in a fund at the beginning of month t is given by

$$S_{o,t} = \frac{1}{NAV_{t-1}}, \tag{23A.1}$$

where NAV_{t-1} is the fund's net asset value at the end of month $t-1$.

An updated share amount was computed following each distribution $i = 1, \ldots, N$, sorted by date, within the month as follows: If the distribution was income or capital gains,

$$S_{i,t} = S_{i-1,t}\left(1 = \frac{XAMT_i}{RENAV_i}\right), \tag{23A.2}$$

where $XAMT_i$ is the per share dollar amount of the income or capital gains distribution and $RENAV_i$ is the reinvestment net asset value on the close of the pay date of the income or capital gains distribution, including reinvestment of the distribution. If the distribution was a stock split,

$$S_{i,t} = S_{i-1,t}SFACTOR_i, \tag{23A.3}$$

where $SFACTOR_i$ is the split factor (e.g., 2 for 1).

The taxes on capital gains and income distributions within a given month t were calculated as

$$\text{Taxes}_t = \sum_{i=1}^{N} S_{i,t}[(XAMT_i^D)(T_d) \\ + (XAMT_i^C)(T_c)], \tag{23A.4}$$

where

$$XAMT_i^D = \text{dollar amount of the dividend}$$
$$XAMT_i^C = \text{dollar amount of the capital gains distribution}$$
$$T_d \quad\; = \text{ordinary income tax rate}$$
$$T_c \quad\; = \text{tax rate on capital gains}$$

TABLE 23A.1   Tax Rates

Year	Income Tax Rate	Capital Gains Tax Rate
1981	63.2%	25.0%
1982	50.0	20.0
1983	50.0	20.0
1984	49.0	19.6
1985	49.0	19.6
1986	49.0	19.6
1987	38.5	28.0
1988	33.0	28.0
1989	33.0	28.0
1990	33.0	28.0
1991	31.0	28.0
1992	31.0	28.0
1993	39.6	28.0
1994	39.6	28.0
1995	39.6	28.0
1996	39.6	28.0
1997	39.6	28.0
1998	39.6	20.0

Note: For years prior to 1993, tax rates are from Dickson and Shoven. For 1993–1998, the ordinary income tax rate is the maximum federal marginal tax rate.

Table 23A.1 lists the tax rates on ordinary income and capital gains used in this chapter for each year in the sample. Although income taxes are a function of an individual investor's personal tax rate, we could not, of course, calculate each individual's rate. For years prior to 1993, the ordinary income tax rates we used to compute taxes correspond most closely to the rates of "high-tax individuals" as determined by Dickson and Shoven (1993). For 1993 forward, the ordinary income tax rate is the maximum U.S. federal marginal tax rate.

Given an initial investment amount of $1, we calculated the after-tax monthly return as

$$r_t^{aftertax} = S_{N,t}NAV_t - \text{Taxes}_t - 1. \tag{23A.5}$$

Several assumptions are inherent in these calculations.

First, taxes are assumed paid at the end of each month, although in reality, they are typically paid on an annual basis. This assumption has only a minor impact on the calculation of after-tax returns.

Second, the capital gains of an investor are not offset by any capital losses of that investor.

Third, all capital gains are taxed at the long-term capital gains rate. To assume otherwise would require information about the investor's holding period and personal tax situation.

Accounting for capital gains taxes individually would change our estimate of the magnitude of returns lost to taxes—our estimate of tax efficiency. But because the estimated premiums are essentially a covariance between the characteristic, such as past *RLT*, and future after-tax returns, a change in the level of return lost to taxes that is driven by a change in the investor's tax rate would not have a big impact on our results.

Fourth, no state taxes are considered. State taxes depend on the individual and will increase the amount of return lost to taxes. Again, an increase in the amount of return lost to taxes does not imply that the estimated premium will change.

Fifth, the calculations ignore any additional taxes resulting from the liquidation of the fund at the end of the period. So, the after-tax returns correspond most closely to those earned by long-term buy-and-hold investors. To assume otherwise, we would have to make assumptions regarding the holding period of each individual investor.

NOTES

1. Past performance is not a guarantee of future results. Principal value and investment returns fluctuate with changes in market conditions, so an investor's shares when redeemed may be worth more or less than their original cost. Small-capitalization funds are subject to greater volatility than funds following other style strategies. For more complete information on a fund's past performance—including management fees, charges, and expenses—investors should obtain and read the prospectus carefully before investing.

2. Prior studies of mutual fund performance did not uniformly conclude that *all* of these characteristics are important determinants of pretax returns, but each characteristic was identified in numerous studies as an important determinant of pretax returns. Many analysts believe that assets under management and/or net cash flow may be important determinants of pretax performance, but the literature contains little evidence to support such a claim.

3. The potential capital gains exposure of a fund might also be an important determinant of future after-tax returns. Unfortunately, data on capital gains exposure were available to us only for the last year of our sample period. We did perform tests for this restricted period and found no relationship between potential capital gains exposure and subsequent after-tax returns. Because of the short sample length, these results are only suggestive, and we thus leave them for future research.

4. Although we do not report results for the case in which returns were measured annually, we did carry out such measurements and found the results to be qualitatively similar to those reported later in this chapter.

5. In tests not reported, we estimated regressions that included past standard deviation together with and in lieu of β and found that past standard deviation did not provide any additional explanatory power beyond that already provided by β. Also, in a test not reported, we tested the hypothesis that funds with a great deal of style purity are less tax efficient than less-pure funds. Our measure of style purity was the standard deviation of the regression error term in Equation 23.1. After controlling for other factors, we found no evidence to suggest that style purity affects after-tax returns or tax efficiency.

6. Measuring *NCF* over the prior quarter did not alter the conclusions drawn from our analysis. Monthly net asset figures are not available in the CRSP database for the entire 1981–98 sample period, so we did not perform tests using *NCF* measured over monthly intervals.

7. We also used a six-month cutoff to define *Mgrturn* and obtained similar results to those reported here.
8. For an example of application of this technique in the mutual fund performance literature, see Carhart.
9. See Malkiel (1995) and Chevalier and Ellison for examples of studies that used pooling in the process of estimating the marginal effects of mutual fund characteristics on return.
10. The average premiums associated with the risk and style variables are a function of more than one regression coefficient. So, the test statistic for the hypothesis that the average premium is 0 is distributed as an *F* random variable. For those non-risk-related and non-style-related variables for which the premium was not allowed to vary over time, the average premium is a function of one regression coefficient. In those cases, the test statistic is *t* distributed. When reporting the results of our tests, we provide the appropriate test statistic.
11. A positive premium on past performance could be the result of performance persistence among the poorest performing funds only. We checked for this possibility and found that performance persisted for both poor performers and good performers.
12. For all funds in 1991, turnover was reported as zero by CRSP. We used turnover in 1990 to proxy for turnover in 1991.
13. We also estimated average premiums for the 1992–98 time period, for which data on tenure and manager turnover became available. The results of this analysis, not shown, are qualitatively similar to those reported here.

REFERENCES

Carhart, Mark M. 1997. "On Persistence in Mutual Fund Performance." *Journal of Finance*, vol. 52, no. 1 (March):57–82.

Chevalier, Judith, and Glenn Ellison. 1999. "Are Some Mutual Fund Managers Better Than Others? Cross-Sectional Patterns in Behavior and Performance." *Journal of Finance*, vol. 54, no. 3 (June):875–899.

Dickson, Joel M., and John B. Shoven. 1993. "Ranking Mutual Funds on an After-Tax Basis." National Bureau of Economic Research Working Paper 4393.

Fama, Eugene F., and Kenneth R. French. 1993. "Common Risk Factors in the Returns on Stocks and Bonds." *Journal of Financial Economics*, vol. 33, no. 1 (February):3–56.

Fama, Eugene F., and James MacBeth. 1973. "Risk, Return and Equilibrium: Empirical Tests." *Journal of Political Economy*, vol. 81, no. 3 (May/June):607–636.

Malkiel, Burton. 1995. "Returns from Investing in Equity Mutual Funds 1971 to 1991." *Journal of Finance*, vol. 50, no. 2 (June):549–572.

Peterson, James D., Paul A. Pietranico, Mark W. Riepe, and Fran Xu. 2001. "Explaining the Future Performance of Domestic Equity Mutual Funds." *Journal of Investing*, vol. 10, no. 3 (Fall):81–91.

ABOUT THE
CONTRIBUTORS

Andrew L. Berkin, Director, First Quadrant, LP

Zvi Bodie, Norman and Adele Barron Professor of Management, Boston University School of Management

Peng Chen, CFA, President and CIO, Ibbotson Associates

Dan diBartolomeo, President and Founder, Northfield Information Services, Inc.

Robert N. Gordon, President, Twenty-First Securities Corporation

Stephen M. Horan, CFA, Head, Private Wealth and Investor Education, CFA Institute

Jeffrey E. Horvitz, Vice Chairman, Moreland Management Company

Roger G. Ibbotson, Professor, Yale University; Chairman, Zebra Capital Management; Founder and Adviser, Ibbotson Associates

Laurence J. Kotlikoff, Professor of Economics, Boston University

Martin L. Leibowitz, Managing Director, Morgan Stanley

Robert C. Merton, John and Natty McArthur University Professor, Harvard Business School

Moshe A. Milevsky, Associate Professor of Finance, Schulich School of Business, York University, Toronto; Executive Director, Individual Finance and Insurance Decisions (IFID) Centre

James D. Peterson, Vice President, Charles Schwab

Paul A. Pietranico, CFA, Senior Vice President, Product Development and Analytics, Allianz Global Investors U.S. Retail LLC

James M. Poterba, Mitsui Professor of Economics, Massachusetts Institute of Technology

Lee N. Price, CFA, President, Price Performance Measurement Systems, Inc.

Clifford H. Quisenberry, CFA, Managing Director, Investment Frontiers Research LLC

William Reichenstein, CFA, Pat and Thomas R. Powers Chair in Investment Management, Baylor University

Mark W. Riepe, CFA, Senior Vice President, Charles Schwab

Chris Robinson, Associate Professor of Finance, Atkinson School of Administrative Studies, York University

Paul A. Samuelson, Institute Professor and Professor of Economics, Emeritus, Massachusetts Institute of Technology

Jason S. Scott, Managing Director, Retiree Research Center, Financial Engines, Inc.

Michael Stutzer, Director, Burridge Center for Securities Analysis and Valuation, University of Colorado

Jonathan Treussard, Lecturer, Boston University School of Management

Mark J. Warshawsky, Director of Retirement Research, Watson Wyatt Worldwide

Scott D. Welch, Senior Managing Director, Fortigent, LLC

Jarrod Wilcox, CFA, President, Wilcox Investment Inc.

Paul Willen, Senior Economist, Research Department, U.S. Federal Reserve Bank of Boston

Fran Xu, CFA, Assistant Vice President, Washington Mutual Bank

Jia Ye, Chief Investment Strategist, First Quadrant, LP

Kevin X. Zhu, Senior Research Consultant, Ibbotson Associates

INDEX

INVESTMENT PERSPECTIVES SERIES

The latest investment research and cutting-edge strategies for financial professionals

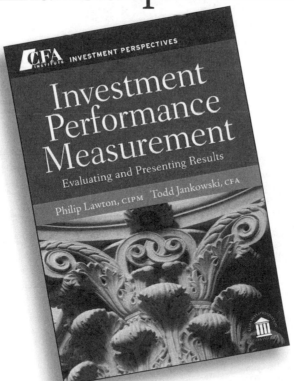

978-0-470-39502-8 • Hardcover • $95.00 US

Available at wiley.com, cfainstitute.org, and wherever books are sold.

Setting the
industry standard

Corporate Finance: A Practical Approach
Michelle R. Clayman,
Martin S. Fridson,
George H. Troughton
ISBN 978-0-470-19768-4

**Corporate Finance:
A Practical Approach, Workbook**
Michelle R. Clayman,
Martin S. Fridson,
George H. Troughton
ISBN 978-0-470-28243-4

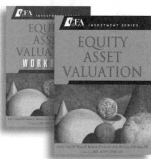

**Managing Investment Portfolios:
A Dynamic Process, Third Edition**
John L. Maginn, Donald L. Tuttle,
Dennis W. McLeavey, Jerald E. Pinto
ISBN 978-0-470-08014-6

**Managing Investment Portfolios:
A Dynamic Process,
Third Edition, Workbook**
John L. Maginn, Donald L. Tuttle,
Dennis W. McLeavey, Jerald E. Pinto
ISBN 978-0-470-10493-4

**Quantitative Investment Analysis,
Second Edition**
Richard A. DeFusco, Dennis W. McLeavey,
Jerald E. Pinto, David E. Runkle
ISBN 978-0-470-05220-4

**Quantitative Investment Analysis
Second Edition, Workbook**
Richard A. DeFusco, Dennis W. McLeavey,
Jerald E. Pinto, David E. Runkle
ISBN 978-0-470-06918-9

International Financial Statement Analysis
Thomas R. Robinson, Hennie van Greuning,
Elaine Henry, Michael A. Broihahn
ISBN 978-0-470-28766-8

**International Financial Statement
Analysis Workbook**
Thomas R. Robinson, Hennie van Greuning,
Elaine Henry, Michael A. Broihahn
ISBN 978-0-470-28767-5

Equity Asset Valuation
John D. Stowe, Thomas R. Robinson,
Jerald E. Pinto, Dennis W. McLeavey
ISBN 978-0-470-05282-2

Equity Asset Valuation Workbook
John D. Stowe, Thomas R. Robinson,
Jerald E. Pinto, Dennis W. McLeavey
ISBN 978-0-470-28765-1

Fixed Income Analysis, Second Edition
Frank J. Fabozzi
ISBN 978-0-470-05221-1

**Fixed Income Analysis,
Second Edition, Workbook**
Frank J. Fabozzi
ISBN 978-0-470-06919-6

CFA INSTITUTE INVESTMENT SERIES
covers core investment topics geared toward
professionals and finance students globally.
Available at wiley.com, cfainstitute.org, and wherever books are sold.